Living at the Borderlines

Living at the Borderlines

Issues in Caribbean Sovereignty and Development

Edited by

Cynthia Barrow-Giles and Don D. Marshall

Ian Randle Publishers
Kingston • Miami

First published in Jamaica, 2003 by
Ian Randle Publishers
11 Cunningham Avenue
Box 686, Kingston 6
www.ianrandlepublishers.com

National Library of Jamaica Cataloguing in Publication Data

Living at the borderlines : issues in Caribbean sovereignty and development / Cynthia Barrow-Giles and Don Marshall (eds)

       p. : ill. ;   cm

    Bibliography : p
    ISBN 976-637-148-2 (pbk)

    I. Barrow-Giles, Cynthia II. Marshall, Don D.

1. Sovereignty   2. Globalization   3. Caribbean Area - Politics and government
4. Caribbean Area - Economic integration   5. Caribbean Area - Economic conditions
6. Caribbean Area - Economic policy

338.9729   dc 21

Published in the United States, 2003 by
Ian Randle Publishers, Inc

ISBN 0-9729358-9-4 (paperback)

Book design by Shelly-Gail Cooper
Cover design by Louis Matalon
Set in Plantin 10pt

Printed in the United States of America

*This book is dedicated to
the people of the Caribbean*

Table of Contents

Illustrations

TABLES

FIGURES

EXHIBITS

CHARTS

Acknowledgements

This book was initially conceptualised by Ian Randle, Cynthia Barrow-Giles and later, Don D. Marshall to focus on the burning issues of the post colonial state in the Caribbean in the hope that it would stimulate debate on Caribbean sovereignty and development and the prospects for survival in a 'globalised world'. We believe that the anthology has achieved its original objectives and to this end the editors would like to thank the many contributors to this book. Indeed, we were overwhelmed by the number of persons who were prepared to make a contribution, several of whom unfortunately we were unable to accommodate at this stage. Like ours, their interest and contributions stem from a combination of their undeniable passion for the region and their frustrations with the ceaseless struggle for global justice and fair play.

A special debt of gratitude is owed to postgraduate student in the department of Government, Sociology and Social Work, Melanie Callender for her assistance in the preparation of the manuscript.

Cynthia Barrow-Giles and
Don D. Marshall

List of Contributors

David Nii Addy is of Ghanaian-German origin and holds a Master's degree in Political Science with a postgraduate specialisation in development studies. His research areas include social development issues in the Caribbean and sub-Saharan Africa, child labour, international migration, racism and anti-discrimination policies. During 1997-2000 he was a Research Officer at the Caribbean Office of the International Labour Organisation. He is currently working with the newly established German Human Rights Institute in Berlin. Some of his most recent publications include the following; 'Restructuring and the Loss of Preferences – Labour Challenges for the Caribbean Banana Industry', in *Journal of Eastern Caribbean Studies*, Vol. 4 No. 4 (2000); 'Poverty Alleviation in Sub-Saharan Africa' in *Asien Afrika Lateinamerica*, Vol. 26, No. 2, 1998 and 'The Quest for Antidiscrimination Policies to Protect Migrants in Germany – An Assessment of the Political Discussion and Proposals for Legislation', ILO Migration Branch, Geneva, 1997.

Michael H. Allen studied at the University of the West Indies, Mona Campus and the London School of Economics. He teaches International Relations in the Department of Political Science at Bryn Mawr College and his fields are International Political Economy and International Law, with special interest in Africa and the Caribbean. He is active in the International Human Rights Exchange. His more recent publications are, 'Globalisation and Contending Human Rights Discourse' *Quarterly Review, Human Rights Committee*, Cape Town, March 2002; 'Women, Bargaining and Change in seven Structures of World Political Economy', *Review of International Studies* (1999)

Winston Anderson is an Attorney & Barrister-at-Law, who received his Ph.D in International Environmental Law from the University of Cambridge in 1988. He has been with the Faculty of Law, University of the West Indies since 1988 and is now Senior Lecturer in Law, having occupied the positions of Head of the Teaching Department, and Deputy Dean. He is the author of numerous publications on international, environmental and commercial law. These include the *Law of Caribbean Marine Pollution* published by Kluwer Law International, in 1997; and *Caribbean Environmental Law Development and Application*, published by the United Nations Environmental Programme Regional Office for Latin America and the Caribbean, in 2002.

Cynthia Barrow-Giles is a lecturer in Political Science, at the University of the West Indies, Cave Hill Campus. She is the author of *Introduction to Caribbean Politics*, published by Ian Randle Publishers 2002. Her current research interests are in the area of Caribbean regional integration, party politics and elections in the Commonwealth Caribbean.

Christopher Chase-Dunn is a Distinguished Professor of Sociology and Director of the Institute on Research on the World System at the University of California-Riverside. He received his Ph.D in Sociology from Stanford University in 1975 and has served as professor in the Department of Sociology at the Johns Hopkins University from 1975-2000. He has authored, co-authored and edited several books. In addition he has published dozens of articles in a number of international journals. His recent research focuses on intersocietal systems, including both the modern global political economy and earlier regional world-systems.

Ann Denis is Professor of Sociology at Université d'Ottawa in Ottawa, Canada, and Vice President, Research of the International Sociological Association (2002-6). In 2001-2 she was a Visiting Research Fellow at the Centre for Gender and Development Studies, University of the West Indies, Cave Hill. Her current research interests include women's paid and unpaid work in the Commonwealth Caribbean and Canada and the effects of globalisation on it; the intersection of gender, class and ethnicity/race; and use of the Internet by women and minority francophones (that is Francophones in Canada). Recent publications include *Femmes de carrières; Carrières de femmes* (co-authored) and articles on feminism's challenges to development, women and globalisation, use of the Internet by women and by students, and the multiple marginalities experienced by Franco-Ontarian women.

Hamid Ghany is a Senior Lecturer in Government and Head of the Department of Behavioural Sciences at the University of the West Indies, St Augustine, Trinidad. He served as a member of the Hyatali Constitution Review Commission of Trinidad and Tobago (1988-90) and also as a member of the Tobago House of Assembly Technical Team for constitutional negotiations with the Central Government of Trinidad and Tobago (1992-95). He was chairman of a Cabinet-approved Task Force on the development of a Code of Ethics for the Public Service of Trinidad and Tobago (1999). His major publications are in the field of Constitutional Studies, Parliamentary Affairs and Judicial Politics.

David Granger is a Ph.D student in the History Department at the University of California, Berkeley. He is currently studying modern imperialism and colonialism in the Atlantic world, integrating diaspora and African American

xvi | *Living at the Borderlines*

studies into an examination of the political and social development of the region. He holds a special interest in the Haitian Revolution and its effects.

Ivelaw L. Griffith is Dean of The Honors College and Professor of Political Science at Florida International University. A specialist on Caribbean and Inter-American security and narcotics issues, he has published six books and is currently working on *Caribbean Security in the Age of Terror*. Ivelaw serves on the editorial board of several journals, including Security and Defense Studies Review and Caribbean Journal of Criminology and Social Psychology, and is a Past President of the Caribbean Studies Association.

Holger Henke received his post graduate education at the University of the West Indies, Mona Campus and is currently employed at the Caribbean Research Center, Medgar Evers College – (CUNY). Among his published books are *Between Dependency and Self-Determination: Jamaica's Foreign Relations, 1972-1989* (The University of the West Indies Press) 2000; *The West Indian Americans* (Greenwood Press) 2001; and co-edited with Ian Boxill, *The End of the 'Asian Model'?*, (The John Benjamin Publishers) 2000. His current research is on New Caribbean Thought; Neoliberalism and legitimacy; and Jamaica's foreign relations.

Taitu A. Heron is Assistant Lecturer in Political Science at the University of the West Indies, Cave Hill campus. Her current research interests include: Caribbean political philosophy, Feminist political theory, and Western political thought. She has published in *Pensamiento Propio*.

Percy C. Hintzen is Professor and Chair of African American Studies at the University of California, Berkeley. He is the author of *The Costs of Regime Survival* (Cambridge Univ. Press), and *West Indian in the West* (New York Univ. Press), and editor with Jean Rahier of *Invisible Others: Active Presences in US Black Communities* (Routledge).

Daphne Jayasinghe completed a MPhil in Sociology at the University of the West Indies, Cave Hill Campus. She has been involved in research with women working in the manufacturing sector in the Caribbean and Sri Lanka and has previously published related work on the training needs of Carribbean women working in manufacturing in the *Journal of Gender and Development*.

S. B. Jones-Hendrickson, is Professor of Economics at the University of the Virgin Islands. Professor Jones-Hendrickson lectured at the University of the West Indies, Mona, Jamaica from 1973-76 and the University of the Virgin

Islands from 1976. As a writer/scholar, Professor Jones-Hendrickson is very prolific. Among his books are *Readings in Caribbean Public Sector Economics* (coeditor, 1981); *Public Finance and Monetary Policy in Open Economies* (1985), and *Caribbean Visions*, (editor, 1990). He has two monographs 'Cross Border Stock Trading in the Caribbean' (1994) and 'Intellectual Property Rights in the Caribbean' (1999). Dr Jones-Hendrickson has also produced several creative works. He has published two volumes of poetry and two novels: the popular *Sonny Jim of Sandy Point* (1991) a quasi-autobiography, and his most recent novel, *Death on the Pasture* (1994). Professor Jones-Hendrickson is currently on leave from the University of the Virgin Islands serving as Ambassador of St Kitts and Nevis to CARICOM, the OECS and the Association of Caribbean States.

Patsy Lewis is a Research Fellow at the Sir Arthur Lewis Institute for Social and Economic Studies, Mona Campus, at the University of the West Indies. She has published in a number of international and regional journals. Among her most recent publications are 'A Future for Windward island Bananas? Challenge and Prospect' *Journal of Commonwealth and Comparative Politics*, vol. 38 (2) July 2000, 'Revisiting the Grenada Invasion: The OECS Role and its Impact on Regional and International Politics', *Social and Economic Studies*, vol. 48 (3), September 1999. The author of *Surviving Small Size: Regional Integration in Caribbean Ministates*, 2003, UWI Press, Dr Lewis' current research area is on regionalism.

Don D. Marshall is a Research Fellow in the Sir Arthur Lewis Institute of Social and Economic Studies, University of the West Indies, Cave Hill Campus, Barbados. He is the author of *Caribbean Political Economy at the Crossroads* (MacMillan Press) 1998 and co-editor of *The Empowering Impulse: The Nationalist Tradition of Barbados* (UWI Press) 2001. Dr Marshall has also published in a number of regional and international journals. He is currently researching issues relating to the fate of (Caribbean) offshore financial services, globalisation, and the state.

Douglas Midgett is an Associate Professor of Anthropology at the University of Iowa. He has conducted research over three decades in the Eastern Caribbean on topics including language and expressive culture, politics and trade union history, land tenure and transfer, and migration.

Keith Nurse lectures at the Institute of International Relations, University of the West Indies, Trinidad and Tobago. His current research area is on cultural industries. He has recently completed studies on The Caribbean Music Industry and Festival Tourism in the Caribbean. He is the co-author of *Windward Islands Bananas: Challenges and Options under the Single European Market* (1996) and *Caribbean Economies and Global Restructuring* (Ian Randle Publishers) 2002, with Marie-Claude Derné.

Dave Ramsaran is an Assistant Professor of Sociology at Susquehanna University in Selinsgrove PA. He earned his degrees from The University of the West Indies, St Augustine Campus, and American University in Washington DC. His current research focuses on the process of globalisation in the Caribbean looking at the intersection of race, class and gender in that process. He has published in a number of international journals.

Lomarsh Roopnarine is Assistant Professor of History at the University of the Virgin Islands, St Croix Campus. His research interests relate to environmental policy challenges and development in Guyana and the Caribbean, and Indo-Caribbean Indenture, Resistance and Accommodation. His publications have appeared in the *Journal of Caribbean History, Immigrants and Minorities, European Review of Latin American and Caribbean Studies, Revista Interamericana, The Encyclopedia of New York State,* among others. Dr Roopnarine's revised doctoral dissertation, 'Indo-Caribbean Indenture: Creating Opportunities out of Adversity' is currently under review for publication.

Hilbourne A. Watson earned his PhD in Political Science from Howard University. Professor of International Relations at Bucknell University, he specialises in international political economy, international relations and political theory. Among his most recent publications are 'Global Finance: the Role and Status of the Caribbean' in *The Political Economy of Drugs in the Caribbean,* edited by Ivelaw Griffith (Macmillan Press) 2000; 'Global Neoliberalism, the Third Technological Revolution and Global 2000: A Perspective on Issues Affecting the Caribbean on the Eve of the 21st Century' in *Contending with Destiny: The Caribbean in the 21st Century,* edited by Kenneth Hall and Denis Benn, (Ian Randle Publishers) 2000; 'Themes in Liberalism, Modernity, Marxism, Postmodernism and Beyond: An Interpretation and Critique of Brian Meeks' Re-Reading the Black Jacobins; James, the Dialectic and the Revolutionary Conjuncture' in *The New Caribbean Thought,* edited by Brian Meeks and Folke Lindhal (The Press, University of the West Indies) 2001; 'Errol Barrow (1920-1987): The Social Construction of Colonial and Post-colonial Charismatic Leadership in Barbados' in Caribbean Charisma: Reflections on Leadership, Legitimacy and Populist Politics, edited by Anton Allahar (Ian Randle Publishers) 2001; 'Theorizing the Racialization of Global Politics and the Caribbean Experience,' in Alternatives, vol. 26, no. 4, 2001, pp. 449-483.

Introduction
Living at the Borderlines

Don D. Marshall and Cynthia Barrow-Giles

Living at the Borderlines arose from the urgent obligation to reevaluate the significance of the 'national option' in a region of small post-colonial societies marked by low levels of capital accumulation and foreign direct investment inflows; diminishing state and institutional capacities; and threats to its security landscape in the context of global restructuring. This necessarily required an exploration of issues of milieu and an interrogation of hegemonic concepts and discourses normally deployed in discussions about Caribbean constitutional development, regionalism, democracy and political economy. While the literature on the macro level has become quite copious, the reader of this anthology will find in these essays many differences in emphasis and perspectives. Some authors sought to broadly outline and analyse the range and complexity of the challenges to Caribbean sovereignty and public policy autonomy. In other cases, the contributors focused discussion on issues relating to small country size, gender and ethnic tensions, discursive understandings of race and democracy, constitutional reform, regional integration and competition dynamics brought about by ongoing globalisation. Overall, quite a number of authors challenged the very constrained terrain of political possibility held for small peripheral societies. While some contributors pointed up the local as a site for resistance and change in the state's international policy bargains, others referred to the scope and range of catalytic possibilities under regionalism. Throughout there is considerable conceptual underclearing taking place. Some of the contributors examined the constitution and legitimation of authority in national constitutions, and through global governance institutions. Others sought to unpack knowledge constructs and discourses on race, sovereignty, legitimacy, globalisation, and marginalisation and inclusivity. Not unexpectedly, there are resonances and discontinuities in the different arguments and perspectives but there are some broad points of agreement in these 24 contributions to the volume. For the intellectual world, this is all to the good as it keeps open our capacity to ask 'different' and more profound questions. Combined, these essays clearly illustrate the breadth and rate of changes in various aspects of the socioeconomic, cultural and political systems and the consequences for systems' maintenance.

The anthology is divided up into six sections featuring a range of themes of a global, regional and domestic in character. Part I of the volume focuses on the theme, *Navigating Globalisation*. Chase-Dunn and Allen speak to the disciplinary nature of neo-liberal global capitalism strongly promoted by the International Monetary Fund and the World Bank. The shared understanding is that the power of capital is being promoted through the extension and deepening of market values and disciplines in social life, under a regime of free enterprise and free trade. Add to this the role of the World Trade Organisation in ensuring legal, institutional and constitutional commitments to the neo-liberal process on the part of member-states and we get a picture of a world in which public policy seems less and less accountable to the interests of the poor. This is particularly in evidence in the Caribbean and other parts of the Third World where governments have had to borrow money in the capital markets or from the international financial institutions (IFIs), yet Chase-Dunn maintains that there is scope for revisiting and mitigating the inevitable adverse effects of global capitalism through the force of globalisation from below.

Allen, Marshall and Barrow-Giles emphasise the importance of using state sovereignty in skillful ways to militate against the harsh effects of neo-liberal programming, Dunn focuses on the anti-globalisation protests around the world and points up the need for broader resistance to austere global governance. He acknowledges the extent to which there has been some success in attempts by progressive forces to assist the state in using its national sovereignty to provide protection from global market forces; and by NGOs in forging new kinds of labour internationalism. It might be strategically more productive, he argues, for progressive groups to make efforts to reform the world system by making alliances and constructing institutions that promote popular democracy on an international, regional or global scale. Keith Nurse's interrogation of the content of Trinidad and Tobago's industrial policy, Barrow-Giles' notion of self-determination and Marshall's discussion on the fiscal sovereignty rights of countries brings the reader back to a reconsideration of Chase-Dunn's argument. It would seem that the politics against austere neo-liberalism and poor developmental planning could simultaneously sit alongside campaigns against the antidemocratic character of global governance institutions. The question is: what are the conditions under which progressives (with an inner-directed gaze) may grasp that international relations might be a meaningful political site to struggle against Anglo-American neo-liberal globalisation and autocratic global governance?

In Part II, entitled *Crisis of Adjustment*, discussion turns towards the impact of neo-liberal regimes on banana workers in St Lucia and St Vincent & the Grenadines (Ramsaran), and ordinary workers in Jamaica and Barbados (Henke & Marshall). Among other issues, we are treated to a prevailing sense of adjustment fatigue on the part of the working majority. This is particularly the case in St Lucia and St Vincent & Grenadines where a sense of despair followed the 1999 WTO ruling requiring a cessation of all European Union quotas and tariffs that allow preferential treatment to ACP banana producers by 2005. Denis and Jayasinghe refer to trends in the restructuring labour market highlighting programmes of work flexibilisation, casualisation and fragmentation. This led to an analysis of the feminisation of work in low-wage jobs in the electronics sector, and in offshore services. From the foregoing, it appears that the demand for a flexible and contingent workforce requires that workers embrace uncertainty and risk as key to survival in a competitive global market place. It is in this context that Henke & Marshall and Jayasinghe, *pace* Chase-Dunn could raise questions about the efficacy of the development models adopted by select regional governments and about how the legitimacy of the neo-liberal ruling order is being mediated and contested in Jamaican and Barbadian societies.

Part III features a number of contributions addressing the theme *Risk and Security in the Contemporary Caribbean*. The security landscape is mined for discussion on the wider Caribbean area in terms of the region's territorial and ecological security, national security, terrorism and sovereignty. Roopnarine argues for an ecologically sensitive approach to public policy formulation in Guyana, but sensitises the reader to the myriad challenges at the socioeconomic and state levels. While Anderson focuses on environmental security risks across Caribbean states he emphasises the legal dimensions. Griffith and Watson in separate contributions take up these and other issues. The former critiques narrow traditional realist understanding of security and questions the security coping measures of Caribbean governments arguing that these have to be 'multidimensional, multilevel, and multiactor'. For Watson, the events surrounding a request in 1997 by the US government for permission to exercise US laws in drug interdiction across the Caribbean waters, bring the efficacy of sovereignty into review. In outlining dominant ways of thinking on state sovereignty, Watson finds realist theory inadequate as an explanatory framework and intones that it functions more as a legitimating 'manual for big power chauvinism'. From Watson's perspective, state-sovereignty must instead be located in discussions about the role and force of transnational capital, property relations, and the capacity of the different states to mediate the diverse constellations of power and authority domestically and internationally.

The regional is a site upon which states seek to effect a restructuring of their political economies given the neoliberal impetus to free trade. Indeed the spectre of increased regionalism and bloc formation in the closing decades of the twentieth century could be read as attempts to recoup sovereignty, meaning, governments' capacity to steer, and/or shape developmental futures. In Part IV

Caribbean Integration Reconsidered, Lewis contemplates the survival of the Caribbean Common Market and the Organisation of the Eastern Caribbean States (OECS). Her central claim is that wider integration processes reflected in the Free Trade Area of the Americas (FTAA) and Regional Economic Partnership Agreements (REPAS) – proposed by the EU to replace the Lome Convention – have rendered the narrower OECS/CARICOM arrangements redundant. Morever, she continues, the goals of the proposed Caribbean Single Market and Economy (CSME) such as building competitiveness in the services sector 'stands to be undermined within the FTAA which has included trade in services as a negotiating area'. Reading Lewis, the functionalist approach to political economic integration in the CARICOM area seems to be outflanked as the task of re-defining and restructuring the region's goals becomes increasingly urgent. While Lewis recommends a political solution that will also serve to lock-in the cultural distinctiveness of the region, we learn from Barrow-Giles' cross-national survey that a high degree of ambivalence exists among ordinary people on deepening the process of integration. While some persons of varying islands recognise the positive synergies possible in a coherent regional order, they also express fear of what free movement of peoples may imply for accustomed levels of national welfare provision and employment opportunities. Addy in his review of migration trends however reminds us that neither globalisation nor regionalism has yet featured unrestricted free movement of labour. Moreover, he maintains that, migratory trends tend often to increase only temporarily in the wake of a regional integration arrangement. The reasons for this relate to the complex range of determinants facing an individual, like wage differentials, employment prospects, and other socio-economic criteria.

In the penultimate section of the anthology, the discussion focuses on governance and constitutional reform (*Constitutional Reform and Caribbean Governance*) set against the backdrop of nationalist/republican responses to identity and systemic challenges posed by ongoing globalisation, and demands for transparency and accountability confronting the various governments. Jones-Hendrickson and Ghany in separate case studies (St Kitts and Nevis, and Trinidad and Tobago respectively) examine the ambiguities that have arisen in prising local constitutions and relying on the judicial structure for clarity on the sovereignty question. In the featured speeches by Prime Ministers Ralph Gonsalves of St Vincent & the Grenadines and Kenny Anthony of St Lucia, we learn that there is a high premium placed on the importance of consensus government, public accountability and civic engagement for ensuring good governance in this adjustment period. Hintzen takes up the issue of governance and sovereignty in a multiethnic society against the backdrop of intensive penetration of the political economy by global capital in Guyana. Midgett draws our attention to two distinct but currently symbiotic perspectives prevalent in the literature on modern Caribbean politics. One is the argument that the legacy of austere rule in the colonial past will continue to render the promise of democratic participation in small Caribbean states illusory. The other relates to the portrayal of 'Caribbean societies as impotent victims of global forces'. These standpoints, he argues, are determinist and, moreover, reflect a refusal to accept that the dynamic of ongoing state formation in the Caribbean simultaneously features perennial modes of resistance and struggle by different social forces. Midgett would later turn his attention to how the first-past-the-post system in Caribbean small-island states often leads to 'majoritarian tyranny', incarcerating minority group expression and dissenting opinion.

The final theme in Part VI, *Recovering Caribbean History – Discourses on Race and Plantation Politics* showcase inquiries intruded upon by a historical mode of thought. We learn from Heron that the quality of democracy in Jamaica is not only affected by austere authoritarian approaches to government by successive administrations, but by historical restrictions to social self-creation. She explains that the battle for 'space', meaning personal development space, extends back to plantation slavery and colonialism where restrictions were placed on the 'freedom and will to express oneself, to eat, to sleep, to worship, to have sex, to work, to think, to create, and to organise society as s/he deems[ed] fit'. While modern Jamaica does not wholly reflect the plantation experience, Heron would have it that 'feelings of defensive entitlement to space' exist. She recommends a kind of constitutional overhauling that would afford a re-distributive justice element, an equal sharing of the country's resources across the ethnic and class groups. Granger on the other hand, confronts modern discourses on race, slavery and revolution and laments their frame of reference relative to the Hatian Revolution example. The continued historical manipulations to the meta-narrative of the Haitian revolution, he argues, effect a silencing on the significance of the event and the dynamic between African born slaves and creoles. As he summarily put it: 'By emphasising the creole element, contributors to the discourse...make the revolution more acceptable, imaginable and conceivable to western observers.'

Summary

The idea that the Caribbean could be devolving downward in wealth, function and sovereignty has become quite overwhelming in popular and academic genres of literary production in recent times. In some cases, a dialogue of disarming woe predominates, producing a sense of powerlessness. As it has turned out, the essays in this volume that address globalisation, sovereignty and self-determination do not feature a hyper-pessimistic interrogation of Caribbean development and fate with trade negotiation authorities. Political agency is afforded a restorative possibility, as concepts such as contingency and conjuncture are elevated in discussions about the global capitalist structure.

In development policy terms, the political leadership in the Caribbean have faced an evolving policymaking environment in which traditional solutions have been deficient, leading the way to the general consensus among elites and social groups across the region that solutions to Caribbean socioeconomic survival and stability lie in among other things, regional initiatives, improved export production in the case of Jamaica and Trinidad and Tobago and a generalised turn towards an export services model of development. Most of these require political will, coherence at the regional level, improvements to skills and technology bases, infrastructural improvements and sea changes within the enterprise culture. Without a thorough makeover, national and regional development could easily become a quagmire. The range of issues featured in this volume is therefore meant to sensitise stakeholders about the complexity of the challenges, the multi-level nature of the changes, the enduring nature of Caribbean societies and the range of alternatives possible. But here we seek to hold on to the unity of theory and policy, and of the human sciences disciplines, sundered from each other by modernity's insistence that things be separated from each other for pragmatic application and simplistic explanation. The net result here has been multidisciplinary conversation, debates on concepts, discourses, prevailing assumptions and redeployment in discussions about the Caribbean life-world. Altogether *Living at the Borderlines* avoids an incarceration of the academic and policy community within regimes of discursive closure and analytical/policy paralysis.

Part I

Navigating Globalisation

1

Toward a Collectively Rational and Democratic Global Commonwealth: Globalisation From Below

Christopher Chase-Dunn

WAVES OF DECOLONISATION

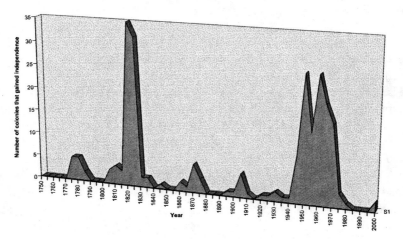

Main Source: Henige 1970. Colonial empires of Britain, Italy, Japan, the Netherlands, Portugal, Spain, France and the United States were coded.

Abstract: This chapter presents a world historical perspective on globalisation and the relationship between capitalist development and anti-systemic movements. It explores the emergence of new popular forces in the world polity, and the possibility of constructing a democratic and collectively rational global commonwealth in the next decades. The idea of 'globalisation from below' is considered in the context of Central American countries and possible contributions by post-communist societies are considered.

(An earlier version was present at the panel on 'Prospects for Democracy and Justice in the Global Economy' at the annual meetings of the American Sociological Association, Washington, DC August 16, 2000).

This essay employs the world-systems perspective on the development of the capitalist world-economy as the framework for analysing globalisation and the possibilities for reorganising the global system.[1] The world-systems perspective is an historical and structural theoretical framework that analyses national societies as parts of a larger stratified sociopolitical and economic system. The focus is on the structural features of the larger system itself. It is a world economy with a hierarchical division of labour for the production of different kinds of goods. There are economically and militarily powerful countries in the core, dependent and dominated regions in the periphery, and a middle sector of countries (the semiperiphery) in which states have intermediate levels of economic and political/military power.

The world market includes both international trade and all the national economies, so the world-system is the whole system, not just international relations. Local, regional, national, international, transnational and global networks of interaction constitute the world-system. This set of nested and overlapping networks of human interaction is itself located in the biosphere and the physical regimes of the planet Earth, the solar system, our galaxy and the larger processes and structures of the physical universe. The world-systems perspective is both materialist and institutional. It analyses the evolution of human institutions taking account of the constraints and opportunities posed by physics, biology and the natural environment (Chase-Dunn and Hall 1997).

The modern world-system is a global set of interaction networks that include all the national societies. But world-systems have not always been global. The modern world-system originated out of an expanding multi-core Afro-Eurasian world-system in which the Europeans rose to hegemony by conquering the Americas and using the spoils to overcome the political and economic strengths of contending core regions in South and East Asia (Frank 1998). The result was a global world-system with a single core region. And, because capitalism had become a predominant mode of accumulation in the European core, European hegemony further extended commodification and markets to the rest of the world. The consequence was a capitalistic and globalising world economy in which states and firms were increasingly focused on competitiveness in commodity production for the global market. Commodification was always much more developed in core regions, whereas in peripheral regions core colonisers used remnants of the tributary modes of accumulation, especially coercive labour control, to mobilise production for profit. Core regions specialised in the production of capital-intensive goods that required skilled and educated labour, and so their class structures and political institutions became more egalitarian and democratic relative to the authoritarianism and much greater internal inequalities of most peripheral and many semiperipheral countries.

Europe's position within, and relations with, the larger Afroeurasian system heavily affected these developments. But the virulent form of capitalism that emerged in Europe was unique in some important respects. For the first time *core* states were dominated by capitalists, and the most capitalist states in the European interstate system were the most successful and powerful states. This restructured the pattern of rise and fall (centralisation/decentralisation) within interstate systems. Earlier systems oscillated between 'universal' states created by semiperipheral marchers and more multicentric state systems. The modern system continued a cycle of centralisation/decentralisation but this took the form of the rise and fall of capitalist hegemons – the Dutch in the seventeenth century, the British in the nineteenth century and the United States in the twentieth century. In this new pattern of rise and fall, formerly semiperipheral capitalist states acted effectively to prevent the takeover of the core region by tributary marcher states (Spain, France and Germany).

The 'capitalism' referred to here is not only the phenomenon of capitalist firms producing commodities, but also capitalist states and the modern interstate system that is the political backdrop for capitalist accumulation. The world-system perspective has produced an understanding of capitalism in which geopolitics and interstate conflict are normal processes of capitalist political competition. Socialist movements are, defined broadly, those political and organisational means by which people try to protect themselves from market forces, exploitation and domination and to build more cooperative institutions. The sequence of industrial revolutions by which capitalism has restructured production and the control of labour have stimulated a series of political organisations and institutions created by workers to protect their livelihoods. This happened differently under different political and economic conditions in different parts of the world-system. Skilled workers created guilds and craft unions. Less skilled workers created industrial unions. Sometimes these coalesced into labour parties that played important roles in supporting the development of political democracies, mass education and welfare states (Rueschemeyer, Stephens and Stephens 1992). In other regions workers were less politically successful, but managed at least to protect access to rural areas or subsistence plots for a fallback or hedge against the insecurities of employment in capitalist enterprises. To some extent the burgeoning contemporary 'informal sector' provides such a fallback.

The varying success of workers' organisations also had an impact on the further development of capitalism. In some areas workers or communities were successful at raising the wage bill or protecting the environment in ways that raised the costs of production for capital. When this happened, capitalists either displaced workers by automating them out of jobs or capital migrated to where fewer constraints allowed cheaper production. The process of capital flight is not a new feature of the world-system. It has been an important force behind the uneven development of capitalism and the spreading scale of market integration for centuries. Labour unions and socialist parties were able to obtain some power in certain states, but capitalism became yet more international. Firm size increased. International markets became more and more important to successful capitalist competition. Fordism, the employment of large numbers of easily organisable workers in centralised production locations, has been supplanted by 'flexible accumulation' (small firms producing small customised products) and global sourcing (the use of substitutable components from widely-spaced competing producers), production strategies that makes traditional labour organising approaches much less viable.

Focusing on the systemic dynamics of this 'modern' Europe-centred world-system produces a model of systemic constants, cycles and trends within which the musical chairs game of geopolitics and economic competition have occurred (Chase-Dunn 1998: xiv-xvi). This model is the structural and dynamic backdrop for this analysis of systemic transformation, the spiral of capitalism and socialism and the roles that transnational social movements are likely to play in the future.

The combination of these structural constants, cycles and trends produces a model of world-system structure that reproduces its basic features while growing and intensifying. I contend contra widely accepted contentions to the contrary that the world-system has not fundamentally changed in recent decades as regards its basic structural features. Most of the events that are depicted as new departures are in fact continuations of cycles and trends long in operation. In *Global Formation* (Chase-Dunn 1998: Chapters 3 & 4) I argued that the 'stages of capitalism' literature could be analytically specified by the model of world-system constants, cycles and trends without the loss of any structural or processual features of importance. The more recent discourse on flexible specialisation and globalisation has failed to alter my view that the modern world-system is continuing on a developmental trajectory that is centuries old. But, Giovanni Arrighi's (1994) study of 'systemic cycles of accumulation' (SCAs) adds an important evolutionary dimension to the basic world-system model by teasing out the important organisational differences that distinguished the Genoese, Dutch, British and United States SCAB. The only thing lacking from Arrighi's analysis is an evolutionary focus on the role played by oppositional forces. With this addition the world-system model will be ready for the next task – how to transform the contemporary system into something more desirable from the point of view of the vast majority of the human species.

Theories of social structure provoke a standard set of criticisms. They are allegedly deterministic and downplay the importance of human agency. They are accused of reifying the idea of society (or the world-system) whereas only individual persons are alleged to really exist and to have needs. Structural theories, it is charged, totalise experience and provide ideological covers for domination and exploitation. And they miss the rich detail of locality and period that only thick description can provide.

The world-systems perspective has been accused of all these sins. In this essay I will describe a model of the structures and processes of the modern world-system and propose a project to transform the contemporary system into a democratic and collectively rational global commonwealth. This involves an approach to structure and action first outlined by Frederick Engels in his *Socialism: Utopian and Scientific* (1935). The point of building a structural theory is to enable us to understand the broad dynamics of social change in the historical system in which we live. This knowledge is potentially useful to those who want to preserve, modify or transform the historical system. For Engels the point was to mobilise the working class to humanise and socialise the world. That is also my intention.

The approach developed here assumes a structural model of the world-system and it identifies the agents who have both the motive and the opportunity to transform the contemporary world-system into a global socialist commonwealth. I also discuss some of the value-bases and the organisational issues that surround the project of transformation. By presenting the model in this way I hope to show the critics of structuralism that structural theories need not be deterministic, nor need they undermine social action. By positively stating the model and its implications for action I hope to get those who would be critical of the modern system to focus on the problems of scientifically understanding and transforming that system.

The scientific approach to world-system transformation needs to avoid the teleological elements of much of Marxism. The ideology of progress has been used to glorify both capitalism and socialism. Progress is not an inevitable outcome of forces that are immanent the world. The idea of progress only means that many humans can agree about the basics of what constitutes a good life. These are value judgments. But by making these assumptions explicit we can determine whether or not social change really constitutes progress as defined.

Inevitabilism also needs to be renounced. Human social change is both historical and evolutionary, but there is nothing inevitable about it. Indeed, another big asteroid or a human-made ecological catastrophe could destroy the whole experiment. Teleology is the idea that progress is inevitable because it comes out of the nature of the universe, or the nature of history, or some other powerful source. For many Marxists the proletariat has been understood to be the agency of progress. It is important to disentangle the scientific from the unscientific aspects of this idea. Workers may have interests that are compatible with and encourage the development of a more humane system, but that is not the same as being a magical source of historical progress. Teleology, inevitabilism, and eschatology are powerful bromides for the mobilisation of social movements, but they are deceptive and counter-productive when the prophesied utopia fails to arrive. What is needed is an open-ended theory of history that can be useful for practitioners of the arts of transformation. The world-systems perspective can serve this purpose.

TYPES OF GLOBALISATION

The discourse about globalisation has used this term to mean several different things. For some globalisation means a new stage of global capitalism that is qualitatively different from a prior stage that recently ended, though the ways in which it is alleged to be different vary from author to author. I will distinguish between two main meanings of the term 'globalisation'

- international integration, and
- the political-ideological discourse of global competitiveness.

Globalisation as international integration needs to be further unpacked as international economic integration, international political integration and international cultural and communications integration. Of course each of these subtypes has many aspects. But the point here is that the question of international integration is an objective problem of the extensiveness and intensity of links in a set of global networks of interaction. We can determine empirically how economically integrated were the societies on Earth in the late nineteenth century and how 'economically globalised' the world economic network is now (Chase-Dunn, Kawano and Brewer 2000). This is a question that is separable from the consciousness that people have about their linkages with one another. The question of consciousness regarding linkages (social cosmology) also needs to be studied, and this second main type of globalisation will also be considered below.

Globalisation as Ideology

Since the 1980s the term 'globalisation' has been used to describe allegedly recent and important changes in the world economy. It generally refers to changes in technologies of communication and transportation, increasingly internationalised financial flows and commodity trade, and the transition from national to world markets as the main arena for economic competition. These ostensible changes have been used to justify economic and political decisions such as deregulation and privatisation of industries, downsizing and streamlining of work forces, and dismemberment of the welfare services provided by governments. The expansion of the global economy has also been painted as the victory of progressive and rational capitalism over the anachronistic ideologies of socialism and communism. People naturally want more and bigger and faster commodities, and global capitalism is alleged to be the most efficient feasible system for providing these.

This discourse about globalisation is itself a phenomenon worthy of social science research. The emergence of neo-liberal political ideology is the topic of Phillip McMichael's (1996) analysis of the 'globalization project'. This phenomenon emerged with Reaganism and Thatcherism in the 1980s and has swept around the world as a justification for attacking and dismantling welfare states and labour unions following the demise of the Soviet Union. How did this somewhat revised and expanded rendition of the private property version of the European Enlightenment become the global hegemonic ideology at the end of the twentieth century?

While political commentators have dubbed this collection of aphorisms about the magic of the market 'the Washington Consensus', the term I prefer for this turn in global discourse is 'neo-liberalism'. The beginning of worldwide decline of the political left may have predated the revolutions of 1989 and the demise of the Soviet Union, but it was certainly also accelerated by these events. The structural basis of the rise of the globalisation project is the new level of integration reached by the global capitalist class. The internationalisation of capital has been an important part of the trend toward economic globalisation for centuries. And there have been many claims to represent the general interests of business before. Indeed every modern hegemon has made this claim. But the real integration of interests of the capitalists in each of the core states has reached a level greater than ever before in the most recent wave of economic globalisation.

This is the part of the model of a global stage of capitalism that must be taken most seriously, though it can certainly be overdone. The world-system has now reached a point at which both the old interstate system based on separate national capitalist classes, and new institutions representing the global interests of capitalists exist and are powerful simultaneously. In this light each country can be seen to have an important ruling class fraction that is allied with the transnational capitalist class.

Neo-liberalism began as the Reagan-Thatcher attack on the welfare state and labour unions. It evolved into the Structural Adjustment Policies of the International Monetary Fund and the triumphalism of the ideologues associated with global corporations after the demise of the Soviet Union. In United States foreign policy it has found expression in a new emphasis on 'democracy promotion' in the periphery and semiperiphery. Rather than propping up military dictatorships in Latin America, the emphasis has shifted toward coordinated action between the Central Intelligence Agency and the U.S. National Endowment for Democracy to promote electoral institutions in Latin America and other semiperipheral and peripheral regions (Robinson 1996). Robinson contends that the kind of 'low intensity democracy' that is promoted is best comprehended as 'polyarchy'– a regime form in which elites orchestrate a process of electoral competition and governance that legitimates state power and undercuts more radical political alternatives that might threaten the ability of national elites to maintain their wealth and power by exploiting workers and peasants. Robinson (1996) convincingly argues that polyarchy and democracy-promotion are the political forms that are most congruent with a globalised and neo-liberal world economy in which capital is given free reign to generate accumulation wherever profits are greatest.

Structural Globalisation

Human societies are composed of interaction networks and the institutions and forms of consciousness that make various kinds of interaction possible. The world-systems perspective asserts that interaction networks have been importantly intersocietal since at least the emergence of cities and states, but comparative studies reveal important intersocietal interaction networks even in systems composed entirely of nomadic hunters (Chase-Dunn and Hall 1997).

While the institutional nature of interaction networks has undergone major transformations with the evolution of social complexity and hierarchy, one important aspect of interaction networks has always been their spatial scale and the relative intensity of smaller and larger nets. Comparative research reveals that all world-systems small and large have exhibited the phenomenon of 'pulsation' in which exchange networks alternately expand and contract. For the modern world-system I will conceptualise globalisation as, in part, *changes in the intensity of international and global interactions relative to the local or national* networks. If both national level and global networks increase in intensity at the same rate, this approach does not see an increase in the globalisation of interaction. Globalisation in this structural sense is both integration and interdependence.[2]

Different kinds of interaction have long had different spatial attributes. Most world-systems are multicultural in the sense that important political/military and trade interactions link groups with very different languages and cultures. The modern world-system is mainly composed of national cultures, though the most powerful countries have long been able to impose, sell or diffuse their cultural characteristics widely, and their may now be emerging a truly global culture that is more than just the cultural reach of the most powerful national states (Meyer 1996; Boli and Thomas 1997).

Structural economic and political globalisation are conceptualised here as the differential density and power of larger versus small interaction networks and organisations. Though we do not contend that politics and economics are separate realms that can be independent objects of scientific inquiry, we do find it convenient to distinguish between political and economic forms of globalisation.

Economic globalisation means greater integration in the organisation of production, distribution and consumption of commodities in the world-economy. We are all aware that our breakfasts have been increasingly coming from distant locations. Sugar has importantly been a global commodity for centuries, in the sense that intercontinental market forces and the policies of competing states have massively affected both its conditions of production and consumption. But fresh grapes have only become global commodities since jets started transporting them between the southern and northern hemispheres. No matter that you do not eat sugar or grapes for breakfast. The energy that was used to produce whatever you eat has long been a global commodity as well, though there have been important changes in the nature of energy production, the organisational structures and ownership of energy-producing firms and the impact of state policies on energy production and consumption (Podobnik 1999).

Political globalisation is here conceptualised as the institutional form of global and inter-regional political/military organisations (including 'economic' ones such as the World Bank and the International Monetary Fund), and their strengths relative to the strengths of national states and other smaller political actors in the world-system. This is analogous to the conceptualisation of economic globalisation as the relative density and importance of larger versus smaller interaction networks.

Economic globalisation is both a long-term trend and a cyclical phenomenon.

If we calculate the ratio of international investments to investments within countries, the world economy had nearly as high a level of 'investment globalization' in 1910 as it did in 1990 (Bairoch 1996). Similarly, if we estimate the degree of trade globalisation, there has been both a long-term trend and three waves of globalisation – one in the last half of the nineteenth century, a small one from 1900 to 1929, and a large upswing from 1950 to the present (Chase-Dunn, Kawano and Brewer 2000) (see Figure 2).

AVERAGE OPENNESS TRADE GLOBALISATION (5 YEAR MOVING AVERAGE)

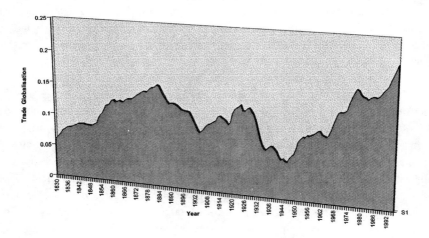

Figure 2: Average Openness Trade Globalisation, 1830-1995 (Weighted)
(Source: Chase-Dunn, Kawano and Brewer 2000).

The point here is that globalisation as international economic integration needs to be understood as part of a long-term set of processes that have characterised the world-system for centuries. This model of the structural constants, cycles and secular trends specifies the basic and normal operations of the system, and I argue elsewhere that this basic schema continues to describe the system in the current period of global capitalism (Chase-Dunn 1998).

THE SPIRAL OF CAPITALISM AND SOCIALISM

In core countries certain sectors of the working classes were able to mobilise political power and raise wages through trade unions and socialist parties. This was made possible by core capital's need for skilled and educated labour. The relatively more democratic political institutions and the development of welfare programmes were mainly based on the political efforts of skilled and organised workers (Rueschemeyer, Stephens and Stephens 1992). In some core countries the relative harmony of class relations was also supplemented by the extraction of profits from peripheral regions and the availability of cheap food and raw materials provided by core domination and exploitation of the periphery.

At some times and places the movements of core workers took a more radical turn and threatened the political hegemony of capital, but the long run outcome in the core states was not socialist revolution, but rather the construction of social democratic welfare states or the sort of business unionism that emerged in the United States.

In the periphery colonial elites used coerced labour (serfdom, slavery, indentured servitude) to produce commodities for export to the core. But resistance in the periphery from peasants and workers, as well as nationalist movements supported by small middle-class groups led to effective anti-imperialist coalitions that were able to achieve decolonisation and the rudiments of national sovereignty. These movements created anti-imperial class alliances that, after World War II, often utilised socialist ideology. But most of the resultant regimes remained quite dependent on neo-colonial relations with capitalist core states. Radical challenges to capitalism in most of the periphery were easily disrupted by overt or covert intervention. Vietnam was a significant exception.

In the world-system framework the Communist states represented efforts by popular movements in the semiperiphery and the periphery to transform the capitalist world-system into a socialist world-system, but also to catch up with core capitalism in terms of economic development. These efforts largely failed because they were not able to transcend the institutional constraints of the capitalist world-economy and because the capitalist core states were spurred to develop new technologies of production, political/military control and global market and political integration in response to the challenges posed by the Communist states. The long run relationship between capitalism and anti-capitalist movements as a spiral in which the contestants provoke each other to ever greater feats of mobilisation and integration (Boswell and Chase-Dunn 2000).

In some countries in the semiperiphery radical challenges to capitalism were able to take state power and to partially institutionalise socialist economic institutions. There were great limitations on what was possible despite the fact that there were true revolutions of workers and peasants in Russia, China, Cuba, Yugoslavia, Korea, Albania and Vietnam.

Socialism in one country was not what the Bolsheviks had in mind. They thought that there would be a world revolution against capitalism after World War I, or at least a revolution in Germany. The decision to hang on in Russia despite the failure of radical regimes to come to power elsewhere may have been a grave mistake. It required the use of both socialist ideology and substantial coercion simply to maintain Communist state power and to mobilise industrialisation, urbanisation and education to catch up with core capitalism. This contradiction was already apparent in the time of Lenin. Stalin did not look back.

It was the military part of this equation that was probably the most costly economically and politically. Military-style mass production became the model for the whole 'socialist' economy in Russia (Boswell and Peters 1990). Building and supporting a Soviet Army that was capable of halting the advance of Germany in World War II meant further concentration of power in the Communist Party, the complete elimination of democracy within the party, and the use of the Communist International as purely the instrument of Russian international interests. The humiliation of the Hitler-Stalin pact and its reversal branded Communism as a form of totalitarianism equivalent to fascism in the minds of millions of democratic socialists all over the globe, as well as playing into the hands of the ideologues of capitalism.

Chirot (1991) and Lupher (1996) argue that Stalinism was mainly a continuation of Russian bureaucratic patrimonialism or oriental despotism. I reject this sort of institutional determinism. I see both structural constraints and historical possibilities. The authoritarian outcome of the Russian revolution was not predetermined, but it was greatly conditioned by Russia's semiperipheral location and the military and economic forces that were brought to bear from the capitalist core states. I agree with Hobsbawm (1994) that this does not excuse the Stalinist repression, but our analysis leaves open the possibility of past and future systemic transformation, while the continuationist frame sees only the end of history.

The Chinese, Cuban, Korean, Yugoslavian, Albanian and Vietnamese revolutions benefited somewhat from the political space opened up by the Soviet Union. The idea that there was a real alternative to the end of history in the capitalist version of the European Enlightenment was kept alive by the existence of the Soviet Union, despite its grave imperfections. The Chinese,

Cuban, Korean, Yugoslavian, Albanian and Vietnamese revolutions were able to learn from Russian mistakes to some extent, and to try new directions and make mistakes of their own. The most obvious example was Mao's turn to the peasantry. While the Bolsheviks had treated peasants as a conservative foe (despite Lenin's analysis), thus putting the Party at odds with the majority of the Russian people, Mao embraced the peasantry as a revolutionary class. The later revolutions also benefited from the maneuverability that Soviet political/ military power in the world-system made possible.

The regimes created in Central and Eastern Europe by the Red Army after World War II are a different breed of cat. In these, socialist ideology and Stalinist development policies were imposed from outside, so they were never politically legitimate in the eyes of most of the population. This major structural fact varied to some extent depending on the strength of pre-existing socialist and communist forces before the arrival of the Red Army. The Soviet Union justified its intervention in terms of 'proletarian internationalism' and creating a buffer zone against the Germans. While the geopolitical justification was plausible from the Russian point of view, it did not help to justify the regimes of the Eastern European countries with their own populations. And the noble ideal of proletarian internationalism was besmirched by its use as a fig leaf for setting up these puppet regimes.

Jozsef Borozc's (1999: Table 1) analysis of these Eastern and Central European 'comprador' regimes details the many compromises that the Soviet overlords introduced in order to increase internal legitimacy. However given the origin of these regimes in world geopolitics, the legitimacy problem was insoluble. Russian tanks crushed the revolts, but the basic problem of legitimacy eventually led to the overthrow of every one of these regimes as soon as Gorbachev lifted the Soviet fist.

Political Implications of the World-System Perspective

Thus class struggles and anti-imperial movements have been important shapers of the institutional structures of modern capitalism for centuries. The waves of globalisation of capitalism in the twentieth century were stimulated in important ways by the challenges posed by the Leninist parties and the Communist states. Contrary to the view that history has ended, anti-capitalist movements will continue to emerge in response to expanding and intensifying capitalist development. The most recent wave of transnational economic integration and the political ideology of neo-liberal restructuring, downsizing and 'competitiveness' is provoking workers, peasants, women, indigenous groups and defenders of the biosphere to mobilise. Some of the resulting movements may employ localist and nationalist organisational structures to protect against market forces and transnational capital, but retreat into xenophobic nationalism might be a recipe for another round of world war. The only effective response will be to organise 'globalization from below' – transnational social movements with the goal of building an Earth-wide collectively rational and democratic commonwealth.

The age of U.S. hegemonic decline and the rise of post-modernist philosophy have cast the liberal ideology of the European Enlightenment (science, progress, rationality, liberty, democracy and equality) into the dustbin of totalising universalisms. It is alleged that these values have been the basis of imperialism, domination and exploitation and, thus, they should be cast out in favor of each group asserting its own set of values. Note that self-determination and a considerable dose of multiculturalism (especially regarding religion) were already central elements in Enlightenment liberalism.

The structuralist and historical materialist world-systems approach poses this problem of values in a different way. The problem with the capitalist world-system has not been with its values. The philosophy of liberalism is fine. It has quite often been an embarrassment to the pragmatics of imperial power and has frequently provided justifications for resistance to domination and exploitation. The philosophy of the enlightenment has never been a major cause of exploitation and domination. Rather, it was the military and economic power generated by capitalism that made European hegemony possible.

To humanise the world-system we may need to construct a new philosophy of democratic and egalitarian liberation. Of course, many of the principle ideals that have been the core of the Left's critique of capitalism are shared by non-European philosophies. Democracy in the sense of popular control over collective decision-making was not invented in Greece. It was a characteristic of all non-hierarchical human societies on every continent before the emergence of complex chiefdoms and states (Bollen and Paxton 1997). My point is that a new egalitarian universalism can usefully incorporate quite a lot from the old universalisms. It is not liberal ideology that caused so much exploitation and domination. Rather, it was the failure of real capitalism to live up to its own ideals of liberty and equality) in most of the world. That is the problem that progressives must solve.

A central question for any strategy of transformation is the question of agency. Who are the actors who will most vigorously and effectively resist capitalism and construct democratic socialism? Where is the most favorable terrain, the weak link, where concerted action could bear the most fruit? Samir Amin (1990, 1992) contends that the agents of socialism have been most heavily concentrated in the periphery. It is there that the capitalist world-system is most oppressive, and thus peripheral workers and peasants, the vast majority of the world proletariat, have the most to win and the least to lose.

On the other hand, Marx and many contemporary Marxists have argued that socialism will be most effectively built by the action of core proletarians. Since core areas have already attained a high level of technological development, the establishment of socialised production and distribution should be easiest in the core. And, organised core workers have had the longest experience with industrial capitalism and the most opportunity to create socialist social relations. I submit that both 'workerist' and 'Third Worldist' positions have important elements of truth, but there is another alternative, that is suggested by the structural theory of the world-system: the semiperiphery as the weak link.

Core workers may have experience and opportunity, but a sizable segment of the core working classes lack motivation because they have benefited from a non-confrontational relationship with core capital. The existence of a labour aristocracy has divided the working class in the core and, in combination with a large middle stratum, has undermined political challenges to capitalism. Also, the 'long experience' in which business unionism and social democracy have been the outcome of a series of struggles between radical workers and the labour aristocracy has created a residue of trade union practices, party structures, legal and governmental institutions, and ideological heritages which act as barriers to new socialist challenges. These conditions have changed to some extent during the last two decades as hyper-mobile capital has attacked organised labour, dismantled welfare states and downsized middle class work forces. These create new possibilities for popular movements within the core, and we can expect more confrontational popular movements to emerge as workers devise new forms of organisation (or revitalise old forms). Economic globalisation makes labour internationalism a necessity, and so we can expect to see the old idea take new forms and become more organisationally real. Even small victories in the core have important effects on peripheral and semiperipheral areas because of demonstration effects and the power of core states.

The main problem with 'Third Worldism' is not motivation, but opportunity. Democratic socialist movements that take state power in the periphery are soon beset by powerful external forces that either overthrow them or force them to abandon most of their socialist programme. Popular movements in the periphery are most usually anti-imperialist class alliances which succeed in establishing at least the trappings of national sovereignty, but not socialism. The low level of the development of the productive forces also makes it harder to establish socialist forms of accumulation, although this is not impossible in principle. It is simply harder to share power and wealth when there are very little of either. But, the emergence of democratic regimes in the periphery will facilitate new forms of mutual aid, cooperative development and popular movements once the current ideological hegemony of neoliberalism has broken down.

Semiperipheral Democratic Socialism

In the semiperiphery both motivation and opportunity exist. Semiperipheral areas, especially those in which the territorial state is large, have sufficient resources to be able to stave off core attempts at overthrow and to provide some protection to socialist institutions if the political conditions for their emergence should arise. Semiperipheral regions (e.g., Russia and China) have experienced more militant class based socialist revolutions and movements because of their intermediate position in the core/periphery hierarchy. While core exploitation of the periphery creates and sustains alliances among classes in both the core and the periphery, in the semiperiphery an intermediate world-system position undermines class alliances and provides a fruitful terrain for strong challenges to capitalism. Semiperipheral revolutions and movements are not always socialist in character, as we have seen in Iran. But, when socialist intentions are strong there are greater possibilities for real transformation than in the core or the periphery. Thus, the semiperiphery is the weak link in the capitalist world-system. It is the terrain upon which the strongest efforts to establish socialism have been made, and this is likely to be true of the future as well.

On the other hand, the results of the efforts so far, while they have undoubtedly been important experiments with the logic of socialism, have left much to be desired. The tendency for authoritarian regimes to emerge in the communist states betrayed Marx's idea of a freely constituted association of direct producers. And, the imperial control of Eastern Europe by the Russians was an insult to the idea of proletarian internationalism. Democracy within and between nations must be a constituent element of true socialism.

It does not follow that efforts to build socialism in the semiperiphery will always be so constrained and thwarted. The revolutions in the Soviet Union and the Peoples' Republic of China have increased our collective knowledge about how to build socialism despite their only partial successes and their obvious failures. It is important for all of us who want to build a more humane and peaceful world-system to understand the lessons of socialist movements in the semiperiphery, and the potential for future, more successful, forms of socialism these.

Once again the core has developed new lead industries – computers and biotechnology – and much of large-scale heavy industry, the classical terrain of strong labour movements and socialist parties, has been moved to the semiperiphery. This means that new socialist bids for state power in the semiperiphery (e.g., South Africa, Brazil, Mexico, perhaps Korea) will be much more based on an urbanised and organised proletariat in large-scale industry than the earlier semiperipheral socialist revolutions were. This should have happy consequences for the nature of new socialist states in the semiperiphery because the relationship between the city and the countryside within these countries should be less antagonistic. Less internal conflict will make more democratic socialist regimes possible, and will lessen the likelihood of core interference. The global expansion of communications has increased the salience of events in the semiperiphery for audiences in the core and this may serve to dampen core state intervention into the affairs of democratic socialist semiperipheral states.

Some critics of the world-systems perspective have argued that emphasis on the structural importance of global relations leads to political do-nothingism while we wait for socialism to emerge at the world level. The world-system perspective does indeed encourage us to examine global level constraints (and opportunities), and to allocate our political energies in ways which will be most productive when these structural constraints are taken into account. It does not follow that building socialism at the local or national level is futile, but we must expend resources on transorganisational, transnational and international socialist relations. The environmental and feminist movements are now in the lead and labour needs to follow their example.

A simple domino theory of transformation to democratic socialism is misleading and inadequate. Suppose that all firms or all nation-states adopted socialist relations internally but continued to relate to one another through competitive commodity production and political/military conflict. Such a hypothetical world-system would still be dominated by the logic of capitalism, and that logic would be likely to repenetrate the 'socialist' firms and states. This cautionary tale advises us to invest political resources in the construction of multilevel (transorganisational, transnational and international) socialist relations lest we simply repeat the process of driving capitalism to once again perform an end run by operating on a yet larger scale.

A Democratic Socialist World-System

These considerations lead us to a discussion of socialist relations at the level of the whole world system. The emergence of democratic collective rationality (socialism) at the world-system level is likely to be a slow process. What might such a world-system look like and how might it emerge? It is obvious that such a system would require a democratically-controlled world federation that can effectively adjudicate disputes among nation-states and eliminate warfare (Goldstein 1988). This is a bare minimum. There are many other problems that badly need to be coordinated at the global level: ecologically sustainable development, a more balanced and egalitarian approach to economic growth, and the lowering of population growth rates.

The idea of global democracy is important for this struggle. The movement needs to push toward a kind of popular democracy that goes beyond the election of representatives to include popular participation in decision-making at every level. Global democracy can only be real if it is composed of civil societies and national states that are themselves truly democratic (Robinson 1996). And global democracy is probably the best way to lower the probability of another way among core states. For that reason it is in everyone's interest.

How might such a global social democracy come into existence? The process of the growth of international organisations that has been going on for at least 200 years will eventually result in a world state if we are not blown up first. Even international capitalists have some uses for global regulation, as is attested by the International Monetary Fund and the World Bank. Capitalists do not want the massive economic and political upheavals that would likely accompany collapse of the world monetary system, and so they support efforts to regulate 'ruinous' competition and beggar-thy-neighbourism. Some of these same capitalists also fear nuclear holocaust, and so they may support a strengthened global government which can effectively adjudicate conflicts among nation-states.

Of course, capitalists know as well as others that effective adjudication means the establishment of a global monopoly of legitimate violence. The process of state formation has a long history, and the king's army needs to be bigger than any combination of private armies that might be brought against him. While the idea of a world state may be a frightening specter to some, I am optimistic about it for several reasons. First, a world state is probably the most direct and stable way to prevent nuclear holocaust, a desideratum that must be at the top of everyone's list. Secondly, the creation of a global state that can peacefully adjudicate disputes among nations will transform the existing interstate system. The interstate system is the political structure that stands behind the maneuverability of capital and its ability to escape organised workers and other social constraints on profitable accumulation. While a world state may at first be dominated by capitalists, the very existence of such a state will provide a single focus for struggles to socially regulate investment decisions and to create a more balanced, egalitarian and ecologically sound form of production and distribution.

The progressive response to neoliberalism needs to be organised at national, international and global levels if it is to succeed. Democratic socialists should be wary of strategies that focus only on economic nationalism and national autarchy as a response to economic globalisation. Socialism in one country has never worked in the past and it certainly will not work in a world that is more interlinked than ever before. The old forms of progressive internationalism were somewhat premature, but internationalism has finally become not only desirable but necessary. This does not mean that local, regional and national-level struggles are irrelevant. They are just as relevant as they always have been. But, they need to also have a global strategy and global-level cooperation lest they be isolated and defeated. Communications technology can certainly be an important tool for the kinds of long-distance interactions that will be required for truly international cooperation and coordination among popular movements. It would be a mistake to pit global strategies against national or local ones. All fronts should be the focus of a coordinated effort.

W. Warren Wagar (1996) has proposed the formation of a 'World Party' as an instrument of 'mundialization' – the creation of a global socialist commonwealth. His proposal has been critiqued from many angles – as a throwback to the Third International, and et cetera. I suggest that Wagar's idea is a good one, and that a party of the sort he is advocating will indeed emerge and that it will contribute a great deal toward bringing about a more humane world-system. Self-doubt and post-modern reticence may make such a direct approach appear Napoleonic. It is certainly necessary to learn from past mistakes, but this should not prevent us debating the pros and cons of positive action.

The international segment of the world capitalist class is indeed moving slowly toward global state formation. The World Trade Organisation is only the latest element in this process. Rather than simply oppose this move with a return to nationalism, progressives should make every effort to organise social and political globalisation, and to democratise the emerging global state. We need to prevent the normal operation of the interstate system and future hegemonic rivalry from causing another war among core powers (e.g, Wagar 1992; see also Chase-Dunn and Bornschier 1998). And, we need to shape the emerging world society into a global democratic commonwealth based on collective rationality, liberty and equality. This possibility is present in existing and evolving structures. The agents are all those who are tired of wars and hatred and who desire a humane, sustainable and fair world-system. This is certainly a majority of the people of the Earth.

GLOBALISATION FROM BELOW OR DELINKING?: THE GUATEMALAN CASE

The strategy of globalisation from below means linking up women's movements, labour struggles, indigenous movements and agrarian reform movements within regions and globally. Labour movements in Guatemala have already been partially successful in forging new implementations of the old notion of labour internationalism, and in mobilising support from the United States and other core countries based on concerns about human rights and the labour provisions of international trade agreements (Frundt 1987; Armbruster 1998).

The problems of cross-border labour organising and international labour solidarity are great, but the new organisational terrain of global capitalism requires new strategies (Stevis 1998). Because the globalisation project has abrogated social compacts between business and labour within core countries, especially in the United States, there are new possibilities for cooperation among Latin American and US workers and their organisations. John Sweeney, the president of the United States American Federation of Labour- Council of Industrial Organizations (AFL-CIO) visited the leaders of independent unions in Mexico City. This willingness to look at new alliances is a welcome relief from the long-standing Cold War approach to labour internationalism that was AFL-CIO practice until recently. Armbruster (1998) reports that help from the AFL-CIO was an important factor in the organising success of the workers at the Phillips-Van Heusen plant in Guatemala.[3]

Women's movements in El Salvador have made important efforts to link their struggles with sympathetic groups in other Central American countries and in the United States. Indeed, these groups have explicitly advocated globalisation from below. In Mexico the resurgent electoral left, the agrarian movements in Chiapas and Guerrero, and independent trade unions have found that common opposition to neo-liberalism is a uniting force. Some of the popular leaders in Mexico have made an effort to mobilise support from the United States, but not many yet see this as part of a larger effort to democratise both Mexico and the global system.

The emerging popular responses to globalisation and neo-liberalism face an important and potentially divisive issue. One possibility for mobilising against global capitalism is 'delinking' and self-reliance. Another, and very different, approach is to respond to global capitalism by building global democracy. The world-systems perspective has much to offer regarding the consideration of the value of these options.

The neo-liberals have pronounced withdrawal from the capitalist world economy as unthinkable and many popular leaders seem to agree. The wonders of technology and communications are alleged to be the highest values, and only by playing the game of competitiveness can a developing country have access to these. But some critics are now questioning whether the 'necessity' of openness to the global economy is worth the costs. This is a healthy response because it unmasks many of the ideological presuppositions of neo-liberalism. People need housing, clean water, and healthy food. It is not necessary to be able to program your hair dryer from your car radio. The hyperbole of workers' needs to be popped, like the financial bubbles that abound in the virtual space of global money.

The notion that self-reliance is an anachronism needs to be examined in historical perspective. In long-run panorama, protectionism and national mobilisation of development have been useful and successful strategies in the past. The semiperipheral national societies that later became hegemons in the Europe-centred world-system all utilised tariff protectionism and state-sponsored mobilisation to move themselves up the value-added hierarchy. The communist states used self-reliance and socialist ideology to try to establish a new mode of accumulation, though they ended in trying hardest to catch up with core capitalism. According to neo-liberal liturgy free trade and the free movement of capital generates the most optimum development for all. But the successful practice of upward mobility in the world-system demonstrates the value that state intervention and protection of certain activities can have (Evans 1995). The trajectories of the communist states are also alleged to prove the worthlessness of state planning and self-reliant economic nationalism.

I would argue that these strategies did indeed work, though the utopias they were intended to forge did not actually result. Instead capitalism expanded and reincorporated the self-reliant. This picture of challenge and response needs to consider the higher degree of economic and political integration of the current world-system. It is undoubtedly more costly to drop out of a more integrated system than to drop out of a less integrated one. So the costs of going it alone have increased. These costs have always been higher for small countries such as those in Central America. This is why small countries have a greater interest in cross-border cooperation among popular movements. But the institutions of nationalism and the existing rules of the interstate system make such cooperation difficult.

Popular movements in Guatemala face the issue of whether or not to focus on local and national-level institutions and alliances, or on international and global ones. Would it be more productive to focus on gaining increasing say in the national state and using national sovereignty as a means of providing protection from global market and geopolitical forces, or on the other hand, to make efforts to reform or revolutionise the world-system by making alliances and constructing institutions that promote popular democracy on an international regional or global scale? The national route has a long history and is supported by the existing institutions, while the international route is little understood and is in great need of imagination. Global democracy seems to be only a pair of words to most people in the world today. It can be defined abstractly, but what would it mean in practice?

As within countries, democracy is a contested concept. Robinson's (1996) critique of polyarchy within countries badly needs to be extended to a critique of global-level political institutions such as the International Monetary Fund and the World Bank. International regional and global political institutions should be governed democratically by the peoples whose lives they affect. This would mean popular participation in the election of representatives and in the decision-making of these institutions. Indeed, though the United Nations verification mission (MINUGUA) has played a valuable role in the Guatemalan peace process, the UN is itself in need of democratisation.

Globalisation from below means spending organisational and movement resources on alliances and institution building at the international regional and global levels. In practice neither a purely national strategy nor a purely global one would work for Guatemala or any other country in the contemporary context. So the real problem is to decide upon the mix and to pursue coordinated and complimentary approaches.

Polyarchy and Beyond in Guatemala

Another issue in the Guatemalan situation is raised by Robinson's analysis. Guatemala has not yet really achieved polyarchy, let alone real democracy. Polyarchy, while it may be largely a smoke screen for continued domination and inequality, is undoubtedly better than a country run by the military and over-run with death squads. The implementation of the Peace Accords has gone very slowly. Some observers have wondered if the current government is seriously committed to implementation. But the main problem is that the neo-liberal elite fraction is weak, so it cannot afford to push too hard on the military or the agro-exporting elite families who have mounted a tremendous resistance to the peace process. And indeed the neo-liberals share many interests in common with the older landed elite. Neither is anxious to pay taxes.

Globalisation from below in concert with popular forces in other Central American countries and in Mexico would naturally be organised around opposition to neo-liberal policies and institutions. Regional-level demands such as a minimum wage for maquiladora workers could be an important component of this strategy. Opposition to neo-liberal policies could also serve as a unifying strategy for different kinds of popular movements within Guatemala.

It might be supposed that in the Guatemalan situation it would make tactical sense for the popular forces to ally with the transnational neo-liberals and the IFIs in the short run in order to attain concessions from the agro-export dynasties regarding the fiscal strength of the state and demilitarisation. The implementation of the Peace Accords has at least the possibility of establishing the trappings of an electoral democracy with substantial participation from popular sectors. Demilitarisation and the establishment of the rule of law may not be true democracy, but they are certainly better for the popular classes than the situation of terror that has long existed and that still exists in some regions of the country. Under these conditions one might conclude that the campaign against neo-liberalism should be postponed.

Like the local/global conundrum discussed above, this problem may seem worse than it actually is. The popular movements can tacitly cooperate with those domestic neo-liberals who are supporting demilitarisation, state solvency and implementation of the peace accords, as well as with the IFIs. Recognition that neo-liberals are better than death squads is not so hard to explain to the grass roots.

This does not mean that popular movements should keep quiet. I do not agree with O'Donnell and Schmitter's (1988) conclusion that popular forces should refrain from pressing socioeconomic or political demands until the transition to polyarchy is consolidated. Robinson (personal communication) argues, and I agree, that strong popular movements in Guatemala can provide the support that the global and local neo-liberals need to push through peace accord implementation.

Once electoral democracy with popular participation is firmly in place the campaign against neo-liberal policies can commence in earnest. In the meantime the popular movements need to learn about the history of the world-system and the globalisation project. This, and the pursuit of further international popular alliances, will make it possible for Guatemalans to benefit from, and contribute to, globalisation from below. Global democracy begins at home.

POSTCOMMUNISM

The demise of the Soviet Union and the adoption of pro-marketisation policies by the Chinese Communist Party led to the declared triumph of Reaganism-Thacherism as global neo-liberalism. The market is the regulator of both first and last resort. Policies of deregulation and privatisation were accepted in nearly every corner of the Earth, and socialism/communism was declared a dead body. At the ideological level this was a massive shift. In most core states the gains of the labour movement and the institutions of the welfare state were rolled back or severely compromised.

The policies of deregulation, privatisation and marketisation were introduced in different ways in the post-communist states. In the Soviet Union Gorbachev's moves toward *glasnost and perestroika* sparked national separatism among the non-Russian peoples of the Soviet Union. A failed coup to replace Gorbachev in 1991 instead led to the fall of one-party rule. It was replaced by a reformist regime that has made some efforts to introduce markets, privatisation and deregulation. To some extent the former Communist managerial elite has transformed itself into a new capitalist class, but this class is also populated by others who have been able to use their political connections to gain control over profitable sectors of the economy.

The former structure of redistribution has mostly not been disassembled, but it is bankrupt. And little in the way of a functioning market economy has replaced it. The political process has succeeded in bringing off some fair popular elections, but these have not resulted in a legitimate government with an effective policy. At least for now the consequence is an economic disaster that may soon lead to a political disaster. The former Communist Party is sufficiently weakened that it cannot lead, but not so weak that it cannot stalemate the reformers. It may be that crisis and corruption will drive the populace to accept the order provided by charismatic nationalism of the sort that Zhiranowsky would provide. That kind of regime would not be likely to make much of a contribution to the construction of global democracy and indeed it might threaten world peace or implode.

In China, it was the Communist Party itself that introduced marketisation policies. The old guard also learned from Gorbachev's mistakes. Rather than trying democracy first, they tried capitalism. To follow this road the gerontocracy found it necessary, in 1989, to order a carefully-picked contingent of the

'Peoples Liberation Army' to slaughter the students on Tienamen Square. Having themselves been on the Long March, the elders had the grit to give these orders, and they eventually found soldiers who would do the dirty work. While the will to rule by force was largely gone from the Communist Party of the Soviet Union in 1991 when their moment came, it was Yeltsin on top of the tank who carried the day.

The Chinese path of reform has been, until now, much more successful in its achievement of rapid economic growth. Some of this has been due to the access that China has managed to negotiate for its goods in the American market. But, much of it has been due to the timing of the reforms in the policy cycle of building socialism that had been the trajectory of Maoist China. Mao had long understood that mobilising millions of people depended on the cyclical shift back and forth between moral and material incentives. Slogans and cheerleading can get people going, but the effect wears off and the campaigners need to rest, and so material incentives return as a method for getting things done. This insight was built into the policy cycles by which socialist industrialisation and agricultural development had been mobilised in China since the revolution. The shift to marketisation and its 'moralization' by Party slogans such as 'Enrich Yourself' unleashed a huge flurry of economic activity at the roots of Chinese society. This was especially true in the countryside where decommunalisation released huge underutilised reserves of rural capital, labour and land. This was a potent combination of both moral and material incentives.

In Russia the Bolsheviks were long dead and the processes of informalisation, the second economy, barter, reciprocity among kin and friendship networks, and the relegation of socialist ideology to ritualistic political and academic rhetoric did not provide such a fertile loam for the seeds of market freedom. In relation to dismal productivity, Soviet incomes were relatively high, even in the countryside. Crime, corruption and disorganisation have prevented productivity gains, leaving real wages to fall where markets spread. After the Soviet demise the Russians expanded upon informalisation of all kinds, but this did not produce a burst of economic growth as it did in China. The irony here is that, to a large extent it was the continuing organisational strength of the Chinese Communist Party that was able to mobilise marketised economic development in China, whereas a much weaker party in Russia could not do the same job.

The prodigious academic literature on postcommunism has attempted to comprehend the social and organisational changes that have occurred within the postcommunist societies in terms of a hypothesised transition from socialism to capitalism, and the implications of these changes for important theoretical issues in economic and institutional sociology (Nee and Stark 1989; Nee and Liedka 1997; Keister 1998). This literature has been quite fruitful for economic sociology, but with a few noteworthy exceptions there has been very little effort to place the phenomena of postcommunism into world historical perspective. The analysis of Chinese business groups within China and in the Chinese diaspora has given new life to the study of economic networks and social capital, as well as considerations of possible newly emergent forms of capitalism that could serve as the organisational model for the next epoch of global capitalism (Arrighi 1994). These topics have also been interwoven with considerations of the possibility of an emergent global hegemony of East Asia. The recent 'crisis' there, and new, or rather renewed, fault-finding about 'croney capitalism', might seem to have put the lid on all this. But the seers of East Asian rise (e.g. Frank 1998) make much of the fact that a global economic crisis began in Asia for the first time in centuries. The argument here is that, as in 1929, global crises begin at the center, not in the periphery.

The best work on postcommunism that utilises world-systems concepts has been done on Central and Eastern Europe (Borocz 1992,1993,1999; Borocz and Smith 1995). While Borocz's analysis is broadly comparative, historically deep and develops important new world-systems concepts such as 'dual dependency', it is unfortunate that equally talented social scientific effort has not also been directed toward the ex-Soviet Union or China. Borocz's (1999) most recent study is careful in the ways that it pays attention to the important differences as well as the analytic similarities of the processes of social change in the Central and Eastern European countries. His pithy characterisation of the postcommunist Eastern European regimes as 'auctioneer states' summarises and compares the literature on emerging combinant property forms and class structures in these countries.

Borocz argues that most of the Eastern European countries are downwardly mobile in the larger core/periphery hierarchy because their former none-to-high situation of dual dependency (caught between Soviet imperialism and dependence on Western finance capital) is being replaced by an even greater degree of penetration by direct investment from global megacorporations. He also emphasises that the breakup of many of the former states, which he argues was mainly motivated by hopes of early entry into the European Union, has increased the geopolitical volatility of the region and exacerbated the economic crisis. Borocz (1999) also cites comparative evidence on declines in life expectancy and the UN's Human Development Index that support his contention that Russia and the Central and Eastern European postcommunist societies are moving down in the core/periphery hierarchy.

I agree that most of the postcommunist states in Central and Eastern Europe and the ex-Soviet Union are likely to experience downward mobility in the core/periphery hierarchy, but some of these states (perhaps the former East Germany, the Czech Republic, Hungary and Poland) may succeed in becoming incorporated into an expanded core region centred in the European Union in the next 20 years. Thus I predict a future bifurcation process in the development of the postcommunist states of Central and Eastern Europe with most experiencing peripheralisation, but with a few managing to successfully move into the European core.

Globalisation from below in the postcommunist societies

The question I pose here is 'what will be the role of the postcommunist societies in the struggle for global democracy?' In general I doubt that the postcommunist societies will be leaders in the future struggle for global democracy. Semiperipheral locations in the world-system have been, and will continue to be, fertile grounds for innovations and organisational implementations that can transform the logic of social development and lead to upward mobility in the core/periphery hierarchy. This phenomenon of transformational action emerging from the semiperiphery can be observed throughout the history of human social evolution, as argued and demonstrated by Chase-Dunn and Hall (1997). In the modern world-system those capitalist states that have expanded and deepened the commodification of the world-system (that is, the Dutch Republic, the United Kingdom and the United States) have all been former semiperipheral countries.

But not all semiperipheral societies are transformative and upwardly mobile. It is our contention that the postcommunist societies are probably less likely to be innovators and leaders in future progressive transformations than other semiperipheral societies that do not carry the political baggage of having gone through a period of Communist government. I also predict that those postcommunist societies that did not have real revolutions of their own will be even less likely to take politically progressive paths. The legacy of having had Communist regimes imposed from without has created a strong antipathy to collectivist-rational organisational forms in these societies. This historical legacy even goes beyond the aversion toward state intervention that is a centerpiece of neo-liberalism.

In addition, the processes of shock therapy in the implementation of market reforms have often led to political changes that are in the wrong direction from the point of view of democratic collective rationality. In Hungary, for example, the Hungarian Workers Party and its government had developed a system of production-based regulation of environmental degradation, a system that has been advocated as a positive move toward sustainable development by industrial ecologists. This approach was dismantled and replaced by a much less effective end-of-pipe system of (de)regulation in the period of transition (Gille 2000).

The efforts by Communist parties to bring about gender equality (e.g. professional jobs for women, child care facilities, etc.) were criticised by feminists for the aspects of patriarchy that remained, but the reactions against these institutions that have accompanied deregulation – example the dismantling of day care for children – have accompanied and facilitated a massive reassertion of patriarchy in most of the postcommunist societies.

Several analysts of postcommunism have feared (or hoped) that the economic crisis of 'transition' might provoke populist or authoritarian movements that would react against the forces of capitalist globalisation (e.g. Przeworski 1991). It has been supposed that the type of IMF (International Monetary Fund) riots that occurred in Latin America (Walton and Seddon 1994) might emerge in Eastern Europe. Greskovits (1997) notes that popular collective resistance to capitalist globalisation has mainly not emerged in Eastern Europe and he seeks to explain the differences in this regard with Latin America.

Greskovits develops ideas from the social movement literature (Tilly 1978; Tarrow 1994) about the historically conditioned nature of popular collective responses to economic crises. The 'repertoire of contention' literature claims that the frames and organisational and tactical alternatives that are employed in resistance are specific to the regional and national histories in each case. Greskovits also utilises Albert Hirschman's typology of 'exit, voice and loyalty' to understand the relatively low degree of contention in the Eastern European postcommunist societies in response to the crisis of 'transition'. It is Greskovits' claim that the historical consequence of patterns of resistance in Eastern Europe formed during the period of Soviet domination have led to the channeling of more recent resistance into individualist and informal 'exit' paths such as capital flight, hoarding, unsecured borrowing and remittance withholding rather than the exercise of public voice.

While I agree that the institutionalisation of informality and the second economy explains a large part of the economic differences between China and the ex-Soviet countries, I am skeptical of Greskovits's claim that this also explains why Eastern European populations have not mobilised against capitalist globalisation. For one thing, the repertoire of contention in Eastern Europe during the Soviet age did include strikes and rebellions, especially in Poland,

Hungary and Czechoslovakia. It is more likely to be the ideological and institutional aspects of historical legacies that better explain Latin American, Eastern European and Russian responses to the increased dependency and peripheralisation that has resulted from capitalist globalisation. Knowledge of organisational strategies and tactics fly around the world rather quickly during the modern age. These are not entirely, or even largely, matters of local habit. But what also flies around the world quickly is the ideology of the dead body of socialism, leaving globalised capitalism as the best world that is possible. This coordinated glorification and vilification resonates differently in distinct political and institutional contexts, and it is these differences that we propose will shape where the strongest anti-systemic movements will emerge within the semiperiphery and the periphery.

It is my contention that democratic socialist ideas for transnational alliances will be more successful in mobilising people in those semiperipheral states that have not experienced Communist regimes. So the main contrast here is between all the postcommunist societies and the other semiperipheral countries. These differences are not ones of tactics, but rather of goals and conceptualisations of shared interests. Transnationally organised labour in coalition with women's, environmental and indigenous movements will eventually coalesce into a coordinated global movement led by a global party of democratic socialists.[4]

The idea of democratic and egalitarian collective rationality is not a new idea. It is basically the Left version of the European Enlightenment and it resonates with populist and egalitarian religious ideologies that are subtraditions of many civilisations and dominant traditions in most tribal and foraging societies.[5] These ideas are not new. And the word we use to label them does not really matter. But the very notion of egalitarian collective rationality is radically contested by neoliberalism. And that challenge resonates differentially with the political cultures that have been created by the historical sequences of different countries in the twentieth century.

It is my main prediction that the next wave of anti-systemic movements will emerge most strongly in the semiperiphery. The most effective of these will be transnational movements that will act to create 'globalization from below' – the construction of collectively rational and democratic global institutions to manage and regulate the world economy, analogous to the nineteenth century movements to democratise national states. A major player in coordinating these movements will be a global political party – some kind of World Party or Network – that is dedicated to the building of a global democratic commonwealth. World citizens from all countries will participate in these movements and this party, but its main organisational support is likely to come from semiperipheral countries such as Brazil, Mexico, Korea and India. These countries do not carry the ideological and institutional baggage that the pioneers (and the victims) of state socialism bear. Their citizens and institutional structures are freer to innovate new forms of organisation and ideology that can benefit from the lessons of the Communist states without being drowned by the heritages that those states bear.

This pattern of uneven development and 'advantages of backwardness' is rather typical of human social evolution. This is part of the reason why old core regions decline and semiperipheral regions emerge, so that the leading edge of evolution moves. The new twist here is that we are differentiating among semiperipheral players themselves rather than contrasting them with core or periphery.

It is also necessary to differentiate success in the global capitalist system from transformational action that contributes to building a more democratic and egalitarian world-system. While Russia and the Eastern European countries are experiencing downward mobility, China is arguably poised to become an important 'emerging market' that some claim might challenge the hegemony of Western capitalism. We are somewhat skeptical about China's possibilities in this regard, especially in the absence of a strong alliance between Japan and China. A Japan-China alliance is unlikely in the opinion of those who are familiar with the history of antagonisms and current public opinion in both of these countries. The careful study by Weede (1999) implies that China has a reasonable shot at moving up in the ranks of the semiperiphery, but we do not see China or East Asia as having a high potential for achieving hegemony in the global system.

As to China's potential for contributing to globalisation from below, it suffers from most of the same problems that the other postcommunist societies do. As marketisation and individualism grows, there will be considerable opposition to socialist ideas because of their association with an authoritarian state. In addition, the ideas of democratic collective rationality are suffering great dilution and confusion because of the current policy of promoting capitalism within an ideological framework that still sanctifies socialism. And the fascination with the slow but eventual establishment of representative Western style democracy and the real possibilities for successful capitalism will make China an unlikely context for the emergence of new antisystemic movements. The same logic applies to those countries in Central and Eastern Europe who may manage to move into the European core in the next decades. The prospect of success within capitalism may undercut support for antisystemic movements.

I do not mean to say that no support for the new wave of global democracy will come from the postcommunist societies. Just as individuals and groups in the core and periphery will contribute, so will some from the postcommunist societies be able to transcend their local historical circumstances. Indeed, these will be needed to provide close testimony and knowledge of the positive and negative aspects of the Communist states and to constitute a representative basis for the World Party Network.

Within the category of postcommunist societies there are also important factors that will affect the strength of support for antisystemic movements. I have emphasised the important differences between those societies who had indigenous socialist revolutions versus those that had Communist regimes imposed from abroad. I suppose the neither of these will be hotbeds of the World Party, but the victims of 'social imperialism' are even less likely to give a balanced consideration to the strategy of globalisation from below. I have already mentioned the effects of upward mobility within global capitalism as negatively impacting antisystemic support. The converse would suggest that downward mobility would, other things equal, produce radical movements. But I can also imagine that a sort of J-curve might operate here, in which those who are near to upward mobility, or those that experience periods in which upward mobility seems to be occurring, might react to a downturn by producing a strong contingent of the global movement. It might also be supposed that recent socialist revolutions might be a differentiating factor, and so perhaps Cuba or Vietnam might be more likely than Russia to support new radical alternatives. More recent revolutions have generally not devolved to corruption to the same extent as older ones, and so disenchantment with collectivist ideas may not be so strong. But these finer points are admittedly controversial, as with all small differences.

In conclusion, the main point is that the semiperiphery remains the weak link of global capitalism – the structural region where the contradictions between core and periphery and between classes intersect powerfully to generate antisystemic movements. But I also add that the legacy of having already generated such movements in the past means that they are less likely to be generated in the same place in the future. I do not expect antisystemic movements to take state power through revolutionary upheavals again. Rather, the much larger proletariats of the non-postcommunist semiperipheral countries and the availability of support from allied groups in the core and the periphery will make it possible for these movements to win legal elections. This path will have a much better chance of avoiding the pitfalls of authoritarianism and war. That is why I am optimistic about the prospects for democratic socialism. But, as before, socialism in one country will not work. The semiperipheral socialist governments of the future will necessarily have to join the transnational movements for globalisation from below.

Endnotes

1. Shannon (1996) provides a helpful overview of the world-systems perspective as applied to the modern system.
2. While integration and interdependence overlap, they are not exactly the same. Two entities may be linked by some kind of frequent interaction, but they may not be interdependent if the frequent interactions are not important. The exchange of food or other strategic raw materials is always more important than the exchange of luxury gods. Thus it is desirable to consider both the amount of exchange and what is exchanged.
3. Unfortunately this instance of proletarian internationalism was undone by Phillips-Van Heusen's recent exit from Guatemala.
4. By socialism I simply mean democratic, egalitarian and collective rationality with regard to human interactions and relations with the biosphere. The word 'socialism' is not necessary, and is itself an oxymoron when applied to the world as a whole. I do not claim that this term is the cause of the differences that we predict will affect where support will come for globalization from below. But perhaps 'global democracy' would be a better short form for democratic collective rationality.
5. Bollen and Paxton (1997) show that, in terms of egalitarian participation in collective decision-making, hunter-gatherer societies were much more democratic than the Athenian state that is alleged to be the institutional ancestor of modern Western democracies. The significance of this is that all human societies are ancestors of hunter-gatherers.

References

Armbruster, Ralph, 'Cross-Border Labour Organizing in the Garment and Automobile Industries: The Phillips Van-Heusen and Ford Cuautitlan Cases' *Journal of World-Systems Research* 4 (1998) pp. 20-41. http://csf.colorado.edu/wsystems/jwsr.html.

Arrighi Giovanni, *The Long Twentieth Century*. (London: Verso, 1994).

Arrighi Giovanni and Beverly Silver, *Chaos and Governance in the Modern World-System: Comparing Hegemonic Transitions.* (Minneapolis: University of Minnesota Press, 1999).

Bairoch, Paul, 'Globalization Myths and Realities: One Century of External Trade and Foreign Investment', in Robert Boyer and Daniel Drache eds., *States Against Markets: The Limits of Globalization,* (London and New York: Routledge, 1996).

Bollen, Kenneth A. and Pamela M. Paxton, 'Democracy before Athens,' in Manus Midlarsky ed. *Inequality, Democracy and Economic Development.* (Cambridge: Cambridge University Press, 1997) p 13-44.

Borocz, Jozsef, 'Dual Dependency and Property Vacuum: Social Change on the State Socialist Semiperiphery.' *Theory and Society,* 21 (1992) pp.77-104.

Bornschier and Christopher Chase-Dunn, eds. *The Future of Global Conflict.* (London: Sage, 1999).

Boswell, Terry and Christopher Chase-Dunn, *The Spiral of Capitalism and Socialism: Toward Global Democracy.* (Boulder: Lynne Rienner, 2000).

Boswell, Terry and Ralph Peters, 'State Socialism and the Industrial Divide in the World Economy: A comparative essay on the rebellions in Poland and China.' *Critical Sociology* 17:1 (1990) pp. 3-35.

Brenner, Aaron, 'International rank-and-file solidarity: labour's democratic response to globalization'. Paper presented at the annual meeting of the International Studies Association, Washington DC, February 20, 1999.

Chase-Dunn, Christopher, ed., *Socialist States in the World-System.* (Beverly Hills: Sage Publications, 1982).

_____, *Global Formation: Structures of the World-Economy* (2nd edition.) (Lanham, MD: Rowman and Littlefield, 1998).

Chase-Dunn, Christopher, Yukio Kawano and Benjamin Brewer, 'Trade globalization since 1795: waves of integration in the world-system'. *American Sociological Review,* (February 2000).

Chase-Dunn, Christopher, 'Guatemala in the global system' *Journal of Interamerican Studies and World Affairs* 42:4 (2000) pp.109-126.

Chase-Dunn, Christopher and Bruce Podobnik, 'The next world war: world-system cycles and trends' in Volker Bornschier and Christopher Chase-Dunn eds. *The Future of Global Conflict.* (London: Sage, 1999).

Chirot, Daniel, ed., 1991 *The Crisis of Leninism and the Decline of the Left: the Revolutions of 1989* (Seattle: WA. University of Washington Press, 1991).

Eckstein, Susan, *Back from the future: Cuba under Castro.* (Princeton, NJ: Princeton University Press, 1994).

Engels, Frederic, *Socialism: Utopian and Scientific. (1935).*

Evans, Peter, *Embedded Autonomy: States and Industrial Transformation.* (Princeton, NJ: Princeton University Press, 1995).

Frank, Andre Gunder, *Reorient: Global Economy in the Asian Age.* (Berkeley: University of California Press, 1998).

Frundt, Henry J., *Refreshing Pauses: Coca-Cola and Human Rights in Guatemala.* (New York: Praeger, 1987).

Gille, Zsuzsa, 'Legacy of waste or wasted legacy?: the end of industrial ecology in post-socialist Hungary' in Arthur PJ. Mol and David A. Sonnenfeld (eds.) *Ecological Modernization Around the World.* (London: Frank Cas, 2000) pp.203-234.

Greskovits, Bela, 'Social responses to neoliberal reforms in Eastern Europe' in Manus Midlasky ed., *Inequality, Democracy and Economic Development.* (Cambridge: Cambridge University Press, 1997) pp.269-289.

Gordon, David, 'The global economy: new edifice or crumbling foundation?' *New Left Review* 168 (1988) pp.24-64.

Harvey, David, *The Condition of Postmodernity.* (Cambridge, MA.: Blackwell, 1989).

Harvey, David, 'Globalization in question.' *Rethinking Marxism* 8:4 (1995) pp.1-17.

Henige, David P., *Colonial Governors from the Fifteenth Century to the Present.* (Madison, WI.: University of Wisconsin Press, 1970).

Jonas, Susanne, *The Battle for Guatemala: Rebels, Death Squads and U.S. Power.* (Boulder, CO: Westview, 1991).

Keck, Margaret E. and Kathryn Sinkink, *Activists Beyond Borders: Advocacy Networks in International Politics.* (Ithaca: Cornell University Press, 1998).

Keister, Lisa A., 'Engineering growth: business group structure and firm performance in China's transition economy' *American Journal of Sociology* 104:2 (September 1998) pp.404-440.

Lipietz, Alain, *Mirages and Miracles: The Crises of Global Fordism* . (London: Verso, 1987).

Lipset, Seymour Martin, 'No third way: a comparative perspective on the Left', in Daniel Chirot ed. *The Crisis of Leninism and the Decline of the Left: the Revolutions of 1989.* (Seattle, WA: University of Washington Press, 1991) pp. 183-232.

Lupher, Mark, *Power Restructuring in China and Russia* (Boulder, CO: Westview, 1996).

Mander, Jerry and Edward Goldsmith, eds., *The Case Against The Global Economy: and For a Turn Toward the Local.* (San Francisco: Sierra Club Books, 1996).

Markoff, John, *Waves of Democracy: Social Movements and Political Change.* (Thousand Oaks, CA: Pine Forge Press, 1996).

McMichael, Philip, *Development and Social Change: A Global Perspective.* (Thousand Oaks, CA: Pine Forge, 1996).

Mittelman, James H., ed, *Globalization: Critical Reflections.* (Boulder, CO: Lynne Rienner, 1996).

Murphy, Craig, *International Organization and Industrial Change: Global Governance Since 1850.* (New York: Oxford, 1994).

Hobsbawm, Eric, *The Age of Extremes: A History of the World, 1914-1991.* (New York: Pantheon, 1994).

Nee, Victor and Raymond V. Liedka, 'Markets and inequality in the transition from state Socialism' in Manus Midlarsky, ed., *Inequality, Democracy and Economic Development.* Cambridge: Cambridge University Press, 1997) pp.206-226.

Nee, Victor and David Stark, *Remaking the Economic Institutions of Socialism: China and Eastern Europe.* (Stanford: Stanford University Press, 1989).

Podobnik, Bruce, 'Global Energy Shifts: States, Firms and Social Unrest in the Evolution of Commercial Energy Industries'. Ph.D dissertation, Sociology, (Johns Hopkins University, 1999).

Przeworski, Adam, *Democracy and the Market: Political and Economic Reforms in Eastern Europe and Latin America.* (Cambridge: Cambridge University Press, 1991).

Robinson, William I., *Promoting Polyarchy: Globalization, US Intervention and Hegemony.* (Cambridge: Cambridge University Press, 1996).

Robinson, William I, 'A case study of globalization processes in the Third World: a transnational agenda in Nicaragua'. *Global Society* 2:1 (1997) pp. 61-91.

Robinson, William I., 'Neo-liberalism, the global elite and the Guatemalan transition: A critical macrostructural analysis' in C. Chase-Dunn, S. Jonas and N. Amaro eds., *Globalization on the Ground: Postbellum Guatemalan Democracy and Development.* (Lanham, MD: Rowman and Littlefield, 2001).

Ross, Robert and Kent Trachte, *Global Capitalism: The New Leviathan.* Albany: State University of New York Press, 1990).

Rueschemeyer, Dietrich, Evelyn Huber Stephens end John D. Stephens, *Capitalist Development and Democracy.* (Chicago: University of Chicago Press, 1992).

Shannon, Richard Thomas, *An Introduction to the World-systems Perspective.* (Boulder, CO: Westview, 1996).

Silver, Beverly 'World scale patterns of labour-capital conflict: labour unrest, long waves, and cycles of hegemony', *Review* 18:1 (1995) pp.155-92.

Silver, Beverly and Eric Slater 'The social origins of world hegemonies', in Arrighi and Silver, *Chaos and Governance in the Modern World-System: Comparing Hegemonic Transitions.* (Minneapolis: University of Minnesota Press, 1999).

Soros, George, *The Crisis of Global Capitalism.* (New York: Pantheon, 1998).

Stark, David, 'Recombinant property in Eastern European capitalism' *American Journal of Sociology* 101 (1996) pp.993-1027.

Stevis, Dimitris, 'International labour organizations, 1864-1997: the weight of history and the challenges of the present'. *Journal of World-Systems Research* 4 (1998) pp. 52 - 75. http://www.csf.colorado.edu/wsystems/jwsr.html.

Tarrow, Sidney, *Power in Movement: Social Movements, Collective Action and Politics.* (Cambridge: Cambridge University Press, 1994).

Taylor, Peter, *The Way the Modern World Works: World Hegemony to World Impasse* (New York: Wiley, 1996).

Tilly, Charles, *From Mobilization to Revolution.* Reading, (MA: Addison-Wesley, 1978).

Tilly, Charles, 'Globalization Threatens Labour's Rights,' *International Labour and Working-Class History,* no. 47 Spring, (1995) pp. 1-23.

Wagar, W. Warren, *A Short History of the Future.* (Chicago: University of Chicago Press 1992).

_____, 'Toward a praxis of world integration', *Journal of World-Systems Research* 2:1. (1996) http://www.csf.colorado.edu/wsystems/jwsr.html.

Wallerstein, Immanuel, *Utopistics: Or, Historical Choices of the Twenty-first Century.* (New York: New Press, 1998, [Tr. Korean 1999].

_____, *After Liberalism.* (New York: New Press, 1995).

Walton, John and David Seddon, *Free Markets and Food Riots: The Politics of Global Adjustment* (Oxford: Blackwell, 1994).

Weede, Erich, 'Future hegemonic rivalry between China and the West?' in Volker Bornschier and Christopher Chase-Dunn eds., *The Future of Global Conflict.* (London: Sage, 1999).

Wilmer, Franke, *The Indigenous Voice in World Politics.* (Newbury Park, CA.: Sage 1993).

2

Containing Globalisation: Rethinking the Dynamic Structural and Ethical Premises of Multilateral Trade Negotiations

Michael H. Allen

INTRODUCTION

Caribbean and other developing states face new rounds of multilateral trade negotiations in the World Trade Organisation (WTO), the Lomé Convention processes and the build-up in the Western Hemisphere to a Free Trade Area of the Americas (FTAA).[1] On current evidence, their negotiating strategies are still being formed and the paradigms of political economy which frame their thinking about development strategies and their associated trading relationships are variants of Neo-Liberalism.[2] While many leaders of thought among developing states are skeptical of neo-liberal free trade models of development, they follow its mandates, either because there are few practical alternatives in the post-Cold War world or because a new theoretical synthesis to replace Dependency Theory as a critical reaction to Northern hegemonic ideas and sources of development models is not yet formed, or some combination of these two factors. There is therefore a need for at least the clarification and consolidation of the negotiating strategies of developing states, in order to minimise the disadvantage that they face under a globalisation that is inspired by neo-liberal approaches. But more fundamentally, there is a need to rethink the political economy of development to arrive at a new synthesis that is at once both critical and practical.[3]

I have been suggesting the outlines of such a synthesis, arguing that globalisation is a relatively new mode of production that is displacing prior forms of capitalism and territorially specific industrialisation.[4]

It is reconfiguring national societies and world society to the point where we live in a gestalt world with some features of the old Westphalian system of production, trade and international law, but also many features of global society with new elements of social structure, collective consciousness, public authority and global rather than multilateral law.[5] This means that states everywhere govern multi-modal relations of production, distribution, nurture and discourse. Their authority is territorial, but other agents, like banks and transnational corporations, who have power to shape the future on their lands, act in global, local and trans-local networks of relationships and can subvert or bypass the states as easily as they can cooperate with them. This has grave implications for human development articulated in territorial units or countries. For example, peoples may exercise democratic choices among competing parties for leadership, and among mixes of public policy, yet find an incoherence between nationally-described policies and trans-nationally driven economic and social dynamics.

If this analysis is correct, it means that Caribbean and other developing states are facing the next rounds of trade negotiations either with Westphalian assumptions about development and trade, or if with recognition of the expanding impact of globalisation, an optimism that it will bring development to their territories as its factors of production and finance flow across the face of the earth.

Much is at stake in these negotiations. It hinges upon whether or not global capitalism is sustainable ecologically, social-structurally and in terms of the ethics and aesthetics of Human Rights, beauty and diversity of human cultures. The optimists say yes and point to the increases in productivity of recent decades, diversity and declining costs of consumer goods, economic growth in most regions of the world and the obvious glitter of the world's major cities.[6] The pessimists say no and point to the ecological and health costs of this voracious production, the increased social inequality and the desperate search for ethical and aesthetic meaning everywhere, but especially among marginalised ethnic groups in the back-streets of the major cities or the distant country sides, all of which became more pronounced during the prosperous 1990s.[7]

Until we know for sure which is right, my critique of political economy suggests a pluralistic approach to development of countries and the world.

On one hand, the power of global forces must be acknowledged but contained. Developing nations should seek such advantages as they can from it, but hedge their bets.[8] This is the top-down side.

On the other hand, the lands and ways of living on which the majorities of people in most countries depend, should be allowed to evolve on their own terms and enjoy equitable terms of exchange with global capitalism in other sectors and regions of their countries. To this end, states should facilitate the redistribution of the capacity to produce: education, credit, market organisation, and public infrastructures.[9] This is the bottom-up side. Multilateral diplomacy, especially for negotiating trade rules, should be geared towards protecting local and indigenous physical, legal and cultural spaces to make bottom-up development possible, as well as to finding opportunities in world markets for the modern sectors.

In what follows, I make the case for a policy of containment of globalisation as a context for multilateral trade diplomacy.

MODELING TRADE DYNAMICS

In the new world political economy, the networks of human relationships that constitute production/trade, financial intermediation and ideological discourses are at least as important as those networks of geography and identity that constitute nations. People are simultaneously citizens of industries, households, faiths, popular identities and nations. But some kinds of citizenship give more power than others. At different times in history, the rules that were meant to order the arbitrageur between these different practical and epistemic worlds were provided by eminent heads of households and clans (patriarchs), imperial states like Rome, the Catholic Church or the Turkish Caliphate, feudal overlords and monarchs, and the Westphalian state. Until recent decades, rules about the spatial and functional boundaries of markets were set by states, since the reach of their industries were still national, or even multi-national. Citizenship of the state bounded the citizenships of other functional networks. Globalisation is overturning all of this, in that the needs of large transnational business organisations in finance, technology and production are reframing the agendas of states and assuming the chairmanship of rule-making in international institutions. Corporate needs are also reframing the parameters of competence of national, productive, consumer, epistemic and other kinds of citizenship.[10] Thus, global business organisations are leading world culture and revolutionising governance.[11] They seek to influence rules making, within states and among them, to facilitate the search for markets, to protect property rights and to accumulate capital.

This dynamic fosters productivity growth and trade, but any socially developmental effects are collateral rather than central. Yet, its spokespersons represent its projects as being essentially developmental.[12] It tends to develop those who are directly involved in production, and to marginalise those that are not. This also helps explain the relegation of rules derived from moral reason, on questions like Human Rights and ecological sustainability, to dependence on their consistency with the search for markets and the protection and accumulation of property.[13] So for example, such rules have enjoyed secondary status, at best, in multilateral conventions and draft rules such as NAFTA, WTO and the once-proposed Multilateral Agreement on Investment (MAI).

Some classes and sectors in most countries are involved in global trade. Roles vary from providers of capital, technology, management and tools, to component suppliers to export-platform labour services, to end-product consumers. Other firms in the same or different sectors produce for local or regional markets in the shadow of global competition. Some households sell labour, services or goods to national or global markets in exchange for all of their consumption needs. Still others supplement consumption from subsistence production. Households in several indigenous cultures meet consumption needs entirely from subsistence and/or hunting and gathering. If, in one sense, development can mean control of the production-consumption cycle and the knowledge and organisation to sustain that control in a given physical environment, then several indigenous cultures are developed at a low level of technology. Their prospects for developing at sustained or higher levels of knowledge might be threatened by disease, displacement or the destruction of the physical environment on which they depend, and these threats have increasingly come from the competing resource needs of modern export industries.[14]

At the level of the trans-regional global mode of production, the production-consumption cycle seems almost concentric. This is development at a high level of technology and organisation. The cycle is not internal to any one national territory, but the most energetic zones of the vortex rest in the rich ex-imperial or former colonising countries.[15] They too, have their marginalised classes and indigenous cultures, but there they are the minority.

But within the global mode of production/trade is an on-going problem of over-capacity or underconsumption and therefore of market reproduction. For development to mean control at this level, there has to be institutionalised order. Conflict among the regions and states within this mode, centres around sharing the costs and benefits of market reproduction, and is organised both ideologically and spatially. Ideologically it pits interventionists against free marketeers, or on some questions, multilateralists against supranationalists.[16] Spatially, the global mode contains three main lobes of interdependence, the Asian, North American and European. These are at once competing spheres of market penetration and reproduction, and competing approaches to market governance.[17] The rules for financial governance and international trade are shaped from the needs of banks, firms and states in this mode of production and are then extended to the developing regions as the price of access to the global market. Under uniform and reciprocal trade rules it is harder for new and technologically inexperienced participants to compete and win market share in global trade, and so even those global players that have a deficit with other global players can be confident in supporting global rules since they can hope to offset those deficits in trade with the emerging regions.

At the level of countries, the production-consumption cycle is disarticulated and control is elusive. Ex-colonial countries typically produce what they do not consume and consume what they do not produce. Opening to global rules of free trade involves abandonment by the state of attempts to control the flow of trade and protect domestic production and employment by administrative means, in exchange for the hope that market forces will result in investment inflows and trade surpluses.

In the prevailing configuration of modes of production in most countries, therefore, development can only occur if the marginal modes of production maintain surpluses with the modern and if residents within the global mode maintain surpluses with non-residents. This is the premise on which I advocate the containment of globalisation.

Containment would involve ethical arguments, legal innovation, cultural resistance, new political coalitions and new uses of the state, particularly in creative diplomacy. But first, the ethical premises.

OF FLYWEIGHTS AND HEAVYWEIGHTS

The Judeo-Christian scriptures record an old rule against the unequal yoking of plough animals.[18] In boxing, while the rules of play are the same for all weight classes, flyweights are not allowed to box heavyweights. These are obvious matters of safety and natural fairness. Yet nations are being asked in the upcoming rounds of trade negotiations to open all sectors of agriculture, services, industry and public procurement to global competition. This would pit huge global firms against small producers who cannot compete in terms of volume, scope, elasticity of production, or in terms of access to technology and credit. Many global firms got their start as national champions in the industrialised countries, benefiting from state-guided industrial policies and continuing subsidies.[19]

While global firms, their lobbyists and academic apologists have captured the public discourses in the industrialised countries, the strength of their voice does not make their positions fair. Making free trade a preemptory norm of post-Cold War international law derives from the power and interests of a narrow class of agents in world society. As a mask for this fact, free trade is represented as derived from positive economic laws and the teleology of modernisation. It denies the historical reality of different modernisations led by a variety of agents in different kinds of politically contained markets. Markets are politically contingent and there is no one script for international trade.[20]

Since markets are politically constructed, either by design or by acquiescence, what is at stake now is the political reconstruction of the world market and not the unfettering of natural economic laws. Since the world economy is articulated in overlapping modes of production more than in Westphalian units, and the modes of production comprise different production-consumption-nurture-governance cultures, the rules should reflect the norms in those cultures. Globalists in all countries should trade under global rules and local cultures should be allowed to develop without disarticulation. The trade negotiations should properly be about organising the mutual access of globalised firms, large and small, not about the obliteration of the remaining vestiges of local autonomy over food cultures, lands, waters and ways of life. On present course, FTAA and WTO negotiations are about re-scripting world society in the image of globalised American capital. Camels, goats and llamas are being asked to graze and plough with buffalo.

LEGAL INNOVATION

It follows from the above that one of the main targets for revised thinking about rules should be the national treatment clauses found in the WTO and in the drafts of the MAI and now FTAA.[21] Under these provisions, all firms, goods and services that are admitted to a country should be treated in the same way throughout that country as local firms, goods and services. The most price-competitive should win contracts and market shares, even for public sector procurements.

Besides being unfair, this is socially dangerous because several local suppliers across a number of sectors could be squeezed out of the market in an environment where there is no guarantee that foreign direct investment will flow in to replace lost production and jobs in similar or different sectors. Whole generations of workers might be too immobile in terms of education or social circumstances to move to new sectors, new cities or to new countries. And unless labour migration is simultaneously liberalised with the markets for goods, services and capital, this discriminates against whole classes of people in a region. If states are at the same time given little latitude of discretion by the World Bank and the IMF for public spending on the human costs of adjustment, then states as a group are courting serious disaster. Globalisation of national markets without globalisation of social obligations is diametrically opposite to the spirit of democracy, which, it is claimed, is the twin of free markets.

The Law of the Sea provides a metaphor for the legal innovations that could be instituted inland. There are demarcated gradations of jurisdiction, from the national territory of Internal Waters and Territorial Sea, through Contiguous and Exclusive Economic Zones, to the Area of the high seas whose surface is for common navigation, and whose seabed resources are the 'common heritage of mankind' administered by a supranational Authority.[22] Here we have adjacent regimes of municipal, public international and supranational authority, based on rules that are appropriate to each context, and reflecting a process of multilateral negotiation and agreement.

On land we already have the fuzzy outlines of this idea. There are embassy premises, which are foreign territory, military bases, which are servitudes, and free zones and export processing zones in which normal tax, customs and currency laws do not apply.[23] In regional arrangements, different levels of factor movements apply across member territories, which do not extend to others. In a sense then, trade liberalisation rules seek to convert entire national territories into free zones, and to bypass regional defense mechanisms like CARICOM.

An alternative in the containment strategy could be to use zoning laws to identify parts of countries that are open to global factor movements under full WTO rules and unrestricted foreign direct investment in fixed assets and land. Other resource areas like forests, prime farmland, mineral deposits and fresh water resources might be zoned for national and regional investment and discretionary extra-regional investment, on a concessionary basis, under rules like UN Resolution 1803 (1963), or the Charter of Economic Rights and Duties of States (1975), and the environmental principles of the Rio Declaration (1992).[24] Ancestral lands of indigenous peoples should be accorded a degree of legal autonomy consistent with the demands of subsistence and the norms of international Human Rights provisions.[25]

Zoning, however, is more appropriate for the management of fixed capital, but less useful for gatekeeping of trade. Market mechanisms would be preferable.

It might not be diplomatically feasible to legitimise logistical trade barriers like special ports or special shops. It might be more feasible to require clear labeling and display that identifies percentages of domestic and regional value-added. This would be consistent with freedom of information rules and would facilitate complementary strategies of cultural resistance. The state would not be interfering in the markets, but would certainly be giving guidance consistent with development objectives.

Another legal provision could be to systematise the use of multiple currencies, by letting domestic firms and households share the burden of finding/earning global or hard currency to pay for global goods and services, even if they are produced in the same country. If firms and households had to do this, it would create incentives to earn the right to global sector goods by 'exporting' to that sector. The freedom to hold and trade foreign currencies would mean that even firms and households that have achieved savings in local currency can have access to global goods, and it would let prices determine what is really worth having in global goods and services. It would also mean continued state vigilance in fundamentals like money supply, interest rates and exchange rates.

Local markets could also be allowed to protect themselves through alternate currencies like store credits, service vouchers and even essential commodities that hold their exchange value. In this way, people in informal activity who do not easily get access to formal money incomes can trade services or recycled materials for essential goods and services.[26] The integrity of such local currencies would depend upon networks of trust that become feasible in small-scale communities. Again, this would mean buttressing formal and informal rules with social capital, in the face of deficiencies in formal capital.

CULTURAL RESISTANCE

Laws designed to contain globalisation cannot be successful if they do not reflect the norms and preferred behaviours of the social forces they are meant to protect. Yet, there seems to be a tension between the long-term interests of marginal populations in employment and food security in a sustainable environment, and the short-term wants of many of them for non-basic consumer goods. Such desires are natural. But they are also inflamed by the inducements of global popular culture via mass media, arts and entertainment, and even formal education. Socially constructed wants shape the patterns of household consumption, which, in turn, aggregate into patterns of trade.[27] Therefore, countervailing values have to be fostered to encourage the free exercise of sustainable consumption. This requires drawing marginalised social groups, especially women, together with critically-engaged people in modern production, into critical discourses in political-economy, gendered justice, Human Rights, ecology and public health, over the same media of radio, television, the internet, theatre and cinema. This kind of leadership should come at least as much from civil society as from the democratic state. Indeed, if the state is seen to follow civil society in the reconstruction of demand for goods and services, this gives it helpful backing in the diplomacy of containment. Where the state is not democratic, the Human Rights aspects of the discourse would be at least as pronounced as that on development. Social coalitions are therefore the essential nursery of critical discourses that underpin the diplomacy of containment.

SOCIAL COALITIONS

Some groups in most countries benefit from globalisation and are likely to be optimistic about its developmental outcomes. Others who are displaced from, or marginalised by it, might aspire to inclusion and therefore be optimists by reason of consciousness, if not by circumstance. Still others might be privileged, but reflective and open to the most humane possibilities. Many are alienated from globalisation as well as from humane responses to the challenges of international order, and become potential terrorists. The majority are objectively marginalised and subjectively distracted with the demands of survival. Different coalitions are possible among all of the above. Class agendas cannot be read-off from social structures, because they are mediated by consciousness, and consciousness is itself shaped by values and contending discourses.

Creative leadership is about assembling the coalitions that are most likely to support pluralistic and complementary approaches to development and the diplomatic postures that result from them.

IMPLICATIONS FOR TRADE DIPLOMACY

Building social awareness and new coalitions takes time, but the next rounds of trade negotiations are imminent. At the very least, ideas such as those suggested here might help to clarify an alternative paradigm in which to frame development objectives and their associated trade policies. I am suggesting that developing states do not have to give away the store at these negotiations just because they are desperate for capital and export markets. They have bargaining power.

It begins with good theory and clear vision that grow out of paradigms that reflect their historical experiences and interests. Ultimately, this power will rest most firmly upon authenticity in their own peoples' material cultures, which allows them to be both cosmopolitan and in control of their material wants.

It is impossible to delink from global capitalism and dangerous to be completely absorbed by its culture, markets and institutions. The real choice for developing nations is between continued marginality in top-down-only growth, and pluralistic approaches that include and protect bottom-up strategies.

The bargaining strategies that grew out of Dependency Theory and framed the New International Economic Order (NIEO) multilateral negotiations of the 1970s depended heavily upon South-South solidarity. This kind of solidarity proved to be permeable under the pressures of competition for markets and capital, and distrust because of ideological and cultural differences.[28] The paradigm offered here takes advantage of solidarity, but does not depend so centrally upon it. Rather, the capacity to negotiate from a position of strength goes to states whose internal coalitions are in control of their wants, creativity, food production and natural resources. These must never be surrendered.

Therefore, in the upcoming rounds of multilateral trade negotiations, representatives of the global South should aim to limit the alienation of their territories and markets, to parts of their countries, reflecting the real modal boundaries of the world economy. They should resist national treatment clauses in the draft treaties and preserve most of their territories and natural resources as sustainable environments held in trust for future generations.

Endnotes

1. On the state of preparation of African, Caribbean and Pacific (ACP) delegations for these talks, see David Jessop 'ACP must ensure involvement in trade talks agenda' The Jamaica Observer Sunday, February 03, 2002. On WTO preparatory talks in Daho, Qatar in the aftermath of the September 11, 2001 attacks in the US, see Naomi Klein 'Daho, the economic frontline' *Guardian Unlimited* Thursday, November 8, 2001.
2. On the framework of thought being applied in Latin America, see Linda Sturm 'Similarities and differences between neostructuralism and neoliberalism' http://tiss.zdv.uni-tuebingen.du/webroot/sp/barrios/themeA3c.html.
3. Norman Girvan has contributed to this rethinking in the Caribbean. See Girvan 'Rethinking Development Out Loud' in Judith Wedderburn, ed., *Rethinking Development* (University of the West Indies, Mona, Jamaica) 1991. See also Don D. Marshall 'NAFTA/FTAA and the new articulations in the Americas: seizing structural opportunities' *Third World Quarterly*, Vol. 19: 4, (1998) pp. 673-700.
4. Michael H. Allen 'Modeling Globalization, Remodeling Democracy' Africana Lecture Series, Bryn Mawr College, April 6, 2001.
5. Michael H. Allen 'Modeling Global, National and Local Dynamics and Some Implications for Trans-Disciplinary Conversation.' Presented to the 2002 International Studies Association Annual Convention, New Orleans, Louisiana.
6. An accessible version of the dialogue between optimists and pessimists is found in 'Dueling Globalizations: A Debate between Thomas L. Friedman and Ignacio Ramonet' *Foreign Policy*, Fall (1999).
7. See *Human Development Report 1999* New York, (Oxford University Press, 1999) especially pp. 38-39.
8. Taking advantages of the openings presented by globalisation has been thought about in a variety of ways. For example, some Caribbean elites

have argued for Strategic Global Repositioning. See Richard L. Bernal 'The Compatibility of Caribbean Membership in Lome, NAFTA and GATT' *Social and Economic Studies* 43:2 (1994), pp. 139-147. Other scholars have pointed to opportunities for penetrating American governance structures and decision-making. See Anthony Payne 'Rethinking United States-Caribbean Relations: Towards a new model of trans-territorial governance' *Review of International Studies* (2000), Vol. 26, pp. 69-82.

9. I argue for this in 'From Marginals to Mentors? Education, Globalization and Democratic Development in Jamaica' under review at Caribbean Quarterly University of the West Indies in Mona.

10. Susan Strange put this observation even more strongly as *The Retreat of the State: The Diffusion Of Power In The World Economy*, (Cambridge: Cambridge University Press, 1996).

11. See David C. Korten 'When Corporations Rule the World' in Bruce Miroff, R. Seidelmann and T. Swanstrom eds., *Debating Democracy: A Reader in American Politics* (Boston, New York: Houghton Mifflin, 2001).

12. This is the message of the American government to Caribbean audiences, through its Ambassador to Jamaica, Sue Cobb 'Trade and Development' *The Jamaican Observer*, April 4, 2002.

13. I argue this point in 'Globalization and Contending Human Rights Discourses' *Quarterly Review*. Human Rights Committee, Cape Town, South Africa, March 2002.

14. For an analysis of aspects of this phenomenon as seen in countries of Asia, Africa and Latin America, see Jessica Tuchman Mathews ed., *Preserving the Global Environment: The Challenge of Shared Leadership* (New York, London: W.W. Norton, 1991), especially pp. 85-88. See also Brian Halweil 'Farming in the Public Interest' Chapter 3 of *State of the World 2002*, (The Worldwatch Institute, New York, London: W.W. Norton, 2002).

15. Most of world trade and foreign direct investment occurs among OECD countries. *See World Development Report 1999/2000* (World Bank and Oxford University Press, 2000) pp. 33-36, 38.

16. There are important institutional differences between the EU and NAFTA, and between NAFTA/OAS and Asian interstate arrangements like ASEAN, which are generally less institutionalised. In NAFTA and the FTAA, the US seems to support supranational models of conflict management, yet resisted these elements in the WTO treaty before finally ratifying that document.

17. For an insightful analysis of the institutional variations of global capitalism, see Colin Hay 'Contemporary capitalism, globalization, regionalization and the persistence of national variation'. *Review of International Studies*, 26: 4, (October 2000) pp. 509-531.

18. Deuteronomy 22:10.

19. I am thinking of leading French firms, such as Pechiney, and American ones in agri-business. On the subsidies and privileges of the latter, see Kurt Eichenwald *The Informant: A True Story* (New York: Broadway Books, 2000).

20. On the politically contingent nature of historical economic systems, see Robert W. Cox 'Social Forces, States and World Orders: Beyond International Relations Theory' in Robert Keohane, ed, *Neorealism and its Critics,* (New York: Columbia University Press, 1986).

21. For useful critical summary of negotiating points in these draft agreements, see Mande Barlow 'The Free Trade Area of the Americas and the Threat of Social Programs, Environmental Sustainability and Social Justice in Canada and the Americas' from Stop the FTAA: http://www.stopftaa.org. Accessed 2/13/2002.

22. See William R. Slomanson, *Fundamental Perspectives on International Law,* (2nd edition), (Minneapolis/St Paul: West Publishing, 1995) pp. 230-26.

23. Again, Slomanson, 1995, pp. 222ff and 289ff.

24. Slomanson, 'New International Economic Order', pp. 589-593; 'Environmental Instruments' (1995) pp. 547-549. Cited in note 22.

25. See Ian Brownlie, ed., *Basic Documents in International Law* (Oxford: Clarendon Press, 1995) and The United Nations Declaration on the Rights of Indigenous Peoples, E/CN. 4/ Sub. 2/1994/Add. 1(1994) accessed at www.umn.edu/humanrts/instree/declar/htm.

26. There have been experiments in some cities in Latin America in which people in informal activity have been given bus passes, food and even theatre tickets in exchange for recycled materials.

27. See Michael H.Allen 'Women, Bargaining and Change in Seven Structures of World Political Economy' *Review of International Studies,* 25 (1999) pp. 451-472. I demonstrated the vulnerability of solidarity strategies among developing states in that period in 'Bargaining and Change: The International Bauxite Association 1973-1977', Ph.D Thesis, London School of Economics, University of London, England. See also Michael H. Allen 'Rival Workers: Bargaining Power and Justice in Global Systems' in Roger Moran and others eds, *New Diplomacy in the Post-Cold War World: Essays for Susan Strange* (London: Macmillan, 1993).

3

Dangerous Waters: Sovereignty, Self-determinism and Resistance

Cynthia Barrow-Giles

The decade of the 1990s has witnessed an ongoing debate and revisionism of the nature of both civil society and the nation state. Central to the debate has been the manner in which both civil society and the nation state must reorganise themselves to pursue the goals which are critical to their survival. Arising from the debate is the elasticity of the twin concepts – independence and international sovereignty. The idea and the practice of absolute sovereignty are even more tattered, more bruised, more bloodied, than a decade ago, and a lot more tarnished than the decade of the 1970s, a decade with which St Lucia's independence is associated. That decade and its forerunner are seen by many nationalists in the developing world as a period when colonialism would be defeated and former colonies would finally achieve self determination. The battering of the sovereignty of small nation states like St Lucia, which stems not only from participation in many international organisations and international obligations, points to the need to reexamine ideas of the nation state, nationalism and national identity. Such reexamination, not withstanding the changes in the global environment that has resulted in the transfer of considerable power away from the nation, should have as its main focus, the need to maintain a search for and the realisation of decolonisation and autonomy. So that while the notion of sovereignty is challenged by global developments and is not as monolithic today as 30 years ago, it should remain important to countries which have experienced centuries of oppression, domination and subordination.

Colonial St Lucia was bound to the international community of states via its vassal connections with the British Empire. Decolonisation partly ruptured that military, political and strategic integration which linked the country with

This is an abridged and revised version of a public lecture delivered in St Lucia, marking the celebration of the 20th anniversary of the country's independence.

Europe. However, the economic system that bound states together in the international community was never effectively ruptured, ensuring strategic economic integration in the community of states.

In 1979 St Lucia became integrated into the international community of states (as an independent country), subjected to the restraints on the independence of all member states which membership to that international community implies. These restraints are of two types. There are those restraints which inclusion in that system imposes which demand that each state takes account of not only the collectivity but also the individual members themselves. Failure to comply with the imperative of the system of states carries with it automatic punishment in various forms, of which the international community has many examples. The second type of restraint faced by states in this interdependent system of states, are those imposed by the hegemony of the strongest powers or power. The mere status of a politically independent nation and the formal recognition of the status accorded to St Lucia on February 22,1979, did not and could not have automatically led to the sovereignty of St Lucia. Such formal decolonisation was but one stage in the road to complete independence, given as I have argued before, the constraints imposed on all independent states. Continuing interdependence and dependence is in fact a hallmark of the interstate system and, some have argued, is indispensable to the economic and social progress of all nations. Constant vigilance and protection of the limited space available to formerly colonised nations are therefore critical. Ironically, such vigilance must take place within a context where the increasing global interconnectedness of the new world order renders more obsolete the thinking of an earlier generation of Third World scholars, which was articulated through the nationalist phase of West Indian development. Indeed, more than at any other time in the history of the globe, societies cannot be regarded as discrete entities. Such discreteness has never been the reality of St Lucia and today has become even more illusionary.

In the more contemporary period, the shift in the global paradigm of development, has seen a 'deconstruction' of the decolonisation era. At the core of this deconstructionism is the attempt to reverse the trend towards a reduction in the integration of the global system. It is this deconstruction that has led to an assault on self-determinism of former colonies such as St Lucia. Such inhibition of sovereignty is facilitated by the inability of the nominally independent state to assume economic independence. Failure to achieve economic independence has permitted the industrialised countries to participate in both the internal and external functioning of the newly independent states. Domestically, such interference has taken the form of international multilateral organisations and direct aid agreements which frequently result in the effective blurring of the lines between colony and nation state. The termination of colonial statehood with the euphoria which accompanied that event has now become questionable with the abuse of hegemonial power that has emerged in the global system, which places new restraints on the ability of independent, particularly developing nations to assert self determinism.

Paradoxically, while the interstate system and globalism are posing threats to the continued survival of small states, the global order is witnessing an unprecedented 'return' of nationalism. In this latest phase of the development of the international liberalism of trade, opportunities are provided for the flowering of nascent nationalism culminating in movements for national and regional autonomy. This new phase of nationalism is marked by the efforts of formerly marginalised, primarily non-black ethnic groups whose identities were smashed by their overlords, to achieve nationhood. This has often taken place at the expense of other groups, as the eastern European ethnic cleansing wars have clearly revealed. In this nationalist phase, national culture is promoted as the primordial source of group and national identity that differentiates the earlier decolonised nationalist struggle from the current period. Neo-liberalists contend that global capital, global reach, and the structuring of a global order, would gradually and ultimately render the nation state and ideas about the sovereignty of the nation state obsolete — too particular to survival in an era of universalism. What therefore, these cultural revolutions, these cultural nationalisms, suggest is that the attachment to the nation and the notion of self determinism is not as obsolete, not as archaic, as neo-liberal scholars would have us believe. Although all nations of the world have been pulled into the vortex of the global capitalist market, it has not yet destroyed the attachment to the nation state, nor has it totally dulled the senses. It is in fact globalism and the global imperative that has revitalised nationalism. While therefore the present, very intense phase of the development of globalism drives the nation state towards supranational integration, it has only damaged the idea of sovereignty, but not destroyed the idea of the independent nation state.

Herein lies the contradictory nature of the process itself. Contradictory because it presents not only challenges and opportunities, but also the spectre of ascending and descending nationality. For our survival, we must focus not only on the challenges but also on the opportunities afforded by the aspect of ascending nationality. Neo-liberalists, of course, would argue that the recent spate in culturalism is but the last burst of life from the dying embers of the nation state; that nationalism is a spent force. I, however, see the moment as an opportunity – an opportunity too signal to be missed by countries of the South to realise their individual and collective identity. While Eastern European nationalism is imbued with ethnic cleansing, motivated in part by decades of suppression, it has nonetheless responded to the opportunities which globalism affords the nation state. Caribbean states, including St Lucia, must also respond; not by compressing the idea of the nation state, but by adopting a more flexible, far broader approach to nationalism, in the direction of the regional. Regional nationalism is preferable to subjugation and recolonisation.

National identity, then, is capable of being manifested in different political clothing at different historical moments. For the Caribbean, traditional nationalism has been confined, specifically after the collapse of the Federation, to the idea of the nation state. It is this loyalty to the nation state that transcended regional nationalism expressed from as early as the 1930s. That regional integration sentiment was reflected and expressed in the resolutions of the British Guiana and West Indian Labour Congress before the Moyne Commission. In their submission before the commission, the regional labour representatives called for a political federation of the West Indies. Ideologically, the labour leaders felt that independence would be forthcoming from the British in a united front, and that political integration would afford the Caribbean states the opportunity to develop economically. The pre-independence nationalism of the region produced as a counter reaction to exploitation – particularly black exploitation and cultural colonisation and its supersession in the decolonisation era with local nationalism – cannot be the same as the nationalism that is being generated today. While there are arguments that global domination by a concert of nations, primarily white nations, requires a pan ethnic response, I do not necessarily hold to that sentiment. The 1990s and the imposed global developments do not afford the opportunities of that precise historical moment. However, a broadening of the definition of identity politics, which partly forestalled the full realisation of a regional state by the 1960s, is central.

Throughout the Caribbean and indeed in every country of the globe, identity politics has led to the emergence of strong groups of formerly silenced and marginalised people. While this has often occurred within the nation state, identity politics can similarly be used and manipulated as a vehicle for the expressed purpose of achieving national consciousness and sovereignty. The old nationalism in St Lucia must, therefore, give way to a new nationalism – one couched within the framework of regional integration – as new opportunities to rewrite our nationalism, our identity, arise. Regionalism must be seen as perhaps a last bid attempt to preserve what little sovereignty is left of nation states like ours. That idea must become hegemonic. It must be supported and advanced by a popularly based movement whose ideology is to give concrete expression to the idea of nationhood, within a unified regional context. This ideology of mini supra-nationalism that infers voluntary erosion of some elements of state sovereignty, must achieve effective prominence despite which political party or groups of individuals control the state. It is based on the awareness that no state can manage alone and that collective capacity is critical to deal with many issues that may overwhelm the individual state. Writing on recolonisation in the Caribbean, George Belle in a paper entitled, *Against Colonialism: Political Theory and Re-colonisation in the Caribbean,* argues that in this present dispensation, false decolonisation, which accompanied the immediate post independence period, will not be the consequence for small states. He contends that if former colonies in the Caribbean do not consciously intervene in global developments to achieve self determinism, then recolonisation will be a condition of the individual ministate. For him, Caribbean individual ministates must establish a:

> ...new socio-historical method and philosophy and a national base transcending the min-state (which) is a minimum requirement for socially challenging the recoloniser (1996, p.26).

The new global political economy is governed by the technological and communications revolution, economic liberalism and the global hegemony of capitalist nations such as the United States. These features, particularly that of the 'disembedded' liberalism, make it difficult for the individual states to actively control global economic actors. The General Agreement of Tariffs and Trade (GATT) are excellent illustrations of unembedded liberalism as they collectively restrict the capacity of the nation state to regulate foreign investment and foreign trade in a direction conducive to the achievement of self determinism. Even the United States finds itself constrained in its ability to insulate its population from the imperatives of the new global ideological consensus.

In this regard, George Belle argues that the global power of capital also inhibits the authority of rich and powerful institutions like the United Nations. It is this capacity of globalism, highly beneficial to the private financial and economic firms that dominate the global economy, which permits opportunities for the recolonisation of formerly colonised nations. These distinctive features, therefore, make the new global paradigm of development infinitely more dangerous for the post colonial world.

Thus, while the current state of global events reduces the capacity of all states to actively intervene to improve local economic conditions, and compels all national governments to play the role of 'Governor' on behalf of *Metropolitan Imperialism,* possibilities for the most powerful to block, and even veto the exercise of authority in some global aspects, exist. It is this capacity to use the objective developments of globalisation which differentiates the more powerful states from the weaker states allowing them the ability to maintain sovereignty and the pursuit of self determinism. While such capabilities are critical for the realisation of the above, it also affords opportunities for the individual powerful states and the transnational global 'metropolitan imperialism' to consciously and deliberately manipulate global developments to disadvantage and subvert the capacity of post colonial nations to sustain self determination. It is against this backdrop, according to Belle, that recolonisation occurs.

It is this sinister action and capacity of powerful global actors, which has led Belle to contend that:

> Former paradigmatic bases, defining colonialism, anti-colonialism and anti-imperialism are in this view inadequate to assisting the addressing of resistance to C21st. Metropolitan Imperialism and recolonisation; because the category firstly, defines developments and characteristics which are not contained in the earlier designations and secondly, because taking account of the quantum leaps in the historical knowledge of mankind, during the second half of the C20th, the tools available in the former paradigms are insufficient to reverse recolonisation. 'False' decolonisation will not be the result this time around. Instead, we will simply fail to prevent recolonisation (1996, p.25).

The broad argument being advanced and outlined above, is that the fate of St Lucia and other member countries of CARICOM lies in any attempt to actively intervene in global developments. Such intervention cannot be achieved on an individual level. The post colonial Caribbean nation state must attempt to reinvent itself in the process. A core foundation stone for successful reinvention, is the need to focus on issues of national consciousness and national pride. As earlier argued, the momentum of the nation state in the post colonial era to achieve self determinism has been defeated, and perhaps the only feasible mechanism for guaranteeing that self determinism is the regional framework.

We are all aware that diplomacy between the European Union, Latin America, the United States of America and the Caribbean is dominated by the issue of bananas in the last few years. At the core of that diplomacy is the future of the banana trade and the banana regimes between the European Union, Latin America and the Caribbean. David Rudder, the Trinidadian calypsonian, has captured the sentiments of the diplomacy with his banana song:

> Well, Uncle Sam used to visit the church of bananas
> He used to go church with a girl name Grenada
> And then he went to church with a girl name Dominica
> He used to bow down to one St. Vincent
> Then he used to go and pray to one called St. Lucia

He say he loved the way they preached in the Caribbean Chapter
But one day Uncle Sammy, he went to South America
And he bounced up a girl, she name was Chiquita
Chiquita Dole is she name and she got plenty power
Them West Indian girls get vexed and the whole thing turn sour.

I do not wish to oversimplify, engage in reductionism, or indeed, to gloss over some details of the present dispute. Nevertheless I will only give skeleton form to that highly controversial issue. In terms of the European banana trade with the rest of the world, Caribbean countries supplied most of the demand for the product in the British market and a small quantity of the Italian market – controlling only three per cent of the entire European market for the product. Latin American producers, dominated by three US transnational corporations – namely Chiquita, Dole and Del Monte – provided over two thirds the European demand. In 1990, they controlled 75 per cent of the world market share for the product, much of which was directed to Germany, Belgium, Denmark, Ireland, Italy, and the Netherlands. With respect to Britain, the Latin American producers provided 12 per cent of the demand of that market. The basis for the agreements that regulated the importation of bananas to the European market is to be found in several regimes that partly stemmed from historical associations.

The banana situation appeared to be politically acceptable to all participating states prior to the late 1980s. However, the decision by the European Economic Community to establish a single European market by the end of 1992 and the rules of the GATT rendered all existing regimes problematic and highly contentious. The problem stemmed from the fact that under the Fourth Lome Convention, Article 1 clearly states that the traditional access of African, Caribbean and Pacific (ACP) states to the European market would be guaranteed at least until the year 2000. On the other hand, GATT rules and regulations demanded the liberalisation of trade in tropical products that would have a major impact on ACP bananas. The short term solution to the problem of economic globalism was to create a new banana regime in 1992, which continued to provide preferential treatment to the ACP bananas.

From the outset the new regime came under attack from within the European Union itself, Latin America and the world's hegemon, the United States. The latter country maintained a solidly hardline position in relation to the issue. It was principally the US that carried forward the political and economic agenda of the US firms that were already in firm control of the world's trade in bananas. A three pronged attack of the Latin American banana concerns took shape. The first strategy was to bring pressure to bear on the European Union (EU). This was done both directly and indirectly. In the first instance formal pressure was brought on the EU through the World Trade Organisation. With respect to the latter approach, the US exploited differences on the issue itself within the European Union, by capitalising on the opposition of Germany and Italy to the regime. This strategy was undertaken by the US government on behalf of the three large banana TNCs operating out of Latin America. On behalf of the transnational banana corporations, the US government immediately lodged an appeal to GATT. The position of the United States government on the new banana regime was that:

> ....The EC banana regime, as proposed is inconsistent with the obligations GATT members have and inconsistent with what we (they) hope would be the outcome of the Uruguay Round, which when terminated will be of benefit to all trading partners (Sutton, 1997, p.21).

In tones, terms and attitudes reminiscent of colonial days, the USA's seemingly benevolent approach towards the Caribbean was expressed in an ideological framework which argued that the EU new banana regime was not in the best long term interest of the Caribbean. The US further stressed that the Caribbean region was in dire need to 'look more seriously at its role in the 21st century' and that 'any country that wants to benefit from free trade will have to look more seriously at what changes it needs to make in its economic structure to accommodate some of the needs of its trading partners'.

The second strategy was to attempt to divide small banana concerns in the islands by fermenting discord and ultimately lessening the solidarity of Windward Island producers internationally and locally. This, like the less direct approach adopted by the Americans is an age-old practice of the divide and rule approach which was so successfully used in the Caribbean by the colonial and neo-colonial powers. It is to be expected that where agents of recolonisation find it difficult to manipulate and control global agreements to their advantage, they would resort to the more devious and more dangerous approach of fermenting discord. The third prong of the strategy was assumed by the Latin and Central American governments in the hemispheric organisation with a formal protest to the Organisation of American States (OAS).

Apparently, it is only the Caribbean and the supporting countries in the European Union that must make accommodations with their trading partners. Indeed, the US government has been unrelenting, immalleable in its attack on the regime, filing suit in 1995 against the new banana regime before the World Trade Organisation. The GATT panels earlier ruled that the new banana regime was in contravention of the international agreements on Tariff and Trade, to which the EU countries were signatories. It also ruled that the Lomé Accord, that bound the ACP countries with the European Union, had in fact been superceded by GATT. The response of the EU was to make further adjustments to the regimes. Thus, a political and economic victory had been scored by the three large Latin American TNCs as the system of country-specific allocations and licensing system was abolished. In essence then, some of the protection offered to the ACP countries, with its 25 per cent market share, was removed.

Notwithstanding these adjustments, further protest on the part of the American Government continued with the American Government threatening trade sanctions against all parties concerned. Like the elephant, the United States was prepared to stamp the ants into nothingness. The question was: 'What would be the next strategy of the Windward Island banana producing countries – the ants – as they attempted to arrive at a solution which would not further damage their capacity to govern?'

Firing my imagination and leading to this paper was the action undertaken by the governments of St Lucia and Dominica. According to the report in the *Barbados Advocate*, the two mini states blocked the adoption of the settlement agenda, which was the result of an attempt to resolve the banana dispute.

In fact, Raghavan likened the action in this way: 'If a banana or a bunch of bananas had been subject to the kind of handling that the banana dispute has been getting at the World Trade Organisation (WTO), by now it would have become a mushy, inedible pulp to be thrown away'.

That defiant action and the consequent delay in instituting WTO rulings could not have occurred without the expressed support of other Caribbean countries in the over five (5)-year dispute between the United States and Caribbean banana producing countries. The point is that regionalism provided the opportunity and possibility for not only a calculated response by the respective governments, but for a protracted negotiation. Could St Lucia and Dominica take such a position without regional support? Should the negotiations not have been long settled in a direction that was beneficial to the United States and harmful to the banana producing Caribbean countries? The fact is that a Caribbean-wide campaign provided both St Lucia and Dominica with the room to manoeuver to carry out a specific campaign, signaling to the global hegemon that the islands were not prepared to dance the dance of the Americans like puppets on a string, but would, instead, resist further attempts at recolonisation and the denial of the pursuit of self determination. Failure to do so would result in the very scenario alluded to by a former World Bank senior economist for Jamaica:

> Look at an island, say, like Montserrat, or the others. If their Governments could be persuaded to sell land for retirement homes for Americans, the place could be another Monte Carlo! The ones (Montserrat citizens) who

stay would have higher incomes. But they don't want it. They regard the land as some sort of birthright.

The Caribbean then would become just another piece of real estate with enclaves where the local population is herded, as the golf courses and retirement villages dot the terrain of the country side.

It is not my intention here to suggest a simplistic one dimensional response to global developments. Globalism, with all its complexities, requires a complex, very flexible approach by all states at all times; but at this precise moment the action undertaken by St Lucia and Dominica in January of 1999 before the WTO suggests three important things. First, that resistance is not futile. Second, that regional support is critical to international negotiation for small states; and finally, that such regionalism can be used or extended to project national consciousness. This is vital for eroding and defeating the pessimism that has accompanied the meta narrative of global developments and its corollary, the seemingly ascendent neo liberalism.

Thus far, it would appear that I have emphasised the political and economic consequences of globalism and its implications for St Lucia. However, globalism is not only an economic and political process. At the core of globalising tendencies is the social dimension associated with the communications technology that spreads western cultural patterns across the globe at an unprecedented level.

Increasingly, globalisation is seen as a mechanism of westernising the world, reducing non-western cultures to the level of mythology. Such westernisation of cultures, a handmaiden of globalisation, is facilitated by the spread of the media, particularly the electronic media, supplanting the traditional roles undertaken by social institutions such as the family, the church and schools. An unbounded electronic medium in the contemporary period exerts an irresistible pull and control over its consumers, who are primarily the young and most vulnerable members of society.

In that context it is necessary for both civil society and state managers to place increasing emphasis on all the barometers of national consciousness which gives flavour to the integrity of the nation state. While it is difficult and clearly romanticised to make a claim for total cultural assertiveness in an era of the bombardment of foreign cultures, renewed emphasis must be placed on all sporting events, local cultural festivals and the creole language, Patois, which partly gives St Lucia its distinctiveness. Richard Allsopp's statement on the creole language to a Guyanese audience, is relevant here:

...creolese and its sister Caribbean creoles were new languages created by the brains of our ancestors, under severe repression, out of the forced mating of their native African language concepts with those of the languages of Europe; you must remember too that our East Indian fellow-labourers adopted and jointly maintained this new language, and it developed as the universal folk language of our country. ...When you understand all this, the logical emotion that will result can only be amazement and full admiration instead of foolish abashment.

The very media that spread western civilisation, which seeks to destroy national cultures, must be manipulated and used as a medium to teach cultural history. That, in itself, would give due recognition to the importance of education and the educational system while creating national identity.

In effect then, resilience is required by both state and civil society to globalising 'homogenising' tendencies. Such resilience must strike a balance between globalising tendencies on the one hand and localising tendencies on the other. Like the idea of sovereignty itself, national identity must and will inevitably bend under the weight of globalism. However, it must not disappear, must not totally rupture and must not wither away. It is, after all, a product of history and the present. The identification of St Lucianhood did not occur in a vacuum and its form and persistence cannot also be perceived in a vacuum.

Bibliography

Allsopp, Richard, *Language and National Unity*, Twelfth Series of the Edgar Mittelholzer Memorial Lectures, (1998).

Anthony, Kenny D., 'Caribbean Integration: The Future Relationship between Barbados and the OECS', *Journal Of Eastern Caribbean Studies*, 23:1 (March 1998) pp.35-50.

Belle, George A. V., 'Against Colonialism: Political Theory and Recolonisation in the Caribbean', (unpublished paper presented at the Conference on Caribbean culture, March 3-5 1996, Faculty of Social Sciences Mona Campus, Jamaica).

Demas, William G., *Critical Issues in Caribbean Development: West India Development and the Deepening and Widening of the Caribbean Community*, (Jamaica: Ian Randle Publishers, 1997).

European Union Newsletter, no.5, 1998.

Hoogvelt, Ankie, *Globalisation and the Post Colonial World: The New Political Economy of Development*, (London: MacMillan Press Limited, 1997).

Lewis W. Arthur, *Labour in the West Indies*, (New Beacon Books, 1977).

Lewis, G. K., *The Growth of the Modern West Indies*, (New York: Monthly Review Press, 1968).

McAffee, Kathy, *Storm Signals: Structural Adjustment and Development: Alternatives in the Caribbean*, (London: Zed Books, 1991).

Munroe, Trevor, *The Politics of Constitutional Decolonisation: Jamaica: 1944–1962*, (Jamaica: ISER, University of the West Indies, 1983).

Raghavan, Chakravarthi, 'Messy Banana Business' *The Barbados Sunday Advocate*, January 31 1999, p.9.

Ramprasad, Frank, ed., *Critical Issues in Caribbean Development: The New World Order: Uruguay Round Agreements and Implications for CARICOM states*, (Jamaica: Ian Randle Publishers, 1997).

Sutton, Paul, 'The Banana Regime of the European Union, the Caribbean and Latin America; *Journal of Interamerican Studies and World Affairs*; 39:2, (summer 1997) pp. 5-36.

Thompson, Pat, *'Europe 1992: Implications for the Caribbean'*; in *Crosswords of Empire: The European Caribbean Connection 1492-1992 ed.* Cobley Alan (The Department of History, Cave Hill Campus, 1994) pp.111-124.

Watson, Hilbourne. A., *The Caribbean in the Global Political Economy*. Boulder, (Colorodo: Lynne Rienner Publishers Inc, 1994).

4

Governance and Re-Regulation of Offshore Financial Centres: (Re)Framing the Confines of Legitimate Debate and Protest

Don D. Marshall

Abstract: This essay highlights the deficiencies and political motives behind global governance processes as they relate to international financial regulation. A case is made for wider public resistance to the arbitrary social hierarchies and exclusions that global financial structures/regimes seemingly encourage. This is especially timely as the September 11 (2001) sneak terrorist attacks in New York and Washington have encouraged a renewed resolve by unaccountable, undemocratic global financial committees to extend the web of surveillance and hasten the pace of regulatory reforms of offshore financial centres.

INTRODUCTION

The power to tax has always been considered one of the cornerstones of state sovereignty. The brazenness of the Organisation for Economic Cooperation and Development's (OECD) approach towards offshore financial centres has been widely criticised. Besides the need for an ongoing dialogue across the Caribbean on the emergence of global governance processes, the politics of global finance, the vagaries of neoliberalism, and the kinds of development challenges facing countries in the Caribbean, what remains necessary are openings for dissent. The resistance by offshore financial centres (OFCs) in the Caribbean and elsewhere to re-regulation pressure from the OECD and other Western dominated institutions beckon civil society engagement and support. Certainly non-governmental organisations (NGOs) have figured with increasing prominence in the recent history of global governance. Countless NGOs have taken initiative to shape global rules and institutions with respect to the following global governance issues: the AIDS challenge, the health of the planet, the status of women, humanitarian relief, trade, and poverty-alleviation. However, in one of the principal areas of contemporary globalisation, namely finance, the forms and intensity of civic activism have varied considerably between different parts of the world. Caribbean NGOs' participation in this regard amounts to nought. This is odd particularly when we consider its activism on other fronts.[1] International re-regulation trends threaten to severely erode the comparative advantage offshore financial centres have over their core onshore rivals. If this and other global governance pressures are to be effectively resisted in the Caribbean, new coalitions of social forces working through governments must be created to effect a new diplomacy of coordination. The resources are limited for each government for what is at stake requires concerted political will, research, skillful negotiation and compromise. The type of organisational capacity suggested here must bear a different feature upon its countenance from the multi-layered committees of CARICOM that deal with post-Lomé negotiations, NAFTA-parity, and FTAA accession. These have tended to simply document and tutor the requirements of transnational neo-liberalism, rather than function as sites for resistance, for feedback, and the positing of alternative paradigms and methodologies.

GLOBALISATION AND GLOBAL GOVERNANCE

Globalisation has become an important signifier of our age marking an increasing interdependence, removal of barriers to trade, and breakthroughs in communications technologies. But too many commentators conflate globalisation with neoliberalism while Caribbean educated opinion nods sagely in assent. The discourse has subsequently become synonymous with the promotion of the interests of capital on a world-wide scale; a tendency towards homogenisation of state policies and state forms; and the evolution of new global ordering structures such as the World Trade Organisation (WTO) and its technocratic-dominated commissions. With the appellation 'globalisation', we are seduced by the myth of its inevitability and historical necessity. But much like its Keynesian-welfare predecessor of the 1960s and 1970s, the neoliberal model of political economy remains shot through with contests as it cannot escape society, the state and political processes. The events and violent protests in Seattle surrounding the WTO conference in late November-early December 1999 betrayed a glimpse into the nature of opposition greeting attempts to enact neoliberal codes of social organisation. The popular slogan both in Seattle and at the 2001 Quebec Summit on the Free Trade Area of the Americas, was for 'de-globalisation', meaning in part, the need to reorient globalisation, to steer the process in a different, socially useful direction. While more humane global futures are being contemplated on the pages of some academic works and in civil society practices, we might be reminded that Seattle and Quebec were as much about a movement of protest against international organisations as well as corporate power. To be sure, each level reinforces the other. For the purposes of this essay, it is necessary to read the protests by Caribbean and other OFCs against OECD strictures as yet another strike against how the world is run.

Certainly many groups are concerned about the way in which the WTO and other international organisations conduct their business, the role within them of NGOs and other representatives of civil society, the transparency of procedures, and, the relation between the more powerful and less powerful states within such organisations. This last concern is not surprising. Already there had been enough in the unfolding of world politics to encourage the view that international law functions as a utopian distraction when national interests among the core appear under threat. A former Secretary of State, Madeline Albright once quipped that 'the US will act multilaterally when we can, and unilaterally as we must'.[2] Her predecessor, George Shultz had indeed argued that 'negotiations are a euphemism for capitulation if the shadow of power is not cast across the bargaining table'.[3] The foregoing prompts the following question: If core countries cannot be trusted to act in accord with treaty obligations and international agreements, how can global governance achieve democratic, accountable, and effective institutional outcomes?

THE INTERNATIONAL FINANCIAL ARCHITECTURE

While it remains empirically suspect to establish contemporary globalisation as unique and driven by a singular logic, what is not in doubt is the far-reaching influence of finance in the world economy. Its scope, reach, and mobility provide an interesting entry-point for discussion on the evolution of global governance regimes, in this case, the governance of global finance. The global financial architecture has been shot through with tensions and challenges. The challenges occur both on the technical side and on the normative side. One is to do with problems of legitimacy, efficiency and coordination, the other points to how intrusive globalist regulatory regimes invariably leads to emancipatory claims-making, meaning demands for greater social justice, democracy, and recognition of (fiscal) sovereignty rights. Indeed the current impasse between offshore financial centres and the OECD demonstrates two things. One: that global governance relations appear ad hoc, experimental and problematic. And two: intractable tensions will persist since there is unbalanced power between the West and the Third World. The centrality of the Western financial system allows key Western states to determine what type of financial activity is acceptable.

There is widespread agreement that territorially discrete states cannot by themselves efficiently handle the many and large global flows that impact on their jurisdictions. This has prompted some shifts in the contours of governance, trends that seem likely to unfold further in the future. Certainly, interstate consultations at the ministerial level have expanded over the last 15 years, including special conferences of the United Nations. The rise of multilateral governance has also occurred through the growth of trans-governmental networks, where civil servants from parallel agencies in multiple states develop close regulatory collabouration in a particular policy area. Supra-state bureaucracies like the International Monetary Fund (IMF), the European Union, and the World Bank have also acquired some initiative and power of their own concomitant with the rise of neoliberalism. Indeed neo-liberal globalisation has encouraged a shift of many regulatory competencies 'upwards' to suprastate bodies, but also various moves 'downwards' to sub state agencies. It has also promoted 'lateral' shifts of governance from the public sector to non-official quarters.[4] This privatisation of governance has transpired, for example, in increased reliance on non-governmental organisations (NGOs) to implement development cooperation projects and several multilateral environmental agreements. Theorists have accordingly dubbed these emergent circumstances as 'multilayered', post-sovereign, post-Westphalian, 'neo-medieval', or 'networked' regulation. Recent developments in the regulation of global finance largely conform to the general trends in contemporary governance, a matter that receives some address in the following paragraphs.

To be sure, states have been a central figure in the de-regulation of capital controls and in contemporary attempts to facilitate cross-jurisdictional cooperation in accounting standards and against money laundering. The view that high levels of capital mobility rob states of their autonomy by compelling them to design macroeconomic and financial policy along the lines demanded by private international investors has become very prominent since the Southeast Asian financial meltdown of 1997/98. Indeed the spiraling devaluation among Southeast Asian countries followed hard on the heels of a collapse of the Russian economy and severe monetary instability in Mexico in 1995. For many policy makers and academics, the merits and demerits of financial deregulation are under active discussion with concerns raised about how to check the increase of risky, speculative investment in the absence of capital controls. But there remains little substantial evidence or research that links money laundering *per se* with market failure, as it does with speculation.

National central banks, national treasuries, national securities and exchange commissions, and national insurance supervisors have also figured prominently in the governance of global finance. However the financial governance architecture has tended to be reflective of both state and substate actors drawn largely from the West. Multiple networks of intergovernmental consultation and cooperation have developed in tandem with the accelerated globalisation of finance during recent decades. For example, central bank governors of core advanced industrialised countries have met regularly at Basle since 1962 to discuss monetary and financial matters of mutual concern. The Basle Committee on Banking Supervision (BCBS) established in 1975, comprise working parties of core countries exploring issues like the capital position of trans border banks and principles for effective bank supervision. In 1989, the OECD has housed the secretariat of the Financial Action Task Force (FATF), a body set up to combat money laundering. In respect of bonds and stock markets, the US based International Organisation of Securities Commissions (IOSC) was created in 1974, but went global in 1983 and now involves nearly 100 national securities authorities. In addition the International Association of Insurance Supervisors (IAIS) was formed in 1994 and has quickly grown to link authorities in over 100 countries. Since 1996, the BCBS, IAIS, and IOSC have convened a Joint Forum on Financial Conglomerates to promote cooperation between banking, securities, and insurance supervisors, given that global financial corporations increasingly operate across the three sectors.

Offshore Financial Services and Political Motives Behind Regulation

Paradoxically the gradual formation of a global financial architecture has not held back the casino character of international finance marked by money laundering, tax evasion, capital flight, speculation, and fierce competition across financial centres both onshore and offshore. Money laundering describes the process through which illicit profits are hidden from authorities, often by using a combination of complex financial transactions and financial secrecy, and re-introduced into the financial system under the guise of legitimate transactions. Usually this money makes its way into real estate prospecting, stock trading and offshore business. OFCs generally offer foreign clients legal, fiduciary, insurance management, financial consultancy, banking and accounting services. Each host government exempts international business from income, capital gains, and inheritance taxes. There is also some measure of discretion and confidentiality on foreign accounts.

It was in the wake of the rise of the Eurodollar market after the late 1950s, the collapse of the Bretton Woods system in 1971, and the relaxation of capital controls that 'tax havens' and other OFCs were spawned. Indeed the incentives to compete through taxes has been a strategy pursued by many Caribbean islands with strong corporate commercial environments, state of the art offshore financial legislation, established reputations in fiscal prudence, political and financial stability, and an influential cadre of lawyers, bankers, management specialists and accountants. Indeed for Caribbean OFCs, Malta and Vanuatu, restructuring global capitalism has reinforced their commitment to capital accumulation strategies centred on the provision of diverse financial services along with holiday-resorting services.

Altogether this is a strike against those that embrace arguments about the structural power of capital, time-space conquering technologies, and loss of territoriality. David Andrews (1994) argues, for example, that states will find it increasingly cost prohibitive to enact monetary policies that run counter to the expectations of the financial system. Other scholars sharing this perspective speak of the structural power of capital noting that it is vested in the fusion of complimentary material and ideological forces within and between states (Gill and Law 1989). Overall this thesis assumes that permanent constraints on states limit their regulatory capacity. This is so as deregulated financial markets provide mobile capital with a greater opportunity to exploit the competitive state dynamic by using differences in fiscal policies to reward some states and punish others. Moreover a combination of economic ideology and well-connected financial interests influence the normative beliefs and mindsets of political and monetary authorities and, thus, reinforce norms favourable to these financial interests. The positive policy result is that even if states want to re-regulate, these structural features can and do force them to accommodate the deregulatory preferences of the financial sector.

But it remains difficult to separate what may be considered the structural behaviour of the financial system from the political interests of dominant states. Two cases in point are important. The political motives for concerted action against money laundering rather than capital flight can be traced to the fact that the West benefitted from capital flight. Indeed Helleiner (1999) and Naylor (1987) argue that the US used the less developed countries (LDCs) flight capital to help finance its deficits. Naylor also claims that, throughout the 1980s, the US budgetary mechanics and its balance of international payments were increasingly dependent on the spread of political instability and economic disorder, and on the flight of capital they engendered (p.15).

The second case in point relates to Western concern over tax evasion, a direct intervention into the market-determining competition between onshore financial centres and offshore equivalents over market share in financial services. The impasse between OFCs and the OECD points to attempts by dominant countries to tilt the stakes in this competition in favour of their respective onshore financial sectors. And this is but an extension of the anti-money laundering regime of the US, France and Britain primarily. Through anti-money laundering activities, core countries can restrict or set conditions upon the operational conduct of financial intermediaries that undertake business on or through their territory. OFCs and states whose current accounts benefit from the influx of money from legitimate and unsuspecting sources will be the losers. Thus far the West's political, legal, and technological resources have been used to exert control over the movement of capital in and out of states with large underground economies. In this sense, *Western political preferences will compliment its comparative advantage so as to capture the indigenous underground capital of less developed economies.*

INTERNATIONAL TAX COMPETITION, ANTI-MONEY LAUNDERING AND THE CARIBBEAN

A two-day meeting (January 8-9, 2001) held at the Sherbourne Conference Centre between the OECD, the Commonwealth Secretariat, Caribbean Community nations, the Caribbean Development Bank and several core countries was significant as it marked the first time that offshore financial centres (OFCs) gained voice in the twilight world of a fading Bretton Woods order. What was under discussion was the content, methodology and implications of the OECD's *Harmful Tax Practice* report of 2000 which blacklisted a number of Caribbean and other OFCs and threatened the imposition of sanctions by July 2001 should these fail to comply with regulatory standards. But there is a wider context to this as it touches upon US hemispheric strategic relations and the competitive stakes involved in international financial services provision.

The combination of twenty-four hour markets and the instantaneous execution of cross-border transactions have allowed for money circulation in unprecedented volumes. OECD member countries claim an unyielding concern with money laundering and instability in the international financial system. Indeed this is a real concern as the 1990s have been attended by an increase in tax evasion as well as a series of spectacular bank failures and financial meltdowns of whole economies. But the motives of OECD member states are beginning to clearly indicate that anti-money laundering regulations are more of a political than technical initiative.

Caribbean OFCs have been implementing state-of-the-art legislation and cooperating in maritime and other drug enforcement agreements to stamp out money laundering since the 1980s. The stimulus for such cooperation can be traced to US geopolitical concerns in the Americas shaped by the threat the narcotics trade poses to its own domestic stability, the international financial system, and governability in the hemisphere with all the attendant illegal immigration problems that can follow state atrophy. The major production centres are reported to be in Central and South America; North America is the principal consumer; while Caribbean sea lanes provide a route to the various markets. Indeed Sea Lanes of Communication in the Caribbean area are of crucial geo-strategic importance to the US. Once ships exit the Panama Canal on the Atlantic side, they must use one of 16 passages in the Caribbean Sea to reach destinations in the US, Europe, Africa, and elsewhere. The Caribbean therefore has multi-dimensional strategic value in the war on drugs. The variety of measures and tactics the US has employed however – from direct military presence, increased military sales, aid, and training, expanding intelligence operations, and regular high-profile military maneuvers, to the signing of Mutual Legal Assistance Treaties and the controversial Shiprider's Agreement (See Chapter 11) – seemed to have had more than a benign objective of simply assisting the region with its security problems. A policy of compliance enforcement has been on the way.

Throughout the 1980s, the US encouraged state action across the hemisphere against money laundering. This has been framed politically as anti-crime and drug policies. Recall that a number of US reports on tax evasiveness and money laundering appeared in the 1980s seeking to investigate the full nature, character and use of offshore banking facilities in the Caribbean. These were *The Gordon Report: Tax Havens and Their Use by United States Taxpayers – An Overview*, (1981); *Crime and Secrecy: The Use of Offshore Banks and Companies* prepared by the US Senate's Committee on Governmental Affairs in 1983; and the 1984 study, *Tax Havens in the Caribbean Basin*, prepared by the US Department of Treasury. The findings were on the whole unflattering, condemnatory and at best suspicious of Commonwealth Caribbean offshore banking operations. But this kind of suspicion extended to OFCs everywhere. A 1985 OECD report entitled *Trends in Banking in OECD Countries* would remark: A Supervisory coverage can no longer stop at national frontiers. Cooperation among supervisory agencies has become a necessity (p.50).

By 1988 a Statement on Prevention of Criminal Use of the Banking System for the Purpose of Money Laundering was issued by the Basle Committee on Banking Regulations and Supervisory Practices, a committee made up of supervisory authorities from core countries. It could be said that a new regulatory regime was thereafter established. These included the creation of the European based, Financial Action Task Force (1989) and the US government's Financial Crimes Enforcement Network (1990). Altogether these investigations, initiatives and reports coincided with deliberate attempts by core countries to remove anti-competitive onshore financial distortions. The intent is to one: position onshore financial centres to attract flight capital escaping the poor economic policies of some Third World countries, and two: blunt the comparative advantage offshore service providers enjoy.

In sum, the war on drugs led to the creation of an international anti-money laundering regime enlisting assistance from the Bank for International Settlements, the Offshore Group of Banking Supervisors and the Offshore Group of Insurance Supervisors. Much like the World Bank, the IMF and the WTO, these would come to function as a centralised chauvinistic authority. It is in this vein that the OECD in its ill-advised *Harmful Tax Practice* reports of 1998 and 2000, could set out to blacklist select OFCs threatening the imposition of sanctions by July 2001 should they fail to comply with regulatory standards. The role of the OECD, in this area as in many other areas, is quite distinctive. It has no formal regulatory powers, it cannot impose its will on states, and it has no sanctioning powers. Nevertheless its influence and prestige are enormous and most OFCs in the world are willing, albeit reluctantly, to comply with its 'recommendations'. Its primary role is that of progenitor of ideas that it successfully spreads through bringing together senior civil servants, business executives and fiscal specialists. Importantly Caribbean officials at the Barbados meeting would counter that if OFCs provide a haven for shady dealings, then the shared solution must be derived from seeking to ensure continued tax competition maximally compatible with regulation against money laundering.

What is missed by most commentators is how neo-liberal de-regulation leads to re-regulation of a specific kind, involving a mix of public, semi-public and private actors and institutions that are brought together in national, regional and global networks and forums. This web of surveillance is legitimising the continued existence of the offshore system for tax avoidance. And tax avoidance depends on facilities such as corporate and banking secrecy, which undermine the scope of Western-led regulatory cooperation.

SUMMARY: WHAT CAN CARIBBEAN NGOs AND NEGOTIATORS DO?

Principally Caribbean NGOs need to engage in public education and raise citizens' awareness and understanding of global finance and its governance. To this end, NGOs can prepare handbooks and kits, organise workshops and seminars, circulate newsletters, maintain websites on the Internet, and develop curricular materials for schools and tertiary institutions. Altogether this may serve to stimulate debate about global finance and Caribbean development options with respect to offshore finance.

The point was earlier made that the implementation of the anti-money laundering regime at the global level features veiled attempts by powerful Western states to tilt the stakes in the financial market competition between core onshore financial centres and their OFC rivals in favour of the former. It is also apparent that the centrality of the Western financial system allows key Western states to determine what type of financial activity is acceptable. There are, of course, rational and clear reasons that help justify the establishment of an anti-money laundering regime. But the media and research institutions must also investigate why flight capital leaving poor countries is neither deemed harmful, nor is it subject to international regulation. A battle by OFCs on points of international law and the sovereign right of states to determine tax policy can only be effective if this is anchored by an understanding of the self-interests and structural power of OECD countries. The Joint Working Group formed in Barbados comprising officials from both the OECD and OFCs is expected to re-examine the terms establishing the recently created Global Forum on Taxation. Should this Forum or any other become truly inclusive, the OFC officials must go beyond tax issues if they are to influence the agenda-setting power of relevant Western dominated bodies. They must test the genuine intent of the OECD by lobbying for regulatory oversight of capital flight. This should be incorporated within what must be a newly constituted anti-money laundering regime. If the OECD cannot be convinced, then OFC representatives should question the inclusion of *tax evasion* within the scope of anti-money laundering regulations. They should also raise the issue of a transfer or lease of software technology if they are to effectively track and monitor financial transactions. Anything less would be akin to effecting a siege without an enemy. Regionally, host governments of OFCs should seek to agree on a minimal threshold of regulations and should make clear their investigative lines of authority. Such a strategy may be best served with support from affiliate NGOs of the Caribbean Policy Development Centre. If global governance institutions are to be inclusive they should comprise representatives from civil society. But these NGOs must be accountable to their respective constituencies, transparent in terms of declaration of objectives, and cognisant of the expense involved in policy formulation, evaluation and advocacy. Inclusion of this sort may assist in promoting legitimacy in global financial governance as well as in the development path pursued. Indeed the benefits that OFC operations offer to host countries do not extend beyond the annual fees and levies paid to government by international business companies and overall image enhancement. Employment opportunities tend to be limited and generally apply only to professionals in accounting, management, law and finance. So there is a creeping legitimacy deficit to meet, helped none by absence of information on the nature of this sector and why it remains important to the economy.

Endnotes

1. Caribbean labour unions feature prominently in the work of the International Confederation of Trade Unions, a civic organisation that has managed to lock in labour issues – such as occupational safety, protection of lower-skilled jobs from undercutting in new trade area deals, and human rights – onto the agenda for hemispheric free trade and security. Women's groups have also been active in administering poverty reduction programmes, micro-enterprise schemes, and women in development schemes. Both the Association of Caribbean Economists and the Caribbean Association for Feminist Research and Action continue to undertake technical studies on matters of political economy and social justice for various agencies like the United Nations and the World Bank. It was in 1991, that a coordinating body was formed, the Caribbean Policy Development Centre, headquartered in Barbados, and currently serving some 34 different civic organisations across the wider Caribbean.
2. This was part of a warning to the UN Security Council on the question of Iraq's non-compliance with UN Resolution 687 of April 3, 1991 demanding inspection of weapons (Chomsky 2000: p.13.). Despite the February 1998 agreement struck between UN Secretary-General Kofi Annan and Iraqi authorities, one supported by the Security Council, the US and UK would launch joint air strikes on Iraq in April 1998 B a clear breach of Articles 41 and 42 of the UN Charter which reposes this authority in the Security Council. For more on this, see N. Chomsky (2000). Only recently, March 18, 2003, the U.S. and Britain defied the letter and spirit of UN resolution 1441 as it relates to developments in Iraq.
3. As cited by Chomsky (2000), p.17.
4. For more on this, see Ronit and Schneider (1999).

Bibliography

Andrews, D. M., 'Capital Mobility and State Autonomy: Toward a Structural Theory of International Relations', in *International Studies Quarterly*, 38: 2, (1994) pp.193-218.
Chomsky, Noam, *Rogue States: The Rule of Force in World Affairs*, (London: Pluto Press, 2000).

Cohen, Benjamin J., *The Geography of Money*, (Ithaca, New York: Cornell University Press, 1998).

Gill, S.R. and D. Law 'Global Hegemony and the Structural Power of Capital', in *International Studies Quarterly* 33: 4, (1989) pp. 475-499.

Friman, H. Richard and Peter Andreas, eds., *The Illicit Global Economy and State Power*, (Lanham, MD: Rowman and Littlefield, 1999).

Haqqani, Husain 'Good Drives Out Bad: Pakistan Awhitens: Black Money Through Bond Issue', *Far Eastern Economic Review*, 19 (September 1998) pp.58-74.

Helleiner, E., 'State Power and the Regulation of Illicit Activity in Global Finance', in H.R. Friman and P. Andreas, eds, *The Illicit Global Economy*, (Lanham, MD: Rowman and Littlefield, 1999).

Marshall, Don D., *Caribbean Political Economy at the Crossroads*, (London and New York: Macmillan Publishers and St Martin's Press, 1998).

Naylor, R. T., *Hot Money and the Politics of Debt*, (Toronto: McClelland and Stewart, 1998).

Pagano, M.and A. Roell, 'Shifting Gears: An Economic Evaluation of the Reform of the Paris Bourse', in V. Conti and R. Hamaui, eds., *Financial Markets - Liberalisation and the Role of Banks*, (New York: Cambridge University Press, 1993).

Pieterse, Jan Nederveen, ed. *Global Futures: Shaping Globalisation*, (London: Sage, 2000).

Ronit, K.and V. Schneider, eds, *Private Organisations, Governance and Global Politics*, (London: Routledge, 1999).

5

Governance, Industrial Policy and the New Global Economy: The Case For Cultural Industries

Keith Nurse

INTRODUCTION

In the debate on governance in the developing world political concerns dealing with human rights, the rule of law and the preservation of democracy tend to dominate the discourse. Other aspects of governance such as the management of a country's economic and social resources for development are consequently shrouded. The primacy of political concerns is not without merit because it is well accepted that good policies in a bad political environment can be counter productive. This paper therefore operates with a wider concept of governance as employed by the UNDP.[1]

Governance is viewed as the exercise of economic, political and administrative authority to manage a country's affairs at all levels. It comprises mechanisms, processes and institutions through which citizens and groups articulate their interests, exercise their legal rights, meet their obligations and mediate their differences.

This chapter starts from the observation that the new global economy is impacting negatively on the development agenda in terms of increasing inequality and the resultant crises of social justice. For example, there are fears that the growth of the internet economy will lead to a 'digital divide' which will widen the income and technological gap between rich and poor nations. These fears are not unfounded as the benefits of contemporary globalisation are proving to be very uneven.

In this chapter I argue that in the contemporary context the role of the state and other key national and regional institutions should be expanded to mobilise the untapped or underdeveloped potential, skills and capacities of individuals and firms. In this regard industrial policy is viewed as a necessary mechanism to reduce uncertainty for small and medium-sized enterprises and to strengthen initiatives towards new forms of specialisation in emerging sectors like the cultural industries, which suffer from market failure.

The paper is organised in five sections. The first section makes the argument for industrial policy in developing countries emphasising the problem of market failure. The second section identifies the special attributes of the cultural industries and outlines specific policy measures. The next section situates the global music industry within the context of the new intellectual property economy. The challenges facing the regional music industry are then analysed. The paper concludes with strategic recommendations for a coordinated industrial policy for the regional music industry.

THE CASE FOR INDUSTRIAL POLICY

In general terms, industrial policy can be defined as 'government intervention in promoting industrialisation' in a context 'where market failures significantly retard industrial development, and where market-driven solutions fail, or take too long, to emerge'.[2] In essence, industrial policy is 'designed to affect the allocation of resources among economic activities and alter what would otherwise have been the market outcome'.[3]

The role of the state is considered critical because it is the largest actor in most national economies and it is the institution that implements the business and legal framework for economic development. Industrial policy can also involve the active participation of non-governmental organisations such as business, trade or industry associations as well as research institutions (e.g. universities) and even trade unions.[4]

Industrial policy includes a wide array of policy instruments; from the traditional trade (e.g. tariffs) tax and credit policies to policies that facilitate technological upgrading and learning, export promotion and human resource development. It could also include ancillary business support services such as in-house technical assistance and trade facilitation in terms of export promotion, marketing, sales and distribution.[5]

Additionally, industrial policy allows for coordination mechanisms and networking opportunities for stakeholders, which are often lacking in free markets, especially in developing countries. This allows transactional costs to be lowered, which ultimately facilitate increased market entry and reduce uncertainty and risk, especially for small and medium-sized enterprises. The goal of industrial policy is to 'coordinate economic change, to promote experimentation, and to preserve diversity'.[6]

In summary, the rationale for industrial policy is premised on the need (1) to assist resource reallocation from declining to rising sectors; (2) to correct externalities associated with specific industries; and, (3) to use 'strategic trade policy' to help firms capture an international pool of profits in globally oligopolistic markets.[7]

The case for market interventions does not accord with neoclassical and neo-liberal economic thought, which gained in ascendancy in developing countries during the structural adjustment years. The argument is that markets optimise resource allocation and that interventions distort resource allocation thus affecting the maximisation of growth. The faith in the market-led approach derives from the 'disillusionment with import substitution, planning and public-sector led development' as well as the neoclassical interpretation of the success of the Asian newly industrialising countries.[8]

On the other hand, it is recognised that industrial policy is not an unqualified success. There are some problems, which have plagued efforts in various countries. It is noted that state intervention can (1) distort relative prices and lead to resource misallocation and a loss of economic efficiency; (2) introduce an additional complex political element since they provide a popular remedy for import-competing firms reluctant to adjust to trade liberalisation; and, (3) inspire countervailing measures and competition among governments to outspend one another thereby squandering resources.[9]

Proponents of industrial policy argue that the assumption of free markets implicit in the neoclassical approach does not accord with the reality of imperfect competition in most global industries. Secondly, the notion that competitiveness flows automatically from 'getting prices right' is not borne out by the experience of most developing countries, including the Asian NICs. And, thirdly the argument that state intervention is necessarily sub-optimal and allows for rent seeking among special interests groups, thereby impeding growth, also does not accord with the Asian NIC experience.[10] The experience of successful industrial policy interventions, however, suggests that:

> It is possible to influence the market place while taking account of price signals in setting priorities and mapping out strategies and, in so doing, serve the long-term interests of the enterprise sector and the economy as a whole.[11]

In the last decade there has been a heightened awareness that the neoclassical paradigm of economic development is inadequate to the challenge of an increasingly volatile global marketplace. The argument is that the neoclassical model does not incorporate the issue of technological development. Industrial competitiveness in the contemporary era of globalisation calls for increased investment in innovation and technological development on the part of firms and national economies. This is because trade liberalisation and new technologies have eliminated the distinction between the home market and the international market for many goods and services. A key component of global competitiveness is innovation, which is based on 'the continuous and incremental upgrading of existing technologies or on a new combination of them'. Additionally, it is argued 'what really matters is a firm's capacity to organise innovation as an interactive learning process'.[12]

Global competitiveness is attained through innovation and a deepening of technological and institutional capabilities and not just through increased capital accumulation, that is, investment.[13] The argument is that enhanced competitiveness is dependent on the stimulation of innovation. This perspective on industrial development suggests that competitive advantage is a dynamic and localised process whereby differences in national values, culture, economic structures, institutions, and histories all contribute to attaining a competitive edge. For instance, Porter argues, 'ultimately, nations succeed in particular industries because their home environment is the most forward-looking, dynamic, and challenging'.[14] He also posits that national prosperity is created and not inherited, states must recognise that a nation's competitiveness depends on the capacity of its industries to innovate and upgrade. In essence, what is called for is an industrial strategy that allows for continuous upgrading, innovation and development of local capabilities.

It is argued that the requirements of technological and institutional innovation are applicable to firms in both developed and developing economies, although it is recognised that the needs are greater in the latter context. It is also noted that critical elements of industrial upgrading, for example, learning and knowledge accumulation, often evade market supply. According to some analysts 'markets are notoriously weak in generating these capabilities, which are subject to externalities'.[15]

Cultural Industry and Industrial Policy

The cultural industries sector refers to commercially viable cultural goods and services that are commodified and distributed to mass audiences. This includes products and services like films, videos, television, musical instruments, sound recordings, commercial theatre, dance and popular music performance.[16] The cultural industries sector, of which the music business is a large component, is one of the fastest growing sectors of the world economy. In the early 1990s entertainment and cultural industries generated a turnover of about US$550 billion of which $380 to $390 billion were accounted for by publishing and printing, $150 billion for the audio-visual sector and $27 billion for music.[17]

The cultural industries are viewed as targets for industrial policy. Industrial policy is largely associated with the manufacturing or goods sector. However, many of the problems and requirements of the goods sector, especially the small and medium-sized enterprise (SME) sub-sector, also apply to the cultural industries sector. For example, the problem of limited access to credit and finance, the high costs of export marketing and inadequate institutional capacity. Where the cultural industries differ relates to the fact that cultural goods and services are genre-driven products built on creativity and reliant on copyright protection. In broad terms the main features of the industrial context for cultural industries can be summarised as follows:

- Intellectual or artistic production is at the heart, while reproduction is a manufacturing process responding to a logic of industrial production.
- Intellectual and artistic production is mainly betting on talent. Market risk is high because consumer taste is volatile and difficult to anticipate, which explains a high rate of failures to successes. Risk can be reduced by concentrating production efforts on a narrow range of universal story lines, which are more likely to appeal to average taste.
- The life cycle of products and services is very short and there is a need for constant innovation. Each entertainment product is typically a 'one-off' and must be perceived as different from previous products, albeit minimally.
- It is difficult to build consumer loyalty. For each product run, consumer taste must be nurtured and channeled. Massive promotional efforts and special mass-marketing techniques, such as the creation of a 'star system' or show business gossip are essential.
- The costs of reproduction are low in relation to initial production costs, which grants high returns to economies of scale in distribution, or audience maximisation.
- Products can be easily reproduced and companies can be considerably hurt by copyright infringement.[18]

The foregoing analysis illustrates the specificity of the industrial challenge facing the cultural industries. It suggests that there are three specific areas for industrial intervention, which differentiates from the traditional goods sector. The first intervention that is required is that of intellectual property protection. The cultural industries cannot survive in the marketplace without adequate protection from copyright infringement. Without such protection cultural entrepreneurs would be at the mercy of piracy, bootlegging, counterfeiting and other forms of infringement such as unlicensed broadcasting. For example, music is one of the easiest forms of art to pirate as a result of the wide diffusion of reproduction technologies such as cassette recorders; recordable compact discs and Internet based file-sharing formats like My.MP3.com, Gnutella and Napster.[19] This calls for the state to comply with and enforce the conventions of the WTO Trade-Related Intellectual Property Rights agreement.

The second key intervention that is required is that of investment in human capital development. This is a critical area because the cultural industries start with creativity. Investing in creative capabilities calls for the establishment of training institutions as well as support mechanisms for young artists and cultural entrepreneurs.

The third key intervention of the cultural industries relates to marketing. As indicated above audience loyalty is difficult to build and predict, hence the need for significant resources in terms of marketing and building a brand. What is also evident is that there is product differentiation based on genre. This calls for lifestyle marketing or niche marketing. Based on this industrial context, analysts argue that:

> To build up a diversified industrial structure and reach a critical mass are essential in order to sustain increasing competition. Maintaining competitiveness requires financial and marketing muscles in order to assemble financing for intellectual and artistic production; to pay the high fees demanded by talented or world famous authors, movie stars, film directors or singers; to bear the relevant risks; to obtain consumer loyalty by promoting massively the product or the brand (the author) over a variety of media; to bundle the rights and protect them; and to be able to gain from ancillary markets such as merchandising. Vast global distribution networks are critical in maximising returns and spreading the risk and cost over larger markets.[20]

MUSIC INDUSTRY AND THE NEW GLOBAL ECONOMY

Perspectives on the music industry have gone through some redefinition because 'what was treated in the 1960s and 1970s as manufacture, an industry primarily selling commodities to consumers, came to be treated in the 1980s as a service, 'exploiting' musical properties as baskets of rights'.[21] This changed view of the music industry is of particular relevance to developing countries since music is one of the copyright industries where they have established some export capabilities.

The convergence of the telecommunications and the media industries as a result of satellite and digital technologies make it 'irrelevant to distinguish between transmission of images from voice, data or text'.[22] The rapid expansion of Internet services illustrates the point. It is suggested, by some industry analysts, that the Internet will revolutionise product sales and marketing, change the nature of piracy and royalties collections as well as upset the balance between the major recording companies and the independents thus giving the consumer greater choice. However, these gains are dependent on wider access to Internet services internationally, improvements in the download capabilities of personal computers and the introduction of world-wide legislation to implement the International Standard Recording Code (a built-in electronic code that identifies all recordings).[23]

Globalising trends signify an expanding market for cultural products and services. The growth of new technologies is also on the viability of the sector in many positive ways. The new digital and telecommunication technologies facilitate a global reach that was impossible before. According to some analysts predictions 'most of tomorrow's entertainment and information products will be recorded digitally, stored digitally, transmitted digitally, and received digitally'.[24] It is anticipated that consumers will have a greater variety of choice in terms of products and service top choose from. Many analysts have likened the emerging scenario to that of 'global jukebox'.[25]

New products and new delivery systems suggest opportunities for new entrants. The issue that arises for developing countries is whether they will be able to develop the expertise and infrastructure to tap into this growth potential. There are essentially two schools of thought on this matter. One school suggests that the new technologies will smooth the entry of small players and promote a democratisation of the marketplace. For example, Paul Goldstein, in his book entitled 'Copyright's Highway', argues that:

> The celestial jukebox, with its enhanced, world-wide access to raw materials of literary and artistic creation and the means to craft them into new products, will reduce the infrastructure costs - printing plants, film studios, distribution channels - that presently exclude less developed economies from creating substantial copyright export industries.[26]

An alternative view suggests that the benefits of the new technologies are not automatic and depend on the structure of the evolving business infrastructure. For instance, it is observable that market control and the profitability of the entertainment industry is moving away from the production side towards distribution and royalties collections. This is the case with technologies like the Internet where a product can be marketed online or downloaded directly to the consumer without a wholesaler or even a retailer. This new business model presents new challenges to the sector:

The problem that needs to be solved is 'who gets the royalties'. Any digital jukebox will have to sort out who gets the revenue, how it's collected and how sales can be properly audited, before they can legally distribute copyrighted music over the Internet.[27]

In the last few years Internet based music services have grown at a rapid rate through firms like CDnow, RealAudio and Liquid Audio, the downloading of music has been made more accessible with file formats like MP3, a2b and Audio 4.0 and the issue of music identification has been addressed through watermarking and other security devices. It is argued that the emerging techno-economic paradigm is likely to result in a radical realignment of the industrial structure of the global music industry. As one analyst put it:

> All previous distributed music carriers – from the wax cylinder to new optical discs systems like Super audio CD and DVD-Audio – have been physical objects requiring manufacturing resources and conventional retailing. But electronic distribution can bypass all this, with music sent direct from record company to consumer. An even more radical possibility is for artists to bypass record companies altogether and sell their music direct.[28]

The threat that the Internet poses has prompted a response from the transnational firms. In December 1998 the Big Five formed a strategic alliance with several technology companies, namely, Sony, JVC, Pioneer, Matsushita, Dolby and Microsoft, to establish the Secure Digital Music Initiative (SDMI), which aims to set a standard system for distributing music over the Internet. The SDMI has yielded little so far. However, industry shifts have been moving at a blinding pace as firms juggle their options. The last few years has seen the major companies jockeying for positions in the Internet race. For example, UMG and BMG have established a joint venture GetMusic.com, IBM and RealNetworks have come together to form a digital downloading system, Microsoft has introduced an alternative downloading solution MS Audio 4.0, AT&T's a2b and Liquid audio have been negotiating with major recording artists like Alanis Morissette and Garbage, and Sony has designed its own digital distribution solution called Magic-Gate.[29]

Another distinguishing feature of the current context is the rationalisation of the industry in terms of corporate takeovers, leading to higher levels of industrial concentration. As table 1 below shows, the six largest firms accounted for close to 80 per cent of the world market back in 1996. The leading transnational firms are: WEA (Time Warner Inc.), BMG (Bertelsmann AG),

EMI (Thorn EMI PLC), CBS (Sony Corporation), Universal (Seagrams formerly MCA) and Polygram (Phillips N.V.). The 'Big Six' became 'Five' after the latter two firms merged in May 1998 when the Canadian firm Seagrams acquired 100 per cent of Polygram to form the Universal Music Group (UMG) (see table 2).

In November 1999 Time Warner merged (vertical integration) with America On Line to form the largest entertainment company in the world. There have been several unsuccessful efforts to purchase EMI by AOL-Time Warner and BMG. In June 2000, in something of a counter strike, Seagrams, the parent company of Universal Studios and the Universal Music Group, was taken over by Vivendi SA, the French utilities, media and telecoms conglomerate. Vivendi owns, among other things, Internet distribution systems and the pay-television channel Canal Plus. The merger establishes Vivendi-Universal as the world's second largest media and entertainment company.

Table 1: World Market Shares of the Major Music Companies, 1996 (%)

BMG	EMI	PolyGram	Sony	Universal	Warner
12.0	14.0	16.5	15.5	6.0	15.0

Source: Music & Copyright, July 16, 1997.

Table 2: World Market Shares of the Major Music Companies, 1998 (%)

BMG	EMI	Sony	UMG	WMG
10.5	14.0	18.0	22.0	13.0

Source: Music & Copyright, July 14, 1999.

The competitive advantage of the major corporations is in the distribution stage: the delivery of finished products to retail markets and the stimulation of consumer demand through advertising and promotion. The large firms have been able to maintain control of this most profitable stage through the 'maintenance of their own wholesale distribution networks and strategic alliances with major retail chains', as well as through 'tight formatting of radio playlists, exclusivity agreements with music video channels such as MTV, and market surveillance systems such as SoundScan'.[30] The vertical integration of music companies and ISPs is a deepening of the corporate consolidation trend as the industry searches for a new business model.

The Caribbean Music Industry

The Caribbean enjoys a competitive capability in cultural production.[31] For example, in the case of Jamaica, reggae accounts for a rising share of global music sales. Jamaica continues to be the primary source for musical innovation in the reggae genre. For Trinidad it can claim that it is the undisputed leader in the globalised Caribbean carnivals. Trinidad is the major supplier of artists, designers, and other forms of cultural capital. Most of the overseas carnivals view Trinidad and Tobago's carnival as the mother of all Caribbean carnivals.[32] The region's contribution to the cultural industries, particularly popular music, has been very significant. It is often noted that the region's impact on the world music scene has been large relative to its size. For example, according to some analysts:

> The many musical styles that have been propagated in these island cultures are among the most dynamic and influential in the world, and their artists - names like Mighty Sparrow, Kassav, Celia Cruz, Ruben Blades, Juan Luis Guerra, and the late, great Bob Marley - have a truly global following.[33]

The Caribbean's long history of involvement in the global music industry and its dynamic contribution to world music through the export of genres like calypso, meringue, son, zouk, dancehall and reggae makes it an interesting case study for examining the prospects for peripheral regions in the emerging world economy. The region's music industry, in spite of its perceived success, has had long-standing problems in relation to manufacturing, distribution, marketing, copyright protection and royalties collections. The argument that is being put forward here is that these problems relate to the fact that the region has spawned great music without putting in place the requisite level of industrial infrastructure to ensure increasing local value added and industrial deepening. This situation has prompted one analyst to argue that:

> Caribbean music, an integral part of culture and tradition, makes money in New York, London, Paris and Amsterdam. More Caribbeannists have earned international recognition from music than from any other pursuit. Living in small countries of little fame, Caribbeans are proud of their music stars. A few have earned millions from recordings that have brought in billions. But so far, this hasn't made their countries any less poor, and the lucrative Caribbean music business has remained far away out of Caribbean control.[34]

The above analysis suggests that artistic production is the strength of the regional music industry but indicates that there is much scope for improvement in professionalism, entrepreneurship and product development. Manufacturing and merchandising are areas that have been plagued by business failure, competition from overseas and the seasonality of some of the art forms, especially in the case of Trinidad and Tobago. Marketing, distribution and retailing are the weakest phase in the music industry, both at the local and international level. Copyright protection remains problematic because of piracy, and, though royalty collections have improved with the establishment of national copyright organisations in Trinidad and Tobago, Jamaica, Barbados and St Lucia, there is still much room for higher inflows from foreign collections. There is also an absence of dedicated training and educational facilities in the area of cultural industries.[35]

The economic and export performance of the entertainment industry illustrates that there is an overseas market for indigenous cultural products and services but the sector is not as competitive as it could be, nor is it marketed appropriately to take advantage of existing opportunities. To expand the export market, the entertainment industry must create and nurture foreign demand through joint ventures or promotional and distribution deals with international entertainment firms. The export thrust will be facilitated by market and media access, human resource development and training, and innovation and industrial upgrading at home. [36]

Building an international image and reputation for quality is important. Participating in international trade fairs, festivals and awards ceremonies can acquaint artists and cultural entrepreneurs with the demands of the overseas market. The entertainment industry in the Caribbean needs to develop an aggressive posture to penetrate the international market. The rationale is that the industry is faced with the task of creating demand for new genres of music and other entertainment products and services. This may require the establishment of strategic alliances in some cases as well direct promotion in others. Foreign direct investment, joint ventures and promotional and distribution deals are avenues that need to be seriously explored given the high barriers to export market entry.[37]

The sector is largely under-researched and suffers from inadequate data. Consequently, policy formulation has suffered from conceptual clarity. In many cases, the music industry is not viewed as a sector by government officials and the corporate elite. A significant part of the problem is that actors in the industry have also rarely organised themselves like other sectors. This has resulted in the blockage of investment and funding to upgrade the competitiveness of the sector.

Strategic Directions for the Caribbean Music Industry

The economic contribution of the Caribbean music industry is not fully captured in existing national and regional statistics nor is it a part of national or regional development or trade policy. This is in spite of the fact that the industry has been proven to have tremendous export capabilities and great demand-pull for the tourism sector in several countries.

From this standpoint it can be argued that the Caribbean has a window of opportunity in the new global economy, where copyright, cultural and media industries are among the fastest growth sectors. In this regard, the Caribbean music industry should be viewed as a prime target for private investment and institutional support in the regional diversification initiative. Based on these criteria the Caribbean cultural industries sector is a good candidate for intervention in that it is an emerging export sector plagued with market failure in key business services and weak institutional support at home and constrained by oligopolistic practices in mainstream markets.

An increasing number of countries have begun to recognise the economic benefits of the music industry and have implemented industrial policies to enhance the competitiveness of the sector. An example of this trend is the increase in the number of national export agencies that participate in the largest annual music trade fair, MIDEM. In countries like Canada,[38] the UK[39] and Ireland[40] active measures have been instituted to deepen the industrialisation of the music industry. A regional initiative, the European Music Office, was established by the European Union in 1997.

Across the various country initiatives there is a general consensus that creating a competitive advantage calls for the continuous upgrading of artistic and entrepreneurial skills, enterprise development, market development, product and service innovation and the strengthening of the home environment. The Irish case is worthy of some mention. The industrial strategy was built on four strands:

1. Developing Irish music
2. Ireland as a location for foreign investment
3. Improved international exposure
4. Public relations/Information campaign[41]

A similar perspective has begun to emerge in the Caribbean. JAMPRO and TIDCO have been engaged in some trade promotion measures. Caribbean Export Development Agency has assisted several firms through their competitiveness programme. In recent times industry players have articulated a position. At a regional meeting at the Caribbean Music Expo (CME), held in Ocho Rios, Jamaica, November 1999, industry stakeholders (for example music producers, artists, distributors, media practitioners, attorneys and industry analysts) identified five critical areas for immediate action to promote the development of the regional music industry. The areas identified were:

1. The removal of customs duties on CDs, cassettes, records, and promotional videos containing performances, sound recordings, or musical compositions by artists from the region, to facilitate free movement of these products in CARICOM.
2. The development of strategic alliances and mergers between small distributors in the region to make Caribbean music more accessible in the global marketplace, and to develop a regional grouping to lobby for further improvements in the music industry.
3. The introduction of content quotas for local and regional music to increase the amount of Caribbean music aired on radio and television throughout the region.
4. The introduction of anti-piracy measures at the national and regional levels to ensure the protection and remuneration of rights owners.
5. The implementation of a regional system for collective management of copyright and related rights to improve the collection and distribution of royalties regionally and internationally.

The issues and strategies identified above are designed to improve local and regional control of the production, marketing and distribution process. Such a strategy, however, calls for a wide range of expertise backed up by an industrial infrastructure, which is not currently in place. This chapter recommends nine key objectives and attendant strategies:[42]

COORDINATED INDUSTRIAL POLICY FOR THE CARIBBEAN MUSIC INDUSTRY

1. EXPAND INCOME GENERATION

- Provide financial support for record producers and labels.
- Upgrade and update record manufacturing.
- Expand earnings from overseas tours.
- Strengthen record publishing.
- Upgrade merchandising
- Introduce Internet based sales techniques.

2. FACILITATE EXPORT MARKETING

- Increase participation in trade fairs.
- Strengthen distribution channels.
- Broaden mass media access.
- Widen circuit of concert tours and festival engagements.
- Develop a joint marketing strategy with tourism sector
- Introduce Internet-based technologies and business practices.

3. INVEST IN HUMAN RESOURCE DEVELOPMENT

- Artist development
- Enterprise development
- Technical skills development
- Professional skills development

4. ENABLE INSTITUTIONAL CAPACITY BUILDING

- Establish a regional organisation
- Establish and upgrade national industry associations
- Offer business support services
- Develop an economic research capability
- Develop a market intelligence capability

5. COPYRIGHT PROTECTION AND COLLECTIVE ADMINISTRATION

- Establish viable national copyright societies
- Strengthen existing national copyright societies
- Implement regional data and rights management centre
- Enhance bargaining leverage with foreign copyright societies

6. IMPLEMENT ANTI-PIRACY CAMPAIGN

- Implement 'banderole' system
- Strengthen enforcement capability
- Introduce private recording levy on blank tape and CD imports
- Develop public awareness campaign

7. UPGRADE THE HOME ENVIRONMENT

- Improve government-industry relations
- Foster public awareness of the contribution of the music industry
- Increase local/regional content on the airwaves
- Establish musicians union
- Improve access to credit

8. DEVELOP INTERNET-READINESS

- Develop market profile of the potential Internet music audience
- Develop a regional Internet marketing and distribution programme
- Conduct training programme for music industry firms
- New product development

9. ALIGN AND HARMONISE GOVERNMENT POLICY FRAMEWORK

- Establish industrial policy
- Establish trade policy
- Establish intellectual property policy
- Establish cultural policy
- Establish educational policy

Conclusion

The paper starts from the premise that the problem of governance is not purely political. There is a critical role for governments in developing countries to impact more positively on their economies. In the context of an increasingly globalised world-economy this calls for enhanced competitiveness. Given the endemic problem of market failure found in most developing countries the paper proposed the adoption of industrial policy interventions. The Caribbean cultural industries sector, specifically the music industry, was selected as a case study for such an intervention based on its export potential in the new global economy.

Throughout the region there is little appreciation and knowledge of the economic, business and legal aspects of the music industry as well as the emerging opportunities offered by the new digital technologies (for example in production, marketing and distribution) and the expansive growth of an intellectual property and services economy. This paper concludes that the Caribbean music industry requires institutional support to upgrade the nascent creative and entrepreneurial capabilities, to facilitate balanced growth in the home market, to maximise on the trade potential of diasporic markets and to make further inroads into global music markets.

The paper identifies a critical role for regional and national organisations involved in enterprise development, business financing and export facilitation. However, it notes that effective lobbying for changes in the industry will only come about through a strong organisational network in the region. Currently, the industry does not have a collective voice or a suitable infrastructure for furthering the development of music and increasing its competitiveness at home or abroad. The small and medium-sized enterprises, which predominate in the music industry, must develop their institutional capacity in areas such as monitoring, documentation and lobbying to achieve many of the stated aims.

Endnotes

1. UNDP, 1997, pp. 2-3.
2. Lall, 1995, pp. 7-8.
3. Leipziger, et al 'Mercosur: Integration and Industrial Policy' *The World Economy* 2015: 585-603. 1997, p. 595.
4. Meyer-Stamer, 1999.
5. Samuels, 1995, pp. 115-116.
6. Kosacoff & Ramos, 1999, p. 44.
7. Leipziger et al, 1997, p. 59.

8. Lall, 1995, p. 7.
9. Leipziger et al, 1997, p. 595.
10. Lall, 1995; Ernst, Ganiatsos & Mytelka, 1998; Wade, 1990.
11. UNCTAD, 1996, p. 78.
12. Ernst, Ganiatsos & Mytelka, 1998, p. 13.
13. Ernst, Ganiatsos & Mytelka, 1998.
14. Porter, M. 'The Competitive Advantage of Nations', Harvard Business Review, March-April: 73-93, 1990, p. 74.
15. Ernst, Ganiatsos & Mytelka, 1998, p. 12.
16. Lewis, 1995.
17. UNCTAD/ILO, 1995, p. 6.
18. UNCTAD/ILO, 1995, pp. 34-35.
19. Nurse, 2000.
20. UNCTAD/ILO, 1995, p. 35 .
21. Frith, 1993, p. ix.
22. UNCTAD/ILO, 1995.
23. Hayes, 1996, pp. 14-15.
24. Goldstein, P. 1994, p. 197, copyright Highway: Frim Gutensberg to the Celestial Jukebox (New York: Hill and Wang).
25. Burnett, 1996.
26. Goldstein, 1994, p. 234.
27. Burnett, 1996, p. 146.
28. Cole, G. 1999, p. 110, 'Music via the Internet' Gramophone, Sept, 110, 112.
29. Haring, 1999.
30. Weber, 1996, p. 5-6.
31. Bourne, C and S.M. Allgrove, 1997; Watson, P., 1995.
32. Nurse, K. 1999 'The Globalisation of Trinidad Carnival: Diaspora Hybridity and Identity in Global Culture', Cultural Studies 13.4: 661-690.
33. Broughton, et al., 1995, p. 473.
34. Kurlansky, 1992, p. 102.
35. Nurse, K. 1997 'The Trinidad and Tobago Entertainment Industry: Structure and Export Capabilites'. Caribbean Dialogue 3.3: 13-38.
36. Nurse, 1997.
37. Nurse, 1997.
38. ACCISS, 1994.
39. Casey et al, 1996; Feist 1996.
40. IMIG, 1998.
41. IMIG, 1998.
42. See figure 1 for further details.

References

Burnett, R, *The Global Jukebox: The International Music Industry* (London: Routledge, 1996).

Del Corral, M. and S. Abada, 'Cultural and Economic Development through Copyright in the Information Age', *UNESCO World Culture Report 1998: Culture, Creativity and Markets* (Paris: UNESCO Publishing, 1998) pp. 210-221.

Goldstein, P, *Copyright's Highway: From Gutenberg to the Celestial Jukebox* (New York: Hill and Wang, 1994).

IMIG, *Raising the Volume: Policies to Expand the Irish Music Industry*, The Irish Music Industry Group of the Irish Business Employers Confederation (1998).

Leipziger, D et al 'Mercosur, 'Integration and Industrial Policy', *The World Economy*, 20.5 (1997) pp. 585-603.

Nurse, K, 'The Trinidad and Tobago Entertainment Industry: Structure and Export Capabilities', *Caribbean Dialogue* 3.3 (1997) pp.13-38.

UNCTAD/ILO, *Media Services: A Survey of the Industry and its Largest Firms* (Geneva: UNCTAD/ILO, 1995).

UNCTAD, *Globalisation and Liberalisation: Development in the face of two powerful currents* (New York: United Nations, 1996).

Part II

❋

Crisis of Adjustment

6

Understanding the Socio-Cultural Dynamics of Globalisation: The Case of Bananas in St Lucia and St Vincent and the Grenadines

Dave Ramsaran

INTRODUCTION

This chapter is a comparative study from a socio-cultural perspective, aimed at understanding the impacts of globalisation on two small island-states St Lucia, St Vincent and the Grenadines. More specifically this paper looks at how people are adjusting and interpreting the process of globalisation as experienced through the reduction in profitability of the banana industry. The study seeks to address certain broad areas of concern. These are: who has been the major casualties as a result of the decline in the banana industry; how do people interpret the challenge to their livelihood; what are the gender implications due to this decline; and what is the relationship between these developments and the overall political process. The major contention is that these questions can only be addressed meaningfully by looking at the unique cultural and institutional arrangements in each society. At a broader level it is suggested that even though globalisation has some uniform processes across countries, the interpretation of those processes and the actions that people take are dependent on their own interpretation of the process through their own cultural lens. To attain these ends, in-depth interviews were conducted with persons who are currently involved in the banana industry in both countries. These were taped interviews that were conducted on-site. To gain access to these persons the various Banana Growers Associations (where they exist) and state ministries in charge of these industries were utilised. The paper is organised into four sections. The first section looks at the theoretical debate that surrounds the process of globalisation and the uniqueness of small island states in that process. Section two looks at the nature of the respective societies and the position of the banana industry in each country, their similarities and differences. Section three looks at how the process of globalisation in the context of the decline of the banana industry unfolded in the late 1980s and early 1990s and Section four looks at the findings.

THEORETICAL POSITION

Globalisation and its impact on society can be viewed from two lenses. One lens note that globalisation has resulted in the emergence of a middle class in some peripheral countries. The implementation of neo-liberal policies is seen as having a positive long-term effect on societies. The other lens shows that globalisation involves increasing inequality between and within nations, increasing environmental degradation especially in the developing world, and deteriorating labour standards. Caribbean realities suggest that both scenarios can be accurate at the same time. The theoretical position adopted here suggest that this process is in fact a contradictory one, and includes three levels – the supra-statal, statal and intra-statal levels, and within each level there are two dimensions; the transnational political organisations and a new global culture. Globalisation involves a dialectical relationship between its economic political and cultural dimensions within each level (Price and Ramsaran forthcoming).

Globalisation is a not a new phenomenon. Capitalism has been global in character since the time Europeans established colonies in what we now know today as the underdeveloped world. Colonial economies were organised to suit the needs of the core countries of the capitalist world system.[1] However even though some elements of globalisation have been around for quite a while, several elements highlight the present phase of global capitalist development. These economic, political, and cultural processes are interconnected through markets, finance, goods and services, and transnational corporate networks.[2] An important dimension of this process is cultural penetration.

The economics of globalisation refers to the contemporary process of capitalist accumulation. This model looks at how this process operates at the supra-statal, statal and intra-statal level. At the supra-statal level this process is propelled by an international elite. Manifested through global commodity chains and a global division of labour, the increasing concentration of industries into a small number of transnational corporations, the development of global regulatory institutions, and a shift in world trade from goods and services to financial instruments. This internationalisation of the world economy under transnational corporations however, is pursued without violating the economic interest of the leading core states.[3] At the statal level the economics of globalisation plays itself out in the context of intra-class struggles between nation elites. Although the relationship between governments in the core states and elements of their respective international elite has been mainly harmonious it is prone to tensions. At times elements of the international elite can run afoul with their respective governments and vice versa. At the intra statal level the economics of globalisation manifest itself within the context of the system of social stratification and can be analysed along the lines of race, gender and class.

The politics of globalisation looks at how decisions are made and how power is distributed. At the supra-statal level this model focuses on the issues surrounding global governance and includes such institutions as the World Trade Organisation, The International Monetary Fund, and The World Bank. Areas of national sovereignty are being redefined since global finance requires global governance. At the statal level this model looks at politics through the world systems arrangement of core and periphery. There are several reasons for the inequality of power between nations the main ones being wealth and military might. At the statal level politics is played out through organisations specific to the local situation. At this level the focus would be on political parties, NGOs and other grassroots organisations.

The culture of globalisation refers to the ideology that drives the process of globalisation. It highlights the increasingly interconnected social world, which weakens the uniqueness of national ways of living, local cultures and non-capitalist values. At the supra-statal level this is the ideology of neo-liberalism and the promotion of the consumer citizen and individualism. At the statal level the ideology is that of civil society and citizenship. This ideology underscores the legitimacy of regional and global treaties, because state power is predicated on the sovereignty of nation-states to engage in international policies that protect national interests. Yet the processes of globalisation at the statal level are squeezing the nation-state between the accountability to market forces represented by supra-statal institutions, and the accountability to 'the governed' represented by domestic political parties and interest groups. This contradiction is intense, because national elites need the state to facilitate entry into the international ruling class, but are constrained by widespread attachment to the ideology of democracy and state sovereignty. At the statal level the culture of globalisation must be seen within the context of meritocracy, equality of opportunity and social justice on the one hand, and the unique cultural and institutional arrangements that allow people to interpret the global process. It must be noted that in this model the three levels and three dimensions within each level is involved in a dialectical relationship. This study is pitched at the statal level so it seeks to ascertain how process at the other levels impact and are interpreted at the local level and in-turn affect process at other levels.

Even though there are some commonalities in terms of how the globalisation process works and particularly the economic assumptions of that process, there are some characteristics that are unique to small-island states. Small states have special issues that must be taken into consideration and one of them is their vulnerability to the international global system. Small states have particular problems with the openness of their economy. There is the general agreement that 'developed countries will sneeze and small states would catch the cold'. Small states also have limited resources in terms of natural resources and human capital. Attaining economies of scale when it applies to production can only be achieved if the commodity is produced mainly for export.[4] Windward Island bananas are also particularly vulnerable to tropical hurricanes that can devastate an entire harvest. Further, small states are particularly vulnerable to instruments that operate outside of the nation state which influence norms and values, namely the media.

THE POSITION OF BANANAS IN THE WINDWARD ISLANDS

The banana industry in the Windward Islands developed at a rapid pace in the post 1950 period under the protection of the British Government. Nurse and Sandiford argues that the promotion of Windward Island bananas was 'viewed as a response to the deplorable conditions of the region's masses... and the rising tide of social discontent and unrest in the Crown Colonies in the depressionary period of the 1930's and 1940's.'[5] Indeed under special arrangements Non-Commonwealth bananas faced import duties that gave preferential treatment to Windward Island bananas.

To a large extent the banana industry allowed for the development of a peasantry that cultivated their lands using mainly family labour thus ensuring some measure of independent development. In the majority of the islands where bananas were cultivated this was undertaken under the auspices of a Banana Growers Association (BGA). These associations were statutory boards that handled all aspects of the banana production process, they provided inputs on credit to the farmers, collected, packaged, shipped the product and paid farmers for their banana. Farmers did not deal with the European companies. The most prominent company in the Windward Islands was Geest.

Some problems arose with the operations of these BGAs. On the one hand there are/were larger farmers who dominated the various growers associations and thus have/had a disproportionate amount of access to credit and fertiliser subsidies.[6] Further, these statutory boards were prone to political manipulation. Since the banana industry was the major contributor to the economies of both St Vincent and the Grenadines and St Lucia in terms of income and employment, political parties sought to influence how these associations operated. Being on favourable terms with participants in the banana sector could result in the mobilisation of many votes. Since it was the respective associations who decided how much farmers were paid for their bananas, governments sought to influence how much was paid to the farmer. Many times the farmer would be paid more than the price fetched for the product on the international market. This resulted in serious indebtedness by these organisations. At the time of this research being conducted the St Vincent BGA was in debt for the sum of $15m EC dollars. In St Lucia because of the problems in the industry the BGA was privatised and no longer operates as a statutory board. The organisational structure of the industry in both islands have significant influence on how those in the industry interpret the process of restructuring that globalisation has forced in the industry.

The organisation of banana production in the Windward Islands has been saddled with particular disadvantages when compared to 'dollar bananas' produced in Latin America and controlled by large US firms. The Windward Island industry has a large percentage of smallholder farms, owned and operated by peasants whereas the industry in Latin America is produced mainly on large plantations. Further the majority of farms in the Windward Islands are on hilly terrain where the soils are not the best for cultivation. The importance of the industry to these islands however, cannot be over-emphasised, it is the largest user of agricultural land, the largest single employer and makes a significant contribution to GDP and foreign exchange earnings.[7]

How the production process was and is organised also has a profound impact on how the globalisation process is felt. Bananas have been, and continue to be a rural crop. Banana cultivation because of the way it is organised provides a fairly continuous source of income. A farmer can plant his/her fields and approximately nine months the trees are grown. With the application of the correct amounts of fertilisers, you can harvest bananas continuously every week for quite a long time. Initially the associations gave credit to the farmers for inputs. At one point in time the respective BGAs had a series of boxing plants located in rural areas. On harvest days the farmers would bring their bananas to these respective boxing plants and the BGA would hire workers and provide cartoons to package the bananas. There was no concern as to what quality of fruit was delivered. So long as one delivered the fruit one was paid. The fruit was then transported to the docks by the association for export to Europe.

The Association would deduct its cost of internal transportation and export cost, and the amount of credit that was extended to the farmer from the money received. If a farmer provided fruit to the Association in this week he/she would be paid for it the following week. It meant then that if one delivered fruit continuously every week one was guaranteed a weekly income. Up to the 1980s the associations had paymasters that took the cash out the rural areas to the respective farmers. Because of the downturn in the industry in both St Lucia and St Vincent the boxing plants are not longer operational, farmers must box their own fruit. They must also provide their own transportation to the port, pay for their cartoons, adhere to certain quality standards, and have reduced access to credit. In the case of St Lucia they have almost no access to credit for inputs as they had in the past, because of privatisation.

The labour organisation in the banana industry also has profound implications for how the restructuring has impacted the society. Among the owners of farms there were large farmers but the majority were small farmers with between three and five acres. Many times the farm was maintained by the farmer's labour along with unpaid family labour from his wife and children. In some instances they would hire some outside help, larger farms were the ones that depended on hired labour. The industry is composed of persons who own their own farms as well as those who hire their labour to the larger farmers. Some small farmers along with cultivating their own land also hire their labour out to other farmers to increase their income. Further, in the banana industry there is a gendered division of labour, some work is considered woman's work and others man's work. Tasks such as digging trenches, transporting the fruit to truck transportation, and fertilising is considered to be men's work. Tasks such as de-flowering the plants and packing, tasks that needs tender hands, are considered women's work. Men's work generally pay more than women's work. Among female farmers their labour demands and cost are different to men-owned farms.

Banana's importance to the employment, income and overall standard of living in both St Lucia and St Vincent is well established. It was the largest employer, the largest contributor to GDP and the largest foreign exchange earner up to the end of the 1980s. In the 1990s however there has been a steady decline. St Lucia's production has fallen from 168,080 tonnes in 1988 to approximately 73,220 tonnes in 1998 and St Vincent's production fell from 64,888 in 1988 to about 39,886 tonnes in 1998.[8] According to an ILO Report (1999) the number of active growers in St Lucia fell from 10,000 in 1993 to approximately 5,000 in 1997. St Vincent also saw a decline in direct growers from 8,000 in 1993 to approximately 6,000 in 1997. These figures relate to those who were active farmers but it had a multiplier effect in employment. So 'whereas the banana industry in St Lucia was said to generate direct employment for some 20,000 people, indirectly some 60,000 people (or over one third of the population) depended on the industry for employment and income'.[9] Further the contribution of bananas to real GDP has also declined significantly. For St Lucia, bananas contribution to real GDP fell from 6.3 per cent in 1993 to 3.2 per cent in 1997 and for St Vincent and the Grenadines for the same period it went from 7 per cent to 1.8 per cent. What precipitated this decline?

The Globalisation of the Banana Market

One of the hallmarks of the globalisation process is rapid trade liberalisation. That process was to be at the center of the decline that the banana industry faced in the 1990s. In the 1980s banana was referred to as 'Green Gold'. To understand the decline however, one has to look externally to the emergence of regionalism and trade liberalisation in Europe and the United States and the role of the WTO in adjudication of world trade practices.

Up to the beginning of the 1990s Windward Island bananas (the Windward Islands include St Lucia, St Vincent, Dominica and Grenada) received preferential treatment for their produce that entered Europe. Europe had made commitments for preferential treatment to many of their former colonies many of which form what is referred to as the African Caribbean and Pacific Group (ACP) under the Lome Convention. Most Western European countries had a 20 per cent common external tariff on bananas, Germany being the exception. In the late 1980s the Europeans announced that in 1993 they would have a common union with unified tariffs and trade rules. This meant that European countries had to deal with the preferential treatment that ACP countries enjoyed which included St Lucia and St Vincent.

The European Union (EU) was faced with a series of contending interest. They had to deal with their own high cost producers (Guadeloupe and Martinique) and former colonies (the Windward Islands) and the demand by Europeans, and in particular Germany and the Benelux countries, for cheaper 'Dollar Bananas' produced by the American multinationals (Chiquita, Dole and Del Monte). They also had to take into account their own companies that were involved in the banana business, British Geest and Irish Fyffes.[10] Trade liberalisation meant the protection and preferential access to markets afforded to these islands had to be reduced and eventually eliminated. The quota and tariff for 'Dollar Bananas' were reduced. It meant that in the long run Windward Island bananas would have to compete on a level playing field with 'Dollar Bananas'.

The US multinational corporations were not happy with the new banana regime and they lobbied the US Government in 1993 to take action in their defence. Initially the US Government was reluctant to take action against some of the lingering protectionist policies of the EU. Caribbean banana producers however, were the pawns in a bigger battle that was being fought between Europe and the United States. In 1989 many European countries placed a ban on all hormone-treated beef from around the world suggesting that it may be a public health issue. To date the ban is still in effect. This ban affected beef supplies from around the world and was particularly harsh on specialty meats.

This dispute led the US Government to take action against the Banana Regime that was instituted by the EU in 1996. The US, Ecuador, Guatemala, Honduras and Mexico all went to the WTO alleging that the EU had violated WTO rules with respect to is banana imports. The WTO announced a panel to deal with the issue in 1996. Only members with substantial direct interest were initially allowed to make their case before this panel. Countries with substantial interest could be considered third parties to the dispute. Initially the Caribbean was not considered a bona fide third party since none of the Caribbean countries had more than a 10 per cent share or more of the European market. After much diplomatic efforts they were allowed to participate but they had to hire legal counsel to represent them. 'Objections were raised to this on the grounds that the legal counsel were not in full time employment of any of the Caribbean countries'.[11] The WTO ruled that the EU was in violation of free trade practices. In 1999 the EU attempted to modify its ruling to comply with the WTO ruling. The new regulations were still not deemed compliant with WTO rules and there were concerns about a trans Atlantic trade war. The US sought to have the WTO 'authorises it to impose retaliatory measures against the EU amounting to more than US$500m since, in its judgment, the EU's modified regime was not in compliance with the ruling of the Panel and Appellate Body'.[12]

The process of liberalisation that began in 1993 continues today. By the year 2005 the EU would have removed all quotas and tariffs that allowed preferential treatment to ACP banana producers. Windward Island bananas would have to compete with bananas produced in Latin America. However they face particularly difficult problems lowering their cost in order to compete. In the first instance because of the hilly terrain farms are much smaller than in Latin America, it severely reduces the use of machinery in the process and therefore limits the benefits of large-scale production. Small size also makes it difficult to standardise products and process. The cost of labour in Central America is also much less than it is in the Eastern Caribbean.

FINDINGS

Persons involved in the banana industry in St Vincent and the Grenadines and St Lucia interpret the process of globalisation through the local lenses and their own cultural experience. In both countries the majority of the persons involved in the industry particularly the farmers, see the decline of the industry more the fault of the internal players, namely the respective BGAs or in the case of St Lucia the privatised banana companies, as well as the governments rather than external sources.

St Vincent and the Grenadines has a more difficult topographical terrain when compared to St Lucia. Almost all of the banana production in St Vincent takes place on very hilly terrain. Some parts of the hilly terrain is very inaccessible to motorised transportation. In St Lucia there are more areas of flat land that are used to cultivate bananas, however larger farmers dominate the flat areas and small farmers tend to cultivate the hilly areas.

In 1998, the population of St Vincent was estimated to be about 111, 224 of which about 52 per cent were considered rural. In terms of poverty estimates about 17 per cent of the population is estimated to be living in poverty but the poverty rate is much higher in the rural areas (21.79 per cent) compared to urban poverty (11.81 per cent). This is directly related to the fact that the banana industry is mainly a rural crop and between 1993 and 1997 the amount of active farmers declined about 13 per cent. Overall St Vincent had a 20 per cent unemployment rate and a dependency ratio of about 1 to 3.3.[14]

The decline in St Lucia has been more precipitous than St Vincent. Between 1993 and 1997 there was a 50 per cent decline in the amount of active growers.[14] Of the 149,621 persons that lived in St Lucia in 1998, 63 per cent were considered rural and 37 per cent urban. A greater percentage of the rural population lived below the poverty line (26 per cent) than the urban population where poverty is placed at 22 per cent. Rural and urban poverty is much closer in St Lucia than St Vincent and may be due to the fact that the collapse is more drastic in St Lucia than St Vincent. Overall the unemployment rate in St Lucia is about 22 per cent and a dependency ratio of 1 to 2.6.[15]

We know from the figures that there is a decline in the number of farmers and persons who are employed in the industry however, as to how many small or large farmers have fallen out is more difficult to ascertain. What is clear is that in both islands larger farmers have cut back the amount of acreage they have under cultivation. It is small farmers who are more likely to fall out of the industry all together however; this is premised on the availability of alternative livelihood earning strategies.

Larger farmers tend to think that the decline in the industry has hit them harder because they had a lot more financial capital tied up in their ventures. The majority of larger farmers depended on hired labour but with the decline in price and labour cost remaining high productivity fell. Labour productivity is a major concern of the larger farmer. One person in St Vincent described the situation in this manner:

> you have people coming to work maybe between 7 and 8 o'clock and by 11 they would be gone, so you really get 3 hours of work out of your labour force. The story is told of workers who would boast that they did 3 days work

in one day because they could work with you from 8 to 11 and go to another
person from 11:30 to 2 and for another person in the cool of the evening ...
So to the worker he got 3 days work, individually however we got only 3 hours
of work out of him and when you look at the 3 hours work he took maybe 1½
(half) hours to prepare his tools and let alone to smoke a cigarette before he
starts to work.

Persons involved in the industry in St Lucia also expressed similar concerns
'we have a problem of labour productivity now, a lot of farmers get 3 to 4 hours
of work from their hired labour and their price is going up'.

Larger farmers in both countries were also concerned about the cost of
labour, 'labour cost here is one of our main problems, now I am not saying
that people are getting too much for a days work but we are not getting what
we should be getting out of the worker in a day's work'. The major impact on
the larger farmers then seem to be a reduction of production and in-turn a
reduction in the number of persons that they hire. The lack of water is one
problem that was identified more by these farmers in St Lucia than St Vincent.
St Vincent has used some funds received from the EU to invest in irrigation.
Some farmers in St Lucia have gone out of banana production all together
because of the lack of water and some have gone into vegetable production.

Small farmers on the other hand are more likely to identify the price they
are receiving for their products and the cost of inputs as their major problem.
Prior to 1993 farmers took their bananas to the BGA and they were paid a
fixed price, there was not concern for quality or the market conditions. With
the coming of the new banana regime however in 1993, the farmers started to
face some elements of competition. Along with the lower prices farmers now
face price fluctuations and the addition of more tasks to their production. In
the 1980s all of the packaging and transportation of their product up to the
port were undertaken by the BGA. With the demands of the global market and
the necessity for traceability by the supermarkets in the UK, most farmers have
more tasks now to undertake. Not only is there the requirement of closer
monitoring of the quality of the product, and standards of pesticides and fertilisers,
but they must also box and transport their products. It was described in this
way:

in the 70s all the farmer had to do was harvest the bunch, he wraps it and
brought it to the reception point, now he has to de-hand it. At one point
he brought that to a central point, not again, now the farmer does everything
even box ... the farmer now does everything and makes it supermarket
ready.

The variability of prices for the small farmers were particularly disconcerting. One farmer put it this way 'sometimes it is good and sometimes it is bad, sometimes you get a good price and sometimes you get nothing at all.' One female farmer in St Lucia expressed her point this way:

> well as you see right now we cannot cook, in the 90s it was better, last year we did not get any money at all, the price was about 20 cents per pound. Whereas I had about 3 workers with me, I could not pay them now it is only me and my son.

Another problem identified by small farmers in the industry is the high cost of inputs meaning fertilisers and pesticides and packaging. In both countries up to a few years ago cartoons for the packaging of their bananas were paid for by the BGA. However because of the financial difficulties farmers must now bear the cost of cartoons for packing. In St Vincent this was a decision taken by the BGA while in St Lucia it came with the process of privatisation. Along with the increasing costs of fertilisers, access to credit that would facilitate the purchase of inputs has been curtailed in St Vincent, and it is almost non existent in St Lucia. In St Vincent the farmer would go to the association's warehouse and credit inputs to his/her account and when the farmer was paid, the cost of those inputs would be deducted. There was a high rate of default on re-payment by some farmers. The BGA in St Vincent over the last five years moved from having a surplus of $25m EC to $15m EC in debt. Now farmers must pay 50 per cent of the cost of their inputs up front. Small farmers complained bitterly about this new practice. One small female farmer in St Vincent said:

> they should give us back the CESS (credit) so that it could be used to buy inputs, that use to help us out better. I have to go and take out a gallon of gramoxone and have to pay down $40, it is $80 for that, it has become too hard now, the cost of inputs are too much.

Another farmer put it this way 'we have to pay a "heaping" set of money to get inputs, if you don't have the money to pay for the inputs you don't get any.' Many perceive that the implementation of the limited credit system is not done fairly. A male farmer contends:

> The BGA say they giving farmers 50% credit on inputs but there are farmers who can get 100% credit who owing the BGA 5 and 6 thousand dollars, and there are farmers who owe $200 and have to come up with 50%.

Small farmers in St Vincent have found ingenious ways around some of this limitation in credit, though this may be only a short-term measure. All farmers have a registration card that they receive from the BGA. This card would be used to credit inputs and to sell bananas. What has happened in the past and continues today, is that the farmer may register himself, his wife and maybe a grown child as a farmer by splitting his small plot into smaller plots. He may then use his wife's or child's card to get inputs and use his card to sell the bananas so that cost of inputs would not be deducted from their income. Because of dual registration the exact number of farmers that exist and the tenure of their land is still an approximation.

St Lucian small farmers address the issue of access to credit and inputs within the context of privatisation. Prior to 1997 St Lucia had a BGA like St Vincent. In 1997 however, the government privatised the industry, now there are four companies. The most dominant company is the one, which took over the assets of the BGA, the St Lucia Banana Company. Farmers could decide to whom they would sell their produce, and for them that generally depended on the price that was being offered by the respective companies. With privatisation credit has dried up. Farmers must purchase up front all their inputs. One male farmer notes:

> Inputs are too expensive, and now you have to pay up front. Sometimes it is
> difficult to buy inputs, before when the association was there you would get
> it on credit but when you privatise it things change, so you have to have to
> get your money cash, so it has become very hard.

Also some of the small farmers were concerned about the quality of the inputs that they got. Topography proves to be a problem for both islands. The small farms in hilly areas are difficult to modernise. These areas cannot be easily mechanised, still the transportation of bananas out of the field to truck transport is done on the head of workers. Further because of the small size of the island new lands cannot be brought into cultivation. It means then that land cannot be left to fallow. In both islands small farms are in constant use. It means that there is more concentrated use of fertilisers. Over time however, the yield of the land will continue to fall. It also means that the cost of producing would continue to increase. The most obvious question then is why does the small farmer not get out of banana production? In a contradictory way the product that contributes to their poverty keeps them in poverty; so long as you deliver some bananas that are of acceptable quality you were guaranteed some income. A small farmer with his wife and children who do not have to pay labour cost see it as their only means of getting a regular income. Many see it as their only way of survival since there are few alternatives for such farmers in St Vincent that would allow them to make a living. This seems to be more prevalent in St Vincent than St Lucia. One government official from the agricultural sector in St Vincent who is working on diversifying the sector and employment notes:

> The problem in agriculture is about 60% are not literate ... can we readily retrain people for other sectors? I don't think so in the short term, because most of the people are not trainable to move into the service sector.

Many of these smaller farmers say that the only thing they have ever been involved in is bananas. Their typical response was:

> In the rural areas we have nothing else to depend on, so regardless we have to stick to bananas – we have to take the blows – there is no market for anything else, people plant other crops but ... banana however is a guaranteed market.

Others note that even though bananas is not profitable in the short run it gives them some cash to deal with day to day problems:

> what would you eat in your house, you have bills to pay, you have water bill, light bill, phone, plus you have your youth (children) to see about and all them things like schooling and books ... it really hard on the farmer.

The response was similar from this St Lucian female farmer:

> I don't know what to do if the banana industry close down, I would have to think about that because it is not that I want to be in this, but there is no alternative – there is nothing that we can do ... I might have to eat rock.

Most people are aware that it is easy to bring banana plantations back into cultivation. One Ministry of Agriculture official in St Lucia noted 'a lot of land is abandoned, but there is still banana on the land ... the thing about bananas you could have an abandoned field and you put 2 or 3 men to work on it and in 2 weeks it is transformed and is ready to produce again.'

Some farmers also remain in bananas because they are in debt to the banks. In the days when bananas earned a lot of money many farmers went to the banks and took loans to build homes and purchase vehicles. Now they are faced with a mortgage to repay so you have the sentiment expressed 'because me owe bank money and thing and if I don't grow banana I don't have no other source of money'. As to why the banana industry is facing the current problems

almost all the farmers but less so the larger ones, think that the local BGA and
the government is responsible for the problems, very few see the problem as
emanating from external sources. This however was interpreted differently in
St Vincent than in St Lucia. In St Vincent the problem was identified as
follows:

> For me (the problem is) management, because from the time I started to
> grow bananas if management was in the right position I think the banana
> industry would have been better off today .... Both government and the BGA
> is management, they are the ones now have the banana industry in the
> condition that it is.

One of the reasons for this maybe the fact that the BGA is attempting to
become more a business venture than one that takes into consideration social
issues. As one official from the BGA in St Vincent notes:

> people still believe that the banana industry is still a social welfare handout,
> and they don't see it as a business, now that we want to run it like a business
> we are having opposition from the people (farmers).

The same official pointed out:

> the farmer has been isolated for quite some time, the BGA was a social welfare
> club, in that when the prices were low and you are suppose to pay the price
> obtained the Board would take a decision to subsidise the price to the farmer.

For St Lucians the industry is in decline because of the privatisation process
and government in-action. There is a sense that farmers may have agreed with
the privatisation process when it was proposed however, they may not have
been fully aware of the consequences. Their general sentiment is that 'it was
better before when we had one association.' There is also a sense of distrust
about some of the operations of the new companies. There is a perception that
the new companies are not being honest with the farmers. One female farmer
made the argument in this way 'I think there are too many companies because
they are saying that banana don't have money yet people fighting to form
companies'. Another farmer express his concern with the honesty of the
companies in the following manner:

> they say your price is determined by the quality you give, sometimes the quality
> system is used to rob the farmers, I know farmers that send good quality they

are trying their best yet the results when it come from England they say it not good, that is impossible...I think the companies do not take care of the farmers well enough, they need the farmer and the farmer needs them but they have to look after farmers better than they have done in the past.

With the existence of four companies rivaling for farmers there has been additional problems in St Lucia. One Ministry of Agriculture official put it this way:

With privatisation you had private companies being formed and one of the unfortunate consequences of that is an extended period of teething problems that those companies experienced where they had problems relating to each other, sharing services. So you had companies with very little resources trying to provide services to the farmers and to woo farmers ... there has not been that cohesion at the ground level, especially in the delivery of services (such as pest control).

How has the people responded and what are the implications of this fall out? One of the direct outcomes of this decline has been the increase in migration both internal and outward. More people are moving out of the rural areas where bananas were being produced, into the urban areas in the hope of finding a job. To this end there has been an explosion in informal sector activity. Informal sector activities vary from very organised to menial labour. Relatives of Vincentians who live in the US and Canada would ship barrels of non-perishable goods, mainly haberdashery and clothing. Some are sent as gifts, others in some sort of business arrangement. Those products are then sold on the streets of the capital city. In other instances some persons would make trips to St Martin and Trinidad and Tobago and purchase items for sale in the informal sector. There is also the explosion of some informal sector activities that are extremely low paying such as washing of cars in the capital city.

The St Lucian government has invested a great amount of time and resources to diversify away from agriculture and to set up other sectors in particular tourism, informatics and light manufacturing. They are particularly concerned about those people in the banana industry that do not have the skills to go into to non-agricultural jobs. Those that had some other types of skills such as masonry or carpentry have sought jobs in the construction sector. Like St Vincent, St Lucia has a high percentage of female headed households. Many of these jobs are not open to women, therefore, many have gone into the informal sector namely vending in the capital city. It may be food and beverage items or items for visiting tourists. Downtown Castries the capital city already has a high number of vendors, however, on the days that cruise ships stop on the island the numbers increase significantly.

External migration to other Caribbean islands and to the US and Canada from both islands seem to be the purview of mostly men. Some have gone abroad to the US and Canada on holiday visas and just not returned. Many are living and working in the US illegally. Others, for example in St Vincent, have sought jobs such as gardening and landscaping in the Grenadines. In the Grenadines some islands and properties are owned by wealthy foreigners who hire labour to take care of their property through out the year. Some have also migrated to places like the Virgin Islands and Trinidad and Tobago to seek employment. In St Vincent there are few employment prospects for those in the 15-24 age group in agriculture. Many have sought jobs in the cruise ship industry and tourism on the whole as well as service sector jobs in urban areas. One male respondent who worked in the banana industry and now migrates to work notes 'they don't have to take on all these things here, when I go out there people call me to do some work and when I am done they pay me good money. I don't have to worry about the banana market falling and price and all of those things.' In both islands there has also been significant out migration of some trained persons such as nurses and teachers to the United States.

This process can also be interpreted with a gender dimension. Both St Vincent and St Lucia have high rates of female-headed household. Men are more likely to migrate to another island or country. They go to seek employment and send money back home to continue to take care of their families. This has increased the number of women that are in-charge of households. Those who hire their labour out continue to do so. Some continue to farm on the plots that they had worked with their mates. One interviewee put it this way 'migration is not an option for women who have children to take care of we have to stay in the community there is just no other option.' Indeed one of the consequences of this practice is summed up in this comment 'well more women are left alone to struggle with their families having to cope not only economically but socially, having to get involved with another man to help subsidise her income'.

The changing nature of banana production has also had significant impact on local rural communities. Banana is essentially a rural crop. Prior to the restructuring which moved many of the activities out of the rural areas, as well as the downturn in the industry, rural communities were thriving economic entities. Many rural shops and 'cook shops' that were once in operation now no longer are in existence. Farmers now have to come to the capital city to do all their transactions so they also shop in the urban areas. Countryside business has grounded to halt; one interviewee in St Vincent identifies the reality this way:

The farmer comes to town and instead of buying 10lbs of flour and sugar in his local shop he can now go to the supermarket in town. So when he goes home he takes the majority of his commodities with him. Also he comes to town for inputs so he can do his business one time. So it is also creating a drain on the local community in terms of clothing, we had tailors and seamstresses in the local community now people buy ready made clothes, you are seeing in some rural communities the small cook shops are being put out of business, the fast foods are here.

In St Lucia the rural economy is also heavily affected. Many of the local shops and community businesses such as local butchers and 'snacketts' are in decline. It is also impacting on the ability of these people to take care of their children. One person who works with some of the farmers notes ' it is difficult for some to send their children to school, they don't have money to pay for transportation and lunches, there are instances where farmers' children have not gone to school for weeks.' One way to really look at the decline in the rural community in St Lucia is to look at one of the most well known community activity what they refer to as a 'blocko'. A blocko is a community party, different districts would have different weekends and there would be music on the streets, stalls for the sale of different items and a festive party atmosphere. One interview explained the chance in this way:

> Blockos in the past you would see the movement of money, when people come on weekends, people would come and collect their checks from the BGA on Friday's, farmers would come to town to collect their money and every rum shop would be full, now there is no such spending, blockos no longer make that kind of money.

There are also other social consequences. Because of the mountainous and in-accessible (to motorised transport) parts of St Vincent many younger persons have resorted to marijuana production. Due to the lucrative nature of the marijuana business the brave at heart have gone into the 'ganga' business. Indeed some of the inputs that were intended to go for banana production end up in the marijuana fields of St Vincent. In a strange way some of the activities of the marijuana trade is also tied to people in St Lucia. Some of the younger persons who once worked in the banana industry have resorted to the drug trade. Some persons in St Lucia have resorted to going to St Vincent to purchase marijuana supplies for resale in St Lucia. One respondent said to me 'there is the temptation to get involved in the drug culture, quick money, ... here they steal the fisherman's boats and use it for drug runs to St Vincent, it is also increasing because of tourism.'

With the increase in marijuana production and the increase in unemployment almost everyone interviewed in both St Lucia and St Vincent felt that there was an increase in illegal activities in the islands particularly an increase in crime, violence and petty theft. One farmer in St Vincent notes 'people already coming to town without a dollar in their pocket and begging, there is also increased prostitution.' In St Lucia the response was the same:

> We are now seeing an element of crime because people are leaving rural areas and coming to the urban areas, they come looking for jobs, but what would happen if someone don't eat in weeks he would thief (steal), a lot of the crime that we see now is the direct result of this fallout.

Almost all the persons involved in the banana industry see the industry as highly politicised. Banana for many years was the mainstay of both economies and control of the industry by a political party was critical for the control of elections and government. In the case of St Vincent the industry is administered by a Statutory Board, which have a board of directors, and includes farmers and government appointed directors. Many see political manipulation as the key reason why the banana industry is in trouble today. Some feel that good business decisions cannot be made because the board is heavily influenced by government. Indeed many felt that the recently concluded elections (elections was held in St Vincent in early 2001) were decided in the particular way because the then opposition promised to solve the problems of the industry.

> In the last election the pressure was on, and politicians in the opposition then was using it. The government was not coming to the rescue of the industry, that they were not doing anything for the industry, they argued that Nero was fiddling while Rome was burning. They said when we get in we would do this or the next, if I am a farmer and I hear government not doing anything and the opposition promising to do I would move in their favour because the government has been given a chance to address the issues.

Government and the politics of the wider society also affected the process of decision making within the BGA in St Vincent. Referring to the deficit position, one BGA official noted that because of interference in the BGA 'our overdraft is now $15m and that came about because the Board refused to reduce the price when they should have, just 3 weeks ago the Board approved an increase in the price at a time when we are struggling'.

As in St Vincent a lot of people of St Lucia agree that bananas and politics have been closely linked. There is a general sense that in the past the fortunes of the banana industry made or broke governments in power. However there is also a sense that the importance of the banana industry to the capturing of political power is reducing. The government has actively sought to diversify the agricultural sector as well as develop new growth sectors particularly tourism. One St Lucian government official made the point in this way :

> There are new Prime Ministers in these countries (Windward Islands) who do not have any sacred cows, the former Prime Ministers came out of the banana struggle and had an attachment to particular modes in that industry. The new ones (Prime Ministers) say we have a problem on our hand and we would use any means necessary to resolve the problem.

Indeed many people think that the block of votes that the banana industry once delivered is no longer there. Another person in St Lucia noted that:

> When you look how they have reduced (the people in banana) so much they cannot be any significant political base again ... it may be why the government is not as driven to get involved in it and get it solved, it is because the large base is no longer there, it has moved somewhere else ... agriculture is no longer the driving force so it is not as important politically.

This indeed seems to be correct for since this research was conducted there has been an election in St Lucia and while the St Lucia Labour Party (SLP) government that presided over the privatisation process – which many people in the industry was not happy with – was returned to office, they fared badly in the banana belt, losing two of the banana constituencies which they had won in the 1997 general elections.

CONCLUSION

Throughout this chapter I have sought to show how people interpret the process of globalisation through their unique sociocultural experience. In the case of St Lucia and St Vincent globalisation has introduced the values of the market into a situation that was governed by other social concerns. It shows the limitation and the devastation that globalisation can have on small societies that are open and have limited resources.

The openness of Caribbean societies have resulted in the continuous pressuring of the indigenous cultural values to the cultural agents of globalisation. In both cases we see that it is the smaller farmers who are the ones that have greatest difficulty in coping with the demise of the industry. Moreover it shows that decisions to leave the industry is linked to the availability of alternative livelihood earning strategies. The demise of the industry has lead to more migration internally and to other countries. Also the changes in the industry have resulted in widespread changes in the rural economy and organisation of both societies. It was also demonstrated that this decline has had a gendered dimension. More women are left to take care of children as men migrate to earn money.

Both societies are at the cross-roads in terms of their development. The banana belt continues to be a powerful force in the political organisation of St Vincent. How the government deals with this group will continue to influence the outcome of the election process. St Lucia however has developed other sectors to cope with a changing global environment. Banana today does not hold the political clout in St Lucia as it did in the past. Both societies must develop alternatives at a rapid rate to absorb people in order to provide a decent standard of living. Failure to do so would result in the escalation of illegal innovative measures to earn a livelihood. The extent to which tourism can become the driving sector is questionable given the amount of leakage that occur on the foreign exchange end of the operations and the continued domination of such sectors by foreign capital. As for bananas the way it was organised in the past is dead. The calypsonian David Rudder puts it this way 'The Future Dread, The Future Dread for Banana'. The extent to which banana would continue would depend on the success of the Fair Trade programme. There would be some banana producers but they would only be those that have incorporated the values of global capitalism, who can therefore boast of market efficiencies.

Endnotes

1. Chase-Dunn, 1989; Frank 1978; Wallerstein 1974, Best et al, 1978.
2. Chase-Dunn, 1999.
3. Arrighi, *The Long Twentieth Century*, 1994.
4. Pantin, D. *The Economics of Sustainable Development in small Caribbean Islands*, 1994.
5. 1995, p. 26.
6. Nurse K. and Sandiford W., *Windward Island Bananas: Challenges and Option Under The Single European Market*, 1995, p. 66.

7. Nurse and Sandiford, 1995, p. 5.
8. Figures taken from Pantin et al.
9. Addy, D.N. 'Restructuring and the Loss of Preferences, Labour Challenges for the Caribbean Banana Industry' 1999, p. 8.
10. Sandiford, W. *On the Brink of Decline: Bananas In the Windward Islands*, 2000, Pantin et al, 1999.
11. Pantin et al, 1999, p. 18.
12. Sandiford, 2000, p. 8.
13. Addy, 1999.
14. Sandiford, 2000.
15. Addy, 1999.
16. Sandiford, 2000.

References

Addy, D. N., 'Restructuring and the Loss of Preferences, Labour Challenges for the Caribbean Banana Industry', *ILO Caribbean Working Papers No 1 1999*.

Arrighi, Giovanni, *The Long Twentieth Century*, (London: Verso, 1994).

Axtmann, R., 'Collective Identity and the Democratic Nation-State in the Age of Globalisation', *Articulating the Global and the Local*, Cvetkovich, A. and D. Kellner, (Westview Press, 1997).

Bahalla, A.S, *Globalisation, Growth and Marginalisation*, (Ottawa: International Development Research Center, 1998).

Best L. and Levitt, K., 'Character of the Caribbean Economy', *Caribbean Economy*, ed., Beckford G.L. (Mona, Jamaica: ISER UWI, 1978).

Bonanno, A. and D. Constance, 'Global Agri-Food Sector and the Case of the Tuna Industry: Global Regulation and Perspectives for Development', *Journal of Developing Areas* 98:14 pp.100-125.

Brenner, R., 'Economics of Global Turbulence: A Special report on the World Economy', New *Left Review*, 1998.

Chase-Dunn, C., 'Globalisation: A World Systems Perspective.' *Journal of World Systems Research* 5:2: pp.187-216.

_____, *Global Formations*, (Cambridge: Blackwell Publishers, 1989).

Copeland, D., 'Globalisation, Enterprise, and Governance', *International Journal* 97:8 pp. 17-37.

Cvetkovich, A., & D Kellner, ed., *Articulating the Global and the Local*, (Westview, 1997).

Frank, A. G., *Accumulation, Dependence, and Underdevelopment,* (New York: Monthly Review Press, 1978).

Friedman, J., *Cultural Identity and Global Processes,* (London: Sage Publications, 1996) .

Levitt, K. P., 'Globalisation Reality or Ideology' Revised version of a paper presented to the Conference Capitalism And Slavery Fifty Years Later: Eric Williams And The Post Colonial Caribbean 1997.

Loker, W. M., 'Grit in the Prosperity Machine: Globalisation and the Rural Poor in Latin America', *Globalisation and the Rural Poor in Latin America,* ed., P.F. Barlett and Lynne Rienner, 1999.

Meyer, J. W et al, 'World Society and the Nation-State', *American Journal of Sociology* 97:103 pp. 144-81.

——————————, 'World Society and the Nation-State' *American Journal of Sociology* 103:1 pp. 144-179.

Nurse, K. and W. Sandiford, *Windward Islands Bananas: Challenges and Options Under the Single European Market,* (Kingston, Jamaica: Friedrich Ebert Stiftung, 1995).

Nandi, P. N. and S. M. Shahidullah, 'Globalisation and Development: The Emerging Dynamics and Dilemmas' *Journal of Developing Societies* 14:1 pp. 1-10.

Oommen, T. K., *Citizenship Nationality and Ethnicity,* (Cambridge: Polity Press, 1997).

Pantin, D., *The Economics of Sustainable Development in Small Caribbean Islands,* (UWI Jamaica: Center for Environment and Development, 1994).

Pantin, D., W. Sandiford, M. Henry, 'Cake, Mama Coco Or? Alternatives Facing The Caribbean Banana Industry in the Light of the April 1999 World Trade Organisations (WTO) Ruling on the European Unions (EU) Banana Regime.' Commissioed by WINFA, CPDC, and Oxfam, Caribbean Revised Report. September 20, 1999.

Poster, W. R., 'Globalisation, Gender and the Workplace: Women and Men in an American Multinational Corporation in India' *Journal of Developing Areas* 14: 1 pp. 40-65.

Price, D. and D. Ramsaran, 'Globalisation: A Critical Ontology' (Forthcoming).

Sandiford, W., *On The Brink Of Decline: Bananas In The Windward Islands,* (St Georges, Greneda: Fendon Books, 2000).

Shahidullah, S. M., 'The Nationality And Globality Of Social Science: The Issues Of Globalising Sociology in America' *Journal Of Developing Societies* 98:14 pp. 164-185.

Stryker, R., 'Globalisation And The Welfare State', *International Journal of Sociology and Social Policy* 98:18 pp 1-49.

UNICEF, 'The Rights of the Child in the Caribbean: Questions and Answers' (Barbados: UNICEF Area Office, 1999).

Uvin, P. Biagiotti, 'Global Governance and the 'New' Political Conditionality' *Global Governance* 2 (1996) pp. 377–400.

Welch, B. M., *Survival By Association: Supply Management Landscapes of the Eastern Caribbean.* (Montreal: McGill-Queen Press, 1996).

7

The Legitimacy of Neo-Liberal Trade Regimes in the Caribbean: Issues of 'Race', Class and Gender

Holger Henke and Don D. Marshall[1]

INTRODUCTION

By now it is a commonplace to state that over the last 15 to 20 years the world economy has undergone a series of significant structural changes. Caribbean countries, part of the New World long at the vortex of global capitalist transactions, once again found themselves in the position of having to respond to the economic, social, and political velocities and countercurrents created by what is nowadays summarily labeled as globalisation. Whichever country in the Caribbean we turn our attention to – be it Haiti, Jamaica, Trinidad and Tobago, St Vincent, Dominica or even Barbados – we find intense public discussions about the benefits, prospects and downsides of neo-liberalism. Indeed the question of the legitimacy of the neo-liberal model – as the current approach to economic growth is often termed – has become an important theoretical and practical challenge for most countries.[2]

Immanuel Wallerstein (1995) suggests that liberalism is in decline, both as a system and as a hegemonic discourse. He contends that with the fall of Communism, untamed progressive forces have posed challenges to globalisation in its current guise, imperiling the survival of liberalism. However, the re-invigoration and rise to prominence of global governance institutions – such as the World Trade Organisation (WTO), the United Nations, the Organisation for Economic Cooperation and Development (OECD), the OECD's Financial Action Task Force (FATF), the IMF and World Bank suggest otherwise. Indeed these institutions serve to reinforce neo-liberal terms of reference for tackling issues ranging from money laundering to poverty alleviation. Consequently it is fair to suggest that market-empowering perspectives remain no less hegemonic now as they did in the 1990s.

For both industrialised and developing countries, adjusting their economic arrangements to the new requirements of global capital, have meant the reorganisation of the social and economic fabric occasioning various tempos of turbulence. To be sure, there has been some resistance to the project. These include the class struggles in the summer of 1995 in France; spontaneous public strikes and unrest in the wake of the financial meltdown of Mexico in 1995 and in several South-east Asian countries in 1997/8; the anti-globalisation protests at Seattle and Genoa in 1999/2000; and more recently, the anti-IMF disturbances in Argentina in 2002. As social and economic displacement became a widespread consequence of the economic restructuring exercise, political regimes began to experience a rapid erosion of the consensus about a professed need to become part of the globalisation carnival. It is in the closing years of the twentieth century that austere free market formats became increasingly discredited even from within World Bank circles as attention turned to the need for a protective and regulatory state to cushion the burden of adjustment on vulnerable groups, and ward off destructive speculative investment. This is what Kees van der Pijl (1998) will refer to as the 'shift to a more cautious attitude.'[3] Consequently it is still premature to speak of liberalism in retreat without noting the range of maneuver possible at the discursive and policy levels.

Here it is important to consider the Foucauldian and Gramscian insight that for power to be effective, it has to be discursively legitimated. The discursive power of neoliberalism is sustained by 1) policy and academic communities that routinely dismiss alternative models of political economy as unrealistic and 2) the policing of legitimate or illegitimate courses of inquiry in the public domain of debate and discussion. Indeed, the many groups and individuals motivated by ethico-political concerns and appealing for inclusion, accountability and transparency are at the same time engaged in an historic open struggle for wider discursive space.[4]

In this chapter, we will first take a closer, albeit by no means exhaustive, look at the notion and content dimensions of political legitimacy *per se*. Secondly, we will assess consensus-formation in Jamaica and Barbados. Here the focus will be on statecraft, and the economic prospects that lay ahead. We also seek to identify the winners and losers of the neoliberal regime as it continues to evolve. To this end twenty-five interviews were conducted in Barbados.[5] The interviewees came from a wide cross-section of Barbadian society and included representatives from the trade unions, media, academia, NGOs, entertainment industry, and regional organisations operating in the island. Our research regarding the situation in Jamaica is based on interviews conducted in the early to mid-1990s, as well as on our close observation of current events and ongoing dialogue with university colleagues in Jamaica. Questions asked pertained broadly to their perceived impact of neoliberal development on society and questions of sustainability of this approach.[6] Based on observation and data gathered from these sources, this chapter will map the levels of legitimacy among different segments of Caribbean society, using a class and 'race' (and, to a lesser extent, gender) focus. Particular attention will be placed on 'subterranean' counter-hegemonic trends as they may be expressed through popular culture and through the existence/performances of counter-publics. We conclude the chapter with some observations about what the current scenario means for the sustainability of the neo-liberal trade regime in the Caribbean.

LEGITIMACY PER SE

The statement that no two people in a car can agree on which window should be shut and how much is probably an exaggeration. Certainly, in more complex and permanent social situations such as modern societies, people with different interests tend to lump themselves in groups to represent these interests. On certain fundamental issues these groups are likely to reach consensus plateaus either by negotiation or by discourse. Legitimacy connotes the existence of a hegemonic consensus among a politically mature population about a subject towards which it (potentially) needs to take a position. We say 'potentially' because consensus can be manufactured through different means and strategies. Thus, legitimacy raises fundamental questions about power, representation, and political leadership. Framing the issue in these terms already points to the role of different groups in society.

In the classical, ideal-typical, elabouration of legitimate rule, Max Weber (1973) distinguished three ideological bases of legitimacy: 1) traditional, 2) charismatic, and 3) legal-rational. His categorisation implies a progressive motion from the first to the third form. While he captured some essential, normative, premises of legitimate rule, Weber's taxonomy failed to consider the more instrumental and utilitarian bases of legitimacy (that is, comparative advantage of one ruler/form of rule over another).[7] As, for example, Habermas' (cf. 1998) Kantian considerations demonstrate, under the conditions of capitalist production the legal-rational basis of legitimacy is largely identified with modern, Western, constitutions and institutions, which draw equally from the presumably universal sources of human rights and the Westphalian notion of sovereignty.

The question is, however, to what extent these legal-rational considerations of legitimacy apply to the contemporary conditions of peripheral capitalism in the Caribbean and Latin America. One does not necessarily have to agree with those who argue that under capitalist conditions legitimacy primarily draws on procedural justifications (as opposed to the moral-legal application of power), or with world systems theorists who would posit that the collusion between internal and external interests generally prevents any level of identification between state and society beyond the social relations of production within the territorial borders of peripheral capitalist social formations,[8] to acknowledge that in many Latin American and Caribbean countries a fundamental disjunction in the political culture tends to obstruct the creation of a generalised political legitimacy (cf. Henke 2001). Volker Lühr (1982, 32), for example, argues that in many Latin American countries the prevalence of social anomie causes a discrepancy between affect and political rationality. In other words, important institutions such as the constitution and the law, parliament and government, the political parties and the process of democratic representation do not inspire emotional affection.

The notion of representation points to yet another dimension of legitimacy. Thus, Michel Foucault (1978) has pointed out that power is not simply a quasi-external force that is traded off between equal or unequal participants of social interaction. Rather, we are all individually shot through with the existing power relationships in our respective environments. As he puts it, 'power is not applied to individuals, it passes through them.'[9] Unfortunately – and Foucault readily admits to that – this conceptualisation of power and representation precludes an understanding of power as a more homogenous complex that can be identified with the rule of one group or class over another. Nevertheless, it is an important corrective to the above mentioned disembodied – that is, de-raced and de-gendered – legal-rational approaches in that it adds a corporeal dimension to the question of power, representation and legitimacy which is not acknowledged by them. Adding this physical dimension to the discussion, however, is immensely important in the context of Caribbean societies, which have been historically conceived and constituted through the racist and colonialist deprivation of people – and nationhood. In fact, by embedding the question of power in the context of body, skin, gestures and so on, Foucault's conceptualisation leads us back to the identification of legitimacy with distinct groups in a given society. Thus, the structures of accumulation and power are often imbricated in the configurations of race, ethnicity and gender.

If we consider legitimacy as a relatively fluid, heterogeneous, hegemonic, yet constantly re-negotiated or discursively (dis-)agreed upon societal consensus, a Gramscian understanding of hegemony appears best suited for an understanding of legitimacy of the neo-liberal model in the Caribbean. In this approach, hegemony is considered as a system of social control, in particular control of subaltern groups and classes, without the open use of force.[10] The representation of capitalist social relations is diffused in ways which induce a partial participation of the subaltern classes in their own political, economic and sociocultural subordination.[11] This is achieved by a portrayal of essentially divergent existential interests and stakes in the existing sociopolitical order as the best (indeed, the only) alternative for a mutually beneficial relationship capable of preventing the descent into poor, nasty, and brutish living conditions. In other words, the ruling class basically 'invites' the subordinate classes to agree to their own submission to the requirements of capital and to the dominant relations of production and capital accumulation. The ultimate rationale of hegemony, therefore, is the normalisation, stability and guaranteed reproduction of the capitalist social order.

As elaborated elsewhere (Henke 2000), developing countries in the Caribbean are in a double dependent situation, as hegemony is exerted by locally resident representatives of international capital, and reinforced by their local (indigenous) counterparts.[12] This does not, however, mean that there is neither an automatic nor a deterministic identification between the specific class interests and a matching ideology. Rather, the formation of a particular ideological and political position is dependent on specific local and circumstantial factors that require further explanation. In the case of Caribbean societies, it may very well be that, because of the populist-driven character of the state, legitimacy waxes and wanes on the charisma variable.

'Populism' is a concept that requires some initial elucidation as it has acquired a variety of meanings when applied in the Americas and Europe. Scholars specialising in Latin America area studies have used the term to speak of a 'personalised' political regime or a set of demands for redistributive economic policies that would benefit 'the masses'.[13] This kind of portrayal holds true over time but the tendency has been to associate this with radical governments of the left in the Americas or extreme right in Central or Eastern Europe. Logical correlations were drawn to a socioeconomic structure fashioned by an industrialising process featuring large movements of workers from rural areas to major cities. It is only with the post-1980s emergence of Jörg Haider in Austria, Alberto Fujimori in Peru and Silvio Berlusconi as Prime Minister of Italy in 2001 that it became clear that it was possible to assemble quite different kinds of socioeconomic coalitions based on free market ideology and economic policies. These recent cases feature a charismatic leader, marked for his/her ability to sway large numbers of people through colourful discourse, appeals to the glorious struggles of history, and the projection of a collective vision of the future. It is fair to note that Caribbean leaders are currently of a technocratic type, certainly not in the charismatic mould of a Michael Manley, Cheddi Jagan, Errol Barrow or Maurice Bishop. But appealing to the popular classes remains a very important feature in these small societies marked by easy social contact. Some of the strategies for reaching the masses directly would include regular appearances on radio and television, regularly commissioning plebiscites, impromptu visits to highly populated districts including garrison/ghetto communities, town hall meetings – tactics designed to bypass existing structures of interest intermediation.[14] Indeed Caribbean governments are not so much defined by their stated commitment to the redistribution of economic wealth or for their support of the 'small man' – as they are by certain aspects of political style and strategy aimed at usurping forms of interest intermediation with direct ties to 'the people'.

To be sure, there is no strong lobbying culture among civil groups in Jamaica and Barbados. Ours is a tradition from which until recently civil society input was notably absent. These societies have known government for a long time. Such was the force with which authority ruled. There remains a limited concept of a civic life without official participation. Every group hopes for a grant or subsidy from the State. In the Barbadian case especially, apart from purporting to act in the interest of the working class, successive populist governments have pursued discursive strategies aimed at shaping public common sense. This has led to the depoliticisation and technocratic routine of political participation even as NGOs and radio call-in programmes proliferate.

The theoretical flip-side of hegemony, however, is the counter-hegemony of the subordinate classes. The persistent (co-)existence of marginalised counter-publics, black or gray markets, and dissenting discourses constantly call into question the dominant discursive consensus described in the pervious paragraph. As Persaud (2001, 49) correctly points out, these counter-hegemonic tendencies are not necessarily mere reactions to the dominant social order, but may very well be preexistent to it; in fact, 'it might be more useful to understand hegemony, and counter-hegemony/resistance, as a simultaneous *double movement*.' Chevannes (2000) seems to hint at that possibility in his distinction of 'two Jamaicas.'[15] Recent works by Meeks (1999), Mars (1998), Scott (1999) and works collected in the journal *Small Axe* have started to more systematically probe and map the nature of this movement in the Caribbean region.[16]

Again, there is no automatic counter-hegemonic project that would be available *prêt-à-porter*. In fact, it may well be that counter-hegemonic strategies – unlike hegemonic practices – are most effective if they proceed in incremental and flexible fashion. Whereas hegemony deliberately tries to create, impose or – at the very minimum – feign unity, subaltern practices of resistance need to focus on glossed-over antagonisms and attempt to replicate and amplify them in a variety of political spaces (Persaud 2001, 50).

UNDERSTANDING THE NEO-LIBERAL GLOBALISATION PARADIGM

There is a need to situate the Caribbean experience within what we mean by neoliberal globalisation. This requires a brief unpacking of the globalisation terminology. Here we use the term as 'short hand' to describe the current phase of world systemic development. This clears the ground for a concrete understanding of what challenges confront the region in this period.

Since the late 1970s, the call by the developing world for greater development chances and more equitable relations in international economic relations, has been countered by a reinvigorated call for economics based on classical liberal free trade ideology which demands unrestricted international flows of money, goods and means of production. In practice, this call translated (as it had in the past) into the intellectual and practical reclamation of unrestricted access by capital in the developed world to the markets of the South. Whereas many countries in the post-World War II period had attempted to define independent, autochthonous, development paths that often relied on import substitution and experimentation with new relations of production, by the early 1980s many found themselves financially exhausted from the combination of an inclement international response to their search for a 'third path' and economic mismanagement. Forced to seek assistance from international financial organisations, they found themselves confronted with demands based on a modified liberal orthodoxy.[17] The orthodoxy reflected a subtle redeployment of classical liberal thought away from modernisation doctrines of development towards an interest in globalisation.

A cottage industry of articles and books appeared over the last twenty years seeking to establish globalisation as an unfolding modern epochal event. Without caricaturing what is a sophisticated body of work, the main claim is that our world's political-economic architecture has changed immensely over the last few decades.[18] The narrative is forged by pointing to the minutiae of observable international interactions as well as shifts in production systems and international business. New information technologies are a large part of it, the flexible specialisation of manufacturing is another big piece, and the timespace compression of fast capitalism also cannot be ignored. The consensus is that the capitalist world system is undergoing yet another restructuring phase.

Globalisation can be understood as a consensus-creating system of (linguistic) rules and codes, mostly rooted in neoliberal imagination, and beckoning an enclosure based on market liberalisation precepts. It is in this sense that it can be said to be an inherently political phenomenon principally as it is nourished by *mobilising* and *ordering* impulses. This can be seen at multiple levels. At the state-level, globalisation girds a normalising rationality of new codes of governmentality. This has led some commentators to take the historical transformation of a particular form of state (the Keynesian-welfare type) to mean the transcendence of the *state* itself. At the global level, recent challenges to the post-war settlement and embedded liberalism have led to the emergence of a consensus favouring deregulation and liberalisation as the only viable way to reorganise and re-embed a new state/market relationship. And at the level of agency, governments face state-splintering movements in all of their cultural, economic, and organisational zones. Here the market reforms, the job instability, the premium placed on competitiveness, flexibility, discipline, speed and risk management lead to 'anti-globalisation' resistance.

Instead of allowing different economic approaches in different social and cultural contexts, the neo-liberal adjustment tends to disallow such flexibility and impose more homogenous practices, standards and rules of production and trade. The generally conveyed assumption is that the homogenisation resulting from these new rules will result in a global convergence without creating new divergences. This belief is based on the economic dictum claiming that a deepening of international division of labour will benefit all parties involved. However, this picture ignores at least three aspects which tend to obstruct convergence in the newly created globalised spaces: 1) As the East Asian crises caused by currency speculations clearly demonstrated, the continuing competition between different currencies tends to create zero-sum scenarios, rather than 'win-win' ones. 2) The international division of labour is selective. While Asia (in particular China) is the major benefactor of international flows of foreign direct investment, other regions (in particular Africa, the Caribbean, and parts of Central Asia) are more or less completely by-passed.[19] Of course this is not to deny domestic culpability in some cases, that is, poor state planning, undeveloped markets, or absence of technical and bureaucratic capacities. 3) The destabilising potential of international finance capital, which occur outside of the trade balance and constitutes 95 per cent of daily foreign currency transactions (Altvater and Mahnkopf 1999).[20]

The reform processes in many countries might, at first glance, betray the impression of a world angling towards an Anglo-American neo-liberal trade and development format. However, the work seeking to empirically test globalisation claims suggests otherwise. Sally (1994) and Ruigrok and van Tulder (1995) observe that national forms persist, that is, of capital accumulation, and of political economy practice. This observation constitutes a strike against those international political economy (IPE) knowledges distorted by the impulse to universalise, or to uncover law-like patterns in world system history. Part of this is at work by those seeking to establish globalisation as an epistemology.

Here globalisation functions as a narrative of closure around the fate of the 'state', the 'market' and 'identity' in the core, with experiences in the periphery read off as epi-phenomena that affirms universal seepage of the same.

However, from the foregoing skeptical literature, it appears empirically suspect to point up the closing decades of the twentieth century as the market triumphing over the state globally. It might be more accurate to step back and fold this historical time-slice into yet another episode in the *perennial tension* between state and market in the various invented spaces of the international. The metaphor of a 'balance-of-power rivalry' between the state and market leaves little room for ambiguity, eliminates complexity, irony and paradox and aspires only to hard and fast truths on the grand scale. We miss the important point that core countries like, for example, the US, China, France, Sweden and Britain each have followed different models of capitalist political economy in the period; and that within the periphery lay treasure troves of experience that have not yet been tapped for IPE or development theory. Despite the putative convergence trends in business standards, fiscal measures, trade laws and labour organisation, each country presents different state-commercial-industrial complexes with institutions and markets jiggered differently.

SITUATING THE CARIBBEAN

Quite often the problem of legitimacy of the neo-liberal approach is cast in terms of a crude 'we-they' dichotomy, which implicitly tends to deny the complexities of both the domestic and international environments.[21] In this interpretation, the question of who profits and who loses from the new orthodoxy is being conceptually glossed over and replaced for positivist categories such as 'sustainability' (of what, anyhow?), stability, social integration and so on, which are now presented as the criteria that imply economic and social growth. However, while a neo-liberal capitalist approach might very well be the only realistic option at this conjuncture, it should be reiterated that there are varieties of approaches that differ from the Anglo-American format or the waning Washington Consensus once avidly promoted by the international financial institutions (Marshall 1996; Henke and Boxill 2000; Fine *et al.* 2001). The question which specific strategy, or combination of approaches serves best the largest number without economically disenfranchising large numbers, however, would be a much more fruitful question to determine economic progress and enhance the legitimacy of neo-liberalism or, for that matter, any other (combination of) economic strategies.

The current acceleration and intensification of neo-liberal practices in the Caribbean and around the globe contributes to a further rift between the everyday material practices and needs of the majority of people in the region and what occurs in the formal economy. Polanyi (1944) has described this chasm as 'disembedding'. While markets existed well before this time, the modern market economy, which transforms nature, labour, and money into commodities, is a post-1700 phenomenon. Disembedding occurs at different levels of social praxis, but most fundamentally it signifies a disconnection between social life and economic activities. The general tendency is to subject modes of social life to the economic rationale of profitability, solvency, and interest. Cultural institutions, social capital and community relations, which in previous times may have fulfilled useful functions (for example, care for children or elderly; education and so on) in the context of community volunteerism, are in this scenario gradually undermined and eroded or, at best, replaced by service industries which may render these functions according to criteria of efficiency, order, and lucre. For 'traditional' societies or 'developing countries' this may be regarded as 'modernisation' and actually provide health and/or life-style improvements.

However, in many instances 'disembedding' creates imbalances, disequilibria, and marginalisation, and falls short of the service functions previously supplied by the community itself. Throughout the 1990s, the burdens of restructuring were felt most strongly by vulnerable members of society. These are persons generally marginalised from privileged circuits of production and consumption under this 'informational global capitalism'. Neo-liberal globalisation accentuates stratification along lines of class, race and gender, with poor women particularly disadvantaged as both commodified labour and provider of care within families. This is worse in those societies where many of the social provisions of welfare states have been dismantled as part of a transitioning to the new world order.

In some ways successive administrations in Barbados have steadfastly maintained social safety-nets where Jamaican governments have relented to market-ideological counsel on the benefits of privatisation. Part of this is to do with a certain deterrence factor, as the Jamaican neo-liberal experience extends back for twenty-five years and has featured successive waves of unrest. Other Caribbean governments would have sought to avoid such an experience. Another explanation can be located in the pragmatic approach to governance, fiscal management and reform under the respective Errol Barrow and JMGM 'Tom' Adams Administrations in Barbados. Here the state provided a variety of social services, not necessarily in keeping with global Keynesian norms as with how this facilitated the government's need to provide 'instant relief' to the masses while facilitating a business-as-usual approach for the traditional elite. Whatever the differences between the Barbados and Jamaica approach, Rodrik (2001) is certain to point out that:

> A sound overall development strategy that produces high economic growth is far more effective in achieving integration with the world economy than a purely integrationist strategy that relies on openness to work its magic. In other words, the globalisers have it exactly backwards. Integration is the result, not the cause, of economic and social development.[22]

The acceleration and increased disembedding of economic processes at the end of the twentieth century in the Caribbean has become one of the main sources for growing resistance against the neo-liberal model enforced in the region. Without doubt, the region is enveloped in the same transition from economic activities in the primary sector to activities in the tertiary sector that can be found in much of the industrialised world and parts of East Asia. One does not have to focus on the recent WTO ruling on Caribbean bananas exports to Europe to see that for this region, like others, raw materials and traditional agriculture will likely no longer be able to provide sustainable growth.[23] And yet, traditional and communal forms of production and trade are deeply ingrained and are (or are perceived as) providing basic necessities for local communities. Thus, recent attempts to privatise communal land – regarded as a precondition for a more direct integration of local farmers into the global economy – run against social traditions and functions that are culturally embedded and have failed due to resistance by local farmers (Dujon 1999/2000).

Even without invoking the 'demand-supply' logic of economic markets, one may recognise that there is even a point to be made for the economic rationality of increased cultivation of illegal drugs in the Caribbean. Thus, for many small farmers who are often extremely hard-pressed to keep up with – (often externally-induced) devaluation of local currencies, growing replacement of local by foreign products, enforcement of higher standards for export and domestic products (and thus, higher production costs), privatisation of previously public services, among others – becoming involved in the cultivation of marijuana (and, possibly, coca) seems the only feasible option. For them, this is a strategy of survival and adaptation to economic hardship. The acceptance of ganja cultivation is not only widespread among those who use it and/or grow it, but as the Vincentian example demonstrates, it even extends to non ganja-using members of the middle classes, 'because they recognise that planting weed has reduced indigence and un(der)employment in several rural areas, it has stimulated commerce at the national level, and it has brought in much needed foreign currency' (Rubenstein 1999/2000, 232). The 1994 United Nations Report, 'Drugs and Development', appropriately underscored this view when it noted that 'the drug trade is sometimes the one which provides the basic necessities for economic survival' (p. 1).[24] Thus, the increasing legitimacy of the illegal market realm is the flip-side of the decreasing legitimacy of the official development doctrine, which is commonly identified with neoliberal globalisation. This delegitimisation process can therefore not be marginalised by claims that it is merely a gut reaction of disenfranchised and 'unsophisticated' poor classes in Caribbean societies who have not been reached by the putative trickle-down benefits of free trade.

The kind of economic development, which immediately resulted from the neoliberal opening of Caribbean markets heavily favoured expatriate investments positioned in quasi off-shore export processing zones (EPZs), sometimes ironically labeled 'Free Zones'. Companies using these sites include garment multinationals such as Liz Claiborne, Hanes, or Tommy Hilfiger, who are targeting the middle to upper consumer echelons in the industrialised economies. The scant job opportunities that they provided, mainly 'benefited' members of the socially marginalised classes with low education, low access to health and other important public services, and minimum family incomes. More often than not, the operators of free zone assembly plants employed women. These types of cut-and-sew and screwdriver assembly production activities were geared toward low-cost labour, and contributed virtually nothing to the local economies. As in South American *maquiladora* production corridors, the lack of back and forward linkages created by the free zones is rendered graphically by the proximity between them and their workers' ghettoised residential areas immediately adjacent to them.

Since the 1990s, however, with increasingly generalised regulations and implementation of neoliberal principles, the EPZ has become an outdated model. The practices of trade liberalisation, the erosion of labour laws, and numerous tax incentives of (foreign) investment and profit transfer, have become more widespread and accepted by governments in the region. There is now a more generalised move under way, which has been described as a trend towards international subcontracting and a partnership between formal and informal modes of production. In other circles this is understood as international production networks (IPNs) or cross-national production networks.[25] According to figures by the *International Conference of Free Trade Unions* (ICFTU), in the mid-1990s about 200 million people were working in semi-formal supplier arrangements for transnational corporations, whereas only 4.5 million were employed in EPZs.[26] In many cases even well-known brand name firms are no longer directly involved in the productive process and in effect have become traders of goods produced for them and marketed in their name.

At the end of this international chain of production are developing countries such as those in the Caribbean region, and – at the micro-level – women. Women in Caribbean countries have been particularly susceptible to rising costs of living, declining wages and unemployment (Enloe 1989, Deere *et al.* 1990, 51ff.). The trends established in the 1980s and 1990s seem to continue. According to new data, labour force participation in the Jamaican labour market continues to decline, with the decrease more pronounced among females, and the youngest and oldest age-groups. Thus, in the 14-24 years age group 42.9 per cent of all females are unemployed, whereas only 23.9 per cent of males are unemployed (Anderson 2001: p.14). Poverty is particularly associated with this vulnerable group positioned at the end of the productive chain, or – as has been said elsewhere – poverty has a woman's face.

Since in many Caribbean countries inequality has been objectively on the rise for the past 20 or so years, when neo-liberalism launched another offensive on the often relatively closed, clientelist, import-substituting, economies in the region, it was rejected particularly among the 'losers' of the 'structural adjustment' exercises. In many countries, particularly in Jamaica, it has given rise to what Meeks (2000, 23) has called a nascent 'Caribbean subalternism'. In other countries – Trinidad and Tobago and Barbados come to mind – the dynamics of economic survival, political legitimacy, ethno-social stridency and acceptance of or resistance to neo-liberalism has been stacked differently. The following section will take a closer look at the Jamaica and Barbados cases, which seem to be located at opposing ends of this acceptance/rejection continuum.

NEO-LIBERALISM IN THE CARIBBEAN: THE CASE OF JAMAICA

Barbados and Jamaica constitute two rather different experiences regarding their insertion into the world economy and their local success/failure at developing an effective strategy of accumulation. For this very reason the subsequent sections will probe the particular responses of both social formations to this experience and draw a number of conclusions pertaining to the relative legitimacy of neo-liberal development in these two countries.

With the regional and local power shifts in the 1980s, the Jamaican State started to embrace neo-liberalism. The policies of the Seaga Administration were largely designed to invite foreign direct investment and to maximise the export opportunities for domestic export manufacturers. At the societal level, the shift reflected strategic realignments in the power structure of local classes from a temporary alliance between the national bourgeoisie and progressive part of the middle class in the 1970s to a comprador-led state-private sector alliance (Henke 1999). It is because of these power shifts that the neo-liberal model has taken relatively firm root among the Jamaican ruling classes, despite occasional official criticism, rhetorical affirmation of sovereignty, and rejection of foreign influence deemed unacceptable for the country.

The unbroken elite support for the neo-liberal project in Jamaica does by no means suggest that they enjoy widespread legitimacy. In comparison to Barbados, the neo-liberal agenda in Jamaican society is clearly on a much less secure footing and appears much more persistently and intensively negotiated. To a large extent this has to do with Jamaica's historical successes of resistance against colonialism and the Jamaican collective psyche that has emerged from these struggles (Sherlock and Bennett 1998; Manley 1982). It is, however, also a function of the fact that during the 1980s and 1990s the Jamaican economy was opened rapidly, with relatively few social security programmes in place, and with largely negative socioeconomic consequences for large sectors of the society. Neo-liberalism in Jamaica is, finally, also strongly contested because it was often projected and perceived as a solely exogenous project implanted through rigorous structural adjustment policies imposed by the IMF and the World Bank. Due to the marginalisation processes and displacements effected by the rapid and often radical opening of the Jamaican economy, clear societal fault lines have emerged.

This became patently clear in April 1999, when – in response to the announcement of a relatively minor increase in gas prices – island-wide protests erupted and roadblocks brought the country to a virtual standstill for three days. Protesters were reported to have targeted businesses, which attempted to remain open during the protests. The drama and intensity of emotions fuelling the protests can possibly be glanced from the following report – somewhat reminiscent of reports received in earlier years from South Africa – from Jamaica's second largest city and one of the tourist centres on the North coast:

> The police remained on top of the situation, responding quickly to reports of looting. But at about 3:00 p.m., the crowd's anger turned against the law officers, with one unit coming under attack on St. James Street in downtown Montego Bay. Scores of rioters surrounded the unit, some of whom hurled heavy stones at the police car, denting it in several places. The policemen were forced to vacate the unit, all the time firing shots in the air to keep the crowd at bay.

Roadblocks sprung up on streets adjacent to economically depressed residential areas, nevertheless often blocked main thoroughfares. While there was no explicit ethnic targeting in these riots, both 'race' and class issues were certainly implied in the targeting of businesses and the prominent involvement of roadblocks by inner-city residents.[27] In an apparent victory for the protesting *hoi polloi* the government was eventually forced to withdraw the proposed price increase. The fact, however, that only in February 2002 the Jamaican government – amidst various financial scandals – again attempted to levy yet another unpopular tax (for public lighting), is evidence for the extremely tight fiscal situation of public finances in the country.

As earlier noted, vulnerable groups, such as women particularly feel the impact of economic austerity. Thus, women's crisis centres in Kingston and Montego Bay show a steep increase from 4,823 calls and visits in 1997 to 5,681 in 1998, which notably fluctuated with periods of economic stress (Ansine 1999). There are also indicators that child prostitution is on the rise in Jamaica, to the extent that even some parents send their children to 'work the beat' (Hyatt 2001). For historical reasons, these vulnerable groups are mostly to be found among the phenotypically darker members of Jamaican society.[28]

In the light of these crudely sketched developments, it is perhaps not surprising that entire sections of the Jamaican society excuse themselves from participating in discourse about national development. Given the victimisation of inner-city areas and abuse by a police force struggling against individual and gang crime, as well as (apparently) internationally organised drug trafficking ventures, citizens resort to historically ingrained patterns of resistance against what they perceive as internal colonisation.[29] Consider, for example, the following statement by a Kingston inner-city resident expressing concerns about the arrest of a community 'don':

> ... there would be some instability in the sense that rape and robbery might take place ... He is ... strongly against the raping a the women. [That was] prevalent until he came along and say look here, dem things must stop ... [...] He provides ... books and other things for school children. There is a basic school ... that he funds [among other things].[30]

In this sociopolitical context, informal non-state institutions are beginning to fill authority vacuums in communities affected by active and passive marginalisation. These vacuums are filled by functions usually firmly located in the State's domain. As Charles (2002, 41) quite correctly observes:

> The garrison communities in Jamaica are usually stable counter societies. They have created their own laws and justice system, which conflict with the laws and justice system of the state. The structural adjustment policies of the 1980s and

full liberalisation in the 1990s have reduced the role of the state as protector and provider, thereby reducing human security.

These aspects of Jamaican public policy and political culture can and have to be read against the lavish support for both domestic and foreign businesses. This support is demanded by the local bourgeoisie and readily dispensed by governments composed by either of the two major parties in Jamaica (Ross 2000). To mention just one example, in 1999 the privately-owned Air Jamaica received for the Jamaican Government, US$100 million in addition to US$114 million paid already to the national carrier (*The Gleaner* 1999).[31] The Government borrowed the cash for this subsidy in international financial markets, in this case from the Belgium finance house KBC Bank N.V. (ibid.). In 2001, the government committed over J$900 million in government subsidy payments to the airline's workers pension fund (*The Gleaner* 2001a). These substantial subsidies are apparently paid despite Air Jamaica's December 2000 court summons for J$184 million in tax arrears and another summons in January 2001 for arrears exceeding J$300 million (*The Gleaner* 2000; 2001b).[32] Beyond mere issues of share ownership, the close cooperation between Air Jamaica and the Jamaican Government is clear evidence of the corporativist relationship between the state and key players in the economy.

From a macro-perspective, then, it seems that Jamaica is precisely in the situation described by Neyer (1996: p.115 – translation by the authors), where it just does not make sense anymore to speak of a *national* economy:

> The innovative and relatively highly developed sectors of the global economy are getting closer to each other and form core regions of the global market. On the other hand one can observe a process of marginalisation in the less developed and only peripherally dynamic sectors, which does not only unfold in Third World countries, but increasingly also in the First World.

It appears that the Jamaican economy has not only become disembedded, but that it and many other Caribbean economies are faced with the prospects of a virtual de-nationalisation and de-territorialisation of their (formerly) national economies.[33] Put another way, governments have become reduced to only partially sovereign (socio-economic) actors within their 'national space'. Clearly, whatever remains of the Jamaican Government's autonomy to make decisions affecting the economy is circumscribed by real and perceived neoliberal imperatives. The reduced autonomy affects not only its ability to steer social and economic development, but also its ability to manufacture consensus.

NEO-LIBERALISM IN THE CARIBBEAN: THE CASE OF BARBADOS

Barbados presents quite a striking case study of the elasticity of neoliberal codes of social and market organisation, and how the tensions associated with such adjustment have been attenuated by populist gestures on the part of the state. However, unlike the Jamaican case, there has not been much work in the field of development studies referring to or discussing the Barbados experience, even as the country remains a point of reflexive, glib reference in international policy-oriented literature. Indeed, the experiences of other Eastern Caribbean countries also continue to be under-researched. It is with this in mind that we decided to attempt a rounded analysis on the Barbadian case as it provides a rich empirical site for situating our discussion on political legitimacy, populist-statism and neo-liberal regime-making.

Barbados implemented a stabilisation programme with the IMF first in 1981, but more substantively from 1991, with the latter featuring a World Bank structural adjustment component and continuous IMF assessment. A brief period of mild disquiet followed popular compliance as the state remained committed to providing public goods, and restoring a semblance of cultural sovereignty. To achieve this, government officials employ(ed) material resources and a welter of discursive strategies to win allegiance and legitimacy from a coalition of class forces. The point about cultural sovereignty is important for understanding how Barbadian civil society processes the 'national' as a cluster of citizenship entitlements and rights, identities, traditions and customs that successive governments have done well to enshrine and protect. For the black Barbadian majority, the franchise, self-government and, later, released political Independence represented significant achievements of post-colonial empowerment and progress.[34] State-managers in the post-Independence period would come to tie their own security as a class to the fate of national sovereignty and the scope for national self-determination. The result would be a populist approach to development and later, neo-liberal reform.

Ongoing global trade rules have been eroding Barbados' fragile manufacturing and agricultural sectors along with the state's monopoly on awarding contracts, and its fiscal and macroeconomic autonomy. Despite these and other competitive challenges, politicians continue to pose as valiant heroes and managers in defense of the island's sovereignty and its policy autonomy. Consequently they exaggerate their capacity to insulate the country's economy and society from the social side effects of neo-liberal transformation and global free trade. This will be especially difficult, if it was ever at all possible, in this historical conjuncture. As will be demonstrated below, where decolonisation presented a challenge for state elites in the area of achieving civilised governance, social/class compliance and economic modernisation, neo-liberal globalisation has since raised the legitimacy ante in societies at the periphery. This has meant an inflation of the politics of statecraft associated with consensus-formation and development planning.

Based on a wide cross-section of opinion from groups and individuals, the consensus among Barbadians on neo-liberalism shifted over time from curious acquiescence to calls for a forestalling strategy and a protective response by the state. Musical entertainers generally welcomed the thrust of liberalisation reforms insofar as it related to reinforcing the intellectual property rights of artistes.[35] The local Chamber of Commerce accepted the arguments emboldening the private sector as the engine of growth, but expressed concern about how far the state should settle for a maximally open economy for foreign competition. Generally, and this includes those NGOs representing popular classes, neo-liberalism arrived on their shores in the 1980s first as a new counsel stressing the need for fiscal discipline and less government spending. By the start of the 1990s, it pointed up the importance building capacity, reducing the size of government and adjusting to increased global competition in goods and services. In these circumstances, most interviewees opined that the state was pragmatically obligated to assist society in its adjustment. However by the year 2000, neoliberalism came to be associated with terms like restructuring, downsizing and labour market flexibility – a sort of double-speak for job losses, low-wage employment options and overall job insecurity. Neo-liberal globalisation for working peoples, fledgling manufacturers and small-business owners, continues to be demonised as inimical to a self-determining nation-building project and many view and accept resistance as the main goal to be pursued by state elites in their bargains with multilateral institutions. This understanding/reasoning is reflected in the gargantuan theatre of electoral politics, a space where a politician's populist credentials are key to survival at the polls. Indeed from the mid-1980s, public perception of foreign oversight of state policy and action meant massive electoral defeats for the two political parties that have alternated in power, the Democratic Labour Party (DLP) and the Barbados Labour Party (BLP).

Thus far the main response by the current Owen Arthur Administration has been to:

1. maintain the welfare and benefits system;
2. set up and regulate rules for reciprocal trade, business investment and offshore financial services;
3. ensure the financing of infrastructural improvements; and,

4. champion the case for special and differential treatment for small states internationally.

In this way, the Barbadian state reinvents itself enough to lay claim to defending the cultural sovereignty of the nation as it engages the international agenda for free trade, and harmonised standards in business and production. However the future of such a strategy is not assured as the social effects of neo-liberal change, made more acute by the 'post 9/11' economic downturn, have begun to unravel internal contradictions in the country's political economy. These contradictions are also woven into the fabric of an uncertain regional integration movement, *pace* the Caribbean Community (CARICOM) and Common Market.

The 'Barbados Model'

Barbados has attracted a fair share of attention in the regional press and among leading international news magazines on its fiscal and political stability, its human resource achievements in the areas of health and formal education and in its capacity to secure social consensus in the wake of neoliberal reforms which began in 1991. Together with a formal tripartite arrangement or social partnership comprising interests from the Government, labour movement and the private sector, Barbados is held to be a model of people-centred development. Indeed it has become commonplace for radio talk-show hosts in Jamaica to point up the Barbados experience as a success story in social change and macroeconomic management. Elites in other Eastern Caribbean countries refer to Barbados' offshore financial sector, its reformed tax policy,[36] its fiscal prudence and the sustained benefits system as features worthy of emulation. And internally, different groups and individuals comprising Barbadian civil society nail at least the benefits system and the stable exchange rate to the mast of national identity.[37]

By global standards Barbados occupies an important position in the United Nations Development Program (UNDP) based Human Development Index (HDI). In all measures of the HDI, including life expectancy at birth, adult literacy rate, mean years of schooling, educational attainment, real GDP per capita, Barbados ranks at the top of Caribbean countries, and thirty-first overall among all the countries in the world.[38] Some international economic pundits have posited that Barbados is the country in the region which is best prepared to participate in the coming Free Trade Association of the Americas (FTAA), while Jamaica ranks in 27th position (see Schott 2001). Making this assertion requires, of course, a neoliberal epistemology and an unquestioned belief in the usefulness of economic theory even in conditions where non-economic, 'human', factors weigh in. Read differently – and still from the neo-liberal perspective – the ranking could also be interpreted as a relative unpreparedness, perhaps even unwillingness, to fully embrace the preconditions and requirements for this hemispheric free trade arrangement. However, the question which is not addressed in this discourse is why a country (that is, Barbados) with an insignificant manufacturing sector – and hence limited domestically produced export goods – would be better able to profit from the FTAA than a country with a larger and better integrated manufacturing sector.[39]

Courtney Blackman, a former Governor of the Central Bank of Barbados has listed the following factors as constitutive of the 'Barbados Model':

a.   the country's open economy;
b.   its historical record of fiscal prudence;
c.   the establishment of a small business soft loan facility;
d.   state-of-the-art legislation specific to offshore business;
e.   and selective state intervention in the direction of maintaining social services such as free health care, a national insurance and pension scheme and free education.

To be sure, he lists these factors to capture the country's political economic strategy since the oil crisis of the mid- to late 1970s. He is also careful to add that notwithstanding similar ideological underpinnings between the 'Model' and the market-liberal precepts of IMF/World Bank programming, the latter was too austere where the Barbados approach had been cautious and people-orientated. As a rule, successive governments have not succumbed to all-out privatisation schemes and where there has been divestment of public enterprises engaged in commercial or entrepreneurial activities, little occurred outside of formal consultation with social partners and/or considerable cost-benefit analyses. This occurred in the sale or divestment of enterprises such as the Barbados Development Bank and Heywoods Hotel in 1991 as well as the Barbados National Bank and the Insurance Corporation of Barbados in 1998. As it is void of a class analysis, Blackman's portrayal of the political economy of Barbados evinces discussion on the politics of consensus-formation and whether such consensus can become unglued as a result of additional anticipated neoliberal reforms or fault lines in the development strategy. We are left unaware of internal contests, tensions, and compromises that occur between one; the Barbadian state and civil society and, two; the state and global governance institutions such as the IMF or the WTO.[40]

Populist Legitimacy and the Erskine Sandiford Administration

In each neo-liberal phase of reform in Barbados, the ruling regimes pointed up their democratic intent, embracing empathy and cooperation as they negotiated with IFIs and the domestic populace. The Erskine Sandiford (DLP) Administration (1987-94) portrayed itself as practising 'consensus politics' where policy was to be considered only after consultation with different groups and the 'wider public'. At times the register shifted to claims about bringing about 'economic democracy' meaning, democratic access for all races and colours to corporate positions and resource allocation to vulnerable groups. The Owen Arthur (BLP) Administration (1994-present) would later shift the parameters of meaning to suggest that theirs is about a 'politics of inclusion'. The current government's stated intent is to rid the country of the negative effects of party tribalism and divisive rhetoric where the globalisation challenge requires the pooling of talents, knowledge and views of individuals, NGOs and oppositional groups in Barbadian society. Notwithstanding the lauding of democratic principles of transparency, fairness and public engagement on the part of successive DLP and BLP administrations, public perception of collusion between established corporate businesses, the senior legal fraternity and the ruling political party of the day nevertheless remains high.[41]

The neo-liberal reforms that were occasioned by a balance-of-payments crisis in September 1991 sat uneasily with the economic democracy rhetoric of the Sandiford Administration. Indeed this was the grand idea, theme and platform of the DLP campaign in the January 1991 elections. The appeals to race and class were clear. Erskine Sandiford, himself a teacher and veteran politician, was careful to establish his hold on the party and public for this was the DLP's first election since the death of its leader Errol Barrow in June 1987. Party members themselves were keen to support a vision that could resonate with Barrow's left-leaning image and extend the association of the DLP with working class opportunity and social mobility. The old capitalist class with roots extending back to the colonial era still constituted the leading factions of the economic bourgeoisie. Economic democracy was about redressing this historical imbalance through legislation to combat insider trading and nepotism in corporate boardrooms, through incentives to promote black businesses and cooperatives and through its allocation of licences and contracts. It was a populist ruse. The wealthy business class was and remains the largest contributor to the campaign funds of the DLP (and indeed the BLP). Moreover, the merchant capitalist predilections of this group had long been supported by both governments through the granting of monopoly import licences, awards of contract and of tender. General Elections occasioned an opportunity for political aspirants to pose as sincere advocates for black economic empowerment in a country where the small white population is at the apex of the socioeconomic class structure. To be sure, such appeals to race employed by both political parties extend back to campaigns in the 1960s. It might have been considered a tired appeal in 1991 except that economic democracy, so coined by a leading historian and champion of such reforms,[42] bore the impression of a movement, a sort of black petit-bourgeois fulfilment of the decolonisation promise.

However building alliances with an expanding black middle class required considerable political savvy. The Barbadian middle class comprises established lawyers, accountants and management specialists who make successful careers servicing the many retail houses, banks, insurance companies, small manufacturing companies and construction firms that are part of two leading merchant capital conglomerates.[43] Those not employed in the private sector are teachers, career bureaucrats, care professionals – all employed directly by the state, and intellectuals, journalists and artisans. Incidentally mass access to primary and secondary education of the mid-1960s led to the significant entry of women into the labour market, equipped to pursue careers across a wide spectrum. Altogether the incomes between each category of middle class occupation vary in large measure, but these persons share their class position by their heavy reliance on their monthly salaries, their consequent lack of collaterisable wealth, and limited decision-making power/influence in corporate investment activity. The fragility of the post-1991 consensus was quickly exposed once middle Barbados learnt of the news of a balance of payments crisis. This was internalised as a crisis of management with dire economic implications.

Altogether the economic enfranchisement rhetoric was inopportunely timed with economic stagnation. What followed was a decision to implement an 8 per cent cut in the wages of public sector workers and job losses for temporary workers in the public sector. The stabilisation measures struck a blow to the middle class both in terms of their bulk location in the public service and in terms of their overall confidence in the economic stewardship of the DLP Administration.[44] A significant amount of those affected were working class women employed as conductors of the National Transport Board and clerical officers in government departments. Private sector firms began downsizing their operations more in anticipation of a deepening economic recession than in foreign competition. One of our interviewees recalled that the situation of reduced spending power was 'made worse by increases in utility rates and house rents in the months after the crisis'. In the months that followed, displaced women joined the informal market mainly as road-side operators selling home-prepared hot meals and snacks. Some women also established small businesses – mostly hair salons and bakeries – from their homes. A few NGO officials point to this period as also marking an increase in the numbers of subcontracted young persons functioning as travelling sales persons of merchandise owned by large wholesale firms. An interviewee would describe the desperate condition of their employment in the following way:

> They [would] pick up their baggage and walk around with no national insurance protection, no job security ... They worked extremely long hours with low wages, and no medical plan.

In sum the initial impact of the 1991 neo-liberal measures was sufficient to undermine the social democratic posture of the DLP government among popular classes. As one calypsonian summarly put it in his 1993 hit, 'Breakdown', the DLP government had seemingly taken 'one step forward, two steps backwards, then trembled'.[45]

While the DLP government would later lose a snap General Election called in 1994 and then fare even worse at the polls in 1999, the Sandiford Administration did manage to broker a formal Incomes and Prices Protocol, and from this initiative, a formal Social Partnership. This Partnership reflected a tripartite social arrangement between the Government, the local Chamber of Commerce and a coalition of bargaining groups, styled the Congress of Trade Unions and Staff Associations of Barbados (CTUSAB). 1993 marked the first year of such a social partnership arrangement. Public sector wages were restored to their 1991 levels, economic stability was being recorded, and mock derision of the DLP government had replaced anger in the prevailing social mood. By this time, Barbados was experiencing a quick recovery based on macroeconomic indicators. A number of social scientists at the University of the West Indies points up this quick rebound in economic growth in Barbados as one of the reasons why the country escaped the kinds of protracted social trauma experienced in Trinidad and Tobago, Guyana and Jamaica in the 1980s. One scholar further argues that 1993 marked a collective sense of vindication as 'the measures of 1991 was marked by a significant Barbadian – and not IMF —— input [read insistence] that the island's currency was not to be devalued'.

Essentially what held the social fabric together was the state's resistance to the IMF austerity programme. Here the Government of Barbados, officials from the Ministry of Finance, and the economists from the Central Bank of Barbados and the University of the West Indies were of single mind. The team managed the 40 per cent reduction in its wage bill without widespread lay-offs and the government convinced IMF officials of the futility of devaluing the Barbados dollar in light of its very limited export portfolio. They also pointed up the social provisions of health-care, water supply, education and national insurance as real investment in human resources, the crucial resource if Barbados was to make good on its future in export-services. One official revealed that the negotiations were intense but that sound research and argumentation ensured a softer approach from the IMF delegation.[46] This strikes a blow to the logic which suggests that countries at the periphery are powerless to positively affect their circumstance with global players.

Populist Legitimacy and the Owen Arthur Administration

The Arthur Administration has been sensitive to the need for a phased liberalisation process. Apart from the social arguments, the reasoning is also linked to the need to 'buy the time' necessary for the CARICOM Single Market and Economy (CSME) to come into effect and local business persons to adjust to open competition in goods and services. Statecraft since 1994 has taken on a liberal populist character rooted in appeals to cultural historical awakening, adjustment to the new rules of international trade and the use of the state to tackle poverty-alleviation and jobs-development strategies. Much of this was possible between 1994 and 2000 as construction-led growth of the Barbadian economy resulted in the country's restoration of a high credit-rating and accessibility to foreign financing in international capital markets. The state could play the expansive role earlier described given the leap in internal revenue gains following the introduction of a value-added tax in January 1997. In a small society like Barbados, the confidence engendered by the state's handling of matters of economy, of international affairs and of community redounded to the appeal of Owen Arthur as Prime Minister and the BLP as the ruling party. The acclaimed 'politics of inclusion' was especially ambiguous appealing both to those constituent groups in search of a participatory social democracy, amelioration and/or accountable governance. Arthur's BLP would record an historic landslide election victory in 1999. The cracks in the overall strategy would only begin to show as the economy slipped into recession after 2000.

Wherever the appellation, 'the politics of inclusion', has been invoked in the local press, it is often employed to capture both the charisma of the current Prime Minister, Owen Arthur and the approach of the BLP in its style of governance. But there is more to the approach of the Arthur Administration than the impression of a benign adoption of a 'style'. Not unlike that that faced the deposed Sandiford regime, the challenge remained as to how to fashion an appropriate statecraft necessary for sustaining popular legitimacy in political economies required to undergo further neoliberal transition.

In order to tease out the ideological lineaments of the Arthur's approach, it might be useful to examine the political personality of the leader himself.

Drawn from the intelligentsia, and a background career in economic planning in the socialist leaning Michael Manley government in Jamaica, Owen Arthur joined the BLP and became a Member of Parliament for the rural parish of St Peter in 1984. His years as chief Opposition spokesperson on financial matters coincided with his academic research and debates on macroeconomic and public policy issues at the local Cave Hill Campus of the University of the West Indies. The period 1986 to 1994 featured a transition in the balance of global sociopolitical forces as the Cold War ended. Socialist experimentation by then lost its moral force and Keynesian demand-management approaches to state management gave way to Hayekian neo-liberal modes across the world. Globalisation, free trade, and multilateral rules-making took on a crusading character in this period. Arthur's speeches and debates at the time often touched on the plight of economies in transition and the need for compensatory financing from global governance institutions. On the floor of the House he advised against introducing neo-liberal reforms too hastily and charged that the divestment programme of the Sandiford Administration often betrayed the public trust.[47] As Prime Minister, he has used various international platforms to defend the sovereignty of small-island states in the globalisation process, to critique laissez faire globalisation approaches, and campaign for small-state inclusion in global governance surveillance organisations.[48] On the domestic front he has managed to tie neo-liberal reforms to social investment and poverty-alleviation initiatives. As he would often put it in the 1999 election campaign, 'no one must be left behind'.

Arthur's orchestration of an enduring politics of inclusion is ultimately a reconstitution of the populist state, with the Office of the Prime Minister (hereinafter, the 'Office') occupying a strategic space within the Cabinet system of government. There has been more money and resources allocated to this Office than under any previous Administration. The argument is that global governance issues, CARICOM matters, local government concerns, and the diplomatic agenda have altogether beckoned the need for decisional speed-up and tighter coordination between government departments. For a Prime Minister to be effective, the argument goes, s/he needs to engage in bilateral dialogues with the different arms of government. This perforce requires that the 'Office' be outfitted with an increased capacity in the area of research, planning and intelligence-gathering. The argument is within reason but it is also a self-serving one as Owen Arthur himself has taken on special responsibility for managing the funds associated with HIV/AIDS research, convalescence and care; Public Sector Reform, and recently, Culture. This is apart from the fact that he also has Lead Responsibility for the implementation of the CARICOM Single Market and Economy, and is the substantive Minister of Finance and

Economic Affairs in Barbados. The Office is additionally served by a Minister of State and Information. An official Commission for Pan African Affairs also operates out of the Office of the Prime Minister. It comprises as well as compromises those elements of the exhausted traditional left – Pan-Africanists, socialists and black nationalists – now dependent upon the state as its stable source of funding and restrained by the terms of the Civil Service Act which debar public servants from active politicking.

The upshot of this is that the Prime Ministership has been magnified to embody the populist state itself. It has become difficult to speak of the Barbadian state without meaning Prime Minister Arthur himself and his Office in Bay Street. It is a new channel through which 'commands' flow in the form of goals framed, directives issued, and policies pursued. Given the myriad responsibilities housed within the Office, it resembles a US Presidential oval office, personifying the Barbadian state in its current function as custodian of the national and cultural interests, guarantor of social investment and welfare, and facilitator of economic enterprise. The Prime Minister or his emissaries reach out to the services of groups and individuals regardless of political affiliation to serve in advisory, administrative and technical capacities. Where this 'inclusion' has extended to members of the opposition DLP the method seems to be absorption. In this regard it is not difficult to understand why 'inclusion' has come to mean a bestowal of 'the gift of grace'.

Double-digit unemployment has been tackled by a growth in the tourism-related sectors up to the year 2000, and the creation of jobs in the National Conservation Commission, Sanitation Service Authority, National Housing Corporation, Welfare Department, Poverty Alleviation Fund, Urban Development Commission or the National Assistance Board. These departments so listed constitute the welfare arm of the state and serve as a superstructure of largesse and patronage. To be sure, successive governments have employed job-development strategies and this has involved the creation of posts and appointments in the public sector. However, the role of the Ministry of Social Transformation is crucial for understanding patronage-distribution in the current temper.

LEGITIMACY VIA THE 'BESTOWAL OF GRACE'

The Ministry of Social Transformation, created in 1999, exposes the clientelist leanings of the state, particularly in its engagement with select community based organisations, and in its unscientific dispensing of benefits and assistance. The Minister of Social Transformation, Mr Hamilton Lashley, is highly regarded as one with sympathies towards the working class given his long association with the Pinelands Community Workshop (PCW), an NGO based in the urban Pine and St Barnabas areas. Since 1999, the Ministry has made poverty-alleviation its principle goal. The repairs to homes, the provision of new houses, indeed the overall use of state resources to alleviate the plight of the aged, the disabled, working poor and the unemployed have been guided more by compassion and paternalism than by rational, means-tested approaches. The paternalism appears quite strong, for example, in the awarding of construction contracts to a group of youths in the Deacons/Ferniehurst urban area.

It was in the early 1990s that the Deacons/Ferniehurst area became associated with drug-related crime and gang violence. The government-owned housing units began to take on the character of inner city projects with graffiti and assemblages of unemployed young men. Following improvements of lighting, and police crackdowns on violence and drug trafficking, Deacons/Ferniehurst became a relatively calm district notwithstanding the steady increase in numbers of unemployed young men. Between December 2001 and January 2002, a group of these men approached local businesses, residents, the sitting (BLP) Member of Parliament for the area and the rival DLP candidate for assistance towards constructing a stall for the sale of fruits, vegetables, and 'itals' (read, vegetarian dishes). There are a variety of versions as to what unfolded thereafter, but when interviewed the young men stated that they received financial assistance from a few businesses, and the rival DLP candidate. It was in late December that construction of the kiosk commenced, albeit without official approval from the Town and Country Department. By mid-January an official order to stop and remove the structure was served. The young men chose to ignore the order citing that they interpreted site visitations by the Minister of Housing and Lands and officials from the Urban Development Commission (UDC) as a vote of confidence in their endeavour. The former is reported to have advised that the group should ensure that the construction was '30ft away from the road', and the latter is reported to have discussed coinciding plans of constructing five kiosks in the district. Moreover, the young men stated that UDC officials advised them to form a company, 'Deacons Construction', and seek to win a contract to construct the five kiosks.[49] On Wednesday January 30, 2002, the young men protested the arrival of bulldozers by refusing to exit the kiosk. The Cabinet of Barbados on the following day ordered that the structure be removed and in a 'show of force unmatched in the history of police response in Barbados', the kiosk was bulldozed and removed.[50] While no violence or resistance occurred, the Arthur Administration was criticised for its lack of sensitivity. One member of the group of young men would state:

> Hamilton Lashley claim he is a man that does look out for poor people and he should make sure that that should never have gone down. Cause if that was in de Pine that would have never got mash down. If that was in the Pine, Hamilton Lashley would have stand up for the Pine youth. Cause the Pine youth does tell we how good Hamilton Lashley does stand up for them.[51]

Not unlike the earlier cited Jamaican case, the apparent powerlessness, frustration and anger of the young men of Deacons/Ferniehurst rapidly transformed into withdrawal:

Interviewer: My last question: so what's your next move?
First young male (1):   Man we done with everything!
Second young male (2):   The next move, we done with everything; we ain't want no stall!
1:   We ain't want no politics! We ain't want nothin'!
2:   We ain't want no politics thing, we done with that! We ain't in politics no more!
1:   Left we out of that!
2:   We ain't want no shop! We ain't want nothing. We ain't want nothing for the BLP, we ain't want nothing from the BLP, we ain't want nothing! We going back suffering man! Till when we dead! That's how we rolling now again, we done with that there man! We ain't want no shop we ain't want nothing from the BLP, we ain't want nothing. ShopSmart and PriceSmart can come here, but we youths can't build nothing??![52]

But the official position of the government was that the rule of law had to be maintained and that it implied no compromise. This was apparently at variance with illegally erected housing structures in the Belle area and illegal extensions to Government-owned housing units in the Pine area. The paternalistic character of the state, or more precisely, the workings of the Ministry of Social Transformation was laid bare when on March 13, 2002, Lashley would grant the aggrieved youth of Deacons/Ferniehurst under the newly formed 'Deacons Community Ventures' a cheque for BDS$ 26,000.00 to rebuild the kiosk. Indeed they were further granted the sum of $100 000 to construct five kiosks, this time under the aegis of the UDC. At the time of writing, these kiosks have been completed, and a $300 000 contract to construct a community center in the area has been awarded to Deacons Community Ventures. What began as an idea in marketing and selling vegetables, fruit and other food items was transformed into an exercise in public relations and political expediency; thwarting the civic-minded impulses and self-help values evidenced by all. Not surprisingly, the new stalls remain idle very much like their counterparts in George Park, St George and in Six Cross Roads, St Philip where the experiment by the Urban Development Commission began. While unemployed youth in other community settings across the country may inquire after such hand-outs from the Government, other salient questions can been raised about the clientelist leanings of the state with respect to select community organisations.

The Israel Lovell Foundation (ILF) and the Pinelands Community Workshop (PCW) have been recipients of government grants and stipends where the criteria for receiving such remains unpublicised and consequently unclear in other community based organisations. This is not to say that NGOs have not received support from the Arthur Administration as women's groups, AIDS awareness organisations, and the Caribbean Policy Development Centre have all been beneficiaries of government assistance. But the ILF and PCW cases are at some variance with the overall practice. Normal standards of accounting do apply, but the assistance to these two organisations run close to (BDS$) two million dollars. Their principals are sitting Members of Parliament in the BLP government. Hamilton Lashley is a leader and member of PCW and sits in Cabinet and Trevor Prescod, a backbencher, is a leader and member of ILF. Both the ILF and PCW have had a track record of service and outreach to their respective communities. But there are other community groups and clubs not seized by such a sense of entitlement simply because there is no clearly defined public policy on the criteria for accessing state funding/donations.

This is where it is possible to refer to the politics of inclusion as both positive and manipulative. The promise of a democratic vista of shared public participation sits uneasily in a two-party system where the ruling party welcomes inclusion so long as it is in conformity or decidedly non-threatening to the Party's or Cabinet's agenda. The Arthur Administration has skilfully used gifts of office, funds, headships and/or chairmanships to win converts as much as to bolster its need for the best talents to serve the country. The politics of inclusion can readily be recruited into a gesture of appropriation or co-optation. Much of this comes into sharp focus when attention turns to the fault lines in the island's political economy, and the threats posed to sustained cohesion among the social groups/classes.

Legitimacy Fault-lines

In a recent assessment of the island's economic performance, officials of the IMF referred to a contraction of the economy by 4.0 per cent during the first three months of 2002.[53] The Central Bank of Barbados would record a 5.7 per cent contraction for the same period.[54] This was the first time since 1993 that real economic activity fell between January and March and it followed three consecutive quarters of decline. The official explanation by Government pointed to the events on September 11, 2001, and their subsequent negative impact on tourist arrivals. With an eye on the country's growing foreign debt which stood at 30 per cent of gross domestic product at the end of 2001, the IMF recommends greater labour flexibility, the elimination of protectionist measures in tourism, agriculture and manufacturing, and the sale of more public enterprises involved in commercial activity in the short-to-medium term. These recommendations at first glance may appear benign, but they reflect a protracted crisis or stasis within the ruling alliance on the competitive way forward for Barbados.

Reference was made earlier of the merchant capitalist character of the local economy. It is important to stress the sense of a delimited economic horizon that pervades historical merchant capitalist thinking in Barbados, because many of the turns taken by modern policy elites can only be understood in the context of this fear of risk and small economic size. Briefly, the commercial circuit gives Barbados its character and its low-risk profile. Real estate and property development, insurance, finance and banking, transport and communications, import-trading and construction predominate in the Barbadian economy with tourism serving as the main foreign exchange earner and, the state, the biggest employer. Agriculture and manufacturing lag behind not only in terms of their respective contribution to the national GDP but at the intersection of global and hemispheric imperatives as well. Despite curriculum reforms and attention paid to information technology, the education system continues to divert an enormous amount of intellectual talent into commerce and tourism (accounting, management, banking, finance, hospitality services) and not necessarily science and technology, the fine and literary arts, and industry. Merchant capitalists, therefore, are not so much part of the ruling class as they are society's leading class. This risk-averse tradition extends back to colonial relations where Britain endeavoured to subsidise local sugar production through the forced supply of labour, cheap extensions of credit, and guarantees in shipping and market share. For most of the post-Independence years the hegemony of commerce over production in Barbados was offset by other factors occurring in the international political economy (IPE): the logic of the Cold War alliance system, easy lines of international credit, preferential market access arrangements, and rising tourism. However the final decade of the twentieth century has come to shatter these IPE arrangements and expose the contradictions of the local economy. As the state continues to negotiate reductions in trade barriers in accordance with international agreements, buying and selling continues to take precedence over production and investment.

This is in the face of broad elite support for a development agenda based on intensified export services development. Leading elements of the private sector, trade unions and government officials vigorously support expansion of the tourism product, and the provision of offshore financial and other international services as key to coping with globalisation. Offshore banking, health convalescence, entertainment, education, and information technology services are held out to be real levers for economic success, even renewal. As the arguments go, success in the export services sector will allow Barbados to withstand the fallout from manufacturing, and the pending loss of preferential market access agreements for bananas, rum and sugar (circa 2009). Confronted by difficulties associated with new trading rules and what this portends for local distributors, manufacturers, and services-providers, the Arthur Administration has pursued a number of local and regional initiatives aimed at consolidating confidence among investors and the public alike. These range from a commitment to further develop the offshore services sector (particularly in the area of international business and software development) and the pursuit of education reform with an emphasis on information technology, to encouraging the implementation of the anaemic CSME of which Barbados could be a part and free movement of labour and capital can be a feature.

Indeed, the new development consensus among Barbadian development planners on the viability of an export-services strategy is problematic on a number of fronts. As Marshall (2002) explains, it reveals a lack of awareness of the complexities associated with information technology access; a particular short-sightedness with regards to the longevity of offshore financial services given current re-regulation trends; and a historical blindness and misreading of say Singapore and Hong Kong's export-services profile.[55] Missing is the sense of how their export services sector is allied to Southeast Asian and mainland Chinese industrial processes respectively, providing for robust manufacturing performance in the region and an exponential rise in the contribution of services to the local economies. Rather than move towards what is globally the most remunerative factors of production: high-level manufacturing and services, a rather curious consensus has emerged which proclaims a solid future for export services without roots and/or ganglia to local manufacturing. The success of such an 'export services' model will not turn as much on the quality of human resources as it will on overcoming the short term horizon of local politicians, and the low-risk predilections of the wealthy, planter-merchant elite. The latter's conscious 'opt out' strategy on the question of manufacturing diversity has made for a quite conservative enterprise culture indeed. More specifically, merchant capitalist societies like Barbados and others in the Eastern Caribbean, insufficiently display the sociocultural attributes required for the creation of high-level services: innovation-mediated risk, research and development competencies, and affinities to industrial processes and networks.

Currently, Barbadian companies do not feature in the shifting geography of production and export services capabilities. None specialise in higher valueadded services and products such as digital design services and semiconductor memory, but there are growing competencies in graphic designs. Nor is there an institute of software technology to assure a cadre of highly skilled persons. Moreover there is very little evidence within relevant Ministries and departments of a strategy for lodging companies anywhere on the earlier mentioned value-chain of international production networks (IPNs). Thus far European, North American, Mexican and Asian companies constitute these networks. For quite some time, in industries like garments, footwear, furniture and toys, it was established practice for 'brand name' companies to depend on contract suppliers for essentially all of their manufacturing requirements. The emergence of contract production and regional arrangements in consumer durable sectors such as electronics turns the phenomenon away from one essentially confined to labour-intensive, low- and middle-skilled locales to those with semi-automated driven infrastructures and cheap, skilled labour. If Barbados hopes to progress beyond marginal participation in export services at the level of data-entry work, the enterprising culture will also have to be transformed. Recently Prime Minister Arthur pointed to the need for the private sector in Barbados to 'correct deficiencies [that include the] absence of research departments, indeed the lack of economists and similarly trained, and [failure] on the part of ... major corporations to seek scientific forecasting as a normal part of business'.[56] But there is more to this.

The business culture, the relationship between business and the state, and the power of commerce in the political economy conspire to stymie an export production ethos and by extension, the innovative and entrepreneurial capacities needed for local nodes in IPNs. Indeed it is not the norm for public sector technocrats to possess expert knowledge, direct technical training or scientific talent in R&D, engineering, or manufacturing technology. The private sector world is also devoid of knowledge gleaned from experience in modern science and technological innovation. An export services strategy that is neither located in burgeoning IPNs, nor in local and regional manufacturing complexes, but spins off primarily in the direction of attracting hospitality and financial services, renders the economy of Barbados hostage to shocks in Wall Street and the flight travel industry. The shocks on the domestic side may imperil the project for as one social worker pointed out, the seasonal character of employment in the tourism industry contributes to the ballooning of the 'working poor' and increasing underclass resentment. Without a thorough makeover, services development as presently conceived and executed could easily become a quagmire.

Other sectoral strategies are also problematic. Where there is an agricultural policy, production centrally rests on sustained traditional agricultural exports. For Barbados, sugar remains its only agricultural export. From 1991, the restructuring programme involved the closure of plants to favour one-factory production. Of the dozen factories then in existence, three remain with Bulkeley Sugar Factory in St George and Portvale in St James scheduled to dismantle operations in August 2002. Andrews Factory in St Andrew will thereafter become the island's production unit, marked by less reliance on extensive mechanical harvesting and more investment in state-of-the-art office and production control systems. Exports of sugar in Barbados and in most of the Anglophone Caribbean countries are largely possible only as a result of preferential arrangements offered by the EU and quota systems devised by the US. The relevant terms of trade for sugar are to be phased out provisionally in 2009. These were part of the market access reforms broadly outlined under Article 20 of the WTO Agriculture Agreement and reinforced in the Doha Declaration of November 2001. It seems strategically wrong-headed, therefore, for governments to focus on sugar as an export commodity. This extends to other cash crops as the Eastern Caribbean small islands face the basic issue of being high-cost producers trying to compete in bulk commodity markets. There are possible agricultural export markets the region should endeavour to pursue such as biological extracts for the nutraceuticals and functional foods markets, and the flavorings and essences markets. These high-value niche markets are characterised by low volumes, high margins, and competition on the basis of quality – unlike commodity markets such as sugar characterised by low volumes, low margins and competition on the basis of cost.

Poultry farmers represent another disgruntled group of local producers. The ongoing elimination of tariff barriers has meant increased price-competition, but the failure of the state to assist is leading to a loss of faith in the BLP Administration. The Barbados Egg and Poultry Producers Association (BEPPA) laments the heavy importation of chicken to the island by the state-run Barbados Agricultural Development and Marketing Corporation (BADMC). In 2001, 746,000 kilos of chicken were imported. By mid-2002, the figure was already

1.2 million kilos. President of BEPPA, Carlyle Brathwaite, explains that the imported chicken is cheaper because of the low tariffs, subsidies and other cheap units of production overseas. He defends their rate of pricing stating:

> Between 1980 and 2000 our prices have increased by 14 per cent. In fact, in 1982 our chicken was $7.62 a kilo and today, in 2002, it is $6.69 a kilo, actually less than what it was, but still you have persons saying how expensive poultry is.[57]

BEPPA seems also to process ongoing globalisation as a challenge that requires a protective response from the state. The following comments by Brathwaite typify how the state's development strategy has come to be internalised. As the neo-liberalism regime gets into full swing, the Arthur Administration will find it increasingly difficult to maintain popular consensus:

> We have people who like to paint bright pictures all the while but we are losing money on a monthly basis. [And] Government has to realise it has a duty to every sector and not just tourism, because when all the other sectors fold and die, the same will be the result for tourism. We can never be competitive because the necessary support is not there. More farmers have come into the BEPPA but they are now crying out, calling me daily complaining.... As it stands there are still lots of work which can be done to the local poultry industry but it makes no sense investing in something which has no certainty.[58]

Altogether calypsonians have used the platform afforded by the local Crop Over calypso competition to register protest against the government's neo-liberal and development programme. Government's land use policy was described as affording foreigners prime agriculture and beach front real estate while reserving 'rab land and the pond-side' for locals by John King in his (1998) 'These Fields and Hills' and David 'Supa D' McCarthy's (1998) 'Barbados Fuh Sale'. Popular calypsonian, Stedson 'Red Plastic Bag'Wiltshire, has consistently crafted songs that take up the globalisation theme and government's response. In each composition he has implored listeners not to confuse the effects of a lack of developmental vision and mis-guided management with that of globalisation.[59]

SUMMARY (BARBADOS)

The local policy community continually asserts that open economies like those in small-island Caribbean states, offer greater scope for surplus accumulation in the area of commercial agriculture, offshore business, import-trading, and international services as high labour costs and lack of economic scale seemingly foreclose on industrial options.[60] This pragmatic reasoning over time has functioned as the prevailing common sense, where it is more appropriately an ideological manual of statecraft to safeguard the social reproduction of the ruling elite. Its intellectual roots lay in positivist problem-solving techniques – techniques that process ongoing globalisation in ways that force a closure on discussion of alternative strategies of accumulation.[61]

This is where the politics of inclusion could be said to have tentacular properties. Beyond questions of intentionality, it is a strategy that unwittingly engenders complicity and self-silencing. Outsiders must either conform or accept isolation. As our interviews in Barbados showed – and in the case of the trade unions, not dissimilar from the Jamaican case – there seems to be little critique from the trade unions and community-based NGOs on the way forward. This is in the wake of uncertainties in the offshore banking and other financial services, the steady closure of electronics companies no longer drawn to the island's basic skills platform, and the proliferation of low value-added, mundane service-related jobs that altogether exert a downward pressure on wages. Increasingly what is lacking is some form of organised community feedback, a framework of induction and involvement in which the politics of an articulate and enduring community would stand in explicit and effective counterpoise to administration and government. The sense of the Pinelands Creative Workshop or the Israel Lovell Foundation as detached, independent organisations was lost in our interviews.[62]

Certainly the question – which new pattern would support a shift away from this exhaustive and ultimately, stymied form of merchant capitalist hegemony – cannot be raised or answered in the prevailing environment. While issues such as gender, identity, race, poverty, ecology, and globalisation have been raised, no challenge is posed as discussion squarely remains within the confines of the existing agenda. If the island's credit rating remains strong, and there is an improvement in tourist arrivals, the government can continue to make good political capital on managing repercussions. However, there is a legitimacy cost associated with rearranging the deckchairs on the Titanic. Already there is a logjam in the labour market for well-educated persons and middle-income earners are decrying escalating land prices. Unless there is an accompanying turn towards encouraging the rise of a new exporter class through tax and other concessions, the pro-status quo leanings of the state may come to beckon wider social resentment, particularly at a time when the economic horizon appears rather clogged.

CONCLUSION: IMPLICATIONS FOR LEGITIMACY

There are significant implications for the legitimacy of the neo-liberal model, which follow from the above described disembedding tendencies acting upon Jamaica, Barbados and the global economy: 1) The capability of the state apparatus to shore up domestic legitimacy is limited and concentrated on the tourism, retail, rum, minerals and specialty goods sectors. Attention to the social sector -- marginalised groups such as youth and the elderly, women, unemployed, temporarily unemployed or seasonal labour – is given sporadically and primarily for narrow partisan advantage and with little sustained dedication of resources.[63] 2) Consequently, as our interviews in Jamaica and Barbados have shown, support for the neo-liberal model is particularly brittle among these groups. When hardships are brought into particular focus this passive resistance may very well translate into street protests of various degrees. 3) To the extent that governments are unable or unwilling to factor the expectations of the entire populace into their public policies framing and supporting the neoliberal trade model, (temporary) counter-globalist 'subalternism' will impact negatively on the overall investment climate and country risk assessments by international agencies. This, in turn, will affect the domestic economic and political elites, as well as – albeit to a far lesser extent -- international capital operating in countries such as Barbados and Jamaica. 4) There appears to be a disconnection between effects of neo-liberalism and globalisation and the way these effects are 'read' locally. Thus, developments emanating from the dynamics in the global sphere are widely perceived in terms of local politics and economics.

This is, for the moment, good news for the globalisation project and the interests of international capital. It is, however, increasingly bad news for the current governments in the region. While some interviewees do not see any serious disenchantment with politics in Barbados, others do, although they may not necessarily see any critical levels of social unrest (as in Jamaica). In any case, however, there may be a point at which businesses and governments may have to re-evaluate the relation between short-term and medium-term profits and long-term profitability or location. Jürgen Habermas (1990, 317-18; see also 271-303) has repeatedly pointed out, legitimacy in conditions of late capitalist development has to be satisfied under formally democratic means. The crisis of legitimacy of the neo-liberal trade regime in the Caribbean is therefore to be seen in the contradiction between this model's privileging of globalised economic and local political elites, and the premises of inclusion implicit in the civil democracy. It is also to be seen in the paradox of the populist state, where Caribbean governments may move steadfastly and in some cases, cautiously, to accommodate neo-liberal imperatives but at the same time remain disinclined to displace the hegemony of merchant dealers by structuring incentives and other initiatives to stimulate and encourage export-orientation.

Ultimately, the growing discrepancies between the economic demands of a slash-and-burn, casino-style, maximum return/minimum expenditure capitalism, and the ethical and moral requirements of a more sustainable development in the context of the 'global village' call for – what Fiona Robinson (1999) terms – a new 'critical ethics of care in the context of international relations.'

Endnotes

1. Research for this article was made possible by a grant of the CUNY-Caribbean Exchange Program at Hunter College.
2. For more on this see for example, See R. Cox (1987) *Production, Power, and World Order*, pp.273-308; and A. Boron (1996) 'Democracy or Neoliberalism'.
3. See Kees van der Pijl (1998) *Transnational Classes and International Relations*. p.134
4. That is, the environmentalists, 'anti-globalisers', leaders of vulnerable Third World countries, NGOs, philanthropists like George Soros, care advocates like Amarta Sen, and the like.
5. In this chapter we will only list the names of interviewees that are of particular relevance to a point made in the text or where we directly quoted from an interview. The full list of interviews can be obtained from the authors upon request.
6. In the process of asking these questions and evaluating the answers, the researchers were of course mindful of the particular socioeconomic position of each of the respondents, as well as the role played by the organisation with which they are affiliated.
7. Weber (1973, 151) is aware of their existence, of course, but considers them not sufficient for the establishment of legitimacy.
8. See for example H. Watson (2000) 'Global Neoliberalism, The Third Technological Revolution and Global 2000: A Perspective on Issues Affecting the Caribbean on the Eve of the 21st Century'. p.391.
9. This is our translation. See M. Foucault (1978) *Dispositive der Macht* p.82
10. As Cox (1993, 52) put it in his article on Gramsci: 'Hegemony is enough to ensure conformity of behaviour in most people most of the time'.
11. We follow here Persaud's (2001, 37ff.) interpretation of Gramsci's concept of hegemony (see also Gill 1993; Henke 2000).

12. See also H. Alavi and T. Shanin (eds.) (1989) *Introduction to the Sociology of 'Developing Countries'*.
13. See for example, J. Lambert (1969) *Latin America: Social Structures and Political Institutions* and; H.J. Wiarda and H. Kline (eds.) (2000) *Latin American Politics and Development*.
14. See K. Weyland (2001) 'Clarifying a Contested Concept: Populism in the Study of Latin American Politics', in *Comparative Politics*, October.
15. B. Chevannes (2000) 'Those Two Jamaicas: The Problem of Social Integration', p.184.
16. See also N. Girvan (2000) 'Globalisation and Counter-Globalisation: The Caribbean in the Context of the South'
17. See for example T.J. Farer (1988) The Grand Strategy of the United States in Latin America; and P. Korner et al (1987) The IMF and the Debt Crisis: A Guide to the Third World's Dilemmas.
18. See for example R.B. Reich (1991) The Work of Nations; K. Ohmae (1990) The Borderless World; and S. Strange (1995) 'The Defective State'.
19. Thus, while in 1998 Asia (without Japan) experienced a net inflow of US$56 billion, Africa's net foreign investment was just US$9 billion (United Nations 2000a, 48).
20. For more on this see, Elmar Altvater and Brigitte Mahnkopf (1999) *Grenzen der Globalisierung*. pp. 47.
21. Interestingly, at the July 2001 G8-Summit in Genoa, U.S. President Bush and Britain's Prime Minister Blair tried a new strategy, which attempts to depict critics of globalisation as enemies of poor nations. Thus, while the dichotomy is perpetuated, there is now a new coalition of rich and poor nations being postulated.
22. Dani. Rodrik (2001) 'Trading in Illusions'. pp. 59.
23. The exception to this may be Trinidad and Tobago, where new oil and gas deposits *may* become the basis for a more diversified, integrated and self-propelling economy.
24. This point was recently reiterated in the U.N. *World Drug Report 2000* (2000b, 11).
25. For more on this see e.g. Thomas J. Peters (1991) *Liberation Management: Necessary Disorganisation for the Nanosecond Nineties*; and Michael Borrus and John Zysman (1997) 'Globalization with Borders: The Rise of Wintelism as the Future of Global Competition'.
26. The last figure does not include Chinese EPZs. These figures are quoted from Altvater/Mahnkopf (1999, p. 348).
27. This picture was also compounded by the sight of tourists being whisked away by tour operators from the scenes where street clashes were imminent.

28. This is so, despite the fact that we have a substantial black middle class and many successful black entrepreneurs in Jamaican society.

29. For more on this see, e.g., Bogues (2002), Gray (2001), Henke (2001), Scott (2001), and Meeks (2000).

30. Quoted in Charles (2002, 36).

31. 70 per cent of Air Jamaica is owned by Air Jamaica Acquisition Group (AJAG), which is led by Gordon 'Butch' Stewart. The other 30 per cent, including five per cent under the Employee Share Ownership Plan (ESOP) are owned by the Jamaican Government.

32. Interestingly, in a press release Air Jamaica's chairman 'Butch' Stewart called reports about the court summons part of an orchestrated campaign 'to discredit the airline to satisfy hidden agendas.' According to the report, he did not point out the source/s of this alleged campaign (*The Gleaner* 2001c). In the same article, the airline's CEO Chris Zacca reportedly had claimed that Air Jamaica had not received any summons. Following the terrorist attacks in the United States, a similar – albeit substantially smaller – Government bail-out was paid to the Jamaican tourism sector (see Simpson 2001).

33. See also H. Watson (1994) 'Global Neoliberalism, The Third Technological Revolution and Global 2000: A Perspective on Issues Affecting the Caribbean on the Eve of the 21st Century.' pp.88-89.

34. This narrative on Caribbean political development, constructed on very broad terms, is not meant to evacuate 'women' to a space in civil society that is nonpolitical and private. While a number of women have been employed in public office, their small numbers, their unequal status to men in Caribbean economies, and their assignment to the private sphere mean that citizens with the fullest entry to recognized politics remain 'men'. As Richard Ashley puts it, 'statecraft' has always been about 'mancraft'. See R. Ashley (1989) 'Living on the Border Lines: Man, Post-structuralism and War'; also E. Barriteau (2001) *The Political Economy of Gender in the Twentieth-Century Caribbean*; C. Enloe (1989) *Bananas, Beaches and Bases: Making Feminist Sense of International Politics*; M. Ringrose and Adam Lerner (eds.) (1993) *Reimagining the Nation*; and, in James Der Derian and Michael Shapiro (eds.), *International/Intertextual Relations: Postmodern Readings of World Politics*.

35. Interview with a key executive member of a local umbrella organisation representing entertainers.

36. This refers to the 1997 introduction of the Value Added Tax (indirect tax) set at 15 per cent on all consumer items outside a basket of basic commodities. Direct income tax was also lowered. These measures are all

in keeping with IMF requirements. Other measures also favoured in recent times are lower corporate taxes, bankruptcy measures and new legal protections for investors from expropriation. The IMF also uses its conditionality to advise on banking law, contract law, company law, the role of the judiciary and judicial review mechanisms.

37. This is based on wide–ranging interviews (January/Februray 2002) with trade unions, youth based- and community based-NGOs, members of the academic community, policy officials, and unemployed youth in the depressed, urban Deacons/Ferniehurst area. Indeed, some interviewees in Barbados vigorously objected to Jamaica and Barbados even being compared in our research

38. See United Nations Development Programme, *Human Development Report 2002*, (New York: Oxford University Press, 2002).

39. See also Watson (1994, 89), who appropriately posits that 'it is unsatisfactory to argue that the economic crisis in the Caribbean is mainly a function of poor economic management.'

40. See also Boxill (2002).

41. This is in spite of a range of activities and initiatives to inspire public trust and confidence. I refer to the following: participation in radio call-in programmes by Cabinet Ministers, the establishment of town hall meetings, Commissions-of-Inquiry, diverse composition of statutory boards and Task Force committees, and the introduction of the Small Business Fund and Youth Entrepreneurship Scheme. Evidence of this perception was drawn from our interviews with young persons between 18 and 27 years of age, NGO officials and academics.

42. I refer to Prof Hilary Beckles who was the intellectual force behind the concept, and a source of scorn and public derision by conservative white elites and some black professionals. His advocacy began in 1988 with a series of public lectures showcasing revisionist historical analysis of the class structure of Barbados. He would later head a pressure group entitled Association of Concerned Policyholders of the Mutual Life Assurance Society, questioning the Mutual's Board of Directors about their investment and other practices. Altogether he became a public figure and symbol of the new educated middle strata demanding transparency and an end to oligarchic practice among wealthy family groups in corporate boardrooms. For more on this see, H. Beckles (1991) *Corporate Injustice in a Political Democracy: The Mutual Affair*.

43. I refer to Goddards' Enterprises and Barbados Shipping and Trading.

44. To be sure, the post-1991 structural adjustment programme included an 8 per cent cut in salaries for 18 months duration and the dismantling of price

controls and import licensing regimes. Gradual financial liberalisation began with the lowering of cash and securities requirements for banks, the abolition of selective credit controls as well as limits on the average lending rate of commercial banks and mortgage rates charged by financial institutions. There has also been devolution of responsibility with respect to the authorisation of foreign exchange transactions and requests. Once under the purview of the Exchange Control department of the Central Bank of Barbados, most daily transactions are processed by commercial banks.

45. See the lyrics of Elonza 'Serenader' Brewster's 1993 calypso, 'Breakdown'.

46. Discussions with Dr Delisle Worrell, former Deputy Governor of the Central Bank of Barbados, over the period October 1997 to March 1998.

47. For more on Owen Arthur's pre-1994 contributions, see his contributions in N. C. Duncan (ed.) (1988) *Public Finances and Budgetary Policy in the OECS*, Kingston, Jamaica: Friedrich Ebert Stiftung and various Opposition Replies to Government Budgetary Statements and Finance Proposals (1987-1994), Hansard, Parliament of Barbados.

48. His latest treatment of these themes was on the occasion of the International Labour Standard meeting in Switzerland, June 2002. After pointing to the social shortcomings of unfettered market forces, he would add:

> [T]he conditions of genuine global development can only be achieved if the existing dominant agenda in support of free trade, the protection of private investment and intellectual property rights and the creation of an environment conducive to financial and capital mobility is counter-balanced and enriched by equal concern for matters pertaining to labour mobility, codes of conduct for transnational corporations, the development of sound rules to govern international competition and the development of compensatory financing mechanisms to sustain the participation of those in danger of being left out or left behind.

In terms of the effect intensified global competition is having on the lives of workers, he stated:

> For across too wide a band of economic activity, the ends of production are now being set only to maximise shareholder value .... [a]nd the shareholder-value driven global corporation has come to enthrone aggressive cost reduction strategies, focusing on layoffs, pay and benefit reductions and a peripatetic approach to hiring as their essential elements. See the *Advocate Newspaper* (17 June 2002) 'PM: Greater Balance Needed'.

49. Interview with young men of Deacons/Ferniehurst. February 1, 2002.

50. See 'Show of Force' by Tim Slinger, *Daily Nation* February 1, 2002. One of our interviewees from the labour movement put it this way: 'Government has served notice as to its recourse to a massive police anti-strike force.'

51. Interview in Deacons/Ferniehurst, February 1, 2002.

52. Ibid.

53. The contents of this report were drawn from an article by Tony Best, overseas correspondent for the *Daily Nation* (July 1, 2002) entitled 'IMF: Sell Some'.

54. See Central Bank of Barbados *Economic Review*, June 2002.

55. See D.D. Marshall (2002) 'At Whose Service: Caribbean State Posture, Merchant Capital and the Export Services Option', in *Third World Quarterly*, Vol.23, No. 4 August (forthcoming).

56. See the transcript: Hon Owen Arthur, 'Structural Adjustment — Phase Two', an Address to the Barbados Chamber of Commerce (Bridgetown: Barbados Hilton Hotel), October 8, 1997.

57. See the comments of Carlyle Brathwaite in 'Chicken Sector Feeling the Heat', *Daily Nation*, July 22, 2002.

58. Ibid.

59. I refer to the lyrics in his 1998 song 'Online: Barbados at the Crossroads dot.com'; his 2001 'I'll Keep on Comin'; and his 2002 composition, 'Ah Seeing Red'.

60. This was best captured in an editorial of one of the leading local newspapers. The *Barbados Advocate*, 'Trade Block: The Future is in Our Hands', 15 May 1999:

> International business has the potential to propel the country forward at a pace which no other sector of the economy can match. Most now recognise that the growth potential of tourism is limited by environmental and sociological constraints; of manufacturing by the realities of open market competition; of agriculture by the amount of land available. No such constraints apply to international business, where the level of foreign exchange earnings and quality employment for a highly educated people can increase dramatically without any negative impact on our environment or society.

p.8.

61. Henke (2000, 69-72) observed a similar development in Jamaica during the early 1980s and has termed the phenomenon 'discursive dependency.'

62. When the interview shifted from matters related to the club's activities, rather than a robust dialogue on the plight of working groups in the wake of the closure of overseas based factories, declining tourism, and advancing free trade reform, we were treated to anemic responses that echoed the views of government. We refer to their confidence in a revitalised

international business sector and tourism sector in terms of restoring employment and maintaining steady inflows of foreign exchange. They also expressed confidence in the capacity community-based training schemes to provide skills for unemployed, undocumented young persons. Interviews here conducted on February 5, 2002.

63. Barbados' sustained commitment to providing mass-based education up to university level, and the state's grants/awards schemes for postgraduate, vocational and retraining programmes however stand in stark contrast to the Jamaica case where state investment in human capital is inadequate.

Bibliography

Alavi, Hamza and Shanin, Teodor (eds.), *Introduction to the Sociology of 'Developing Countries,'* (London: Macmillan, 1989).

Altvater, Elmar and Brigitte Mahnkopf, *Grenzen der Globalisierung. Ökonomie, Ökologie und Politik in der Weltgesellschaft,* (Münster: Westfälisches Dampfboot, 1999).

Anderson, Patricia, 'Social Risk Management, Poverty and the Labour Market in Jamaica,' (Paper presented at the conference 'Re-inventing Jamaica,' Columbia University, Institute for Research in African-American Studies, February 2), New York, 2001.

Ansine, Janice, 'Economic Hardships Hike Domestic Violence Rate,' in: *The Gleaner,* (March 8, 1999).

Ashley, Richard, 'Living on the Border Lines: Man, Post-structuralism and War', in: Der Derian, James, and Michael Shapiro (eds.), *International/Intertextual Relations: Postmodern Readings of World Politics,* (Lexington, MA: Lexington Books, 1989).

Barriteau, Eudine, *The Political Economy of Gender in the Twentieth-Century Caribbean,* (New York: St Martin's Press, 2001).

Beckles, Hilary, *Corporate Injustice in a Political Democracy: The Mutual Affair,* (Bridgetown: Lighthouse Publications, 1991)

Blackman, Courtney N., 'The Barbados Model,' in: *Caribbean Affairs* 8:1, 61-68, 1998.

Boron, Atilio, 'Democracy or Neoliberalism,' in: *Boston Review* Vol. 21 No. 5 (October/November 1996), (also available on the internet at http://bostonreview.mit.edu/BR21.5/boron.html).

Bogues, Anthony, 'Politics, Nation and Postcolony: Caribbean Inflections,' in: *small axe: a caribbean journal of criticism* No.11 (March), 1-30, 2002.

Borrus, Michael and John Zysman, 'Globalization with Borders: The Rise of Wintelism as the Future of Global Competition', in: Berkeley Roundtable on the International Economy (BRIE) Working Paper 96B, (Berkeley: University of California 1997).

Boxill, Ian, 'Barbados and the Myth of British Conservatism,' in: *Ideaz*, Vol.1 No.1 (May 2002), 44-52.

Burchell, Graham, Colin Gorden and Peter Miller, (eds.) *The Foucault Effect: Studies in Governmentality*, (Chicago: University of Chicago Press, 1991).

Castells, M., *The Rise of the Networked Society*. 3 Volumes. Vol.1, *The Information Age: Economy, Society and Culture*, (London: Blackwell Publishers, 1996).

Charles, Christopher, 'Garrison Communities as Counter Societies: The Case of the 1998 Zeeks' Riot in Jamaica,' in: *Ideaz*, Vol.1 No.1 (May, 2002), 28-43.

Chevannes, Barrington, 'Those Two Jamaicas: The Problem of Social Integration', in: Kenneth Hall and Denis Benn (eds.), *Contending With Destiny. The Caribbean in the 21st Century*, 179-184. (Kingston: Ian Randle Publishers, 2000).

Cox, Robert W., *Production, Power, and World Order. Social Forces in the Making of History*, (New York: Columbia University Press, 1987).

Cox, Robert W., 'Gramsci, Hegemony and International Relations: An Essay in Method,' in: Stephen R. Gill (ed.), *Gramsci, Historical Materialism, and International Relations*, 49-66. (New York: Cambridge University Press, 1993).

The Gleaner, 'Air Jamaica set for US$100m,' (September 3, 1999).

The Gleaner, 'Air Jamaica summoned - For arrears of $184m travel tax returns,' (December 7, 2000).

The Gleaner, (a), 'Government short-changes Air Jamaica pension fund,' (April 29, 2001).

The Gleaner,(b), 'Air J summoned again,' (January 11, 2001).

The Gleaner, (c), 'Stewart defends Air Jamaica,' (January 15, 2001).

Dujon, Veronica, 'Caribbean Peasants in the Global Economy: Popular Resistance to the Privatization of Communal Land in the Twentieth Century and Beyond,' in: *Global Development Studies* Vol.2 Nos.1-2 (Winter-Spring, 1999/2000), 199-221.

Enloe, C., *Bananas, Beaches and Bases: Making Feminist Sense of International Politics*, (London: Pandora Publishers, 1989).

Farer, Tom J., *The Grand Strategy of the United States in Latin America*, (New Brunswick, NJ: Transaction Books, 1988).

Fine, Ben, Lapavitsas, Costas, and Pincus, Jonathan (eds.), *Development Policy in the Twenty First Century: Beyond the Post-Washington Consensus*. (New York: Routledge, 2001).

Foucault, Michel, *Dispositive der Macht. Über Sexualität, Wissen und Wahrheit*, (Berlin: Merve Verlag, 1978).

Gill, Stephen R. (ed.), *Gramsci, Historical Materialism, and International Relations*, (New York: Cambridge University Press, 1993).

Girvan, Norman, 'Globalisation and Counter-Globalisation: The Caribbean in the Context of the South,' in: Denis Benn and Kenneth Hall (eds.), *Globalisation. A Calculus of Inequality*, 65-87. (Kingston: Ian Randle Publishers, 2000).

Graham, Burchell, Colin Gorden and Peter Miller (eds.), *The Foucault Effect: Studies in Governmentality*, (Chicago: University of Chicago Press, 1991).

Gray, Obika, 'Cultural Forces and the Criminalization of Jamaican Politics,' in: *Wadabagei. A Journal of the Caribbean and its Diaspora*, Vol.4 No.2, 2001, 51-67.

Habermas, Jürgen, *Zur Rekonstruktion des Historischen Materialismus*, (Frankfurt a.M.: Suhrkamp Verlag, 1990).

Habermas, Jürgen, 'Zur Legitimation durch Menschenrechte,' in: Jürgen Habermas, *Die postnationale Konstellation. Politische Essays*, 170-192. (Frankfurt a.M.: Suhrkamp Verlag, 1998)

Henke, Holger, 'Jamaica's Decision to Pursue a Neoliberal Development Strategy. Re-alignments in the State-Business-Class Triangle,' in: *Latin American Perspectives* 108, No.5 (Sept. 1999), 7-33.

————, *Between Self-Determination and Dependency. Jamaica's Foreign Relations 1972-89*, (Mona: University of the West Indies Press, 2000).

————, 'Freedom Ossified: The Public Use of History and the Political Culture of Jamaica,' in: *Identities: Global Studies in Culture and Power* (Vol.8 No.1, September, 2001).

Henke, Holger and Ian Boxill, (eds.), *The End of the 'Asian Model'?*, (Amsterdam/ Philadelphia: John Benjamins, 2000).

Hyatt, Stephen-Claude, 'My Parent and My Pimp - Child Prostitution in Jamaica,' in: Daily Gleaner, (December 6, 2001).

Van der Pijl, Kees, *Transnational Classes and International Relations*, (London and New York: Routledge, 1998).

Körner, Peter, Maass, Gero, Siebold, Thomas, Tetzlaff, Rainer, *The IMF and the Debt Crisis: A Guide to the Third World's Dilemmas*, (London: Zed, 1987).

Lambert, J, *Latin America: Social Structures and Political Institutions*, (Berkeley: University of California Press, 1969).

Lühr, Volker, 'Legitime Herrschaft an sich,' in: Klaus Lindenberg (ed.), *Lateinamerika. Herrschaft, Gewalt und internationale Abhängigkeit*, 29-47. (Bonn: Verlag Neue Gesellschaft, 1982).

Manley, Michael, *Jamaica. Struggle in the Periphery*. (London: Third World Media, 1982).

Mars, Perry, *Ideology and Change. The Transformation of the Caribbean Left*, Detroit: (Wayne State University Press & The Press – University of the West Indies, 1998).

Marshall, Don, D., 'National Development and the Globalisation Discourse: Beyond `Imperative' and `Convergence' Notions', in: *Third World Quarterly*, Vol.17, No.5, 1996

——————, *Caribbean Political Economy at the Crossroads: NAFTA and Regional Developmentalism*, (London: MacMillan Press, 1998).

——————, 'At Whose Service: Caribbean State Posture, Merchant Capital and the Export Services Option', in: *Third World Quarterly*, August (forthcoming, 2002).

Neyer, Jürgen, *Spiel ohne Grenzen. Weltwirtschaftliche Strukturveränderungen und das Ende des sozial kompetenten Staates*. (Marburg: Tectum Verlag, 1996).

Ohmae, K., *The Borderless World: Power and Strategy in the Interlinked Economy*, (London: Harper Collins, 1990)

Persaud, Randolph B., *Counter-Hegemony and Foreign Policy. The Dialectics of Marginalized and Global Forces in Jamaica*, (Albany: State University of New York Press, 2001).

Peters, Thomas, J., *Liberation Management: Necessary Disorganisation for the Nanosecond Nineties*, (New York: A.A. Knopf, 1991).

Polanyi, Karl, *The Great Transformation*, (New York: Farrar & Rinehart, 1944).

Reich, R, B., *The Work of Nations: Preparing Ourselves for 21st Century Capitalism*, New (York: Knopf Inc., 1991)

Ringrose, M, and Adam Lerner (eds.), *Reimagining the Nation*, (Buckingham: Open University Press, 1993).

Robinson, Fiona, *Globalizing Care. Ethics, Feminist Theory, and International Relations*, (Boulder: Westview Press, 1999)

Rodrik, Dani, 'Trading in Illusions,' in: *Foreign Policy* (March/April, 2001), 55-62.

Ross, Charles, 'Globalisation and the Private Sector,' in: Denis Benn and Kenneth Hall (eds.), *Globalisation. A Calculus of Inequality*, 143-146. (Kingston: Ian Randle Publishers, 2000).

Rubenstein, Hymie, 'Ganja and Globalization: A Caribbean Case Study', in: *Global Development Studies* Vol.2 Nos.1-2 (Winter-Spring, 1999/2000), 224-250.

Ruigrok, W. and R. van Tulder, *The Logic of International Restructuring*, (London and New York: Routledge, 1995).

Sally, Razeen, 'Multinational Enterprises, Political Economy and Institutional Theory', in: *Review of International Political Economy* Vol.1, No.1, (1994) 161-192.

Schott, Jeffrey J., *Prospects for Free Trade in the Americas*, (Washington, DC: Institute of International Economics, 2001).

Scott, David, *Refashioning Futures. Criticism after Postcoloniality*, Princeton: (Princeton University Press, 1999).

Scott, David, 'The Dialectic of Defeat: An Interview with Rupert Lewis,' in: *Small Axe: a Caribbean Journal of Criticism*, 10, (2001) 85-177.

Sherlock, Philip and Hazel Bennett, *The Story of the Jamaican People*, Kingston and Princeton: (Ian Randle Publishers and Markus Wiener Publishers, 1998).

Simpson, Lynford, 'Tourism, Air J bail-out - Government announces measures to avert more damage,' in: *The Gleaner* (September 26, 2001).

Strange, S., 'The Defective State', in: *Daedalus: Journal of the American Academy of Arts and Sciences* Vol.124, No. 2, (1995) 55-74.

United Nations, *Drugs and Development* (Discussion paper prepared for the World Summit on Social Development, UN International Drug Control Programme), (1994), New York.

United Nations, (a), *World Economic Situation and Social Prospects 2000*, New York: (Department of Economic and Social Affairs & UNCTAD). 2000.

United Nations, (b), *World Drug Report 2000*, New York: (Office for Drug Control and Crime Prevention), 2000.

Wallerstein, Immanuel, *After Liberalism*, (New York: New Press, 1995).

Watson, Hilbourne A., 'Global Restructuring and the Prospects for Caribbean Competitiveness: With a Case Study from Jamaica,' in: Hilbourne A. Watson (ed.), *The Caribbean in the Global Political Economy*, p. 67-90. (Boulder & Kingston: Lynne Rienner Publishers & Ian Randle Publishers, 1994).

_____, *Women and the New Trade Agenda* (New York: UNIFEM 1994)., 'Global Neoliberalism, The Third Technological Revolution and Global 2000: A Perspective on Issues Affecting the Caribbean on the Eve of the 21st Century,' in: Kenneth Hall and Denis Benn (eds.), *Contending With Destiny. The Caribbean in the 21st Century*, 382-446. (Kingston: Ian Randle Publishers, 2000).

Weber, Max, *Soziologie. Universalgeschichtliche Analysen. Politik*. Stuttgart: Alfred Kröner Verlag, 1973).

Weyland, Kirk, 'Clarifying a Contested Concept: Populism in the Study of Latin American Politics', in: *Comparative Politics*, Vol.34, No.1 October, 2001.

Wiarda, H, J. and H. Kline (eds.), *Latin American Politics and Development*, (Boulder, Colorado: Westview Press, 2000).

8

A Gendered Analysis of the Impact on Women's Work of Changing State Policies in Barbados

Ann Denis*

Abstract: From the theoretical perspectives of feminist theories of citizenship, of appropriation, and of gender systems, this chapter examines the effects of state policies on work by women in Barbados since the 1970s. 'Work' is conceptualised broadly, including not only revenue producing activity in the formal and informal sectors, but also, for instance, family and community responsibilities and study. State policies include those relating to personal autonomy, to employment, including entrepreneurship, to the provisions of social programmes (including education and the social safety net), to structural adjustment measures and to the organisation of Women's Affairs. It is concluded that there have been significant improvements in the political and civil components of women's citizenship and, to a lesser extent, in the social components, all of which have repercussions on women's paid and unpaid work. Changes have, however, been more significant in the material dimensions of the gender system than in the ideological dimensions. Women's appropriation continues to be evident and state policy does not guarantee either gender equality or gender equity, an outcome one would anticipate if women enjoyed full citizenship rights.

I wish to acknowledge and thank Dr Eudine Barriteau, Head, Centre for Gender and Development Studies, UWI, Cave Hill Campus, for her support, advice and friendship particulary during 2000-1, when she made me very welcome as a visiting research fellow at CGDS. I also wish to acknowledge with thanks the very helpful comments of the editors and the anonymous reviewer on earlier drafts of this manuscript.

INTRODUCTION

This chapter examines the effect of state policies on work carried out by women in Barbados since the 1970s. Although it is a truism to posit that men and women constitute distinctive status groups, each of which intersects with groupings based on such factors as class, ethnicity/race and age, state policies have often been gender blind, with the result that ostensibly neutral policies may, effectively, have differential effects on men and women, frequently with a negative impact on women. Even in the absence of explicit exclusion, policies which are formally neutral may be effectively excluding for the members of certain political categories, due to the latter's differential access to resources and the predominant ideological climate. In societies, such as Barbados, which obtained political independence in the latter half of the twentieth century, the constitution typically accords women political citizenship, including the right to vote and hold political office. In fact, in Barbados universal adult suffrage, introduced in 1951, predates political independence. Neither the constitution nor other national laws, however, necessarily accord women full rights of civil citizenship, including property rights and liberty of person, or of social citizenship, which includes rights to education, economic welfare and security. Civil and social citizenship are the other two components of citizenship, or full membership in the community that T. H. Marshall (1950) has identified, in addition to social citizenship. After briefly elaborating on the theoretical and conceptual underpinnings of our analysis and the hypotheses these entail, I will then describe my methodology and examine how state policy in Barbados during the past quarter century has related to various aspects of women's lives which impact on the work they do.

Theoretical and conceptual underpinnings

Extending Marshall's insights, feminist scholars (for example, Yuval-Davis and Werbner 1999; *Feminist Review* 1997) stress the importance of the impact of gender on citizenship. The analysis of the ways in which women may be excluded from full citizenship must also include, they argue, examination of how other categorical groupings intersect with gender. Other feminist theorists, who espouse materialist feminism, argue (Guillaumin, 1995 ; Juteau and Laurin, 1988), argue in fact, that women remain not merely subordinated in society but appropriated: their whole being becomes the property of another, their husband, in the case of individual appropriation or the society, in the case of collective appropriation. These authors argue that the material appropriation is reinforced and perpetuated by ideologies which legitimise the situation as 'natural' and therefore not subject to change: based on such an analysis, women can be, at best, second class citizens. Without adopting the appropriation model, Barriteau (1998a, 1998b) also distinguishes between the ideological and material dimensions of a gender system, arguing, in the case of Barbados, that the effects of formal changes towards equality on the material level have been mitigated by the perpetuation of patriarchy on the ideological.

In this analysis we adopt a feminist conceptualisation of 'work', which includes not only revenue generating activities in the formal and informal sectors ('productive' work), but also activities which maintain the society ('reproductive' work, including biological and social reproduction and maintenance within the family, volunteer community activity, study ...). Unlike more traditional social (and economic) analyses, this conceptualisation acknowledges that productive work does not occur in a vacuum, and it also takes account of the existence of revenue generating activities in the informal sector, something that analyses informed by advanced capitalism tend to overlook.

Methodology

Our examination of state policies will draw mainly on the constitution (Government of Barbados 1966) and other laws of Barbados, along with the Development Plans (Government of Barbados, n.d.(a), n.d.(b), n.d.(c), n.d.(d), n.d.(e), n.d.(f), n.d.(g)) which have informed government policy.[1] We will also consider selected recommendations by the National Commission on the Status of Women (NCSW) (1978a) and women's organisations (for example in NCSW 1978b), on some of which the government has chosen not to act, at least to date.

State policy related to women in Barbados

1.   Overview

Barbados presents a mixed situation regarding the impact of state policy on women: while important measures which acknowledge the principle of gender equity have been introduced, there are also significant gaps.

The NCSW (1978a) concluded the historical background in its *Report* by observing that:

> [t]he status of women in Barbados has certainly been elevated in the twentieth century and particularly in the last thirty years or so, but the attitudes of a male dominated society are still affected by the past; the law of the eighteenth century has been radically altered but the customs and attitudes of that age have died harder and in some cases are not dead at all. In addition there is no doubt some men resent and fear the wave of female progress and try to erect breakwaters

against it. The man does not want to give up his position of domestic dominance nor does he feel easy about the professional progress of women as accountants, engineers, doctors and the like. The attitude is morally indefensible while ... being emotionally understandable. (1978a: 4-5)

This analysis supports Barriteau's thesis that changes in the ideological dimensions of the Barbados gender system have not kept pace with changes in the material dimensions. What is also noteworthy about Barbados is the lack of explicit references to women in either the Constitution or the successive development plans since independence. The Barbados constitution does allow persons to make claims against the State regarding rights (T. Robinson, personal communication, June 2001), but, in Antoine's estimation, this offers women insufficient protection (1997: 547-549). Similarly, a perusal of the Barbados *Development Plans* since the late 1960s underlines the lack of explicit attention to women (see also Barriteau 1994), even when they make up significant proportions of target populations – notably of the poor and the unemployed. Discussions of the reduction of inequality of wealth and income do not include a gendered analysis of these phenomena.

In 1992 Cabinet approved a National Policy Statement on Women (Bureau of Women's Affairs 1992; Government of Barbados n.d. (g): 235-6) which included among its principles the equal and complementary partnership of women and men, the redress of any lingering disadvantage by women by providing 'equitable citizenship rights under the Constitution'. Despite these impressive principles, few concrete measures seem to have been enacted during the intervening years to implement them. In addition, statistics on programme implementation – for instance on those supporting the establishment or expansion of small businesses – do not routinely provide gender disaggregated data.

We will now consider selected aspects of state policy related to women and work under the following headings: personal autonomy, education, employment, maternity, family responsibilities and the place of women's affairs within the State system.

2. *Personal autonomy: facilitating and constraining work*

Civil rights include those related to property ownership and liberty of the person (Marshall 1950). Until about the 1980s there was a clear distinction between the rights of unmarried and married women: married women continued, in some respects, to be legal minors, unable, under Common Law, to make binding contracts on their own behalf (NCSW 1978b: ch 8) and thus lacking full civil citizenship. In this respect materialist feminists would argue that they remained subject to private appropriation by their husbands. A number of the subsequent changes in state policy reflect the recommendations of the NCSW

Report of 1978. Although since 1879 married women have shared equal rights to landownership with men and single women in Barbados (Momsen 1998: 123), it is, for instance, only since 1980 that a married woman could acquire property and sue and be sued with respect to property in her own right (Married Persons Act 1980 - cap 219). In the same year a married woman obtained the right to have an independent domicile (Domicile Reform Act 1980 - cap 266), rather than being constrained, as a dependent, to have her husband's domicile. Practically this meant that a women domiciled in Barbados whose husband acquired a domicile of choice in another country could petition Barbados courts for divorce (NCSW 1978b: ch 8). Women also obtained the right to completely separate income tax assessment (Income Tax (Amendment) Act, 1980- cap 73), thus 'emphasizing her unlimited legal control of her financial affairs' (Bureau of Women's Affairs n.d.: 4). While, as a result of these changes, women have become less appropriated, legal inequalities remain: whereas the wife of a Barbadian citizen acquires citizenship by virtue of marriage, the husband of a Barbadian citizen does not.[2] Nor can a Barbadian mother confer citizenship upon her legitimate children: only the father can. On the other hand, only the mother, but not the father, can convey citizenship on illegitimate children. Between 1978 (NCSW 1978a: 103-106) and 1997 the Infants Act (Minors Act - cap 215) was changed, so that either parent of a legitimate child can give consent for the child's medical treatment and sign for the issuing of a passport for the child. Previously only the father could provide these authorisations.

A woman's right to determine whether she will have an abortion, as well as her more general right to safe choices regarding reproduction have widely recognised since the UN Population conference in Cairo in 1994. While overall improvement of *maternal* (rather than *women's*) and child health has been a government priority in Barbados throughout the period under review, the question of abortion has been more litigious and reflects ambivalent public opinion (NCSW 1978a: 315-330, 414-21). Without fully endorsing abortion on demand, the Commission recommended abortion at the sole request of the woman up to the twelfth week of pregnancy and a liberal interpretation of indications for termination after that date in the case of those under 18 or over 40 and those with at least four children. These recommendations would still have constrained women's autonomy regarding reproductive choice, but to a lesser extent than the Medical Termination of Pregnancy Act (cap 44a), the law which was actually passed in 1983, and which only permits termination 'where there is grave injury to the physical and mental health of the woman and where there is risk to life' (Women's Bureau n.d.: 3). That doctors interpret this clause liberally is probably why there has not been pressure from the women's movement for further change. Despite its liberal interpretation, the law itself is an example of the appropriation of women: a third party, the doctor, is mandated to make the decision about the fate of a product of the woman's body, the fetus, rather than the woman herself having the right to do so.

The changes in state policy during the past twenty odd years have significantly reduced the inequities associated with the status of 'married woman', and thus facilitate women's full exercise of personal autonomy, with both the associated rights and obligations.[3] Thus married and single women now share with men almost all of the same formal political and civil rights in relation to choices related to or impacting on paid and unpaid work (participation in political processes, choice of domicile, ownership of property), although women still do not have full reproductive choices and, in practice, remain a minority in Parliament. Thus women continue to be somewhat appropriated. We now turn to issues related to women's social citizenship rights.

3. Education and training: preparation for work

State policy extending access to education by both girls and boys has had an important impact on women's labour force participation by allowing them to obtain secondary and tertiary level qualifications in a wide range of subject areas. Secondary schooling and much post-secondary schooling is tuition free, with a minimum school leaving age of 16.[4] The introduction of co-educational schools has equalised funding to schools (boys' secondary schools were previously both more numerous and more generously funded) and has equalised access to science and technology subjects, which were formerly unavailable in the girls' secondary schools. These measures, although clearly necessary, are insufficient. Girls continue to be required to have a higher average to enter secondary school. Furthermore, both in their choice of subjects of study and, to a greater extent in their eventual occupations, women remain segregated in a much narrower range of activities than men, and in substantially less remunerative positions (de Alburquerque and Ruark 1998). Proactive measures have not been initiated by the Ministry of Education to counter the strong ideological pressure against women entering 'non-traditional' (and lucrative) work within the less routine aspects of information technology and within the construction trades, for instance. What is also striking – and reflects the strong persistence of patriarchal values – is the preoccupation by politicians and the media with the lack of academic success of (some) young men, in combination with an absence of concern about gender segregation in trades and technology studies, persistent high rates of unemployment for young women, the lack of equivalence between women's qualifications and remuneration when compared with men's. With lower average levels of education, men's average earnings are nevertheless significantly higher than women's: whereas 22.8 per cent of all male employees and 13.6 per cent of self-employed men earned less than $200 a week in 1990, the percentage of women in both cases was more than double (Barbados 1994: table 8.02). This inequality obtains at each level of completed education. In addition, although education largely escaped being the object of structural adjustment cuts to social services in 1991, for some types of post-secondary education tuition fees are charged. The effects of this measure on differential access in terms of gender and social class remain to be analysed.

In summary, although state policy has successfully extended women's educational access through the introduction of co-educational schools, differential entry requirements for secondary school and the lack of proactive policy regarding subject choices mean that inequality persists. What should be of particular concern is that public attention is now being focussed on 'marginalised men' to the exclusion of any concern about women who may remain marginalised. Here, again, ideological changes have not kept pace with material ones.

4. *Employment and self-employment: work for pay or profit*

What Antoine has called the ECONSOC rights (economic, cultural and social rights) in relation to paid work can be seen as components of Marshall's 'social' citizenship. She suggests (1997: 535) that these include:

(1) The right to work - which encompasses such subsidiary rights as equal access to employment without discrimination on the basis of gender, the right not to be prevented from full-time employment, and the right not to be discriminated against in relation to job opportunities

(2) The right to just remuneration for such work - which includes the right to equal remuneration for work of equal value and provision of job-related benefits.

(3) The right to health - which encompasses the right to safe and healthy working conditions including holidays, rest-periods, maternity leave and protection against disease and hazards which are detrimental to women.

Noting the difficulty of enforcing such rights as legitimate human rights under the constitution (Antoine 1997: 540), she argues pragmatically for the use of other legal strategies to protect these employment-related rights. While some of these rights are the subject of laws in Barbados, this is not the case for all, and the exceptions and exclusions are also worthy of note. Despite the fact that it is government policy in Barbados to prevent sex discrimination in employment (Antoine, 1997: 553), women's unemployment rates are consistently and substantially higher than men's (16.4 per cent for women and 8.4 per cent for men in 1998 (Barbados 1999), for instance), there are significant sex differences in occupational distribution and in average wages, and it is only in relation to the public service that there is equal pay legislation. While there are general equality of employment provisions, there are no legal provisions prohibiting denying women work on the basis of their gender (Antoine 1997: 554). Antoine goes on to argue that other aspects of equal access to employment could include equal access to opportunities within the job, including training and promotion up into management.

In the 1983-8 *Barbados Development Plan* (Government of Barbados n.d. (c): 153-4), while no longer providing the gender disaggregated labour force and unemployment data which in earlier *Development Plans* highlighted women's disadvantage without commenting on it, the government did acknowledge that it was 'aware of the high unemployment among women' - 23.0 per cent for women compared with 13.1 per cent for men in 1986 (Stuart 1998: 36-7) - and was 'committed to ensuring that as many women as possible participate in the productive sectors of the economy'. That it would 'act as a channel for funding' given an amenable funding agency implied, however, that such endeavours were at best secondary in establishing funding priorities.

Despite the fact that small business entrepreneurship became a development priority during the 1980s, in her doctoral research Eudine Barriteau (1994) discovered that government officials seemed unaware of the extent to which women already owned and managed small business. Barriteau's research documented ways in which the assumptions of neoclassical economics result in a masculinist state climate, which, despite its formal measures of equality, operated to the disadvantage of women entrepreneurs. It is not clear that the promises to change this state of affairs which have been made in the most recent *Development Plan* (Government of Barbados n.d. (g): 237) have resulted in any substantial modifications. In fact my own, limited inquiries in search of gender disaggregated statistics indicated that at least one person in a position to mandate the collection of relevant data refused to do so.

The lack of attention in the *Development Plans* to the informal sector, despite its importance for women, particularly in times of economic crisis (de Albuquerque and Ruark 1997; Mondesire and Dunn 1997, Stuart 1998), suggests that their coping strategies are considered to be of marginal interest to national planners.

When concern first focussed internationally on the inequalities experienced by women in the work place, the concept of equal pay for equal work was invoked. Further analyses of the causes of inequalities resulted in a shift to the concept of equal pay for work of equal value. In this way the problems of unequal pay for the same job, or substantially similar ones, and the effects of occupational segregation by gender can both be addressed. The shift to evaluation in terms of work of equal value is clearly important in Barbados which continues to share with other societies in Latin America and the Caribbean very high levels of occupational segregation (Antoine 1997: 563; Lynch 1995:68; Mondesire and Dunn 1997). At the moment, however, although it has signed the ILO Convention on Equal Pay, Barbados does not have legislation explicitly addressing the issue of equal remuneration (Antoine 1997: 563), except within the public service. Within the latter, the use of the same pay scale for women and men has been a long-standing principle, but equal access to benefits has been more problematic. It was only in 1990 that legislation was passed entitling the spouse of a female public officer who qualifies for leave passage to accompany her on this leave (Bureau of Women's Affairs n.d.: 5), although the inequity of wives but not husbands having this right had been raised, clearly not for the first time, in the NCSW's *Report* in 1978 (1978a: 195). Tables 1 and 2 provide evidence of gendered occupational distributions, unequal wage rates, and the impact of category of employer on women's and men's earnings in 1990. The positive effect of equal pay legislation in the public sector is somewhat offset by occupational segregation by gender. Half of the female labour force was in occupations – sales and service, skilled agriculture, operatives and elementary occupations – in which the median earnings for women were $100-199 per week. In contrast, almost half the male labour force was in occupations – managers, professionals, technicians and skilled craftsmen – in which the median weekly earnings were $300-499. Except for clerks (where they are equal), the median weekly earnings in each occupational group was one income category higher for men than for women.

i   The economic trials of the 1990s

In the early 1990s Barbados introduced a number of structural adjustment measures, including cutbacks in wages under the 'social partnership' (Barbados Workers Union 1998), reduction in expenditures on public services, privatisation, increases in the cost of publicly supported services, such as bus fares. The retrenchment in the public service had a particularly negative effect on women, since this is one of the few sectors, as Table 1 shows, in which they achieve wage parity and where there is a concentration of their better paying jobs.

During the same period of the early 1990s offshore manufacturing and data entry companies began to withdraw, as their concessionary tax regimes ended. Unemployment, and particularly the unemployment of young women skyrocketed during the early 1990s. Although Barbados has stood out by its insistence that workers in EPZs be covered by Barbadian labour law, such employers are fickle, and when they close their doors without paying their workers, the latter seem to have no means of recourse. That there seems to have been an informal agreement by the unions (Freeman 2000) not to organise EPZ workers increases the latter's vulnerability to poor working conditions.

Unionisation attempts in the late 90s resulted in at least two companies leaving the island (Barbados Workers Union 1998).

Although unemployment rates have now dropped, as we have seen the rates for women remain higher than those for men. In general, during times of retrenchment it seems relatively harder for women than men to re-enter formal sector employment, with men being seen as the breadwinner (and therefore needing employment more), despite the significant proportion of female household heads in the society (Antoine 1997: 583 Stuart 1998). Casual labour – seasonal or temporary – and work in the informal sector have become widespread for women, with the attendant low wages and absence of benefits. Multiple casual jobs and increasing self-employment, often associated with decreased earnings, are characteristic strategies of women for coping with retrenchment in regular jobs in the formal sector. These types of non-standard work do not seem to be perceived as a social problem in Barbados, although Antoine argues that this

> casualisation of labour is no substitute for women achieving their full potential in employment. The right to work, to equal opportunity in employment and to access to employment, can never be interpreted to mean a right to the lowest paid and weakest protected jobs in the economy (1997: 585).

ii. Protective legislation ... and insurance

Protective labour legislation for women can arouse ambivalent reactions from feminists. On the one hand is the acknowledgement that, associated with pregnancy, actual or eventual, are legitimate health concerns, such as those related to exposure to radiation or to chemicals which may harm their fertility.[5] On the other hand, protective legislation contradicts the principle of equality and has often served as a mechanism for policing women's morality and for obliging them to adjust their behaviour and their presence so that men do not have to exert some self-control over their sexual urges. Both exemplify appropriation of women, on behalf of their actual or eventual partner. Protective legislation can also serve, implicitly, as a mechanism for excluding women from competing with men in the work place. Prohibition, for women only, of night work – especially when the prohibition is applied, for instance, to factory work but not to nursing, is a case in point. In Barbados there was a shift in 1977 (Employment (Miscellaneous Provisions) Act) from the protective exclusion of women from night work in industry to the protective exclusion of all – except in specific circumstances. The revised prohibitions, along with the terms of the Factories Act of 1984, require safe and salubrious working conditions for all, not exclusively for women. The frequency of protests related to working conditions suggests, however, that enforcement – for the benefit of men as well as women – could be improved.

An aspect of 'working in salubrious conditions' whose existence is barely acknowledged officially and on which legislation is lacking is that of workplace harassment, particularly sexual harassment (Robinson 1999). Although both men and women may experience harassment, where the existence of the problem is acknowledged, women are recognised as more frequently being the victim.

A rather different type of work-related protection is offered by National Insurance. Initiated in 1966 for employees, and based on contributions by both employer and employee to cover sickness, maternity leave, long term disability, employment related injury, old age and survivors' pensions, and funeral grants, the National Insurance Scheme was extended to the self employed in 1971 (Government of Barbados n.d. (c)). By the end of the 1970s it was estimated that between 80 and 90 per cent of the employed population, including the self employed, were covered by the scheme (Government of Barbados n.d. (d)). This estimate, however, probably does not take account of those working exclusively in the informal sector.

5.   *Maternity: at the intersection of paid and unpaid work*

Child bearing can be analysed as the provision of a social good, not merely an individual act. Both the ILO and the *UN Convention on Women* specifically mention that maternity and pregnancy benefits should be rights for all working women (Antoine 1997:554-5). In Barbados no law forbids the refusal to hire a women because she is pregnant, or might become pregnant. Once employed, however, the Employment of Women (Maternity Leave) Act 1976 stipulates that a woman may not be fired because she is pregnant. Women with at least twelve months' service with one employer may benefit from maternity leave of 12 weeks on a maximum of three occasions from the same employer. On resuming her work, the woman maintains her seniority and the calculation of continuous service, returns to the same or equivalent position and does not receive lower wages due to the maternity leave. The requirement of a year's service with the employer for entitlement to maternity leave assumes what could be described as a middle-class male pattern of regular, continuous employment, one that is at odds with the employment experience of much of the female labour force. Furthermore the Act excludes those working at home for wages (NCSW 1978:112). The restriction to three periods of maternity leave from the same employer clearly impinges on women's free exercise of reproductive choice, whether it reflects the State's encouragement of family planning – although there seems to be no formal State policy on child-bearing (Antoine 1997: 559) – or its acceptance of limits to the costs of social reproduction which a single employer can reasonably be expected to bear. That there are no provisions for paternity leave[6] indicates the assumption that a significant role in early parenting, and assistance for the new mother do not fall within the purview of a husband's (or partner's) responsibilities.

Participation in remunerative activities outside the home is problematic for mothers in the absence of affordable day care, from infant care through after school programmes. Barbados has introduced, and over the years extended, publicly funded day care. As successive development plans (for example, Government of Barbados n.d.(g)) attest, however, the number of places remains clearly insufficient, and the nurseries can neither accommodate infants nor sick children. The high incidence of female headed households, coupled with low average wages for women, particularly those who are household heads, and the expectation that it is mothers who take responsibility for infant and child care, militate against women's equal participation in the labour force, and are an indication of women's collective appropriation.

In an effort to reduce the imbalance of the negative effect of parenthood on school aged young people, teenaged mothers may now return to school after giving birth, either to their former school or a different one. The lack of day care facilities for infants, is, however, a deterrent to their doing so, unless a relative or friend (usually a woman) cares for the baby without pay during school hours, yet another example of the social expectation of women's collective appropriation.

6. Family responsibility: unpaid work in the private sphere

In view of the belief in societies influenced by Western political philosophy, as Barbados is, that the private sphere, most notably the family, should be largely exempt from State regulation, it is not surprising state policy impinges to a much lesser extent than in the public sphere. The introduction of laws relating to domestic violence and the protection of children from abuse (Prevention of Cruelty to Children Act 1981, Domestic Violence (Protection Order) Act 1992 and the Sexual Offences Act 1992, all referred to in Women's Bureau n.d.: 1, 6-7), which require police or welfare intervention in the case of suspected abuse, even in the absence of a complaint by the alleged victim, has represented a quite radical philosophical change (NCSW 1978a; National Consultation 2000, Robinson 2000). Although it could be argued that the philosophy is one informed by protection of women rather than their autonomy, the change is positive in the recognition it affords of women's right to physical (and emotional) safety within the confines of their home, the right to not be a man's chattel which he can treat as he pleases. It eliminates the formal legitimation of this aspect of women's individual appropriation, at least in theory.

The day-to-day care and maintenance of the family continue to be socially defined as primarily women's responsibility, whether men contribute financially or not. In the case of female-headed households in Barbados, significant financial contributions by men seem to be the exception rather than the rule. Instead, women often develop a network of support, both material and emotional, of other women (Barrow 1996). In fact, despite its concern with public health issues affecting children, the State provides only limited direct or indirect support to the exercise of family responsibilities. A notable gap is the fact that full-time, unpaid housewives can not be covered under national insurance, despite representations to this end (NCSW 1978b). Thus, they can not be insured for illness, disability or death. The level of welfare payments, which offer, to some extent, a social safety net, is low, and there is no automatic financial support for the raising of children. As already noted, the nursery school care available remains insufficient to meet demand. In recognition that, with smaller nuclear families and increased labour force participation by women, the women of the society are less able to provide informal care and assistance to their extended family and neighbours in times of illness or old age, limited means-tested home help is now available under welfare provisions. This assistance is, however, provided by other women, at relatively low wages. The allocation of these responsibilities illustrates, yet again, society's collective appropriation of women, who are expected to care for the young, the infirm (and able-bodied men) either for free or for low wages.

7. *The place of women's affairs in the State system*

The locating of the Bureau of Women's Affairs, once it was established, in Community Development, rather in a ministry dealing with Economic Development is, perhaps, an unconscious indication of the ideological location of women – removed from the 'important', 'productive' components of national development.[7] For instance, the 1983-88 *Plan* (Government of Barbados n.d.(e): 153-4) states that government assistance to women's organisations will continue to be for 'socially desirable programmes'. Women's Affairs should be part of Community Development (not Economic Development) and should provide input to 'agencies of Government especially concerned with women'. By 1988-93 Community Development had become part of 'other social services', with youth and women's organisations linked. Concrete proposals in that *Development*

Plan, in fact, relate to 'youth entrepreneurship'.What is unclear is whether, as is often the case, 'youth' here was code for 'young men', even though young women's unemployment is about twice as high as young men's.

Despite government promises to promote women's affairs through a restructured Bureau, the Bureau has remained underfunded and therefore less effective than the 1992 *National Policy Statement on Women* would lead us to expect. Channels of communication and consultation between the State and the women's NGO community seem less well developed in 2000-1, when I was doing the research on which this article is based, than they had been in the past. That the Bureau of Women's Affairs had been without a Director for over a year as it went through a slow transformation into the Bureau of *Gender* Affairs lends credence to the conclusion that women's affairs are not a high priority. Furthermore, although a gender-sensitive analysis of the country's budget was carried out by the Ministry of Finance with the collabouration of the Bureau of Women's Affairs as part of a Commonwealth Secretariat initiative, the outcomes of this pilot project were not evident.

It also seems that women's voluntary organisations are again being expected to take on responsibility for the support of women and children in the community, just as they were praised for doing by the NCSW (1978a: 315-330). This emphasis on women's altruistic service to others suggests to me that the expectation remains that women should (and will) continue to be collectively appropriated through the targeting of their time and energy - their work - to service to the less fortunate in the community, and to supporting organisations (such as political parties) which are dominated by men.

Concluding analysis

Using the critical lenses of gender analysis, this overview of the impact of state policy on women's paid and unpaid work acknowledges the important contributions made by the Barbadian state since the 1970s to the promotion of gender equality, notably to the material dimensions of political and civil – and to a much lesser extent, social – citizenship. At the same time it also demonstrates that the effect of gender blind or ostensibly gender neutral policies do not, alone, necessarily result in either equality or equity. The silence about the inequality women continue to experience in their paid and unpaid work, the contradictions between stated goals of gender equality or equity and allocation of means (whether legislative or financial) to promote their achievement, the absence of public outcry about these contradictions, and the shift to a preoccupation with 'marginalised males' lend support to Eudine Barriteau's thesis that the material changes towards gender equity in Barbados have not been not supported by accompanying ideological changes. Instead there has been a backlash against women, exaggerating their gains and ignoring or denigrating the inequality they continue to live. Moreover, I would argue, despite (or perhaps as part of) the popular image of the Caribbean matriarch, we find evidence of the past and continuing appropriation of women in Barbados. Materially it is now primarily collective rather than individual in form, although ideologically both types of appropriation remain important. Further research is needed to tease out more fully the details about women's differential experience of appropriation, depending on their social class, colour and age, and about the continuing contribution of state policies to the ways this specifically affects women in their paid and unpaid work.

Table 1 : Percentage Earning Less than $200 Gross per Week and Median Gross Weekly Earnings by Type of Employer, for Women and Men, 1990. 1

	Women Gross Weekly Earnings			Men Gross Weekly Earnings		
	% Earning < 200	Median Earnings	(Total Number in Category)	% Earning < 200	Median Earnings	(Total Number in Category)
	%	$		%	$	
Worked for						
Employer	48.2	100-199	(34,270)	22.8	200-299	(40,153)
Government	26.4	200-299	(9,801)	19.4	200-299	(12,143)
Private Enterprise	46.0	100-199	(21,846)	23.9	200-299	(27,108)
Private Household	81.2	100-199	(2,594)	35.2	200-299	(877)
Worked for self	30.0	200-299	(2,653)	13.6	400-499	(6,460)

1. Calculated from Barbados 1994: Table 8.02.

Table 2: Percentage of the Labour Force and Median Gross Weekly Earnings by Occupation, for Women and Men, 1990. 2.

	Women Gross Weekly Earnings		Men Gross Weekly Earnings	
	% of Female Labour Force	Median Earnings	% of Male Labour Force	Median Earnings
	%	$	%	$
Legislators, Managers	5.0	300–399	7.8	400–499
Professionals	11.6	300–399	7.2	400–499
Technicians & Associated Professionals	4.4	200–299	8.1	300–399
Clerks	22.4	200–299	5.3	200–299
Service, Sales & Market Workers	19.2	100–199	11.1	200–299
Skilled Agriculture & Fishery Workers	0.7	100–199	3.6	200–299
Craft & Related Workers	3.4	200–299	23.3	300–399
Plant & Machine Operators & Assemblers	5.3	100–199	10.1	200–299
Elementary Occupations	25.0	100–199	19.9	200–299
(Total Number)	(47,114)		(58,516)	

2. *Calculated from Barbados 1994: Table 8.01.*

Endnotes

1. I am indebted to E. Barriteau (1994 and personal communications) for the idea of using Development Plans as a resource, and to T. Robinson for bringing R. M. Antoine's article (1997) analysing the constitution and laws to my attention.

2. This law has now been changed, but not yet gazetted, which means that the change has not yet (June 2001) come into effect. I understand that the delay was due to administrative decisions which remained to be taken. This change was originally part of the proposals for Constitutional reform (Barbados Constitution Review Commission 1998) which were still being debated in June 2001. The reason why it had been separated and 'fast tracked' is unclear.

3. For instance liability to pay maintenance for children or partner in the case of divorce.

4. With the possibility of grants for books, uniforms, bus fare and school lunches in cases of need for secondary school students.
5. It is now becoming recognised that the fertility of men, too, may be vulnerable to work place health hazards.
6. Although proposals for very limited paternity leave have been part of contract negotiations by public sector unions, no such benefits have been won and it was not my impression that such a clause had very high priority in the negotiations.
7. This assertion is made on the basis of the very heavy concentration on – gender blind – economic concerns in all the *Development Plans* consulted, despite the claim in each that the government's preoccupation is with development rather than with economic growth.

References

Antoine, R.M.B., 'Constructing a legal framework for securing economic, social and cultural rights for women workers, with particular reference to structural adjustment and the Caribbean', *The Caribbean Law Review*, 7: 2 (1997) pp. 534-87.

Barbados, *Digest of Statistics 1998* (Bridgetown, Barbados: Ministry of Labour, Sports and Public Sector Reform, 1999).

Barbados, *1990 Population and Housing Census, I* (Bridgetown, Barbados: Statistical Service, 1994).

Barbados Constitution Review Commission, *Recommendations Contained in the Report of the Constitution Review Commission* (St Michael, Barbados: Government Printing Dept., 1998).

Barbados Workers' Union, *57th Annual Report* (Bridgetown, Barbados: Barbados Workers' Union, 1998).

Barriteau, Eudine, 'Liberal Ideology and Contradictions in Caribbean Gender Systems' in *Caribbean Portraits. Essays on Gender Ideologies and Identities*, Christine Barrow, ed. (Kingston, Jamaica. Ian Randle Publishers in association with the Centre for Gender and Development Studies, University of the West Indies, 1998a) pp. 436-456.

Barriteau, Eudine, 'Theorizing Gender Systems and the Project of Modernity in the Twentieth-Century Caribbean', *Feminist Review*, 59 (1998b) pp. 186-210

Barriteau, V. Eudine, 'Gender and Development Planning in the Post Colonial Caribbean: Female Entrepreneurs and the Barbadian State' (unpublished doctoral dissertation, Howard University 1994).

Barrow, Christine, *Family in the Caribbean: Theories and Perspectives* (Kingston: Ian Randle Publishers and Oxford: James Currey Publishers, 1996).

Bureau of Women's Affairs, *National Policy Statement on Women*. Formulated in collaboration with the National Advisory Council on Women. Approved by Cabinet 1992 (Mimeo 1992).

Bureau of Women's Affairs, *Major Legal Provisions for Women in Barbados* (Mimeo n.d.).

de Albuquerque, Klaus and Sam Ruark, 'Men Day Done: Are Women Really Ascendant in the Caribbean?' in *Caribbean Portraits. Essays on Gender Ideologies and Identities*, Christine Barrow, ed. (Kingston, Jamaica: Ian Randle Publishers in association with the Centre for Gender and Development Studies, University of the West Indies, 1998) pp. 1-13.

Feminist Review, Special issue on 'Citizenship: pushing the boundaries', No. 57 (1997).

Freeman, Carla, *High Tech and High Heels in the Global Economy* (Durham N.C. & London: Duke University Press, 2000).

Government of Barbados, *Constitution of Barbados* (No publisher or place of publication given, 1966).

Government of Barbados, *Development Plan 1965-1968* (No publisher or place of publication given, n.d. (a)).

Government of Barbados, *Development Plan 1969-1972* (No publisher or place of publication given, n.d. (b)).

Government of Barbados, *Development Plan 1973-1977* (Bridgetown: Ministry of Finance and Planning, n.d. (c)).

Government of Barbados, *Development Plan 1979-1983. Planning for Change* (Bridgetown: Ministry of Finance and Planning, n.d. (d)).

Government of Barbados, *Development Plan 1983-1988. Change plus Growth* (Bridgetown: Ministry of Finance and Planning, n.d. (e)).

Government of Barbados, *Development Plan 1988-1993. A Share for All* (Bridgetown: Ministry of Finance and Economic Affairs, n.d. (f)).

Government of Barbados, *Development Plan 1993-2000. Prosperity Through Increased Productivity* (Bridgetown: Ministry of Economic Affairs, n.d. (g)).

Guillaumin, Colette, *Racism, Sexism, Power and Ideology* (London: Routledge, 1995).

Juteau, Danielle and Nicole Laurin, 'L'évolution des formes de l'appropriation des femmes: des religieuses aux "mères porteuses" ', *Canadian Review of Sociology and Anthropology*, 25, 2 (1988) pp. 183-207. (In English translation as: 'From Nuns to Surrogate Mothers: Evolution of the Forms of the Appropriation of Women', *Feminist Issues* (1989)).

Lynch, Roslyn, *Gender Segregation in the Barbadian Labour Market 1946 and 1980* (Mona, Jamaica: Consortium Graduate School of Social Sciences, University of the West Indies with Canoe Press, 1995).

Marshall, T. H., *Citizenship and Social Class* (Cambridge: Cambridge University Press, 1950).

Momsen, Janet H., 'Gender Ideology and Land' in *Caribbean Portraits. Essays on Gender Ideologies and Identities* Christine Barrow, ed. (Kingston, Jamaica: Ian Randle Publishers in association with the Centre for Gender and Development Studies, University of the West Indies, 1998) pp. 115-132.

Mondesire, Alicia and Leith Dunn, *An analysis of Census data in CARICOM countries from a gender perspective* (Trinidad & Tobago: Central Statistical Office Printing, 1997).

National Commission on the Status of Women, *Report*, Vol. 1 (Bridgetown: Ministry of the Attorney General, 1978a).

National Commission on the Status of Women, *Report*, Vol. 2 (Bridgetown: Ministry of the Attorney General, 1978b).

National Consultation on the Rights of Women and Children in Barbados for the III Summit of the Americas, *Report* (Pinelands, St Michael: Women and Development Unit, University of the West Indies and Invesp/Participa, c 2000).

Robinson, Tracy S., 'Naming and Describing it - The First Steps Towards the Development of Laws relating to Sexual Harassment in the Caribbean', *Caribbean Law Bulletin*, 4 (1999) pp.50-66.

Robinson, Tracy S., 'Fictions of Citizenship, Bodies without Sex: the Production and Effacement of Gender in Law', *Small Axe*, 7: March (2000) pp. 1-27.

Stuart, Sheila, *The Gender Implications of Trade Policies in the Caribbean with Special Reference to Women and NAFTA. A Case Study of Barbados and St. Lucia* (Bridgetown, Barbados: UNIFEM, 1998).

UNIFEM, *Progress of the World's Women 2000* (New York: UNIFEM, 2000).

Yuval-Davis, Nira and Pnina Werbner, eds., *Women, Citizenship and Difference*, London and NY: Zed Books, 1999.

9

Changing Skill Demands in Manufacturing and the Impact on Caribbean *Female Workers.* *

Daphne Jayasinghe

INTRODUCTION

Women throughout the world have been drawn into the manufacturing labour market to produce goods for export. The propensity for female workers to be employed in labour intensive, low skilled, low paid assembly jobs have occurred globally. Evidence of high numbers of women relegated to monotonous, routine assembly work in poor conditions is abundant.[1]

However, as international trade escalates, global competition is increasing and Caribbean countries are facing a market where cheap labour no longer provides any comparative advantage in the global economy. Policy makers advocate a shift in manufacturing away from low cost, labour intensive production towards the output of goods and services where high productivity, high value and improved technology produce provide the competitive edge. I review some of these policy recommendations in section one. In section two I assess to what degree this shift has taken place in three Anglophone Caribbean countries, Barbados, St Lucia and Trinidad and Tobago. I review the changes in output from high skilled manufacturing and female dominated manufacturing sectors in the three countries. This is followed by a theoretical analysis of the ways in which gender issues have shaped women's experience of employment in the manufacturing sector. I end by exploring the implications for women of the changes in the nature of industry in the Caribbean. If women are to retain their share of employment in manufacturing in the future, they not only need access

A version of this paper is due to be published in the UWI Cave Hill Centre for Gender and Development Studies working paper series. A version was also presented at the Caribbean Studies Association Twenty Sixth Annual Conference in St Martin. The field research for this study and attendance at the conference was funded by a research award from the Leverhulme Trust and should be acknowledged, although the views expressed in this document are those of the author and do not necessarily represent those of the Leverhulme Trust.

to training to enable them to adapt to the changing working environment, but gender biases in skill evaluation and terms and conditions of employment must be overcome.

From labour intensity to skill intensity – 'low road' and 'high road' options. As competition for the lowest labour costs and the most favourable tax incentives for foreign investors intensify globally, some developing countries have found that they can no longer compete in manufacturing where low wages are the key determinant. In the Caribbean, a combination of Mexico's low wages and preferential access to the US market provided by the North American Free Trade Agreement (NAFTA) has also proved detrimental for manufacturing.[2] Between 1994, the year of the introduction of NAFTA, and 1998, it is estimated that over 150 companies and 123,000 jobs have been lost in the Caribbean apparel industry, and many of these firms relocated to Mexico.[3] Moreover, export-manufacturing competitiveness globally is increasingly defined by skill, technology intensity and high quality output. [4]

Policy makers across the English speaking Caribbean, where the cost of labour is relatively high, recommend a shift away from labour intensive manufacturing and a shift towards skill-intensive manufacturing where high productivity and high value added produce provides the competitive edge.[5] In his analysis of the restructuring of Caribbean markets in the context of globalisation and trade liberalisation, Momm simplifies the trade options available for open Caribbean economies. He differentiates between the 'low road' option, where the competitive advantage is low cost labour and the 'high road' approach where high productivity and high value produce provide the competitive edge.[6] Momm argues that the low road option caters for firms that seek high returns from low investment '…often forcing countries to sacrifice labour standards and workers to accept low pay, low social protection and abject working conditions'.[7]

Even aside from the social costs, Momm asserts that owing to the low volume of production of much of the Caribbean economy, even with low cost labour, high rates of return are not guaranteed. He therefore promotes the high road approach to trade as the suitable approach for the Caribbean. Trade in goods and services will be of higher value, demand will shift from low paid unskilled labour, to a highly productive skilled workforce. Thus Momm joins Ould El-Hadj in highlighting the required restructuring of the Caribbean workforce. Both commentators point out that changes in demand in the global market and the increased competition from other developing countries necessitate a movement away from labour intensity and towards, increased skill, value and technological competencies: '…the current supply structure of the Caribbean labour markets focusing on providing basic skills for labour market entrants is no longer sufficient.'[8] Ould El-Hadj asserts the need for improved training and education for the labour force in order to ensure their flexibility and adaptability to the fast changing needs of the market.[9]

The change occurring in manufacturing for export in developing countries as well as its impact upon female employment has been highlighted by a number of commentators.[10] Export manufacturing in a globalising world calls for increasingly high quality goods at high volumes, with stringent specifications, rapid turnaround and timely delivery.[11] Therefore even low-tech manufacturing calls for increasing skills and changing work practices.

The Anglophone Caribbean Context: Export Development in Barbados, St Lucia and Trinidad and Tobago

Aside from sharing the legacy of British colonisation, Barbados, St Lucia and Trinidad and Tobago have all historically experienced dependency on one traditional primary export – sugar in Barbados, bananas in St Lucia and petroleum and petroleum produce in Trinidad and Tobago. Primary resource and non-manufactured exports are vulnerable and susceptible to swings in world demand and price.[12] During the 1980s, world market prices fell for nearly all non-manufactured exports from the Caribbean.[13] The consequential contraction in export earnings coincided with rising debt repayment obligations and trade deficits, which made foreign exchange requirements increasingly important.[14] In a bid to diversify exports and increase foreign exchange, all three countries under analysis pursued 'industrialisation by invitation' policies. These were inspired by the Arthur Lewis model, which aimed to stimulate industrialisation through abundant low cost labour and foreign capital.

All three countries signed Fiscal Incentives Acts in order to encourage foreign investment, export growth as well as employment and foreign exchange generation. Development and investment corporations were established in each of the three countries to promote, support and facilitate foreign investment. The Barbados Development Board, (now known as the Barbados Investment and Development Corporation – BIDC), the National Development Corporation of St Lucia (NDC) and the Export Development Corporation in Trinidad and Tobago pursued industrialisation with three fundamental aims: to increase employment opportunities, to improve the external balance of trade and to promote industries manufacturing for export. Foreign investors, taking advantage of the proliferation of incentives and concessions established factories producing clothing, paints, paper products, furniture and electronic components for markets outside the region. Low wages for labour intensive manufacturing were an attraction to foreign investors. The majority of low wage labour in light manufacturing was provided by women.

Post independence, the Barbados apparel-manufacturing sector grew significantly. Between 1968 and 1978, exports of clothing and textiles expanded at 38 per cent annually and led the growth in overseas sales of manufactured goods during this period.[15] Female workers took up most of the new employment opportunities in apparel manufacturing and the lowest average wage rate could be found in this sector.[16]

In the earliest phases of export manufacturing development in St Lucia, operations were limited to food and beverage processing and some electronic component assembly. During the mid 1980s, there was an increased focus on garments and textiles. Trade was reoriented to the American market and United States foreign investment was targeted so that special access provisions of the 9802 US tariff provision or the Caribbean Basin Initiative could be exploited and goods could be sold to North America.[17]

In the second half of the 1980s, exports from Barbados and St Lucia contracted due in part to a fall in regional trade. This was caused by economic crisis and increased protectionism in Trinidad and Tobago and Jamaica, two key regional export markets. Trinidad and Tobago emerged from the petroleum fuelled boom of the 1970s in deep recession. When oil prices collapsed after 1982, Trinidad and Tobago experienced a decade of contracting output, falling per capita income and high unemployment. Foreign exchange reserves were falling, current account deficits were rising and debt grew rapidly.[18] Serious adjustments were made to the economy in the mid 1980s many of which had ramifications for trade across the region. For example, tightening of import and exchange controls and devaluation affected import potential. Stabilisation policies included public sector wage and workforce reductions and increased taxation on public utilities and services.

As part of the efforts to increase exports and foreign exchange whilst diversifying the economy away from petroleum through foreign direct investment, the Export Development Corporation was established in 1984 and the Free Zone Act was signed in 1988. Along with energy intensive industry and chemicals, large-scale garment, electrical goods and electronic component manufacturing for export became priority investment areas.[19] When the IMF intervened in 1989, the policy of state ownership gave way to divestment and increased privatisation.

It became apparent that technology and entrepreneurial transfers, increased global competitiveness and export earnings were not as significant as originally anticipated. In an analysis of manufacturing in Barbados during the second half of the 1970s, the 1979 to 1983 development plan suggested that '[t]he new [export oriented and foreign owned] manufacturing enterprises [had] not transmitted much managerial skills to the domestic population and transfer of technology [had] been disappointing'.[20] The limited use of local managerial skills in foreign owned enterprises had further serious ramifications when considered in relation to increasing 'footloose' investors who shut down operations and left at the end of tax holidays, often with debts of capital and rent unpaid and employees' National Insurance contributions owing. In Barbados and St Lucia a number of large manufacturing plants closed down in the late 1980s and early 1990s, displacing thousands of workers, due to the relocation of foreign investors.[21] A number of civil society groups in Trinidad and Tobago raised the potential threat of footloose investors and deteriorating working conditions in response to the proposed establishment of Free Trade Zones . In response, the government stressed that Trinidad and Tobago would not compete on a cheap labour agenda, the government's aim was to attract more technologically advanced enterprises, thus exploiting the abundance of natural gas in energy intensive industries as well as facilitating advanced technology transfer.[22] In Trinidad '…comparative advantage resides in abundant supplies of cheap energy rather than labour….'[23] and therefore capital intensive, heavy industry and petrochemicals predominate. The government restated its commitment to increased global competitiveness through increased skill development in the 1997 to 2001 *Trade Policy for Trinidad and Tobago*. Enhanced competitiveness in the non-oil sector is included as a strategy for trade reform and export promotion. The Ministry of Trade and Industry asserts the importance of human resource development and technological improvement as catalysts for export market penetration.[24] With this in mind, the government has engineered extensive skills development programmes targeted towards heavy industry and advanced technology.

Similarly, Barbados and St Lucia express a commitment to targeting high-skilled manufacturing sectors and improving labour force skills and technology in a bid to increase global competitiveness. The 1983 to 1988 development plan for Barbados pledged to '…promote a strategic shift from "labour" to "skill" intensive industries….'[25] During the 2001 Budget debate, Prime Minister Owen Arthur stressed that manufacturers in Barbados needed to 're-tool and re-equip themselves with the latest technology' in anticipation of the impact of regional and hemispheric change.[26] A recent report argued that through industrial deepening and technological advances, combined with swifter responses to changes in global market demand, St Lucia could achieve a competitive advantage in areas of high quality goods and services. The report also recommends technical upgrading and the movement of manufacturing into technologically complex activities such as the high-end informatics services already operating in St Lucia.[27]

It is possible to determine the extent of a shift towards high-skilled manufacturing and away from labour intensive, female dominated manufacturing by analysing the respective sectors' contributions to total output. Table 1 provides an indication of the changes in skilled [28] and female dominated manufacturing [29] outputs between 1985 and 1995. With the exception of Barbados, there has been an increase in the share of output from skilled sectors and a decline in the share of female dominated manufacturing in total output. Although there was a small overall decline in the share of skilled manufacturing output in Barbados between 1985 and 1995, skilled sectors evidently made a recovery from contractions in trade in the early 1990s. On the other hand the share of female dominated manufacturing declined significantly throughout this period. During the mid 1980s, the share of female dominated manufacturing in St Lucia exceeded that of skilled manufacturing. However, by 1995, the share of female dominated manufacturing output has almost halved and the share of skilled manufacturing output has increased significantly. Although, labour intensive female dominated manufacturing is not well represented in total manufacturing output in Trinidad and Tobago, a decline has occurred during the recorded period and an increase in the share of skilled manufacturing output is also evident.

Table 1: Percentage of Skilled and Female Dominated Manufacturing (FDM) Represented in Total Manufacturing Output

	1985		1990		1995	
	Skilled	FDM	Skilled	FDM	Skilled	FDM
Barbados	47.3	8.6	42.7	3	45.7	2.2
St Lucia	10.5	12.8	12.3	9.7	17.7	7.3
Trinidad &Tobago	17.4	2.1	23.2	1.8	29.6	1

Source: United Nations Industrial Development Organisation Industrial Statistics Database 2000

Although all three countries under analysis have had distinct experiences of export oriented growth and trade liberalisation, all three at some point in their history have promoted labour intensive manufacturing sub-sectors in a bid to generate employment and foreign exchange. Textiles, apparel, electronics assembly and food processing are industries once active in all three countries that are recorded as female dominated. [30] As global competition accelerates and Caribbean export markets receive goods at a higher quality, higher volume and lower cost from competitors in Asia and Latin America, countries in the region are choosing to take the 'high road'. In Barbados, St Lucia and Trinidad and Tobago skill-intensive areas of export manufacturing are prioritised in development plans, consultancy reports and trade policy, and labour intensive manufacturing is experiencing a decline.

The 'Nimble Fingers' Debate: The Preference for Women in the Light Manufacturing Labour Force

Elson and Pearson (1980) investigate the predominance of women in the labour intensive sections of the international production process. They argue that the preference for female labour is determined by the lower unit costs of production provided by women workers. Women are viewed as having 'natural' dexterity or 'nimble fingers'. Defining the tasks done by women as 'natural' and therefore innate reduces the *acquired* skill level and justifies a lower wage. The manufacturing labour market preference for female labour is based on socially constructed perceptions and norms regarding women's biological and psychological traits and assumptions regarding their economic conditions.[31]

Employers and policy makers alike articulate essentialist concepts of biological traits determining women's prevalence in labour intensive industry. The manager of an electronics assembly company in Barbados suggested that '…females make better use of their hands than males who tend to put their arm into work. Women tend to manipulate their fingers and wrists better'.[32] An official from BIDC reported that the concentration of women in electronics assembly '…has to do with finer technical things that they do, men are clumsy with these parts'.[33] Psychologically, women are generalised as being more compliant. As one Trinidadian supervisor put it, women are characterised as 'more receptive to taking instructions', in other words, more docile or easily manipulated. They are also described as more tolerant of monotonous, tedious, repetitive work. A Barbadian plant manager suggests that:

> [Women] are more suited to the kind of work we do, more inclined to sit and spend a day doing repetitive work, males get restless and bored with repetitive work, females are more conducive … in this business, men tend to be more disruptive than women[34]

Sexual divisions of labour, existing in many of the factories, reflect the gendered assumptions regarding the embodiment of femininity and masculinity, namely feminine physical restraint, discretion and concealment and masculine physical mobility and independence. Socially defined gender ideologies and hierarchies contribute to determining the location of women in the labour market. Women are concentrated in jobs where tasks are repetitive, monotonous and often detailed and where dexterity and patience is required. The men are concentrated in any technical jobs as mechanics as well as those jobs requiring physical strength such as truck loaders, cutters, or jobs involving dangerous chemicals.[35] This sexual division of labour is explained by employers using social definitions of tasks, which are appropriate for men and women. Such gender constructs are also defined using essentialist interpretations of men and women's 'natural' abilities, whereas they are in fact abilities deemed socially appropriate, learnt by men and women. Embroidery, needlework and tailoring skills are not inherent to all women, they are taught in the private realm of the home. Similarly women are not naturally dextrous, nor do they naturally have more patience or tolerance of routine work than men. However, they are familiar with performing routine tasks such as cooking and cleaning, peeling and de-seeding vegetables, all of which are tasks delegated to women by the sexual division of labour, tasks performed in the confined private space of the home and tasks socially defined as natural female tasks. Private, domestic labour is socially and economically invisible and is thus transferred to the workplace as 'unskilled labour'.[36]

Women's tolerance, dedication and responsibility in the workplace are not understood by employers in isolation. Many articulate the importance of a regular income to women with financial responsibilities and suggest that this obligation guarantees a reliable, stable workforce. The financial responsibilities of lone female breadwinners and women bringing up families are understood as contributing to the dedication of women workers. A Barbadian manager points out that:

> Females are prepared to work hard because they have more responsibilities, they are more dedicated because they need the job more. Females have families and children that they have to provide for. Males aren't interested.[37]

And a St Lucian manager argues that:

> ... the majority here aren't married, they have boyfriends and they have kids, you'll find that the boyfriend don't take care of the kids ... that plays a very important part in why ladies come out and work, whether they like it or not, because men are not taking care of their responsibility. If they do give, they give a little but not enough to take care of a home.[38]

Despite such acknowledgements, women's acceptance of a lower wage is still interpreted as related to their status as secondary earners, as a male garment factory supervisor in Trinidad put it, '[m]en are more heads of households, women are supplementing the [family] income'. On the other hand financial burdens of women or the absent or unreliable father of the children are recognised as the reasoning behind women's acceptance of the low wage. An official of the BIDC suggested that the concentration of women in labour intensive manufacturing could be explained by their willingness to '...work for the low wages offered. They are keen to earn their own living and not depend so much on men'.[39] Marxist and Socialist feminist analyses help to explain women's location in low paid and 'unskilled' employment. The sexual division of labour in the private domestic realm, which is seen as both functional for and created by capitalism,[40] is reflected in relations of production. The productivity of the workforce (and the surplus value) can be increased if the production process is subdivided into component parts. This process removes the craftsmanship and reduces the skill content from the workers' tasks thus allowing the capitalist to pay wages at a lower rate. Marxist and Socialist feminists argue that this 'de-skilling' process is pitted against women ideologically in that gender assumptions regarding women's 'natural' or 'in-born' skills are re-interpreted and redefined in the workplace to further de-skill women.[41] Capitalism has proved to be discriminating beyond the logic of surplus extractions and, in attempts to assert command; it builds upon those social relations, which make some workers more subordinated than others.

The work done by women in industries located in the Caribbean is described as tedious, routine and monotonous.[42] Despite the dexterity and patience required, the actual transferable skill content of many of the tasks performed by women is limited. In the female dominated garment and electrical assembly plants operating in the Anglophone Eastern Caribbean, the bulk of produce is assembled from pre-cut or pre-fabricated produce.[43] Many of these enclave factories produce exclusively for the US market under the 9802 provision, more commonly known as the Caribbean Basin Initiative. It is only the labour intensive assembly stage of production that is located locally and thus design, seamstress, marketing and packaging skills are often absent.[44] In her study of female employees of electronics factories in St Lucia, Kelly (1987) found the skill level of production to be low, '[a]ll jobs could be classified as either unskilled or semi-skilled. According to managers and workers alike, a person could usually learn her task in a matter of minutes – or at most a day'.[45] Production in electronics factories includes occupational categories such as coil winding, coil inserting, hand assembly of parts and soldering. Due to the specific nature of the job, training in skills is limited. As one female St Lucian electronics production worker put it, 'Nothing you can learn. They're not telling you "that is to make that" You are just working. You don't know what you are doing so you don't get improved in anything'.[46] Marxist and Socialist feminist commentators also point out that gender ideologies defining women as secondary earners, supplementing the income of an assumed male breadwinner provide employers with a further justification for paying women a low wage.

However, the Marxist and Socialist feminist theoretical framework does not help in assessing the complexities and contradictions inherent to Caribbean women's location in the manufacturing labour force. Social definitions of gender relations are historically, politically, economically and socially located. By limiting the analysis of the subordination of women to an investigation into the exploitation of female wage labour, an overemphasis is placed on wage and production relations.

Furthermore, it is assumed that capital captures and reinforces gender relations in identical ways throughout the world. The sexual division of labour, relevant to the European model of the nuclear family, is far from applicable in many cultural contexts. In the Caribbean labour market, in which women workers are simultaneously defined as both the 'strong matriarch' willing to accept low wages in order to provide for her family and the 'dependent girl' who supplements the salary of a male breadwinner, the underlying social and historical specificity of gender relations needs to be understood. Aiwah Ong in her analysis of the gender and labour politics of postmodernity suggests that '[r]ather than a homogenous spread of Fordist production and "despotic" labour regimes, we find local milieus constituted by the unexpected conjectures of labour relations and cultural systems, high tech operations and indigenous values'.[47] The interaction between capital, labour and gender relations is a dynamic and changing process. Gender relations are both transformed and reinforced under changing social and economic contexts and existing gender relations cannot be understood through an analysis of capital-labour relations alone.

As Durant-Gonzalez points out, women are the preferred workforce in labour intensive industries in the Caribbean (1987). However, capital reinforces and replicates historically and contextually located gender relations unlike those posited in the early literature. For example, in South and East Asia, preference for young, unmarried women is based on the intense social stigma attached to illegitimacy and pre-marital sex.[48] This cultural determinant guarantees employers of young women a stable workforce, unlikely to require maternity leave. In contrast, it is recorded that some employers in the Caribbean express a preference for older women with children.[49] They are defined as 'reliable' and 'committed' due to their socially determined responsibilities to care for and provide for their children. Furthermore, they are considered stable and less likely to get pregnant and require maternity leave.[50] The historically high incidence of female-headed households in the Caribbean and the corresponding income generating responsibilities are recognised by employers. These factors guarantee that a female labour force will accept low wages, work under poor and unfair conditions, and avoid (or have little time for) union activity. In the early phases of manufacturing in the Caribbean, an abundance of low wage, female labour provided countries with a comparative advantage and opportunities were created for women in female dominated manufacturing. The division of labour on the production line and the limited nature of individual tasks reduced the level of transferable skills gained by female employees. It is in the interests of employers to 'de-skill' female employees through 'scientific' management and 'Fordist' production techniques. Not only does this increase efficiency, but also women can be paid less for a skill considered easily acquired.

Since export manufacturing in the Caribbean can no longer compete on the basis of low wage labour, manufacturing is reoriented to high efficiency, high technology and skill intensive manufacturing, and as shown earlier, there has been a decline in female dominated manufacturing in all three countries under analysis. Due to the gendered nature of women's entry into the first phase of manufacturing, these shifts are likely to have a negative impact on women workers unless gender biases are challenged.

De-feminisation of the Manufacturing Labour Force

As the 'skill' content of tasks or jobs is transformed in manufacturing, the gender composition of the labour market is changing and a 'de-feminisation' of the manufacturing labour force is occurring. In their analysis of the global changes of women's employment, Mehra and Gammage (1999) argue that the demand for female labour is declining in manufacturing as export production is restructured and becomes more technologised and as increases in specialised skill requirements leads to an increased demand for male labour. In Korea during the 1980s, there was a shift from garments, radios and shoes to more capital intensive and sophisticated semi-conductor communications and computer products. Although the total number of employees fell, the fall was more significant for women than for men. Similarly, as technology improved in the Malaysian semiconductor sector during the 1980s, the demand for multi-skilled operators increased. However, female representation, which was 80 per cent in the first phase of the industry, fell to 67 per cent in 1986 and even lower by the 1990s. [51]

A number of those manufacturing branches described as 'skilled' can also be described as capital intensive, for example, transport equipment, industrial chemicals and fabricated metal products. As already discussed, such heavy, capital-intensive industrial manufacturing tends to be socially defined as masculine work due to social constraints on women defining them as 'unsuited' to heavy manufacturing. For example, upgraded capital intensive and technological processes require continuous use, and workers often work night shifts. Night work is sometimes considered socially inappropriate for women, and in some countries is prohibited by law. Cultural norms suggest that women are unsuited to industries which involve heavy lifting, for example the metal and transport sectors, or where dangerous work is involved, such as industrial chemicals. Moreover, women are considered to be 'unstable' workers who are likely to withdraw from the workforce for child rearing purposes.[52] Thus, male workers are more likely than women to be recruited into jobs in capital and skill-intensive industries where they benefit from improved in-firm training provisions.

In order to ascertain whether or not a de-feminisation of manufacturing has occurred in the countries under analysis, it is necessary to analyse labour force composition. An analysis of the composition of plant and machine operators and assemblers by sex in Trinidad and Tobago in Figure I and St Lucia in Figure II show two very different patterns. In Trinidad and Tobago, where manufacturing has been consistently concentrated in energy intensive, heavy manufacturing sub-sectors over the last ten years, the majority of plant and machine operators have (Figure I and Figure II) consistently been male. In 1997 this majority came to 88 per cent of plant and machine operators representing 12 per cent of all male workers.

In St Lucia, where there has been a steady decline in overall manufacturing as well as a sharp decline in garment exports, we can see a very different pattern of male and female employment. During 1994, female plant and machine operators outnumbered their male counterparts, however, from 1995 onwards; female plant and machine operators were on the decline whilst male plant and machine operators were on the increase. According to the director of the St Lucia government Statistical Department, the steep decline in numbers of women employed as plant and machine operators may be related to the high numbers of factory closures during the second half of the 1990s.

The predominance of men employed as plant and machine operators in Trinidad and Tobago, an economy where the majority of manufacturing is made up of capital intensive, skilled sub-sectors, leads to the conclusion that skilled, heavy manufacturing is male dominated. In St Lucia where manufacturing is moving away from labour intensive, female dominated manufacturing and towards skilled manufacturing, there is not only a decline in female plant and machine operators but also a commensurate increase in male counterparts. Thus, assuming a similar segregation by sex of manufacturing in St Lucia as in

Trinidad and Tobago we can infer that men are being absorbed into the increasingly technical manufacturing activities and that women are being displaced from the manufacturing labour market.

We can analyse this segregation by sex and skill in further detail using available data on employment by manufacturing sub-sector and by sex in BIDC assisted industries. This shows the distribution of male and female employees in the various manufacturing sub-sectors. Figures III and IV shows the numbers of men and women employed in skilled manufacturing and female dominated manufacturing sectors. Employment data on data processing sectors is also included. Although this is a service sector, the information and data processing sector is the largest employer of women in BIDC assisted industries. The data processing sites are located in industrial parks alongside garment factories and assembly plants and the recruitment processes and employment practices share similarities with those found in female dominated manufacturing industries.[53]

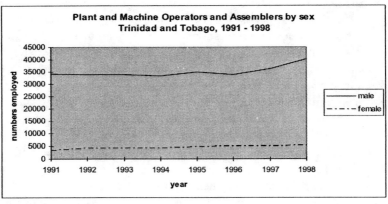

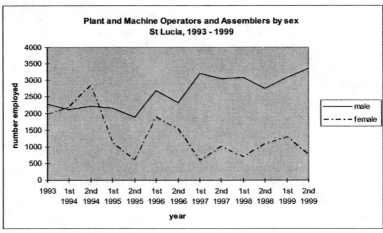

Although there was a growth in numbers of women employed in the data processing industry between 1995 and 1997, the sector is now on the decline.[54] Over the last decade there has been a decline in numbers of women employed in all sub sectors under review. However, the industries which I have thus far defined as female dominated, textile, apparel and leather, have done extremely badly in Barbados, experiencing a fall from 1,674 female employees in 1990 to 905 in 1999.

A detailed analysis of employment by sex and manufacturing sub-sector in Barbados suggests that men do dominate in the skilled areas of manufacturing. Fabricated metals, chemicals and toiletries and paper products and printing, are, as anticipated, dominated by male employees, although, there is a slight growth in the number of women employed in paper products and printing.

Figure III also shows that female employees dominate the electronics sector in Barbados. Similarly high numbers of women have been recorded as being employed in electronics in St Lucia.[55] This sector is defined as a skilled sector by the ILO,[56] however, as mentioned earlier, women tend to be employed in the assembly sections of this industry. In a survey of 99 St Lucian female electronics assembly workers, women were asked if they had learned skills on the job that would help them find other work. Of those responding, 59 per cent said no or that they were not sure, while 41 per cent said yes. Of those who said they had learnt skills, most said they could only find work in another electronics factory.[57]

Thus despite large numbers of women being employed in the electronic equipment manufacturing sector, which is defined as a skilled manufacturing sector, they are occupied in monotonous routine jobs with minimal training, little scope for advancement and poor workers' rights.

The reinforcement of gender stereotypes and inequalities in the labour force perpetuate biases against female employment in skilled manufacturing sectors. Therefore it is not enough to simply increase women's access to skilled manufacturing sectors. Evidence suggests that once within the male domains of scientific institutions or capital-intensive industry, women continue to be concentrated in the lower levels of the hierarchy of these organisations in contrast to their male counterparts, despite being equally qualified.[58] Education and training also remains highly gendered with a shortage of women taking technology-related subjects. For example, 91 per cent of the students who enrolled into the technology division of the Barbados Community College in the 1999 – 2000 academic year were male.[59] Yet technology subjects are of relevance to technological skill development required in globally competitive industry.[60]

Therefore in order for more women to contribute to the development of globally competitive manufacturing, the gender stereotypes which were reinforced in the interests of capital in the early phases of export manufacturing need to be challenged. The social and economic obstacles to technological training faced by women need to be uncovered and challenged. Low enrolments of women in technological fields need to be accounted for, and programmes should be devised to reverse gender asymmetries.[61]

SUMMARY AND CONCLUSION

Anglophone Caribbean economies have experienced an adjustment away from inward looking, protectionist industrialisation policies, towards export-oriented policies and trade liberalisation. For many countries, cheap labour and proliferating incentives defined their competitive advantage and female dominated assembly manufacturing fuelled the initial stages of export manufacturing development during the 1970s and 1980s.

However, the Anglophone Caribbean is facing escalating global competition and a global market where its relatively high wages cannot compete. Therefore the recommendations amongst policy makers to increase international competitiveness by shifting manufacturing towards capital intensive, high skilled industry are being adhered to and there is evidence of an increase in skilled manufacturing in all three countries under analysis.

Caribbean women had been absorbed into assembly manufacturing through complex and subtle negotiations between the labour market and gendered society. Low pay is justified by essentialist connections between light manufacturing work and gender roles socially constructed as 'natural' women's work. A reliable workforce has been identified amongst female household heads dependent on a steady income and the division of labour and routinisation of tasks creates an obstacle to women furthering skills and advancing. As Joekes (1999) points out, '[b]eing unable to find jobs in increasingly important technology-intensive production in the same proportion as in basic manufacturing operation, women are unable to consolidate the foothold in that sector that trade expansion initially brought to them by drawing them into the workforce'.[62]

The entry of women into the labour force is by no means a new phenomenon and Caribbean women will continue to require access to wage labour. However, due to the nature of light manufacturing work, the development of female employees skills and capabilities have been stunted and thus, I would argue, the employment created through a growth in manufacturing has not contributed to sustainable human development.

It must be recognised that labour markets reflect gender subordination found in wider society, and this acts as an obstacle to the development of women's skills. In the interests of human development and economic growth, it is essential that male and female workers are given access to training.[63] However, it must be recognised that women face obstacles to employment in skilled work that men do not face and such gender biases must be uncovered and inequalities challenged.[64]

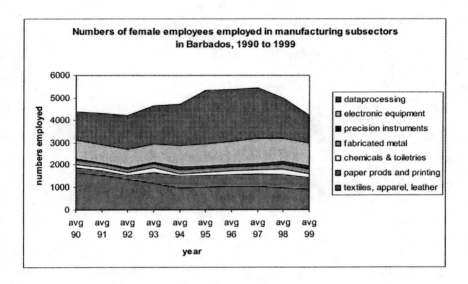

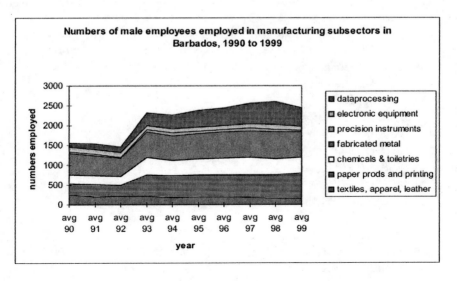

Endnotes

1. Nash and Fernandez-Kelly, 1983; Ong, 1987; Green, 1990; Stuart, 1998; Joekes, 1999.
2. Stuart, 1998.
3. Caribbean Textile and Apparel Institute cited in ILO, 1998a.
4. Lall, S., 'Skills, Competitiveness and Policy in Developing Countries,' Queen Elizabeth House workingpaper no 96, 2000.
5. Momm, 1999; Abbatte 2000.
6. Momm, 1999.
7. Momm, 1999, p. 50.
8. Momm, 1999, p. 51.
9. Ould El-Hadj, 1999.
10. Joekes, 1995; Horton, 1999; Joekes, 1999; Mehra and Gammage, 1999; Lall, 2000.
11. Lall, 2000.
12. Paus, 1988.
13. McAfee, K. 1991.
14. Paus, 1988; McIntyre, 1995.
15. Cox, 1986, p. 56.
16. Cox, 1986.
17. Green, 1990; Stuart, 1998. All of the countries under analysis can take advantage of the 'production sharing' mechanism of the United States Tarriff code. This HTS 9802 provision allows United States apparel inputs to be assembled offshore and payment of tarrifs on re-entry into the USA is based on the value added which is mainly labour costs. See Mortimore, 1999 for an analysis of the Caribbean Basin Initiative.
18. World Trade Organisation, 1998.
19. Friday, 1988.
20. Barbados Ministry of Finance, 1979, p. 82.
21. Green, 1990; Wilmore, 1996; BIDC 1996.
22. Friday, 1988, p. 30.
23. Long, 1989, p. 129.
24. Ministry of Trade and Industry, 1996.
25. Barbados Ministry of Finance, 1983, p. 94.
26. *Daily Nation*, March 15, 2001.
27. Abbatte, 2000.
28. Skilled sectors defined by the International Labour Organisation Employment Report 1998–1999. The high-skilled manufacturing sectors are: Printing and publishing, industrial chemicals and other chemicals,

fabricated and metal products, machinery, non-electrical and electrical transport equipment, professional and scientific equipment.

29. Textiles, wearing apparel and leather and fur products.
30. Kelly, 1988; Green, 1990; Lewis, 1998; Stuart, 1998; Harris, 2000.
31. Durant-Gonzalez, 1987.
32. Interview, Barbados, December, 2000.
33. Interview, Barbados, December, 2000.
34. Interview, Barbados, December, 2000.
35. Mies, 1986; Beneria and Roldan, 1987.
36. Beneria and Roldan, 1988.
37. Interview, Barbados, December, 2000.
38. Interview, St Lucia, June, 2000.
39. Interview, Barbados, December, 2000.
40. Barrett, 1988.
41. Phillips and Taylor 1980.
42. Kelly, 1986; Durant-Gonzalez, 1987; Green, 1990; Yelvington, 1994.
43. Green, 1990.
44. Mortimore, 1999.
45. Kelly 1986, p. 828.
46. Female electronics production worker cited in Kelly, 1987, p. 40).
47. Ong, 1991, 280.
48. Ong, 1991; Jayasinghe, 1997.
49. Joekes, 1987; Green, 1990.
50. Green, 1990.
51. Narayan and Rajah 1990, cited in Mitter 1995).
52. Joekes 1995, 13.
53. Dunn and Dunn, 1999; Pearson, 1993; Freeman, 2000.
54. The industry has come under media scrutiny over the last two years as two large foreign owned informatics companies faced highly publicised union attack when they refused to acknowledge the Barbados Workers Union as the workers mediator. An intolerence of union activity and relatively high wages by Caribbean standards has driven a number of companies out of Barbados and a large number of women out of the informatics labour market.
55. Kelly, 1987.
56. ILO, 1998b.
57. Kelly, 1987.
58. Borque and Warren 1990; Mark 1991; Mitter 1995.
59. Barbados Community College Book Of Facts 2000, 53.
60. Lall, 2000.

61. Borque and Warren 1990.
62. Joekes, 1999, p. 45.
63. Tzannatos Z. 1999.
64. Fine and Howard, 1994; Ong, 1991.

Bibliography

Abatte, F., *Enhancement of the Competitiveness of the Manufacturing Sector in St Lucia*, (Geneva: UNCTAD, 2000).

Barbados Community College Book of Facts 2000, unpublished report.

Barbados Ministry of Finance, *Barbados Development Plan 1979 – 1983* (Bridgetown: Ministry of Finance, 1979).

Barbados Ministry of Finance, *Barbados Development Plan 1983 – 1988* (Bridgetown: Ministry of Finance, 1983).

Barbados Investment and Development Corporation, *History of BIDC* (Bridgetown: BIDC, 1996).

Beneria, L and Roldan, M., *The Crossroads of Class and Gender: Industrial Homework, Subcontracting and Household Dynamics in Mexico City* (Chicago: University of Chicago Press, 1987).

Bolles, L., 'Kitchens Hit by Priorities: Employed Working-Class Jamaican Women Confront the IMF', in Nash, J. and M.P. Fernandez-Kelly, eds., *Women, Men and the International Division of Labour* (Albany: State University of New York Press, 1983).

Borque, S and K. Warren, 'Access is not enough: Gender Perspectives on Technology and Education', in Tinker I. ed., *Persistent Inequalities* (New York: Oxford University Press, 1990).

Branford, A., 'Arthur's Rebuke. PM: Manufacturers not preparing for change', Daily Nation, March 15, 2001.

Buitelaar, R., Padilla, R. and Urrutia, R., 'The in-bond assembly industry and technical change,' in *Economic Commission for Latin America and the Caribbean Review* 67 (1999), pp. 137-157.

CARICOM, *CARICOM's Trade: Aggregate and Principal Domestic Exports* (Georgetown: Caribbean Community Secretariat, 1998).

Cox, W., 'The Manufacturing Sector in the Economy of Barbados 1946 – 1980' in Worrell, D., ed., *The Economy of Barbados 1946 – 1980,* (Bridgetown: Central Bank of Barbados, 1986).

Durant Gonzalez, V., 'Women are Better Suited', in *Women's International Resource Centre ed., Women in the Rebel Tradition: The English Speaking Caribbean* (New York: WIRC, 1987).

Elson, D. and Pearson, R., 'The latest phase of the internationalisation of Capital and its implications for women in the Third World,' *Institute of Development Studies*, Sussex, Discussion Paper 150 (1980).

Fine, J. & Howard, M., 'Women in the Free Trade Zones of Sri Lanka', in *Dollars and Sense*, November/December (1995) pp. 26-7, 39-40.

Green, C., *The World Market Factory. A Study of Enclave Industrialisation in the Eastern Caribbean and its Impact on Women Workers* (Kingstown: CARIPEDA, 1990).

Friday, G., *The Caribbean Basin Initiative and Industrial Development in Trinidad and Tobago* (Ontario: Queens University, 1988).

Harris, M., 'The Current Situation of Small and Medium-sized Industrial Enterprises in Trinidad and Tobago, Barbados and St Lucia', Economic Commission for Latin America and the Caribbean Working Paper No 69 (2000).

Hilaire, A., 'Caribbean Approaches to Economic Stabilization', IMF Working Paper WP/00/73 (2000).

Horton, S., 'Marginalisation Revisited: Women's Market Work and Pay, and Economic Development', *World Development*, 27:3 (1999) pp. 571-582.

International Labour Organisation, *Labour and Social issues relating to Export Processing Zones* (Geneva: ILO, 1998a).

International Labour Organisation, *World Employment Report 1998 – 1999 Employability in the Global Economy: How Training Matters* (Geneva: ILO, 1998b) *International Labour Organisation Statistical Yearbook for the Caribbean* (Port of Spain: ILO, 1998c).

Jayasinghe, D., 'Machine Girls', (unpublished dissertation, Cambridge University 1997).

_____., 'More and more technology, women have to go home': changing skill demands in manufacturing and Caribbean women's access to training', *Gender and Development*, 9:1 (2001) pp.70–81.

Joekes, S., *Women in the World Economy: An INSTRAW Study* (Oxford: Oxford University Press, 1987).

_____, *Trade Related Employment for Women in Industry and Services in Developing Countries* (Geneva: UNRISD, 1995).

_____, 'A gender analytical perspective on trade and sustainable development', in *UNCTAD Trade, Sustainable Development and Gender* (Geneva: UNCTAD, 1999).

Joekes, S and A. Weston, *Women and the New Trade Agenda* (New York: UNIFEM 1994).

Kelly, D., 'St Lucia's female Electronics Factory Workers: Key Components in an Export Oriented Industrialisation Strategy', *World Development*, 14:7 (1986) pp. 823–838.

Kelly, D., 'Hard Work, Hard Choices: A Survey of Women in St Lucia's Export Oriented Electronics Factories', *Occasional Paper* No. 20, (1987) Barbados: Institute for Social and Economic Studies, EC, University of the West Indies.

Lall, S., 'Skills, Competitiveness and Policy in Developing Countries', *Queen Elizabeth House Working Paper* No. 96 (2000).

Lewis, D., 'Gender Implications of Trade Policies in the Caribbean with special reference to Women and NAFTA: A Case of Trinidad and Tobago', unpublished report (Bridgetown: UNIFEM, 1998).

Long, F., 'Manufacturing Exports in the Caribbean and the New International Division of Labour', Social and Economic Studies, 38:1 (1989).

Lim, L., 'Women Workers in Multinational Companies in Developing Countries – The Case of the Electronics Industry in Malaysia and Singapore', Women's Studies Program, *Occasional Paper* No. 9, (1978) University of Michigan.

Massiah, J., *Women as Heads of Households in the Caribbean: Family Structure and Feminine Status* (Paris: UNESCO, 1983).

Mark, P., 'Status Attainment and Gender in Scientific and Technological Institutions in Trinidad and Tobago. in Ryan S. ed., *Where to next? Social and Occupation Stratification in Contemporary Trinidad and Tobago* (St Augustine: Institute of Social and Economic Research, University of the West Indies, 1991).

McAfee, K., *Storm Signals: Structural Adjustment and Development Alternatives in the Caribbean* (Boston: South End Press, 1991).

McIntyre, A., *Trade and Economic Development in Small Open Economies: The Case of Caribbean Countries* (Conneticut: Westport Press, 1995).

Mehra, R. and S. Gammage, 'Trends, Countertrends, and Gaps in Women's Employment,' *World Development*, 27:3, (1999) pp. 533–550.

Mies, M., *Patriarchy and Accumulation on a World Scale* (London: Zed Books, 1986).

Mitter, S., 'Does New Technology Bode Well for Working Women?: An Evaluation and Analysis', The United Nations University, Institute for New Technologies, *Discussion Paper Series* No.9512 (1995).

Momm, W., 'Restructuring Caribbean Labour Markets in the context of Globalization and Trade Liberalization', in W.Momm ed., *Labour issues in the context of economic integration and free trade – A Caribbean Perspective* (Port of Spain: ILO Caribbean Office, 1999).

Mortimore, M., 'Apparel-based industrialisation in the Caribbean Basin: A threadbare garment?', *Economic Commission for Latin America and the Caribbean Review*, No 67, (1999) pp. 119–136

Nash, J. and M.P Fernandez-Kelly, *Women, Men and the International Division of Labour* (New York: State University of New York Press, 1983).

National Development Corporation, *St Lucia Country Profile* (Castries: National Development Corporation, 1999).

Ong, A., *Spirits of Resistance and Capitalist Discipline: Factory Women in Malaysia* (Albany: State University of New York Press, 1987).

_____., 'The gender and labour politics of postmodernity', *Annual Review of Anthropology*, 20 (1991) pp. 279–309.

Ould El-Hadj, S., 'Trade Liberalisation and its implications for labour markets in the Caribbean,' in Momm, W. ed., *Labour Issues in the Context of Economic Integration and Free Trade – A Caribbean Perspective* (Port of Spain: ILO, 1999).

Paus, E., ed., *Struggle Against Dependence, Nontraditional Export Growth in Central America and the Caribbean* (London: Westview Press, 1988).

Phillips, A. and Taylor, B., 'Sex and Skill: Notes towards a feminist economics', *Feminist Review*, 6, (1980) pp. 79-88.

Rosa, K., 'The conditions and organisational activities of women in Free Trade Zones: Malaysia, Philippines and Sri Lanka, 1970 – 1990,' in Rowbotham, S. and M.Swasti eds., *Dignity and Daily Bread, New Forms of Economic Organising Among Poor Women in the Third World and First* (London: Routeledge, 1994).

Safa, H and P. Antrobus., 'Women and the Economic Crises in the Caribbean' in Beneria L. and S. Feldman eds., *Unequal Burden: Economic Crises, Persistent Poverty and Women's Work* (Colorado: Westview Press, 1992).

St Cyr, J., 'Participation of women in Caribbean development. Inter-Island Trading and Export Processing Zones', Report prepared for the Economic Commission for Latin America and the Caribbean, Caribbean Development and Co-operation Committee Kingston (1990).

Stuart, S., *The Gender Implications of Trade Policies in the Caribbean with Special Reference to Women and NAFTA. A Case Study of Barbados and St Lucia*, unpublished report (Bridgetown: UNIFEM, 1998).

Trinidad and Tobago Ministry of Trade and Industry, *Trade Policy for the Republic of Trinidad and Tobago, 1997 – 2001* (Port of Spain: Trinidad and Tobago Ministry of Trade and Industry 1996).

Tzannatos, Z., 'Women and Labour Market Changes in the Global Economy: Growth Helps, Inequalities Hurt and Public Policy Matters,' *World Development*, 27:3, (1999) pp. 551-569.

Wilmore, L., *Export Processing in Saint Lucia: Ownership, Linkages and Transfer of Technology* (Economic Commission for Latin America and the Caribbean, 1993).

World Trade Organisation Secretariat, Trade Policy Review, Trinidad and Tobago (Geneva: WTO, 1998).

Yelvington, K., *Producing Power: Ethnicity, Gender and Class in a Caribbean Workplace* (Philadelphia: Temple University Press, 1995) *United Nations Industrial Development Organisation Industrial Statistics Yearbook* (Geneva: UNIDO, 2000)

Part III

※

Risk and Security in the
Contemporary Caribbean

10

Security and Sovereignty in the Contemporary Caribbean: Probing Elements of the Local-Global Nexus

Ivelaw L. Griffith

Today it seems that the heads of governments may be the last to recognize that they and their ministers have lost the authority over national societies and economies they used to have.

Susan Strange[1]

INTRODUCTION

Susan Strange's observation highlights the increasing recognition by scholars and statesmen, albeit a reluctant acceptance by some of the latter, of the changing dynamics of international relations and, correspondingly, the changing vicissitudes of power on the part of state and non-state actors in the contemporary geopolitical and geoeconomic milieu. The resonance of the statement is, however, greater at the dawn of the year 2002 than when Susan Strange wrote it in 1996. This is so because the dramatic terrorism episode of September 11, 2001 in the United States has removed any ambiguity among the doubtful about the power transformations the world is undergoing, the security and sovereignty limitations of large and powerful nations, the potency of non-state actors, and the need to rethink both conceptual and operational approaches to internal and external security.

Needless to say, the salience of Susan Strange's remark is not confined to large and powerful nations; it extends to states that are small and vulnerable, like those in the Caribbean. Indeed, it is even more relevant to states in the latter category when they are subordinate states[2] and subject to both direct consequential and collateral damage, even though they may not be intended targets or in the planned theatres of operations. Thus, it is important that for a discussion on the Caribbean security landscape to examine not only the nature of the security arena, but also some of the linkages between things local and regional, and hemispheric and global. In other words, there is a local-global nexus that is central to understanding the nature of the region's security landscape as well as the strategies that may be employed to cope with it.

This chapter offers a modest attempt at doing this. It looks first at the conceptual and operational meaning of security and then examines some of the key security challenges facing citizens and governments in the region. It ends by raising some policy and operational issues that are germane to appreciating how Caribbean leaders might approach pursuit and protection of the security and sovereignty of their states, especially in the context of the changed dynamics occasioned by the terrorist attack by non-state actors on the world preponderant power.

THE CONVENTION OF NON-CONVENTIONALITY

For the entire post-World War II period until about a decade ago there was wide consensus among political scientists that traditional Realist theory provided *the* appropriate conceptual architecture to examine questions of security. Among other things, Realist theory emphasises the military and political aspects of security, focuses on the state as the unit of analysis, and views security as 'high politics' – power-based, state-centred, and oriented towards the international arena. Moreover, it postulates that states are rational actors pursuing their own national interests, and that military force is the most effective way to cope with threats. However, international political dynamics since the end of the Cold War have led many scholars to replace the traditional Realist conceptual lenses used to examine security with other, non-conventional, ones.[3]

Yet, the conceptual adaptation has not been as striking for Caribbean security scholars, as non-conventionality has long been their convention.[4] In the Caribbean security has never really been viewed merely as protection from military threats. It has not been just military hardware, although it has involved this; not just military force, although it has been concerned with it; and not simply conventional military activity, although it certainly has encompassed it. Thus, in the context of the Caribbean, security may be defined as protection and preservation of a people's freedom from external military attack and coercion, from internal subversion, and from the erosion of cherished political, economic, and social values.[5]

Consequently, security in the Caribbean is multidimensional, with military, political, and economic dimensions. Moreover, it is concerned with both internal and external threats. Further, the state is not the only unit of analysis; non-state actors are equally important. Indeed, some non-state actors own or can mobilise more economic and military assets than some states. Jorge Domínguez suggests some of the historical continuities in this regard:

> The international relations of the American Mediterranean have never been just limited to relations among states. Since the sixteenth century, the powers and the pirates have helped shape the international environment of the lands and peoples around the contours of the Caribbean Sea and the Gulf of Mexico. In doing so, they have interacted with each other and with 'local' actors in and around the American Mediterranean. These local actors have been quite varied as well, ranging from states to individuals.[6]

The following proposition by two scholar-observers of the Caribbean is hardly disputable:

> In the Caribbean, as around the world, security concerns regarding state-based military conflict have been replaced by less institutionalized transnational threats … These dangers constitute a new security agenda for the region, and require the revision of traditional concepts of national and regional security with a view to new ones that include but are no longer centered around traditional state-based threats.[7]

Neither can one credibly object to the following observation from a policy maker within the region:

> Security can no longer be achieved by merely building walls or forts. The very large and the very small states of this hemisphere have found that security, in an age of globalization, is rather complex. Security includes the traditional notions of yesteryear, but today, security must now be extended, in the case of the small-island state, to encompass several non-traditional aspects. Natural disasters, for example, pose a greater threat to our security than does the loss of national territory to an enemy.[8]

Security Issues

With security viewed in this way, the nature of the Caribbean security landscape could be seen as including both traditional and non-traditional concerns. Territorial disputes and hemispheric geopolitics are the core traditional concerns, the former being relatively more important than the latter. The most serious disputes involve Venezuela and Guyana, Guatemala and Belize, Suriname and Guyana, Venezuela and Colombia, and France (French Guiana) and Suriname. As this list indicates, a few countries are involved in several disputes. For example, Guyana is facing a claim by Venezuela for the western five-eighths of its 214,970km² territory and one by Suriname for 15,000 km² to the east. Drugs, crime, political instability, economic vulnerability, illegal migration, and environmental degradation are part of the non-traditional security matrix.

There is no uniformity in the importance statesmen and scholars ascribe to these concerns, but a comparison of the two categories – traditional and non-traditional – would reveal that more countries place a higher premium on the non-traditional area. Of course, some states, such as those in the Eastern Caribbean, have no traditional security concerns; some also have no overt external threat from other states. Especially in this context, issues of internal security take a place of primacy. Although attention cannot be paid to all the salient security concerns, a few areas deserve some mention. This discussion tilts in the direction of military and political security aspects, not because economic and environmental ones are unimportant, but because of the relatively greater contemporary currency of the former areas.

Drugs and Crime

What generally is called 'the drug problem' in the Caribbean really is a multidimensional phenomenon with four problem areas: drug production, consumption and abuse, trafficking, and money laundering. However, the drug phenomenon does not constitute a security matter simply because of these four problem areas. It does so essentially because:

- These operations have multiple consequences and implications – such as marked increases in crime, systemic and institutionalised corruption, and arms trafficking, among other things;
- The operations and their consequences have increased in scope and gravity over the last decade and a half;
- They have dramatic impact on agents and agencies of national security and good governance, in military, political, and economic ways; and
- The sovereignty of many countries is subject to infringement, by both state and non-state actors, because of drugs.[9]

Two decades ago most Caribbean leaders found it impolitic to accept that their countries were facing a drug threat. But over the years the scope and severity of the threat increased and became patently obvious to observers within and outside the region. Leaders could, therefore, no longer deny it. At the special CARICOM drug summit of December 1996, leaders issued a statement indicating acknowledging that: 'Narco-trafficking and its associated evils of money laundering, gun smuggling, corruption of public officials, criminality and drug abuse constitute the major security threat to the Caribbean today'.[10]

In June 2000, at a multinational high level meeting on criminal justice in Trinidad and Tobago, that country's Attorney General made the following declaration in speaking on behalf of the Caribbean:

> There is a direct nexus between illegal drugs and crimes of violence, sex crimes, domestic violence, maltreatment of children by parents and other evils. ...Our citizens suffer from drug addiction, drug-related violence, and drug-related corruption of law enforcement and public officials. The drug lords have become a law unto themselves. ... Aside from the very visible decimation of our societies caused by drug addiction and drug-related violence, there is another insidious evil: money laundering. ...It changes democratic institutions, erodes the rule of law, and destroys civic order with impunity.[11]

The statement by Attorney General Maharaj points clearly to the nexus between drugs and crime. Indeed, crime is a component of the drug phenomenon. Crime could be viewed in several ways typologically. One study sees two basic categories of drug crimes: 'enforcement' crimes, and 'business' crimes. The former involves crimes among traffickers and between traffickers and civilians and police, triggered by traffickers efforts to avoid arrest and prosecution. The latter category encompasses crimes committed as part of business disputes, and acquisitive crimes, such as robbery and extortion. Another typology posits three types of crime: 'consensual' ones, such as drug possession, use, or trafficking; 'expressive' ones, such as violence or assault; and 'instrumental' or property crimes, examples being theft, forgery, burglary, and robbery.[12]

Irrespective of the typology used, there is a wide range of drug-related criminal activity in the Caribbean. There is no firm evidence of region-wide causal linkages between drug activities, on the one hand, and murder, fraud, theft, and assault on the other. However, three things are noteworthy. First, murder, fraud, theft, and assault these are precisely the crimes likely to be associated with drugs. Second, in a few countries, notably Jamaica, Puerto Rico, Haiti, the Dominican Republic, and Trinidad and Tobago, there is clear evidence of a linkage. Moreover, the countries with the high and progressive crime reports in the theft, homicide, and serious assault categories are the same ones featuring prominently over the last decade as centers of drug activity. These countries include the Bahamas, the Dominican Republic, Puerto Rico, Jamaica, Trinidad and Tobago, Haiti, the US Virgin Islands, Guyana, and St Kitts-Nevis.

Dudley Allen, a former Jamaican Commissioner of Corrections, once remarked:

> It is no longer possible to think of crime as a simple or minor social problem ... Mounting crime and violence have been declared leading national problems, and the issue of law and order has assumed high priority in national planning and policymaking. Fear of crime is destroying ... freedom of movement, freedom from harm, and freedom from fear itself.[13]

Allen first made this statement in 1976, but it is still relevant a quarter-century later, now even more dramatically so. He also was speaking mainly in the Jamaican context, but the observation now has region-wide validity, because, for a variety of reasons that cannot be explored here, crime has skyrocketed in many countries.

There is a local-global nexus in the region's drug-related crime, reflected in the fact that the crime is not all ad hoc, local crime; some of it is transnational and organised, extending beyond the region, to North America, Europe, and elsewhere.[14] Groups called 'posses' in Canada, the Caribbean, and the United States and 'yardies' in Britain perpetrate some of the most notorious organised crime. They are organised criminal gangs composed primarily of Jamaicans or people of Jamaican descent, but increasingly involving African-Americans, Guyanese, Panamanians, Trinidadians, Nigerians, and Dominicans. Although the posses are known most for the trafficking of drug and weapons, they also have been implicated in money laundering, fraud, kidnapping, robbery, burglary, prostitution, documents forgery, and murder.[15] Some of this crime is possible because of corruption.

The Inter-American Convention Against Corruption states the impact of corruption on societies cogently: 'Corruption undermines the legitimacy of public institutions and strikes at society, moral order, and justice, as well as the comprehensive development of peoples'.[16] Thus, crime and corruption, whether ad hoc or organised, but more so if organised, have deleterious effects on democratic governance, in which Caribbean peoples and governments have justified self-interest. Two scholars presciently observe:

> The threat of organized crime to democracy is basic. While it rests upon many supports, democracy depends upon the faith of people in the institutions and practices that sustain and operationalize it. Integrity and a sense of fair play are

critical components of that faith. It is precisely these that criminal organizations challenge.[17]

The Realities of Terrorism

Brian Jenkins calls terrorism 'violence for effect'. It is 'not only, and sometimes not at all, for the effect on the actual victims of the terrorists. In fact, the victims may be totally unrelated to the terrorists' cause'.[18] Compared to other regions of the world states the Americas have witnessed relatively little terrorism. However, the contemporary salience of terrorism has less to do with this fact and more with the scale and impact of terrorist actions over the last decade, especially in the United States. For many people in the United States terrorism ceased being a foreign phenomenon following two major incidents in the early-mid 1990s.

One was the World Trade Center bombing on February 26, 1993, which killed six people and injured over 1,000. The other was the bombing of the Oklahoma Federal Building on April 19, 1995, which killed 168 people and injured hundreds of others. And, undoubtedly, the events of September 11, 2001 have etched the destructive power of terrorism indelibly in the minds of all Americans and, indeed, citizens elsewhere. Terrorism – and the consequences of state action to cope with it – has become an unwelcome, but undeniable, reality for citizens of the United States and elsewhere, including the Caribbean.

The terrorist attack against the United States on September 2001 has affected the Caribbean in several ways, both as a direct consequence of the economic and military fallout from the impact on the United States and as a result of region's security vulnerability as a subordinate area in global terms. For one thing, according to the US Department of State, some 160 Caribbean nationals were victims of the actions against the World Trade Center and the Pentagon. Moreover, the domino effect on tourism has been deleterious to the economic security of the region. A few examples should suffice.

In Jamaica, where tourism earns some US$ 1.2 billion a year and employs over 30,000 people the impact has already been very dramatic, with Air Jamaica losing US$ 11 million within the week following the attack. In Barbados, where tourism contributes about US$ 1 billion to the economy, the authorities anticipated a US$30.3 million decline in receipts, a 30-35 per cent reduction in the cruise enterprise, US$ 857,000 less in the head tax, and a drop in tourist spending of US$9.2 million.[19] Indeed, the tourism impact is expected to be so far reaching that the Second Caribbean Tourism Summit, held in The Bahamas on December 8-9, 2001, decided on a package of special measures to salvage the industry, which in 2000 provided gross foreign exchange earnings of US$ 20.2 billion and employed an estimated 1 in 4 persons in the Caribbean.[20]

The impact on the region goes beyond tourism, though. As the CARICOM leaders acknowledged at the special summit held in October:

> We are concerned that the attacks and subsequent developments have been especially devastating to our tourism, aviation, financial services, and agricultural sectors, which are the major contributors to our GDP, foreign exchange earnings and to employment in our Region. We are particularly conscious that our ongoing efforts to combat money laundering must now take specific account of the potential for abuse of financial services industries by terrorists, their agents, and supporters in all jurisdictions.[21] Indeed, although some impact areas have already begun to reveal themselves,[22] both statesmen and scholars feel it is still too soon for a meaningful assessment of the multiple economic, political, military, foreign policy, migration, and other impact and implications for the Caribbean.[23]

Still, it should be remembered that although the Caribbean was not the target of the dramatic September 2001 terrorist operation, the region has not been immunised against terrorism; neither by state actors – in Cuba, Haiti, Grenada, and Guyana, for example – nor by non-state actors. As a matter of fact, the Caribbean was the scene of one of the most dramatic non-state terrorist acts in the hemisphere in the mid-1970s.

On October 6, 1976 a Cubana Air flight from Guyana to Cuba was detonated shortly after departing Barbados, where it had made a transit stop. All 73 people on the flight – 57 Cubans, 11 Guyanese, and five North Koreans – were killed. Anti-Castro exiles based in Venezuela later claimed responsibility for the action. (On August 1, 1998, while on a visit to Barbados, President Fidel Castro dedicated a monument to the victims of the incident.)[24] Moreover, Cuba suffered a dozen bombings of tourist locations during 1997, allegedly perpetrated by anti-Castro Cuban exiles in Miami and Central America.[25]

Terrorism, whether in the United States or the Caribbean, often is transnational, multidimensional, and organised. The extent of these features depends on variables such as the history of the actor(s), motives, size, funding, ideology, organisation, and the political-institutional environment involved. It is, however, fairly easy to appreciate that the frequency and scope of action by groups within the Americas, such as the Revolutionary Armed Forces (FARC) and the National Liberation Army (ENL) of Colombia, and the Popular Revolutionary Army (EPR) of Mexico, and by an individual such as Ramzi Ahmed Yousef (World Trade Center bombing), could not be accomplished without transnational linkages – often beyond the Americas – and often skillful organisation. Paul Wilkinson's decade-and-a-half-old assertion about terrorism is certainly true today: 'Terrorism is inherently international in character, so that, paradoxically, the more individual states improve their national measures, the more it becomes attractive for the terrorists to cross national frontiers'.[26]

Beyond all this, terrorism is a salient issue partly because of the high premium placed on the (re)construction and maintenance of democracy by statesmen and scholars around the world, and because terrorism serves to undermine democracy by threatening the exercise of various civil and political rights that are fundamental to it. David Apter captures the essence of why many leaders view terrorism as antithetical to democracy: 'In democratic societies, political violence suggests institutional weakness and blockages, or normative insufficiencies, injustices, or inequities, that is wrongs to be righted'.[27]

Coping with the Challenges

Some of the drugs, crime, and other challenges are both a function and reflection of the dynamics of globalisation. In relation to drugs, for instance, quite correctly the *World Drug Report* states:

> The illicit drug phenomenon cannot be viewed outside the context of contemporary economic, social, and political developments. Changes in the world political economy and advances in technology over the past three decades have had a significant impact on the scope and nature of the illicit drug problem. It is now recognized that rapid growth in the trade of goods and services has resulted in a more interdependent world. Yet, [continues the report,] despite the positive implications which the increase in world trade has for prosperity and efficiency, sustained growth in international trade can complicate efforts to control the illicit problem.[28]

International affairs scholars generally agree that globalisation is a defining moment in the history of international relations, coming in the wake of the collapse of the world order that defined almost the entire second half of the twentieth century, a world order that itself was precipitated by a defining conflagration called World War II; it denotes fundamental change in the structure of global power and the operation of the inter-state system. Yet – and this is quite understandable – scholars disagree about how to capture the defining moment called globalisation in conceptual terms.[29] However, some scholars are persuasive in suggesting the value of *The Great Transformation* by Karl Polayni both in helping contemporary analysts capture globalisation conceptually and in locating some of the security elements involved.[30]

In this respect, a proposition by Mittleman and Johnson is worthy of replication:

> Like the conjuncture of the 1930s marking the socioeconomic transformation analyzed by Polanyi, contemporary globalization represents unprecedented market expansion accompanied by widespread structural disruptions but now at a world level. The rise of transnational organized crime groups is spurred by technological innovations, especially advances in commercial airline travel, telecommunications, and the use of computers in business, allowing for increased mobility of people, some of them carriers of contraband, and the flow of illicit goods. Central to this process are innovations in satellite technology, fiber-optic cable, and the miniaturization of computers, all of which facilitate operations across frontiers. Closely related, hypercompetition is accelerating cross-border flows and thereby challenging sovereignty. Deregulation, in turn, furthers borderlessness, because it lowers state barriers to free flows of capital, goods, services, and labor.[31]

Caribbean statesmen are obliged to act to deal with the impact and consequences of globalisation for their nations' security and sovereignty. Moreover, they need to act both in policy and operational terms. Thus, a few observations on this subject are warranted.

In the policy area, there are some truisms that should inform the pursuit of policy options. One is that security is always relative – to problems (or threats), perceptions, capabilities, geopolitics, and geoeconomics, among other factors. Hence, all states exist with a certain margin of insecurity. Small states in the Caribbean and elsewhere have to accept to exist with a relatively wide margin of insecurity compared with, say, big powers. Thus, there are aspects of their external security circumstances with which Caribbean states will simply have to live because they are powerless to alter them.

Included here is their military vulnerability and political penetrability because of geography and capability limitations, even with some low-level collective security efforts, such as the Regional Security System (RSS). Yet, it should be possible for most Caribbean nations to prevent or resolve internal instability precipitated by political or racial factionalism, and some aspects of crime and corruption. Hence, avoiding false expectations is just as important as preventing fatalism.

Given the nature of the region's security landscape and the hemispheric and global context in which it exists, security coping measures have to be multidimensional, multilevel, and multiactor.

For example, in relation to drug, something that is true for terrorism and other areas, security coping measures need to be multidimensional because drug operations and their impact are multidimensional. They also need to be multilevel – national, regional, and international – as drug operations and many of the problems they precipitate are both national and transnational. Moreover, countermeasures have to be on a multiactor basis, for the two above reasons plus the fact that individually Caribbean states lack the necessary individual capabilities to meet the threats and challenges facing them. Hence, countermeasures need to see the reaction and proaction not only of governments, but also of corporate entities, non-governmental organisations, and international governmental organisations, such as the RSS, the OAS, and the United Nations International Drug Control Program (UNDCP).

In so far as regional and international cooperation are concerned there are some sub-text realities that warrant consideration. Caribbean leaders should recognise that the adoption of multilateral security measures does not preclude the adoption of bilateral ones. Indeed, some bilateral measures may very well be more desirable from the stand point of political expediency, given that generally they can be designed and implemented more quickly, which means that policy makers can showcase their efforts to resolve problems and salvage, if not bolster, the confidence of local citizens, tourists, and potential investors in their credibility as governmental actors.

However, this very reality of bilateral and multilateral options requires Caribbean policy makers to:

- determine the combination of measures that best suits their national interests, bearing in mind the nature and salience of the issues (threats), their capabilities, and the time factor;
- pursue bilateral measures that do not contradict or undermine multilateral efforts initiated earlier; (of course, they are free to revisit multilateral deals);
- be cognisant of the institutional capacity requirements of initiating numerous bilateral mechanisms or several combinations of bilateral and multilateral ones, considering that bilateral and multilateral initiatives outside the security area will also have been initiated and be in need of implementation.

In terms of operational action one example should suffice. In relation to internal security, many nations with defense forces deploy those forces to cope with internal security challenges, particularly crime. This is done within constitutional and legal parameters, as Caribbean defense forces have aspects of internal security as part of their legal missions. Indeed, in the case of Trinidad and Tobago, both the number (11) and specificity of the mandate related to internal security are noticeable. The mandate includes internal security; control of terrorism and religious fundamentalism;[32] assistance in times of natural disaster; assistance in the maintenance of essential services; and support of the police in maintaining law and order.[33] Hence, over the years, defence forces have been deployed for a variety of internal security operations in Barbados, the Dominican Republic, Guyana, Haiti (before the army was abolished in 1995), Jamaica, Suriname, and Trinidad and Tobago. Even in Puerto Rico and the U.S. Virgin Islands, with no armies because of their special relationships with the United States, there has been the deployment of the surrogate army – the National Guard.

Some joint operations are conducted on an ad hoc, needs basis, while others are run on a structured, long-term basis. One such operation in the latter category is Operation Intrepid in Jamaica. National Security minister explained:

> Operation Intrepid was introduced on July 7, 1999. The objective of the joint police military [exercise] is to specifically target communities in which where was a upsurge of criminal activities and violence and implement law enforcement strategies to bring the situation under control. Since beginning the operation has conducted a total of 100 curfews, 358 cordon and search actions, 2,272 snap raids, and 5,055 road blocks, 9,612 joint foot patrols, and 4,900 joint mobile patrols.[34]

Given the gravity of the internal drugs and crime-driven situation I anticipate continuance of joint operations, although with appropriate modification (and in some cases, introduction) of joint procedures. Needless to say, while defence and police forces are the main security institutions maintained by Caribbean states, they are not the only ones. Important too are courts, intelligence agencies, prisons, immigration agencies, customs outfits, and other entities. Moreover, as the capacity of the state is challenged in many places, public security is increasing being outsourced to the private sector.

The jury is still out on how the exercise of power and discretion by state (and private) security institutions is helping to reduce insecurity within Caribbean countries, especially since a decade-old observation by one scholar still rings true:

> Challenges to the established order have been met with appeals for law and order and by increased coercion. Jails are full, but the level of violence and crime does not diminish. More and more repression simply begins to undermine the very values it was intended to protect, and a sense of failure is promoted.[35]

CONCLUSION

The justifiable concern about sovereignty in relation to national security tends to result in almost exclusive focus on formal-legal sovereignty, central to which is the precept that a state is (should be) free from outside interference, and that no authority is legally above a state except that which the state voluntarily confers on international agencies it joins.

However, it is noteworthy that formal-legal sovereignty is not the only aspect of sovereignty that requires attention; also important is what Robert Jackson called 'positive sovereignty', which enables states to take advantage of their independence or formal-legal sovereignty. A government that is positively sovereign not only is able to enjoy rights of non-intervention, but it has the ability to provide 'political goods' for the society it governs. Positive sovereignty includes having the economic, technical, military, and other capabilities to declare, implement, and enforce public policy.[36]

For various reasons having to do with size and subordination, Caribbean nations face considerable limitations in exercising both formal-legal and positive sovereignty. Indeed, sovereignty in the Caribbean seems to be perennially under siege. Nevertheless, both the changing reality to which the Susan Strange epigraph adverted and the national interest dictates of Caribbean nations suggest the need for Caribbean policy makers to continuously assess how they pursue and protect both formal-legal and positive sovereignty. Whether or not Caribbean leaders know it or like it, the importance of this task has been buttressed by the changed international realities occasioned by the September 11, 2001 terrorist incident in the United States.

Endnotes

1. Strange, Susan. *The Retreat of the State: The Diffusion of Power in the World Economy* (Cambridge MA: Cambridge University Press, 1996), p. 1.
2. For a theoretical and empirical assessment of subordinate states, see Brecher, Michael, 'The Subordinate State System of South Asia,' in Rosenau, James N., ed., *International Politics and Foreign Policy* (New York: The Free Press, 1969); Cantori, Louis and Steven Speigel, *International Politics of Regions: A Comparative Approach* (Englewood Cliffs, NJ: Prentice Hall, 1970); and Harden, Sheila, ed., *Small is Dangerous: Micro-states in a Macro World* (New York: St. Martin's Press, 1985). For a work that examines the Caribbean as a subordinate state system, see Griffith, Ivelaw L., *The*

Quest for Security in the Caribbean: Problems and Promises of Subordinate States (Armonk, NY: M.E. Sharpe, 1993).

3. See, for example, Buzan, *Peoples, States, and Fear* (Boulder: Lynne Rienner, 1991); Rohm, Joseph J., *Defining National Security* (New York: Council on Foreign Relations Press, 1993); and Legro, Jeffrey W. and Andrew Moravcsik, 'Is Anybody Still a Realist?' *International Security*, 24 (1999) pp. 5-54.

4. For evidence of this see Young, Alma H. and Dion E. Phillips, eds., *Militarization in the Non-Hispanic Caribbean* (Boulder: Lynne Rienner, 1986); Bryan, Anthony T., J. Edward Greene, and Timothy M. Shaw, eds., *Peace, Development, and Security in the Caribbean* (London: Macmillan, 1990); Griffith Ivelaw L., 'Caribbean Security: Retrospect and Prospect,' *Latin American Research Review*, 30:2 (1995) pp. 3-32; and Beruff, Jorge Rodríguez and Humberto García Muñiz, eds., *Security Problems and Policies in the Post Cold War Caribbean* (London: Macmillan, 1996).

5. This definition is developed in chapter 1 of *The Quest for Security in the Caribbean*.

6. Jorge I. Domínguez, 'The Powers, the Pirates, and International Norms and Institutions in the American Mediterranean,' in Desch, Michael C., Jorge I. Domínguez, and Andres Serbin, *From Pirates to Drug Lords* (Albany: State University of New York Press, 1998), p. 79.

7. Tulchin, Joseph S. and Ralph H. Espach, 'Introduction: U.S.-Caribbean Security Relations in the Post-Cold War Era', in Tulchin, Joseph S. and Ralph H. Espach, eds., *Security in the Caribbean Basin* (Boulder: Lynne Rienner, 2000), p. 5.

8. 'Statement by Minister Henderson Simon of Antigua and Barbuda to the Third Defense Ministerial', Cartagena, Colombia, November 1998, available at http://www.oas.org.

9. For a discussion of the drug threat, see MacDonald, Scott B., *Dancing on a Volcano* (New York: Praeger, 1988); Griffith, Ivelaw L., *Drugs and Security in the Caribbean*; (University Park: Pennsylvania State University Press, 1997); Beruff, Jorge Rodríguez, ' "Narcodemocracy" or Anti-drug Leviathan: Political Consequences of the Drug War in the Puerto Rican High-Intensity Drug Trafficking Area', in Griffith, Ivelaw L., *The Political Economy of Drugs in the Caribbean* (London: Macmillan, 2000), pp. 162-82; Gabriel Aguilera Peralta, 'Fighting the Dragon: the Anti-drug Strategy in Central America,' in Griffith, *The Political Economy of Drugs in the Caribbean*, pp. 218-229; and U.S. Department of State, *International Narcotics Control Strategy Report*, March 2001.

10. *Communiqué, Fifth Special Meeting of the Conference of Heads of Government of the Caribbean Community*, Bridgetown, Barbados, December 16, 1996, p. 2

11. *Remarks by the Hon Ramesh Lawrence Maharaj, Attorney General and Minister of Legal Affairs of the Republic of Trinidad and Tobago at the Opening of the Caribbean-United-States-European-Canadian Ministerial (Criminal Justice and Law Enforcement) Conference*, Port of Spain, Trinidad, June 12-13, 2000. Available at http://usinfo.state.gov/regional/ar/islands/maharaj.htm The conference was attended by Attorneys General from The Bahamas, Barbados, Belize, Canada, Dominica, the Dominican Republic, France, Grenada, Guyana, Jamaica, St Kitts-Nevis, St Lucia, Suriname, The Netherlands, the United States, the Netherlands Antilles, Aruba, Guadeloupe, and the United Kingdom (including the Cayman Islands and Montserrat). Observers also attended from the Organization of the American States, the UN International Drug Control Program, CARICOM, and the Caribbean Financial Action Task Force.

12. See Kleiman, Mark A.R., *Marijuana: Costs of Abuse, Costs of Control* (Westport, CT: Greenwood, 1989), pp. 109-17; and Anglin, M. Douglas and George Speckart, 'Narcotics Use and crime: A Multisample, Multimethod Analysis', *Criminology* 26:2 (1988) pp. 197-231.

13. Allen, Dudley, 'Urban Crime and Violence in Jamaica', in Brana-Shute, Rosemary and Gary Brana-Shute, eds., *Crime and Punishment in the Caribbean* (Gainesville, FL: University of Florida, 1980), p. 29.

14. For a discussion of organised crime in the Caribbean, see Douglas Farah, 'Russian Mob Sets Sights on Caribbean', *Miami Herald*, September 29, 1997, p 8A; Maingot, Anthony P., 'The Decentralization Imperative and Caribbean Criminal Enterprise', in Farer, Tom, ed., *Transnational Crime in the Americas* (New York: Routledge, 1999), pp. 143-170; and Bryan, Anthony T., *Transnational Organized Crime: The Caribbean Context*, The Dante B. Fascell North-South Center, University of Miami, October 2000.

15. For more on posse and yardie operations, see Gunst, Laurie, *Born Fi' Dead: A Journey Through the Jamaican Posse Underworld* (New York: Henry Holt, 1995); Small, Geoff, *Ruthless: The Global Rise of the Yardies* (London: Little, Brown, and Company, 1995); and Serge Kovaleski and Douglas Farah, 'Organized Crime Carries Clout in Islands', *Washington Post*, February 17, 1998, p. A1.

16. 'Inter-American Convention Against Corruption', OEA/Ser.K/XXXIV.1.CICOR/doc14/96rev.2. March 29, 1996, p. 1.

17. Godson, Roy and Wm. J. Olson, *International Organized Crime: Emerging Threats to U.S. Security* (Washington, DC: National Strategy Information Center, 1993), p. 22.

18. Jenkins, Brian, *International Terrorism: A New Mode of Conflict* (Los Angeles: Crescent Publications, 1975), p. 1.

19. Anthony T. Bryan and Stephen E. Flynn, 'Terrorism, Porous Borders, and Homeland Security', *North-South Center Update*, October 22, 2001, p. 5.

20. See 'Meeting the Challenge of Change: Address Delivered by the Secretary General of the Caribbean Tourism Organization, Mr. Jean Holder, at the Second Caribbean Tourism Summit, Nassau, December 8-9, 2001', p. 1. Holder provides a comprehensive analysis of the travails of tourism.

21. *Nassau Declaration on International Terrorism: The Caricom Response Issued at the Conclusion of the Special (Emergency) Meeting of Heads of Government of the Caribbean Community, 11-12 October 2001, The Bahamas, p. 1.*

22. See, for instance, 'Caribbean Drug Traffic up 25%: U.S. Law Enforcement Focusing on Terrorism', *The Baltimore Sun*, October 18, 2001; Greg Fields, 'Caymans to Share Information on Bank Customers with U.S.', *Miami Herald*, November 28, 2001.

23. See, for example, Miller, Billie A., 'Managing Foreign Policy in an Interdependent World', *Honors Excellence Occasional Paper*, 1:1, (2001).

24. For an examination of the incident, see Phillips, Dion E., 'Terrorism and Security in the Caribbean: the 1976 Cubana Disaster off Barbados', *Terrorism*, 14:4, (1991), pp. 209-19. On the 1998 dedication, see 'Castro to Dedicate Monument to Cubana Crash Victims', *Barbados Nation*, August 1, 1998, p. 1.

25. See Larry Rohter, 'Cuba Arrests Salvadorean in Hotel Blasts', *New York Times*, September 12, 1997; and Ann Louise Bardach and Larry Rohter, 'Bombers Tale: A Cuban Exile Details a "Horrendous Matter" of a Bombing Campaign', *New York Times*, July 12, 1998.

26. Wilkinson, Paul, 'Trends in International Terrorism and the American Response', in Freeman, Lawrence et al, eds., *Terrorism and International Order* (London: Routledge and Kegan Paul, 1986), p. 49.

27. Apter, David, 'Political Violence in Analytic Perspective' in Apter, David, ed., *The Legitimation of Violence* (New York: New York University Press, 1997), p. 7.

28. United Nations International Drug Control Program, *World Drug Report* (New York: Oxford University Press, 1997), p. 17.

29. See, for example, Sakamoto, Yoshikazu, ed., *Global Transformation: Challenges to the State System* (Tokyo: United Nations University Press, 1994), especially chapters 1, 2, 6, 14, 16, and 18; and Rosenau, James N., *Along the Domestic-Foreign Frontier: Exploring Governance in a Turbulent World* (Cambridge: Cambridge University Press, 1997), especially chapters 3, 4, 5, 6, 8, and 11.

30. See, for instance, Gill, Stephen, 'Structural Change and Global Political Economy: Globalizing Elites and the Emerging World Order', chapter 6 of Sakamoto, *Global Transformation*; and Mittleman, James H. and Robert Johnson, 'The Globalization of Organized Crime, the Courtesan State, and the Corruption of Civil Society', *Global Governance*, 5, (1999), pp. 103-26.

31. Mittleman and Johnson, 'The Globalization of Organized Crime', p. 110.

32. This, no doubt, is related to the efforts of a Black Muslim fundamentalist group – Jamaat al Muslimeen – to seize power in July-August 1990. The six-day coup attempt left 31 people dead, 693 wounded, some 4,000 people unemployed, and over $US 120 million worth of damage. For more on this, see Ryan, Selwyn, *The Muslimeen Grab for Power: Race, Religion, and Revolution in Trinidad and Tobago* (Port of Spain, Trinidad and Tobago: Imprint Caribbean, 1991).

33. See Phillips, Dion E., 'The Trinidad and Tobago Defense Force: Origin, Structure, Training, Security and Other Roles', *Caribbean Quarterly*, 43 (1997), pp. 13-33.

34. Parliament of Jamaica, *Presentation of the Hon K.D. Knight, Minister of National Security and Justice*. Budget Sectoral Debate, June 13, 2000, pp. 29-30.

35. Duncan, Neville C., 'Political Violence in the Caribbean', in Ivelaw L. Griffith, ed., *Strategy and Security in the Caribbean* (New York: Praeger, 1991), p. 55.

36. See Jackson, Robert H., *Quasi-States: Sovereignty, International Relations, and the Third World* (New York: Cambridge University Press, 1990), pp. 28-29.

11

The 'Shiprider Solution' and Post-Cold War Imperialism: Beyond Ontologies of State Sovereignty in the Caribbean[1]

Hilbourne Watson

INTRODUCTION

Violence in the form of robbery, organised oppression, and exploitation, including the annexation and colonisation of the Caribbean marked the rosy dawn of capitalism. Those forms of violence featured in the evolving security strategies of European states in the Caribbean region long before the global reach of capitalism and the European national states model became a reality. Violence was at work in the construction of colonial fortifications to expropriate the lands and subjugate and/or exterminate the indigenous populations: terror and genocide were part of the colonising project, such that traces of fascist tendencies scarred the landscape of life and memory in the Caribbean long before fascism took hold in modern Europe. The building of Spanish fortifications at Hispaniola and the introduction of the Encomienda System involved a great deal of violence and exploitation that continued with African slavery, Asian indenture, and a variety of other colonial strategies in the Caribbean. Modern national security strategies have involved a complex of territorial, military, economic, political, and cultural forms of domination under the aegis of the territorial state and it successor national state forms. Yet the dominant tendency within national security studies has been to assign organic rights to states as though states have existed outside of the material practices and historical forms of power and spatio-temporal social relations of production. Such a move constitutes a deceptive way of dehistoricise state making and war making which comprise an indissoluble couplet within modernity.

I view the 'Shiprider Agreement',[2] as one of the latest United States (US) strategies for dominating the Caribbean. Much of the academic debate about drugs and money laundering in the Caribbean emphasises cooperation between the US and Caribbean states in ways that mask the substantive aspects of the US project (see essays in Tulchin and Espach 2000). Historical capitalism has been based on processes of territorialisation, deterritorialisation, and reterritorialisation around commodity production, market competition, the appropriation of the surplus value, the anarchy of production, and the global mobility of capital and capital accumulation. Four key principles – Manifest Destiny, Expansionism, Invincibility, and Exceptionalism – have featured in the evolution of the ideological consciousness of United States strategies of nation building and world domination. This idea does not sit well with the Jeffersonian ideology of the 'empire of liberty' (see Foner 2002), given how the realist-liberal project has replaced imperialism with the right of the American imperial state to base its national security interests on organic rights of the state, with the effect of privileging the retrospective illusion of the organic personality of the national state. The US implemented a number of security programmes in the wider Caribbean around the Monroe Doctrine, Teddy Roosevelt's Big Stick Policy, Taft's Dollar Diplomacy, F.D.R. Roosevelt's Good Neighbor Policy, the Truman Doctrine, the Kennedy-Johnson Alliance for Progress, Ronald Reagan's Caribbean Basin Initiative (CBI), and Bill Clinton's Partnership for Prosperity. The 'Shiprider Agreement' formed an integral part of Clinton's Partnership for Prosperity.[3]

Under the Shiprider proposals, the United States (US) presented a 'Model Shiprider Agreement' to Caribbean states as a mechanism for counteracting maritime drug operations. Without exception, all Caribbean countries participate in counternarcotics activities, so that when most Caribbean states, except Barbados and Jamaica, signed the Model Shiprider Agreement (MSA), this did not signal their opposition to narcotics countermeasures in the region. Barbados and Jamaica saw the MSA setting a dangerous precedent by deepening the erosion of the territorial integrity of state sovereignty. For this and other reasons they asked that issues like development aid, immigration, trade, and anti-gun smuggling provisions be linked to a negotiated version of Shiprider.[4] As such, Barbados and Jamaica did objected to the attempt to extend the scope and reach of American power in the airspace and territorial waters of Caribbean states to the detriment of the already highly circumscribed sovereignty of Caribbean states. Ostensibly, shiprider – the 'Agreement Concerning Maritime Counter-Drug Operations' – is to counteract illicit trade in narcotics, but substantively shiprider is an integral part of the strategy for restructuring American hegemony within global capitalism, national states and sovereignty (see Watson 1993) with reference to the ongoing processes of deterritorialisation and reterritorialisation (Harvey 1995: 5-7).

Kathy-Ann Brown links Shiprider to a 'growing body of international agreements concerning the illicit traffic of narcotic drugs', with precedents in 'nineteenth and twentieth century treaties governing piracy, slave trading and contraband traffic in alcoholic liquor', including 'the 1924 Convention between the US and Great Britain for the Prevention of Smuggling', which influenced the 'drafters of the 1981 Exchange of Notes on Co-operation in the Suppression of the Unlawful Importation of Narcotics Drugs into the United States' (1997:1-2). Brown says the '1981 US/UK Agreement, ... sets a clear precedent for high seas interdiction within the context of the ...Shiprider agreement'. Even though the 1981 Agreement between the United States and the United Kingdom required the UK to 'make ... concessions with respect to its sovereignty without the provision of any quid pro quo', and permitted 'officials on board US vessels to board, search, and detain UK vessels in certain waters, to determine whether illicit drugs may be among the cargo', the United Kingdom did not see it '... setting a precedent for the conclusion of any further agreement affecting the freedom of passage of British ships on the high seas' (1997: 12).

In this light, Shiprider is not unique. There are bilateral Interdiction Agreements between the US and most Caribbean states, ranging from provisions for entry to investigate to shipriding. There are treaties between several Caribbean states that deal with narcotics: treaties between Suriname and Colombia, Suriname and Guyana, Cuba and Guyana, Venezuela and Guyana, Cuba and Jamaica, Jamaica and Mexico, and Trinidad and Tobago and Venezuela (Griffith 1997: 214-15). Caribbean states are signatories to the '1988 United Nations Convention Against Illicit Traffic in Narcotics drugs' which, addresses '... the issue of maritime interdiction on the high seas *and* contemplates police cooperation to suppress illicit traffic even within the territory of Contracting States.' The 1988 UN Convention commits states to 'cooperate in the suppression of the international trade in illicit narcotics drugs'. Shiprider might very well reflect 'the spirit and intent of the 1988 Convention' (Brown 1997: 2-3), but there are other precedents, such as the 1961 Single Convention on Narcotic Drugs and its 1972 Protocol, the 1971 Convention on Psychotropic Substances, and the 1986 'narcotics: Interdiction of Trafficking Agreement between the United States of America and the Bahamas ...' all of which predated the 1988 United Nations Convention. The 1988 UN Convention stressed the urgency of international cooperation to suppress illicit maritime drug traffic (see, the United States/Dominican Republic Agreement). Other related agreements that predate Shiprider include agreements between the US and the Kingdom of the Netherlands on behalf of the Netherlands Antilles and between the US and the United Kingdom for the British Virgin Islands.

Brown views Shiprider as legally problematic and suggests that

> a unified regional approach which embraces some level of cooperation with the United States in the context of a reciprocal arrangement in accordance with the rules of international law is the path Caribbean leaders must take in the effort to suppress the illicit drug trade' (1997: 3; 65-71).

She claims that the impact of the global narcotics problem on the exercise of state sovereignty makes the crime of drug trafficking increasingly '… subject to universal approbation' of the 'universal jurisdiction of all states over the crime of piracy on the high seas' (1997: 5). It is necessary to place Shiprider in its proper context which requires treating it as part of a strategy to reconfigure the global framework of US national security. The global reach of capital and capitalism conditions how the US defines national security. It is impossible to understand the US national security project without an appreciation of global capitalism and the mobility rights of capital. Territoriality, mobility and 'rightful' property income are at the heart of national state sovereignty that begins from property relations in terms of exclusionary territorial property rights in the means of production. While this is not to assert that state sovereignty is reducible to private property relations, it is important to see that early historical globalisation was set in motion by the nationalisation of property relations within the process of the formation and internationalisation of the national states system: the nationalisation of territories, state power, societies, identities, languages, and so on has been central to the making of national states. Since this historical process is not the final outcome of social evolution the national state should not be taken to be the absolute container of the human community (Watson 1993). The nationalisation of society contributed to a global context within which each 'nationalized' state and territory came to understand and appreciate its national identity (see Holloway 1995: Burnham 1995; Burch 1994, 1997): nation-states presuppose a system that is greater than each national state and within which all states are embedded. Part of the problem stems from how national security academic and policy approaches give security studies an artificial autonomy from the very spaces through which it gets its articulation.[5] This problematic tendency rivets mainstream international relations scholarship in the Commonwealth Caribbean and locks it in atheoretic concepts and formulations.

This essay examines Shiprider as an issue in post-Cold War imperialism. Neoliberal notions of globalisation announce the arrival of post-ideological capitalism with vistas of global change unfolding on 'level playing fields' marked by transparency of rules that are said to benefit all actors. The neo-liberal notion of globalisation reflects a 'win-win' logic of new realignments between states, bureaucracies, civil society, empowered individuals, 'free markets' and unfettered capital. The emphasis on exchange relations derives from the practice of treating prices, money, and markets as autonomous of social relations of production. This flawed logic reiterates the destiny of reason in the rediscovery of the liberal subject/agent with the aim of uniting capital and civil society in a singular identity. Global neo-liberalism works at externalising all forms of domination with the effect of silencing the *direct producer of value* (Ebert 1996: 286; italics mine).

In reality, imperialism is a competitive global class process of reproduction and appropriation of surplus value in which global practices of capital accumulation are masked by nationality and culture via territorial particularism. Of necessity, imperialism spawns chauvinistic theories and ideologies like 'Realism' and national 'Security Studies' in international relations (see Waltz 1959; Rosenberg 1994). By equating capitalism with the culmination of the historical destiny of reason, global neo-liberalism announces the end of history much like the final flight of Hegel's 'owl of Minerva' which flies 'only with the falling of dusk' (Hegel 1942: 13).

ANALYTICAL FRAMEWORK

In this essay I approach Shiprider as an integral aspect of the ongoing restructuring of US hegemony under the 'Partnership for Prosperity'. I locate Shiprider within global neo-liberalism. I make a number of claims about the nature of the relationship between the global economy and national states. I treat sovereignty foremost as a property relation and the core mechanism through which national states process global capitalist relations. I discuss a number of Shiprider agreements between the US and Caribbean states to clarify the issues and specify the crisis of the national state model and sovereignty. My perspective on the crisis of the national states model suggests that states and their power are being restructured as part of global restructuring. This makes restructuring a political class and power process at the core. I do not assert that all states have equal capacities to deal with the contradictions of global restructuring, but I insist that states are integral to global social relations of production as they participate in and process restructuring from their varying capabilities and capacities. I stress that states attempt to use restructuring to enhance their positions, but they realise different outcomes, depending on the relationship between the state, capital, and other forces at the domestic and global level. Hence, the degree to which certain aspects of national policy are shifting to the global level does not necessarily reflect the desires or initiatives of all states. By arguing that states process use sovereignty, which is foremost the expression of a property relation between states, to process global social relations of production, I am able to show that the issue of restructuring has less to do with giving up power in any narrow sense and more to do with shifting key areas of national decision-making to the world level where those social relations and being mediated on an increasing scale. As such states move in this direction to become more active in the global arena, hoping to enhance their capabilities to affect outcomes around production, trade, migration, financialisation, and other initiatives in regionalisation via the World Bank Group, the World Trade Organisation, and other key institutions (see Weiss 1997). Of course, not all states are equipped to exploit the global environment to their advantage, given the way the West dominates and/or monopolises the key areas of raw materials and their substitutes, the media and communications, science and technology, finance and money, and weapons of mass destruction. This monopoly power gives the corporate capitalist interests and imperialism more broadly a strategic advantage from which to leverage power over the world. I analyse a number of hypotheses and arguments that have been posed by academics, technocrats and others around the Shiprider controversy, and I provide explanatory critiques of those and other perspectives.

I approach explanatory critique as:

> that knowledge-practice that historically situates the conditions of possibility of what empirically exists under patriarchal-imperialist-capitalist labor relations and, more importantly points to what is suppressed by the empirically existing: Critique indicates that 'what is' is not necessarily the real or true but rather only the existing actuality that is transformable. The role of critique ... is...: the production of historical knowledges that mark the transformability of existing social arrangements and the possibility of a different social organization, ... free from exploitation.... (Ebert 1996: 294).

The knowledge-practice of explanatory critique grows out of 'a mode of knowing that enquires into what is not said, ... in order to uncover the concealed operations of power and underlying socioeconomic relations connecting the myriad details and seemingly disparate events and representations of our lives.' Such a critique exposes how 'seemingly disconnected zones of culture...are ...linked through the ...differentiated and dispersed operations of a systematic... exploitation and international division of labour informing all practices in societies globally under...late capitalism' (Ebert 1996: 294). Contradictions have a way of seeming to be distant, hidden away from themselves, out of sight so to speak, and even nonexistent to the unsuspecting observer (see Gramsci 1971: 277-315 passim). Shiprider is integral to this very domination that must be explained by unearthing the mechanisms of global capital and national states within the restructuring of global capitalism.

MODEL SHIPRIDER AGREEMENT & THE US/TRINIDAD AND TOBAGO SHIPRIDER AGREEMENT[6]

Under the Model Shiprider Agreement:

1. The United States government shall have 'the right to designate US Coast Guard officials to embark on government ships of the specific Caribbean country to advise and assist in boarding suspect vessels to enforce the country's laws, to enforce US laws outside the country's territorial sea and to authorise the country's vessels to assist in enforcing US laws outside the country's territorial sea...

2. The Caribbean state shall also have the right to designate its own shiprider(s) to travel on US ships and shall have the power to authorise the US ships to pursue suspect vessels and aircraft fleeing into the country's waters and to conduct counter-drug patrols in the country's territorial sea ...

3. In the event that the Caribbean country's shiprider(s) is/are unavailable to embark on a US ship the ship may nonetheless enter the country's territorial sea in order to investigate any suspect or board and search any suspect vessel ...

4. The government of the Caribbean state shall allow US aircraft to overfly its territory and waters and order any suspect aircraft to land in the country .

5. US law enforcement officials involved in the Shiprider programme are granted a certain level of diplomatic privileges and immunities ...

6. The agreement may be terminable at any time by either party, such termination taking effect one year after the date of notification' (Ferguson 1997: 9; from Proposed Agreement Between the Government of the United States of America and the Government of State X Concerning Maritime Counter-Drug Operations).

The US/Trinidad and Tobago Shiprider Agreement (US/T&T Agreement) shows that Shiprider begins from the reality of unequal power between the United States and Caribbean states. Sovereign equality of states does not imply that all states have the effective means to defend and/or protect their territory from threats to its integrity. Shiprider calls for enforcing the laws of a particular Caribbean state in its territorial waters, and requires the 'country's vessels to assist in enforcing US laws outside the country's territorial sea' (Ferguson 1997: 9), with the effect of giving the US primary jurisdiction on the high seas and contingent jurisdiction in a country's territorial waters.

Brown (1997: 35) says, in 'light of the tremendous latitude granted the US Coast Guard to take enforcement action in Trinidad and Tobago territorial waters, possibly even entailing the liability of the coastal state, the point is not an unimportant one'. She raises concerns about the implications of article 12 of the Agreement which 'allows for the enforcement of US law in circumstances which raise questions as to the consistency of the Agreement with general rules of international law' (1997: 39). Shiprider might possibly serve as a precedent in respect of which the global reach of the illicit drug trade is forcing tendencies toward the universalisation of 'jurisdiction in such matters as narcotics drugs,...' (1997: 41; see Kerry 1997b), thereby reinforcing the precedents for which the Caribbean has been used to test initiatives of imperialism from colonial times to Clinton's 'Partnership for Prosperity.' In light of 'controversies generated by the assumption of jurisdiction over foreign troops in circumstances unacceptable to the sending state, the US/T&T Shiprider Agreement is fraught with difficulties'[7] (1997: 66). Brown's recognition of the unsettled nature of 'customary international law' contrasts with Griffith's assertion that 'a central principle of international law' lies in the fact that 'no authority is above the state except that which the state voluntarily confers on international bodies it joins'. A basic truism in international law neither validates nor verifies questionable ontological claims on behalf of sovereignty, even when Caribbean states have 'protested loudly' against 'sovereignty infringement' (Griffith 1997: 20, 21).

The US/T&T Agreement extends to full cooperation between the US and Trinidad and Tobago, and recognises the responsibility and authority of Trinidad and Tobago over its territorial sea, internal waters, and the air space over those waters. Under the US/T&T Shiprider, Trinidad and Tobago designated 'qualified law-enforcement officials to act as law enforcement shipriders,' who may embark - on United States Coast Guard and navy vessels with Coast Guard law-enforcement detachments embarked in the 'pursuit' by the US vessels on which they are embarked of suspect vessels fleeing into Trinidad and Tobago waters. 'Under the Model Shiprider Agreement, the designated Caribbean law-enforcement officials may authorise 'the vessels on which they are embarked to conduct counter-drug patrols...' in the 'exercise of hot pursuit'. US designated Coast Guard law-enforcement officials are authorised to act as law-enforcement shipriders who may embark on vessels of the Caribbean state and advise and assist 'in the boarding of vessels to enforce the laws of the Caribbean states' and 'enforce the laws of the United States seaward of the territorial sea' of Caribbean states. The 'special nature of the problem of illicit maritime drug traffic' summons an 'urgent need for international cooperation in suppressing illicit maritime drug traffic' (see also Kerry 1997b).

The US/T&T Agreement does not preclude 'the Government of the Republic of Trinidad and Tobago from otherwise expressly authorising United States counter-drug operations in Trinidad and Tobago waters or involving Trinidad and Tobago flag vessels or aircraft suspected of illicit traffic' (US/T&T Agreement, 3).[8] In jurisdiction over vessels detained in operations seaward of the territorial sea of a Caribbean state the Model Shiprider Agreement would authorise the US Coast Guard officials to board and search any vessel, including any flag vessel of a Caribbean state, suspected of engaging in illicit drug traffic. Any Caribbean state, whose law-enforcement operations or operations in support of law enforcement, are engaged in 'hot pursuit' may 'subject to its Constitution and the laws, waive its primary right to exercise jurisdiction and authorise the enforcement of United States law against the vessel and/or persons on board' (Model Shiprider Agreement, 4). This does not make Shiprider unprecedented. Rather, it is its scope, range, and the lack of specificity of the limits to the 'authorization' given to the US Coast Guard that constitutes grounds for the abuse of the sovereignty of Caribbean states by the US Shiprider confirms that sovereignty expresses a relation of power, including property relations between states; sovereignty cannot be quantified, nor is it a thing with an organic ontological essence that states possess.[9]

Peculiarities of the Barbados and Jamaica negotiated agreements with the US

The Preamble to the Barbados/US Agreement[10] reiterates all the conventions, agreements, laws and other measures that are precedents to Shiprider. The Preamble stresses the need for cooperation between the US and Barbados to combat 'illicit traffic by sea on the basis of mutual respect for the sovereign equality and territorial integrity of States' (Preamble, 2). Barbados and the US agreed that operations are to be done with 'the prior express permission of the law enforcement authorities of the Party on whose behalf the operation is to be carried out' (Article 3: 4). This specificity contrasts with the US/T&T Agreement. The Barbados/US Agreement uses the term 'coordinator' instead of Shiprider, conveying the notion of a joint and equal sharing of authority. The Barbados Coordinator is to 'designate qualified law enforcement officials who may embark on United States law enforcement vessels' to authorise pursuit, 'of suspect vessels and aircraft fleeing into Barbados waters' and 'authorize ... law enforcement vessels ... to enter Barbados waters'. The laws of Barbados are to be enforced in Barbados waters or seaward therefrom in the exercise of the right of hot pursuit or ... in accordance with international law:

Barbados Coordinator may seek the 'assistance of the United States law enforcement officials in the enforcement of the laws of Barbados.' The US/T&T Agreement does not specify that the laws of Trinidad and Tobago are to be enforced seaward from its territorial waters.

In relation to the enforcement mechanisms and provisions for both Parties, primacy is accorded to the 'law enforcement vessels or aircraft from the flag state' (Article 3: 5-6). The principle of the sovereign jurisdiction of the state on whose behalf law enforcement officials are acting is to apply when 'any boarding, search or seizure of property, any detention, of a person, and any use of force pursuant to this Agreement, whether or not involving firearms,' occurs, except where specified to the contrary (Article 4: 6). Article 5 on 'Operations in and over the Territorial Sea' upholds the principle of sovereignty where 'a Party exercises sovereignty' such that its law enforcement officials shall have jurisdiction. Like other Shiprider agreements, the Barbados/US Agreement provides for pursuit and entry, including when the Party exercising sovereignty does not have a 'law enforcement vessel ... immediately available to investigate', but law enforcement vessels of the other party may enter the territorial sea of the sovereign party to monitor the suspect vessel and 'keep it under surveillance until the law enforcement officials' of the Party with sovereign jurisdiction 'take control of the situation' (Article 6; 7).

Article 7, 'Assistance by Aircraft', prohibits arbitrary use of the airspace of the sovereign Party. Law enforcement officials of both parties are to comply with 'such air navigation instructions as are given by the aviation authorities of the Party within whose airspace such aircraft are operating. A Party may request assistance by aircraft from the other Party in suppressing illicit traffic within its waters or airspace'. Other Shiprider agreements share this general provision, including the observance of safety (see Article 7: 8). Article 9 defines operations to suppress illicit traffic against 'Suspect Vessels and Aircraft,' including vessels with the 'nationality of the Party in which it is registered' and 'vessels without nationality.' Fishing vessels licensed in Barbados qualify as vessels having Barbadian nationality (Article 9: 9).

Law enforcement officials are to follow 'national laws and procedures, international law and accepted international practices' when 'conducting boardings and searches pursuant to the Agreement', and they may carry firearms, and may 'discharge them only in accordance with Article 13.' In Article 13 – 'Use of Force'[11] – the 'inherent right of self-defense by law enforcement or other officials of the Parties' is to prevail. The exceptions to the use of force in any way, 'including the use of firearms', extend to when a suspect vessel fails to stop after it has ignored stop warnings,[12] and when there is 'disorder, resistance, impeding boarding and search activities, destruction of evidence of illicit traffic, or an attempt to flee during the boarding and search or the period of detention'.[13] The law enforcement or other officials are to safeguard 'life at sea, the security of the suspect vessel and its cargo' and the 'commercial and legal interests of the flag State or any other interested Party' (Article 11: 9- 10). Brown notes that the US/T&T Agreement is problematic in relation to 'jurisdiction over foreign troops in circumstances unacceptable to the sending state' (1997: 66). Prompt notification and reporting of investigations, prosecutions, and judicial proceedings are expected when a Party boards and/or searches a suspect vessel where evidence of illicit traffic was found (Article 12: 10).

Article 16 pertains to the implementation of the Agreement and presupposes the availability and knowledge of the laws and procedures of both Parties especially those that pertain to the use of force. Operations by law enforcement officials and vessels or aircraft in the territorial sea or territory of the Party with sovereign jurisdiction are subject to the 'laws, and naval customs and traditions of the *sovereign* Party'(Article 16: 12).[14] Respectively, Articles 20, 21, and 22 pertain to the 'Settlement of Disputes', 'Consultation and Review' and 'Preservation of Rights and Privileges', respectively. Article 20, provides for 'negotiation, enquiry, mediation, conciliation, arbitration, recourse to regional bodies, judicial process or other peaceful means of their own choice'. Article 21 applies to periodic consultation between the two Parties to enhance 'the effectiveness of this Agreement', and Article 22 safeguards the 'rights and privileges due any individual in any legal proceeding'. Article 23 addresses 'Entry into Force and Termination': written notification through normal diplomatic channels is required for termination which shall take effect '3 months after the date of such notice'.[15]

The Barbados/US Agreement differs in a number of ways from the agreements that were signed by other Caribbean states like the Dominican Republic, Grenada, Guyana, and Trinidad and Tobago. Coordinator replaces Shiprider as used in the US/T&T Agreement. The term 'maritime counter-drug operation' does not appear in the title. It carries a much shorter termination requirement of 3 months in contrast with all the other Shiprider agreements that carry a one year termination notification. The Barbados/US Agreement stipulates the sovereign equality of the Parties in specific ways that are left ambiguous in the US/T&T Agreement (Brown 1997; Sheppard 1997a). The Prime Minister of Barbados, Owen Arthur, saw the Model Shiprider in a very different light than Trinidad and Tobago Prime Minister, Basdeo Panday.[16] Arthur treats as a 'dangerous doctrine' the argument that sovereignty 'does not matter;' he insists that sovereignty was 'not divisible' and could not be 'circumscribed' (see Dumas 1997c: 9).

In contrast with other CARICOM member states that signed shiprider agreements without consulting with member states, Barbados and Jamaica 'collaborated in their negotiations with the US for the separate agreements that have been worked out' (*Trinidad Guardian*, May 9, 1997: 15), a move that is consistent with the cooperation in foreign policy aspects of the 1973 Treaty of Chaguaramas[17] (see Sheppard 1997a). Barbados insisted that the 'drug issue be tied to aid, immigration and trade' and measures to combat gun running (*Trinidad Guardian*, May 29, 1997: 13).

The US/Jamaica[18] Shiprider Agreement also differs from the US/T&T Agreement in a number of ways. Jamaican Prime Minister P.J. Patterson stressed that Jamaica would never accept the 'standard Shiprider model', and he insisted that Jamaica signed an agreement that protects the sovereignty of the Jamaican state, observes principles of reciprocity, protects the rights of individuals, and provides for consultation and the 'granting of permission as to leave little room for misunderstanding' (*Trinidad Express*, May 7, 1997: 13). Not only did Jamaica link sovereignty, development, immigration, and gun running to Shiprider, but it also succeeded in establishing 'inextricable linkages between gun smuggling and maritime narcotics trafficking'. Reportedly there is a 'separate instrument for the USA to waive sovereign immunity in relation to any claims which may be made against it or its agents, in any case of loss or injury sustained during operations in which they are involved' (*Trinidad Express*, May 7, 1997: 13; see also Article 19 of the Barbados/US Agreement).

Like Barbados, Jamaica rejected the standing authorisation contained in the MSA for US flag vessels to enter its territorial waters. The US/Jamaica Agreement requires 'the consent of the flag state on a case-by-case basis'; it forbids 'random patrolling' of its 'airspace and territorial waters, and insists on the primacy of Jamaican law' whenever 'law enforcement measures are taken within our territorial waters' (*Trinidad Express*, May 7, 1997: 13). Jamaica specified a linkage between the trade in arms, partly by securing 'pre-and post-shipping verification of licensed arms' and by obtaining US commitments for continued technical assistance to combat illegal trade in arms, given the high incidence of gun violence in that country, especially during election time (*Trinidad Guardian*, May 29, 1997: 13; May 9, 1997: 15). Jamaica succeeded in linking the granting of consent to enter its territorial waters and airspace to the 'provision of all relevant information including information as to reasonable grounds for suspicion of involvement in drug trafficking' (see also Article 16 of the Barbados/US Agreement). [19] Since states have sought assistance 'from other states in maintaining their territorial integrity and enforcing their laws', the problem of Shiprider lies in the 'unprecedented level of cooperation envisaged

238 | *Risk and Security in the Contemporary Caribbean*

in the ... arrangement *that* threatens traditional perceptions of sovereignty (Brown 1997: 28).

The narcotics problem is a problem of global capitalist organisation, production, distribution, marketing, and capital accumulation that copies aspects of processes of reterritorialisation in the global capital-national states conjuncture. It is the juridical-legal ways national states treat narcoproduction and trafficking that makes it a problem of international law: the complete outlawing of narcotics is what mystifies its place in global capitalism (Uprimny 1995; Watson 1997a). Like other small states Caribbean states lack the effective means to deal with the illicit drug problem on their own, and they have accommodated themselves to a combination of initiatives and programmes that incorporate United Nations, US, and regional strategies. Brown is very concerned that the Shiprider agreement opens to question that 'most basic principle of international law ... that a foreign sovereign has no enforcement jurisdiction in the territory of another sovereign state', and she feels the politicisation of Shiprider has been due to the 'sovereignty issue' (1997: 27, 67).

Caribbean states may have the formal sovereign authority to exercise jurisdiction but they lack the resources and enforcement capabilities. Griffith says that while Caribbean states readily accede to international treaties and agreements to counteract narcotics, they are mostly ineffective in eradication measures for reasons of 'administrative lethargy and technical, financial and other resource limitations' (1997: 211-12). The US has a strategic advantage in technological cost imperatives to deal with eradication, a fact that is conveyed in Basdeo Panday's frustration about the inability of his government to patrol the country's territorial waters (Viarruel 1997). Often shifts in US budgetary priorities affect the level of consistency with which Caribbean states are able to pursue countermeasures. Ironically, their nervousness about the limitations of sovereignty comes out in protests to the US against the heavy-handed tactics of its drug enforcement officials (Griffith 1997: 222, see Tulchin and Espach 2000). Shiprider is silent on the matter of 'disciplinary and criminal jurisdiction and liability for third party claims' [20] (Brown 1997: 68), with the exception of the Barbados and Jamaica agreements. The Regional Security System (RSS) provides for the mutual equality of states principle in relation to rights, powers, duties, privileges and immunities, but such a provision is absent from Shiprider, such that 'RSS service personnel ... enjoy fewer immunities than US Shipriders under the proposed model agreement' (1997: 70). [21]

Brown concludes that a regional approach to combating the illicit drug trade is preferable with respect to a 'sublimation of sovereignty in selected areas for the common good'. Such an approach 'permits lesser developed countries to deal from a position of greater equality with outside forces' and it 'reflects that whereas the crime itself may be localised, it is also an international problem that often spans several jurisdictions' (1997: 70-71). Brown prefers a cooperative reciprocal arrangement that accords with the 'rules of international law' beyond the issue of sovereignty. The rules of international law may mediate contradictions around the imbalances and inequalities in the social and material power of state, but it can neither resolve them nor render sovereignty ontological.

The Shiprider Solution: National Security as Imperialism

Abrams' (1996: 86-92) essay on the 'Shiprider Solution' elicited rejoinders from a number of Caribbean academics (Demas 1996, Ferguson 1997, Lewis 1996, Parris 1997, Ramphal 1997). Abrams offers a strategy for the US to bring Caribbean states and societies into conformity with its counter maritime drug policy. Abrams [22] contends that there is an economic and geopolitical predicament in the Caribbean that shows 'reliance on a foreign power for security and prosperity may be the most sensible form of nationalism' and 'the only available foreign power is the United States' (1996: 86; see Maingot 1997: 103).

Abrams' argument about how Caribbean states, beset by the crisis of illicit drug trafficking, ought to respond draws on realist ideological presuppositions about the nature of the world and the nature of power to buttress the expressed and implied national security imperatives of the US. His argument draws on familiar national security discourses with which Griffith's (1997) and Maingot's (1997) arguments are very compatible. Abrams redefines Caribbean nationalism to suit the 'new' global reality, by depicting the power, rights, and security interests of the United States as the universal perspective from which the Caribbean should reexamine its predicament.

Maingot is at one with Abrams, when he says 'the notion of a "dominant ... nation", which uses persuasion much more than force, diffusing a world-view that the rest of the world comes to regard as "common sense" is applicable to the contemporary Caribbean' (1997: 103). This diffusionist logic is about more than cold war doctrinal policy of anti-communism. It is a principle of faith that abides beyond reason, law, and empirical verification; it self-indulgently displaces Manifest Destiny and the other structuring ontologies of US imperialism and appeals to persuasion to mask all the excesses of the self-referential imperative of social control. It is about exercising hegemony by co-opting, controlling and otherwise making subordinates accept consensus as the displacement of domination. Maingot does not appreciate the relationship between displacement and preservation: domination was the battering ram that shaped persuasion into a shared world-view, long before the US national security project invented anti-communism as its core project.

Persuasion is the 'mobilization of bias' working through 'repressive tolerance' to denigrate those who are made into the threat to state and society. Maingot has great difficulty understanding that a persuasive state must have the material, military and other aspects of social power that make persuasion possible. Maingot's positivism is informed by an instrumentalist logic that cuddles an aversion to theory; it is typical of the discursive strategies found in mainstream Commonwealth Caribbean international relations scholarship. Maingot buries the socially produced asymmetries of power in national security discourses and locates Caribbean self-realisation within an intuitive acceptance of big power chauvinism, while he elides social contradictions and equates the unsaid with the unreal in a disingenuous attempt to separate history from domination as a social practice of imperialism.

Maingot does not seem to appreciate that persuasion is compatible with the logic of the 'empire of liberty' with its grounding precepts of Manifest Destiny, Expansionism, Exceptionalism, and Invincibility. Persuasion is a concept that masks the construction of an inverse identity in the negative sociability of the ethos that he so eagerly defends. Maingot makes it imperative for the Caribbean to avoid committing acts that are objectionable to the US, in order to avoid endangering US security interests. In effect, it is not the 'economic or political success or the openness of their political systems, but by their degree of affinity for US that other countries are judged by the US (Landau 1988: 40). Terms like cooperation produce the pragmatic effect of immobilising theoretical consciousness.

Abrams criticises Caribbean states for having limitations that pose national security problems for the US. He captures those limitations in chauvinistic terms. Demas characterised Abrams' depiction as symptomatic of 'the arrogance of power and a certain contempt for the West Indian people' (Demas 1997: 92; see Ramphal 1997). US national security doctrine and interests are historical constructions; it is problematic to treat the national security interests of any one state as the uncontested terrain on which to analyse relations between states. Early American concepts about Manifest Destiny, Divine Providence ('Zion in the wilderness'), expansion beyond the national frontier to secure national prosperity, the close links fostered between business, state militarism, and other structural factors presaged the evolution of an expansionist conception of a national security doctrine in the US (see Landau 1988: 13-18, Foner 2002). The postwar US national security doctrine is special because the Cold War provided a comprehensive rationalisation for the ethics and morality of the national security state that repressed opposition politics to the Cold War, the national security state, and the broad political economy strategies for restructuring global capitalism under US hegemony.[23]

The conjuncture of the National Security Act (1947), the Taft-Hartley Act (1947), and McCarthyism was strategic for setting up a 'repressive tolerance' machinery that was used to stifle domestic opposition to the hegemonic dispensation in the US. Specifying the historical context of the US national security state helps us to transcend the claim that US national security policies provide the cover to promote, protect, and secure democracy for the world at large. Maingot's suggestion that American historical particularism can offer the ultimate universality for global humanity is unacceptable because that universality is really an exclusivist particularism that is grounded in a necessity that expresses the fundamental historical contradiction between capital and labour on a global scale.

Postwar realism was created to rationalise and articulate the imperatives of American hegemony, such that realism is less a theory of international relations and more of an ideological 'manual of statecraft' to gird big power chauvinism (Rosenberg 1994). Mainstream versions of international relations 'discourse' in the Commonwealth Caribbean show no sensitivity to these realities (see Griffith 1993; 1997; Braveboy-Wagner 1989; Maingot 1997). Their logic is informed by positivist problem-solving techniques that accept the assumed limits of the system they defend as the absolute limits of the historically possible. This pragmatism relies on notions of power that mask the social relations of power between classes and states. This technique processes cultural imperialism in ways that force a closure on the development of theoretical consciousness. The negative cultural sociability in this scholarship makes it indifferent to the social metabolic control that capital enforces over the world and insensitive to the social and political oppositional struggles that statecraft attempts to externalise or neutralise through repressive tolerance, or otherwise destroy.

Griffith's nervous disposition to serious theorising also reflects a narrow organicist view of change. He remains unruffled by how the national security technique has structured the principles of freedom and democracy around the four freedoms – freedom of expression, conscience, freedom from fear and want – that in turn mask capital's foremost freedom to 'rob and exploit' under the national security state (Landau 1988: 40). It matters not that Griffith acknowledges that the US employs coercive strategies in the region to deal with countermeasures and protests by Caribbean states (1997: 219). In reality, the real test of any useful social theory lies in its validation before its consumers: the real purpose of politics should be the emancipation of humanity from domination. National security 'discourse' validates inequality of wealth and power between states and classes; it rationalises the systematic and deliberate production, sale and use of all types of weapons, big power chauvinism, large-scale human rights violations, ecological degradation, and other violent acts against nature, including human society.[24]

Abrams blends US security imperatives into the ideological landscape of mainstream international relations, by asking pragmatically how to protect US national security in an 'unstable' region of national states without the means to solve their 'own' problems, much less America's regional security problems. There is no inside-outside dichotomy at work here. Abrams' shiprider solution introduces migration, drugs, democracy, and human rights as issues in US security relations with the Caribbean. In fact, the migration problem is an integral part of the contradictions that unfold around the global capital-wage labour relation. The global neo-liberal strategy works through financial globalisation to aggravate labor flows and other migration problems (see Watson 1997a). Abrams uses Haiti and Cuba to highlight the impact on US foreign policy of illegal immigration into the US, and the overflow into domestic politics and public policy. Caribbean societies do not create the problems Abrams dumps on them, rather those problems express global capitalism's structural contradictions.

With respect to illicit drugs, Abrams defines the Caribbean as a bridge to the cocaine-producing countries of South America, and to drug trafficking and money laundering activities that plague the US. But Abrams cannot afford to connect the global drug business to global capitalism. In an attempt to displace America's role as the leading consumer of narcotics, Abrams asserts that the interests of the US are inseparable from the 'maintenance of democracy and respect for human rights in this border region' (1996: 87). Contrary to Abrams reasoning, democracy is a particular classed-based model for the organisation and exercise of power within national states. Democratic processes unfold around contradictions and struggles of social, political, and economic forces that are structurally unequal in their access to property, income and political power. Most of the ontological constructs of democracy that dominate most Caribbean writings on the subject are theoretically and epistemologically sterile.

Abrams argues that freedom and democracy 'in the Caribbean cannot be taken for granted' (1996: 87). He separates the limits of political democracy for Caribbean states and societies from the domestic bases of state sovereignty. He means that definitions of democracy and domestic sovereignty in the Caribbean cannot be left to Caribbean states; he derives definitions of democracy and sovereignty from the universalistic presuppositions of the US national security project. Abrams denies that Caribbean people have created reliable 'intersubjectively constituted' means out of their experience to inform ways to govern themselves, at least none that Washington must respect. He depicts the

Caribbean in pathological ways as a place where instability is rampant: democracy is uncertain: ethnic strife and chaos are pervasive; economic decay is setting in from the erosion of preferential trading arrangements and the transition to a new 'level playing field' – 'the new organizing principle of international trade' (1996: 88) – that aggravate threats to U.S. national security. His idea of a level playing field derives from the social physics of disembedded market logic, as it has no relevance to concrete reality under imperialism. The level playing field concept is intended to make accommodation to domination more tolerable.

From NAFTA, textiles, bananas, and declining official development assistance (ODA) flows to corruption, drug-trafficking, chronic unemployment, and a lack of the means to provide effective forms of security, Abrams sees a protracted crisis looming across a Caribbean that 'export little, save little, have few resources but sand (except for Trinidad, which has oil), and need far more new jobs than they are creating', with those states and societies becoming 'virtually defenseless' in the face of 'powerful drug and criminal groups...' (1996: 89). But there is a contrasting Caribbean where leading global corporations still realise surplus value from banking, finance, mining, advertising, construction, transportation, public utilities, communications, printing, publishing, shipping, insurance, tourism, retail outlets, real estate, agriculture, ... dairy farming, ... management services, ... manufacturing, accountancy and consultancy' (Thompson 1997: 152).

Abrams believes the crisis of 'viability' compromises sovereignty and demands a pragmatic 'continuing dependency on a larger, richer, stronger nation....' He concedes that 'while [F]ull colonial status may be a non-starter,... a voluntary, beneficial erosion of sovereignty should not be'. He offers Caribbean states a choice between having 'the sovereignty invaded by Americans under treaty' and seeing it usurped 'by drug runners at will' (1996: 90). He tries to make them an offer they should not refuse: swap enervated juridico-legal sovereignty for assured protection under the US security umbrella, now that narcotics have replaced Communism: even if the Cold War has ended, the cold war project is yet alive, as it undergoes restructuring.

Abrams is groping for a way to deal with the crisis manifestations of the national state model in the Caribbean in terms of how the crisis undermines the capacity of Caribbean states to process global capitalist relations and in relation to how the contradictions affect the competitiveness of American capital in the region. This seminal issue has escaped all mainstream responses to the shiprider controversy, and it applies equally to Demas (1997), Ramphal (1997), Parris (1997), Ferguson (1997) and others. Neither Abrams nor his Caribbean critics know how to locate US security interests in the global mobility of capital problematic. In contrast, Dupuy argues that 'Washington has never equated stability and security with legitimate government; the only concern is whether, elected or not, the government in power maintains the status quo. For many countries ... in the twentieth century, the status quo could be maintained and "stability" achieved only with strong and repressive military governments' (1996: 161-62) and the status quo includes the requirements of the reproduction of capital. Washington's concept of democracy and human rights is linked to the primacy of private property in capital and capital's right to property income on a global scale.

The main link between liberal democracy, sovereignty and stability is an environment that is conducive to the global mobility of capital,[25] without which capital's existence and reproduction become threatened, along with US global domination. The trick lies in how the US has systematically equated capitalism with democracy, by burying civil society inside bourgeois property relations, such that wherever capital predominates democracy is said to exist or on its way back. The global mobility of capital has its code in terms like free markets, direct foreign investment, privatisation, unrestricted repatriation of profits, the subsumption of labour under capital, and the global deployment of US military power, in conjunction with political arrangements as varied as liberal democracy, autocracy, or other right-wing strategies.

BEYOND THE LOGIC OF SOCIAL PHYSICS: 'NARCOCAPITAL' AND SOVEREIGNTY AS PROPERTY RELATION

The United Nations International Drug Control Programme (UNIDCP) reports that 'illegal drug dealing is a US$400 billion-a-year business, equal to about 8 per cent of all international trade', exceeding 'worldwide exports of iron and steel, or cars, and about equal to the entire worldwide trade in textiles'. The $400 billion figure represents '8 per cent of total global exports of $4.95 trillion in 1995, and dwarfs ... foreign investment, $240 billion, and foreign aid, $69 billion'. It would require the successful interception of three-fourths of 'all drug shipments ... to seriously cut into the profitability of the business.' The UNIDCP report estimates that there are 'about 140 million users, or about 2.5 percent of the world population' late in the 1990s (*Trinidad Guardian*, Friday, June 27, 1997: 27). The illegal narcotics problem is deeply rooted in the sociospatial and scalar reorganisation of the political economy of global capitalism.

The Paris-based Geopolitical Drug Watch Annual Report highlights the large-scale restructuring within the global narcotics business, with smaller and more specialised operations being created around a global division of labour. Leading drug lords have entered into new relationships with some states to share the profits from the drug business, a development that helps drug producers to transform their drug receipts into capital. Areas like the former Soviet Bloc are being integrated into the globalising drug business. It is by now difficult to target and neutralise the drug enterprise as it becomes more deeply integrated with the global capitalist reproduction processes.

According to Senator John Kerry (D-Mass.), who chaired the Senate Subcommittee on Terrorism, Narcotics and International Operations, five big powers make up the 'global crime axis', including 'the Italian mafia, the Russian mobs, the Japanese yakuza, the Chinese triads and the Colombian cartels' which work closely with 'smaller but highly organised gangs with distinct specialties in such countries as Nigeria, Poland, Jamaica, and Panama, which remains a significant transshipment and money-laundering point even after the arrest of General Noriega'. The drug groups have formed strategic alliances through which to coordinate their activities and alleviate some of the competitive conflicts (1997b: C4; 1997a).

Sicilian drug lords specialise in acquisition and marketing; Russian mobs, who handle shipping and distribution in the former USSR, are building new links with the American mafia; and the Chinese, Japanese and Colombians share an alliance in which Colombians exchange their cocaine with the Chinese for heroin that is smuggled into the US. The Chinese ship cocaine to Japan where the yakusas coordinate distribution, while the Asian mafiosi launder most of their drug money in Europe (Kerry 1997b: C4).

Senator Kerry notes that drugs are linked to other illegal activities such as 'gambling, prostitution, robbery, contract murder, and gasoline tax fraud and gasoline bootlegging'. He is blunt about moving 'beyond traditional notions of national sovereignty when those notions benefit only the bad guys'. This argument resonates with assertions by Abrams and a number of Caribbean leaders (see Viarruel 1997). Kerry recommends the creation of minimum standards of international law to achieve uniform global provisions for punishment for drug crimes in areas like money laundering and banking activities worldwide. He feels this is necessary to break up the new global division of labour that links bankers and other money launderers to drug producers, narcoproducers and certain insurgency groups and traffickers, and to disrupt the ties between drug trafficking and gun running activities.

These issues require a more adequate conceptual framework than the notion of 'geonarcotics' that remains theoretically inadequate (see Griffith 1997: 21). It is necessary to develop new theoretical insights to grapple with the major global changes that are afoot and that condition the strategies of the drug industry. Griffith expresses skepticism toward theory, generally, and with reference to how to situate the global narcotics problematic. He acknowledges that a 'comprehensive approach offers the best possible prospect for meaningful understanding of both the phenomenon as a whole and the dynamics of its individual parts' but does not think a 'comprehensive analysis is either absolutely necessary or the only credible approach' (1997: 14). He seems more comfortable with the realist-liberal problem-solving positivist approach to international relations. A comprehensive analysis demands a 'knowledge-practice that historically situates the conditions of possibility' and transcends the conceptual limits of 'what empirically exists under ... capitalist labour relations' with the aim of exposing 'what is suppressed by the empirically existing' methodology that equates unsaid, suppressed meanings with the unreal or undesirable. Only a praxis that unearths the hidden tracks of capital and those seemingly aleatory 'zones of culture' that are actually connected by means of 'highly differentiated and dispersed operations of a systematic ... exploitation and international division of labour informing all practices in societies ... under ... late capitalism' (Ebert 1996: 294) will suffice. Indeed, the 'dialectical/relational approach' has the virtue of revealing 'all sorts of possibilities that might otherwise appear foreclosed'; in fact, it is 'our embeddedness in nature, space-time, place and a particular kind of socio-ecological order (capitalism) that regulates the material conditions of daily life' (Harvey 1996: 12).

Distancing one's scholarship from theoretical rigour desensitises intellectual consciousness and celebrates commonsense at the expense of theoretical rigour (Ariffin 1996: 133). Kerry advocates monitoring all electronic money transfers to bring banking into full compliance, and the enactment of ...laws allowing domestic and foreign law enforcement to seize and share the property of convicted criminals'. He proposes '... a system of special courts to try at home cases involving victims abroad' with trials taking 'place wherever the evidence and witnesses were located, applying the law of the country where the crime took place.' He urges the US to 'add 1000 officers to the 2000 already stationed abroad. Every US embassy should have a law enforcement team' (1997b: C4) to reterritorialise the police and security functions of the US in the post-Cold War. Kerry wants to speed up the global reach of American law to make it easier to deal with the challenge from hypermobile information technologies that make it easier for drug barons to confront states and transform their money into capital. Kerry's recommendations highlights the property relations dimensions of state sovereignty.

Abrams' Shiprider Solution proposes to intensify in the Caribbean the very process Kerry proposes for the world. The Cuban Democracy Act of 1992 and the Cuban Liberty and Democratic Solidarity Act of 1996 provide ample evidence in support of this claim. [26] To his credit, Abrams identifies legitimate concerns about the illicit drug problem, which bear directly on the future direction of the national state and sovereignty in the Caribbean and beyond. The task of conceptualising the problematic of sovereignty in the Caribbean is made more difficult by the fact that the anti-colonial and anti-imperialist struggles have left deeply etched ideological and intellectual traumas and traces of modernity such as the effects of slavery that are hard to erase. The abstract universality in liberalism that informs concepts like the state, self-determination, sovereignty, freedom, justice and democracy are assumed to share a common ontological grounding that is at once legitimating and mediatory (see Henke 1997).

I challenge such assertions by arguing that sovereignty is an integral aspect of global (bourgeois) property relations that have their most concrete articulation at the global level, where capital accumulation takes place, though sovereignty appears as a property of national states that are embedded in geographical particularism. I agree with David Harvey who argues that 'historical-geographical processes of place and community' are constructed, and 'cultures are just as relationally (and "dialogically") constructed as individuals and a good deal more porous' (1996: 352). As such, the treatment of sovereignty as a purely national phenomenon is the result of the 'merciless separation' and freezing of global territorial space into hardened national zones of culture. It is this that leads many to take spatial scale of states for granted by reducing scale to a physical thing. Understanding this misrepresentation of sovereignty is key to deciphering why sovereignty is treated as an irreducible ontological phenomenon that is made independent of the historical moment of the bourgeois state and capitalism where we locate the nationalisation of the state, society, language, culture, property relations, and other symbols of national identity (see Reuten and Williams 1989).

The reality is that private property as capital is essentialised and made into an organic object coextensive with nature via the metaphor of an inalienable right to assets, or claim to assets by a person, company, or even a state. This fetishisation of property masks the social nature of private property which substantively expresses a social class relation to and in the means of production. As such, private property is privatised nature that is organised as a social property (power) relation between persons around the possession, use, and disposal of socially necessary objects (Teeple 1995: 76). Capitalist private property therefore expresses an antagonism with nature as society. Inevitably, all bourgeois notions of freedom, justice, equality, and democracy mask this antagonism in the peculiar and distinctive forms of civil society that bourgeois society reproduces.

The survival of capital demands mobility rights across the whole earth. Capital has no choice but to rupture and destroy as far as possible all types and forms of time-space constraints on its mobility and social reproduction (Marx 1952: 72, Harvey 1995: 2). Global capital and national states are connected by bourgeois property relations and civil society that are masked by the social power of money and the market, nationally and globally. Of course, bourgeois ideology asserts the principle of fictive sovereignty as derived from the will of the people. The notion of the will of the people is premised on the separation of civil society from the state, economy, market, and capital, and of coercion from the economy, while sealing off the power of capital from popular accountability. No wonder bourgeois civil society turns up again and again in the collective national identity that presupposes objectified bourgeois property relations. It is the separation of coercion from the economy that generated the bourgeois notion of individual freedom as a derivative of market constructs.

Collective identity at once displaces and preserves the tension between unity-in-separation and separation-in-unity which refer to the origins of the bourgeois state in society and its separation from society to return as the force that rules over society (see Reuten and Williams 1989). The 'sovereign will' harnesses the social relations under the state to make it such that the sovereign will could delegate power to a peculiar state that Montesquieu at once invented and imbued with a democratic nature to fulfil the destiny of reason in history, by giving the European world a peculiar natural disposition toward freedom and democracy.

In order to decipher sovereignty one must understand that capital revolutionises the productive forces to 'accelerate the turnover time, to speed up the circulation of capital, and to revolutionise the time horizons of development', to rupture all spatial obstacles, and 'annihilate space through time' though capital 'can do so only through the production of a fixed space' (Harvey 1995: 6). When demystified, the national state is revealed as the site where states use sovereignty to process global capitalist relations. Capital mobility registers a sociospatial scalar destructiveness that unfolds along trajectories of uneven and unequal development. As Swyngedouw notes, creative 'destruction is always an already social process. It is a metabolic transformation that takes place in association with others and extends over a certain space.' In effect,

> spatial scale is ... something that is produced; a process that is always deeply heterogeneous, conflictual, and contested. Scale becomes the arena and moment, ... where sociospatial power relations are contested and compromises are negotiated and regulated. Scale, ... is both the result and the outcome of social struggle for power and control (1997: 143).

In the revolutionisation of the productive forces capital intensifies the demand for material and juridical rights of global mobility, in order to reproduce itself in spatial scale terms in the process aggravating processes of deterritorialisation and reterritorialisation. Shiprider helps to adjust these imperatives.

Sovereignty may be tied juridically to a fixed space via the national state, but it also legitimates the right of capital to mobility and to appropriate 'rightful property income' (see Reuten and Williams 1989). It is this relational property right that is masked by the idea of sovereignty as an ontological category that is tied to the inside of national states. National sovereignty became the core ingredient of the global system of national states that replaced the old empires of the period eighteenth century in Europe (see Tilly 1992). National states are a recent historical form but some thinkers tend to base the state's claims to authenticity in appeals to historical time (Balibar 1990).

The question of the limitations of state sovereignty in the Caribbean is not in dispute. Commonplace realist assertions about the supposedly anarchical nature of the world essentialise the logic of the primacy of the national over the global, according to which stability and order prevail on the inside (the US) and disorder and chaos threaten from the outside (the Caribbean). Realist logic normalises and naturalises big power chauvinism and hegemony. In the hands of realists, anarchy is to the 'international states system' what the market is to the capitalist economic process. Anarchy is the law of social physics that makes the quest for power the anchoring principle of the international system of national states (Waltz 1959; see Rosenberg 1994). Abrams offers Caribbean states the option to submit to the security that only the US can provide because, especially the small '... states ... are nearly defenseless if their territory, sovereignty, and democratic institutions are attacked by criminals and drug traffickers. Their ... fragile democratic institutions cannot survive without help from outside powers which means, – ... the United States who ... cannot evade its role as the ultimate guarantor of peace, stability, and, nowadays, democracy.' Abrams displaces imperialism by justifying 'American intervention ... in exchange for certain economic and trade benefits' (1996: 90, 91).

By posing the problem in such stark binary terms Abrams displaces the embedded relationality that characterises the global capital-national states problematic (see Rosenberg 1994: 92). He is looking for additional space in which to facilitate the restructuring of hegemony, by enticing Caribbean states to cede sovereignty rights under the legal invasion of sovereignty. He says '...Caribbean micro-states have a most uncertain future, and may prove to be politically and economically unviable', and since 'geography forces them to associate with the United States', two choices remain, namely 'sporadic intervention or permanent cooperation'. Abrams' 'postnational' Caribbean state trades sovereignty for democracy to bolster protection from potential coup plotters and the drug barons, coupled with increased levels of aid, NAFTA parity, a defence treaty that ties economic assistance to military aid, a new arrangement that gives the US 'control over national security affairs,' and with 'some Caribbean nations voluntarily link themselves with the United States' (1996: 91; see Caribbean/United States Summit 1997). In the process Caribbean states could become new model states with more democracy and less sovereignty. Considering that national state sovereignty expresses a property relation, it follows that independence could not abolish global capitalism's own negative sociability. Why should any serious scholar embrace this logic, especially now that globalisation deconstructs the historical linkages between sovereign states and representative democracy?

A number of Caribbean leaders cast sovereignty in a different light, in view of how narcotrafficking and the corruption it engenders within the state apparatuses affect their ability to govern, protect the territorial and external bases of the state from the drug barons and their operatives, and respond to the international pressures they face from powers like the US. For example, when he was Prime Minister of Trinidad and Tobago, Basdeo Panday, ridiculed those who asserted the primacy of national sovereignty in the face of the drug threat (*Trinidad Guardian*, June 17, 1997:6). The Prime Minister of Grenada was even more emphatic: 'We are not in control the drug lords are, so far as I am concerned the territorial integrity issue is about drug lords....controlling it' (quoted in Ferguson 1997: 5). Part of the problem is that the personal and official views of Caribbean leaders about sovereignty and its relationship to shiprider do not necessarily tell us anything significant about the relationship of sovereignty to global capitalist relations of production.

'SHIPRIDER SOLUTION' AS RECOLONISATION: LIMITS OF A PLAUSIBLE HYPOTHESIS

I want to challenge a number of assertions that the 'Shiprider Solution' is a US strategy for recolonisation. An editorial in the Barbados Advocate depicted Shiprider as an

> obscene and cowardly assault on the integrity of some of the smaller states in the community of nations by our erstwhile ally in the north, acting i n pursuit of some obscure and questionable notion called national interest and disguised as a generous and unselfish offer of assistance to states unable to help themselves (*Barbados Advocate*, December 15, 1996).

Sir Shridath Ramphal echoed that sentiment when he said the '...proposal essentially was to turn back the clock of history and remove from West Indian hands the right to determine the nature of our engagement with the wider world. It was a proposal for recolonisation ...' (1997: 7; see Demas 1997: 92; Dumas 1997).

In part, the plausibility of recolonisation stems from Abrams' suggestion that 'American control of national security' could 'coexist with local control over all other matters, at least for the smallest islands', because 'developments in the world economy ... have made full independence tantamount to full vulnerability for the smallest states'. Abrams suggested the possibility of 'new forms of Commonwealth status, under which some ... Caribbean nations might voluntarily link themselves with the United States' (see Dumas 1997). But recolonisation is hardly the key issue. The United States does not have to return to old-fashioned colonialism to promote its interests as it negotiates the terms for ending the Cold War partly by restructuring hegemony. The real issue has to do with US responses to the particular features of the crisis of global capitalism and the national state model in the Caribbean region under globalisation.

In the Caribbean the United States relies on a combination of factors such as open regionalism, trade and investment strategies, structural adjustment programmes, the 'shiprider agreement', and a new national security policy to inform the logic of partnership between unequal states. The adoption by the Organization of American States of Resolution (OAS) of Resolution 1080 of 1990 at Santiago, Chile signalled the restructuring of the Inter-American Treaty of Reciprocal Mutual Assistance of 1947 (Rio Treaty) with capitalist market norms as the guiding factor in Western Hemisphere restructuring (Bloomfield 1998). Resolution 1080 requires each OAS member state to make the protection of capitalism and free markets the first line of defence of its national security, under which economic development and capital accumulation are subsumed.

There are conjunctural, structural, and ideological factors to consider. Conjuncturally, globalisation encompasses spatial, ideological, and class formation dynamics that have to do with the restructuring and expansion of capital into the former Soviet Union and Eastern European countries, the entry of more than one billion new workers and consumers into the capitalist world market, the embrace of bourgeois strategies by the Communist parties and party elites in China and Vietnam, and the collapse of national liberation revolutions in the post-colonial states (see Panitch 1997). These conjunctural shifts have modified the geopolitics of international relations, and helped to align the transnational bloc of the dominant capitalist ruling forces through the dominance of money and finance capital, and adjusted the dialectic of hegemony (see Van der Pijl 1998, Rupert 2000: 43-49).

The ideological reach and scope of capitalist ideas and values reflects the intensity of the global neo-liberal turn. Globalisation points to the deepening of the integration of certain components of heterogeneous transnational capitalist class fractions through the new patterns of the concentration and centralisation of old and new forms of capital around the world. Structurally, the expansion of global capital accumulation is conditioned by the transition from postwar military Keynesianism to contemporary 'post-Keynesian militarism', in the wake of the breakdown of the Bretton Woods system, the growth of foreign direct investment, production, trade, exchange, the growth of international credit, the expansion of the circuits of money and currency flows, the intensification of financial speculation, the rapid expansion of private corporate and public debt, and the nationalisation of private debt. Of course, the integration of the national state with the global movement of capital and the shifting upward and outward to the world level of aspects of state decision-making are integral to the shifts.

Mainstream Caribbean international relations specialists do not normally integrate these structural and conjunctural issues in their analyses. Ferguson (1997: 5) stresses the historical basis of sovereignty, its contemporary crisis, and the associated contradictions of national states as he thinks of ways to 'effectively battle the scourge of drugs'. Largely, Caribbean academics fail to locate illicit drug trafficking in the political economy of global capitalism (see Watson 1997), though this is absolutely necessary to redirect the argument beyond the nationalist responses to Abrams account. The contradictions of state sovereignty in the Caribbean are not caused by participation in illicit trafficking in narcotics, though narcotrafficking brings into sharper relief the contradictions in the relationship between national states and global capitalism. The US is actively restructuring its hegemonic control over the entire Western Hemisphere, including the Caribbean where its 'tendency toward nonconsultative, unilateral decision-making in bilateral or multilateral affairs' (Ferguson 1997: 6) is very pronounced.

The crisis of state sovereignty is inseparable from the crisis of the national states model. The tendency to give sovereignty an organic ontological base (Henke 1997) reflects how nationalism keeps alive the 'retrospective illusion of the national personality', by naturalising metaphors like autonomy, citizenship, unity, democracy, and belonging. Preoccupation with these symbols and institutions undermines efforts to decipher the contradictory formation and development of national identity within social relations of production. Such aspects comprise:

> an interrelated language or discourse that has its expressive ceremonials and symbols... *that* include the ... attributes of nations - flags, anthems, ... coinage, ..., oaths, folk customs, ..., war memorials, ..., remembrance of the national dead, passports, frontiers, as well as ... popular heroes and heroines, ..., styles of architecture, ..., legal procedures, .., and military

codes - all those ... ways of acting and feeling that are shared by members of the historical community' (Smith 1991: 77).

These and other symbols yield to an identification with a 'militant particularism' of place that nationalises 'tangible solidarities' (Harvey 1996: 32-33) and eschews the global as an unwanted foreign intrusion. The 'imagined community' is one of the ontologies that recondition the 'vestigial skin' of the nation-state and freeze spatio-temporality and scale into the fixity of the territorial exclusivism and regulatory power of the state in matters such as currency, law, politics and the monopoly over 'coercion and violence according to a sovereign territorial (and sometimes extraterritorial) will' (Harvey 1995: 7). The perspectivism of the 'particularism of place' masks the contradictions that are thrown up by global capitalism.

The recolonisation thesis deflects attention from the real problem of the crisis of the national state system around the world, and the restructuring of US hegemony and imperialism, partly through a competitive hemispheric expansionist strategy called the 'Partnership for Prosperity (see Caribbean/US Summit 1997). The issues are more complex than Ramphal (1997), Abrams (1996) Demas (1997), Parris (1997), and others have depicted them. The making of national states in the Caribbean was a very violent process,[27] and global capitalism continues to restructure the moorings of the national state (Harvey 1996: 40-41; Holloway 1995).

It is important to look at how and where Shiprider enters the picture in order to 'deconstruct' the recolonisation hypothesis. Sovereignty reflects 'processes of state formation and dissolution' that inform 'the unstable processes of globalisation/territorialisation'. Most Caribbean international relations scholarship ignores the 'process of territorialisation, deterritorialisation, and reterritorialisation continuously at work throughout the historical geography of capitalism' (Harvey 1995: 7; see Watson 1993; 1997a). Harvey's concept of 'spatial scale and temporal horizon' (1996: 41) is useful for examining the extent to which Abrams' 'Shiprider Solution' represents a test case with broader geopolitical and economic significance than may be inferred from how the Caribbean participates in the global drug industry. Does restructuring within the global drug industry along lines of strategic alliances among drug barons signal new spatio-temporal departures around political reorganisation and the much more comprehensive processes of capitalist restructuring? Can customary concepts of national sovereignty accommodate the spatial scale shifts that accompany the dissolution of customary spatio-temporal configurations?

Questions such as these make it easier to question Parris' plausible attempt to situate Shiprider in an 'Atlanticized Brezhnev Doctrine' which, he says, depicts a 'state of "low intensity" belligerency between the Great Powers and selective areas of the Third World, with the exercise of "limited sovereignty" at its epicenter' (1997: 2). US imperialism has long conducted high and 'low intensity belligerency' against selective areas of the Third World: global restructuring is marked by coercive strategies of capitalism's 'production of uneven temporal and geographical development'[27] (Harvey 1995: 8). Parris says a 'revamped, creeping version of the concept of "limited sovereignty" is back ..., with hardly a face-lift ... under the guise of enlightened foreign policy, entangled as it were, in the debates over "free trade" and "globalisation" ' (1997: 2, 3).

The fact is that the Western Hemisphere has lived with 'limited sovereignty' since the days of the Monroe Doctrine. It was vigorously and coercively reconfigured by the Truman Doctrine and the postwar national security state. All interventions, invasions, and occupations of Latin American and Caribbean countries by the US since the nineteenth century have reinforced the assertion that Caribbean sovereignty has implied '... asking US permission before making changes in ...foreign policy (Landau 1988: 17). It is not that the partial and/or total abrogation of the sovereignty of the independent states of the Caribbean might be necessary for globalisation as Parris asserts, rather it is that the crisis of the national state model, including state sovereignty, is itself reflective of global restructuring. Parris and Abrams are operating from broadly common presuppositions, but Abrams is forthright about reterritorialisation within global capitalism, while Parris privileges the moral and ontological aspects of sovereignty, without reference to its property relations basis. Griffith seems completely unaware of this important point in his notion of 'positive sovereignty' (1997: 20-22).

Parris blames Caribbean states for failing to '... arrive at a concerted strategy which obeys the endogenous logic of survival', and he insists that failure to 'delimit a specifically Caribbean sphere of influence within the ... world system has created a dangerous void that exogenous forces now are more than willing to fill' (1997: 13). The reality is that Commonwealth Caribbean states follow a globally constituted 'endogenous logic' that comports with the US national security framework. They deploy sovereignty to support capital accumulation strategies. They embrace the Enlightenment Project via the nation-state model with all its impedimenta. They adopted admixtures of import substituting industrialisation, the Keynesian welfare state strategy, and export-led growth, and they look to tourism and other services to find the new pistons in the engine of growth under global neo-liberalism (Enloe 1989: 41).

Parris' 'endogenous logic' does not seem to be mindful that the global and national constitute a complex, heterogeneous totality that becomes more integrally connected as states become more deeply integrated with the global movement of capital (Holloway 1995, Watson 1997b). His argument ignores expanding foreign currency and capital markets that function increasingly beyond national state control, of course, with the state's endorsement. It does not take into account global credit systems, money supply, exchange rates, investment policies, taxation, and debt-management and other processes and shifts that states aid and abet, by exploiting them to attract global capital for reproduction and capital accumulation. The dominant bourgeois interests have in conjunction with the states they dominate embraced global monetarism even when they foster the myth that supranational finance capital is autonomous of the social relations of production.

Under restructuring global capital continues to demand greater freedom from national controls and regulation, and rulers of states have taken measures to convince capital of their reliability and dependability in this and other respects. Capital expresses a global social class relation and as such it lacks of allegiance to national space and shows defiance toward its own bourgeois state as it increasingly asserts its own globality. Corporate capital's global interests increasingly crystallise beyond national spatial scale demonstrating that its interests cannot be adequately accommodated at the national level, even when its cultural prejudices may reflect certain national biases. Such biases are without a doubt tied to big power chauvinism, racism and other features of imperialism. National space is but one component in capital's complex global interests and its production and accumulation imperatives; substantively corporate capital's idea of a home market is the global economy which reinforces the point that the real economy today is the global market economy. Broadly, central banks are instrumental in this context, especially in their capacity as the handmaidens of global monetarism, and central banks, which regulate national political money supply, are the first to become unglued from the national priorities as they become reconfigured via global neo-liberalism. Central banks increasingly call for autonomy for themselves by separating monetary policy and economics from politics (Teeple 1995: 71).

Parris would have to explain the relevance of the endogenous logic where the restructuring of science, technology, industry, production, trade, labour processes, consumption, and the global reach of direct foreign investment have long intensified the economic, industrial, commercial, financial, and monetary integration of the Caribbean into global capitalism. To hold to this position Parris must mercilessly and arbitrarily separate space into autonomous national components and conclude that the real economy is the national economy, an untenable position indeed. The migration of global capital significantly reconfigures labour by restructuring the demographic and cultural parameters of Caribbean nations into the 'metropoles', giving the region the character of 'nations unbound' (Basch, Schiller, and Blanc 1994). Self-determination and sovereignty are not definitive outcomes of decolonisation, but rather integral parts of a contradictory process of the becoming and reshaping of nationhood and identity over time within contradictory processes of global restructuring.

Parris blames Caribbean leaders for missing the opportunity to craft a 'specifically Caribbean approach to regional socio-economic development, foreign policy, security..., or,..., educational strategy' because he fails to see the historical limits of the national state model unfolding around contradictions like those that have been posed by Shiprider. He attributes the failure to 'doubts regarding the capacity of Caribbean states to uphold their own sovereignty' (1997: 13). Parris must also explain why Caribbean states relate to global capital as they do and how transnational capital features in their development strategies, as this point is important for any useful analysis of how national states employ sovereignty to process global capitalist relations of production. The shiprider controversy has stimulated very little useful analysis of the global capitalism and the limits of the national state and sovereignty in the Caribbean. It is necessary to advance the intellectual debate by locating the shiprider arrangement in its proper historico-social context.

SOVEREIGNTY, SHIPRIDER, AND GLOBAL CAPITALIST RESTRUCTURING

Shiprider signals the disconcerting reality of the reconfiguration of the nation-state and national sovereignty. The associated contradictions of this process are far more traumatic in small and weak states than they seem to be in large and powerful states, but they are more or less evident in all states across the global spectrum. Shiprider and the narcotics industry must be situated in the relationship between global capital and national states, around capitalist reproduction and global capital accumulation. Shiprider privileges particular representations of national security in its use of diplomacy to help restructure interstate relations.

When there is no clear sense of the dialectics of spatial scale all notions of social relations between humans tend to be reduced to technical relations between things which is how liberalism and realism see reality. The logic of sovereignty is evident in Ferguson's contention that the 'cumulative impact' of the 'realities of interdependence and globalisation', understood via 'information technology, the formation of mega-economic blocs ... ' and such, 'has been to collapse national borders, to dissipate the primacy of the state-actor and the resultant sharing of authoritative space by a host of non-state actors (MNCs, NGOs,

IGOs) and, ultimately to question the sovereignty of the state,...' (1997:12-13). National borders have not been tightly framed under modern capitalism and imperialism. Ferguson's argument reflects anxieties about the status of the ontological fixedness of state sovereignty as prescribed by realism. In order to resolve the epistemological problem about the future of the national state, we must proceed from the historical nature of national states and not from their functions. This calls for abandoning functionalist notions of 'transhistorical essentialisms' from which the organic theory of the state is derived.

To derive the state and sovereignty from the logic of national identity is to reduce history to idealist reflections in which the state and sovereignty assume mythical proportions in the retrospective illusion of a collective organic 'national personality'. Ferguson is concerned that the flows of capital, mega-bloc formation, technology, and other forces dislodge the state, almost conspiratorially collapsing national borders, dissipating the 'primacy of the state-actor' and forcing the state to share 'authoritative space' with non-state actors, with the effect of ultimately questioning 'the sovereignty of the state ...' He does not seem to appreciate that the symbols of the national imaginary are not 'finished products' that have their base in some 'past tense' of an archaic originary (Williams 1977: 128-29).

Ferguson's argument does not tell us anything about the national state or sovereignty beyond a repetition of the metaphor of realist centrism that appropriates history without providing the theoretical tools for a more critical explanation of the issues. He does not give the state historical or theoretical grounding; nor is there any appreciation of anarchy as a specific representation of the fundamental process of capitalist modernity (see Rosenberg 1994). The rhetoric that anarchy is the absence of a superordinate global authority to rule over the international system is problematic. It is necessary to understand that anarchy is a specific configuration of the fundamental capitalist process in its historical articulation. Mainstream international relations suffers from a certain theoretical impossibility that is at once derived from the logic of the balance of power, itself an ontological premise, and from the mediation of the balance of power by aleatory — non-logical, random and unique — homeostatic events. (Aron 1967, Griffith 1997; see Ariffin 1996, Sinclair 1996: 7, and Rosenberg 1994 for critiques).

It is impossible to provide an adequate conceptual framework to study international relations phenomena without a critical knowledge of capitalist modernity and with particular reference to nation-states, classes, self-determination, sovereignty, nationalism, balance of power, anarchy, comparative advantage, free trade, war making and state making, and the relationship between nation-sates and capital, in the context of the world market and capital accumulation (Rosenberg 1994: 89-90). Sovereign states presuppose the development of a modern world market, uneven spatial scale differentiation, the mobility of capital linked to 'rightful property income', and the appropriation and disposal of that income as surplus value without respect to national space. The market and private property relations are central to thinking about state sovereignty because state sovereignty expresses a peculiar historical 'abstraction from civil society, an abstraction which is constitutive of the private sphere of the market, and hence inseparable from capitalist relations of production' (Rosenberg 1994: 123-24). Market hegemony is a subset within bourgeois hegemony that subsumes civil society under the private sphere of capital around the separation of coercion from the economy. As such, Ferguson's lamentation against the intrusions from the global market economy and other non-state actors that are taken to dislodge the sovereign state is problematic, historically and theoretically, for its devotion to Newtonian-Cartesianism prejudices that obstruct his view to the location of the state within the global space of capital.

Indeed nationalism expresses the state's own cultural sensibility and its sovereign authority over society, a fact that engenders the view that the state and capital constitute an irreducible unity around the state's own collective identity. In reality the division of labour between the state and capital is a technical division of labour but this does not mean the state and capital comprise an irreducible national oneness. Ferguson concedes that it is necessary to 'realistically adjust to changing sovereignty' as a functional problem to arrive at a 'notion of shared sovereignty on a regional basis among CARICOM countries, ... signifying the aggregation of individual national sovereignty in defined areas to strengthen our capacity to function and to withstand pressure and threats from whatever sources' (1997: 13). Clearly, sovereignty is not cumulative in this quantitative way precisely because what is at issue is the bourgeois property relation through which Caribbean national states process global capitalist relations. This notion begs the question via the medium of the European Union (EU) that represents a very different model of capitalist integration of states and markets, such that there is very little in common between CARICOM and the EU for making comparisons.

Parris and Ferguson want to rescue the Caribbean national state and sovereignty from the ravages of globalisation, the former by privileging an 'endogenous logic of survival' and the latter by pooling sovereignties; both of these notions are trapped by the logic of the populism of particularisms. As with the contributions by Fergusson and Parris there are questions about the underlying assumptions about the nature and self-images of international law that inform Kathy-Ann Brown's account of Shiprider. Brown provided a useful way to look at the shiprider problematic through the lens of international law.

But international law offers clarifications that it also masks in its own self-images through which it arrives at its conception of sovereignty. International law sets out from those very positivist premises that mask the 'inextricable singularity of capitalism and the state system', a problem that Brown does not even consider. Brown provides important accounts of the historical antecedents and precedents of shiprider and shows how international law has treated the problem of narcotics drugs by associating it with broader issues such as piracy. In Brown's account of the universalisation of narcotics drugs there is no sense of the way international law separates the national territorial state from the social relations of production of global capitalism. There is nothing in her argument to connect international law to the rationalisation and normalisation of capital and the nation-state.

Brown does not say it but she leaves the impression that international law may be autonomous of the historical knowledge-practice around the uneven production and accumulation processes in the geographies of global capitalism. Brown betrays no sense of the property relations embodiment of state sovereignty: to connect sovereignty with private property and explain the connection via international law would be certain to destabilise the imperial basis of international law itself. Her treatment of Shiprider is undisturbed by the dialectic of global capitalist restructuring and, intentionally or otherwise, she leaves the impression that international law is the prime mover behind politics, the state, sovereignty, and, by implication, capital accumulation. The strength of her argument lies in the descriptive detail she provides rather than in any new departures she suggests for understanding United States-Caribbean relations under contemporary imperialism.

Brown stresses the need for cooperation between the US and Caribbean states, and concludes that the 'appropriate legal framework for cooperation is one based on a reciprocal arrangement in accordance with the rules of international law' (1997: 72). International law is an historical knowledge subject that informs certain juridical and political (power) norms and practices around the primacy of property in the making of the international system on which sovereignty depends. Shiprider is about renegotiating the territorial and mobile property rights basis of US-Caribbean relations. The sovereign subject and empire of modern international law is global capital and the anarchy of sovereignty. Brown's interpretation of Shiprider through the medium of international law autonomises international law with the effect of preserving the spirit of imperialism whose own seeing eye is international law.

State sovereignty could not invent or make national states rather the swivel of the international system that comprises national states required something to gird self-determination – something more modern than the sovereignty of absolute monarchies – to lend feasibility to the modern international system and international law has been pivotal in this respect. The deepening of globalisation engenders the transfer of important national decision making to the world level, a shift that signals how national states have been reconfiguring their global responsibilities and some of their national obligations under the discipline of supranational finance capital. This shift is marked by a lessening of the state's control over the mobility of certain types of capital such as money and finance capital with the complicity and participation of states. It is the semblance of the autonomy of money and supranational finance capital from social relations of production that lends the market its seductive power and appearance of being tucked away from exploitation around the 'imaginary networks' of bourgeois power.

To decipher sovereignty calls for a 'knowledge-practice that historically situates the conditions of possibility' that are masked by Ferguson's notion of pooling CARICOM sovereignties. Situating the 'conditions of possibility' requires getting past the conceptual limits of 'what empirically exists under patriarchal-imperialist-capitalist labour relations' to discover 'what is suppressed by the empirically existing'. This requires uncovering the tracks of capital in the seemingly disconnected global 'zones of culture', but which are 'linked through the highly differentiated and dispersed operations of a systematic ... exploitation and international division of labour informing all practices in societies ... under ... late capitalism' (Ebert 1996: 294). This is where we begin to discover that the principle of sovereign equality of all national states at once masks the real substantive material (property) inequality of those states, and validates the real socioeconomic inequality of the classes comprising the societies that are ruled by those states. Ferguson's 'fundamental guiding principle' of sovereignty masks the contradictions of the neocolonial state.

In view of the fact that sovereignty expresses historical social relations under global capitalism, and since capital's global mobility is central, it is impossible to restrict sovereignty to national space: sovereignty is conditioned by the spatiotemporal momentum that characterises the production of global scale. Hence state sovereignty reflects the heterogeneity and contradictoriness around domination, exploitation, and the historical violence and bloody origins and processes of bourgeois property relations based on capitalism. Here we must keep in mind that capital accumulation is a global process. By extension, to deal with crisis that unfolds around the inability of some states to accommodate changes around externalisation, states have been shifting to the world level more of the regulatory power they use for processing global capitalist relations. This externalisation reflects reterritorialisation processes that generate the political and ideological adjustments that are justified under what passes for the legitimising logic of market objectivity. The transnational bourgeois forces now promote the idea of market impartiality and attempt to tuck it away from the political and social contradictions that states cannot by their class nature escape. Of course, displacement is a form of preservation. The related contradictions are embedded in the United States militarist strategy in Afghanistan and the Persian Gulf region and in the larger rhetoric about waging a war against terrorism when in fact the basis of terrorism lies within capitalism and imperialism. The war against terrorism is a war to intensify and centralise the control of capital over all the key resources and spaces that are important for capitalist reproduction and global capital accumulation (see Pilger 2002).

The tendency to reduce the fluidity, mobility, spatiality, transferability, and exchangeability necessary for the production and reproduction of capital as property to the sovereign and supreme territoriality or the geographically based landed property of the national state obstructs the view to the substantive meaning of sovereignty. In contrast, Burch locates property relations in the genealogy of national sovereignty when he says: 'the "state" represents the territorially grounded property rights of sovereign monarchs, especially as these rights and holdings were fundamental in the development of institutional-legal structures for ruling and controlling society.'

> [The] "crown state" emerged from the "crown" when monarchical families became the purveyors of property rights as part of their alliance with the bourgeoisie in order to organise and administer institutional structures for public governance and rule .... real property was significant because it provided the foundation for the claims by states' rulers to be territorial rights-bearers – that is, landholding sovereigns (1994: 44, 47).

This is what makes '... territoriality ... solely a function of property rights of a settled and exclusionary sort and such rights are a product of society not inherent in nature' (Harvey 1996: 162) and they have been bound up with the production of massive forms of violence that shape the 'constitution of the political world,' and it is inseparable from forms of 'control, domination, exploitation, production, and exchange ... which are ... structural features of social relations' with which we associate 'the transition to state-building and nascent capitalism' (Burch 1994: 44-45, Tilly 1992).

Largely, because Caribbean social theory, including mainstream international relations theory, is yet to grasp the proper relationship of state sovereignty to global capitalism, it settles for commonsensical interpretations of the sovereignty-global capital issue and excludes any reference to sovereignty as a property relation that is expressed in the intercellular junctional complexes that depict the heterogeneous and dynamic global reality. The tendency has been to fetishise and idealise sovereignty by equating it to a disembodied category of autonomous 'national will'.

The acceleration of mobility of supranational finance capital reduces the turnover time of various forms of capital with consequences for the production and location of sovereignty. This is the point that Blackman Associates imply in their argument that some companies in a number of CARICOM countries are diversifying their investment strategies and practices away from the local and regional level to the wider world, in a bid to compete for market share in Europe and the Western Hemisphere, consistent with the deepening of strategic alliances on a global and regional scale (Blackman Associates 1996: 76, 82-86; Bernal 1996).

> [In the] patterns of financial intermediation.... Life insurance companies are buying commercial banks, and commercial banks are acquiring industrial and commercial enterprises. The financial system has ... increased in complexity with the arrival of merchant and investment banks, and ... the branching of financial institutions throughout CARICOM and even into the USA (1996: iv).

Recent initiatives by the Dominican Republic and CARICOM states to develop and/or broaden economic and trade relations with Cuba also reflect a transition in business practices that are intended to strengthen the competitive position of private capital in certain countries in the region (see Gonzalez Nunez 1997). The deepening of the integration of certain old and new capitalist strata in the Caribbean into the global economy via business alliances with extra-regional interests is also changing the sense of Caribbean value structures and the idea of time-space (see Bernal 1996). This transition is very disconcerting in relation to the restructuring of Caribbean states and the surrounding class relations.

The ways the US used to exercise leverage over Caribbean states around Cuba with extremely harmful effects on Cuba and the Caribbean (see Figueros and Plasencia 1994: 113-14) are being questioned by several Caribbean states. U.S. punitive strategies against Cuba via the Cuban Liberty and Democratic Solidarity Act, (Helms-Burton Law), signal continuing efforts to apply Cold War measures of economic warfare against Cuba, [29] the Caribbean, and major allies for economic and political ends (see Cox 1996b: 33-34). The Caribbean has been attracting a much smaller portion of global foreign direct investment resources than in previous years (Watson 1997). Caribbean businesses have to search for new ways to exploit the space created by some of the decentralising effects of reterritorialisation in the 'residual Cold War'.[30] Indeed, 'the separation of the political and the economic indicates ... the central institutional linkage between the capitalist economy and the nation-state: that is the legal structure of property rights which removes market relationships from direct political control or contestation and allows the flow of investment across national boundaries', thereby revealing that 'the economy is not, ..., a nationally constituted instrument ready at the disposal of the state' (Rosenberg 1994: 14). Clearly, power relations between states routinely mask the fact that class relations are at the heart of property-based relations that are dependent upon the 'inextricable singularity of capitalism and the state system' (Burch 1994:52; Holloway 1995; Burnham 1995). With respect to the United States and its role as the unsurpassed imperialist state in the world the riddle can be solved as soon as we discover that 'the imperial character of American world power is least visible' when international relations scholarship concentrates on 'the purely political world of sovereign equality and anarchical competition' (Rosenberg 1994: 172).

CONCLUSION

Metaphors are important in representing and articulating the historical differences between states and societies but the real problem around such differences lies in their social and political construction. Geographical and territorial compartmentalisation foster the impression that the natural order of the human species is competition and conflict as opposed to dialectical interrelationships. This study has shown that to understand the shiprider controversy we must begin with an explanatory framework that is grounded in a rigorous 'theoretical practice' of global capitalism. I approached capitalism as a global system that undergoes periodic restructuring in ways that reconfigure capitalist reproduction and capital accumulation and the broader social relations. The study has challenged the dominant propositions and presuppositions of international relations and security studies approaches found in mainstream academic scholarship in the Caribbean.

Space like sovereignty is relational and is produced under contradictory conditions. Hegemony is relational and contingent, and US foreign policy towards Caribbean states is bound to be open to contestation at different moments. The key contested issues around Shiprider are the nation-state, sovereignty, and security, each of which has been treated in inadequate ways that mask the substantive problems. I have attempted to excavate the underlying problems, by starting from the historical nature of the state, sovereignty, and security rather than their functional aspects. I argued that sovereignty expresses foremost a property relation, as opposed to an inherent ontological property of national states. I linked sovereignty as an historical phenomenon to national states and global capital which is the expression of a global social relation.

I insisted that the academic response to the Shiprider controversy has failed in its empiricist articulation to recognise and appreciate the crisis of the national state model with special reference to the Caribbean. This failure is made more apparent by the tendency to relate to the state, sovereignty, and nationalism through retrospective illusions. My critique suggests that the crisis of the national state model is one of the core issues to be addressed in deciphering the Caribbean problematic in the contemporary global context. By extension, the responses to Abrams' depiction of the Caribbean have been lacking in originality partly because of a failure to see that Abrams' thesis conveys a national security strategy to deal with the reality of the crisis of the state model in the region. Abrams does not isolate the crisis parameters of the US national state in spite of the fact that the same global restructuring the US now promotes also disciplines and constrains the US state and capital in their ability to dictate to the rest of the world. The contradictions that follow from this situation come to the fore in a highly militaristic response by the US to problems, a sign of the deepening crisis of its own hegemony. I located the illegal narcotics problematic within global capitalism, in order to tie it to the crisis of global capital accumulation based on the dominance of money and finance and issues of the state and sovereignty.

My critique of the arguments around Shiprider suggest a way to place Shiprider where it belongs within global capitalist restructuring, generally, and within the restructuring of American hegemony, specifically, in the immediate context of the intensification of competition between the dominant capitalist classes in the world. The US is restructuring its national security state doctrine and apparatuses, as the global bourgeoisie pursues more transparent rules for capital accumulation based on the primacy of the economic civil rights of capital on a global scale. From this angle it is easier to locate the Helms-Burton Law within the restructuring of the cold war national security state apparatus in anticipation of what some would seem to wish for Cuba. Those who desire to force Caribbean states to isolate Cuba are pandering to a neocolonial nostalgia about Cuba also miss the point. Helms-Burton is explicit about the property relations basis of sovereignty, but it also reveals the weakness of the US state to act intelligently on Cuba, considering how cold war imperialism made Cuba into a domestic issue in American national life. The US has been at a strategic disadvantage to deal with Cuba, because the US state lacks an integral domestic capability around state-capital coalitions to deal with this contradiction. Even where the US may project its power globally, it has to confront the contingent nature of its own hegemony. The competition between the global forces of capital also conditions and constrains the effective reach of US power in the post-Cold War. The new capitalist strata in the Caribbean have no choice but to push their states to challenge the political basis of US policy toward Cuba as they attempt to restructure their role in the global division of labour, and this is why they have to become globally oriented by finding niches in places such as Cuba, Latin America, Europe and North America.

Those who want to 'take back Cuba' are blinded by the maelstrom that is being churned by the seismic forces of contemporary globalisation. The global thrust of US power contrasts with a lack of 'domestic capacity (public-private coalitions)' to act decisively, including when the objectives are explicitly militaristic around securing control of strategic global resources like oil reserves (Weiss 1997: 25, Cox 1996: xi). Like capital, sovereignty is becoming increasingly unglued from its traditional moorings in national states. Globalisation is about the restructuring of social class relations of production; it is not about the decline of the state in favour of the enhancement of the power of capital, considering that state and capital are integral to those social relations of production. Shiprider exposes the weaknesses of Caribbean states in the material and other means to shape the regional agenda, and it is the sense of this inadequacy that underlies the frustration that emerges in nationalist responses to Shiprider.

The arguments I developed in this essay build on and in some ways transcend those I advanced in Watson (1993), which serves as a critique of the ideological consciousness of social theory and the mainstream international relations scholarship in the Caribbean. Caribbean intellectual culture cries out for a paradigmatic shift in relation to a range of issues around the impact of modernity on the evolution of ideological consciousness in the region, and the inadequacies of the modernisation constructs of the nation, nation-state, sovereignty, nationalism, democracy, freedom, and market economy. The challenge is to overturn the embedded logic of the Newtonian-Cartesian prejudices that inform the most cherished metaphors found in the study of the international relations of the Caribbean. I view this contribution as another installment to a 'theoretical practice' that is conscious of the heterogeneous social totality of the global/local dialectic.

Endnotes

1. Research for this article was funded by a grant from Bucknell University.
2. Herein after called Shiprider Agreement or Shiprider. The term shiprider(s) refers to a person(s) designated by a State(s) to ride on a designated vessel of another state in the performance of duties defined under the 'counter maritime drug operations' between the US and a Caribbean state.
3. See Caribbean/United States Summit. Partnership for Prosperity and Security in the Caribbean. Bridgetown, Barbados. The White House, Office of the Press Secretary, Bridgetown, Barbados May 10, 1997.

4. The Shiprider Agreement signed by CARICOM member states like St Lucia and Trinidad and Tobago is identical to the one signed between the US and the Dominican Republic in March 23, 1995. See Agreement between the Government of the United States of America and the Government of the Dominican Republic Concerning Maritime Counter-Drug Operations.

5. Griffith (1997: 6-13) divides security into four aspects, military, political, economic, and environmental. But Griffith does not make any connection between how security has been redefined and the new departures in contemporary capitalist globalisation.

6. I use the US/Trinidad and Tobago Agreement (US/T&T Agreement) as a case study, considering that all CARICOM states, except Barbados and Jamaica, signed the Model Shiprider Agreement with the US. The Dominican Republic also signed the Model Shiprider Agreement in March 1995. The US/St Lucia Agreement is identical to the US/Dominican Republic Agreement. My discussion of Trinidad and Tobago holds for the Dominican Republic and CARICOM states, except Barbados and Jamaica.

7. Brown argues that 'an international obligation imposed on the sending state to indemnify the receiving state for any claims attributable to its forces resulting from counter-drug operations, is suggested as a preferable alternative' (1997: 66).

8. Trinidad & Tobago Prime Minister Basdeo Panday makes light of opposition to the Shiprider Agreement when he says: 'We can't even guard the north coast, but they want the right to chase traffickers into Key West. Great. Great.... And if the Americans are chasing drug runners on reaching the 12 mile limit with Trinidad waters I imagine they must pull brakes, stop, take the phone and ring to get permission to come in' (Viarruel 1997:7).

9. When the US/T&T Agreement was signed in 1996, there was no public outcry or controversy. The controversy erupted when opposition from Barbados and Jamaica to aspects of the Model Shiprider Agreement became public and it was learnt that Trinidad & Tobago and other CARICOM states had signed without due regard to the foreign policy consultation provisions of the Treaty of Chaguaramas which created CARICOM. Patrick Manning argued that 'the CARICOM Treaty' provides for 'member states to consult with each other on foreign policy issues' and that by 'failing to following (sic) that arrangement, this country had violated the CARICOM Treaty.' For other details see Sheppard (1997a-b); Dumas (1997a-d); Viarruel (1997); Cezair (1997); and Horne (1997).

10. There are differences in the titles of the Shiprider Agreements between the US and Trinidad and Tobago and between Barbados and the US. The

US/T&T Shiprider Agreement is titled: Agreement Between the Government of the Republic of Trinidad and Tobago and the Government of the United States of America concerning Counter-Drug Operations. The Barbados/US Agreement is titled: the Agreement Between the Government of Barbados and the Government of the United States of America Concerning Co-operation in Suppressing Illicit Maritime Drug Trafficking.

11. See Article 14, pp. 11-12 for 'Verification of Registration' provisions of the Agreement.

12. Article 19 deals with Claims for 'damage, injury, or loss resulting from a boarding and search carried out under the Agreement...' (p. 13).

13. See Article 15, p. 12 for details about Jurisdiction over Detained Vessels. While the Party under which a suspect vessel is registered may exercise jurisdiction over the vessel cargo. and persons aboard, the Party may 'subject to its Constitution and laws waive its right to exercise jurisdiction ...'

14. See Article 18 for information about Asset Sharing 'by the respective Parties and the rights of the seizing Party in waters seaward of the territorial sea of a given State'.

15. Termination of the US/T&T Shiprider Agreement shall occur one year after 'written notification to the other Party through the diplomatic channel' (US/T&T Agreement, p. 6).

16. According to the *Trinidad Express* of May 15, 1997, p. 2, Leader of the Opposition People s National Movement (PNM) in Trinidad, Patrick Manning suggested that Trinidad and Tobago signed the Shiprider Agreement 'in that form only because of a problem one of your Ministers has with a relative in Miami'.

17. In December 1996, a special drug summit was held in Barbados to deal with the issues that surfaced in the Barbados/Jamaica negotiations with the US over the Shiprider Agreement. See Communique. Fifth Special Meeting of the Conference of Heads of Government of the Caribbean Community, Barbados. December 16, 1996:2.

18. The Agreement Between the Government of Jamaica and the Government of the United States of America Concerning Cooperation in Suppressing Illicit Maritime Drug Trafficking makes specific reference to the 1988 Convention: 'Recalling further that paragraph 9 of Article 17 of the 1988 · Convention requires the Parties to consider entering into bilateral arrangements to carry out, or to enhance the effectiveness of the provisions of Article 17'.

19. Arguments about how the Shiprider Agreement has affected or is affecting the CARICOM regional integration process may be gleaned from statements by Trinidad and Tobago PNM Opposition Leader Patrick Manning see Sheppard (1997); Ramphal (1997); Demas (1997); Dumas, (1997). The main issue areas stressed by these sources include implications of globalisation for West Indian unity and identity; trade, aid and WTO issues around US banana policy; recolonisation and other concerns. None of the media coverage cited in this article mentioned shiprider agreements with Haiti or the Dominican Republic or any of the special agreements between Cuba and the US on counter-drug interdiction. Hence the widening of CARICOM implications do not seem to have surfaced in the controversy over Shiprider in the CARICOM area.

20. That the US is not a party to the 1982 Law of the Sea Convention, and the fact that the US opted out of the 'dispute settlement resolution mechanism of the 1988 Convention as it relates to other State Parties' (Brown 1997: 33) was of real concern to Barbados and Jamaica.

21. Brown (1997: 65-71) discusses the Regional Security System (RSS) in the Eastern Caribbean in connection with Shiprider. She stresses sub-regional cooperation between RSS member states in areas that include control over fisheries, immigration, pollution, customs, and excise and the 'prevention and interdiction of traffic in illegal narcotics drugs'. She notes the RSS arrangement may yet provide a 'contrasting and preferable approach to ... the Shiprider agreement' (1997: 65, 66).

22. Elliott Abrams, a senior fellow at the Hudson Institute, was Assistant Secretary of State for Inter-American Affairs under Ronald Reagan. Reginald Dumas, who was Ambassador of Trinidad & Tobago to the US in the late 1980s, describes Abrams as an 'unreconstructed hawk,..., given to right-wing rigidities and to cheerful prevarication in the defense of those rigidities'. See 'The Shiprider Solution' *Trinidad Express*, May 21, 1997:9.

23. Maingot's (1997) simplistic notion of hegemony is at one with the logic of mainstream international relations ideology. His argument comports with the 'mobilization of bias', without a semblance of bias because it expresses the 'rules of the game', around the seemingly pragmatic, predominant values and institutional procedures. His tendency to represent the dominant view without appearing to do so is also transparent in the international relations writings by Griffith (1997) and Braveboy-Wagner (1989).

24. The US has opposed signing the anti-land mine treaty being negotiated in France. US opposition is based on typical national security claims.

25. Capitalism presupposes the ability of capital to be mobile in material and juridical terms, but this does not presuppose that each and every capitalist

can move his capital around the country or world at will. Notwithstanding the relevance of his criticism of mainstream globalisation arguments on capital mobility, Cox (1997) strikes me as confused about the meaning of the mobility of capital in Marxist terms. His idea of the mobility of capital is heavily constrained by the logic of the primacy of national states/space. Though Cox appreciates the primacy of production relations in the fundamental capitalist process, an essentialist (geographical determinist) construction of national states informs his notion of capital mobility. Holloway (1995) and Burnham (1995) offer compelling interpretations of the relationship between global capital and national states. Swyngedouw (1997) offers a more useful concept of spatial scale.

26. See Landau 1988: 71-72 for a discussion of US reactions and policy responses to the nationalisation strategies of the Cuban Revolution. There is clear evidence of the US strategy to reinforce the global power of capital to secure the mobility rights of capital across national borders. The US embargo against Cuba has much to do with protecting global capitalism against a new wave of revolutionary options in the neocolonial world. The Cold War was used to mask US led counterrevolutionary offensives against revolutionary alternatives to capitalism and imperialism.

27. See Davidson (1992) for a pertinent elaboration of what he calls the 'curse of the nation-state' in relation to the 'black man's burden' in Africa.

28. According to Landau, former General Smedley Butler (U.S. Marine Corps) summed up his experience as protector of US imperialism in Latin America and the Caribbean this way:

> During [my thirty-three years in the Marine Corps] I spent most of my time being a high-class muscle man for Big Business, for Wall Street, and for the bankers.... I was a racketeer for capitalism.... I helped make Haiti and Cuba a decent place for the National City Bank.... I helped purify Nicaragua for the international banking house of Brown Brothers in 1909-1912. I brought light to the Dominican Republic for American sugar interests in 1916. I helped make Honduras 'right' for American United Fruit Companies in 1903. *These and other activities allowed the US to establish* a tacit protectorate over the region" (Landau 1988: 19, italics mine).

29. Robert Cox argues that the passing of the Cold War between the US and the USSR changed the form of the Cold War, but does not negate the 'substantive meaning of the Cold War', in relation to the national security state and doctrine, intelligence and surveillance systems, and the co-optation of the political leadership of subordinate states, etc. (Sinclair 1996: 4-5).

30. Gonzalez (1996: 91) argues that 'Cuba has begun to see the other Caribbean nations more as potential economic and commercial partners than as possible allies in its conflict with its northern neighbour.' Gonzalez (1996: 92-93) discusses trends in Cuba-Caribbean trade since the 1960s. Cuba-Caribbean trade has never exceeded the $57.6 million level (1974-1978). In 1994, trade between Cuba and the Caribbean was $35 million. Gonzalez acknowledges that Cuba-Caribbean trade is not likely to 'absorb considerable proportions' of the exports of both sides.

Bibliography

Abrams, Elliot 'The Shiprider Solution: Policing the Caribbean'. *The National Interest,* (Spring 1996) pp. 86-92.

Ariffin, Yohan 'The return of Marx in international relations theory', *Economy and Society,* 25: 1 (1996) pp. 127-135.

Aron, Raymond 'What is a theory of international relations?' *Journal of International Affairs,* 21: 2 (1996) pp. 185-206.

Balibar, Etienne 'The Nation Form: History and Ideology' *Review,* XIII: 3 (Summer 1990).

Basch, Linda, Nina Glick Schiller, and C. Szanton Blanc, *Nations Unbound: Transnational Projects, Postcolonial Predicaments and Deterritorialized Nation-States.* (Langhorne, PA: Gordon and Breach Science Publishers, 1990).

Bernal, Richard Strategic Global Repositioning and Future Economic Development in Jamaica. *The North-South Agenda Papers,* Number 18. (A Publication of the North-South Center Press, University of Miami, Coral Gables, Florida, 1996).

Blackman Associates Comprehensive Review of CARICOM Investment Climate. Commissioned by Caribbean Community Secretariat, Georgetown, Guyana (February (1996).

Bonefeld, Werner and John Holloway, eds *Global Capital, National State and the Politics of Money.* New York: St Martin's Press, 1995).

Brown, Kathy-Ann, 'THE SHIPRIDER MODEL: An Analysis of the U.S. Proposed Agreement Concerning Maritime Counter-Drug Operations in its Wider Legal Context,' *Contemporary Caribbean Legal Issues* Issue No: I. (Faculty of Law, University of the West Indies, Cave Hill, Barbados, 1997).

Burch, Kurt, 'The "Properties" of the State System and Global Capitalism' in *The Global Economy as Political Space;* ed. by Stephen J. Rosow, Naeem Inayatullah, & Mark Rupert. (Boulder: Lynne Rienner Publishers, 1994).

Burch, Kurt, *'Property' and the Making of the International System,* (Boulder: Lynne Rienner Publishers, 1997).

Burnham, Peter, 'Capital, Crisis and the International state System' in *Global Capital, National State and the Politics of Money*; eds. Werner Bonefeld and John Holloway. New York: St Martin's Press, 1995).

Callari Antonio and David F. Ruccio, *Introduction: Postmodern Materialism and the Future of Marxist Theory in Postmodern Materialism and the Future of Marxist Theory* (Hanover, NH: University Press of New England, 1996).

Cezair, P. L., 'Sovereignty debate – to be or not to be?' *Trinidad Guardian*, May 20, 1997, p. 9.

Cox, Kevin, 'Globalization and the Politics of Distribution: A Critical Assessment' *in Spaces of Globalization: Reasserting the Power of the Local* (New York: Guilford Press, 1997).

Cox, Kevin, ed., *Spaces of Globalization: Reasserting the Power of the Local* (New York: Guilford Press, 1997).

Cox, Robert W., 'Preface' in Robert W. Cox with Timothy J. Sinclair, *Approaches to World Order*. (Cambridge: Cambridge University Press, 1996a).

Cox Robert W., 'Influences and Commitments' in Robert W. Cox with Timothy J. Sinclair, *Approaches to World Order*, (Cambridge: Cambridge University Press, 1996b).

Cullenberg, Stephen, 'Althusser and the Decentering of the Marxist Totality' in *Postmodern Materialism and the Future of Marxist Theory*, edited by Antonio Callari and David F. Ruccio, (Hanover, NH: University Press of New England, 1996).

Davidson, Basil, *The Black Man's Burden; Africa and the Curse of the Nation-State*, (New York: Times Books, 1992).

Demas, William G., Critical Issues in Caribbean Development. Number 1: *West Indian Development and the Deepening & Widening of the Caribbean Community*. (Kingston, Jamaica: Ian Randle Publishers, 1997).

Dumas, Reginald, 'Many issues still to be clarified', *Trinidad Express*, May 15, 1997, p. 9.

_____, 'The Shiprider Solution', *Trinidad Express*, May 21, 1997, p. 9.

_____, 'What did T&T gain from Shiprider', *Trinidad Express*, May 27, 1997, p. 9.

_____, 'Maritime cowboy notion', *Trinidad Express*, May 30, 1997, p. 8.

Dupuy, Alex, *Haiti in the New World Order: The Limits of the Democratic Revolution*. (Boulder: Westview Press, 1996).

Ferguson, Tyrone, 'Sovereignty. Shiprider and Small States' Department of Government, University of the West Indies (St Augustine. Trinidad and Tobago, 1997).

Figueros, Miguel Alejandro and Plasencia Vidal, Sergio, 'The Cuban Economy in the 1990s: Problems and Prospects' in *The Caribbean in the Global Political Economy*, ed. Hilbourne A. Watson (Boulder: Lynne Rienner Publishers, 1994).

Gonzalez Nunez, Gerardo, 'International Relations between Cuba and the Caribbean in the 1990s: Challenges and Perspectives' in *Latin American Perspectives*, 24: 5 (September 1997) pp. 81-95.

Gramsci, Antonio, *Prison Notebooks*. Translated by Quentin Hoare, (New York: International Publishers, 1971).

Harvey, David 'Globalization in Question' in *Rethinking Marxism*, 8: 4 (Winter 1995) pp.1 - 17 .

Hegel, Georg W., *Philosophy of Right* (Oxford: Clarendon Press, 1942).

Henke, Holger, 'Toward an Ontology of Caribbean Existence', *Social Epistemology*, 11: 1, (Jan.-March 1997) pp. 39-58.

_____., 'Re-alignments in the State-Business-Class Triangle and the Negotiation of Foreign Policy Priorities in Jamaica during the 1980s'. Paper delivered at the 51st Annual New York State Political Science Association Conference, John Jay College of Criminal Justice, CUNY, (April 18-19, 1997).

Holloway, John, 'Global Capital and the National State' in *Global Capital, National State and the Politics of Money*, Ed. Werner Bonefeld and John Holloway. (New York: St Martin's Press, 1995).

Horne, Louise, 'Shiprider Reeks of Bases Agreement' *Trinidad Express*, May 19, 1997, pp. 30-31.

Ingo, Walter, *The Secret Money Market: Inside the Dark World of Tax Evasion, Financial Fraud, Insider Trading, Money Laundering and Capital Flight*, (New York: Harper and Row Publishers, 1990).

Jessop, David, 'Can the Caribbean cope with free trade?' *Trinidad Sunday Express*, 26 April, 1996, p. 10.

Kerry, John, *The New War*, (New York: Simon and Schuster, 1997).

_____, 'Organized Crime goes Global While the US stays Home', *Washington Post*, Sunday, May 11, 1997: C1. 4.

Lewis, Patsy 'The Caribbean and the Restructuring of the United Nations: Alternatives to Abrams' Shiprider Solution' Journal of Commonwealth and Comparative Politics, 34: 3, (November 1996) pp. 235-247.

Maharaj, Kathleen, 'AG defends Shiprider ... as T&T sign new treaty with UK', *Trinidad Express*, May 15, 1997, p. 2.

Maingot, Anthony P., 'The Sovereignty versus Security Paradox in the Caribbean' in *Cuba and the Caribbean: Regional Issues and Trends in the Post-Cold War*, Eds J. Tulchin, A. Serbin and R. Hernandez(Wilmington, DE.: Scholarly Resources Inc, 1997).

Marx, K. and F. Engels, *Manifesto of the Communist Party* (Moscow: Progress Publishers, 1952).

Parris, Carl, 'A Limited Sovereignty for Caribbean States' (Institute of International Relations, University of the West Indies, St Augustine, Trinidad and Tobago, 1997).

Pilger, John, *The New Rulers of the World*. (London: Verso Books, 2002).

Ramphal, Sir Shridath, 'The West Indies in the Wider World: Compulsions of Regional Engagement' Address by Sir Shridath Ramphal, Chancellor. Distinguished Lecture Series of the University of the West Indies, April 14, 1997, Mona, Jamaica.

Richards, Peter, 'Panday: Shiprider "sails on"' *Trinidad Guardian*, May 9, 1997: 1.

Rosenberg, Justin, 'A non-realist theory of sovereignty? Giddens' "The nation-state and violence"', *Millennium*, 19, (1997) pp. 249-59.

Rosenberg, Justin, *The Empire of Civil Society: A Critique of the Realist Theory of International Relations*, (London: Verso Books, 1994).

Rosow, Stephen J., N. Inayatullah, and M. Rupert, eds, *The Global Economy as Political Space* (Boulder: Lynne Rienner Publishers, 1994).

Sheppard, Suzanne, 'C-26 no part of Shiprider Agreement, says Maraj' *Trinidad Sunday Express* May 18, 1997, p. 14.

Sheppard, Suzanne, 'Manning: Shiprider signing violation of CARICOM treaty' *Trinidad Sunday Express*, May 18, 1997 p. 3.

Sinclair. Timothy J., 'Beyond international relations theory: Robert W. Cox and approaches to world order' in Robert W. Cox with Timothy J. Sinclair, *Approaches to World Order*, (Cambridge: Cambridge University Press, 1996).

Smith, Anthony D., *National Identity* (Reno: University of Nevada Press, 1991).

Sunday Express (Trinidad), 'Manning: Shiprider signing violation of CARICOM treaty,' May 18, 1997 p. 3.

Swyngedouw, Erik, 'Neither Global nor Local: Glocalization and the Politics of Scale' in *Spaces of Globalization: Reasserting the Power of the Local*, Ed. Kevin Cox. (New York: Guilford Press, 1997).

Teeple, Gary, *Globalization and the Decline of Social Reform* (Toronto: Garamond Press, 1995).

Tilly, Charles, *Coercion, Capital, and European States. AD 990-1992* (Boston: Blackwell Publishers, 1990).

Trinidad Express, 'Jamaica: New agreement different from old Shiprider', May 7, 1997, p.13.

_____, 'More Shiprider talks in B'dos', May 9, 1997 p. 15.

_____, 'Manning: Take Shiprider to Parliament for debate,' May 15, 1997, p. 2.

_____, 'Shiprider an odious treaty', May 17, 1997, p. 8.

_____, 'Manning gets copy of the shiprider agreement', May 17,1997, p. 6.

Trinidad Guardian, 'J'ca parliament ratifies shiprider', May 29, 1997, p.13.

Tulchin, Joseph S. and Ralph Espach, Eds. *Security in the Caribbean Basin: the challenge of regional cooperation*. (Boulder, Colo.: Lynne Rienner Publishers, 2000).

Viarruel, Alva, 'Panday: Shiprider a vital tool in drug fight' *Trinidad Express*, June 17, 1997, p.7.

Walker, Robert, *Inside/Outside: International Relations as Political Theory* (Cambridge: Cambridge University Press, 1993).

Waltz, Kenneth, *Man, the State and War,* (New York: Columbia University Press, 1959).

Watson, Hilbourne A., 'Globalization, Liberalism and the Caribbean: Deciphering the Limits of Nation, Nation-State and Sovereignty under Global Capitalism'. *Caribbean Studies,* 26:3-4:, (July-December 1993) 213-264.

_____, 'The Globalization of Finance: The Role and Status of the Caribbean' in The Political Economy of Drugs in the Caribbean. Edited by Ivelaw L. Griffith. (London: Macmillan Press) forthcoming.

_____, 'Global Change: Restructuring the Enterprise Culture and Power in Contemporary Barbados' in *Journal of Eastern Caribbean Studies,* 22: 3 (December, 1997).

Williams, Raymond, *Marxism and Literature*. (Oxford 1997).

12

Environmental Policy Challenges and Growth in Guyana

Lomarsh Roopnarine

Without any doubt, natural resources such as gold, diamond, bauxite, manganese and timber hold great possibility for development, providing these resources are carefully and skilfully mobilised. Some countries like Israel and Switzerland have become advanced precisely because they have exploited their human and natural resources wisely, while others, despite the lack of indigenous resources, have managed to become prosperous, like for example, the 'Asian Tigers'.[1] Unlike most countries in the developing world – India, Brazil, and Nigeria – where there are demographic pressures and shrinking natural resources, Guyana is fortunate to have an abundance of natural resources, many of which are still largely untapped and unexplored. It is widely assumed that if Guyana utilises these resources the country would be better positioned to deal with the throes of underdevelopment, stagnation and poverty. Guyana has accepted this responsibility, especially since the early 1990s, and implemented a host of environmental development strategies intended to embrace sustainable development and environmental protection goals.[2] However, economic growth has resulted in skewed management practices and increased pressures on the environment. Guyana's predicament to use its natural resources and turn around a slumping economy has been largely due, *inter alia*, to the asphyxiating bonds of colonialism, political corruption, administrative neglect, shortages of skilled environmental personnel, indebtedness, and above all, a lack of financial resources to monitor and regulate uncontrolled practices of foreign and domestic companies.[3]

Under colonial rule, a host of challenges – tropical heat, diseases, inhospitable terrain, and Amerindian resistance – prevented the colonisers from exploiting Guyana's environment successfully and putting in place effective environmental regulations. Alvin Thompson noted that the Dutch as well as the British never fully exploited Guyana's interior resources, except for a small export trade in timber and limited attention paid to small-scale gold and diamond operations from the 1880s.[4]The colonisers were careful not to divert the labour force from plantation agriculture along the narrow coastal strip, and thus designed policies to prevent the development of a population movement away from the plantation system. The consequence of all this was that Guyana became a mono-cultural cropping system, and little was done to open and develop the interior of the country, though few efforts were made to exploit gold and diamonds on the river-beds and to raise cattle on poor quality grasslands in the south.[5] The limited attention paid to developing Guyana's interior resources meant that colonisers made no genuine efforts to put in place environmental laws to protect the interior.[6]Thus, environmental regulations and laws were practically absent during the colonial period in Guyana.

Post-independent Guyana inherited a legacy of environmental problems regulated mainly to the coastlands. The European colonisers pulverised Guyana's wealth with no guiding environmental standards and left behind a corpus of environmental problems that still exist to this day. But, as for reasons mentioned earlier, the colonisers never fully tapped into the country's interior resources. Cut off from the coast, the interior was considered to be another country. The environmental problems that post-independent government (Peoples National Congress, PNC) inherited were mainly restricted to the coast. From 1970-85, the PNC under the leadership of Forbes Burnham, instituted a policy of Cooperative Socialism that was bent in severing ties with colonial powers. Cooperative Socialism was designed to develop Guyana's economy along indigenous routes, and as a consequence, the government nationalised most foreign companies and assumed control of eighty per cent of the economy. Monopolisation of the economy discouraged foreign investment in Guyana and this led indirectly to the protection of interior resources without any environmental specialists and procedures. The PNC administration, however, engaged in a series of development initiatives, which were not guided by safe environmental planning. Cooperative Socialism neglected environmental responsibilities and promoted unsound environmental projects. The government was too busy trying to hold on to dictatorial power and environmental concerns were suppressed and ignored and economic growth was marginal.

If the period under Cooperative Socialism experienced administrative environmental policy neglect and dictatorial rule, the ensuing years (1985-92) under Desmond Hoyte, were marked by environmental policy weakness and unethical managerial practices. The Hoyte administration opened Guyana to foreign investment in order to generate foreign exchange and deal with a crumbling, cash-starved economy. Generous concessions were given to foreign companies with rapacious environmental track records when Guyana did not even have an environmental stature or environmental regulations to remotely monitor large foreign companies. Moreover, there was a torrent of claims alleging rampant corruption and unethical practices among top officials in the Hoyte administration.[7] Marcus Colchester demonstrated skilfully that Guyana's economy registered growth rates because of the influx of foreign companies but it was achieved with tremendous environmental costs.[8]

The return to democracy in Guyana under the aegis of the Cheddi Jagan's People's Progressive Party (PPP) in 1992 sparked a ray of hope among majority of Guyanese.[9] After an interlude with allegations of corruption, the PPP administration has 'taken remedial actions toward existing environmental problems and to avert potentially adverse environmental effects [and] decided to embrace sustainable resources management and environmental conservation'.[10] Realising the quagmire of environmental problems in Guyana, the government in 1996 implemented the Environmental Protection Agency (EPA), which has been supported by a host of international agencies. These institutions, though influential, have not alleviated Guyana's environmental problems and the challenge of implementing more frontline policies to ensure that the balance of economic development and ecological preservation is practised is still alive.

DICTATORSHIP, ENVIRONMENTAL POLICY NEGLECT AND GROWTH

Various studies have put forward the thesis that authoritarian regimes seem to be unfriendly to the environment.[11] Authoritarian regimes generally are conducive to long-term environmental planning and law-making but legislations when implemented are only symbolic and are never fully enforced because authoritarian regimes do not expect to be removed from power.[12] Along with this retentionist view, authoritarian regimes are guided by policies of command and control in which power is essentially centralised in the hands of a few individuals. Government undertakings, especially on environmental matters, are notoriously secretive, and the general public is excluded from decision-making, or their concerns are not seriously taken into consideration. The government does accept some degree of cooperation but is recalcitrant on issues of widespread public participation in problem solving, including environmental matters.

Another equally salient characteristic of authoritarian regimes in regards to the environment is that they embrace what John Dryzek calls the 'Promethean Discourse', that is, natural resources are infinite, and there are no limits to economic growth.[13] According to this view, nature is there to be dominated and environmental concerns are not intentionally brought into the core of society's political, economic, and social systems. Rather, environmental matters are seen as sources of problems and are pushed and treated outside of these systems. Where there is a lack of openness and information about government policies coupled with a lack of freedom of speech as well as a muzzled press, the ramifications are that economic growth occurs at the expense of environmental degradation. The consequence is that the general public becomes ignorant and voiceless against environmental destruction while the government only accepts or observes environmental regulations in their breach. Guyana under Forbes Burnham's Cooperative Socialism is no exception.

Soon after Guyana's independence in 1966, and after a brief experiment with St. Lucian economist Sir Arthur Lewis' 'industrialisation by invitation' development model, Forbes Burnham embarked on an ambitious plan through the policy of cooperative socialism. The incantations of cooperative socialism were that it would reduce Guyana from colonial dependency and Guyanese would run the political, economic and social systems in the interest of Guyanese. Such policy was promoted by state ownership of the economy and central planning. Burnham and his development planners purported that the vehicle for development lies in the exploitation of natural resources, agricultural diversification, nationalisation of foreign assets and self-reliance.[14]

Within a decade, cooperative socialism failed dismally to live up to its vision and as Harry Dyett puts it, from the 'mid-1960s to the mid-1980s was a dark period in Guyana's history.'[15] Professor Clive Thomas observed that cooperative socialism never matched its objectives primarily because it never put the people at the centre of development and the main impediment to progress lay in its design. He further reiterated that political corruption intermixed with production crisis over two decades resulted in a widespread national crisis.[16] Distrust, disillusion, despair, marginalisation, poverty and unemployment, engulfed Guyana, and a generation of highly skilled, highly educated class of Guyanese emigrated to other Caribbean countries and further afield.[17] Although the Forbes Burnham administration repeatedly echoed sentiments of cooperative efforts and cooperative building, the reality was that a majority of Guyanese were excluded from the development process.[18] Cooperative socialism supported the interest of those who acquiesced to its demands and objectives in exchange for its survival, and opposing factions such as political and human rights organisations were systemically suppressed. Furthermore, Guyanese citizens' rights-to-know about government's undertakings were subverted. To this day, Guyanese are misinformed about the extent of environmental risks associated with certain chemicals used in their environment. Noxious substances, when used, are not generally disclosed to the public. Hazardous and toxic substances have assumed a secondary role, especially under the Burnham administration, since media coverage about potential risks of dangerous chemicals was downplayed. There was little or no public apprehension about risks chemicals might have posed to Guyanese society.

Another equally important caveat of cooperative socialism was that because it was so dictatorial, there were absences of opportunity for readjustment and reform concerning important issues such as environmental responsibilities. Meanwhile, the government continued to promote projects and institute environmental laws intended to preserve and protect the environment. At one level, these environmental laws were simply put in place to force the government to consider environmental values, which might otherwise be overlooked or ignored. At another level, these environmental laws were merely symbolic because the country's weak economic position impaired its ability to carry out environmental policy objectives.

In the absence of standards, it is difficult to assess correctly, in quantitative terms, the harmful impact development projects under cooperative socialism had on Guyana. Certainly, development projects under cooperative socialism and environmental concerns always pointed in the opposite direction. Lakhan et al (2000) stated that:

> An examination of national development plans of Guyana for the periods 1966-1972, 1972-1976, 1976-1981 and 1983 reveal that all the plans were devoid of ecological measures and no funds were allocated for environmental protection. The various plans stipulated the development of many large-scale land, water, and forestry resources projects, which degraded or destroyed ecological communities throughout the coastal and interior environments.

To this analysis, Lakhan et al added some more interesting information of how cooperative socialism approached environmental issues. They claimed that cooperative socialism engaged in a number of projects with little regard to the environment and in some ways replicated the closed systems of authoritarian governments. Moreover, the Forbes Burnham administration never embraced the sustainability debate sweeping through the world in the 1970s and 1980s. Guyana neglected to sign many multilateral treaties such as 'the 1971 Convention of Wetlands of International Importance Especially of Waterfowls Habitat, and the 1983 International Tropical Timber Agreement'.[19] Domestically, Guyana's environmental policy was also laggard. Economic constraints and mismanagement led to environmental policy neglect and irresponsibility. Under cooperative socialism (1966-85), real GDP grew only at 0.4 per cent a year. Statistics for the decade between 1970 and 1980 have shown that per capita growth was 0.2 per cent; agriculture, forestry and fishing registered at 0.1 per cent, while mining and quarrying were at a minus 4.3 percent. Except for manufacturing (4.8 percent), all major sectors of the economy showed marginal growth.[20] The reason for this sluggish growth was that the 'economy was plagued by dismal macroeconomic performance linked to the prevailing fiscal imbalance, foreign trade disequilibrium, and suppressed foreign exchange market. State intervention in major economic activities was rampant and prices, credit and foreign exchange was controlled'.[21] There was a direct correlation between dismal economic growth and lax environmental regulations. Except for the interior, all along the narrow coastal strip, especially in urban areas, the infrastructure broke down, roads were left unattended, seawalls, sewage and water systems collapsed, garbage piled up almost everywhere, and dumping in rivers and drains were a common occurrence.[22] 'All the basic social services: health, education, housing and social welfare, collapsed as well. Worse still, by the end of the 1980s, income inequality was marked'.[23]

Several explanations can be proffered as to why environmental policies were neglected during the period of cooperative socialism. Although Forbes Burnham stated repeatedly that Guyana was a cooperative republic, the administration was structurally hierarchal. Each tier within the hierarchy was too busy looking out for their spheres of interest and therefore forestalled the long-term interests of the nation. As important information (money included) ascended from the top echelon of the administration, and disseminated to the desired level, vital aspects of it were inevitably lost. The personnel who were responsible for this information were obliged and disciplined to maintain the status quo and subsequently were less open or willing to acknowledge anything different unless there were opportunities for bribes and kickbacks. Government officials were not scrutinised and Guyana was reeling in lawlessness. So environmental matters were faced with a conundrum: the more the Burnham administration became corrupt, the less it was opened to other issues such as environmental policies. One major setback of cooperative socialism was that it stifled views from various directions. Foremost was the suppression of interactive problem solving that involves individuals from within and outside the government. Effective environmental policies invariably require, *inter alia,* debate, hearing, investigation, and questioning. But Burnham was adamant about not allowing room for alternative opinions because he believed that it would ultimately weaken his power base, and therefore never embraced environmental policies seriously. Environmental affairs were subsequently decentralised among various departments within the government, causing much confusion as to who should be addressed when specific issues arose. Because of this, the Burnham administration is sometimes regarded as anti-environmental, but it was more than that. The personnel who set the government's responsibility for the environment had in mind to solve environmental problems but it turned out a problem displacement, leading to an implementation policy deficit. The structure of the government created many characteristic processes and problems associated with the management of environmental matters. Cooperative socialism operated behind an opaque exterior and the protection of the environment depended on moods rather than the law and responsibility. Not only was it difficult to bring critical environmental issues to the government but it also was impossible to hold the government accountable for environmental recklessness. The repercussion was that there was never a petulant national mood about environmental matters as noticed elsewhere in the world, although it should be noted that the international environmental grass roots movement was hardly conceptualised before the 1960s. Guyanese were subdued and ignorant about environmental issues and Guyana as whole was deprived of what environmentalists call a 'learning curve'.

Paradoxically, under cooperative socialism Guyana's forest resources remained almost unexplored not because of design but because of deprivation. The administration did not have the financial means and technologies necessary to exploit the country's forest resources to its fullest potential. Guyana was constrained by the closed door of cooperative socialism that de-emphasised and discouraged the role private investment could have played to develop the country's interior resources. One must emphasis, however, that the role of private investment must be combined with a favourable environment for development. To do otherwise, might run the risk of promoting inefficient and irreversible environmental destruction and even fuel a decline in overall welfare of the host country. Some studies have put forward the 'Pollution Holas' thesis that foreign firms are forced to use cleaner technologies and practice safe environmental standards at home, which they diffuse to host countries.[24] Two World Bank studies (Wheeler et al 1997; Pargal and Wheeler 1995) rebutted this hypothesis and showed that other forces such as effective national regulations and community pressures can actually lead to safer environmental practice.

Under cooperative socialism, Guyana succeeded in offloading many of its environmental problems onto a concentrated area, the coastlands, while leaving the interior somewhat undisturbed. Reduced to the essentials, Guyana sacrificed one area of the country for the protection of the other. Interestingly, this is what actually occurs at the international level. A clean environment, for example, in the United States or Britain may be due in part because dirty manufacturing industries are bought or transferred to poor countries.[25] Likewise, deforestation in Brazil occurs to meet the needs of developed nations.

There is clear evidence that, even though full environmental costs are not internalised, certain resources and intensive pollution industries have a locational preference for areas of low environmental standards. There is also evidence that host countries do not enforce domestic standards in order to attract and retain investors, and that international investors have often encouraged such behaviour.'[26]

Alongside this 'pollution haven hypothesis' – companies will move their operations to less developed countries to take advantage of slack environmental regulations and countries may deliberately under value their environment to attract new investment – there has been growing involvement of NGOs and community groups against the influx of suspected and dirty foreign firms and industries in their neighbourhood. They have adopted the NIMBY (not in my back yard) phenomenon exercised by rich communities in developed nations. The World Bank (2000) has documented cases in Indonesia, Brazil, Korea, Columbia and Mexico where communities have organised themselves and prevented the installation of dirty industries. 'Although these groups [communities] vary from region to region, the pattern is similar everywhere: Factories negotiate directly with local actors in response to threats of social, political or sanctions if they fail to compensate the community or reduce emissions'.[27]

While the practice of 'communities as informal regulators' against pollution is encouraging and forward-looking, it has been slow in reaching Guyana. Except for Guyana Human Rights Association (GHRA), local autochthonous oppositional groups against environmental malpractice are largely far and few between; and even the ones that do exist have not turned the corner in their fight against environmental degradation. Non Governmental Organisations (NGOs) and civil society in Guyana need greater access to information about dirty industries and government transactions if they are to scrutinise them and protect themselves and the environment. Certainly, this lack of local community solidarity against environmental ills allowed Forbes Burnham to some degree to practise in Guyana a new form of 'internal environmental colonialism'. This trend, however, was radically reversed under the Desmond Hoyte administration.

REFORM, ENVIRONMENTAL POLICY CONFLICTS, CONTRADICTIONS AND GROWTH

The widely shared perception that Guyana's environment under cooperative socialism was neglected presented a major challenge to the Desmond Hoyte administration. Interestingly, comprehensive reforms based on coherent policies that would have encouraged innovative change were not pursued fully. The administration introduced liberal economic reforms reminiscent of the former Soviet Union's *perestroika* and Great Britain's *Thatcherism*. Hoyte declared that his 'single ambition is to put this economy right. I want to put it on the path to recovery'.[28] Yet, this was mostly a matter of expedience and comprise. Although the Hoyte years did see a retreat from the excesses that so epitomised the Burnham era, corruption, mismanagement, and thievery still prevailed. Among the reasons for this was that Hoyte was moulded and anointed by Forbes Burnham. According to the *Financial Times*, 'even the President [Hoyte] had wanted to reform the creaking political machinery of the country, powerful party bosses might not allow him to threaten the hegemony of the PNC'.[29]

Desmond Hoyte brought Guyana again into mainstream Caribbean economics and broke tradition with the Burnham era, especially with the nationalisation of foreign companies and the restriction on private investment and ownership.[30] The main locus of Hoyte's liberalisation plan was to revive Guyana's economy through foreign investment and maximise the use of the country's natural resources. Given the country's history of dependence on the state-owned sugar and bauxite industries for most of its foreign exchange, the development of the country's interior resources was not surprising. Since Guyana was undermined by two decades of cooperative socialism, international financial agencies such as the International Monetary Fund (IMF) and the World Bank were invited to guide the privatisation and development process. The process of reform was carried out with much mendicancy and commitment to the IMF and World Bank prescriptions.[31] The nature of the 'IMF medicine' caused Guyana to slump into a parlous economic state: poverty, unemployment, crime, and mass emigration increased to unprecedented heights.

The liberalisation policy of the Hoyte administration was discomfiting for scientific professionals and environmentalists since it was bereft of any meaningful environmental laws and regulations. Without much pre-planning, without much research, and without much debate, the Hoyte administration committed itself to leasing Guyana's natural resources to foreign companies to bring in foreign exchange reserves. The main environmental problem the Hoyte administration faced was that it had increased the flow of foreign investment and exacerbated the inefficient allocation of Guyana's natural resources, while urban areas were neglected. Economic benefits were achieved with environmental and social costs – rapacious mining and increased poverty, especially to the disadvantage. Colchester conceded that the administration handed generous concessions to foreign companies, many of which have been known to have terrible environmental track records in the world, especially in Southeast Asia.[32] Nick Mabey and Richard McNally identified one key interaction between foreign investment and the environment: 'Natural resource seeking investors have a poor record of environmental management relative to global best practice. Often investors prevent host countries maximising returns from their resources, encouraging over-exploitation and unsustainable use'.[33] Much the same environmental carelessness was identified in Guyana as critics charged that the government did not have the resources to monitor and control foreign companies. Guyana did not have an environmental protection agency (EPA) nor were there any genuine efforts to install an Environmental Impact Assessment (EIA), an institution renowned, when applied effectively, to resist the multitude of environmental derangements (nipping pollution problems in the bud). Conventional wisdom and common knowledge dictate that since the Hoyte administration lacked the environmental mechanism and wherewithal to protect the interior resources large foreign companies did not obey the meagre environmental regulations ostensibly in force. The result was that wanton marauding of forest resources went unchecked. Worse still, the Hoyte administration's approach to environmental standards punctuated the sometimes misguided, predatory view developed nations have about Third World governments. Proponents of developed nations claimed that Third World governments are not genuinely interested in carrying-out sustainable development and would not modify their development plans for the sake of the global environment.[34]

Apart from the problems of institutional capacity, mismanagement, ineptitude, and insurmountable economic obstacles, there were testimonies that members of the Hoyte administration allocated concessions in a veil of secrecy, particularly to the two largest foreign investors in Guyana: Omai Gold Mines and Barama Timber Company. Prime Minister Sam Hinds remarked that 'his government [Hoyte administration] never made public, nor ever laid in Parliament any agreements signed by OGML, Demerara Ltd., Barama, or Aroamiama Mining Company. It was left to the PPP/Civic government to take these agreements to the National Assembly'.[35] Government officials were accused of plundering the public purse for their own material interests and benefits and were thoroughly indifferent to environmental values. Conspicuously missing from these individuals were concerns to remedy environmental problems. Corruption leads to economic and social underdevelopment as well as undermining the public trust and confidence towards governance. One of the most disturbing characteristics about corruption is that natural resources are generally undervalued. Colchestor concluded that 'under the liberation policies of the Hoyte administration, foreign companies investing in forestry were accorded extraordinarily generous terms to exploit enormous timber concessions. Most of the agreements they reached with the government are secret.'[36] Even more controversial were problems surrounding the Guyana Forest Commission (GFC) and Guyana Geology and Mines Commission (GGMC), institutions bearing the heaviest burden of responsibility for forest resource protection.

The *Catholic Standard* wrote that these institutions shouldered too many responsibilities that translated into broad mandates, posing serious challenges.[37] The GFC and the GGMC embraced a large and complex set of programs ranging across a wide spectrum of environmental management. The staggering range of responsibilities was perhaps one major reason why environmental policy implementation was elusive and repudiated, although one cannot overlook that laggard environmental policy enforcement was a continuing inheritance from the Burnham years. The World Bank remarked that the GFC and the GGMC lacked transparency and most transactions were regarded as confidential and not opened to the public.[38] There is hope that this attitude will probably change in the future in light of the US Foreign Corruption Practices Act, which makes bribery of a foreign official a criminal offence. In February 1999, this discipline was extended internationally as an agreement was struck between the Organisation of American States and the Organisation for Economic Co-operation and Development (OECD) Convention on Combating Bribery of a Foreign Public Officials in International Business.[39] As has been so evident in most developing countries, under the Hoyte administration, there was also a mismatch between responsibilities assigned to environmental departments and financial resources required for their accomplishment. Environmental-marginal departments were poorly funded and poorly staffed, and many deficiencies within these institutions led to malpractice, impropriety and unethical practices.

A different, but equally contentious problem was the use of thallium sulphate as a rodenicide on sugar cane. According to Jang Singh, the Guyana state-owned sugar corporation (Guysuco) used thallium sulphate on sugar cane crops along Guyana's populated coast when the World Health Organisation (WHO) recommended against the use of thallium in 1973. The Hoyte administration bought and used thallium because it was economically feasible. Singh insisted that the 'amount [of thallium] kept in storage by Guysuco is enough to kill the entire population of Guyana....'[40] The *Stabroek News* on March 6, 1987 ran a headline titled the entire 'Country [was] placed on Alert'. Although researchers found thallium and other chemicals in soils and sediments of coastal Guyana,[41] the latency and impact of these chemicals on Guyanese would not become clinically evident until some time later. Hazardous chemicals whose malignancy has been documented in the United States illustrate that it takes sometimes 15 to 50 years after exposure for signs of illness to appear. Given the nature of Guyanese politics, conclusive evidence about thallium use and its effects on Guyana's population may not appear in the lifetime of any Guyanese living today.

The environmental policy challenge the Hoyte administration faced in 1980s and early 1990s has not been peculiar to Third World governments. Poor governments generally give out reasonable concessions to foreign investors on the basis that they would bring in foreign exchange, technologies, skills, jobs, and perhaps with hope that foreign investment would lead to the mushroom of ancillary industries. Poor governments also are generally impatient and oscillatory when negotiating with foreign investors and therefore bargain from a position of weakness. Foreign investors argue that they are the risk-takers and poor host countries are the risk-avoiders since the latter do not invest the capital.[42] An examination into the Hoyte administration policy towards foreign investment reveals these characteristics. The Hoyte administration rubbed shoulders with foreign investors and overlooked two important economic/ environmental nemeses: the function of the scarcity of Guyana's natural resources on the world market should have allowed the country to bargain from a position of strength; and 'concession contracts' should have been viewed as a 'concession process' subjected to change because of the country's weak environmental standards and weak currency.[43] The absence of these two fundamental principles meant that Guyana settled for low environmental standards and sold itself short when handing concessions to foreign investors; this is national prostitution. Not all foreign investors contribute to environmental ills, but to rely on, or place environmental responsibilities on foreign investors to safeguard the environment certainly increases the likelihood of national security threats and environmental problem proliferation; it is no different than putting the fox to guard the chicken coop. In this regard, the Hoyte administration became a victim of circumstances. The large foreign companies the government was intended to regulate, regulated it.

Under the Hoyte administration, Guyana's economy was in perilous straits, especially in the 1980s. Per capita growth between 1980 and 1990 was minus 3.9 per cent per annum. No sectors of the economy experienced growth rates during this period.

At the macroeconmic level, price inflation, which had grown by two percent per annum in the 1960s and 10 per cent in the 1970s, had jumped to 33 per cent per annum in the 1980s. Massive increases in the domestic money supply became the order of the day. The external current account deficit rose to an extraordinary level, averaging 50 per cent of export earnings in the 1980s. External borrowing led to a situation where per capita external debt was US$2,800 (one of the highest in the world).[44]

But in 1991 and 1992, the economy registered positive growth rates at 6.0 and 7.3 percent respectively. Liberal policies, in particular, the Economic Recovery Programme (ERP) had certainly contributed to the growth of the economy. The ERP embraced a market-oriented economy, dismantled state controls, abolished price controls, eliminated most import prohibitions, and divested public enterprises.[45] While it was encouraging that the Hoyte administration had such positive growth rates, nuanced circumstances conspired to prevent the integration of economic growth with sound environmental practice. The sinews of economic growth were cancelled out by the huge national debt (US$2.2 billion in 1992) and the harsh impact the IMF structural adjustment programme had on Guyanese. If the quality of life is used as a proxy for environmental performance, the Hoyte administration is seen to have a mixed performance. While the situation at international level had improved (debt forgiveness and debt rescheduling in particular), and income at home had risen, 'poverty increased, health and educational standards fell, and infrastructure crumbled. Many of Guyana's brightest talents chose to emigrate rather than continue to suffer the straitened circumstances of the domestic economy', and 'nearly 75 percent of the population sinking below the poverty line'.[46]

Unfortunately, the negative relationship between struggling economic growth (that favours the richest groups in society) and environmental recklessness has been noticed globally. The World Bank (1997) remarked that liberalisation has caused the world per capita output to increase from US$614 to US$4,908 in the last 30 years. But this growth has not been free from social and environmental costs. Mabey and Richard (1999) wrote that the World Resources Institute (WRI), United Nations Environmental Programme (UNEP) and the United Nations Development Programme (UNDP) in 1997 found:

> Global poverty and inequality continues to rise: the number of people in absolute has grown to 1.3 billion (though the proportion in poverty has fallen). Many of the less developed country, especially in Sub-Saharan Africa, have become locked into economic stagnation fuelled by falling commodity prices, conflict and debt. Between 1960 and 1994 the ratio of the income of the richest 20 percent to the poorest 20 percent increased from 30:1 to 78:1.

The World Wildlife Fund (WWF) in 1998 claimed that the environment had also deteriorated over the past quarter of a century. It estimated that global freshwater ecosystems have declined by 50 per cent, the world forests by 10 per cent, and global energy has increased by 70 per cent. Why this discrepancy in performance? Partly, it lies in what drives environmental policy globally. As noticed in Suriname and in other developing countries, matters of economic development were also accorded a higher priority under the Hoyte administration than benign environmental practice. Desmond Hoyte was graded more on the performance of the economy than his success to balance economic growth with environmental protection. The government glorified development goals, and as long as these development goals showed some signs of progress, the government faced no political or public challenge to commit itself to environmental activities. The Hoyte administration anticipated that environmental regulations would rise above expectations, and therefore reasoned that this would defeat the purpose of having large foreign firms operate in Guyana. The country experienced a 'race-to-the bottom' environmental standard and adapted a 'pollute now-clean up later' attitude as evidenced by the clear absence of political allure to introduce cost-effective, cost-saving devices, and cost-benefit analysis to guide environmental policy protection. The government was slow and loath to respond to environmental challenges and environmental matters were evanescent, lacking a constant course.

DEMOCRACY, ENVIRONMENTAL POLICY AWARENESS AND GROWTH

The passing of rule from the PNC to the PPP in 1992 under the first free and fair election since independence was a turning point in Guyana's political history. Most independent analysts concurred that Guyana actually became independent in 1992, not in 1966, since the latter date exuded more theory than practice. The Jagan administration in 1992 inherited a desk full of problems: Guyana was politically corrupt; economically bankrupted; socially polarised along racial lines; and environmentally inimical. The Jagan administration began to rule Guyana with little experience and repertoire, especially in the domain of democracy partly because of long years of political isolation by the ruling PNC and partly because the PPP was Marxist-oriented.[47] But Guyana did improve substantially both at the micro and macro level. Yet despite these achievements, the sense of malaise was not lifted, and new policy initiatives have not brought a dramatic change. Guyana is still reeling from political corruption, bribery, crime, poverty, and mass migration, although it should be emphasised that Guyana is better off today than when it was under 28 years of PNC rule.

The PPP administration chose to maintain the liberalised Economic Recovery Program (ERP) put in place by the Hoyte government and also handed out generous concessions to foreign investors, many of who have been reputed to comply minimally with environmentally acceptable standards. The PPP government, however, has displayed more transparency and openness, and is more pragmatic about environmental issues. There has been over the past nine years an explosive growth of environmental legislation in Guyana demonstrating that the government has begun to embrace environmental values more seriously, even though the enforcement of environmental regulations has been at a plodding pace. The three-year moratorium declaration in 1995 on issuing of new logging concessions and the implementation of the National Environmental Action Plan (NEAP) are manifestations of this growing ecological sensitivity. But, as we have seen so often in Third World countries where there is an accomplishment or a local success story, it follows naturally that there are hidden problems elsewhere. In 1995 one of Guyana's major environmental mishaps occurred when cyanide from Omai Gold Mines Ltd spilled into the Essequibo River threatening the security of communities and exposing not only the fragility of Guyana's environmental regulations but also showing how ill-prepared Guyana was in regards to environmental protection.[48] No doubt this environmental mishap arose from Guyana's maladroit monitoring capacity and the blatant disregard of foreign companies to take the environment more seriously. Environmental policy is the most complex of all government transactions because it requires, *inter alia*, a diverse array of information to be collected, arranged, analysed coherently, and then placed into the ambit of decision-making process. Additionally, sound environmental policy does not only call for experience, resource, cooperation, and technical experts, but above all, environmental policy remains beyond the ability of politics to manipulate. Guyana up to this point never had a grip on these issues and environmental policy seemed to be ad hoc, running on a continuum from ambiguity to dissension without a clear, defined agenda. The PPP administration vacillated between these entanglements because it has been incapacitated by financial problems, limited by vital skills, constrained by pressing economic needs, derailed by lingering border disputes with Venezuela and Suriname, and whittled by violence and crime. The Omai cyanide spill, however, was a wake-up call, if not an apocalyptic environmental concern, that forced the Guyanese government to revise muddled laws and bring environmental consciousness into the inner sanctums of policy making. The PPP responded by establishing the environmental protection agency (EPA) in 1996 and promoting sustainable development, a process although ill-defined, has been assisted by a host of international agencies, including Britain Overseas Development Administration (ODA), Global Environmental Facility (GEF), United Nations Development Programme (UNDP), Canadian International Development Agency (CIDA), German Technical Assistance Agency (GTZ), Inter-American Development Bank, and World Bank, Commonwealth Secretarial, World Wildlife Fund (WWF), and the Smithsonian Institution. The country also became a signatory to many international environmental conventions.

While Guyana ought to be commended for making strident strides in the direction of environmental protection, and the condominium with international as well as domestic agencies is expected to result in valuable environmental improvements, the country must address the current disposition associated with managing its forest resources. Sizer (1996) pointed out that Guyana does not have a structured comprehensive plan on land use and the supervision of natural resources is the responsibility of many governmental departments, causing overlaps and conflicts between these departments. To deal with the land use conflict, the government has set up two committees: the Natural Land Use Committee (NLUC) and the Natural Resources and Environment Action Committee (NREAC). According to Patrick Williams, 'these committees comprise the heads of such agencies as the GGMC, GFC, EPA, and Land and Surveys', and while they are intended to solve land use conflicts, one weakness is that 'these two bodies do not always have statutory powers, but instead are advisory, and as such this limits the extent to which they can influence the implementation of policies'.[49] In addition to these ambiguities and challenges, the Environmental Protection Act of 1996, of which its main thrust has been to utilise Guyana's resources without damaging or depleting them, has yet to come to grips with its broad mandate. Rovin Deodat noted that:

> EPA's comprehensive approach to environmental management is built around five main components: Development of regulations, standards, codes of practice and technical guidelines; undertaking an environmental awareness, education and capacity building programme throughout the country; promotion of environmental management systems (EMS) which integrate environmental aspects into general practices in public and private sector agencies and activities; encouraging and facilitating environmental friendly technology and cleaner production techniques and practices; and promotion of the concepts of market-based incentives for best environmental practices which can lead to a product or country achieving 'green' label status and 'green' certification and access in the global market.[50]

Notwithstanding some significant achievements, especially in raising the level of environmental awareness, the EPA together with other environmental administrative organisations has been confronted with daunting problems. Many of these problems arose from the volume and complexity of work entrusted on the EPA in a few years. The numerous failures in programme implementation have been due mainly to the lack of resources and institutional capacity as well as foot-dragging. Moreover, the EPA has not adapted well to the increasing responsibilities. The result has been that the EPA has plunged into a demoralised, acrimonious state while environmental problems abound: unmanageable burden of unrestrained logging,[51] catastrophic mining practices,[52] continued slaughter of turtles through poor fishing techniques,[53] and solid waste problems.[54] Further findings indicate that only the most blatant cases are being brought to the forefront and other cases of environmental disturbance and destruction generally go undetected and unpunished. The *Stabroek News* remarked that Guyana's main waterways have become a sponge for uncontrollable hazardous waste laced with cyanide and mercury from mining operations that affect riverrain Amerindian communities and aquatic life.[55] Research done on water and soil samples from the Wemanu River in western Guyana confirmed that the river area was contaminated with cyanide. Another study conducted by the Institute of Applied Science and Technology (IAST) in the Upper Mazaruni River found that the villagers, mostly Amerindians, 'may be at risk for mercury contamination'.[56] A separate study by the World Wildlife Fund (WWF), Canadian International Development Agency (CIDA), United Nations Development Programme (UNDP), and the Organisation of the American States (OAS) showed 'significant levels of contamination among the human and wildlife population due to occupational use and residual mercury in the aquatic systems'.[57]

The Amerindian People Association (APA) has often expressed concern about the impact of mining operations, especially illegal mining by Brazilians (*Garimperios*), on their communities. Dredging and mud washed into rivers with the use of mercury from mining activities have caused a lot of silting and decolourisation. Residents have complained of skin rashes, diarrhoea, vomiting, and even death from *Minimata* disease as a result of using the rivers for domestic purposes.[58] Researchers have warned that HIV has reached these remote Amerindian communities due to the encroachment of gold mining and increased contact with outside communities.[59] Mining has scarred Guyana so much in the recent past that Prime Minister Sam Hinds was forced to close down 20 mining dredges in the upper Mazaruni.[60] Along with mining problems, the GFC noted that timber companies have not complied with environmental standards, and rampaging, skidding and extractive practices have caused damage to the forest.[61] The Guyanese government and the GFC have taken remedial actions and introduced national zonation and certification standards.[62] Although this move is forward looking, serious doubts have been raised about its likely efficacy. Powerful stakeholders' interest in logging may prove too dominant for environmental planners unless zonation and certification are backed by strong, enforceable sanctions. Meanwhile, it is expected that the government will continue to hand out concessions and expand mining and forestry operations since they contribute to 25 per cent and eight per cent of the Gross National Product (GNP), respectively.

Paradoxically, alongside these environmental challenges, Guyana improved overall under the PPP administration. From 1992 to 1997 the GDP grew averaging 7.1 per cent per annum but dropped between 1998-2000 averaging four per cent per annum for the entire period. Guyana's Minister of Finance in the 2000 National Budget 'highlighted the difficulties faced by the economy in 1998. He attributed them to the contagion effects of the Asian financial crisis, the unfavourable weather conditions that were occasioned by the El Nino weather phenomenon, and political instability which disrupted various facets of the society'.[64] The national debt was reduced from US$2.2 billion in 1992 to US$1.2 billion in 2001. Per capita income rose to over US$800, up from around US$500 in the 1980s. Inflation was brought down to single digit; social welfare improved, especially in the areas of education and human rights; more jobs were created. Contributions from forestry to the GDP as a raw material were $71M in 1990; $72M in 1991; $88M in 1992; $117M in 1993; $197M in 1994; $228M in 1995; $229M in 1996; $246M in 1997; $200M in 1998 and $226M in 1999 (all in Guyanese dollars).[65] Contributions from the Omai Gold Mines was also impressive as yearly production from 1993 to 1999 were: 206; 539; 250; 642; 175; 080; 254; 950; 338; 496; 327; 546; 306 and 060 ounces respectively.[66] In addition, the National Development Strategy stated that Guyana's 'environmental policy is founded in the belief that economic growth and environmental sustainability are compatible, that indeed the latter is one of the bases for ensuring that enduring prosperity can be achieved for all Guyanese'.[67] Such goals were complimented when Guyana was ranked recently as one of the top 20 countries in the world by the Swiss-based World Conservation Company in balancing the demands of economic growth with protection of the environment.[68] The *Guyana Review*, however, wrote that 'Public disorder has become commonplace [in Guyana]. Interest groups and aggrieved individuals quickly resort to street violence in order to grab the attention of government to address their complaints' and '[n]ine years into its tenure in office, the PPP-C is yet to deliver on its promise'.[69]

Whatever is the real story in Guyana, this development paradox forces one to entertain the possibility whether the need to meet target economic growth rates and the challenge to protect the environmental has more to do with the Environmental Kuznets Curve (EKC), and the stage of development than the mismanagement of the country's resources. The EKC stipulates that economic growth is consistent with environmental quality in the long-term, but in the short-term environmental mishaps and social costs are necessary prerequisite for long-term prosperity. There is an inverted U shaped relationship between income and the environment: as the economy develops, so too do the use of energy, materials as well as the acceleration of environmental degradation. But when countries reach per capita income of $5,000 and more, environmental degradation will level off and eventually decline.[70] In other words, the EKC suggests that ecological ruin may worsen over the initial stage of development before environmental standards improve to acceptable or safer levels of income.

Higher incomes invariably bring greater incentives to pay for environmental improvements. Rich nations spend more on the environment and enforce environmental regulations more than poor countries. There is empirical evidence to support the EKC hypothesis for some regions and some environmental problems. Grossman and Krueger (1995) found an inverted U shaped between per capita GDP and urban sulphur dioxide (SO_2) concentrations:

> Contrary to the alarmist cries of some environmental groups, we find no evidence that economic growth does unavoidable harm to the natural habitat. Instead we find that while increases in GDP may be associated with worsening environmental conditions in poor countries, air and water quality appear to benefit from economic growth once some critical level of income has been reached. The turning points in these inverted U-shaped relationships vary for the different pollutants, but in almost every case they occur at an income of less than $8000.

Shafk and Bandyopadhyay (1992) identified a similar relationship for annual deforestation and national income. Despite these findings, the EKC hypothesis has its limitations and cannot be applied to the universal law of development, at least not at the present time. Kaufmann et al (1997) found an opposite result when EKC for income and SO_2 concentrations are compared mainly because critical variables such as the density of economic activity was excluded from previous studies.[71] Moreover, research has been limited to a class of environmental problems for which data exist. We are still puzzled about the relationship between income and ecological destruction of key resources. EKC applicability appears limited when contrasted to the environmental gains in developed nations. The Clean Air Act in the United States, for example, had more to do with the enforcement of command-and-control legislation than rising incomes. The World Bank (2000) stated that:

> At best, environmental Kuznets curve provide snapshots of a dynamic relationship between pollution and development that is evolving in response to experience. To understand the forces underlying this evolution, we need to pay closer attention to the complex factors driving environmental progress in developing countries.

Even if the EKC holds, economic growth will not bring about the desired environmental improvements for vast majority of Guyanese as the average income was US$800 in 2001. It will take many years of environmental destruction, with potential irreversible effects, before Guyanese can reach the income level of $8000, not to mention if this can ever be achieved.

From the aforementioned evidence we can discern that in spite of the fact that the PPP has endorsed a number of environmental regulations, both processes and objectives have been sluggish and challenging. Amongst the reasons for this has been that regulatory bodies have been under-staffed, under-funded, under-trained for their mandated responsibilities. Apart from the administrative structure and organisational inefficiencies, regulatory bodies are located outside the spheres of environmental interests (posh offices in Georgetown) and therefore are in a disadvantaged position to enforce and ensure preventative actions against environmental damage, especially in far-flung areas; interior-monitoring outposts should be established. Further, the recent post-election violence and incendiary actions have whittled away the gains made in the direction of environmental values. There is a fear that ethnic violence may be transformed into ecological ruin (sections of Georgetown already look like a war-torn zone). Violent campaigning aimed at derailing the democratic process has plunged Guyana into a tailspin. Critics assert that the PNC/REFORM party's quest for power by any means possible would definitely forestall economic and environmental progress. It is expected that resources set aside to develop sound environmental standards will be diverted to other areas. The recent budget shows little concern for environmental protection and the protection of the environment is expected to operate on a marginally improved environmental policy.

CONCLUDING REMARKS

Guyana's environmental policy has been examined to emphasise the daunting scope and complexity of the challenge of growth and ecological restoration, and to illustrate how short a distance the country has travelled since independence towards that goal. Since independence Guyana has suffered from neo-colonialism, political corruption, indebtedness, economic backwardness, and ethnic polarisation, but the country has moved from environmental neglect to environmental conflicts to environmental awareness. Alongside these movements, there have been significant gains in the direction of environmental values and developments: the implementation of the EPA and regulatory environmental bodies, and cooperation and commitment to a multitude of international and domestic agencies. Yet, Guyana has been struggling to monitor and regulate its natural resources without inflicting damaging or depleting them. Among the reasons for this struggle has been that environmental policy has been too laggard, under-staffed, under funded, and under trained for their broad mandates. Consequently, there has been runaway logging, rapacious mining, disturbance and destruction to habitats, mercury and cyanide pollution of waterways, and health risks to Guyanese. No doubt, the paucity of resources and skilled personnel, unethical management practices, indebtedness, post-election violence, crime, etc., have handicapped and constrained the current administration in carrying out sound environmental standards. Guyana has few choices but to overcome these hurdles and chart a positive course to ensure that the balance between economic development and ecological preservation is practiced. To do otherwise would run the risk of repeating the mistake so experienced by other tropical forests in the world where ecological ruin is a common occurrence.

Environmental policy in Guyana needs long-term political commitment supported by a holistic analysis of economic and environmental processes rather than short-term focus on environmental abuse as they appear. In addition, environmental policy calls for cooperation and commitment on the part of the entire society, not merely by industry and government. As Dryzek has pointed out 'these commitments include foresight, attacking problems at their origins, holism, greater valuation of scarce nature and the precautionary principle.'[72] Part of the process of establishing safe environment standards requires accepting mistakes as a consequence of learning and accepting negative feedback since it has a tendency to create awareness and equilibrium when the environment is disturbed. Moreover, sound environmental policy involves debate, bargaining, even conflicts at the local, regional, national, and international levels. Few environmental problems lie within one agency, and most ecological ills are products of diverse factors involving government, business, technology, and the inherent character of the environment itself.[73] In this regard, environmental management should be a shared responsibility. The return to democracy in Guyana may allow these options to be realised.

Guyana can relinquish itself from its present predicament by resisting dependency from 'foreign exploiters' (since they are too large to monitor and can easily circumvent environmental regulations) to generate foreign exchange and embrace eco-tourism and nature swap for debt relief and conservation concessions. Why eco-tourism and nature swap and conservation concessions instead of foreign investment? As Phillip Da Silva has pointed out since Guyana is endowed with an abundance of diverse natural and biological resources plus a few protected areas, 'Eco-tourism and Protected Areas [can be] Mutually Beneficial Tools', because they have proved to be 'economically, ecologically and culturally' viable.[74] Guyanese politicians, however, must be the cognisant of challenges associated with these endeavours since they require a carefully planned 'systematic framework encompassing environmental, economic and social objectives as well as appropriate legislative, fiscal and institutional mechanism…'[75] In tandem with this, Guyana needs to recognise the rich tapestry of local talent and work in partnership with it. Amerindians, for example, can serve as a guide to eco-tourism. Nature swap has been slow to materialise but this option cannot be ignored. The recent signing of an exploratory lease for some 200,000 acres of state forest as a 'Conservation Concession' between the Guyana government and Conservation International (CI) has been forward looking.[76] Conservation Concession of Guyana's forest is expected to 'prove that viable economic benefits could flow from sustainable non-timber uses and conservation of the rainforest….'[77] Finally, it should be noted that environmental problems can be inherently refractory under the best management, and new problems may emerge as the management becomes more efficient through technology and otherwise. Moreover, existing environmental regulations and problems may be maligned for failures with little consideration how the environment would have been had there not been environmental laws.[78] It is important, then, to recognise that Guyana has come a long way in environmental matters, and it is in a unique position to learn from the environmental mistakes made by other countries in the world.

Endnotes

1. Editorial, 'Indices of development and the wealth of a nation'. *Guyana Chronicle*, May 19, 2000, p. 2.
2. *Guyana National Development Strategy*, 1996, Chapter 3.
3. Lakhan, V. C., A. S. Trenhaile & P.D. LaValle. 'Environmental Protection Efforts in a Developing Country: The Case of Guyana', *Electronic Green Journal*, 13: December (2000), pp.1-11.
4. Thompson, A., 1987, pp. 62-176.
5. Mckitterick, T.E.M., 'The End of a Colony: British Guiana 1962', *The Political Quarterly*, 30: January (1962), p. 31.
6. Thompson A., p. 176.
7. See Colchestor, M., 1997, p. 102.
8. See Colchestor, M., 1997.
9. 'From Jagan to Jagdeo: The People's Progressive Party's nine years in Office', *Guyana Review*, 9:105 (October 2001), p. 24; Colchester, 1997, pp. 42-43.
10. Lakhan, at el, 'Environmental Protection', p. 4.
11. See Areola, O., 1998, pp. 229-269. & Cribb, R., 1998, pp. 65-86.
12. Desai, U., 1998, p. 301.
13. Dryzek, J. S., 1997, pp. 46-60.

14. See Nascimento, C.A and R.A Burrows, ed, 1970.

15. Dyett, H., 'Enigma of Development – Guyana 1900-1989: An Unrealized Potential', *Transition*, 22-23: (1994), p. 88.

16. Thomas, C., 'The Economics of the Cooperative Republic', *Guyana Review*, 8:86 (March 2000), p. 38.

17. 'Desperate Guyanese flocking to Canada as depressed homeland nears total collapse', *Toronto Star*, March 21, 1984, p.A21; Dyett, 'Enigma of Development, 1900-1989', 1994, p. 87.

18. Lapper, R., 'Guyana Wakes Up', *South* (London) 95: (September 1988), p. 33.

19. Lakhan, et al. 'Environmental Protection', p. 3.

20. Thomas, 'Economics', p. 38.

21. 'Socio-economic Trends in Guyana and Priorities for Development Assistance', http://www.sdnp.org.gy/odag/l-socio-trends.html.

22. Roopnarine, L., 'Politics, Economics and Environmental Policy in Guyana', *Journal of Caribbean History*, 34:1&2 (2000), p. 184

23. Thomas, 'Economics', p. 38.

24. See Mabey, N. and R. Ncnally, Foreign Direct Investment and the Environment: From Pollution Havens to Sustainable Development, *WWF-UK Report*, August 1999.

25. Dryzek, 1997, p. 98.

26. Mabey N., and R. Ncnally, 'Foreign Direct Investment', p. 2.

27. World Bank, 2000, p. 59.

28. Dawnnay I., and C. James, 'Guyana: Financial Times Survey', *Financial Times* (London), May 26, 1989, p.22.

29. Dawnnay I., and C. James, 'Guyana', p. 19.

30. See Government of Guyana, 'Statement on Guyana Investment Policy', Georgetown, 1988.

31. Thomas, 'Economics', p. 38.

32. Colchestor M., 1997, p. 102.

33. Mabey N., and R. Ncnally, 'Foreign Direct Investment', p. 2.

34. Rosenbaum W., 1998, pp. 340-345.

35. 'Other major investors started up the same way as Beal – Hinds criticizes Hoyte's attack', *Stabroek News*, July 15, 2000, pp. 1-4.

36. Colchestor, 1994, p. 45.

37. 'Forest: Guyana's Great Assets – Use with Care', *Catholic Standard*, (Georgetown) November 24, 1991, p.1.

38. World Bank, 1993, p. 71.

39. See *Organisation for Economic Co-operation and Development (OECD), Convention on Combating Bribery of Foreign Public Officials in International Business Transactions, OECD,* Paris, December 1997.

40. Lakhan, et al. 'Environmental Protection', p. 3.

41. Lakhan, et al. 'Environmental Protection', p.3.

42. Singh C., 1989, pp. 1-17.

43. See Smith, D. N., and L.T. Wells, 1975, p. 3.

44. Thomas, 'Economics', p. 38.

45. World Bank Group Countries: *Guyana, Trends in Developing Economies,*
http://www.worldbank.org/html/extdr/offrep/lac/gy2.ht

46. *Guyana National Development Strategy,* 1996, chapter 1.

47. Guyana Review, 'From Jagan to Jagdeo', p. 24.

48. Editorial, 'Lessons from the Omai Spill', *Stabroek News,* September 15, 2000, p. 1.

49. Williams, P., 'How long will Guyana's bountiful forest resource last? *Guyana Review,* 8:89 (June 2000), p. 16

50. Deodat, R., 'Protecting the environment', *Guyana Review,* 8:95 (December 2000), pp. 56-57.

51. Editorial, 'Forest Management', *Stabroek News,* December 12, 2000, pp.1-2.

52. Pearce, F., 'Caught in the gold rush', *New Scientist,* 150: 2029 (May 1996), pp. 14-15. 'GGMC symposium: Unrestrained pollution of rivers seen as big problem', *Stabroek News.* February 22, 2000, pp. 1-2.

53. La Rose, M., 'Extension of Olive Ridley at Shell Beach feared — turtle conservation official', *Stabroek News.* March 12, 2000, pp. 4-6, 'Slaughter of marine turtles in some areas on the rise, Olive Ridleys return, strange markings seen', *Stabroek News,* July 5, 2000, pp. 5-8. 'Turtles found dead on Shell Beach', *Guyana Chronicle,* March 4, 2000, pp. 12-13.

54. Deodat, 'Protecting the environment', pp. 56-57.

55. Editorial, 'Environment at risk', *Stabroek News,* March 20, 2000, pp. 1-2. M. Ramotar, 'Gold mining under scrutiny at key conference', *Guyana Chronicle,* June 19, 2000, pp. 2-4.

56. Richards, A., 'Isseneru villagers face of mercury contamination-reports finds', *Stabroek News.* June 19, 2001, pp. 6-8.

57. Richards, 'Isseneru villagers face risk of mercury contamination-reports finds', pp. 6-8.

58. 'Interior mining pollution worrying Amerindians group', *Stabroek News,* February 9, 2001, pp. 3-4.

59. 'How HIV spreads into the wilderness', *New Scientist,* 167: 2249 (July 2000), p. 15.

60. 'Turbidity in Mazaruni: Some 20 gold mining dredges closed down', *Stabroek News*, March 15, 2001, pp. 1-2.
61. 'Timber companies' environmental compliance way below standard – GFC', *Stabroek News*, July 7, 2000, pp. 1-3.
62. Lall, S., 'Forestry to conduct zonation exercise', *Guyana Chronicle*, July 26, 2000, p. 1; A. Kippins. 'Forestry Commission moves to advance certification process', *Guyana Chronicle*, June 10, 2001, pp. 1-3.
63. 'Forestry Contributions on the Rise', *Guyana Chronicle*, January 10, 2001, pp. 3-4. M. Jacobson & A. Kratochvil. 'Guyana's Gold Standard', *Natural History*, 107:7(September 1998), p. 51.
64. *2000 National Budget*, 2000, chapter 1.
65. 'Forestry Contributions on the Rise', *Guyana Chronicle*, January 10, 2001.
66. Davidson,Wendella, 'On Tenth Anniversary: Omai Optimistic about future in Guyana', *Guyana Chronicle*, September, 2001, pp. 1-4.
67. *Guyana National Development Strategy*, 1996, chapter 18.
68. 'Guyana gets good environmental protection rating', *Guyana Chronicle*, October 27, 2001.
69. 'From Jagan to Jagdeo', pp. 24-25.
70. World Bank, 2000, p. 8.
71. See Rothman, D. S., 'Environmental Kuznets curves—real progress or passing the buck?', *Ecological Economics*, 25: 2 (1998) pp. 177-194; Kaufmann, R. K., B. Davidsdottir, S. Garham, and P. Pauly, 'The Determinants of Atmospheric SO_2 Concentrations: Reconsidering the Environmental Kuznet's Curve', *Ecological Economics*, 25, pp. 209-220, 1998; Suri, V., S and D. Chapman, 'Economic growth, trade and energy: implications for the environmental Kuznets curve', *Ecological Economics*, 25:2 (1998) pp. 195-208; Tisdell, C., 'Globalisation and sustainability: environmental Kuznets curve and the WTO', *Ecological Economics*, 39:2 (2001) pp. 185-196.
72. Dryzek, 1997, p. 143.
73. Rosenbuam, 1998, p. 7.
74. a Silva, P., 'Protected Areas and Ecotourism: conserving Biological Diversity in Guyana', *Transition*, 26: (1997), p. 102. Tharay, B., 'Tourism For Guyana', *Mirror*, June 6, 2001. pp. 1-2.
75. Da Silva, P., 'Protected Areas', p. 98.
76. Lall, S., 'Conservation group gets forest management concessions', *Guyana Chronicle*. October 13, 2000, pp. 5-6.
77. 'Conservation body to prove non-timber uses of forest really pays – Waldron' *Stabroek News*. October 27, 2000, pp. 5-6.
78. Rosenbaum, 1998, p. 6.

References

Areola, Olusegun, 'Comparative Environmental Issues and Policies in Nigeria', in *Ecological Policy and Politics in Developing Countries: Economic Growth, Democracy, and Environment*, ed., Uday Desai, pp. 229-268 (Albany: State University of New York Press, 1998).

Colchestor, Marcus, *Guyana, Fragile Frontier: Loggers, Miners and Forest Peoples* (London: Latin American Bureau; Gloucestershire: World Rainforest Movement; Kingston: Ian Randle Publishers, 1997).

Colchestor, Marcus, 'The New Sultans: Asian Loggers Move in on Guyana's Forests', *The Ecologist*, 24:2 (March/April 1994) pp. 45-52.

'Conservation body to prove non-timber uses of forest really pays – Waldron', *Stabroek News*, October 27, 2000.

Cribb, Robert, 'Environmental Policy and Politics in Indonesia', In *Ecological Policy and Politics in Developing Countries: Economic Growth, Democracy, and Environment*, ed., Uday Desai, pp. 65-86 (Albany: State University of New York Press, 1998).

Da Silva, Phillip, 'Protected Areas and Ecotourism: Conserving Biological Diversity in Guyana', *Transition*, 26: (1997), pp. 99-110.

Davidson, Wendella, 'On Tenth Anniversary: Omai Optimistic about future in Guyana', *Guyana Chronicle*, September, 2001.

Dawnnay, Ivo & Canute James, 'Guyana: Financial Times Survey', *Financial Times* (London), May 26, (1989), pp. 17-22.

Deodat, Rovin, 'Protecting the environment', *Guyana Review*, 8:95 (December 2000), pp. 56-57.

Desai, Uday ed., *Ecological Policy and Politics in Developing Countries: Economic Growth, Democracy, and Environment* (Albany, State University of New York Press, 1998).

'Desperate Guyanese flocking to Canada as depressed homeland nears total collapse', *Toronto Star*, March 21, 1984.

Dryzek, John, S, *The Politics of the Earth: Environmental Discourses* (Oxford: Oxford University Press, 1997).

Dyett, Harry, 'Enigma of Development – Guyana 1900-1989: An Unrealized Potential', *Transition*, 22-23: (1994), pp. 1-148.

Editorial, 'Indices of development and the wealth of a nation.' *Guyana Chronicle*, May 19, 2000.

Editorial, 'Lessons from the Omai Spill', *Stabroek News*, September 15, 2000.

Editorial, 'Environment at risk', *Stabroek News*, March 20, 2000.

Editorial, 'Forest Management', *Stabroek News*, December 12, 2000.

'Forest: Guyana's Great Assets – Use with Care', *Catholic Standard* (Georgetown), November 24, 1991.

'Forestry Contributions on the Rise', *Guyana Chronicle*, January 10, 2001.

'GGMC symposium: Unrestrained pollution of rivers seen as big problem', *Stabroek News*. February 22, 2000.

Guyana National Development Strategy, Georgetown, Government of Guyana, 1999.

Government of Guyana, 'Statement on Guyana Investment Policy', Georgetown, 1988.

'From Jagan to Jagdeo: The Peoples Progressive Party's nine years in office', *Guyana Review*, 9:105 (October 2001), pp. 24-25.

Grossman, Gene. M. & A. B. Krueger, 'Economic Growth and the Environment', *Quarterly Journal of Economics*, 110:2 (May 1995) pp. 353-378.

'Guyana gets good environmental protection rating', *Guyana Chronicle*, October 27, 2001.

'How HIV spreads into the wilderness', *New Scientist*, 167:2249 (July 2000) p. 15.

Jacobson, Mark and Antonin Kratochvil ,'Guyana's Gold Standard', *Natural History*, 107:7 (September 1998), pp. 46-59.

'Interior mining pollution worrying Amerindians group', *Stabroek News*, February 9, 2001.

Kaufmann, R. K, B. Davidsdottir, S. Garham, and P. Pauly, 'The Determinants of Atmospheric SO_2 Concentrations: Reconsidering the Environmental Kuznet's Curve', *Ecological Economics*, 25, pp. 209-220, 1998.

Kippins, Abigail, 'Forestry Commission moves to advance certification process',*Guyana Chronicle,* June 10, 2001.

Lakhan, V, Chris, A. S. Trenhaile and P.D. LaValle. 'Environmental Protection Efforts in a Developing Country:The Case of Guyana', *Electronic Green Journal*, 13: (December 2000) pp.1-11.

Lall, Sharon, 'Conservation group gets forest management concessions', *Guyana Chronicle*. October 13, 2000.

_____, 'Forestry to conduct zonation exercise', *Guyana Chronicle*, July 26, 2000.

Lapper, Richard, 'Guyana Wakes Up', *South* (London) 95: (September 1988), pp. 33-34.

La Rose, Miranda, 'Extension of Olive Ridley at Shell Beach feared- turtle conservation official', *Stabroek News*. March 12, 2000.

_____, 'Slaughter of marine turtles in some areas on the rise, Olive Ridleys return, strange markings seen', *Stabroek News*, July 5, 2000.

Mabey, Nick and Richard Mcnally, *Foreign Direct Investment and the Environment: From Pollution Havens to Sustainable Development*, WWF-UK Report, August 1999.

Mckitterick, Thomas, E, M, 'The End of a Colony: British Guiana 1962', *The Political Quarterly* 30: (January 1962), pp. 30-40.

Nacimento, C. A and R. A. Burrows, eds., *A Destiny to Mould: Selected Speeches by the Prime Minister of Guyana* (London: Longman Caribbean, 1970).

Other major investors started up the same way as Beal – Hinds criticizes Hoyte's attack', *Stabroek News*, July 15, 2000.

Pearce, Fred, 'Caught in the gold rush', *New Scientist*, 150:2029 (May 1996), pp. 14-15.

Ramotar, Mark, 'Gold mining under scrutiny at key conference', *Guyana Chronicle*, June 19, 2000.

Richards, Andrew, 'Isseneru villagers face of mercury contamination-reports finds', *Stabroek News*. June 19, 2001.

Roopnarine, Lomarsh 'Politics, Economics and Environmental Policy in Guyana', *Journal of Caribbean History*, 34:1&2 (2000) pp. 178-217.

Rosenbaum, Walter, *Environmental Politics and Policy* (Washington DC: Congressional Quarterly, 1998).

Rothman, Dale S. 'Environmental Kuznets curves – real progress or passing the buck?', *Ecological Economics*, 25: 2 (1998) pp. 177-194

Shafik, Nemant, & S. Bandyopadhyay, 'Economic Growth and Environmental Quality:Time Series and Cross-Country Evidence', *World Bank Policy Research Working Paper* WPS 904, 1992.

Singh, Chaitram, *Multinationals, The State, And The Management of Economic Nationalism: The Case of Trinidad* (New York, Westport, Connecticut, London: Praeger,1989).

Sizer, Nigel, *Profits Without Plunder: Reaping Revenue From Guyana's Tropical Forests Without Destroying Them* (Washington DC: World Resource Institute, 1996).

Smith, David N., Louis .T.Wells, *Negotiating Third World Mineral Agreements: Promises as Prologue* (Cambridge, Mass.: Ballinger Publishing Co.,1975).

'Socio-economic Trends in Guyana and Priorities for Development Assistance', http://www.sdnp.org.gy/odag/l-socio-trends.html.

Suri, Vivek, Duane Chapman, 'Economic growth, trade and energy: implications for the environmental Kuznets curve', *Ecological Economics* 25:2 (1998) pp. 195-208.

Tisdell, Clem, 'Globalisation and sustainability: environmental Kuznets curve and the WTO', *Ecological Economics*, 39:2 (2001) pp. 185-196.*2000 National Budget*, http://www.sdnp.org.gy/mininfo/budget2000.htm.

Tharay, Bhoj. 'Tourism For Guyana', *Mirror*, June 6, 2001.

Thomas, Clive, 'The Economics of the Cooperative Republic', *Guyana Review*, 8:86 (March 2000) pp, 37-39.

Thompson, Alvin, *Colonialism and Underdevelopment in Guyana, 1580-1803* (Bridgetown: Carib Research and Publications, 1987).

'Timber companies' environmental compliance way below standard – GFC', *Stabroek News*, July 7, 2000.

'Turbidity in Mazaruni: Some 20 gold mining dredges closed down', *Stabroek News*, March 15, 2001.

'Turtles found dead on Shell Beach', *Guyana Chronicle*, March 4, 2000.

Williams, Patrick, 'How long will Guyana's bountiful forest resource last?' *Guyana Review*, 8:89 (June 2000), pp. 14-17.

World Wildlife Fund-International. *Living Planet Report 1998: Overconsumption is driving the rapid decline of the world's natural environments*, WWF-International, Gland, Switzerland.

World Bank Group Countries: Guyana, Trends in Developing Economies, http://www.world bank.org/html/extdr/offrep/lac/gy2.htm

World Bank, *Guyana: Public Sector Review* (Washington DC: World Bank, 1993).

_____, *World Bank Development Indicators* (Washington D.C: World Bank, 1997).

_____, *Greening Industry: New Roles for Communities, Markets, and Governments* (New York: Oxford University Press, 2000).

World Resources Institute, United Nations Environmental Programme and the United Nations Development Programme, *World Resources 1996-1997*, (New York Oxford University Press, 1997).

13

Environmental Security Risks for Caribbean States: Legal Dimensions

Winston Anderson

INTRODUCTION

Environmental Risks From Military or Quasi Military Sources

The notion of environmental security is receiving widespread attention as the international community grapples with the task of ensuring minimum environmental integrity for individuals. At one level there is an obvious relationship between military security issues and environmental protection. Warfare is inherently destructive of the environment and, more particularly, sustainable development. The vulnerability of the environment and natural resources to the ravages of war and oppression has been recognised in the 1972 Stockholm and the 1992 Rio Declarations,[1] as well as in general state practice.[2] In 1992, the United Nations Security Council took the decision to regard ecological instability as a potential threat to international peace and security such as could provoke the enforcement powers of the Council under Chapter VII of the Charter.[3]

Caribbean states have a long history of seeking to reduce environmental risks from military as well as quasi-military sources. Adopted in 1967, the Treaty for the Prohibition of Nuclear Weapons in Latin America[4] (including the Caribbean)[5] was premised on the realisation that military forces and civilian population alike suffered the terrible effects of nuclear weapons. These effects were suffered 'indiscriminately and inexorably'.[6] The persistence of the radioactivity released by these weapons into the environment constituted an attack 'on the integrity of the human species and ultimately may even render the whole earth uninhabitable'.[7]

In more recent times, there has been trenchant opposition to the trans-Caribbean shipment from France to Japan of plutonium extracted from the spent nuclear material.[8] Official reports have suggested that an accident or hijacking could result in an unmitigated disaster; an individual shipment probably contain material emitting 15 times as much radiation as was vented during the Chernobyl disaster.[9] The difficulty of reconciling the strident calls for the prohibition of the passage of such hazardous materials with the fundamental principles of innocent passage and freedom of navigation[10] has led to the adoption of a new approach.

At the II Summit of Association of Caribbean States in Santo Domingo, April 1999, Caribbean states adopted a Resolution to have the United Nations System recognise the Caribbean Sea as 'a Special Area within the context of Sustainable Development'. This initiative, which overlaps with but goes beyond UNEP's Caribbean Environment Programme (CEP) on the protection and development of the marine area of the wider Caribbean,[11] was stymied in negotiations at the General Assembly.[12] It was supported by the Group of 77 and China, but was rejected by some developed countries precisely on the grounds of its implications for freedom of navigation in relation to traditional rights of navigation through Caribbean Sea. France, Japan, United States all expressed concern that the declaring of the Caribbean sea as a special area was the first step towards obtaining a halt on the transshipment of nuclear waste and other hazardous cargoes through the region.

A watered-downed Resolution was eventually adopted at the 87th plenary meeting and formally approved on February 15, 2000.[13] The Resolution recognises the importance of 'an integrated management approach to the Caribbean sea in the context of sustainable development' and encourages 'further development of integrated management' taking account of Agenda 21 and the SIDS-POA. No mention is made of transshipment of nuclear materials.

Environmental Risks From General Environmental Degradation

A second level at which environmental security is threatened is both more mundane and more pervasive. It is the level of general environmental degradation. Here the risks may arise from industrial activity, as for instance, where there is pollution of such environmental media as air, water, land, and sea. Treatment and disposal of hazardous wastes are also productive of possible endangerment of the environment. Depletion of natural resources is also cause for concern as evident in the saga of fisheries management, despair over deforestation and disenchantment over destruction of wetlands. Grant of permission for development in the context of less than a rigorous environmental impact assessment, and the policy governing the change of land usage, create further areas of concern.

The First CARICOM Ministerial Conference on the Environment was held in Port of Spain Trinidad May 31 – June 2, 1989 and produced the Port of Spain Accord.[14] The Conference had the primary objective of increasing 'appreciation of the significance of the issues and needs relevant to management and protection of the Caribbean environment'. It acknowledged the worldwide transformation in attitudes and perspectives on environmental issues that had been spawned by the historic 1972 Stockholm Conference and the 1987 Report of the World Commission on Environment and Development (which led to the 1992 Rio Conference). Ministers of the environment perceived their mandate as providing political impetus to the coordination, identification, development and execution of activities that would address deficiencies in traditional arrangements for environmental management.

Fourteen priority issues and problems were identified[15] and one of the strategic approaches to their solution as highlighted was the 'development of legislative frameworks adequate to the requirements of sound environmental management, and the required machinery for their enforcement.' The recommendations from the Port of Spain Accord, as well as its partner Port of Spain Consensus agreed in 1991 were to have been carried forward by the regular meetings of the Caribbean Environment Ministers as augmented by a CARICOM Task Force on the Environment. Whilst these regional declarations probably gave some impetus to the development of national legislation, the regional institutional arrangements have, unfortunately, become virtually moribund.

However the Accord and Consensus did receive virtual ratification at the 1994 United Nations Global Conference on the Sustainable Development of Small Island Developing States (UNGCSIDS) held in Barbados from April 25 to May 6, 1994. This Conference, which adopted the Barbados Declaration and Programme of Action (POA),[16] was a follow-up to the 1992 Rio Conference, and Caribbean states, along with the other participants, committed themselves to the principle of sustainable development as embodied in the Rio Declaration and Agenda 21.[17] In 1997, Caribbean ministers held a follow-up meeting on implementing the POA[18] and declared that they would do a number of things at the national level to ensure the adoption of the 'sustainable development paradigm throughout the Caribbean region'. These included (a) using new innovative mechanisms to mobilise financial resources to support implementation of sustainable development programmes, and (b) enhancing of inter-sectoral collaboration through establishment of multi-sectoral, multi-disciplinary mechanisms.

In relation to the latter, one of the outcomes of the UNGCSIDS-POA was the Capacity 21 Project undertaken by UNDP and formulated in collaboration with CARICAD and CDB. The Project assisted Caribbean capacity building and institutional strengthening through establishment of 'Sustainable Development Councils' (SDC) or 'Sustainable Development Commissions' (SDC). These bodies were established in several Caribbean countries including Barbados, Jamaica, and Trinidad and Tobago. Membership on the Council or Commission is broad-based and includes representatives of Government, NGOs, and the business sector as 'the major stakeholders'. The functions appear to be facilitation of public information (encouraging a national dialogue on the importance of sustainable development); research (identifying gaps in policy and legislation); and institutional management (coordinating sustainable development activities).

REDUCING ENVIRONMENTAL RISKS BY THE USE OF LAW

In accordance with the global and regional mandate Caribbean states have sought to reduce the risk to environmental security through use of the law. The effort has been multifaceted and the space available in a paper such as this allows for the highlighting of only two aspects. First the passage of legislation to provide the institutional and enforcement framework for environmental preservation; second, the ability of individual citizens to seek the court's assistance in ensuring that the institutions of government properly execute their obligation to regulate human impacts on the environment.

Institutional Mechanism

A major criticism of traditional environmental law was its domination by sectoral statutes that were unsupported by any overarching policy-making institution.[19] The corpus of environmental statutes inherited from the British displayed an approach of responding ad hoc to environmental challenges. The lack of modern regulatory tools was also very much in evidence. A litany of regulatory problems ensued of which lack of judicially enforceable environmental standards, insufficient coordination with related legislation, lack of policing and enforcement, and inadequate penalties were among the most prominent.[20] Institutional difficulties arose from the multiplicity of administrative responsibility and the resultant problems of overlap, duplication, 'gaps' and the administrative fighting over 'turf'.[21] Absence of an institutional focal point therefore became synonymous with a fragmentary regulation, ineffective management, and lack of serious intent.

TYPES OF EXECUTIVE AGENCIES

Creation of a central executive agency with overall competence for environmental matters was the *raison d'être* for the development of comprehensive environmental legislation but as the legislation evolved, two distinct types of agencies were seen to emerge. The state agency is the traditional type agency established within the existing civil service establishment. Into this category fall the Department of the Environment (DOE) within the Ministry of the Environment in St Kitts and Nevis,[22] and Belize.[23] So too do the Department of Health Services, (DEHS) established in the Ministry of Health in The Bahamas[24] and the Environmental Health Board (EHB) and Environmental Health Division (EHD) of the Public Health Department are established in the Ministry of Health in St Vincent and the Grenadines.[25]

Alternatively, parastatal institutions have emerged; these are bodies with governmental responsibility for the environment but which are established and operated outside of the strict public service establishment. The best known parastatals are the Natural Resources Conservation Authority (NRCA) in Jamaica,[26] the Environmental Management Authority (EMA) in Trinidad and Tobago[27] and the Environmental Protection Agency (EPA) of Guyana.[28]

Autonomy

Assessment of the merits of the institutional arrangements within the state as opposed to outside of it tends to focus on issues of administrative convenience, autonomy and resource availability. The choice of an agency within the public service has two main advantages. It enhances the profile and standing of the parent ministry (often the Ministry of the Environment) and makes for easier sectoral legislation to be articulated into the existing administrative structure where environmental management remains largely in the hands of other government departments. Often there may even be an overlap of personnel. Far less violence is therefore likely to engendered than with the creation of a separate statutory body with executive-type functions as in the case of the NRCA, EMA or EPA.

On the other hand the government agency approach suffers precisely from over-identification with government. There is often a perceived lack of autonomy that can be of particular concern when the issue of governmental breach of environmental norms arises. In such circumstances the bare provision that the Act binds the Crown[29] might not be sufficient. A further consequence relates to the loss of control over recruitment of officers, ability to negotiate and settle levels of salaries thereby attracting desirable staff, and general control over financial management. Moreover, governmental control of agency action is evident. This is hardly surprising where the agency is a department of government, although in the view of one commentator, functional independence in environmental regulation 'is more likely to be achieved within the civil service than without'.[30] A government agency located within has no power to employ staff outside the civil service and is financially dependent upon governmental support. In this connection, however, an interesting provision may be highlighted from the EPA of Belize. Section 3 (4) requires that the Public Services Commission 'shall' appoint such environmental officers, inspectors and other staff as may be necessary to carry out the provisions of the Act and any regulations made thereunder.

The parastatal lead agencies in Jamaica, Trinidad and Tobago, and Guyana, established as bodies corporate outside the strict public service structure, do have greater power over their budget and staff recruitment. However, government remains a significant financial contributor to these agencies and the major guarantor of its loans. Salaries payable to staff, as well as pension schemes, and arrangements for medical or death benefits, may be subject to the minister's approval. In Guyana, ministerial directions may extend to the size of the establishment of the agency, the employment of staff and the terms thereof, the provision of equipment and funds.[31] Governmental control is also evident in the power to appoint and dismiss persons comprising the board of the agency. Except in Trinidad and Tobago, this power lies in the hands of the minister. While the minister in Guyana can only dismiss for one of a number of specified causes, and must grant the person concerned a reasonable opportunity to be heard, the power to dismiss in Jamaica is apparently unrestricted. Governmental control is also exerted by the subservience of the agency to ministerial direction. Legislation expressly provides that the agency is subject to general and special directions given by the minister.[32] Other provisions empower the minister to give to the agency directions of a general character as to the policy to be followed by the agency in the performance of its functions, and require the agency to 'give effect thereto'.[33]

Immunity

Parastatal agencies may be at a peculiar juridical disadvantage. In *Natural Resources Conservation Authority v. Seafood and Ting International Ltd.*,[34] the applicants succeeded against NRCA for injunctive relief and threatened individual employees of the Authority with forfeiture of private assets if the court orders were not obeyed. But ancient common law rules prevent the award of injunctive relief against the Crown and on this basis the minister of agriculture made regulations under the Fisheries Act empowering himself to issue quotas to conch exporters. The absence of immunity from prosecution may become an important deterrent from the enthusiastic exercise by parastatals of state power over the environment.

BASIC FEATURES OF AGENCIES

More interesting than the comparisons between the types of institutions are the common features shared by these various institutions. There are some five features of institutional organisation that warrant mention.

Broad environmental mandate

The lead agency is generally given numerous specific functions in relation to environmental management. Greatest specification is achieved in Belize where the DOE is assigned 27 specific functions. The gist of the mandate is however, captured in a broad sweep-up provision assigning overall environmental competence. For example, the DOE in Saint Christopher and Nevis is mandated 'to initiate, oversee, co-ordinate, *integrate*, regulate, facilitate, and monitor environmental protection and conservation strategies, and to initiate and implement policies, programs and projects to achieve sustainable development'.[35] The NRCA in Jamaica is required 'to take such steps as are necessary for the effective management of the physical environment of Jamaica so as to ensure the conservation, protection and proper use of its natural resources'.[36]

An important legal consequence to flow from this broad environmental mandate was debated in the Australian case of *Phosphates Co-operative v. Environmental Protection Agency*.[37] There the lead environmental agency in Australia, having a similarly broad mandate to those described above, refused to grant permission for a proposed development. The courts decided that the agency could act on purely environmental considerations and need not take into account the economic benefits of the proposal.

Priority in environmental decision-making

The impression conveyed by reading the legislation is that the decisions of the executive agency take priority over the decisions of other environmental bodies. Thus, a general obligation is placed upon all persons having environmental functions to consult with the lead agency before determining those matters.[38] Although the requirement here is not one of receiving the Authority's approval, the responsibility of the other agencies to initiate the consultation process appears strong enough to allow the lead agency to be kept abreast of developments in the various sectors and thereby to exert a coordinating and harmonising influence.

Another formulation addresses the primacy issue even more starkly: persons vested with power in relation to the environment are required to defer to the lead agency. Thus, the agency might enjoy a right akin to the power of veto in respect of certain decisions of other government agencies related to developmental activities. Where the agency requests an environmental impact assessment, it must inform any government agency having responsibility for the issuing of any license, permit, approval or consent in connection with any matter affecting the environment that a request has been made. However, once that information has been given such government agency 'shall not' grant the relevant license, permit or approval or consent 'unless it has been notified' by the agency that the request has been complied with and that the agency 'has issued or intends to issue a permit'.[39]

Although the intention might be to make sure that decisions of executive body prevail over decisions of other environmental bodies the question arises whether this can be achieved in our present constitutional context. It is basic constitutional law that subsequent legislation prevails over earlier legislation.[40] Accordingly, it is a relatively easy matter for Parliament to enact legislation making decisions of executive body subservient to those of other bodies.

Articulation of Institution into Infrastructure

A central problem that emerges, concerns the methodologies for articulating the insurgent institutions into the pre-existing legal infrastructure of multiple institutions having segmented environmental functions. Two approaches have been adopted. First, allied to the grant of a comprehensive environmental mandate is the consolidation of substantive environmental regulation in the lead agency. The new agency may be given administrative control over the previous sectoral legislation and thus brings together previously fragmented sectoral legislation, while making provision for their administration. For example, the Act in Jamaica provided that the NRCA would be the executing authority for sectoral legislation passed before 1991[41] including the Beach Control Act, the Wildlife Protection Act and the Watershed Protection Act. Similarly, in St Kitts and Nevis, The Forestry Act, The Beach Control Act and The Wild Birds Protection Act were all repealed and reenacted into the NECPA 1987.[42]

Again, in some regards, the parent statute might create a double track system in making clear that regulation is to be exercised by both the newly created authority and the pre-existing agency. This occurs in those areas where the jurisdiction of the pre-existing agency is too deeply entrenched or relates to specialised functions or areas not yet ripe for assumption of responsibility by the agency. For example the jurisdiction exercised under the *Town and Country Planning Act 1958*[43] is not abolished. The statute makes clear that developmental activities in prescribed areas require permission from both the authority and the Town and Country Planning office.[44]

Revision of environmental law

Revision and replacement of obsolete legislation follow ineluctably from the approach of synchronising and identification of regulation revolving around functional segments. NCEPA repeals and replaces out-moded legislation relating to forestry, beaches and wildlife. The repealed *Beach Control Act 1956*[45] prohibited the use of the foreshore and floor of the sea for any industrial or commercial enterprise except with a license contravention were punished by a fine of $50 per violation day or a maximum of 12 months imprisonment. The minister was empowered to make regulation for the observance of sanitary and cleaning conditions and practices of the beaches habitually frequented by the public. The Act vests all rights in and over the beach in the Crown and provides for a public right of access and use and enjoyment. Duties and functions of the minister and the Conservation Commission in respect of coastal conservation are specified. The Act specifies and prohibits activities, which would undermine beach preservation or foul or pollute beaches and institutes a modern permit system for sand mining. The minister is given power to declare protected beaches in which activities such as fishing, sand-mining, waste disposal, waterskiing are prohibited. Violations are publishable by fines and/or imprisonment and there are provisions for the confiscation of vehicles used in connection with the commission of offences. The *Wild Birds Protection Act*[46] contained archaic provisions relating to the protection of wild birds and was repealed by the NCEPA. New and extensive provisions were introduced to deal with the subject in the appropriate functional segment.

Ministerial oversight

A central harmonising role is played by the assignment of ministerial oversight. The minister may give general policy directions to the Authority and is a part of the appeals process. Where a person is aggrieved by a decision of the agency in relation to a permit or a license there is a right of appeal to the minister. The provision that the minister's decision is final does not, of course, abrogate the rules relating natural justice and general administrative law standards. This ministerial 'override' *ipso facto* creates a mechanism for inter-ministerial conflict resolution in relation to overlap of jurisdiction. Such an overlap could occur, for example, in relation to the statutory power of the minister who may, on the recommendation of the Authority, take any emergency action to protect any aspect of the natural environment of Jamaica (or the whole Island) without, presumably, reference to sectoral jurisdictional concerns.

Similarly the minister may make regulations on natural resources conservation, development activities in relation to which impact assessment is required, emission of pollutants and hazardous substances, public safety at beaches, protection of fauna and flora etc; presumably, jurisdictional conflict are resolved through inter-ministerial cooperation. But the Act goes beyond voluntary cooperation between the ministries, however. Under the Act, the minister may, by order, alter any enactment if he considers such alteration to be necessary or expedient on account of anything contained in this Act.[47] This remarkable power, which could raise important constitutional considerations, is only restricted by the requirement that the order is subject to an affirmative resolution of the House.

CONTINUING PROBLEMS

Not all the difficulties associated with the integration of the executive agency with new and sweeping powers into the existing fragmented system of environmental management have been resolved. The present situation in Guyana,

Jamaica, and Trinidad and Tobago is characterised by no little confusion as the various governments departments come to grips with loss of autonomy and turf, and as the agency finds itself constrained within the limits of its resources. One view gaining ground in Jamaica is that the Authority has simply been granted too great a role to play without the exercise of the required surgery on the pre-existing institutions and without the committal of the required resources. Another suggests legislative modification to that would lead to consolidation with related institutions, such as planning.[48] Ultimately a great deal will depend upon the wisdom and sagacity of the leadership in the agency and its ability to forged new linkages and partnerships with the other arms of government having jurisdiction in the field.

JUDICIAL REVIEW OF INSTITUTIONAL REGULATION

The heavy reliance placed on 'framework' legislation, fleshed out by guidance, regulations and decisions of the enforcing authorities means that many of the everyday rules of environmental protection are made without the scrutiny of parliament. Similarly, statutory requirements, such as that the environmental agencies consult with other authorities or the public, publish documents, require the environmental impact assessments, are not supervised by the legislature. Scrutiny of administrative regulation must therefore be undertaken by the courts, which ensure, through the mechanism of judicial review, that the authorities properly perform their duties.

Recent developments in the law support the thesis that the way in which judicial discretion is exercised to interpret legal standards is directly proportional to the usefulness of judicial review as a mechanism for environmental protection. A particularly vexing issue concerns the judicial interpretation of the standards applicable to the question of standing to seek judicial review.

THE STANDING REQUIREMENT

In order to have standing to bring an action for review, the applicant must demonstrate that he or she possesses a 'sufficient interest' in the matter to which the application relates. Until recently the courts over the common law world all adopted a restrictive interpretation to the standing requirement and ruled, in a number of cases, that environmental pressure groups or public spirited individuals did not satisfy the *Boyce v. Paddington Borough Council* [49] test so as to obtain review. For example, in *R. v. Secretary of State for the*

Environment ex p. Rose Theatre Trust,[50] an interest group specifically formed to defend the remains of an Elizabethan theatre, was refused standing. It was held that, as individuals, none of the group had any special interest in the matter over and beyond the general interest of the public. The case resulted in a great deal of criticism and was a blow to the notion of environmental litigation in the public interest. Among other things, *Rose Theatre Trust* appeared unconcerned, or at least not overwhelmed by the probability, that no one could sue in such a situation, leaving the decision of the government agency beyond rebuke.

CARIBBEAN TRILOGY

A similar criticism may be leveled against the first three Caribbean attempts to seek judicial review of environmental decision making. The trilogy of cases began in March 1993 with *Spencer v. Canzone Del Mare and the Attorney General of Antigua and Barbuda (Spencer No. 1).*[51] The applicant was a member of parliament of Antigua and Barbuda and leader of the opposition. He alleged that the acting chief town planner, acting on behalf of the Land Development Control Authority, had ordered the defendants to halt all development activities at its Coconut Hall site because the work there was environmentally unfriendly and required an environmental impact assessment, which had not been done. It was further alleged that the prime minister had improperly written to the developer allowing the continuation of construction. The application for declaratory orders and an injunction was dismissed on the grounds that the plaintiff lacked standing because he had not shown 'sufficient interest' in the matter to be litigated.

In June and August 1996, the High Court of Barbados considered the standing issue in *Scotland District Association Inc. v. Attorney General et al.*[52] The applicant was a recently formed corporation whose objective was to foster and promote the preservation and improvement of the ecologically sensitive Scotland District. Its application for a declaration that the decision of government to site a sanitary landfill for the deposit of waste materials and refuse in the Scotland District was unlawful was rejected. Although there was not much discussion of the *locus standi* point, the court appears to have agreed with the defendants' argument that members of the association had no individual interest in the matter and that joining themselves into a company created no better right than they enjoyed as individuals.

Finally, *Spencer v. Attorney-General of Antigua and Barbuda et al (Spencer No. 2),*[53] decided in April 1998, rejected an application from Mr Spencer for a declaration that the agreement between the government and a private developer for a tourist development on Guiana Island was unconstitutional. One ground advanced by the applicant was that the proposed development was harmful to the ecology and was contrary to common law principles that protect the environment. At first instance, Saunders, J. found that the applicant had standing but rejected his arguments on the merits. This decision on standing was overturned on appeal. In the view of the Appellate Court, the applicant had failed the constitutional requirement that he should have 'a relevant interest' in order to be granted standing.

Admittedly, there are important differences between applications by genuine environmental organisations or pressure groups to seek judicial review and applications by professional politicians who may have other axes to grind. The court clearly has an interest in not becoming a forum for political debate, particularly in circumstances where the applicant has access to parliament.

However, the broader problem concerns interpretation of the 'sufficient interest' criterion. Parliament was not a possible venue to the applicants in the *Scotland District* case but they were nonetheless deemed not to have sufficient interest. This was despite the fact that Barbados has special legislation in the form of the *Administration of Justice Act 1980*,[54] which specifically allows for litigation in the public interest. Indeed, even more recent decisions have continued the now ingrained tradition of a restrictive approach to standing, requiring, virtually, that the applicant possesses a property interest in the subject matter of the litigation as a condition precedent for standing.[55]

SHOULD THE BOYCE TEST APPLY?

Whether the *Boyce v. Paddington Borough Council* test, developed in the context of a private action for public nuisance, is appropriate to determine standing for judicial review of environmental decision-making seems debatable. It seems entirely reasonable that in nuisance, where the plaintiff is attempting to recover compensation or to halt damage to an interest in land, that special loss should be the measure of compensation and of whether an injunction is appropriate. But in situations where the applicant sues to ensure sound environmental management, the paramount concern is the vindication of the public interest. This is reflected in the fact that the remedy sought tends to be one of the prerogative remedies rather than an award of damages. From this it would seem to follow that the criterion of standing based on special loss and injury might not necessarily be appropriate to review actions.

RELAXATION OF STANDING IN FOREIGN JURISDICTIONS

Whatever may be the final decision on this issue, it appears clear that recent English decisions have relaxed the meaning attached to 'sufficient interest' as the requirement for standing in review applications. In *R. v. Pollution Inspectorate, ex p. Greenpeace (No. 2)*,[56] Otton J. allowed Greenpeace standing to challenge a government decision to grant permission for the handling of nuclear waste. He held that Greenpeace had sufficient interest in the matter because it was a well-established and responsible body, acknowledged as such by international agencies, and because its members included many people living in the area of the proposed activities who would be affected by them. Otton J. took the view that Greenpeace could assist the court by providing expertise, and noted that if Greenpeace were refused standing, there might be no other way in which the issues in question could be brought to the attention of a court.[57]

The trend towards recognising the standing of pressure groups was given further support in the case of *R. v. Secretary of State for Foreign Affairs, ex p World Development Movement*.[58] Rose LJ held that the World Development Movement had sufficient interest to challenge the British government's aid for the Pergau Dam scheme in Malaysia, on the basis that there were few other parties that could challenge the decision, and also because of the prominence of the Organisation. It is important to note that the World Development Movement was granted standing even though its members had no direct personal interest in the issue before the court. Rose LJ stated that the real question 'is whether the applicant can show some substantial default or abuse, and not whether his persona rights or interests are involved'. Unlike *Rose Theatre Trust*, the court made it clear that it would not rule against the applicants' standing because so to do would mean that a clear illegality would not be subject to challenge.

Another recent decision shows that judicial review decisions concerning environmental law issues need not be brought by environmental pressure groups. Individuals may also have the right to seek judicial review, even if the *Boyce* test is not satisfied, provided they are personally affected. *R v. Secretary of State for Trade and Industry, ex p Duddridge and Others*[59] involved parents concerned about the risk to their children contracting leukemia from the electromagnetic fields (EMFs) off high voltage underground cables. The secretary of state took a decision not to limit the levels of EMFs, although he had the power to do so under the provisions of the Electricity Act. Standing was granted to the parents to argue that the secretary of state should be forced to exercise his statutory powers.

RELATIONSHIP BETWEEN JUDICIAL REVIEW AND ENVIRONMENTAL MANAGEMENT

It is not being contended that judicial review will necessarily ensure sound environmental management and consequent elimination of risks to environmental security. Even if the recent more liberal approach to standing were adopted in the Caribbean, there would still remain clear limitations to what judicial review could achieve. As Thorton and Beckwith state,[60] in judicial review actions, the role of the court is confined to ensuring that public authorities perform their functions properly. The court cannot substitute its own views on the merits of a decision for the views of a public authority. So, in the words of Smith J. in *Duddridge:*

> It is important to make clear at the outset that it is not the function of this court to decide whether there is in fact an increased risk of leukemia. The Court appreciates that the parents of these children are deeply concerned about these issues and it is not through lack of any sympathy with that concern that the court must decline to decide them. The only issue before the court is whether the Secretary of state acted unlawfully. [61]

The decision to stop short of reviewing the merits of environmental decisions, is, quite apart from the constitutional doctrine of the 'separation of powers', based upon substantial grounds. A court is not necessarily suited to assume the role of environmental decision-maker. In making environmental decisions, the administrative agency will rely on information from a variety of sources such as industry, scientists, environmental groups, consumer protection groups, and (perhaps wishful thinking) academics. The objectivity of each group's viewpoint will be assessed. A number of technical questions will need to be considered. Costs of enforcement must be taken into account, as must the effects of the legislation and the decision on market competition. The final decision will probably represent a compromise between the viewpoints held by different stakeholders.

Clearly, then, the institutional constraints on the court means that they cannot hope to have access to the same information. Accordingly, most of the commentators – those at any rate who do not support the American Public Trust doctrine [62] – agree that it is right that the court's role should be confined to ensuring whether the administrative authority's actions are consistent with the principles of administrative law. *The importance of the recent trend in liberalising the standing requirement is that the courts themselves are enabled to perform their role of keeping administrative bodies within the limits of the powers assigned.* Easier access also comports with international admonitions, found in Principle 10 of the 1992 Rio Declaration, that governments should provide 'effective access to judicial proceedings' for litigation of environmental issues.

CONCLUSION

Caribbean states have awoken to the task of reducing the risks to environmental security. At the international level they have adopted treaties and resolutions designed to prevent catastrophic harm to the environment from the use of nuclear weapons and the transshipment of nuclear materials. At the national level, Caribbean legislatures have been enacting framework type legislation to provide an institutional focal point for policy-making, standard setting, and law enforcement. There is some hesitancy in opening up the courts to individuals and pressure groups seeking judicial review of how environmental agencies discharge their functions. It is to be hoped that this reluctance is transient as Caribbean courts become more aware of the contemporary trends to liberalisation in this regard. For the use of all available means to ensure a minimum level of environmental security is central not just to creature, social and spiritual comfort. It is also essential to the discharge of international obligations incumbent upon Caribbean nation states.

Endnotes

1. Stockholm Declaration 1972 (11 ILM 1416); preamble, Principles 1, p.26; Rio Declaration 1992 (31 ILM 876), preamble, Principles 1, p. 24.
2. *Certain Phosphate Lands in Nauru-Nauru v. Australia,*1992, ICJ Report, p. 240.
3. See Declaration adopted January 31, 1992, (UN Doc. S/23500), esp. at p. 2.
4. Text in Winston Anderson, *Caribbean Instruments on International Law,* 1994, p. 71.
5. Note in particular that the following Caribbean states are parties to the Treaty: Antigua and Barbuda, The Bahamas, Barbados, Grenada, Jamaica, Trinidad and Tobago. Ibid., p. x.
6. Ibid., Preamble.
7. Ibid.
8. See generally, Winston Anderson, *The Law of Caribbean Marine Pollution,* 1997, pp. 282-287.
9. Ibid., pp. 282-283, describing the CEP/Greenpeace Report.

10. Ibid., pp. 283-284.

11. Ibid., chap. 2.

12. The Resolution, drafted by Guyana and endorsed by a CARICOM Heads of Government Meeting in Trinidad in July 1999, was introduced at the Twenty-Second Session of the General Assembly (September 1999). See Permanent Secretary, (Foreign Affairs), Ministry of Foreign Affairs & Foreign Trade. 15/B57/9-15 (1999-10-18). For a chronology of events see: 3rd INFORMAL COFOR, New York Helmsely Hotel, September 26, 1999. It was supported by the Group of 77 and China, but was rejected by some developed countries. The latter were concerned over (a) the legal implications of accepting the concept in relation to traditional rights of navigation through Caribbean sea, and (b) the precise parameters of the concept.

13. 'Promoting an integrated management approach to the Caribbean sea area in the context of sustainable development'. UNGA Res. A/RES/54/225, February 15, 2000.

14. Winston Anderson, supra, (note 4), p. 502.

15. These were: (a) orderly land use planning and coordination; (b) housing and human settlements; (c) degradation of the coastal and marine environment; (d) prevention and mitigation of the effects of oil spills; (e) solid and liquid waste management; (f) management of toxic and hazardous substances including the control of agri-chemical residues; (g) dumping of extra-regional, hazardous and toxic wastes in the Region; (h) water quality and supply; (i) forest and watershed management; (j) preservation of genetic resources; (k) vector control; (l) disaster preparedness; (m) preservation of cultural, archaeological and historical resources; and (n) air and noise pollution. *Ibid.*

16. Earth Summit: Programme of Action for Small Island, *Global Conference on the Sustainable Development of Small Island Developing States, Bridgetown, Barbados, 26 April-6 May 1994* (United Nations Publication).

17. Ibid., Declaration of Barbados.

18. Caribbean Ministerial Meeting on the Implementation of the Programme of Action for the Sustainable Development of Small Island Developing States, Barbados, November 10-14, 1997; SIDS97/CONF.27/Rev.1

19. Carnegie, A. R., 'Governmental Institutional Organisations and Legislative Requirements for Sustainable Development', and Griffith, Mark, 'Governmental Arrangements and Legislative Requirements for Sustainable Development in the Caribbean' With Special Emphasis on Governmental Institutional Arrangements'. Both articles are published in Dr. Mark Griffith & Professor Bishnodat Persuad, *Economic Policy and the Environment:*

The Caribbean Experience, (UWICED, 1995), pp. 105-120, and 121-146, respectively.

20. The deficiencies are evident, for example, from an analysis of the various *Beach Protection Acts*, prevalent throughout the region. See generally, *Caribbean Law Institute,The Environmental Laws of the Commonwealth Caribbean* (CLI, 1992).

21. For a good example of sectoral legislation leading to institutional fragmentation, see the case study of the Barbados situation presented in article by Mark Griffith, supra, (note 19).

22. The *National Conservation Environmental Protection Act 1987 (No. 5 of 1987)* ('NCEPA') was enacted on 27th April 1987 by the National Assembly of Saint Kitts and Nevis. Brought into effect on 3rd July 1989 by SRO 14 of 1989. See, too, the *National Conservation and Environmental Protection (Amendment) Act, 1996. Act No. 12 of 1996.*

23. The *Environmental Protection Act 1992 (No. 22 of 1992)* (BEPA) was enacted on 14th October 1992. The BEPA is composed of a statement of policy and eight parts. Part I deals entirely with preliminary issues such as the title of the statute and interpretation of words and phrases used in the body of the legislation. Part II establishes the institutional arrangements for the management of the environment. Parts III - VI concern substantive regulation and adopts the approach of regulation by functional segments/ units. Parts VII and VIII relate to general and miscellaneous matters such as investigations, proceedings, penalties and the making of regulations

24. *Environmental Health Services Act* 1987 (No. 4 of 1987, Bahamas).

25. *Environmental Health Services Act* was enacted 4th July 1991 (Act No. 14 of 1991) by the Parliament of Saint Vincent and the Grenadines.

26. Act 9 of 1991.

27. Act No. 3 of 1995; replaced by Act No. 3 of 2000, which is basically to the same effect.

28. Act No. 11 of 1996.

29. There appears to be no provision in the Act in Belize that the Act binds the Crown.

30. See A.R. Carnegie, *supra* (note 19) at p. 114.

31. EPA 1992, sect. 8.

32. NCEPA, 1987, (St Kitts & Nevis), s. 3 (2); EMA 1995, 2000 (Trinidad and Tobago), s.5.

33. NRCA (Jamaica), s. 7.

34. Unreported Judgment of the Court of Appeal of Jamaica: Suit No. C.L. 1999/S-134; dated July 1, 1999. See generally, Winston Anderson, 'Implementing MEAs in the Caribbean: Hard Lessons' from *Seafood and Ting*' (2000) Vol. 10 No. 2 *Review of European Community & International Environmental Law* 227.

35. Amendment Act, 1996 (St Kitts & Nevis) s. 2B (i) (ii).
36. Ibid., sect. 4 (1), (a).
37. (1977) 18 ALR 210.
38. See e.g. NRCAA, Jamaica, sect. 8.
39. See e.g., NRCAA Jamaica, sect. 10 (3).
40. *Ellen Street Estates Ltd., v. Minister of Health* [1934] 1 KB 590.
41. Ibid., sect. 43.
42. Ibid., sect. 58.
43. *56 E/1986 (L.N.)*
44. NRCAA 1991 (Jamaica), sects. 9 & 31.
45. 480/1973 (L.N.)
46. *(Cap. 113)*
47. NRCAA 1991 (Jamaica), sect. 40.
48. The merger of the Natural Resources Conservation Authority with Planning into the National Environmental Planning Agency (NEPA) was, at the time of writing, imminent.
49. [1903] 1 Ch. 109.
50. [1990] 1 All ER 754.
51. Unreported Judgement of the High Court of Antigua and Barbuda, No. 7 of 1993, dated March 12, 1993. See also Winston Anderson, 'Locus Standi in Commonwealth Environmental Law: Caribbean Perspectives' in (1994) Vol. 4 No. 2 *The Caribbean Law Review*, 379, pp. 383-387.
52. (1996) 53 WIR 66.
53. Unreported Judgement of the Court of Appeal (OECS), Civil Appeal No. 20A of 1997; dated April 8, 1998
54. Cap. 109, 63/1980.
55. See *The Historical and Archaeological Society of Antigua and Barbuda v. Colonial Ventures Limited,* Unreported Judgment of the High Court of Antigua and Barbuda, Suit No. 156 of 2000 (In Chambers), dated June 22, 2000 (Georges J.). But see encouraging developments in the Cayman Islands case of *National Trust For the Cayman Islands, Burns Conolly v. The Planning Appeals Tribunal* Cause No 368/2000 and 378/2000 (Sanderson J.).
56. [1994] 4 All ER 329. See further: Justine Thornton & Silas Beckwith, *Environmental Law* (Sweet & Maxwell, 1997), p. 15.
57. Thornton & Beckwith, *ibid.*, p. 15.
58. [1995] 1 All ER 611.
59. [1995] Env. LR 151; 7:2 (1995), p. 224.
60. Ibid., (note 56), p.15.
61. Ibid.
62. Winston Anderson, supra (note 51), pp. 408-410.

Part IV

❋

Caribbean Integration
Reconsidered

14

Is the Goal of Regional Integration Still Relevant among Small States? The Case of the OECS and CARICOM

Patsy Lewis

Abstract: This chapter focuses on the experience of the OECS, a sub-regional grouping within the CARICOM regional integration scheme, in an effort to highlight some of the challenges confronting micro-states in the regional integration process. It examines the extent to which the shift in the theoretical underpinnings and goals of regional integration processes in the 1960s and 1970s, from the creation of protected markets among countries of like size and resource endowments, to one of 'open regionalism' based on the ideology of free trade amongst countries of widely difference size and resource endowment which affords no privileges to small size, has undermined the viability of the OECS and, ultimately, CARICOM itself. Specifically, it questions whether this shift has derailed the process in the Caribbean region; whether it is worthwhile for such schemes to continue to focus on economic goals over political processes; and whether the OECS experience does not mirror the future of CARICOM.

'In a divided world
That don't need islands no more
Are we doomed forever,
To be at somebody's mercy.
Little keys can open up mighty doors'

INTRODUCTION

This verse from popular calypsonian David Rudder's 'Haiti I'm sorry',[1] speaks both to the despair small Caribbean states, and indeed small states in general, feel in contemplating a world that appears to limit the options previously open to them. But it also speaks to the potential that such states hold, despite their small size, to shape their own fortunes. Rudder's perspective on smallness provides an appropriate framework for analysing the integration experience of some of the world's smallest island states, drawn together as the Organisation of Eastern Caribbean States (OECS). The OECS constitutes a sub-grouping within the Caribbean Community (CARICOM). Its members are the four independent states of the Windward Islands — Grenada, Dominica, St Vincent and the Grenadines and St Lucia; two independent states of the Leeward Islands – Antigua and Barbuda and the Federation of St Christopher and Nevis (St Kitts/Nevis); and Montserrat, which remains a British dependency. CARICOM includes these states as well as Jamaica, Barbados, Trinidad and Tobago, Guyana, Belize, The Bahamas (which is a part of the Caribbean Community but not common market, nor is, strictly speaking in the Caribbean) and Suriname.[2] The OECS represents some of the world's smallest independent states the largest being Dominica, covering a mere 750 km[2] and with a combined population of a little over a quarter of a million people (Table 1).

Most of these states emerged as independent entities in the 1980s, a decade of prosperity for them, but are now facing serious challenges to their economic well being epitomised, in the Windwards by the challenges to the survival of the banana industry, central to most of their economies, and, in the Leewards, by the attack on their offshore financial sector by the OECD. For the OECS, the world has changed significantly since their independence. Notions of colonial responsibility for their economic development, which underpinned preferential arrangements embedded in the ACP/ EU relationship, and an acceptance by the international community of the need for special and differential treatment for small states, have been replaced by assertions that it is possible for all states, despite size and resource endowments, to succeed in an international environment of global free trade. This acceptance of the neo-liberal perspective that free trade was good for all countries, which, paradoxically for some,[3] has encouraged the growth of regional arrangements, has had consequences for the region's older integration movements. Specifically, the movement towards a hemispheric Free Trade Area of the Americas (FTAA), of which these countries are a part, has serious consequences for their integration movements, both because the perceptual underpinnings are different, and because it threatens to weaken their own development processes.

This paper uses the OECS integration movement, within the broader context of CARICOM integration, to illuminate some of the issues the neo-liberal trading regime poses for integration processes among small states. It discusses the reasons for the formation of the OECS within CARICOM, in the context of the theoretical considerations guiding the formation of the wider integration movement, their experiences so far, and ways in which their economic processes have been affected by the prospect of an FTAA. The paper raises the question of whether these wider integration processes, reflected in the FTAA and Regional Economic Partnership Agreements (REPAS) proposed by the EU to replace the Lomé Convention, have rendered the narrower OECS/CARICOM arrangements redundant and what, if anything, can be rescued from the process.

BACKGROUND

The Caribbean Community and Common Market (CARICOM) emerged out of the failed West Indies Federation, which had been perceived, by the British, as a mechanism for granting independence to countries too small to achieve this on their own. The failure of the Federation[4] formalised the division between two broad groups of countries that comprised it.[5] On the one hand, the larger and more resource-endowed countries – Jamaica, Trinidad and Tobago and Barbados (Barbados here being the exception both in terms of size and endowments) – proceeded to independence after its collapse, while the smaller resource poor islands of the Windward and Leeward chain were forced to remain British dependencies. This division between the two groups was formalised in the regional integration movement, expressed in CARICOM, with the recognition of More Development Countries (MDCs) and Lesser Developed Countries (LDCs), the latter embracing all the Windward and Leeward Islands and Belize, finding form in special treatment and provisions for the LDCs in the treaty of Chaguaramas that established CARICOM.

The OECS which was formed among the LDCs (excluding Belize) in 1983 was both a reflection of the different experiences of its members as well as a perception of weakness by the LDCs in relation to the more advanced MDCs. After the Federation's collapse, the Windward and Leeward islands were forced to forego independence and settle instead for 'Associated Statehood', a truncated and controversial form of independence, where they were given control over functions that fell within their domestic jurisdiction, while the conduct of their foreign affairs and defence remained with the British government.[6] During this period, however, they developed structures and relationships, which later provided the basis for the OECS. These included a currency board and common currency, the Eastern Caribbean dollar which had served the Federation; a common judicial system with a single High Court; and, significantly, a forum for consultation at the Heads of Government level in the WISA (West Indies Associated States) Council. The WISA states, in advance of their accession to CARIFTA (Caribbean Free Trade Area), which preceded CARICOM,[7] proposed their own common market arrangement, the East Caribbean Common Market (ECCM), with the goal of removing barriers to trade, movement of capital and establishment of services and the free movement of people within the area. The ECCM served to consolidate their special economic interests within the broader grouping. It represented a more encompassing form of regional integration with a common market and goals for harmonisation of regulations and policy than CARIFTA and a free trade area, which promoted trade over other forms of integration. Although CARICOM embraced the goals of a common market, the WISA states continued with the ECCM.

The ECCM and WISA were eventually transformed into the OECS, now among independent states (with the exception of Montserrat), which brought together the economic and political areas of cooperation, strengthened by provisions for cooperation in security, and functional cooperation on a wide range of issues. The OECS gained international notoriety when its members attempted to provide legal justification for the 1983 US invasion of Grenada under Article 8 of the Charter, which addresses security cooperation. OECS countries emerged in the post-independence era as a more coherent group, strengthened as a regional organisation, in party, by the ideological affinity of its leaders coming out of their role in the Grenada invasion.[8]

THE OECS AND CARICOM

The integration movement in the Commonwealth Caribbean was influenced by the European integration process, modified by Latin American and Caribbean dependency theory to suit the perceived developmental needs of the region. Integration theory developed to explain the European experience that was based on the creation of a customs union among its members and functional cooperation that was expected to spill over into the political sphere. European interest in integration lay, not only in its possibility for strengthening economic performance, but more importantly in its potential for contributing to European peace by integrating national economies so closely that it would make war among its members difficult.

In Latin America and other developing countries, the movement's appeal lay in its development potential, which went beyond issues of specialisation and competitiveness of firms. In Latin America, following the failure of national Import Substitution Industrialisation (ISI) strategies advocated by ELCA and pursued in Latin America and the Caribbean, regional integration was viewed as an avenue for creating larger markets for national production. This held special appeal for the Commonwealth Caribbean given the small size of their internal markets. The underlying aim of this process was to reduce the dependency such countries had on developed countries in preference for a more autonomous type of development based on the creation of indigenous industrial capacity and control over national resources. Integration was attractive for Caribbean countries, therefore, because of the scope it provided for enlarged markets, its promotion of an industrial base and transformation of structures of production, which, ultimately, would be reflected in a change in its relationship with Europe and the US, and its potential for saving foreign exchange.

In the Caribbean integration process, modifications were made to traditional customs union theory, which was premised on free trade among participants, to address the reality of differing economic strengths and prospects of its members and the potential this had for economic polarization. This was reflected in the formal designation of the Windward and Leeward Islands and Belize as LDCs and Barbados, Guyana, Jamaica and Trinidad and Tobago as MDCs, which had concrete implications for the former's treatment in the process. This was expressed in special provisions allowing them more generous time periods for opening their markets to trade (20 years as opposed to five for MDCs) and for removing duties on goods not immediately subject to free trade, and to protect their industries from competing industries in MDC countries, even when the latter were established first. The Caribbean Development Bank was established to provide, *inter alia*, soft loans for the establishment of industries in the LDCs.

The OECS worked alongside CARICOM, but represented a much more closely integrated process reflected in stronger institutional arrangements that included two secretariats (later reduced to one), focusing on economic integration,[9] the other functional activities, regular meetings of the Authority of Heads of Governments, a concerted effort at coordinating and harmonising policies, laws and regulations, *inter alia*. This process, particularly the tendency to treat the OECS as a distinct sub-regional entity, was encouraged by the desire to secure greater benefits than the MDCs under the Lome Convention, which were more likely for projects of a regional rather than national nature.

Despite the classification of OECS countries as LDCs, the first decade of their independence saw steady economic growth and a generally favourable economic performance outstripping that of their MDC counterparts. OECS economies grew in the 1980s by an average of 5.76 per cent, with no OECS country or Belize experiencing negative growth during this period. The situation was different for the MDCs, with most experiencing years of negative growth during this period. Although the 1990s were a period of lower growth for OECS economies, the trend of a more favourable performance in relation to the MDCs continued with OECS economies growing at an average of 2.88 per cent compared to 1.23 per cent for Barbados, 0.12 per cent for Jamaica, and 2.41 per cent for Trinidad and Tobago.[10] Significantly, OECS countries also performed well on the UNDP's Human Development Index Ranking of countries, performing better than Jamaica and Guyana, although other MDC countries such as Barbados, The Bahamas and Trinidad and Tobago scored high (Table 3).

The OECS states' strong economic showing, however, masks a fragile economic base, reflected in their continued dependence, in three of the four Windward islands on bananas and tourism, and in the Leewards on tourism and the financial services sector.[11] Their economic performance has been attributed to the existence of preferential access to the British market for Windward Islands bananas which experienced expanded production and favourable prices in the 1980s; concessionary financing from international financial organisations; aid flows from the US and EC; and the development of the services sector, particularly tourism, in the Leeward and some Windward Islands. However, early trends in globalisation influencing the move towards regionalism, reflected in the EC's transformation to the European Union and the establishment of a Single European Market and the formation of NAFTA, suggested that their traditional approach to development, premised on preferential access to their major export markets, was threatened. The EU's SEM, in particular, and the likelihood of reduced protection under a new banana regime, threatened the very foundations of Windward Islands economies, already plagued by high levels of unemployment and rural poverty (Table 3).

By its own measure, CARICOM had little effect in transforming the character of its economies, especially those of the LDCs. The CARICOM market never achieved the significance as an outlet for national production as hoped, despite protective mechanisms for local and regional enterprises. Intra-regional trade did show some growth since CARICOM was established in 1973.

Intra-regional imports as a percentage of total imports showed modest improvement, moving from 7.1 per cent in 1974 to 9.5 per cent in 1998.[12] Intra-regional exports as a percentage of total exports fared better, moving from 7.2 per cent in 1974 to 22.9 per cent in 1998. The picture here is heavily skewed, however, in favour of the MDCs, who alone account for 90.4 per cent of intra-regional exports as opposed to 8.4 per cent from the OECS. Trinidad and Tobago alone accounted for 75.2 per cent of intra-regional exports, mainly in petroleum products, followed by Jamaica with 10.8 per cent (Table 4). If Trinidad and Tobago were excluded, the picture would be far less impressive.[13]

Despite their minimal contribution to intra-regional exports, OECS states showed a greater reliance on intra-regional trade than the MDCs, with intra-regional exports, in 1998, comprising 22.8 per cent of total exports for the

MDCs, compared with 37.6 per cent for the OECS.[14] Even here, the picture is uneven, with intra-regional exports accounting for only 3.3 per cent of total exports from Jamaica, but 43.3 per cent of Barbados', and 31.5 per cent of Trinidad and Tobago's (Table 4). Among the OECS countries, Dominica relies most on the regional market, with its exports to the region accounting for 78.3 per cent of its total exports, while St Kitts falls at the other end of the spectrum, with its exports to the region accounting for a mere 3.3 per cent of its total exports (Table 4).[15] These gains in intra-regional trade must be balanced by a broader perspective which shows CARICOM exports growing by a mere 4 per cent between 1990-1998 and its total imports by 55 per cent, reflecting, as CARICOM notes, 'a large imbalance in the growth of trade with extra-regional markets'.[16]

Despite these gains in intra-regional trade, however, CARICOM trade remained skewed towards traditional markets of Europe and the US, which suggested that the character of production within the region had remained largely unchanged. CARICOM countries continued to rely on the US and EU as chief sources of imports, with 46.2 per cent and 13.7 per cent respectively, in 1998, and exports, with 35.2 per cent and 16.9 per cent, respectively. The EU market was particularly important to the OECS countries as an outlet for their primary products, primarily bananas. This is reflected in their continued dependence on the sale of bananas to Europe and the economic and social dislocation they have begun to experience with a reduction in protected access.[17] Although exacerbated in the Windward Islands' economies, the point holds true for all CARICOM states: the integration process, although strengthening intra-regional trade, was unable to transform the character of regional economies from primary producers to manufacturers hence, primary exports continue to dominate regional economies – oil in Trinidad and Tobago,[18] bauxite/alumina in Jamaica, gold in Guyana, and bananas in the Windward Islands. This is also evident in the fact that the region remains a high importer of food – 15.7 per cent of total imports – pointing to an economic structure that privileges export agriculture over production for domestic consumption.[19]

Various reasons have been proposed for the failure of both CARICOM and the OECS to transform the character of the economies of member states. One explanation points to the sameness of production activities and resource base across the region, and the smallness of the regional market. Attempts to develop industries within the OECS were undermined by the tendency for OECS governments to protect their own industries at the expense of the regional process, thus ultimately undermining their own viability. The process was also negatively affected by the downturn in the economic fortunes of the MDCs in the 1980s and 1990s that led to currency devaluations in all MDC countries, except Barbados. This encouraged the erection of barriers against regional competitors and affected the regional trade in agricultural products from the Windward Islands. It also led to the collapse, in 1983, of the Multi-lateral clearing facility which had been established to facilitate intra-regional trade by making cross-country settling of accounts easier, when Guyana, highly-indebted to the facility, defaulted on its obligations.[20]

OECS

The late 1980s and early 1990s marked a period of change for the regional integration process. Developments in the global political and economic arena suggested an environment less conducive to the development goals of small Caribbean states. The specific harbingers of these changes were the EC's decision to strengthen its integration process with the formation of a single market; and a general movement towards free trade agreements with the consolidation of existing regional blocs and the formation of new ones, such as the US/Canada Free Trade Agreement and the negotiation of a US/Mexico free trade arrangement. Other important indicators were the beginning of the Uruguay Round talks on global trade liberalisation, which, added to the collapse of communism throughout Eastern Europe and the Soviet Union, suggested the full embrace of free market principles at the international level. The Uruguay Round, in particular, appeared particularly threatening, reflected in the observations of the West Indian Commission – established in 1992 to review CARICOM – that the GATT talks 'continue with no sure benefits, and holding a number of serious potential threats, for countries like our own'.[21] The insecurities these developments engendered were reflected in a comment by Trinidad and Tobago's prime minister, ANR Robinson, in his paper calling for a reform of CARICOM, when he noted 'the real danger of the Caribbean becoming a backwater at a time of historic change when the central reality in international affairs lay in the fundamental restructuring which was taking place in the world'.[22] It is in this context that both the attempts to form a political union of some, if not all OECS states, and the decision to review CARICOM's goals and operations, and the subsequent adoption of measures to strengthen the regional process, were taken.

The OECS, because of the importance of the European market to their economic well being, were the first to respond to the negative effects that globalisation posed to their economic stability. This was met with a call, in 1986, originating from the Windward Islands, to radically transform the integration process from its economic and functional focus to a full embrace of political union of all OECS countries as a means of responding to the challenges confronting their survival.[23] CARICOM responded a little later, in 1989, with measures to implement a Single Market and Economy (CSME).

By 1987, when the proposal for a political union of OECS countries was made, the OECS had eliminated most barriers to trade within the ECCM, operated a common external tariff, common rules of origin, common trade policy which included quantitative restrictions to protect specified industries. Freedom of movement, however, and barriers against the establishment of services remained elusive goals. They operated CARICOM's fiscal incentives programme in relation to foreign enterprises, and had made good progress toward harmonising laws and regulations in areas of taxation, incentives and customs, inter alia. They were even discussing moving towards creating a customs union. In terms of their goals of coordinating foreign policy and pursuing joint representation and accreditation to states and international organisations, they had limited success, particularly in foreign policy coordination. They did, however, operate common high commissions in London and Canada, although not all countries were represented, and housed their separate embassies in New York in a single building, saving on overhead costs. These modest achievements, however, represented a significant advance over what had been achieved within CARICOM. OECS cooperation extended to functional areas of health, education and sports. The Organisation established a Legislative Unit that advised individual governments on draft legislation, drafted common legislation for all member states, and kept records of international treaties to which member states were a party.

The OECS' main achievement, however, can be viewed as its ability to present its members as a distinct sub-grouping within CARICOM. This had favourable consequences for aid disbursement, their ability to secure technical and financial assistance and to keep their special needs on the regional agenda, reflected in their ability to keep the markets of MDC countries open to their exports in periods of economic downturn. One of its main weaknesses, however, was the inability to transform regional agreements into national laws. This has been attributed to an absence of political will on the part of OECS leaders, reflected in a tendency to succumb to national pressures to the detriment of the regional process.[24] The problem has plagued the implementation of freedom of movement, which had been adopted by the Heads in 1989 and the effective operation of the industry allocation programme, which aimed at rationalising the development of national industries and reducing inter-island competition thus enhancing the possibilities for such industries to be competitive. The OECS failed to resolve the issue of uncoordinated shipping and airline services into the region, the latter moving in the direction of competing foreign-owned 'national' airlines of questionable viability. This failure, however, is a broader failure of CARICOM which also aimed at addressing the absence, particularly in shipping, of a reliable service for the region, and which provides the more logical forum for addressing this intractable problem.

The call for the OECS effort to be shifted from an economic one, characterised by a functionalist approach to decision-making, was based both on a dissatisfaction with the pace of progress within the arrangement, and the perceived threats to the economic viability of member states from the shifts in the global economy towards greater free trade, but within the context of mega-blocs. The main arguments made by the proponents of union, who all hailed from the agricultural-based Windward Islands, was that changes in the world economy signaled an erosion of the elements which had so far sustained regional economies: these included an expected decline in foreign inflows and difficulties in securing non-governmental financial inflows, the possible loss of concessionary financing because their status as middle-income countries, and a loss of export markets. They feared that preferential access to the US market, under the Caribbean Basin Initiative, would be eroded by the creation of NAFTA, and, in the case of the UK, that the SEM would replace their banana protocol with the UK with a far less favourable arrangement. They strongly believed that their difficulties were directly related to their small physical size. They argued that, given the region's poor record with implementation, political union provided the only solution for pooling their various strengths to combat the threats they foresaw.

The political union initiative, which originated with St Vincent and the Grenadines' prime minister, James Mitchell, failed to interest the governments and people of the Leeward Islands who felt that Windward Islands leaders were responding to the perceived threat to their banana industry. Given their service-based economies, they did not perceive their vulnerability in the same way. The initiative proceeded until 1992 among the Windwards as a more limited affair, but became dormant after internal political change in St Lucia prevented its adoption by parliament there. It was revived briefly in 1998 when Barbados Prime Minister, Owen Arthur, expressed interest in entering into a Confederation with the OECS countries. The issue remains dormant, though not dead.

In the absence of a political union OECS countries responded to external challenges by agreeing to strengthen their integration process with the formation of a single market by 1993, which would include the free movement of goods and services, labour and capital and macro economic policy coordination. Monetary union already existed within the OECS with a common currency, the Eastern Caribbean dollar, and central bank. The OECS' decision to establish a single market, in the context of a broader push by CARICOM to achieve a single market and economy, would suggest that its members continued to perceive their relationship with CARICOM as a competitive one. The OECS Secretariat noted that the 'principal' objective of establishing a single market was 'the strengthening of the economic position of the sub-regional economies in the global economic system and in the CARICOM area'.[25]

CARICOM's responses to the identified global challenges was for a strengthening of the integration process and, at the behest of Trinidad and Tobago's prime minister, ANR Robinson, a review of the entire package. This led to the 1989 Grand Anse Declaration, which agreed, *inter alia*, to the formation of a CARICOM Single Market and Economy (CSME),[26] the details of which were formally accepted by member states in 1992. Specific measures adopted included the free movement of people in certain occupations (UWI graduates, sports and media), the formation of a monetary union guided by specific criteria for the performance of national economies, the implementation of a common external tariff and the adoption of common incentives programme. The review led to a revision of the Treaty of Chaguaramas through the adoption of nine protocols governing the establishment of services and movement of capital, industrial, trade, agricultural, transportation policy and competition policy, dispute settlement and institutional reform of CARICOM institutions and organs. Significantly, the new measures reduced the distinction in place between LDCs and MDCs, which now less justifiable in light of the former's more favourable economic showing in the previous decade. The LDCs were required to adopt the same CET on final good within the same time frame as the MDCs. Some concessions were made, however, in allowing them tariffs between 0-5 per cent as opposed to 5 per cent for MDCs on non-competing inputs, and in the Rules of Origin.[27]

The CSME was expected to increase the competitiveness of regional firms in the context of what was viewed as 'an increasingly open and competitive global environment'.[28] It sought to establish a more favourable environment for firms to operate, especially in terms of facilitating the development of firms of a regional character, and those geared towards export. It sought to privilege the service sector over the productive sectors, given the increasing role of services in the international economy. The elements which were viewed as important to the development of competitiveness of such firms included the reduction of government involvement in productive enterprises; the removal of restrictions on certain categories of workers so as to make skilled labour available to firms across the region; removal of restrictions on the establishment of CARICOM firms in national markets such as Alien Witholding Laws common to OECS countries; the creation of a capital market and monetary union to facilitate the smooth operations of these firms.

Central to the CSME was the agreement to institute a Caribbean Court of Justice to arbitrate in disputes among member states in matters arising from implementation of the CSME. The court has proved controversial, however, as its jurisdiction goes beyond matters arising from the CSME. It is also expected to serve as the court of final appeal for the region, abolishing the appeal to the UK Privy Council. The Revision to the Treaty of Chaguaramas, reflected in the protocols, also sought to address widespread dissatisfaction with the progress of change and the ability to transform regional agreements into national action – the same issues which plagued the OECS process – with the establishment of a Community Council to oversee the implementation of decisions taken by CARICOM heads (The Conference); and Ministerial Councils in the major areas of economic cooperation to support the Council. CARICOM governments addressed the elusive goal of cooperation in foreign affairs with the establishment of a Regional Negotiating Machinery (RNM). Coordination of foreign relations was now viewed with particular urgency in light of the new challenges thrown up on the international scene, especially in the negotiation of a new relationship with the EU to replace the Lomé Conventions and the free trade area of the Americas. The RNM was vested with the authority, not only to coordinate a regional response to these developments, but also to lead the negotiating process.[29]

From Regional Integration to Regionalism

While the initiatives to strengthen the CARICOM process did not reflect a departure from the Organisation's original goals, it was clear that the context had changed. Regional Heads recognised, and accepted, that regional integration involved a different kind of process than originally conceived. The central goal of the movement, the need to compensate for small size and a sense of insecurity to meet the challenges they faced as small states in the international arena, remained unchanged. What had changed was the acceptance that economic viability could be achieved within the framework of a protected regional market for firms in the early stages of development from international competition, to an acceptance that such industries could only become competitive if immediately subjected to open competition.

The wave of regional integration schemes being established in the early 1990s, which acted as a spur to the reassessment of CARICOM, has been coined by Bhagwati as 'the Second Regionalism', suggesting a break with the earlier integration movements of the 1960s and 1970s.[30] These groups emerged in a different global context of the triumph of the free-market version of capitalism, over Communism and statist economics. As noted earlier, economies in Latin America and the Caribbean were already being subjected to IMF

BRYN MAWR COLLEGE BOOKSHOP

www.brynmawr.edu/bookshop

- Textbooks
- General books
- Special order books
- School supplies
- Greeting cards
- Imprinted gifts
- Imprinted clothes
- College rings
- College chairs
- Snacks, candy
- Health and beauty aids
- Magazines

Hours
Monday through Friday
9: 30 a.m.-5 p.m.

Saturday
12-3 p.m.
(when classes are in session)

We accept Mastercard,
Visa, Discover, and
American Express.

610-526-5323

Bryn Mawr College
Bookshop is College
owned and operated.

Bryn Mawr College Bookshop

Last day to return textbooks for Spring

Wednesday, January 27, 2010

1. Returns must be accompanied by a cash register receipt.

2. New books must be in mint condition—absolutely new and unmarked. Books that are purchased with shrink-wrap or poly-wrapped must be returned with the wrap intact.

DO NOT WRITE OR MARK IN YOUR BOOKS UNTIL YOU ARE POSITIVE YOU ARE KEEPING THEM!

BRYN MAWR

978
BH

structural adjustment policies geared at opening their economies. This process was not occurring within the broader context of regional integration schemes, but in the realm of national policy. In the Caribbean, therefore, CARICOM's initiatives to reassess the integration process was a belated response to developments already occurring at the national level under the auspices of international financial organisations.

The second wave of regionalism has been attributed to initial stalls in the Uruguay Round on international free trade, and the US' interest in developing alternative forums for advancing global free trade. It is because of this commitment to free trade and the opening of national economies that ECLAC has dubbed the new regionalism 'open regionalism'. Its development has also been viewed as an attempt, particularly by the US and Europe to achieve competitiveness vis-à-vis each other.[31] Open regionalism, therefore, is viewed, by some, as an integral part of the movement toward global free trade, or as a 'third-tier' in the liberalisation process, the first being the unilateral opening of economies in the late 1980s, early 1990s, followed by the multi-lateral opening represented by the Uruguay Round.[32] In this framework open regionalism represents an ever-greater degree of liberalisation than was possible at the multi-lateral level.[33]

Open regionalism differs from regional integration of the 1960s and 1970s in its assumptions that competitiveness was possible only in the context of open markets, and that this holds for all economies regardless of size or resource endowments. Within these assumptions, there is little patience with arguments for special and differential arrangements for small countries arising from concerns about the negative effects of trade liberalisation in aggravating regional differences among countries. As Burke et al note, the debates around regionalism have shifted from concern about its ability to advance the welfare of its member to whether or not it advances global free trade.[34] This perceptual shift has already had specific consequences for CARICOM countries. The most obvious instance of this was the WTO's rejection of the EU's banana regime, and its lack of response to pleas from OECS micro-states that they faced severe economic dislocation in the context of reduced protection on the EU market. Generally, the WTO has few provisions for small states in the process of opening their markets, limited to provisions for a delay in applying certain clauses of the WTO agreement and a call on developed countries to provide them with technical assistance. A similar attitude has been adopted within the FTAA, which has made few concessions to regional arguments relating to small size. CARICOM's call for the establishment of a separate negotiating group for small states was rejected in favour of a more limited Consultative Group on Small Economies, restricted to monitoring the negotiating process and reporting to the Negotiating Council matters affecting small countries.[35] The trend of full reciprocity between partners of unequal size and resource endowments has also been embraced by the EU as a formula for its Regional Economic Partnership Agreements (REPAs) with ACP countries.

Regionalism and its Challenges to Caribbean Integration

The CARICOM region has been caught up in this new wave of regionalism because of its decision to participate in the negotiation of a Free Trade Area of the Americas (FTAA), and the likelihood of its post-Lomé relationship with Europe taking the form of REPAs, based on fully reciprocal access to markets. CARICOM states are reluctant participants in these processes, their involvement based on a psychological sense of their inevitability and their own inability to influence the direction of change, especially in relation to their traditional trading partners. It is also a response to failings in their integration process, certainly in its ability to transform their economies and bring about growth. As Table 3 shows, the Caribbean remains a region high in unemployment.

The Caribbean's participation in these broader processes has two implications worth noting. The first lies in the tremendous strain on human resources arising from the need to engage in the simultaneous negotiation of these arrangements covering a wide arena. Both FTAA and REPAs are expected to be negotiated by 2005. This also does not take account of the effort required to implement the CSME and other initiatives such as the establishment of trade agreements with the Dominican Republic, Canada and Cuba, among others, and to fulfill their obligations under the WTO. The region has responded to this challenge with the establishment of the Regional Negotiating Machinery (RNM) to guide the negotiating process on their behalf. While this addresses the challenges to each member state of providing individual negotiators for all areas of these agreements, the reality is that CARICOM countries are at a disadvantage, certainly in terms of the sheer number, if not quality, of personnel that large countries such as the US and Brazil have at their disposal.[36]

The second challenge these countries are already facing from their experience in negotiating the FTAA arises from the pressures powerful countries can bring to bear in advancing the process beyond what is possible within the wider multi-lateral process. NAFTA, which included regulations on labour and the environment, not possible to achieve within the WTO, has set a precedent for what can be expected under the FTAA. The commitment for the FTAA to be 'WTO-plus', adopted as a general principle of the negotiations, suggests that CARICOM countries may well find themselves subject to far greater opening of their economies than they are ready for, or required by the wider international trading regime, while their appeal for special measures to address the challenges arising from the small size of their economies is treated superficially. Nor does CARICOM find the option of opting out of these arrangements feasible, as this would have negative consequences for access to their most important markets.

CARICOM's commitment to participate in these processes raises the question of how useful is its own regional integration scheme, given the fact that the ultimate aim of both FTAA and REPAs is the complete removal of barriers to trade among member states. The first challenge to CARICOM's CSME would be the maintenance of the CET that it is busily trying to achieve before the FTAA comes on stream in 2006.[37] The CET provides for a reduction in tariffs within the community from 35 per cent to a maximum rate of 20 per cent between 1993 and 1998.[38] Although most countries have implemented phase IV (the final phase) of reductions, not all have done so.[39] This is being treated with some urgency as CARICOM hopes to be able to negotiate within the FTAA to keep its CET for a transitory period as a concession to the small size of its member states.

The implications of the embrace of open regionalism and CARICOM's response in the formation of a CSME, has had more obvious implications for the OECS integration process. The OECS' decision, in particular, to form its own single market has been derailed, to some extent, by CARICOM's CSME. The OECS has had to shelve its plans for establishing its own CET because the CSME, which requires OECS countries to adopt the same tariffs as other CARICOM states, has removed the basis for a separate CET among OECS countries. An OECS commissioned study noted these difficulties, pointing out that possibilities for an OECS single market remained for joint or integrated approaches to the production of goods and services, the full removal of restrictions to intra-OECS travel, and the suspension of provisions of the Aliens Land Holding Regulations that exist in OECS countries.[40]

Even these limited areas for providing a distinctive OECS arrangement within the CSME appear optimistic. The goal of the CSME is also the integration of production and services across the region. So far, such moves have emerged from the services sector, led by Trinidad and Tobago and Jamaica – financial services in the former, and tourism in the latter. Trinidadian firms have penetrated the banking and insurance industries, as well as the productive sector in both MDC and OECS countries. The favoured route for penetration has been through the purchase of shares in national banks in OECS countries open to divestment, the acquisition of assets in Jamaican insurance companies following a crisis in the financial sector in the 1990s.[41] One Trinidadian company has even bought out the Jamaica cement company. Jamaican tourism companies have also extended their fields of operation not only to other CARICOM countries, but also outside the region. For example, the Sandals Group, headed by Butch Stewart, has established hotels across the Caribbean, from Cuba to St Lucia, and the Issa Group in Brazil. The trend suggests that investments in productive and service enterprises will come from areas in the CARICOM region most equipped to establish such firms, most likely in the MDCs, and will go anywhere in the region where opportunities present themselves. The OECS has been the primary beneficiary of most of CARCOM cross-border investments, which CARICOM attributes to the generally low levels of technology and entrepreneurship coupled with a medium level of capital income.[42] It is also likely that the strength of the EC dollar, which, unlike other major regional currencies, has not experienced devaluation, and the resulting economic stability of these countries, has contributed to their attractiveness. The suspension of Alien Landholding laws within the OECS may provide greater encouragement to OECS firms to branch out within the sub-region, but, as CARICOM is committed, under the CSME, to the removal of all such restrictions vis-à-vis the wider community, this advantage may be short lived.

The possibility of OECS opening its doors fully to labour movement throughout the sub-region remains an area in which the OECS could move beyond the more restricted provisions of the CSME which limits movements to certain categories of workers. This could provide a fillip for OECS businesses to branch out from the national to the sub-regional sphere. It would also address labour imbalances that exist between the Leeward and Windward islands.

The challenges to maintaining a distinctive grouping with defined areas of cooperation and a distinct identity within a broader integration process is of relevance, not just to the OECS, but to CARICOM as well.[43] As noted earlier, it is not yet clear that CARICOM will be allowed to maintain its own CET within the FTAA and, even if allowed to do so, for how long. The absence of a CARICOM CET would remove some of the advantages for CARICOM firms to operate within the narrower region, as opposed to the wider FTAA. The obvious inducements to doing so would be language and familiarity of other member countries. In terms of broader market access and resources, however, there is no obvious advantage to firms wishing to integrate production processes to limit their involvement to firms within CARICOM. Other CSME objectives such as removals to restrictions on certain categories of workers remain unaffected by the FTAA. However, CARICOM's emphasis on developing competitiveness in the services sector, as a primary goal of the CSME, stands to be undermined within the FTAA which has included trade in services as a negotiating area. Significantly, the preference for NAFTA countries for a negative list approach to restrictions, which allows for greater degrees of liberalisation, as opposed to a positive lists approach adopted by the WTO, which gives countries greater choice in protection, makes it more difficult for CARICOM to protect its fledgling industries.[44]

The regionalisation process has already thrown up challenges to the unity of the CARICOM arrangement. CARICOM countries have negotiated their major trading agreements with external parties under the regional umbrella. These include the Lomé Conventions between the ACP/EU, the Caribbean Basin Initiative with the US, and CARIBCAN with Canada. The intensification of regional groupings has clearly provided the impetus for CARICOM countries to consider trading arrangements with their Latin American neighbours. So far, most of these initiatives, since the 1990s – the establishment of the Association of Caribbean States,[45] a free trade area with the Dominican Republic, preferential access arrangements with Venezuela and Columbia, a trade cooperation agreement with Mexico, and the negotiating of a free trade area with Canada – have been CARICOM led.[46]

There is another trend, developing alongside this, however, for individual member countries to seek autonomy from the CARICOM arrangement to pursue their own trading arrangements with third parties. Earliest pressures in this direction came from Jamaica's and Trinidad and Tobago's bid, in the early 1990s, to gain fast-track accession to NAFTA, on the ground that their economies had achieved a greater degree of openness, making their membership in NAFTA more likely than was the case for other CARICOM states. This threatened to undermine CARICOM's unity, because it meant that had these states may have had to extend at least the same degree of market access as enjoyed by CARICOM countries, which would have undermined the effectiveness of a CET against third countries, and the competitiveness of regional companies. Girvan notes that in the end, pressures from those countries in their bid to join NAFTA resulted in a significantly lowered CARICOM CET with no concessions in return.[47] This trend continues with Trinidad's interest in trade negotiations with Mexico, Costa Rica and Panama. CARICOM has made some concessions towards this desire for greater autonomy in trade with the adoption of Article 14 of Protocol IV on Trade Policy, which amended Articles 33 and 34 of the Treaty of Chaguaramas, making it easier for countries to pursue such arrangements.[48]

Trinidad and Tobago's desire to diversify its trade relations with Latin America suggests some of the pressures the integration arrangement will increasingly face once the FTAA becomes a reality. Not only does CARICOM embrace member states of different size and resource endowments, but its members cover a wide geographical area, extending from the North to the

South of the Caribbean Sea. Jamaica, for instance, is much closer to Cuba than to any of its CARICOM counterparts, Trinidad to Venezuela than most other CARICOM states, and Belize, Guyana and Suriname are all located on the Central American/South American mainland. In terms of transportation costs, resources and so on, production integration may be more possible for these countries to achieve with their closest neighbours, than more far flung CARICOM counterparts. The FTAA, despite language difficulties, will aggravate this tension within CARICOM. CARICOM's trade relations with Latin America, serves as an indication of how these relations are likely to develop. Trinidad has emerged as a dynamic country in CARICOM, penetrating the South American market more than any other member state. Trinidad's position, within sight of South America, has made this possible. In addition, the diversification in its economy, which has led to the development of steel products, along with more traditional petrochemicals, has given it an entrée into the Latin American market. Trinidad now runs a trade surplus with Mexico, the Dominican Republic and Costa Rica.[49]

These developments may not be entirely negative, but it requires CARICOM to recognise that they require a reassessment of the goals of the CSME and how to achieve them. It may also require CARICOM states to consider the possibility that the FTAA may render some aspects of the CSME's outmoded or ultimately redundant. Vaughan Lewis, former Director General of the OECS, has questioned the very viability of the CARICOM Common Market, asking:

> whether the pace of liberalisation within the Caribbean Common Market will be sufficiently great and persistent, to permit them (Jamaica and Trinidad) to see the liberalised single market as an extension of their own liberalised individual economic systems ... or ... whether the push towards trade liberalisation, including deeper tariff cuts matching international levels, will negate the necessity for a formal arrangement such as the Caribbean Common Market.[50]

If this scenario holds, CARICOM may well lose its distinctiveness and find its very existence threatened. Regional governments could anticipate this happening and initiate a rethink of the main goals of the integration movement, and how these should be achieved. So far, CARICOM has shied away from considering a more directly political integration process, shunning even initiatives adopted within the EU to institutionalise the arrangements for negotiating trade with countries outside of the arrangement, or for formulating broad policy and strategy.[51]

CARICOM's response to the challenges confronting its member states in the late 1980s fell short of the political sphere. The West Indian Commission, established to solicit a broad perspective on CARICOM's future, rejected political union as a means of addressing the region's difficulties, arguing that the Federal experiment 'must be allowed to settle in its niche in history',[52] although they allowed for the possibility for member states within the group to pursue such arrangements among themselves. The Commission's report reflected some ambivalence on the question of political unity: while the report observed strong interest among CARICOM nationals in a political union, reflected in their observation that 'the majority of people seemed to despair that they would see full-scale West Indian political union in their lifetimes', it concluded, nevertheless, that West Indians would not accept a 'centralised authority'.[53] Rather than pursuing the clear interest expressed in a political union of some sort and the possible forms these might take to both fulfill that desire, and avoid some of the more negative experiences of the Federation, the Commission settled, instead, for the functionalist approach of close cooperation in specified areas. In the end, a proposal for the creation of an Assembly for Caribbean Community Parliamentarians that predated the Commission, but which it endorsed, was rejected by regional leaders.[54] It received most hostility in Jamaica, where opposition leader, Edward Seaga, dismissed it as bringing Federation 'through the back door'. This variance between popular interest in some form of political union and hostility at the political level, lends credence to the view that emerged out of the Windward Islands' political union initiative that the failings of the integration process can be laid at the feet of regional politicians who were unwilling to concede political power.[55]

The weakening of the economic rationale for CARICOM integration may well lead to a reassessment of attitudes to a more political movement. On the economic front, it can remain a bargaining group to ensure regional difficulties are aired.[56] The rationale for a political approach, however, will continue to lie in their shared insecurities, arising from their small size, but no less in their desire to maintain a distinct cultural region based on a shared history in the context of a broader hemispheric movement.[57]

CONCLUSIONS

The CARICOM and OECS integration schemes have experienced difficulties in achieving rapid progress in the economic sphere, especially on measures, which have broader political implications, such as freedom of movement, and economic initiatives which negatively affect certain national interest groups. The smaller size and similarity of Windward Islands' economies, on the one hand, and Leewards on the other, has not made this more possible than within CARICOM, as might be expected. The painful pace of advancing the process continues with a reluctance to remove barriers to achieving the CSME, evidenced in the shifting deadlines in the adoption of the CET. Paradoxically, countries which face full opening within the FTAA remain worried about opening within the smaller, more intimate context of CARICOM.

The problem with CARICOM and the OECS is that they have relied on economic rationalisations to justify action required in the political sphere, with implications for the viability of ruling parties and national politics generally. Many of CARICOM's CSME objectives would benefit from a frontally political response, which takes on board divergent political views and constituencies. This approach should allow for a coalescence of interest groups across the region, augmenting forces favourable to facilitating the integration process. But it would also allow for opposing groups to gain strength. The importance of a directly political approach (whether or not this means a political union) is that it should allow for openly addressing fears/reservations, which can happen only in the context of a democratic process. This process of democracy is crucial as the CARICOM and OECS, with their heavily technocratic focus, has meant that democracy has not been considered important in the integration process. CARICOM has moved to addressing this democratic deficit with its incorporation of the need for broad-based consultations although, in the absence of specific guidelines as to what measures would be acceptable as achieving this, it may end up being neither consultative nor democratic.

A political approach must also allow for a change in the direction of the process. This means an acceptance that a democratic approach may well lead to a shifting in goals and change in the focus on the integration movement. In other words, its outcome may not be predictable. This process may result in an integration movement far different from what now exists. This may not be a bad development if it addresses the expressed interests of significant sections of CARICOM's population for a more people-centred approach and integration in the popular sphere.

The challenges to CARICOM's survival goes beyond ways of achieving its objectives under the CSME, to the very heart of its viability based on economic approaches that may shortly be rendered redundant. This requires a more forceful rethink of what basis, if any remains for its existence. This has to move beyond narrow economic concerns to wider issues of the survival of Caribbean people, more broadly defined to include a distinct cultural identity that embraces shared historical experiences, including their experiences as small states. It also requires a reassessment of the role of political union, especially in terms of its potential to fulfill these objectives, and the creative forms it might take to consider not only their existence for long periods as separate states, but their far-flung

Diaspora who, in many instances, continue to cling to a perception of themselves as 'West Indians' and of the West Indies as a homeland.

Table 1: CARICOM Countries Geographic size and population (1997)

Country	Area (km^2)	% of total	Population (1997)
LDCs			783468
Belize	22,966	5.28	230000
OECS			553468
Antigua/Barbuda	422	0.1	69747
Dominica	750	0.17	76000
Grenada	345	0.08	99500
Montserrat	103	0.02	5000
St. Kitts/Nevis	269	0.06	42600
St. Lucia	616	0.14	149621
St. Vincent	389	0.08	111,000
MDCs			5,269,914
The Bahamas	13,864	3.19	288,000
Barbados	431	0.1	265,350
Guyana	214,970	49.42	775,143
Jamaica	10,991	2.53	2,540,500
Suriname	163,830	37.65	418,921
Trinidad/Tobago	5,128	1.18	1,270,000
Total	435,084	100.00	6,341,382

Source: Caribbean Trade and Investment Report 2000. Tables 1.1 and 1.2.

Table 2: Real Rates of Growth of GDP of CARICOM Countries 1991-1999

Countries	1991	1992	1993	1994	1995	1996	1997	1998	1999
The Bahamas	-2.7	2.1	-2.1	2.0	1.1	4.2	3.3	3.0	6.0
Barbados	-3.9	-5.7	0.8	3.9	2.9	3.8	3.0	4.4	3.1
Belize	3.1	9.5	4.3	1.4	4.0	1.1	4.0	1.5	6.2
Guyana	7.8	7.7	8.3	8.5	5.1	7.9	6.2	-1.3	3.0
Jamaica	0.7	1.5	1.5	1.0	0.7	-1.4	-2.0	-0.5	-0.4
ECCB Area	2.3	4.2	2.1	3.0	0.7	2.7	3.2	3.9	3.9
Suriname	3.5	5.8	-4.5	-1.2	-3.8	7.0	5.6	2.7	0.8
Trinidad and Tobago	2.9	-1.1	-2.6	5.0	2.6	2.9	2.9	4.0	5.1
Average	1.7	3.0	1.5	2.8	1.6	3.5	3.2	2.0	3.5

Source: Caribbean Trade and Investment Report 2000: Dynamic Interface of Regionalism and Globalisation, Table 1.5, p. 10.

Table 3: Development Indicators for CARICOM Countries

Country	HDI 1991	HDI 2000	Real Per Capita Income ($US 1999)	Poverty levels*	Unemployment Rates+ (1999)
LDCs					
Belize	67	58	2730	22.6	12.8 (1999)
OECS					
Antigua/Barbuda	46	37	9410		6.0 (1991)
Dominica	53	51	3170		23.1 (1997)
Grenada	64	54	3450	31.8	17.0 (1996)
Montserrat					
St. Kitts/Nevis			6420		
St. Lucia	68	88	3946	18.8	17.7 (1997)
St. Vincent	79	79	2941	32.7	19.8 (1991)
MDCs					13.8 (1999)
The Bahamas	28	33			9.8 (1997)
Barbados	22	30	8660	11.6	10.4 (1999)
Guyana	89	96	760	30.5	11.7 (1992)
Jamaica	59	83	1980	18.7	16.0 (1999)
Suriname	55	67	1660		10.5 (1997)
Trinidad/Tobago	39	50	4230		13.1(1999)

Poverty levels refer to assessments done in 1995, except for Jamaica, which represents 2000.

Source: Elsie Le Franc et al (2000) *Poverty in the Caribbean, vol. 1.*

+ Sources: *Caribbean Trade and Investment Report 2000: Dynamic Interface of Regionalism and Globalisation,* Table I.8, p.13 (Unemployment rates for 1999); ILO Caribbean Office, *Digest of Caribbean Labour Statistics 1999* (Port of Spain, Trinidad) – all other years.

Table 4: CARICOM Intra-Regional Trade 1998

	Intra-Regional Exports as % of Total Exports (1998)	% distribution of Intra-Regional Exports by country (1998)	% distribution of Intra-Regional Imports by country (1998)
CARICOM	22.9	100.0	100.0
MDCs	22.8	90.4	74.3
Barbados	43.3	10.8	20.8
Guyana			
Jamaica	3.3	4.4	40.0
Suriname			
Trinidad & Tobago	31.5	75.2	13.6
LDCs	24.6	9.6	25.7
Belize	7.1	1.2	1.4
OECS	37.6	8.4	24.3
Antigua & Barbuda			
Dominica	78.3	3.7	
Grenada	25.1	1.0	7.2
Montserrat			
St. Kitts/Nevis	3.3	0.1	2.0
St. Lucia	19.5	1.1	9.1
St. Vincent & Grenadines	49.1	2.5	6.1

Source: Caribbean Trade and Investment Report 2000: Dynamic Interface of Regionalism and Globalistion, Tables III.4, p. 54, III.6, p. 57 and III.5, p. 56.

Endnotes

1. Rudder, David, 'The Gilded Collection', *Lypsoland*, 1993.
2. Haiti is expected to become a member of CARICOM and The Bahamas to enter into some of the Common Market arrangements.
3. See note 34.
4. For perspectives on why the Federation failed see Mordecai, John, *The West Indies: The Federal Negotiations*, (London: Allen and Unwin, 1968); Springer, H., *Reflections on the Failure of the West Indies Federation*, (Cambridge, Mass: Harvard University, Center for International Affairs, 1962).
5. The division was already manifest before the Federation, as reflected in the sentiment that they should proceed in the federation as a single group rather than separate entities.
6. For details of this arrangement see Ann Spackman, *Constitutional Development of the West Indies 1992-1998: A Selection from the major Documents* (Barbados: Caribbean Universities Press, 1995).

7. The Caribbean Free Trade Association (CARIFTA) was the first attempt at economic integration after the collapse of the Federation. It was limited to trade. It was established in 1968 and gave way to CARICOM in 1973. CARICOM includes the Caribbean Community and Common Market. The latter became operational in the early 1980s.

8. See Patsy Lewis, 'Revisiting the Grenada Invasion: the OECS' Role, and its Impact on Regional and International Politics', *Social and Economic Studies*, 38:3 (September 1999) pp. 85-120.

9. The Economic Affairs Secretariat, located in Antigua, was previously in place to implement the ECCM.

10. CARICOM Secretariat, *Caribbean Trade and Investment Report 2000: Dynamic Interface of Regionalism and Globalisation*, (Caribbean Community Secretariat Economic Intelligence and Policy Unit: Guyana: Georgetown; Kingston: Ian Randle Publishers, 2000), pp. 10, 11.

11. In the Windward Islands, bananas was estimated as employing 45-55 per cent of the workforce in 1998 and was a major source of foreign exchange to all, except Grenada.

12. Figures for 1974 are taken from Ian Boxill, *Ideology and Caribbean Integration*, (Jamaica: Consortium Graduate School of Social Sciences, 1993), Appendices II and III; and for 1998 from *Caribbean Trade and Investment Report 2000*, Tables III.3 (a) and III.3 (b), p. 53. The figures for 1998 include Suriname, which joined CARICOM in 1995.

13. See *Caribbean Trade and Investment Report 2000: Dynamic Interface of Regionalism and Globalisation*, p. 52.

14. *Caricom Trade and Investment Report 2000*, p. 54.

15. Mitchell notes that intra-OECS trade improved between 1982-1991 increasing by an average of 9.1 per cent, compared to a 0.5 per cent average growth for OECS-CARICOM trade during the same period. He attributed this to the elimination of most trade barriers within the OECS, low levels of economic disparity and high degree of complementarity among the Windward and Leeward islands (agriculture and tourism), a labour surplus in the Windwards and deficit in the Leewards, and similarities in the structure and performance of their manufacturing sectors. See Carlyle Mitchell, 'Historical Perspectives of OECS economic integration over the past 10 years', *OECS Occasional Paper no. 2*, July 1992, p. 9.

16. See *Caribbean Trade and Investment Report 2000: Dynamic Interface of Regionalism and Globalisation*, p. 53.

17. See Cargill Technical Services Ltd., 'Socio-Economic Impact of Banana Restructuring in St Lucia', September 1998, and Patsy Lewis, 'A Future

for Windward Islands' Bananas? Challenge and Prospect', *Journal of Commonwealth and Comparative Politics*, 38:2 (July 2000) pp. 51-72.

18. Trinidad's economy has undergone a great degree of economic transformation, experiencing rapid growth in the 1990s, resulting in its accounting for one-third of CARICOM's GDP. This is partly attributable to high FDI in its manufacturing and petrochemical sectors. It currently enjoys a trade surplus with all CARICOM countries. See *Caribbean Trade and Investment Report 2000: Dynamic Interface of Regionalism and Globalisation*, p. 92.

19. See *Caribbean Trade and Investment Report 2000: Dynamic Interface of Regionalism and Globalisation*, Table X.2, p. 306.

20. See *Caribbean Trade and Investment Report 2000: Dynamic Interface of Regonalism and Globalisation*, p. 24.

21. The West Indian Commission, *Time for Action: The Report of the West Indian Commission*. (Barbados: The West Indian Commission) 1002, p. 21.

22. Quoted in *Time for Action: The Report of the West Indian Commission*, p. 9.

23. For a detailed account of this process see, Patsy Lewis, *Surviving Small Size: Regional Integration in Caribbean Ministates*, (Jamaica: UWI Press, 2002).

24. See Lewis, *Surviving Small Size: Regional Integration in Caribbean Ministates*.

25. OECS Economic Affairs Secretariat, *The OECS Single Market and Economy: National Consultations April-June 1996*, p. 1. (Antigua: OECS EAS, 1996).

26. The Grand Anse Declaration has been published in full in *Time for Action: The Report of the West Indian Commission*, as Appendix A, 'Grand Anse Declaration and Work Programme for the Advancement of the Integration Movement', pp. 525-528.

27. See *Caribbean Trade and Investment Report 2000: Dynamic Interface of Regionalism and Globalisation*, Chapter 3.

28. *Caribbean Trade and Investment Report*, p. 74.

29. For a critique of the RNM see Cedric Grant, 'An Experiment in Supra-National Governance: The Caribbean Regional Negotiating Machinery', in Kenneth Hall and Denis Benn, *Contending with Destiny: The Caribbean in the 21st Century*, (Jamaica: Ian Randle Publishers, 2000), pp. 447-499.

30. See Burki, Shahid Javed; Guillermo E. Perry; Sara Calvo, eds., *Trade: Towards Open Regionalism*, Annual World Bank Conference on Development in Latin America and the Caribbean 1997, (Washington, D.C: World Bank, 1998), appendix 2, 'Background on Regionalism vs. Multilateralism in East Asia', p. 46.

31. See Robert O. Keohane and Stanley Hoffman, 'Institutional Change in Europe in the 1980s', in Keohane and Hoffman, eds., *The New European Community: Decisionmaking and Institutional Change*, (Colorado: Westview Press, 1991).

32. See Enrique V. Iglesias, 'The New Face of Regional Integration', in Burke et al, *Trade: Toward Open Regionalism*, p. 24.

33. There is another view represented by Jagdish Bhagwati and L. Alan Winters that regionalism may not necessarily promote free trade. See Jagdish Bhagwati, 'The FTAA is not Free Trade' and L. Alan Winters 'Assessing Regional Integration', in Burki, Shahid Javed; Guillermo E. Perry; SaraCalvo eds., *Trade: Towards Open Regionalism*, Annual World Bank Conference on Development in Latin America and the Caribbean 1997, (Washington, D.C: World Bank, 1998); and L. Alan Winters, 'Regionalism versus Multilateralism, World Bank Policy Research Working Paper Series, No. 1687'.

34. Burki, Shahid Javed; Guillermo E. Perry; Sara Calvo eds., *Trade: Towards Open Regionalism*, Annual World Bank Conference on Development in Latin America and the Caribbean 1997, (Washington, D.C: World Bank, 1998), appendix 2, 'Background on Regionalism vs. Multilateralism in East Asia', p. 46.

35. See Norman, Girvan, 'Caribbean-Latin American Relations and the FTAA', p. 4.

36. Girvan points to some of the difficulties the FTAA negotiating process, in particular, pose for small CARICOM states in, Girvan and Hatton, CARICOM and Central America and the Free Trade Agreement of the Americas, pp. 9-11.

37. See *CARICOM View*, July-August 2001, 'On the Home Stretch: Final Round of CSME Restrictions Talks Set for September', p. 3.

38. *Caribbean Trade and Investment Report 2000: Dynamic Interface of Regionalism and Globalisation*, pp. 46-47.

39. For an update on the state on implementation of the various protocols, including the CET, see the CARICOM website at http://www.caricom.org.

40. OECS, 'The OECS Single Market and Economy – Issues Related to its Future Direction', December 1999.

41. For details on intra-regional investments see, *Caribbean Trade and Invest Report 2000: Dynamic Interface of Regionalism Globalisation*, Chapter VIII.

42. *Caribbean Trade and Investment Report 2000: Dynamic Interface between Regionalism and Globalisation*, pp. 231-2.

43. Vaughan Lewis also raises the question of whether CARICOM's CET could survive as an 'identifiable entity' within the FTAA. See 'Regional

and International Integration and Modes of Governance: The Caribbean Case', mimeo, March 2001, p. 9.

44. For a discussion of the implications of this to OECS states see, OECS Secretariat, 'the OECS and Trade in Services: Multilateral and Hemispheric Imperatives', Trade Policy Brief, vol. 3.

45. CARICOM was central in the formation of the ACS, which was one of the proposals coming out of the CARICOM for widening the integration process to include the wider Caribbean. See The West Indian Commission, *Time For Action: The Report of the West Indian Commission*, pp. 446-451.

46. See *Caribbean Trade and Investment Report 2000: Dynamic Interface of Regionalism and Globalisation*, Chapter iv.

47. See Norman Girvan and Miguel Ceara Hatton, *CARICOM Central America and the Free Trade Agreement of the Americas*, (Kingston, Jamaica: Freidrich Ebert Stiftung, 1998), p. 7.

48. See *Caribbean Trade and Investment Report 2000: Dynamic Interface of Regionalism and Globalisation*, p. 91.

49. For a discussion of Trinidad's trade with Latin America, see *Caribbean Trade and Investment Report: 2000: Dynamic Interface of Regionalism and Globalisation*, pp. 91-101.

50. Vaughan Lewis, 'Caribbean Countries: Transiting to New Regimes of International Economic Governance', mimeo. p. 8.

51. See Vaughan Lewis 'Regional and International Integration and Modes of Governance: The Caribbean Case', mimeo, March 2001, p. 9.

52. The West Indian Commission, *Time for Action*, p. 14.

53. The West Indian Commission, *Time for Action*, p. 14.

54. The West Indian Commission, *Time for Action*, p. 485.

55. Havelock Brewster points out that interest in political union extended beyond the Windwards with Trinidad's Prime Minister, Patrick Manning, at the CARICOM summit in 1992, urging CARICOM members to 'to take the incremental approach to Caribbean unity', followed in 1994 with Guyana's Prime Minister, Cheddi Jagan suggesting that the Federation did not suggest that political union was a lost cause, but that sensitivity to the 'nature and character of that concept' was required. See Havelock R.H. Ross-Brewster, 'The Future of the Caribbean Community', in Winston C. Dookeran ed., *Caribbean Choices and Change: Reflections on the Caribbean*, (Washington D.C: Inter-American Development Bank, 1996), p. 38.

56. A colleague, Ian Boxill, argues that CARICOM's role as a bargaining unit within the FTAA, increases its rationale for survival. Conversation with author, December 7, 2001.

57. Brewster argues for a more political process on similar ground of cultural identity and functional cooperation. See, 'The Future of the Caribbean Community'. See also, Patsy Lewis, *Surviving Small Size: Regional Integration in Caribbean Ministates.*

15

From National Independence to a Single Caribbean State: Views on The Barbados-OECS Initiative

Cynthia Barrow-Giles

This chapter contributes to the literature on the failure of regional integration by addressing two specific issues. Firstly, it attempts to document the extent and nature of the support for one specific regional integration proposal namely, the Barbados-OECS Initiative, by drawing on the findings from opinion polls conducted between November 1998 and April 2001. While several works including the much celebrated Time For Action Report published by the West Indian Commission, alludes to the low level of support for regional political integration among Caribbean people, none of these works have attempted to rigorously examine the extent and nature of the support of citizens across the Caribbean for regional integration. Drawing from the cross national survey in four eastern Caribbean countries, this chapter seeks to supplement the literature that treats regional integration by addressing the issue of support for closer collaboration/unity between Barbados and the Organisation of Eastern Caribbean States. Secondly, in so doing the chapter also examines the extent to which attitudes on sub-regionalism are shaped by the respondents socio-economic background, and their perceptions of the likely impact and performance of the socioeconomic sectors in their respective countries. For the most part reference is made to the views of the committed respondents. Generally, the study found that while sub-regional integration finds favour, there is considerable reservation. Nonetheless the research reported here, contributes to our understanding of national impulses and their implications for regional integration.

THE BARBADOS-OECS INITIATIVE

The Barbados-OECS Initiative represents a response at governmental level to the challenges imposed by the forces of globalism. The Initiative itself,

The data discussed in this paper forms the basis of work for my PhD. The field research was partly funded by a grant from the Ford Foundation and the University of the West Indies, Cave Hill Campus, School for Graduate Studies and Research.

followed a series of recent developments between Barbados and the Organisation of Eastern Caribbean States. The initiative also represents the latest in a number of initiatives since the mid 1980s, to reactivate interest in sub-regional integration. The most recent of which, was the bid on the part of the OECS governments, and, later the Windward Islands to politically integrate.[1] Unfortunately the OECS countries have failed to make any substantive progress towards the 1992 final report of the Constituent Assembly and have yet to table the motion before parliament. This not only signals the unwillingness of the political leadership to give substance to decisions taken, but, also the weaknesses of the OECS as the implementation of such decisions require political will. Kenny Anthony also alluded to apathy and indifference in 1995, when he posited the view that the regional political leadership cannot be entirely blamed for the failure of the regional integration movement. Rather, according to him;

> ... there is a fundamental problem among the people of the region themselves. There is considerable pessimism about anything to do with integration. It is not restricted to the CARICOM region as a whole, but it applies with equal force and measure to the OECS states. Many doubt that it is desirable even on its own merits.[2]

The earlier thrust towards sub-regional political integration in the form of OECS political integration, had, come from St Vincent and the Grenadines. In 1987, Prime Minister James Mitchell called for the formation of a political union of the OECS on economic grounds. Mitchell argued that there were;

> .... thousands of reasons why we should unite, ranging from the hopeless limitations and fragility of the present system to the fulfilment of our most ambitious dream.[3]

The Tortola Declaration which emerged from the urging of Prime Minister James Mitchell did not receive unanimous political support across the sub-region. Former prime minister of Antigua and Barbuda, himself an early advocate of regional economic integration, argued that political integration was not a major priority for Antigua and Barbuda on the following grounds;

> We fought years to put away being a colony. Forty-eight until we were able to stop Britain from making us a colony. And now that the people have won and got the right to turn their own affairs you coming and telling them that they should have one government.... Antigua and Barbuda is not interested in that.[4]

The call for a consideration of closer collaboration between Barbados and the OECS comes in the wake of the August 1995 signing of an 'Agreement for Economic Cooperation between Barbados and the OECS which identified several areas of cooperation between Barbados and the member states of the organisation.[5]

The prevailing view therefore, is that the sub-regional integration movement must proceed in a gradualist, incrementalist fashion, but that ultimately political integration between Barbados and the OECS is imperative.

Table 1: Demographic profile of interviewees in the four countries

DEMOGRAPHIC PROFILE	FREQUENCIES	PERCENTAGE %
1 AGE RANGE		
18-25 years	626	18.6
26-35 years	756	22.5
36-45 years	928	27.6
46-55 years	519	15.5
over 55 years	526	15.7
Non-Responsive	03	0.1
2 EDUCATIONAL ATTAINMENT		
None/primary Complete	224	6.7
Completed Primary/Incomplete Secondary	1057	31.5
Completed Secondary/ Incomplete University	1739	51.8
University Completed	325	9.7
Non-Responsive	13	0.4
3 EMPLOYMENT STATUS		
Employed	2232	66.5
Unemployed	699	20.8
Pensioned	249	7.4
Student Employed	75	2.2
Student unemployed	94	2.8
Non-Responsive	09	0.3
4 GENDER		
Male	1671	49.8
Female	1686	50.2
5 RANGE OF ANNUAL INCOME		
Under $15,000.00	923	27.5
$15,001.00 - $30,000.00	837	24.9
$30,001- $45,000.00	339	10.1
Over $45,000.00	183	5.4
Unemployed	793	23.6
Non-Responsive	283	8.4

Source: Cross National Survey in the four countries conducted between November 1998 and April 2001.

Demographic Profile of Interviewees (the sample).

The data examined is drawn from a survey of persons conducted in Barbados and three member countries of the Organisation of Eastern Caribbean States, namely; Barbados, St Lucia, Antigua and St Vincent between November 1998 and April 2001. The survey was administered to a representative stratified random sample of citizens aged 18 and over. The sample was therefore designed to represent the population in the four countries that form the focus of the discussion. A combined total of 3358 persons interviewed. Table 1 gives a breakdown of the demographic profile of the interviewees. Cross tabulating some of the data provided additional insights into the attitudes of civil society in the four countries.

It should be noted that the cross national survey of the four countries, took place over a twenty eight month period (28), beginning with Barbados in 1998 and culminating in Antigua in April 2001. Of interest too is the fact that it was in Barbados that the more focused discussion of the proposed Barbados-OECS Initiative took place. Among the most obvious aspects of the debate on the issue was the public lecture delivered by Prime Minister Kenny Anthony of St Lucia in Barbados in 1998. We should therefore bear in mind that the greater public discourse on the Barbados-OECS Initiative that occurred in Barbados would necessarily correlate with a greater appreciation of the proposal when compared with the other eastern Caribbean countries. The higher level of awareness of the initiative of the sampled population in Barbados is therefore not startling, though the low level of awareness in St Lucia is somewhat dismaying given the central role which Prime Minister Kenny Anthony of St Lucia played in promoting the idea of a Confederation between Barbados and the OECS.

Chart 1 shows that the general public in the OECS and Barbados was largely unaware of the Barbados-OECS Initiative, with 63.9 per cent of the sampled population displaying ignorance of the proposal. However, when we dis-aggregate the data, in Table 2, the Barbadian respondents showed a higher level of awareness of the initiative, with 49.0 per cent of the interviewees indicating knowledge of the proposal, compared to 42.7 per cent, 20.9 per cent and 22.9 per cent in St Lucia, St Vincent and Antigua respectively. This can be compared to the sub-regional average of 31.9 per cent. The percentage awareness level of the Initiative in Barbados is well above the regional average by 17.1 percent. Not surprisingly therefore the Barbadian respondents were more likely to be aware of the initiative, with Barbadians twice as likely to be aware of the Initiative than the respondents in St Vincent.

Chart 1
Level of Awareness of the Barbados-OECS Initiative

Level of Awareness of the Barbados-OECS Initiative
(All four countries)

Yes
36.1%

No
63.9%

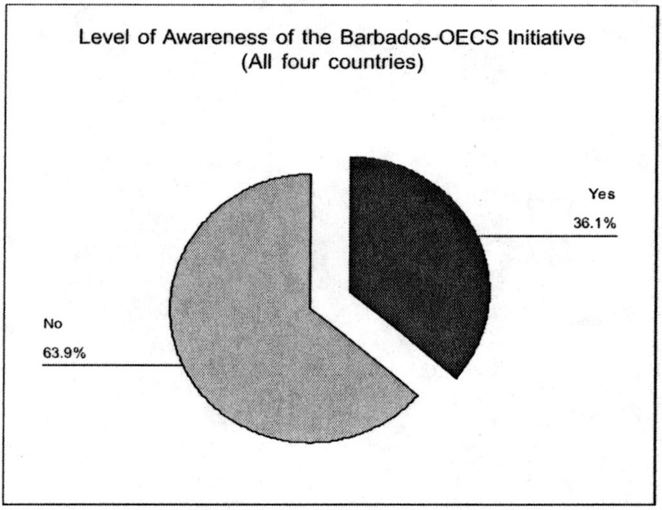

Source: Cross National Survey conducted between November 1998 and April 2001.

Quite apart from the macro level awareness of the Initiative and the country differences that exists, the survey also attempted to assess the role played by other socio-demographic factors.

Table 2 shows a number of significant factors. Firstly, the male respondents were slightly more aware of the Initiative than their female counterparts, with an eight per cent gap between the two groups. More importantly however, is the fact that employment status, educational achievement and income are far more important socio-demographic factors determining awareness of the Initiative than gender. Indeed the Table shows that the employed and better educated respondents showed a higher level of awareness of the initiative than the less educated and unemployed respondents. 55.4 per cent of the university graduates, 39.8 per cent of the employed individuals, and 54.1 per cent of those individuals earning between $45,001.00 and over $60,000. 00 annually were aware of the initiative. In contrast, those individuals who were unemployed, had low incomes and were less educated were also less aware of the initiative. Here 30.2 per cent of those earning under $15,000.00 annually, 23.6 per cent of the unemployed and 22.8 per cent of the respondents who had not completed primary level education were aware of the Barbados-OECS Initiative. Thus literacy levels, education attainment and affluence were far more important indicators of awareness of the Initiative than was gender.

Table 2: Degree of Awareness of the Barbados-OECS Initiative

Extent of Awareness of the Initiative	Yes	% No	%
1 Country of Origin			
Barbados	49	51	
St Lucia	42.7	20	
St Vincent	20.9	26.1	
Antigua	22.9	25.8	
Combined Total	36.1	63.9	
2 Gender			
Male	40.1	59.9	
Female	32.1	67.9	
Unresponsive	-	0.03	
3 Age			
18-25 years	30.5	69.5	
26-35 years	37.6	62.4	
36-45 years	39.9	60.1	
46-55 years	38.2	61.8	
Over 55 years	31.9	68.1	
Non-Responsive	33.3	66.7	
4 Employment Status			
Employed	39.8	60.2	
Unemployed	23.6	76.4	
Pensioned	33.7	66.3	
Student Employed	42.7	57.3	
Student Unemployed	42.6	2.5	
Non-Responsive	33.3	66.7	
5 Range of Annual Income			
Under $15,000.00	30.2	69.8	
$15,000.001-$3,000.00	43.4	56.6	
$30,001.00-$45,000.00	52.5	47.5	
$45,001.00-Over $60,000.00	54.1	45.9	
Unemployed	26	74	
Non-Responsive	30.7	69.3	
6 Educational Attainment			
None/Primary Incomplete	22.8	77.2	
Primary Complete/Secondary Incomplete	26	36.4	
Secondary Complete/University Incomplete	40.4	59.6	
Completed University	55.4	44.6	
Non-Responsive	23.1	76.9	

Source: Cross National Survey conducted between November 1998 and April 2001.

Despite the relatively low level of information by the respondents regarding the proposed Barbados-OECS Initiative, more than half of the sampled population showed support for the Initiative. Overall, 53.2 per cent of the population supported the Initiative. This is in keeping with the views expressed by the Time For Action Report that the 'people of the region desired closer integration'.[6] In terms of the geographical spread of that support, 53.6 per cent of Barbadians supported the Initiative, compared to 54.9 per cent, 62.5 per cent and 41.4 per cent of the respondents in St Lucia, St Vincent and Antigua respectively. Of interest therefore is the disjuncture between prior information on the initiative and the support for the proposal. As the data clearly show, while more Barbadians indicated that they were aware of the initiative, the highest level of support for the proposal was in St Vincent with a 62.5 per cent support level compared to its 20.9 per cent awareness level. Thus an important discovery here is the fact that sub-regional proposals of the type of the Barbados-OECS Initiative is seen as a valuable commodity in its own right. While therefore information is critical, on its own it does not automatically lead to interest and support for regional integration enterprises.

Chart 2
Support for the Barbados-OECS Initiative

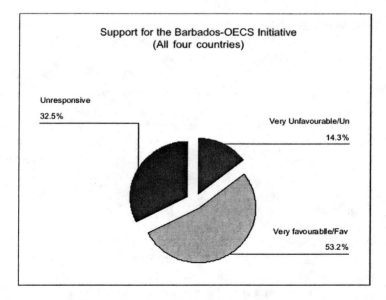

Source: Cross National Survey conducted between November 1998 and April 2001.

With respect to the socio-demographic breakdown of support for the initiative, within the total sample, gender does not factor significantly in the equation. It is quite clear that there is little gender difference among the respondents, with 56.0 per cent of males and 50.4 per cent of females supporting the initiative. It is in fact educational attainment that differentiates the respondents with respect to support for the initiative. Table 3 shows that support for the initiative increases with higher levels of educational achievement, so that university graduates exhibit a 58.5 per cent compared to 46.4 per cent support by the respondents with only minimum levels of education. As far as age, employment status and income status are concerned, the data here suggest that the employed is slightly more inclined to support the initiative than the unemployed, but it is the students, both employed and unemployed who show a greater level of support. Secondly in so far as income is concerned, it is clearly not as critical as educational attainment, though the respondents earning the highest level of income are slightly more supportive than those earning the lowest level of income. Table 3 shows that nearly 60.0 per cent of persons earning between $45,001.00 to over $60,000.00 annually responded affirmatively to the question of support of the initiative compared to the 54.9 per cent affirmative response of persons earning under $15,000.00 annually. The result also suggests that age in this respect is not as important as educational attainment. Though the younger respondents showed a lower level of support for the initiative than the older respondents, the differences are not significant. What however, is significant is the fact that persons within the lowest income bracket and the younger respondents were less committed in their responses than the other socio-demographic categories.

As observed, the data reveal a moderate level of support for the Barbados-OECS Initiative among the respondents. The survey also attempted to assess the level of support among the population in the sub-region to the idea of the expanded OECS with Barbados as a member. Table 4 and Chart 3 summarise the attitudes of the respondents. In so far as national support is concerned, again the data is consistent. It is in St Vincent that the strongest support for the inclusion of Barbados in the OECS can be found while the lowest level of support is found in Antigua. 75 per cent of the respondents in St Vincent showed support for Barbados compared to 54.0 per cent in Antigua. St Lucia also shows a slightly higher per cent for Barbados than the sub-regional average. Overall however, as Chart 3 shows the sub-regional support for membership to the OECS by Barbados is 62.3 per cent.

Again, an analysis of the data presented in Table 4 show that both education and income are strongly associated with support for membership to the OECS by Barbados. Here, among the committed respondents, 68.0 per cent of university

Table 3: The Level of Support for the Barbados-OECS Initiative

How Favourable	Very Unfavourable/ Unfavourable %	Very Favourable/ favourable %	Unresponsive %
1 Country of Origin			
Barbados	12.6	53.6	33.8
St Lucia	13.4	54.9	31.8
St Vincent	13.8	62.5	23.7
Antigua	18.7	41.4	39.9
2 Gender			
Male	15.3	56	28.7
Female	13.4	50.4	36.2
Unresponsive	-	-	
3 Age			
18-25 years	12.9	48.6	38.5
26-35 years	15.3	51.9	32.8
36-45 years	15.4	55.9	28.7
46-55 years	13.3	55.7	31
Over 55 years	13.5	53	33.5
Non-Responsive	33.3	66.7	-
4 Employment Status			
Employed	14.9	54.7	30.3
Unemployed	12.3	48.2	39.5
Pensioned	14.5	51.8	33.7
Student Employed	16	57.3	26.7
Student Unemployed	12.8	55.3	31.9
Non-Responsive	22.2	22.2	55.6
5 Range of Annual Income			
Under $15,000.00	12.4	54.9	32.7
$15,000.001-$3,000.00	14.9	56.3	28.8
$30,001.00-$45,000.00	18.3	54	27.7
$45,001.00-Over $60,000.00	18	59.6	22.4
Unemployed	12.4	49.1	38.6
Non-Responsive	17.3	44.5	38.2
6 Educational Attainment			
None/Primary Incomplete	12.9	46.4	40.6
Primary Complete/Secondary Incomplete	13.9	49.7	36.4
Secondary Complete/University Incomplete	14.3	55.3	30.4
Completed University	16.6	58.5	24.9
Non-Responsive	23.1	30.8	46.2

graduates were supportive of Barbados' membership, compared to 54.9 per cent support level of those respondents with the lowest educational achievement. While the employed were only marginally more supportive of the prospect of an enlarged OECS with Barbados, the more highly paid respondents indicated overwhelmingly their support. Whereas 63.4 per cent of the respondents earning under $15,000.00 annually were supportive, 80.3 per cent of the highest income bracket showed positive support. There is little significant difference among the age groupings with all age categories indicating around 60 per cent support.

Chart 3
Level of Support for Barbados' Inclusion in the OECS

Level of Support for Barbados' Inclusion in the OECS (All four countries)

Non Responsive 26.8%

No 11.0%

Yes 62.3%

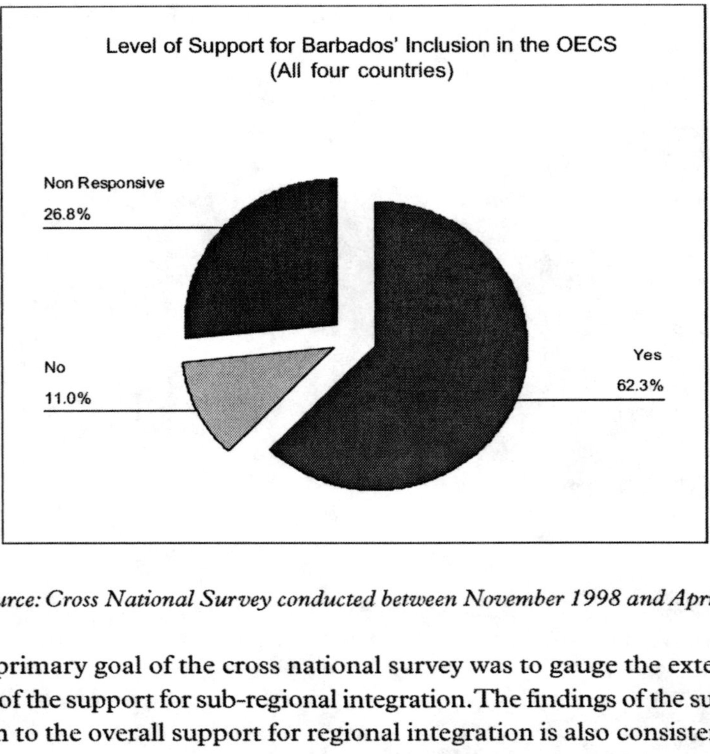

Source: Cross National Survey conducted between November 1998 and April 2001

A primary goal of the cross national survey was to gauge the extent and nature of the support for sub-regional integration. The findings of the survey in relation to the overall support for regional integration is also consistent with the previous findings. As seen in Chart 4 and Table 5, approximately half the sampled population (53.8 per cent) were supportive of regional integration, with St Vincent displaying significantly higher levels of support than the other three countries. 67 per cent of the population in St Vincent showed an inclination to regional integration, with the affirmative response divided between economic and political integration. Surprisingly, 42.9 per cent of the respondents in St Vincent showed a preference for political integration. Again it was in Antigua that the lowest level of support for regional integration was seen, with a 41.8 per cent support, indicating a 12 per cent lower support level than the sub-regional average of 53.8 per cent. In both St Lucia and Barbados with 55.0 per cent and 52.5 per cent respectively, there is moderate support for regional integration. Whereas however, the St Lucian respondents who showed a preference for regional integration showed a higher level of support for political

Table 4: Views on Barbados' Inclusion in the OECS

Barbados' Inclusion into the OECS	Yes %	No %	Non-responsive %
1 Country of Origin			
Barbados	58.4	12.3	29.2
St Lucia	66	5.7	28.3
St Vincent	73.2	10.6	16.2
Antigua	54	14.5	31.5
2 Gender			
Male	64.6	11.7	44
Female	60	10.2	29.8
Unresponsive	-	-	-
3 Age			
18-25 years	59.1	9.9	31
26-35 years	61.1	11.4	27.5
36-45 years	64.9	10.5	24.7
46-55 years	63.6	11.8	24.7
Over 55 years	61.6	11.8	26.6
Non-Responsive	100	-	-
4 Employment Status			
Employed	63.8	11.3	24.9
Unemployed	57.9	8.6	33.5
Pensioned	62.2	13.7	24.1
Student Employed	60	13.3	26.7
Student Unemployed	60.6	11.7	27.7
Non-Responsive	55.6	11.1	33.3
5 Range of Annual Income			
Under $15,000.00	63.4	10.8	25.8
$15,000.001-$3,000.00	63.1	11.6	25.3
$30,001.00-$45,000.00	62.8	13.3	23.9
$45,001.00-Over $60,000.00	80.3	9.3	10.4
Unemployed	58.3	9	32.8
Non-Responsive	55.1	13.4	31.4
6 Educational Attainment			
None/Primary Incomplete	54.9	8.5	36.6
Primary Complete/Secondary Incomplete	60.5	11.4	28.2
Secondary Complete/University Incomplete	63.6	10.6	26.1
Completed University	68	12.9	19.1
Non-Responsive	61.5	15.4	23.1

Source: Cross National Survey conducted between November 1998 and April 2001.

integration (31.5 per cent), the opposite is the case with the Barbadian respondent. In that case, 28.7 per cent of the respondents supported economic integration which is slightly higher than the indicated support for political integration.

Chart 4
Choice of Sub-regional Integration Among Respondents

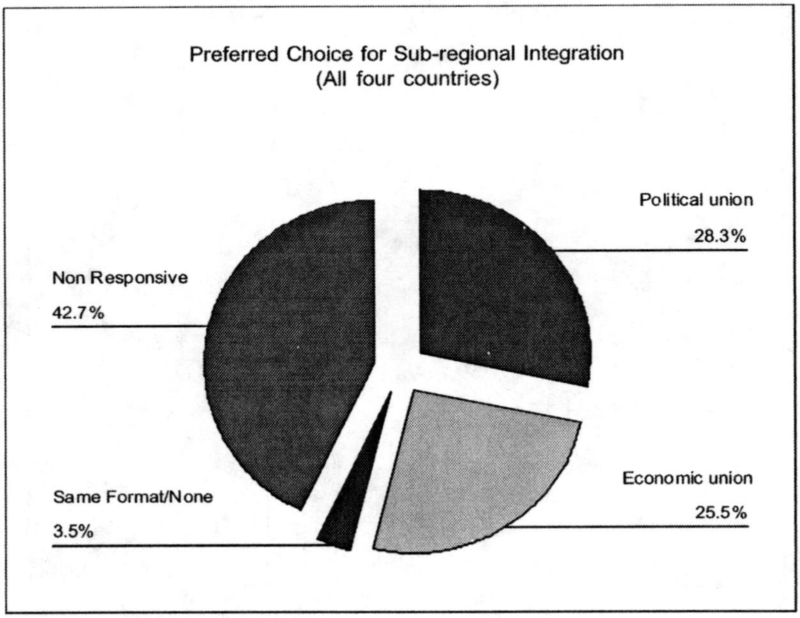

Preferred Choice for Sub-regional Integration
(All four countries)

Political union
28.3%

Non Responsive
42.7%

Economic union
25.5%

Same Format/None
3.5%

Source: Cross National Survey conducted between November 1998 and April 2001

There is no doubt that the data presented in Table 5 positively show that there is considerable difference between generations in relation to the efficacy of regional integration. No doubt this can be partly explained by the different formative experiences of the people of the sub-region. In keeping with this, it is the younger and older generations that show the lowest level of support for regional integration, with less than 50 per cent showing any real interest. As far as the older generation is concerned, that is, persons over 55 years of age, the regional failure of the 1958 Federation provided the context within which that grouping came of age. In keeping with the view expressed by the West Indian Commission, representations of regional political integration is seen by the older generation as a return to federation. Thus memories of the failed collective action of the British Caribbean may explain the low preference for regional integration. However, while this may partly explain their overall reticence to support regional integration, it cannot account for the significantly higher level of support for political integration (30.8 per cent) among that grouping compared to their significantly lower support for economic integration (18.1 per cent). Thus the younger and older the population, the lower the level of support for regional integration. Having said this however, it is important to note that the support for regional integration does not show a major difference among the groups. Indeed the major difference exists between the over 55 age grouping (48.9 per cent) support and the 26–35 generation group with a 57 per cent support, indicating a differential of 8.1 per cent.

Three other results deserve comment here. Firstly, support for political integration across the region is higher than that for economic integration with the exception of three socio-demographic groupings. Namely, persons between the ages of 26–35 years (30.4 per cent for economic integration compared to 26.6 per cent for political integration), students, both employed and unemployed and persons with the highest income and educational achievement.

Secondly, employment is positively related to support for regional integration, with a 9.2 per cent difference between the employed and the unemployed. Similarly, the employed students are more inclined to support regionalism than the unemployed student, as 64.0 per cent of the former and 52.2 per cent of the latter supporting regional integration.

Thirdly, income is also associated with differences in opinions on the question of regional integration. It is the lower income bracket that is less likely to support regional integration. While 74.8 per cent of the highest income earners supported regional integration, those in the lowest income brackets only showed a 51.8 per cent support, reflecting a differential of 23 per cent.

The findings in relation to income and regional integration are mirrored in the data on education attainment, with a 36.5 per cent difference between the two groups at polar ends of the education stratum. Consistent with earlier findings it is the university graduates (76.7 per cent) who indicated the highest level of support for regional integration. Indeed the largest differential is to be found here. Thus it can be concluded that higher levels of education and the improvement of education throughout the region will contribute to an increased level of support for regional integration, whether economic or political.

The data analysed here also debunks the idea that regional integration has faltered due largely to middle-class conservatism. Overall however, while there is moderate support for regional integration there is still a deep adherence to traditional national identities.

Table 5: Range of Support for Regional Integration

Support for Regional Integration	Political Union %	Economic Union %	OECS Format %	Non-responsive %
1 Country of Origin				
Barbados	23.8	28.7	8.1	39.4
St Lucia	31.5	23.5	0.9	44.1
St Vincent	42.9	24.1	0.1	32.9
Antigua	18	23.8	1.7	56.5
2 Gender				
Male	29.8	27.4	3.9	38.9
Female	26.9	23.7	3.0	46.4
Unresponsive	-	-	-	-
3 Age				
18-25 years	24.9	24.3	2.7	48.1
26-35 years	26.6	30.4	4.2	38.8
36-45 years	29.7	26.7	2.8	40.7
46-55 years	29.9	25	3.7	41.4
Over 55 years	30.8	18.1	4.2	47
Non-Responsive	33.3	66.7	-	-
4 Employment Status				
Employed	29.1	27.2	3.6	40.1
Unemployed	27.6	19.5	1.7	51.2
Pensioned	25.7	22.5	6.4	45.4
Student Employed	26.7	37.3	6.7	29.3
Student Unemployed	24.5	27.7	3.2	44.7
Non-Responsive	22.2	33.3	-	44.4
5 Range of Annual Income				
Under $15,000.00	29.7	22.1	4	44.2
$15,000.001-$3,000.00	27.5	28.9	4.5	39.1
$30,001.00-$45,000.00	31.3	30.7	3.8	34.2
$45,001.00-Over $60,000.00	31.1	43.7	4.4	20.8
Unemployed	27.4	20.6	1.9	50.2
Non-Responsive	23.7	22.6	1.8	51.9
6 Educational Attainment				
None/Primary Incomplete	29	11.2	1.8	58
Primary Complete/Secondary Incomplete	29.1	17.1	3.3	50.4
Secondary Complete/University Incomplete	27.7	29.4	3.6	39.3
Completed University	28.9	41.8	4.6	24.6
Non-Responsive	23.1	23.1	-	53.8

Source: Cross National Survey conducted between November 1998 and April 2001.

So far, the data presented above reveal a measure of support for regional integration and while interesting do not provide a holistic picture of the perceptions of the respondents. Therefore in order to assess the underlying reasons why levels of support varied across the region and within groups, the survey attempted to focus on perceptions of respondents of the general and economic impact that regional corporation would have on the individual units.

The survey therefore sought to understand the attitudes of the respondents to the idea of free mobility of persons across the region implied by regional economic and political integration. This is especially critical in the circumstances where CARICOM Heads of Government in July 2001, made provisions in the Revised Treaty of Chaguaramas for the free movement of persons, capital and services and the right of establishment to facilitate the establishment of the CARICOM Single Market and Economy. What the data reveal in Table 6 is most interesting. Certainly, it can provide some insight into the seeming reticence of the sample population to regional integration and the consequences for the CSME.

There are in fact good reasons to assume that a support for regional integration would be matched by a corresponding level of support for free mobility of persons within the region. Equally so, the expectation is that a belief that such cooperation would improve the well being of a country would automatically lead to increased support. Indeed the West Indian Commission Report of 1992 indicated that while interest in regional integration existed among the people of the region, such interest was based primarily on the assumption that regional integration would serve to improve their lives and that of their children.[7] It is clear from Table 6 that there is a general assumption that improved regional cooperation in the form of the Barbados-OECS Initiative would confer tremendous benefits on the countries, however there are mixed feelings on some of the collateral developments that must necessarily flow from it. At the macro-level while two-thirds of the respondents supported the idea of non nationals residing in any country that is associated with the regional integration enterprise, the same cannot be said of their position vis-à-vis free mobility of labour. In fact an overwhelming 40 per cent of the population in the four countries were opposed to the idea of free mobility.

Table 6: Macro Level Views on Residency, Employment, and Effect of Closer Collaboration

Issues	Percentage Support (%)
Support for Residency	
Yes	66.7
No	19.0
Employment Opportunities	
Yes	46.4
No	40.1
Impact of Joining	
Better/Much Better	73.6
Worst/Much Worst	7.0
General Economic effect	
Good/Very good	75.9
Bad/Very bad	9.6

Source: Cross National Survey conducted between November 1998 and April 2001.

If indeed the West Indian Commission was correct, then the question still remains, why is it that although the dominant view among the respondents is that closer collaboration among the sub-region would lead to an improvement of the affairs of the countries within the sub-region, such belief cannot translate into a similar level of support for regional integration. The answer may lie in assessment of the data presented in Tables 7-10.

It is clear that there is some dilemma here. As I have argued, regional cooperation is seen as having the capacity to improve the conditions in the individual countries. In fact Table 6 shows a 66.7 per cent support for nationals of one country being able to reside permanently in any country of the sub-region. The same cannot be said of the position in relation to the possibility/right of non nationals ability to work throughout the sub-region.

What emerges here very clearly from the sub-regional macro-level picture is that there are fears that such openness and the removal of national barriers may in fact worsen the personal position of many respondents. Further light can be thrown on the issue when an examination of how structural factors such as education and income impact perceptions on these critical issues.

Tables 7 and 8 show the regional distribution of views with respect to perceptions of the economic and general impact of Barbados' membership to the OECS. In all four countries there is the general impression that only a positive outcome is likely from an expanded OECS that includes Barbados. Secondly, as the data have consistently shown, it is in Antigua that the lowest positive rating is to be found. While Barbados, St Lucia and St Vincent show positive perceptions of between 70-82.4 per cent, in Antigua only approximately 60 per cent of the sampled population felt that the relationship would have positive outcomes. Further analysis of the data only confirm earlier findings that structural factors such as education, income and employment status are critical dynamics informing the respondents. Tables 7-8 show very clearly that on average while approximately 70 -75 per cent of the respondents agreed that the impact on the individual countries will be a positive one, it is the university graduates, the employed and the highest income earners, averaging around 80 per cent, who show the greatest conviction that the impact would be to the benefit of the individual countries.

The results here therefore make the position on regional integration even more puzzling and continue to beg the question that was posed earlier. For on the basis of the data presented in Tables 7-8 it does not appear that anticipated negative impact on the individual countries is the factor that contributes to the seeming reluctance of the respondents to support regional integration. I attempted to arrive at a possible answer to the mystery by evaluating the responses of the interviewees on the issue of residency and free mobility of labour; issues that continue to bedevil the region.

Table 7: Views on Impact of Barbados' Membership to the OECS

Impact of Barbados' Joining the OECS	Better/Much better off %	Worse/Much worse off %	Non-responsive %
1 Country of Origin			
Barbados	79.7	11.1	9.2
St Lucia	70	4.3	25.8
St Vincent	80.1	3.5	3.5
Antigua	60.8	6.6	32.6
2 Gender			
Male	74.1	8.2	17.7
Female	73.1	5.8	21.1
Unresponsive	-	-	-
3 Age			
18-25 years	73.6	6.1	20.3
26-35 years	75.7	8.2	16.1
36-45 years	74.6	5.9	19.5
46-55 years	74	8.3	17.7
over 55 years	68.3	7	24.7
Non-Responsive	100	-	-
4 Employment Status			
Employed	75.8	7.4	16.8
Unemployed	68	4.9	27.2
Pensioned	67.1	8.8	24.1
Student Employed	78.7	5.3	16
Student Unemployed	77.7	9.6	12.8
Non-Responsive	55.6	11.1	33.3
5 Range of Annual Income			
Under $15,000.00	73.1	7.9	19
$15,000.001-$3,000.00	76	6.9	17.1
$30,001.00-$45,000.00	79.6	8.8	11.5
$45,001.00-Over $60,000.00	83.6	6.6	9.8
Unemployed	69.4	5.4	25.2
Non-Responsive	66.1	6.7	27.2
6 Educational Attainment			
None/Primary Incomplete	59.8	4.5	35.7
Primary Complete/Secondary Incomplete	67.9	7.4	24.7
Secondary Complete/University Incomplete	77.6	6.8	15.6
Completed University	80.6	8.6	10.8
Non-Responsive	61.5	-	38.5

Source: Cross National Survey conducted between November 1998 and April 2001.

Table 8: Views on the General Economic Effect of Barbados' Inclusion in the OECS

General Economic Effect	Very bad/ Bad %	Very good/ Good %	Non - Responsive %
1 Country of Origin			
Barbados	13.1	80.6	6.3
St Lucia	8.3	82.4	9.3
St Vincent	6.9	77.9	15.2
Antigua	7.7	59.7	32.6
2 Gender			
Male	10.2	76.7	13
Female	8.9	75.2	15.9
Unresponsive	-	-	-
3 Age			
18-25 years	9.1	76.2	14.7
26-35 years	10.4	78.3	11.2
36-45 years	9.1	76.5	14.4
46-55 years	9.1	77.1	13.9
Over 55 years	10.3	70	19.8
Non-Responsive	-	100	-
4 Employment Status			
Employed	9.4	77.2	13.4
Unemployed	10.2	72.4	17.5
Pensioned	10.8	70.7	18.5
Student Employed	8.7	80	13.3
Student Unemployed	9.6	83	7 .4
Non-Responsive	-	77.8	22.2
5 Range of Annual Income			
Under $15,000.00	10.5	76.1	13.4
$15,000.001-$3,000.00	8.1	77.3	14.6
$30,001.00-$45,000.00	9.7	79.9	10.3
$45,001.00-Over $60,000.00	7.7	82.5	9.8
Unemployed	10.1	73.8	16.1
Non-Responsive	10.2	68.6	21.2
6 Educational Attainment			
None/Primary Incomplete	9.4	68.8	21.9
Primary Complete/Secondary Incomplete	11.5	72.7	15.8
Secondary Complete/University Incomplete	8.9	77.7	13.3
Completed University	6.8	83.1	10.2
Non-Responsive	7.7	46.2	46.2

Source: Cross National Survey conducted between November 1998 and April 2001.

Tables 9-10 summarise the position of the population to issues of the ability of non-nationals both residing and working in the respective countries. The respondents in the three OECS countries were asked to indicate whether or not Barbadians should be able to work and live without restriction in the event that Barbados became a member of the OECS. Similarly Barbadians were asked to indicate their position on the issue. The findings are dramatic and perhaps hold the answer to the very modest level of support for regional integration. It is obvious that the general public in the four countries is divided over the question of free mobility of persons implied by regional cooperation and integration. It is also clear that tension exist between what respondents at the level of cognition believes is in the best interest of the respective nations and in their personal interest. Nowhere was this disjuncture more dramatised than in the response of the student unemployed, with over three quarters of the respondents in that category indicating that the effects on the respective countries of closer collaboration would be a positive one. Yet as Tables 9-10 show, only 33 per cent showed support for free mobility of labour with a 70 per cent support for residency by non-nationals.

While the earlier findings that education, employment status, income and age to a lesser degree continue to exert powerful influences on the respondents, the micro level differences here are less acute. Table 9 is most striking, given the fact that in almost every category less than 50 per cent of the sampled population would support the idea of free mobility of labour in the sub-region. Indeed the exceptions to this general pattern are in the case of Barbados (52.2 per cent) and St Vincent (62.5 per cent), the age group 36-45 years (51.1 per cent), university graduates (52.3 per cent), and the two highest income earners with a support level of 51.3 per cent and 52.5 per cent. Indeed the lowest support for free mobility of labour is to be found within both categories of students, whether employed or unemployed, Antiguans, St Lucians, and those with the lowest level of education. In all of these cases under 40.0 per cent of the respondents were favourably disposed to the idea of free mobility of persons. Half of the unemployed students were not in favour of free mobility with 56.0 per cent of the employed students expressing similar views. Indeed the two lowest level of support is to be located among Antiguans and the unemployed students.

Table 9: Support for Persons Working in Country

Support for persons working	Yes %	No %	Non-Responsive %
1 Country of Origin			
Barbados	52.2	36.7	11.2
St Lucia	36.2	39.8	24
St Vincent	62.5	30.2	7.3
Antigua	31.8	56.1	12.1
2 Gender			
Male	49.6	38.4	12
Female	43.3	41.9	14.8
Unresponsive	-	-	-
3 Age			
18-25 years	41.2	46.2	12.6
26-35 years	48.5	39.4	12
36-45 years	51.1	37.0	12
46-55 years	43.0	40.8	16.2
Over 55 years	44.9	38.8	16.3
Non-Responsive	33.3	66.7	-
4 Employment Status			
Employed	48.9	39.6	11.5
Unemployed	42.9	40.2	16.9
Pensioned	43.8	36.5	19.7
Student Employed	34.7	56.0	9.3
Student Unemployed	33.0	50.0	17
Non-Responsive	11.1	33.3	55.6
5 Range of Annual Income			
Under $15,000.00	47.5	39.5	13.0
$15,000.001-$3,000.00	48.9	41.9	9.2
$30,001.00-$45,000.00	51.3	36	12.7
$45,001.00-Over $60,000.00	52.5	37.7	9.8
Unemployed	41.7	41.2	17.0
Non-Responsive	39.2	40.3	20.5
6 Educational Attainment			
None/Primary Incomplete	34.4	37.1	28.6
Primary Complete/Secondary Incomplete	44.6	39.6	15.8
Secondary Complete/University Incomplete	48.2	41.7	10.1
Completed University	52.3	34.5	13.2
Non-Responsive	23.1	61.5	15.4

Source: Cross National Survey conducted between November 1998 and April 2001.

Table 10: Support for Non-National Residency

Support for residency	Yes %	No %	Non-Responsive %
Country of Origin			
Barbados	59.7	27.3	13
St Lucia	62.6	14.0	23.4
St Vincent	79.1	13.0	7.9
Antigua	70.3	16.3	13.4
2 Gender			
Male	70.2	17.6	12.2
Female	63.3	20.3	16.4
Unresponsive	-	-	-
3 Age			
18-25 years	63.3	22.4	14.4
26-35 years	65.6	20.6	13.8
36-45 years	71.8	17.2	11
46-55 years	65.3	18.1	16.6
over 55 years	64.6	16.5	18.8
Non-Responsive	100	-	-
4 Employment Status			
Employed	69.1	18.7	12.2
Unemployed	61.1	19.5	19.5
Pensioned	63.1	19.3	9.1
Student Employed	61.3	24.0	14.7
Student Unemployed	70.2	18.1	11.7
Non-Responsive	22.2	11.1	66.7
5 Range of Annual Income			
Under $15,000.00	66.6	21.1	12.2
$15,000.001-$3,000.00	70.1	18.6	11.2
$30,001.00-$45,000.00	68.1	15.9	15.9
$45,001.00-Over $60,000.00	77.6	14.8	7.7
Unemployed	62.0	19.4	18.5
Non-Responsive	61.1	18.0	20.8
6 Educational Attainment			
None/Primary Incomplete	57.6	16.1	26.3
Primary Complete/Secondary Incomplete	63.6	20.0	16.5
Secondary Complete/University Incomplete	69.1	19.6	11.3
Completed University	70.8	14.8	14.5
Non-Responsive	53.8	7.7	38.5

Source: Cross National Survey conducted between November 1998 and April 2001.

When the respondents' views on free mobility are compared with their views on persons' ability to reside in each other's countries, there are stark differences. As Table 10 shows, in almost every category of respondents more than half of the sample was supportive. It is in St Vincent that the highest level of support is to be found with 79.1 per cent. Again persons within the age category 36-45 years (71.8 per cent), highest income earners (77.6 per cent), university graduates (70.8 per cent) were more disposed towards the idea. Interestingly while Antiguans were quite opposed to the idea of free mobility of persons, 70.0 per cent of them were supportive of persons outside of Antigua taking up residency in the country.

Conclusion

The article sought to both gauge the level and nature of sub-regional support for closer collaboration and regional integration and identify the socio-demographic influences that informed the above. A number of factors stand out. First, the data analysed above show considerable evidence to suggest that more than half the sampled population supported initiatives (specifically the Barbados-OECS Initiative) for closer cooperation among sub-regional countries. However, only moderate support is evidence for regional proposals that would advance the movement towards regional integration. In effect therefore the evidence presented does validate the view of Kenny Anthony that there is much pessimism about regional integration. However, there are mixed signals in relation to his latter contention that across the region there is doubt as to the desirability of integration itself. Second, while I have argued that the data presented do not suggest the existence of macro-level gender based differentials with respect to the various issues discussed above the same is not true of other structural factors. Third, what emerges is a picture of significant income, age and education based differences among the respondents.

Surprisingly while the data indicated a positive evaluation of the capacity of regional cooperation to improve the health of the nations involved in the cross national survey and indeed in all the member states of the OECS, such evaluation is not matched by an equal or similar level of support for regional integration. Finally therefore, it appears that the respondents' position in relation to regional integration is also informed by the fear that regional integration would merely serve to worsen the prospect for personal employment opportunities. This is informed by the low support for the free mobility of labour expressed by the respondents in comparison to support for persons taking up residency. Certain groups are therefore reluctant to allow citizens of other nations to participate in the labour market. As a consequence, it seems reasonable to interpret the data as tentative evidence that opposition to regionalism springs from a view that the presence or potential influx of citizens from member states of any sub-regional grouping would limit job opportunities and therefore impact negatively on the personal welfare of the individuals. Thus regional cooperation is viewed by many respondents as a two way street, one that can afford considerable benefits to the nation state, while simultaneously having the capacity to limit and constrain personal opportunities among some groups. Personal economic loss therefore remains a central issue in the regional integration enterprise.

Endnotes

1. *The Fourth and Final Report of the Windward Island Consultative Assembly.* (Castries, St Lucia: OECS Secretariat).
2. Kenny Anthony, 'Reflections on the RCA Experience' in Neville C. Duncan (ed), *Caribbean Integration: The OECS Revisited* (Kingston, Jamaica: Friedrich Ebert Stiftung, 1995) pp.113-118.
3. Voice Focus. *From Tortola to Kingstown: A Report on Eastern Caribbean Political Union.* (Castries, St Lucia: Voice Press, 1991).
4. P. K. Mennon (1988) unpublished. 'Eastern Caribbean States: Institutional Arrangements to Promote Cooperation Among Member States'. (A paper presented at the 29th Annual Convention of the International Studies Association held in St Louis, Missouri) pp. 26.
5. The main areas of cooperation agreed upon under the Agreement for Economic Cooperation focused on the development of the services sector, particularly that of the financial and informatics sectors. Two other areas of cooperation were, the participation of Barbados in the OECS single market and the negotiation of double taxation agreements and trade promotions.
6. *Report of the West Indian Commission: Time for Action Report.* 2nd Edn (Kingston, Jamaica: The Press, 1993) p. 24.
7. Ibid. *Report of the West Indian Commission: Time for Action Report.*

16

Trends in Labour Migration and its Implications for the Caribbean

David Nii Addy[1]

This chapter presents an overview of current patterns in international migration, recent developments within the Caribbean and a discussion of some of the socioeconomic consequences migration can entail. It highlights changes in the character of regional migration as well as the emergence of non-traditional forms of population movements in an attempt to call for a forward-looking management of migration. Encouraged by the demands of enhanced regional integration, the chapter argues that such a new Caribbean migration regime should respond to the growing policy challenges by building upon the existing international framework for the protection of migrants' human rights.

MIGRATION IN THE ERA OF GLOBALISATION AND INTERNATIONAL INTEGRATION

Migration has existed throughout the history of mankind, but has gained tremendously in importance and recognition at the beginning of the twenty-first century. Today international migration has been recognised as a major element of international relations and a key development issue that needs to be addressed in any discussion about the impact and characteristics of globalisation. For, more and more states are affected by migration, either as sending, transient or receiving countries. Global estimates put the total number of migrants, who live outside their countries of origin, at over 120 million people, of which the International Labour Organization (ILO) counts roughly 80 million as migrant workers. An estimated 30 million migrant workers are found in irregular situations. In addition, the United Nations High Commission for Refugees (UNHCR) points to the existence of over 20 million cross-border refugees and many more internally displaced people.

As a result of these dynamic migratory movements, some traditional migrant-sending countries face the challenge of developing new migration policies as they themselves change to becoming major migrant-receiving countries. Further, the universality of migrants' basic human rights requires not only the development of policies that serve to protect nationals abroad but also to guarantee the fair treatment of non-national immigrants domestically. Given its transnational nature, international migration thus cannot be dealt with unilaterally and clearly demands multilateral cooperation between states. Finally, the accelerated integration of commodity and capital markets is generally expected to fuel large-scale population movements in the years to come. From all indications, expanding wage and income differentials, persistent poverty and unemployment, changing manpower needs, further liberalisation in trade and capital flows, and the rapid developments in communication and transport infrastructure will all collude in maintaining a high propensity to migrate for work.[2]

Today's global migration systems tend to be influenced by a wide range of push- and pull-factors, such as current unemployment levels, active overseas recruitment to fill labour shortages, comparative wage rates, standards of living and other socioeconomic prospects, which eventually determine decisions to migrate. Current migration trends include the diversification of source countries, a growing importance of private recruitment agents and a *rise in skilled labour migration,* reflecting the global demand for highly educated specialists associated with the growth of trade in services and the transition towards knowledge-based economies.[3] At the same time, an ongoing demand for relatively low-skilled migrant work persists in many of the expanding 'new economies', which indirectly tends to encourage the presence of undocumented migrants in segmented labour markets.

Furthermore, the increasing *participation of women migrants* occurs at a time, when restrictive immigration policies in traditional migrant-receiving countries have effectively put an end to many forms of permanent settlement migration. Finally, persistent refugee crises, the rapid growth of international crime networks and limited opportunities for legal migration, enabled the *phenomenon of trafficking* to take on dangerous dimensions.[4]

Migration and its consequences

Most of these significant migrant groups make up extremely vulnerable social groups that are often at risk of abuse – both during the migratory process and, in the case of migrant workers, when at work in their final destination. In fact, large numbers of migrants have to work in dangerous occupations that are often shunned by nationals and frequently do not benefit from protective legislation in the informal labour market, as domestic servants or as child labourers. Contrary to the popular belief that migrants represent dangerous competition for scarce jobs, they are often simply relegated to jobs nobody else wants to do or even denied employment altogether. Widely held social stereotypes, xenophobic forms of racism and other mechanisms of social exclusion often limit their access to decent employment. Recent ILO research confirmed widespread labour market discrimination as being largely responsible for high unemployment rates among migrants and their descendants.[5]

Hence, there is no doubt that migration flows can entail very different implications in terms of socioeconomic, political and demographic consequences for all sides involved. While recent comparative studies suggest that the impact of migration may well produce 'small net gains in terms of per capita output to the host country', in most cases it has no obvious influence on domestic unemployment rates.[6] However, the distribution of benefits needs not to be even. On the economic side, therefore, any cost-benefit analysis will have to carefully measure the diffusion of business linkages and to assess the sector-specific impact of migration on employment, wages and the social welfare system. The contribution of migrants will also depend on their skill level, their age and gender as well as their role as oftentimes-creative entrepreneurs and highly significant remittance providers.[7] At the same time, international migration and its transnational networks have been credited with the 'denationalizing of urban space' in what have become truly 'global cities' in major migrant-receiving countries, whose socioeconomic dynamism created many uniquely positive economic and cultural spin-off effects.[8] The complex social impact of migration can thus range from an increased cultural diversity interacting with dynamic Diaspora communities to new demands placed on existing health and education systems, all of which will require a new policy framework to manage migration.

Increasingly during the 1990s, major migrant receiving countries were looking at ways in which to deal with real or perceived 'emigration pressure' from major migrant sending regions.[9] Apart from increased trade and foreign direct investment, official development assistance targeted at employment creation was discussed as a potential tool in reducing domestic push factors. However, based on the experiences so far, no clear empirical evidence could be established to support that thesis. Quite to the contrary, it seems that, at least in the short run, increased aid and economic growth associated with integrated trade blocs might actually fuel out-migration.[10]

In any case, it is clear that the current 'age of migration' has not yet succeeded in replacing the movement of people with that of goods, as some globalisation proponents had hoped. Rather, this phase of rapid global change has been characterised by accelerated population flows and a new complexity of migration types based on dynamic migratory chains that challenge rigid distinctions and old-fashioned notions of homogenous nation states.[11] In many traditional migrant-receiving countries, the one-time illusion that temporary migrant labour would never become a permanent reality has slowly been vanishing, at times reinforced by the demographic concern about aging populations and a desire for a migration-induced 'replacement population'. These countries are now challenged with devising effective integration policies for citizens of migrant origin, who are already present. At the same time, the protection of human rights for newly arriving migrants has to be guaranteed by a flexible policy-mix that would incorporate domestic labour market needs, which will often facilitate an upsurge in labour migration during economic boom cycles or sectoral labour shortages.

Migration in the Caribbean

Historically, migration has most likely shaped the formation and development of the Caribbean more profoundly than any other region of the world. Up to the 1850s, the transatlantic slave trade forcibly transported at least 15 million African slaves to the Caribbean, with many more not surviving the deadly 'middle passage'. In the aftermath of the Haitian Revolution, thousands of 'French Creoles' sought to reestablish their privileged position in plantation agriculture by intra-Caribbean migration to islands such as Jamaica and Trinidad. Both intra- and inter-island migration of free African descendants further accelerated with the abolition of slavery, when the labour demand in some of the expanding plantation economies had to be met through immigration. The resulting large-scale immigration of indentured labourers from the Indian sub-continent and China impacted profoundly on the social structure of countries such as Guyana, Suriname, Jamaica and Trinidad and Tobago in the aftermath of Emancipation.[12] The cosmopolitan population mix of the modern Caribbean is a direct result of migration.

Major migration waves occurred also during the early twentieth century, for instance during the construction period of the Panama Canal, when construction workers from Jamaica, Barbados and other Caribbean states migrated to Panama and other Central American countries. During the 1930s, Aruba, Curacao, Trinidad and Tobago and Venezuela imported migrant workers for their oil sectors. A continuous flow of women migrant workers often followed these newly established trade routes and continues up to today through much of the region. Accounts of the difficult working conditions of domestic worker communities from the anglophone Eastern Caribbean in Aruba highlight the many subtle barriers to social mobility reproduced by existing division of class and race.[13]

The 1950s and early 1960s, then, saw the departure of thousands of Caribbean people migrating to Britain to fill positions in the health and transportation sector.[14] With an annual average of some 30,000 anglophone Caribbean immigrants entering Britain, an estimated 50 per cent of the natural population increase in the region during 1950-1970 was effectively 'cancelled out' according to some estimates.[15] Similarly, several thousand Caribbean citizens of the French Overseas Departments moved to metropolitan France every year. In the aftermath of its independence, more than 100,000 Surinamese migrated to the Netherlands and, in 1997 represented there a community of 182,000 in the stock of the foreign-born population.

Finally, with the tightening of most European immigration regimes by 1971, Caribbean migrants increasingly sought opportunities in Canada or North America, where with the advent of new immigration legislation, migration opportunities had begun to be less nationality-dependent and more skill-based. As a result, Caribbean migrants were well represented during the 1990s in both the inflows of temporary workers and permanent settlers. More and more Caribbean women migrant workers participated in these movements. In 1998 alone, as noted by the *World Migration Report* some 75,000 Caribbean migrated to the USA, the majority of which came from the Dominican Republic (20,000), Cuba (17,000), Jamaica (15,000) and Haiti (13,000).[16] By the mid-1990s, more than two million people who were born in the Caribbean resided in the USA. In Canada, too, the census results for 1996 showed a growing Caribbean immigrant population with nearly 116,000 Jamaicans as the biggest group. The overall size of the Caribbean Diaspora is estimated at over five million people worldwide and represents a great potential in terms of ethnic niche markets, transnational networks and political lobbying groups.

Given the multiple migratory routes, past research often tended to characterise Caribbean migration as a natural 'safety valve' regulating both surplus labour and unmet aspirations of small island societies. Migration is therefore largely seen as a successful mechanism for social mobility and status that produced an increasing complexity of circulatory population movements within the region.[17] Especially women migrants hereby often maintain strong family responsibilities in both the old and new countries of residence, reflecting important gender differences in the process.[18] Furthermore, in view of prevalent discrimination patterns, migration also entails the danger of 'downward occupational mobility' and presents no long-term solutions to structural unemployment.[19] Consequently, the over-representation of young and educated migrants increasingly led critical observers to warn against the depletion of human capital through emigration.

Recent migration trends in the region

Despite the significance of migration to the region, current accounts of contemporary Caribbean migration practices are rare and there is a remarkable absence of comparative studies dealing with new forms of inter-island migration or the determinants of recent return migration.[20] Most data used in Caribbean migration research is fairly outdated and limited in scope. Much of it originated from the 1990 Regional Census and today's data collection methods still make it difficult to distinguish between permanent emigrants, temporary visitors, returning migrants, students pursuing higher education abroad and ordinary tourists.

As a notable element in traditional *extra-regional movements*, a large number of the Caribbean emigrants to the USA and Canada occupied low or semi-skilled positions. However, the available occupational listings for Jamaican nationals who migrated to Canada during the second half of the 1990s, show a clear trend towards departing migrants with extensive skills in business, finance and service occupations, which is followed by Jamaicans with occupational backgrounds in natural and applied science. Other Caribbean nationals migrating to the USA or Canada in the 1990s tended to equally possess higher educational attainments or entered their new destinations as students pursuing higher studies. This seems to indicate a clear trend towards a greater proportion of skilled migration in the total number of Caribbean migrants, with men still accounting '...for a larger percentage than females in the skill worker categories, but females (...) well represented in all occupations, and especially students'.[21]

At the same time, regular migration opportunities for unskilled labour migrants have become much more difficult to obtain. One exception is seasonal or *temporary labour recruitment*, which regularly leads to circular migration movements of Caribbean labour migrants hired to work in the agricultural sectors of the Unites States or Canada. Despite periodic reports of discrimination and few possibilities for skill-upgrading or permanent settlement, these schemes remain attractive throughout the region. Available data for the inflow of temporary Caribbean migrant workers to the United States range from an annual figure of 12,000 to 19,000 during the period of 1985 to 1995.

In Trinidad and Tobago, for instance, according to statistics provided by the Manpower & Employment Division of the Ministry of Labour, the number of workers who migrated to Canada for participation in the temporary farm worker programme stood at 1,475 during the year of 1999. This is a considerable increase in the number of workers who actually participated in the programme, when compared to the figures for 1994. During the latter, only 799 workers out of 4,730 who had applied for participation in the programme, actually left Trinidad and Tobago. Similar seasonal programmes are nowadays combined in many Caribbean countries with temporary schemes for hotel workers and attractive scholarship programmes of major universities. While these opportunities respond to both demand and supply, and thus are generally welcomed, a recent spate of aggressive campaigns by private recruitment agents aimed at experienced teachers and health personnel has given reason for great concern. As an example and within just a few weeks of May 2001, several hundred teachers from Trinidad and Tobago as well as from Jamaica signed up for employment with the New York City Council, as the result of a direct recruitment campaign. [22]

Other current forms of *intra-Caribbean migration* involved migrants moving to micro-destinations such as St Kitts & Nevis, the Turks & Caicos Islands, the Caymans, Anguilla or St Martin, which recently experienced labour shortages and economic expansion due to booming construction and tourism sectors. Some of these territories have now very high percentages of foreign-born populations, which in the case of Saba, St Eustatius and St Maarten of the Netherlands Antilles, reportedly rose to over 80 per cent during recent times. [23] According to another source, migrant labour from Dominica, Guyana, Jamaica, Montserrat accounts for 23 per cent of the labour force in Antigua, enhancing the local skill levels in domestic service, construction, agriculture and the hospitality industry. [24]

More traditional movements take place between Haiti and the Dominican Republic [25] or between Creole-speaking migrants from St Lucia, Haiti and Dominica to the French Overseas Departments of Guadeloupe and Martinique. In addition, each year, the ailing sugar and banana industries of St Kitts & Nevis and Dominica attract small numbers of seasonal labour migrants from the Eastern Caribbean. Barbados and Trinidad and Tobago have also remained attractive destinations for migrants from smaller neighbouring islands, such Grenada and St Vincent & the Grenadines. Finally, The Bahamas is home to some estimated 60,000 Haitians and continues to experience the immigration of other Caribbean nationals, such as an estimated 100 Cubans per month, and also Jamaicans and Dominicans in search of work. This steady influx creates very real challenges in terms of language instruction and the provision of social services for the local authorities. It might equally hamper the extension of CARICOM's free movement of labour policy, when Haiti becomes a member of the regional body. Nevertheless, cutting across language barriers and paving the way for new intra-Caribbean trade patterns, these existing migration networks in the Caribbean should eventually be recognised as a powerful integration force.

At the same time, the presence of non-Caribbean migrants in the region is equally growing. In Suriname, during much of the 1990s the vast majority of work permits for migrant workers were given to Brazilians. By 1997 these had numbered over 3,000 per year, a figure that subsequently dropped to 1,500 in 1999. However, other estimates put the number of (irregular) Brazilian migrant workers involved in mining activities at some 15,000, which increased to 60,000 if the family members were included. According to official work permit statistics, the majority of other migrants in Suriname came from Guyana, China, Haiti and Indonesia. Further north, Trinidad has once again become a major study centre for Venezuelan students and its booming natural resource-based industries attract other migrants, as well. Among the 37,000-strong workforce of Bermuda, there are 8,000 foreign work permit holder, who hold important positions in the insurance and tourism sectors, which prompted the Government recently to introduce a six-year limit on work permits for foreigners.[26]

Despite these national differences, common questions regarding the future management of migration and the provision of social services, land ownership and citizenship rights for settled migrants will need to be addressed throughout the Caribbean. In view of the greater vulnerability of mobile population groups to HIV/AIDS, improved access to health services and targeted education programmes will also be crucial.[27] Interestingly enough, though, concern about the social situation of migrants within Caribbean territories often remains much weaker than the one aimed at the protection of Caribbean nationals abroad.

Non-traditional forms of migration

Another significant feature of temporary population movements in the Caribbean is *return migration,* which is expected to grow, as more and more post-war migrants reach retirement age. As a matter of fact, moving back to the country of origin can also confer additional status for working-age returnees and often facilitates upward social mobility, since it often occurs after newly acquired skills and additional educational attainment have led to valuable experiences of a transnational nature.[28] Some Caribbean countries, such as Jamaica and St Kitts & Nevis, have begun to actively promote the reintegration of returning citizens by setting up offices or programmes facilitating the return of their nationals. With well over 1 million Jamaican migrants living abroad, it is estimated that some 16,000 nationals returned to the island over the last eight years.

On the immigration side, the experience with *Economic Citizenship Programmes* in countries such as St Vincent & the Grenadines, Dominica and Belize is rather mixed, as the economic benefits expected from the investment necessary to obtain citizenship often did not appear to be sustainable. At times, it is even alleged that several of the new citizens, most of which are of Chinese origin, seem to have been more interested in using the geographical proximity and existing migration networks to plan their eventual migration to the United States – rather than to contribute permanently to the economic and social development of their new homes. However, further research and empirical analysis need to verify such allegations and prevent existing xenophobic sentiments from growing.

Similarly, the forced return of so-called *'deportees'* has caused much controversy in receiving countries. Hereby the descendants of Caribbean migrants from the Dominican Republic, Jamaica, Guyana or Trinidad and Tobago, who often lived most of their adult life in the United States, are returned to the Caribbean after serving time for criminal offences of different nature. Apparently, some of these returnees are subsequently responsible for masterminding serious crimes and trafficking in drugs or firearms. Be that as it may, Caribbean countries need to urgently establish programmes aimed at assisting these involuntary 'returnees' with socioeconomic integration. Bilateral negotiations should also lobby for improved humanitarian treatment of these offenders in the US, which might then include the right to remain in the country of residence.

Moreover, it appears from growing numbers of irregular entries involving, among others, Chinese, Nigerian, Colombian and Mexican nationals, that *trafficking* in migrants from outside the region through Caribbean transient points is on the rise. In addition, the presence of undocumented migrants seems to be on the rise in a number of countries. Increasingly, therefore, some immigration authorities have expressed concern about irregular migration that – for instance in the case of the Bahamas – led to the expulsion of no less than 5, 801 persons during the year 2000.[29] Indeed, it is estimated that up to 40,000 undocumented migrants already live in the Netherlands Antilles and that other states such as Antigua have 'become a transient point in the trafficking of migrants, including the trafficking of women as sex workers'.[30] Other smuggled Caribbean migrants and victims of trafficking include nationals from Haiti, the Dominican Republic and Jamaica, attempting to enter the United States or wealthier micro-states of the Northern Caribbean.

While recognising these non-traditional forms of migration and the special constraints of small island states, the regional discourse about migration issues in general is not yet sufficiently focussed and rationalised. In fact, both sides of the Caribbean migration equation, whether it is the emigration outside of the region or the immigration to the region, have to be informed by a careful analysis of labour market realities and undivided respect for basic human rights of migrants. Experience from other regions has shown that when 'sending workers abroad', emigration countries can actually do a lot to regulate foreign employment: by setting minimum standards for employment contracts, by screening job offers, by establishing improved banking facilities for the development-oriented transfer of remittances and by promoting the movement of migrant workers to sectors and countries with comparatively good employment conditions.[31] Similarly, other creative policy responses are needed for those Caribbean countries that have become countries of immigration.

Human Rights of migrants

While governments have the right to regulate conditions of entry as part of their national immigration regime, international human rights have to govern the domestic treatment of migrants. Several international instruments provide a framework for the protection of migrants. The United Nations adopted the most recent and most comprehensive *International Convention on the Protection of the Rights of All Migrant Workers and Members of Their Families* in 1990. It recognises the fundamental human rights of all migrant workers, including those with an irregular status, and reaffirms equality in treatment with regard to terms and conditions of work, including the minimum age for admission to employment and remuneration. These rights are accorded 'without distinction of any kind such as to sex, race, colour, language, religion or conviction, political or other opinion, national, ethnic or social origin, nationality, age, economic position, property, marital status, birth or other status'. As such, the Convention protects against arbitrary arrest, forced labour or the unlawful confiscation of identity documents. It defines a migrant, regardless of the legal status, '… as a person who is to be engaged, is engaged or has been engaged in a remunerated activity in a State of which he or she is not a national'.[32]

Prior to this, the ILO had developed the *Migration for Employment Convention* in 1949 and the *Migrant Workers Convention* in 1975 plus its respective Recommendations, which address the protection of migrant workers in two corresponding instrument.[33] The main provisions of these ILO labour standards aim at improving migration conditions in abusive conditions as well as at ensuring the principle of non-discrimination and equality of opportunity between nationals and (legal) migrant workers in areas such as remuneration, membership in trade unions or social security. They further encourage more exchange of information between states, the reduction of clandestine migration and comprehensive protection for migrants from unjustified withdrawals of work permits or residence rights.[34] The non-binding Recommendations provide detailed policy suggestions for the development of fair recruitment and contract conditions as well as a model agreement on migration for employment. While some Caribbean countries[35] have ratified the ILO Migration for Employment Convention, it seems much more needs to be done in the region to guarantee migrants' equal rights and improve their access to employment, education and health care facilities.

Indeed, no Caribbean country has so far ratified the comprehensive UN Convention, which eleven years after its adoption is still not in force due to the lack of the 20 mandatory ratifications. Furthermore, many Caribbean states, such as Barbados, Cuba, Guyana, Grenada or Trinidad and Tobago, have also not acceded to the 1951 Refugee Convention and its 1967 Protocol. Even where these international instruments for the protection of refugees have been adopted, as in the case of The Bahamas, the Dominican Republic, Haiti or Suriname, corresponding legal and institutional arrangements are often missing. As a result, irregular migrant workers and especially refugees and their children are often without proper protection, at times face detention and are in general in need of regularisation programmes. According to the UNHCR, many Caribbean states are in urgent need to improve the policy framework, as countries such as the Bahamas, Jamaica or Trinidad and Tobago would most likely 'be one of the countries most affected by any future Caribbean refugee emergency'.[36] In this regard, the experience of Central American refugees in Belize, who benefited from specific naturalisation provisions in the Immigration Act and the Constitution, should be further analysed. For instance, its 1999 Amnesty Programme offered irregular immigrants and unregistered refugees permanent resident status.

In 1999, the UN Commission on Human Rights appointed a special rapporteur on the human rights of migrants, reflecting the growing concern with the lack of protection of this vulnerable group, especially when in irregular (undocumented) situations. The second report of the *Special Rapporteur on the human rights of migrants* expressed serious concern about the living and working conditions of the 500,000 Haitian migrant workers in the sugar cane fields of the Dominican Republic.[37] The report also urged governments to ratify the International Convention on the Protection of the Rights of All Migrant Workers and Members of their Families.[38]

Finally, to combat the growing incidence of trafficking and cross-border smuggling of migrants, the *United Nations Convention against Transnational Organized Crime* was recently adopted with two important protocols that now need to be ratified.[39] For instance, many thousand women from the Dominican Republic have been trafficked into countries of the European Union for commercial sexual exploitation. Various other forms of abuse can victimise trafficked migrants from the point of departure, during the transitory process and after arrival in the destination country. Recent reports even indicate a growing number of irregular migrants, who are washed ashore dead in places such as St Martin and The Bahamas. New preventive measures are urgently needed to reduce such incidents of trafficking in the region and, more importantly to protect the human rights of the victims, in particular when they are vulnerable due to their age, sex or (irregular) status.

THE ISSUE OF BRAIN DRAIN

The loss of skilled manpower through emigration has been a long-standing concern of Caribbean policy-makers. Generally, the 'brain drain' was seen as foregone investment in education and training, which in the case of the Caribbean mostly affected the health and education systems. For instance, in *Jamaica*, earlier studies estimated the lost training output for Jamaican doctors and nurses during the period of 1978-1985 at 78 per cent and 95 per cent respectively.[40] A recent survey on migration of skilled health personnel in the Caribbean by the Commonwealth Secretariat reported that the

> main problem was retention of nurses/midwives, but shortages were also noted in all other categories of health workers ... namely, medical laboratory technologists, pharmacists, physicians, public health inspectors, and radiographers. Barbados indicated that it also had problems retaining physiotherapists and occupational therapists, and Trinidad and Tobago was experiencing problems retaining scientific assistants. The survey revealed a clear perception that there were three main reasons for this loss of trained health personnel: poor conditions of service, poor conditions of work and much more attractive opportunities in the private sector and elsewhere.'[41]

Consequently, some countries experience shortages of skilled professionals, resulting in the recruitment of experienced health care personnel from other regional providers, such as Cuba, or even West Africa.

Equally in *Suriname*, the 'brain drain' among civil servants has been a major concern throughout the post-independence period. In the 1990s, the

National Planning Bureau has conducted several studies in an attempt to monitor the situation and to identify solutions for the preponderance of unqualified teachers in the education system.

> In the Civil Service the brain drain of desk personnel is estimated at 40% of all the highly educated who have left the service. For the Education Sector the brain drain is approximately 32% of all highly educated persons who have left this service. (...) The brain drain in the Health Sector during 1990-1995 stands at 33%. (...) The professions that suffer greatly from brain drain are the highly educated nurses (62%) and the medical specialists (34%).[42]

Recognising the need to urgently improve both the retention of qualified staff and the larger human resources planning process, bilateral agreements for temporary migration or 'ethical recruitment' should be promoted between sending and receiving countries. However, critical voices have also pointed to the fact that the circular patterns of (skilled) migration does not simply represent permanent losses in human capital, but rather the foundation for complex transnational households, capable of producing a multitude of positive socioeconomic effects in past, present and future locations.[43] Recent comparative research confirms that skilled migration can indeed have multiple impacts. Empirically it remains unclear whether out-migration necessarily hampers development and slows growth or whether it actually boosts productivity by facilitating investment as well as knowledge and technology transfer. Increasingly, the diverse effects are therefore characterised as 'brain exchange', which is seen as integral and largely beneficial part of globalisation, rather than as a linear 'brain drain'.[44]

Indeed, even if skilled migration presents a loss of human capital in the short run, it can actually produce important incentives to invest in education and thus benefit the local skill base, if better domestic opportunities are created. Sending and receiving countries need to cooperate by targeting economic development in the sectors at risk of skill depletion in the source countries. Further, voluntary codes of practices could impose restrictions on recruitment from countries at risk. Once again, creative migration policies are needed to manage these movements and to harness the benefits of both (temporary) out-migration and (voluntary) return migration of nationals with important skills. Finally, abusive practices of recruitment agencies need to be monitored and curtailed, all of which might go a long way in reducing the negative effects of otherwise potentially beneficial migration.

REGIONAL INTEGRATION AND THE FREE MOVEMENT OF LABOUR

Economic integration requires the removal of formal and informal barriers that prevent the free movement of capital, goods, services and people. Within the Caribbean, so far, only certain skill categories of Caribbean migrants were exempted from work permits and, in principle, guaranteed free movement.[45] However, further research would be required to determine, if there are any informal obstacles for the implementation of the regional Action Plan for skilled labour mobility and how the current phased approach to skill-based free movement can be extended to all categories of migrant workers.

Indeed, in July 2001 at the Twenty-Second Meeting of the Conference of Heads of Government of the Caribbean Community (CARICOM) in The Bahamas, the revision of the Treaty of Chaguaramas was completed by making provision for the free movement of persons, capital and services and the right of establishment. The establishment of the Caribbean Single Market and Economy (CSME) now further underlines the need to review regional migration policies and to enact laws and administrative regulations that guarantee the non-discrimination of CARICOM migrants. This should eventually include access to employment, residence rights, the transferability of welfare and social security benefits as well as the mutual recognition of educational qualifications.

Given the relatively high unemployment rates and wide income disparities in the region, concerns about the likely migratory impact of these provisions are common, especially among the wealthier states of the region. However, the labour market impact of a free movement of labour policy is hard to predict. Assuming a temporary increase in intra-regional migration, the effects for receiving countries can be very positive, if the skills brought by the migrants are complementary and help to enhance competitiveness. For those countries that loose skills through out-migration, investment in education and training will become necessary to replenish the loss and to boost the chances of creating sustainable economic growth, which in turn would reduce the propensity to migrate. Theoretically, in the long run, it is then expected that economic integration will diminish existing income levels and balance skill shortages.

It is important to note, however, that fears expressed elsewhere in anticipation of major migratory flows as a result of regional integration have mostly proven to be exaggerated. Rather, it seems safe to say that the existence of income differences and divergent poverty rates alone does not automatically lead to migration. Actually, in most cases it is not the poor who migrate and it appears that the decision to migrate is not necessarily a direct outcome of economic integration. Instead, it is a complex function of different determinants based on existing migration networks and trade relations, the likelihood of finding employment and by taking into consideration wage differentials and other socioeconomic criteria. The experiences of other regional integration schemes, such as the EU or NAFTA tend to confirm these complex migratory linkages,[46] and could thus provide important reference points for CARICOM's envisaged Free Movement of Labour policies.

Conclusion

The limitations to the free movement of labour are increasingly seen as serious contradictions restricting the effective operation of international labour markets and international competition. While some countries have in the past successfully developed comprehensive foreign employment policies, often based on bilateral agreements between the sending and receiving country, most Caribbean states are only now beginning to realise the full implications of existing migration dynamics. More and more countries, however, now recognise the need for properly managed migration and the development of forward-looking policies. The future management of international migration therefore presents challenges to all involved: the individual migrant but also the migrant-sending and -receiving states. Key issues that need to be addressed urgently in all important migrant regions, with the Caribbean being a small but important one, are:

- The development of forward-looking migration policies
- The protection of basic human rights of migrants, including their non-discrimination in domestic labour markets
- The reduction of the 'brain drain' phenomena
- The optimisation of remittance flows
- The implications of migration for citizenship and national identities
- The regulation of irregular immigration.

Endnotes

1. Associate Research Officer at the Caribbean Office of the International Labour Organization (ILO) in Port of Spain/Trinidad and Tobago. The views expressed here are entirely those of the author and do not represent official statements on behalf of the ILO. Piyasiri Wickramasekara provided helpful comments on an earlier draft.

2. Peter Stalker: Workers without frontiers – *The impact of globalisation on international migration*, ILO, Geneva 2000.

3. Migration Policy Group & Institute for the Study of International Migration: Transatlantic Round Table on High Skilled Migration – A Report on the Proceedings, Brussels, March 4-6, 2001.

4. OECD: *Trends in International Migration*, Paris 2000; IOM/UN: World Migration Report 2000, Geneva 2000.

5. Roger Zegers de Beijl: *Documenting discrimination against migrant workers in the labour market – A comparative study of four European countries*, ILO, Geneva 2000.

6. J.Coppel, J.C. Dumont & I. Visco: Trends in immigration and economic consequences, OECD Economics Department Working Papers No. 284, February 2001, p.4.

7. Peter Stalker: *The work of strangers – A survey of international labour migration*, ILO, Geneva 1994, p.53.

8. Saskia Sassen: *Globalization and its Discontents* – Essays on the new mobility of people and money, New York 1998.

9. For a review of the US discussion see Christopher Mitchell: 'Restricted Migration and Caribbean Development – Policies and Prospects' in: *Free Markets, Open Societies, Closed Borders? Trends in International Migration and Immigration Policy in the Americas*, ed. by Max Castro, University of Miami, 1998.

10. Roger Boehning & M. Schloeter-Parades (Eds.): *Aid in place of migration?* Selected contributions to an ILO-UNHCR meeting, ILO, Geneva 1994.

11. Stephen Castles & Mark J. Miller: *The Age of Migration – International Population Movements in the Modern World*, London 1993.

12. Peter Fryer: *Black People in the British Empire*, London 1988, p.26.

13. Paula Aymar: *Uprooted Women – Migrant Domestics in the Caribbean*, Westport 1997.

14. The Race Today Collective: The arrivants – A pictorial essay on blacks in Britain, London 1987.

15. Stalker (1994): op. cit., p.115.

16. IOM/UN: *World Migration Report 2000*, op. cit., pp.256-258.

17. Dennis Conway: 'The complexity of Caribbean Migration' in: *Caribbean Affairs* Vol.7 No. 4 (1994).

18. Karen Fog Olwig: The Migration Experience – Nevisian Women at home and abroad' in: Janet Momsen (Ed.): *Women and Change in the Caribbean*, London 1993, pp. 150-166.

19. Jorge Duany: 'Beyond the Safety Valve – Recent Trends in Caribbean Migration' in: *Social and Economic Studies* 43:1 (1994).

20. Aaron Segal: 'The Political Economy of Contemporary Migration' in: Thomas Klak (Ed.): *Globalization and Neoliberalism – The Caribbean Context*, Oxford 1998, pp. 211-225.

21. Elizabeth Thomas-Hope: 'Skilled Labour Migration from Developing Countries – The Caribbean Case', Draft Report, ILO, April 2001, p.9.

22. 'US hiring 600 Jamaican teachers' in *The Gleaner*, May 25, 2001; '400 nurses leaving' in *Trinidad Express*, 23.04.01; Teachers flood Hilton looking for US jobs' in *Newsday* April 22, 2001.

23. ECLAC: Report of the Ad Hoc Expert Group Meeting on Intraregional Migration, November 9-10, 2000 in Port of Spain, p.20.

24. Jessica Brown: 'Migration, National Identity and Regionalism in the Caribbean – Leeward Islands Case Study' in: Kenneth Hall & Denis Benn (Eds.): *Contending with Destiny – The Caribbean in the 21st Century*, Kingston 2000, pp.80-90.

25. The Dominican Republic is home to an estimated one million Haitians, half of which are said to be undocumented, living and working under extremely difficult circumstances.

26. Latin America Monitor - Caribbean, Vol. 18, No. 4, April 2001, p.6.

27. UNAids: 'Population Mobility and Aids, Technical Update', February 2001.

28. See the case of return migration to Trinidad & Tobago presented by Roger-Mark De Souza: 'The Spell of the Cascadura – West Indian Return Migration' in: Thomas Klak (Ed.): *Globalization and Neoliberalism – The Caribbean Context*, Oxford 1998, pp.227-253.

29. Repatriation statistics produced by the Enforcement Unit of Immigration in the Bahamas.

30. ECLAC: op. cit., p. 17.

31. Manolo Abella: *Sending workers abroad – A manual for low- and middle-income countries*, Geneva 1997.

32. Article 2 and 7 of the International Convention on the Protection of the Rights of All Migrant Workers and Members of Their Families. See http://www.unhchr.ch/html/menu3/b/m_mwctoc.htm.

33. The full titles are: *The Migration for Employment Convention* (Revised), 1949 (No.97) and its accompanying *Migration for Employment Recommendation* (Revised), 1949 (No.86); the *Migrant Workers (Supplementary Provisions) Convention*, 1975 (No.143) and the *Migrant Workers Recommendation*, 1975 (No.151).

34. Piyasiri Wickramasekara: 'Recent trends in labour migration, standards and policies', Paper presented at the International Migration Policy Seminar for the Caribbean Region, Kingston, Jamaica, 28-31 May 2001.

35. To date, these countries are The Bahamas, Barbados, Belize, Dominica, Grenada, Guyana, Jamaica, St Lucia and Trinidad and Tobago.

36. UNHCR: Mid-Year Report 2000 – North America and the Caribbean. http://www.unhcr.ch/world/amer.htm.

37. UN Economic and Social Council: Report of the Special Rapporteur, submitted pursuant to Commission on Human Rights resolution 2000/48, E/CN.4/2001/83, January 9, 2001.

38. For a similar appeal see: Communique of the First Ecumenical Conference on Migration in the Caribbean, June 1-5, 1998, Santo Domingo.

39. This was recently also recommended at the International Migration Policy Seminar for the Caribbean. See IMP Summary Report and Conclusions, Kingston/Jamaica, 28-31 May 2001.

40. Stalker (1994): op.cit. pp. 118-121.

41. Commonwealth Secretariat: *Migration of Health Workers from Commonwealth Countries – Experiences and Recommendations for Action*, London 2001, p.11.

42. Stichting Planbureau Suriname: Hooggeschoolden bij de overheid – Onderzoegksrapport, Paramaribo 1997, pp. 43-44.

43. Elizabeth Thomas-Hope: 'Caribbean Skilled International Migration and the Transnational Household' in: *Geoforum* Vol. 19 No.4 (1988), pp. 423-432.

44. B. Lindsay Lowell & Allan M. Findlay: 'Migration of Highly Skilled Persons from Developing Countries – Impact and Policy Responses, Draft Synthesis Report', ILO/DFID, June 1, 2001.

45. The respective skill categories included university graduates, media personnel, artists and musicians as well as sports persons.

46. Elmar Hoenekopp & Heinz Werner: 'Eastward Enlargement of the European Union – a Wave of Immigration?', IAB Labour Market Research Topics No. 40, 2000, Institute for Employment Research of the Federal Employment Services, Germany; Alan B. Simmons: 'NAFTA, International Migration and Labour Rights' in: *Labour Capital and Society* Vol. 31 No. 1+2 (1998), pp.10-43.

Part V

※

Constitutional Reform and Caribbean Governance

17

Democracy and Electoral Reform in the Anglophone Eastern Caribbean

Douglas Midgett

Prelude: Two events, occurring at different times and in different places, suggest some fundamental problems of the democratic process in the small islands of the Eastern Caribbean. The first occurred in 1979 in Antigua. At a sitting of the House of Representatives a bill was to be introduced allocating funding for a scheme that would resuscitate the sugar industry in the island.[1] The scheme was motivated by partisan political considerations, since the Government party, the Antigua Labour Party, had made a campaign promise to reintroduce sugar, an industry abandoned by the opposition party during their term of office from 1971-76. The expected debate would presumably address the merits of the scheme, for its cost, approximately EC$9 million, was to be funded by the Caribbean Development Bank. In 1979 this represented a substantial sum for a small island economy.

At the opening of the session the first order of business was a motion from the Government side to suspend the rules – to undertake all three stipulated readings of the bill during the present sitting of the House. This would mean no serious and considered public airing of the issue, and that any debate that would attend the consideration of the bill would take place during the one sitting. The bill was controversial; the Government-owned sugar industry had incurred a heavy debt before its closure; and studies undertaken at various times had concluded that the island was not naturally well-endowed for the growing of cane, and that reintroduction of sugar would not be economically viable.

The motion to suspend passed easily with the eleven ALP members of the seventeen-seat House voting in favour. As they said, in Antigua, 'The ayes have it', a statement not simply a representation of a vote, but a recognition that the Government party will typically eschew any significant public airing of measures that constitute their agenda. The ensuing debate reflected the realisation of the measure's foregone conclusion. Some spirited and fact-laden statements from the Opposition were greeted with derision from Government supporters in the gallery, and some government representatives, themselves. Little in the way of justification for the enactment of the measure was offered. At day's end, the bill was passed and the process set in motion for the fulfillment of the campaign promise.

The second insight came in 1994 during a viewing of C-SPAN's weekly broadcast of 'Prime Minister's Questions', the exchanges in the British parliament. The usual spirited banter between the government and opposition benches was suspended on this occasion in the aftermath of the death of the Labour Party Leader, John Smith. Parliamentarians from both sides and representatives of minor parties took the opportunity to celebrate the career of their deceased colleague, and the discourse was uniformly laudatory and obviously heartfelt. Smith was extolled especially for his dedication to the institution of parliament and his conduct as a parliamentarian. I was struck by the willingness of all to abjure party differences and to give due praise for one whose contributions had been noteworthy and sustained.

I have tried to imagine this kind of suspension of usual oppositional banter by politicians in the eastern Caribbean, and I cannot. The absence of rancour evidenced in the House of Commons on that occasion would be quite unlikely in my experience of West Indian political discourse. The events surrounding the recent demise of Rosie Douglas in Dominica might provide an example to the contrary, but I cannot say that for sure.

INTRODUCTION

Events of recent Eastern Caribbean elections and the controversy occasioned by new constituency boundaries in St Lucia before the island's recent poll are indicative of problems of democratic representation and process that appear common to the region. In this paper I want to address these under two headings: 1) voter participation as it is expressed in the definition of constituencies, and 2) parliamentary representation, especially of third (or fourth) parties, in a system based on single-member constituencies where winners are determined on a first-past-the-post basis.[2]

With respect to the first issue I review the method for determining size and boundary definitions for constituencies in the Eastern Caribbean, particularly in the years since the states have become constitutionally independent. With respect to the second, I look at a number of recent elections where highly skewed results have raised again the question of appropriateness of the electoral mechanism for these small states. In the latter case it is not my intention to suggest alternative systems, a topic beyond my expertise. It is the purpose of this exercise to indicate problematical aspects inherent in the current systems.

Before examining these two issues, let me address some other arguments made about the possibilities for democratic participation in the English-speaking Caribbean. A decade ago a spate of books and articles appeared addressing the state of democratic institutions and conditions for their maintenance in the Anglophone Caribbean.[3] These were representative of great interest, especially by political scientists, in processes of democratisation following the break-up of the Soviet Union, the transformation of eastern European polities and similar efforts in numerous developing countries. These arguments generally dealt with three issues, with some overlap:

1. political practice is dominated by the privileged classes in these societies, allowing for only limited participation by the masses;
2. the political culture emerging from the colonial episode is riven with clientalistic arrangements where benefits are awarded according to nepotistic criteria; and
3. within the global structure of domination hegemonic outside forces inhibit and frustrate impulses toward democratisation.

With respect to the Caribbean, Percy Hintzen has made a case for domination of the system by middle-class interests, effectively excluding the masses. He writes of a 'statist organisation ... designed to serve the power and accumulative interests of a particular segment of the middle class'. This, he says, results in 'oligarchic control by the representatives of this middle class'.[4] He sees this class segment emerging from the colonial epoch to assume control of the state mechanism relinquished by the colonial power. In addition it assumed domination of the trade union organisations that emerged in the 1940s. For Hintzen this domination was and is legitimised by middle-class ideological hegemony. This ideology stems from 'a vision rooted in their own middle-class culture but couched in terms of the appropriated culture of the lower class. Nationalism and developmentalism are at the core of this ideology'.[5]

Hintzen goes on to suggest that an ideological construct is promoted in the legitimisation of middle-class dominance, political practice depends upon a clientalistic relationship between classes.[6] The assertion of clientalistic relations in Caribbean politics is frequently made, and its demonstration is provided in numerous examples. Discussion of this phenomenon draws attention to two factors that produce this kind of political practice. The first is the economies of these small states, situations in which many livelihoods depend upon perceptions of political support for parties and politicians. In these conditions nepotism and clientalism flourishes and becomes the commonplace practice.[7] The second factor is the allegation that such relationships and the features of the social contracts that sustain them have become the substance of political culture in these small arenas.

For a number of observers these structural and cultural features are not separable from the international context of Caribbean political life. This view recognises a fundamental weakness of Caribbean polities, marginal to international sources of power and perpetually called upon to service the needs of mostly poor constituents.[8] Some of these observations indicate rather dismal prospects for the enactment of meaningful democracy in Eastern Caribbean states. If, for example, agency of Caribbean peoples is so compromised by the constraints of their marginalisation in the international scene, then discussion of the mechanisms of elections appears a spurious exercise. These are issues to which we will return, but first we examine those very mechanisms.

CONSTITUENCY SIZE AND BOUNDARIES

In addressing the conduct of elections I intend to augment an earlier study by Lijphart, which examined the utility of the Westminster model for small eastern Caribbean states.[9] The six states in question include St Kitts-Nevis, Antigua and Barbuda, Dominica, St Lucia, St Vincent and the Grenadines, and Grenada. Beginning with Grenada in 1974, all have become constitutionally independent. The introduction of mass-based electoral politics was effected by constitutional changes in 1950-51 that legislated universal adult suffrage. The translation of the Westminster system resulted in single-member electoral districts geographically demarcated, with representatives to parliaments elected on a plurality (first-past the-post) basis. The law-making body is made up of the elected members, with the party that can command a majority forming the government. The parliaments are very small – from 11 to 21 members. Party politics have become the rule following an earlier period when independent candidacies were occasionally viable in some of the polities.[10]

The question of boundary determination has two aspects. First is the constitutional charge given to Constituencies Boundaries Commissions, the bodies established by statute in all of the states according to their constitutions. As we shall see, there is some variation among the constitutions. Second is a consideration of the manner in which this boundary definition is carried out in practice. Here we examine issues of voter parity among constituencies and the possibility of gerrymandered boundaries.

The relative size and definition of constituency boundaries is an exercise that may take into account singularly, or in combination, the following factors: 1) population size, with a view to approximating equal numbers of voters; 2) maintaining the integrity of communities; and/or 3) geographical features that would mitigate against access of some voters to polling stations. In states that have multi-ethnic or multi-racial populations, as example Fiji, other considerations may be taken to ensure representation of all groups. This is not an issue in the Eastern Caribbean. Examining the constitutions of the six states yields a few differences with respect to the determination of electoral districts. In Table 1 the relevant passages of the constitutions are indicated.

We see that there is no difference in the constitutional direction provided for commissions in Dominica, Grenada and St Lucia. St Vincent and the Grenadines' constitution does not relegate the significant language to an appended schedule, and it stipulates 13 constituencies (enlarged to 15 in 1989). The St Kitts/Nevis constitution reflects the two-island nature of the state and is a product of the unique federal arrangement under which the state was formed at independence. Only Antigua differs significantly from the general instruction, stating only the Barbuda must be represented. The other multi-island entities, Grenada and St Vincent and the Grenadines make no special provision for representation of the smaller islands that comprise the state.

How, then, does this play out in practice? Noting that, except for Antigua, the first principle in all of the constitutional stipulations is that 'All constituencies shall contain as nearly equal numbers of inhabitants as appears to be reasonably practicable', we can assess the degree of numerical parity in practice by applying a coefficient of variability test (V) to each of the islands' distributions of voting lists by constituency (see Table 2).[11]

The examination of relative size of constituencies suggests that the application of the stipulations contained in the constitutions varies considerably form island to island. Recall that only the Antigua and Barbuda constitution does not state as a first principle that 'all constituencies shall contain as nearly equal numbers of inhabitants as appears to be reasonably practicable'. However the V values range from 0.155 in the 1979 St Vincent and the Grenadines election to 0.482 for Dominica in 1980. There are also some noteworthy within-state variations – St Kitts-Nevis, 1980-89, and St Vincent and the Grenadines, 1979-89.

Table 1: Constitutional Stipulations Regarding Constituency Boundaries

Antigua and Barbuda	'shall be divided into such number of constituencies, **at least one of which shall be within Barbuda**' (sect. 62)
Dominica	'should be divided in order to give effect to the rules set out in Schedule 2 to this constitution' (sect.57) **Schedule 2:** 'All constituencies shall contain as nearly equal numbers of inhabitants as appears to the Constituency Boundaries Commission to be reasonably practicable, but the Commission may depart from this rule to such extent as it considers expedient to take account of the following factors, that is to say :- a. the density of population, and in particular the need to ensure the adequate representation of sparsely-populated rural areas ; b. the means of communication ; c. geographical features ; d. the boundaries of administrative areas.'
Grenada	'should be divided in order to give effect to the rules set out in Schedule 2 to this constitution' (sect.56) **Schedule 2:** (same as Dominica)
St Kitts/Nevis	'should be divided in order to give effect to the rules set out in Schedule 2' (sect. 50) Schedule 2: **1. There shall be not less than eight constituencies in the island of Saint Christopher and not less than three constituencies in the island of Nevis and if the number of constituencies is increased beyond eleven, not less than one-third of their number shall be in the island of Nevis.** **2.** All constituencies shall contain as nearly equal numbers of inhabitants as appears to the Constituency Boundaries Commission to be reasonably practicable but the Commission may depart from this rule to such extent as it considers expedient to take account of the following factors, that is to say – **(a) the requirements of rule 1 and the differences in the density of the populations in the respective islands of Saint Christopher and Nevis;** (b) the need to ensure adequate representation of sparsely populated rural areas; (c) the means of communication; (d) geographical features; and (e) existing administrative boundaries.
St Lucia	'should be divided in order to give effect to the rules set out in Schedule 2 to this Constitution' (sect. 58) **Schedule 2:** (same as Dominica)
St Vincent and the Grenadines	**'shall be divided into thirteen constituencies,** "All constituencies shall contain as nearly equal numbers of inhabitants as appears to be reasonably practicable, but the Commission may depart from this principle to such extent as it considers expedient to take account of the following factors, a. the density of population, and in particular the need to ensure the adequate representation of sparsely populated areas. b. the means of communication c. geographical features, and d. the boundaries of administrative areas.' **(sect. 33)**

Table 2: Eastern Caribbean – Relative Size of Constituencies

Island State	Year	Voters on Rolls	Mean (X)	Standard deviation (s)	Coefficient of Variability (V)
Antigua and Barbuda	1980	28903	1700.18	656.77	0.386
	1984	31480	1851.76	678.92	0.367
	1989	36875	2169.12	797.74	0.368
Dominica	1980	38452	1831.05	882.11	0.482
	1990	52547	2407.48	1022.09	0.409
	2000	60165	2865.00	1265.95	0.442
Grenada	1984	48158	3210.53	927.12	0.289
	1999	73682	4912.13	1361.13	0.277
St Kitts/ Nevis	1980	19921	2213.44	489.87	0.221
	1989	26482	2407.45	829.08	0.344
	1993	28987	2635.18	939.01	0.356
St Lucia	1979	67909	3994.65	1801.32	0.451
	1987	83153	4891.35	2079.87	0.425
	1997	111330	6548.82	2753.34	0.420
St Vincent and the Grenadines	1979	52073	4005.62	620.31	0.155
	1989	61091	4072.73	852.74	0.209
	1998	76469	5097.93	1099.10	0.216

When we turn to the actual boundaries and the changes effected through time, the variations become understandable. For the following island states the criteria for boundary definition appear to apply:

Antigua: Until 1980 parish integrity was maintained, with additional constituencies carved out of existing parishes. In 1980 and again in 1984 new boundary changes did not follow parish boundaries, even though the number of constituencies remained at 17. Changes likewise do not appear to have been effected in the service of increasing parity among the Antigua districts. Most rural districts continue to bear parish names.

Dominica: Dominica continues to evidence greatest discrepancy in constituency size. An overriding criterion here appears to be maintenance of community integrity at the expense of numerical parity. Dominican districts bear the names of villages and towns.

Grenada. Grenada districts are defined strictly along parish lines. Increased numbers of constituencies have been created by intra-parish divisions, attempting equal representation within the sub-parish districts.

St Kitts-Nevis. Prior to 1983, when St. Kitts-Nevis became independent the nine constituencies evidenced considerable numerical parity except for an inordinately large Central Basseterre district (see 1980). The constitutional arrangement that created a federal system, granting Nevis significant autonomy, also changed the balance of representation, giving Nevis proportionally more representation per voter than St Kitts (see 1989). This would seem to be perpetuated in the provision for Nevis to have no less than one-third of the seats, a proportion unlikely to ever be met by its share of voters in the state.

St Lucia. Community integrity has been the rule in St Lucia. Constituencies are named for communities and, for the most part, new districts have resulted by dividing previously existing ones. The disparity is largely a result of numerically large districts in the Castries-Gros-Islet area in the north and smaller districts elsewhere, plus the maintenance of the very small Central Castries constituency.

St Vincent and the Grenadines. More than any of its neighbours St Vincent has observed the parity rule (see 1979). In the past this has resulted in divided communities – Colonarie from 1951-57, and Barrouallie, 1961-67. Prior to the 1989 election, however, two constituencies were added, one in St Vincent, proper, and one in the Grenadines, the latter dividing this group of small islands into Northern and Southern districts. Although the subsequent divisions within St Vincent actually enhanced numerical parity (V=0.078 in 1989), the Grenadines districts, especially the Southern, are much smaller than those on the main island.

Two considerations emerge from these data. One is the obvious recognition that all voters within a state do not see their votes count equally. In states like St Lucia and Dominica where constituency size variation is greatest, a vote in the largest district may be worth less than one-fourth that in the smallest. This is one issue that the St Lucian Commission addressed prior to the 2002 poll. In the 1997 election Central Castries contained just 2,615 voters, while neighbouring Castries East and Castries Northeast, which it abuts, had more than 12,000 each. The issue of disparity of districts within states has been raised sporadically precisely on these grounds, but little has been done to create districts of relatively equal size in the most disparate cases.

The second consideration is that changes that have been effected, whether as a result of an increase in the number of districts or not, have often been done to the advantage of one party at the expense of rivals. Although mandated by the Independence Constitution of 1983, the changes in St Kitts-Nevis clearly advantaged the coalition PAM/NRP government by adding a seat in Nevis and carving out a safe seat in Sandy Point, St Kitts.[12] The addition of a new seat in the Grenadines for the 1989 Vincentian election resulted in an additional safe seat for the governing NDP. In other cases individual candidates appear to have been targeted by boundary changes that had no effect on parity. In Antigua successive changes in 1980 and 1984 whittled away a stronghold that had been held by one-time premier, George Walter, and later contested by his wife. In Dominica Rosie Douglas saw his constituency altered to the extent that he was defeated in 1990. Gerrymandered boundaries can tip the balance in close elections in these small polities where one or two seats may spell the difference in a close contest.

DETERMINING WINNERS

The results of some recent elections have raised again the question of the appropriateness of the first-past-the-post or 'plurality' system of determining winners and the compositions of parliaments. The severely skewed nature of parliamentary representation in a number of outcomes causes understandable alarm when large numbers of voters are not represented by anything close to their weight in the electorate. In one case, Grenada in 1999, voters for minority party candidates are not represented at all. A contrasting situation has appeared in two cases where governments have been elected by a minority popular vote. Both of these kinds of results are illustrated in Tables 3A and 3B.

**Table 3A: Selected Elections
Votes and Representation**

St Lucia, 1997					
Party	Candidates	Elected	%	Votes	%
SLP	17	16	94.1	44153	61.3
UWP	17	1	5.9	26325	36.6
Ind	7	0	0.0	1494	2.1

Grenada, 1999					
Party	Candidates	Elected	%	Votes	%
NNP	15	15	100.0	25850	62.2
NDC	12	0	0.0	10337	24.9
GULP/UL	9	0	0.0	4998	12.0
MBPM	7	0	0.0	252	0.6
GOD	3	0	0.0	69	0.2
Ind	2	0	0.0	42	0.1

Table 3B: Selected Elections
Votes and Representation

St Kitts-Nevis, 1993					
Party	Candidates	Elected	%	Votes	%
LP	8	4	36.4	8405	43.8
PAM	8	4	36.4	6449	33.6
UPP	6	0	0.0	605	3.2
CCM	3	2	18.4	2100	10.9
NRP	3	1	9.1	1641	8.5

St Kitts-Nevis, 1995					
Party	Candidates	Elected	%	Votes	%
LP	8	7	63.6	10722	49.6
PAM	8	1	9.1	7530	34.8
UPP		0	0.0	71	0.3
CCM	3	2	18.2	1777	8.2
NRP	3	1	9.1	1521	7.0

St Vincent and the Grenadines, 1998					
Party	Candidates	Elected	%	Votes	%
ULP	15	7	46.7	28052	54.6
NDP	15	8	53.3	23258	45.3
PWP	1	0	0.0	45	0.1

Table 3A, showing the representation resulting from the 1997 St Lucian and 1999 Grenadian elections, illustrates the point made above with reference to disproportionate representation. In the St Lucian case the UWP lost control of the government but their supporters, representing more than one-third of the votes cast had but a single parliamentarian in the House of Assembly. The outcome in Grenada was even more skewed. Opposition parties that collectively polled more than one-third of the votes were left with no elected representation.

The converse situation is illustrated in Table 3B. In St Vincent in 1998, ULP candidates were given a substantial majority of the popular vote, but in losing some close contests, failed to win a majority of the seats in the House.

The situation was perhaps exacerbated by the fact that they won over 60 per cent of the vote in St Vincent. The St Kitts-Nevis results for 1993 and 1995 perhaps best illustrate this problem for small Caribbean states. In 1993 the LP carried St Kitts by a substantial plurality over their rivals, PAM. In Nevis CCM won a majority of the vote and two of the three seats. However, because the LP won only four of the eight Kittitian seats, splitting them with PAM, and because the CCM had made it a part of their platform that they would not enter into a coalition with any Kittitian-based party, the government was formed by the existing PAM/NRP coalition, a minority arrangement that eventually failed. The outcome, where majority parties in both islands of the Federation found themselves outside the Government suggests some serious flaws in the system.

The subsequent election only further illustrates the point. In 1995 LP candidates won seven of the eight Kittitian seats and formed the Government. PAM, with more than one-third of the vote and by far the second highest vote total, did not even have enough parliamentary representation to form the Opposition. The dramatic swing in the representation of the parties far overshadowed the rather modest swing in voter support. The volatility in the fortunes of parties in the cases illustrated above, in part produced by the system of representation, raises some serious questions as its utility.

Table 4: Legislature Sizes and 'Cube Rule' Sizes

	Legislature Size	
	Actual Size	**Cube Rule Size**
Antigua and Barbuda (1989)	17	33
Dominica (2000)	21	39
Grenada (1999)	15	42
St Kitts-Nevis (1993)	11	31
St Lucia (1997)	17	48
St Vincent and the Grenadines (1998)	15	42

Another methodological approach addresses particularly the problems associated with extremely disproportionate representation, especially when successive elections result in very large swings in representation. This examines the appropriate size of parliaments. It would seem to be commonsensical that if the number of representatives and thus, constituencies, increases that possibilities for the outcomes noted in Tables 3A and 3B would be mitigated.

The operationalisation of this observation into a formula for determining appropriate size of parliaments derives from the 'cube law', a predictor of parliamentary outcomes. The derivation of the cube law applied to parliamentary size yields for Eastern Caribbean states significantly enhanced legislatures (Table 4). Moreover, with electorates that have grown appreciably in the past two decades, application of the rule suggests that legislatures would have had to grow in some proportion to the expanded electors' lists – as much as seven additional seats in the case of St Lucia between 1979 and 1997.

SUMMARY

In summarising and concluding this discussion let us examine the problems of democracy in the Eastern Caribbean employing a hierarchical argument. That is, we move from a premise where the possibilities for meaningful democratic participation are most remote to one where they are seriously compromised, and finally to one where we admit possibilities for enhanced participation and representation.

According to the first scenario there is no possibility for democratic participation in this class-dominated, extraverted political and economic climate. Such a premise follows from the characterisation of Caribbean societies as impotent victims of global forces that have their representation in the local context. This argument suggests that in a world where 80 per cent of the population is superfluous, condemned to perpetual marginality, most of the citizenry of the islands are included in this category, and that the island societies, themselves, are beyond a redemption of their own making. This is a characterisation that denies to Caribbean states any agency in controlling their destinies, either individually or collectively. It is a vision of a future that may be realised, if only because it would seem to fulfil a present trajectory. It is also a crushingly pessimistic view.

A second scenario would begin with the premise that Caribbean states have it within their power to affect their destinies, but that they have yet to develop the political culture necessary to exercise this responsibility. This is a view that comes close to the pessimism expressed in the vignettes that commenced this paper. The prevalence of what has been termed the tyranny of the majority – expressed as 'the ayes have it' – continues to deny participation to sizeable minorities in every island. Once the issue of governance has been decided, an election ceases to be of any consequence, even when the outcome is decidedly mixed. In such a political climate a one-vote majority in parliament is as good as a complete rout. The views of the minority cannot be countenanced. We have seen over the decades how this leads to a hardening of positions, to a disregard and disrespect for opponents, a situation characterised by the late Michael Manley as political 'tribalism'.[13] Again, should such a state of political culture prevail we understand that it cannot be changed simply by incremental electoral reform. Possibly the latter changes may influence such cultural change, but we must realise that this culture is informed by and sustained by some of the conditions alluded to in the discussion of the first scenario.

As to the third scenario, despite the possible validity of some aspects of the first two, we can still posit that some mechanisms work better than others – expanded parliaments, experiments with modifications toward proportional representation, attempts at some kind of constituent representation/voice. What is patent is that these are changes that are within the power of governments and legislatures to effect. They are structural changes that are unaffected by outside forces and they do not depend on some kind of nebulous behaviour modification on the part of politicians.

To take each of the three innovations mentioned above, let us look at possibilities and previous attempts. Each of the island states under consideration has expanded its elected legislature since 1960, some twice. These have taken no consistent form and it is not evident that the numbers determined are any more than arbitrary. In a couple of cases the expansion has resulted in boundary definitions that were clearly designed to benefit the governing party. At the same time legislators have rewarded themselves with escalating salaries and perks such that a significant expansion of any parliament – as, in keeping with a cube-root rule – would likely be opposed as a financial burden. Nonetheless, the possibilities of mitigating frequently disproportionate representations suggest that consideration be given to these changes.

Proportional representation has been long discussed but, aside from its cynically self-serving institution by the Peoples National Congress in Guyana, it has never been seriously pursued. Ironically, the recurrent criticism of the governmental system as a colonial implant often includes discussion of the problems of a first-past-the-post electoral mechanism. Despite the apparent validity of the critique and a rather general acceptance of the flaws of the present system, the introduction of some form of proportional representation remains a chimera for the politicians.

Finally, some kind of constituent representation also receives occasional lip service. The Senates of many islands are theoretically to embody such representation but, as they exist at the will of the government, their representative function is ephemeral. The Senator who is appointed as a government party representative cannot act independently of this affiliation. A Constituent Assembly structure was one of the early proposals of the New Jewel Movement in Grenada before the revolution in 1979, but following their ascendance, rigid central control was instituted. In like measure, occasional proposals for 'governments of national unity' always come from parties in opposition who, when achieving power, conveniently forget about such innovations.

The latter two approaches, if implemented in some form, would presumably result in what has been termed 'consensus democracy'. The case for such an alteration in Caribbean political structure and practise is persuasively made in Lijphart's article. As he notes, '(T)he proponents of plurality (first-past-the-post) make their case on a variety of grounds except that plurality is the more democratic method; they usually concede that proportionality is, at least in principle, more democratic'.[14]

To conclude this discussion I suggest that the politics of majoritarian tyranny are outmoded and dysfunctional, that creative approaches to representation and governance need to be pursued, and that in a world increasingly dominated by hegemonies having little regard for ministate considerations, Caribbean peoples and their political representatives had best adopt much more of a 'lifeboat ethic' in the way they conduct their political lives. Perhaps the recurrent discussion and planning that have gone into schemes for political integration have precluded serious consideration of some of these alternatives. But the integration attempts have either foundered or have benefited the few, and perhaps time is growing short and solutions diminishing for these societies.

Endnotes

1. The context of this debate is dealt with in Douglas Midgett, 'Distorted Development: The Resuscitation of the Antiguan Sugar Industry', *Studies in Comparative International Development* 19(2):33-58 (1984).
2. This discussion is prefigured in an article by Arend Lijphart a decade ago. See 'Size, Pluralism, and the Westminster Model of Democracy: Implications for the Eastern Caribbean," in Jorge Heine, *A Revolution Aborted: The Lessons of Grenada* (Pittsburgh: University of Pittsburgh Press, 1990). I disagree with one feature of Lijphart's article – the characterisation of Eastern Caribbean states as 'plural or deeply divided societies' (p. 321). Deeply divided they frequently appear to be, but this is not because of fundamental social and cultural pluralism in Furnivall's sense. The divisions reflect class conflict, and, important for this discussion, political party struggles that have emerged in the past half-century. Michael Manley saw these in light of the influence of a pervasive and lengthy colonial experience (see Richard S. Hillman, 'Interviewing Jamaica's Political Leaders',

Caribbean Review 8(3):28-31, 53-55 [1979]). In the Eastern Caribbean there is nothing like the communal segmentation represented in party affiliation found in Trinidad and Tobago or Guyana.

3. See two volumes, similarly titled: Carlene J. Edie, ed., *Democracy in the Caribbean: Myths and Realities* (Westport, CT: Praeger, 1994); and Jorge I. Dominguez, Robert A. Pastor, and R. Delisle Worrell, eds., *Democracy in the Caribbean: Political, Economic, and Social Perspectives* (Baltimore: Johns Hopkins University Press, 1993). Also of note are Donald Peters, *The Democratic System in the Eastern Caribbean* (Westport, CT: Greenwood Press, 1992), and Lijphart, 'The Westminster Model'.

4. Percy Hintzen, 'Democracy and Middle-Class Domination in the Anglophone Caribbean', in C.J. Edie, ed., *Democracy in the Caribbean*, p. 13.

5. 'Democracy and Middle-Class', p. 21.

6. Ibid.

7. Selwyn Ryan, 'Problems and Prospects for the Survival of Liberal Democracy in the Anglophone Caribbean', in C.J. Edie, ed., *Democracy in the Caribbean*, pp. 236-41.

8. See Evelyne Huber, 'The Future of Democracy in the Caribbean,' in J.I. Dominguez, et al., eds., *Democracy in the Caribbean*, pp.74-95. See also, Paget Henry, *Peripheral Capitalism and Underdevelopment in Antigua* (New Brunswick, NJ: Transaction Books, 1985).

9. Lijphart, 'The Westminster Model'.

10. For a more detailed examination of the history of party politics in these islands see Patrick Emmanuel, 'Parties and Electoral Competition in the Anglophone Caribbean, 1944-1991: Challenges to Democratic Theory', in C.J. Edie, ed., *Democracy in the Caribbean*, pp. 251-26.

11. The coefficient of variability is a measure of the standard deviation relative to the mean in each case, a statistic that allows us comparability across islands and from one election to the next.

12. Douglas Midgett, 'St Kitts-Nevis', in Jack W. Hopkins, ed., *Latin America and Caribbean Contemporary Record*, Vol. III (New York: Holmes and Meier, 1985). pp. 868-74; and 'An Analysis of the 1984 General Elections in St Kitts-Nevis', *Bulletin of Eastern Caribbean Affairs* 10(6):18-28 (1985).

13. Hillman, 'Jamaica's Leaders', p. 54.

14. Lijphart, 'The Westminster Model', p. 338. A recent contribution to this discussion suggests that a 'high consensus' approach was implemented in St Kitts-Nevis after 1980 (see Clifford E. Griffin, 'The Opposition and Policy Making in the Caribbean: The Emergence of High Consensus Politics

in St Kitts and Nevis', *Journal of Commonwealth and Comparative Politics* 32:230-43 [1994]). This argument distorts the reality of that case in which the apparent 'consensualism' resulted from a political convenience that allowed the formation of a PAM/NRP coalition government in order to wrest power from the Labour Party. Subsequent events have illustrated the cynicism underlying that arrangement.

Bibliography

Dominguez, Jorge I., Robert A. Pastor, and R. Delisle Worrell, eds., *Democracy in the Caribbean: Political, Economic, and Social Perspectives* (Baltimore: Johns Hopkins University Press, 1993).

Edie, Carlene J., ed., *Democracy in the Caribbean: Myths and Realities* (Westport, CT: Praeger, 1994).

Emmanuel, Patrick, 'Parties and Electoral Competition in the Anglophone Caribbean, 1944-1991: Challenges to Democratic Theory', in C.J. Edie, ed., *Democracy in the Caribbean*, pp. 251-26.

Griffin, Clifford E., 'The Opposition and Policy Making in the Caribbean: The Emergence of High Consensus Politics in St. Kitts and Nevis', *Journal of Commonwealth and Comparative Politics* 32:230-43 (1994).

Henry, Paget, *Peripheral Capitalism and Underdevelopment in Antigua* (New Brunswick, NJ: Transaction Books, 1985).

Hillman, Richard S., 'Interviewing Jamaica's Political Leaders', *Caribbean Review* 8(3):28-31, 53-55 (1979).

Hintzen, Percy C., 'Democracy and Middle-Class Domination in the Anglophone Caribbean', in C.J. Edie, ed., *Democracy in the Caribbean*, pp. 9-23.

Huber, Evelyne, 'The Future of Democracy in the Caribbean', in J.I. Dominguez, et al., eds., *Democracy in the Caribbean*, pp. 74-95.

Lijphart, Arend, 'Size, Pluralism, and the Westminster Model of Democracy: Implications for the Eastern Caribbean', in Jorge Heine, ed., *A Revolution Aborted: The Lessons of Grenada* (Pittsburgh: University of Pittsburgh Press, 1990), pp. 319-340.

Midgett, Douglas, 'St. Kitts-Nevis', in Jack W. Hopkins, ed., *Latin America and Caribbean Contemporary Record, Vol. III* (New York: Holmes and Meier, 1985). pp. 868-74.

Midgett, Douglas, 'Distorted Development: The Resuscitation of the Antiguan Sugar Industry', *Studies in Comparative International Development* 19(2):33-58 (1984).

Midgett, Douglas, 'An Analysis of the 1984 General Elections in St Kitts-Nevis', *Bulletin of Eastern Caribbean Affairs* 10(6):18-28 (1985).

Peters, Donald, *The Democratic System in the Eastern Caribbean* (Westport, CT: Greenwood Press, 1992).

Ryan, Selwyn, 'Problems and Prospects for the Survival of Liberal Democracy in the Anglophone Caribbean', in C.J. Edie, ed., *Democracy in the Caribbean*, pp. 233-250.

Party Acronyms

Antigua and Barbuda
ALP   Antigua Labour Party
Grenada
GULP/UL   Grenada United Labour Party
MBPM   Maurice Bishop Patriotic Movement
NDC   National Democratic Congress
NNP   New National Party
St Kitts-Nevis
CCM   Concerned Citizens' Movement
LP   (St Kitts-Nevis) Labour Party
NRP   Nevis Reformation Party
PAM   People's Action Movement
UPP   United People's Party
St Lucia
SLP   St Lucia Labour Party
UWP   United Workers Party
St Vincent and the Grenadines
NDP   New Democratic Party
ULP   Unity Labour Party

18

Race, Ideology, and International Relations: Sovereignty and the Disciplining of Guyana's Working Class

Percy C. Hintzen

NATIONALISM AND NEO-COLONIAL ACCOMMODATION

As an ideology, nationalism has proven to be quite amenable to the interests of global capital. As a construct, it easily accommodates the changing technical and social conditions of economic capital without losing its power as a symbol of national sovereignty and self-determination. In the post-war era, new forms of capitalist organisation began to emerge, creating conditions for the demise of colonialism and the emergence of new neo-colonialism forms of dependency. Colonialism was rapidly becoming an impediment to the development of more intensive forms of exploitation in the peripheral economies. By challenging colonial domination, nationalism began to lay the groundwork for the accommodation of these new forms of neo-colonial exploitation in the political economies of the European colonies. As colonialism was giving way to the new nationalist movements these new forms of economic organisation began laying the groundwork for post-colonial formation.

Embedded in notions of nationalist self-determination were the ideas of sovereignty and the autonomy of the state.[1] These have acted to hide a reality of the post-colonial condition where global capital has maintained and intensified its active presence. Either this, or its agents have increased their capacities for retaliation against those who choose to resist. The ex-colonies of Britain in the West Indies provide typical examples of these new forms of interventionism that hide behind nationalist ideologies of self-determination and sovereignty. These ideologies, rather than presaging a break with colonial patterns of dependency, effected a transfer of their positions of economic, political, and social subordination from Britain to the United States. The anti-colonial agenda of the West Indian nationalists fit well with decisions to establish closer relations with the United States. There was an inherent contradiction between the quest for sovereignty and continuation of the exclusive pattern of economic relations with Britain. Absolute dependence upon the former colonial power was inconsistent with ideas of national self-determination as a critical component of sovereignty. West Indian nationalist leaders had to seek alternatives to economic relationships with the British colonial metropole. But given the absolute dependence of their economies on commodity exports, they were trapped in conditions of economic dependence on the industrialised North. The emergence of the United States as the dominant global economic power led the way out of this dilemma. A shift in the focus of economic and political relations away from Britain and to the United States had both symbolic and practical value. It was consistent with nationalist assertions of sovereignty while allowing the newly independent countries to retain relations of economic dependency in the global capitalist economy. These new relations did not come with the taint of colonial domination. The establishment and intensification of economic and political ties with North America were justified, also, by the quest for developmental transformation, another of the pillars of nationalism. As the dominant, richest, and most technologically advanced economic power, the United States became the ideal partner in such a quest.

Thus, anti-colonialism in the West Indies became rapidly transformed into an instrumentality for the penetration of neocolonial forms of global capital in the region. The latter came with the need for significant changes in the political economies of the former colonies. The emergence of the United States as the financial and technological superpower of the industrialised capitalist world and as the world's major market was the force driving these transformations. Anti-colonialism, by attacking relations of empire between the European colonial powers and their non-European colonies, acted to accommodate new patterns of international relations centered upon the United States. The discourse of sovereignty freed the new postcolonial leadership from obligations imposed and maintained by colonial power. It facilitated the reorientation of economic relations toward the United States. This came with the tremendous benefits derived from closer relations with the world's newly dominant economic, financial, and military power.

The reorientation began during the fifties, even before independence was granted. West Indian nationalist leaders began to employ their increasing autonomy, derived from reform of colonial political organisation, to effect a gradual shift in their economic and political relations toward the United States. A potent signal of the shift was the development of plans to introduce a 'Puerto Rican' type economic model into the region. This was patterned after forms of 'industrialization by invitation' through which the bootstrap policies of the United States were being implemented in Puerto.[2] This predictable outcome of the deepening of ties of dependence with the United States was intensified even further by a developing tourist industry based on North American visitors that was becoming indispensable to the economic well being of islands such as Barbados and Jamaica. Additionally, the United States was beginning to absorb a growing number of West Indian immigrants under conditions of escalating unemployment and underemployment in the region. North American migration was becoming critical to the region's efforts at poverty alleviation. Remittances from these migrants were proving important as additional sources of income, revenue, and economic support.[3]

Nationalism and the Cold War Agenda[4]

The United States began to provide significant support to West Indian nationalist political leaders sympathetic to its economic, political, and strategic interests. This shored up its anti-colonial image and convinced many of the region's radicals to shift their ideological position. At the same time, there was a high price to be paid for challenging US hegemony in the region. Soon after the end of World War II, the United States became consumed by a virulent anti-communism, fed by the dogma of McCarthyism sweeping the country. Combating domestic and international communism became the primary concern in its corridors of power. This produced an absolute intolerance for nationalist movements overseas even mildly critical of the West.

The nationalist movement in British Guiana was formalised in the crucible of the two imperatives of economic dependency upon the United States and commitment to its ideology. Unlike the rest of the region, the class dynamics of the country were dictating an alternative path that challenged the tenets not only of colonialism but also of neo-colonial dependence upon the United States. By 1950, the colony's anti-colonial movement had formalised itself into a radical class-based nationalist party called the People's Progressive Party (PPP). It was organised and led by a group of anti-capitalist radicals who were strongly supported by the colony's black and Asian Indian working class, the two ethno-racial groups that together comprised over 90 per cent of the country's population. From the very beginning, the stated goal of the party, contained in its manifesto, was the establishment of an independent socialist state:

> Recognising that the final abolition of exploitation and oppression, of economic crises and unemployment and war will be achieved only by the socialist reorganisation of society, (the party) pledges itself to the task of winning a free and independent Guiana, of building a just socialist society,

in which the industries of the country shall be socially and democratically owned and managed for the common good, a society in which security, plenty, peace and freedom shall be the heritage of all.[5]

While the socialist populism of the party generated tremendous support among the colony's working classes, it placed its leadership on an inevitable collision course with Britain. The party was formed at a time when arch conservative Winston Churchill, as prime minister, was reviving Britain's colonial appetite. His Conservative Party was using executive authority to wage a campaign against the thrust toward decolonisation of its progressive Labour Party predecessor. The interests of British capital rested as much in the preservation and prolonging of colonial dominion as in the containment of communism. And Britain's political leadership viewed the PPP's strident advocacy of self-government and socialism as a considerable and direct threat to its political, economic, and strategic interests.

A PPP victory in 1953 in the first national election to be held under universal suffrage was interpreted as a threat to Britain's colonial interests. The British Colonial Office wasted little time before embarking on efforts to secure the PPP's ouster. Cold war definitions became superimposed upon nationalist politics and inserted into popular interpretations of political and labour organisation. Even before the elections, cold war slogans and images were deployed in a vicious assault against the People's Progressive Party. This shift to cold war terminology was important because it brought the United States into the picture. Concerns were raised that events in British Guiana foretold the direction of the emerging nationalist anti-colonial movements in the region.[6]

Britain managed to use the PPP's election to office to convince the United States of the need for collaboration in shaping the conditions and terms of West Indian nationalism. Its entreaties fell on fertile ground. It provoked considerable alarm as a harbinger of the future of Britain's other West Indian colonies. The Eisenhower administration was more than willing to be convinced of the danger to American interests posed by British Guiana's nationalist movement. In October 1953, the American Consul General cabled the Department of State over concerns about the consolidation of a 'communist bridgehead in the area'. He advocated that this 'menace' be 'firmly met'.[7] With the groundwork laid and with the approval if not active support of the United States, Britain intervened militarily on October 9, 1953, suspended the colony's constitution, and ousted the PPP from office. The party had lasted only 133 days in office. With the PPP's ouster, British Guiana took its place with Iran and Guatemala as the first of the political economies of the global south to have cold war categories imposed upon their domestic politics. In all three instances, the indictment of communism was used against a legitimate elected government to justify direct foreign intervention. In the wake of the suspension of the new constitution, the United States increased its involvement in the region significantly. This presaged a new globalisation that compromised significantly any possibility for the exercise of sovereignty and self-determination in the region.[8]

With colonialism under attack, Britain sought to justify its intervention by claiming to act on behalf of domestic representatives of the population to forestall a 'communist takeover'. This claim of intervention in response to domestic appeals is consistent with discourses of sovereignty. Intervention serves to protect the domestic political economy from 'subversive' 'foreign' ideologies. The pragmatics of a nationalist discourse that accommodated a new dependency upon the United States functioned to normalise this form of intervention in the region. The result was a pro-capitalist agenda that placed severe limits and imposed strict conditionalities upon domestic and international policy. West Indian nationalist leaders began to line up behind the United States across the Cold War divide. Once their countries became inserted into the arena of cold war contestations, they were quick to impose the litmus test of anti-communism as a legitimising principle of political participation at any level. In the process, the neo-colonial forms of global capitalism came to be cast as the national will. And nationalist leaders became its active agents.

Without exception, anti-Communist leaders led the governments of the region to independence during the sixties and seventies. They were able to count on covert, and sometimes overt, support by the United States in their quest for power. Supported by persistent and pervasive efforts of destabilisation directed at radical movements, these leaders acted to keep the region free from radical expression. The radical nationalist leadership found itself isolated and abandoned as the new anti-Communist agenda began to unfold. Those who attempted to break out of the ambit of the regional superpower and of the strictures of anti-communism found themselves under attack.[9]

Creole Nationalism and Regional Interventionism

The PPP's ouster ushered in an era where interventionism was deployed to discipline and punish nationalist aspirations for sovereignty and self-determination. The party came to be perceived not merely as anti-capitalist, but anti nationalist. To be West Indian is to occupy the hierarchical, hybridised 'Creole' space between two racial poles. These serve as markers for civilisation and savagery. It is to be constituted of various degrees of cultural and racial mixing. At the apex is the white Creole as the historical product of cultural hybridisation. The Afro-Creole is located at the other end of the Creole continuum. The 'creolisation' of the latter derives from the contingencies of separation from Africa and the civilising influences of transformative contact with Europeans. Creoleness is central to the social construction of nationalist belonging and 'peoplehood' in the West Indies. It does not accommodate the indigenous groups of the region and the diasporic communities with cultural and racial origins outside of Africa and Europe. In representation and practice, they remain marginal to Creole reality unless amalgamated through individual practices of cultural and sexual immersion. As such, these groups were excluded from the new imageries of nationalist belonging.[10] Soon, these Creole definitions of national belonging began to dictate the terms of alliance between political leaders in British Guiana and the West Indian nationalists.

Unlike the rest of the English-speaking Caribbean, valorised Creole cultural forms were less important than institutional solidarity in representations of national belonging in British Guiana. The historical absence of white Creoles in the colour class order of Guyanese social construction lessened significantly the need for idioms of belonging that bridged the divide between white coloniser and colonised. Thus, class solidarity became much more potent a force in the organisation of the nationalist movement. While no racial grouping in Guyana enjoyed a numerical majority, Asian Indians, by virtue of their numbers, comprised the largest of the ethno-racial groupings. Africans, mixed Creoles and considerably smaller groupings of Amerindians (indigenous native groups), Portuguese, and Chinese followed them.

SOVEREIGNTY, INTERVENTIONISM AND RACIALISED POLITICS

Ideological fissures within the PPP after its ouster from power, instigated by Britain with the promise of support to the more moderate leaders, produced competing claims to the party's leadership. Unable to resolve these claims, the nationalist movement split into two factions, one led by the more radical and the other by the more moderate of its co-leaders. The former, an Asian Indian dentist, Cheddi Jagan, had a support base in the rural predominantly Asian Indian plantation proletariat and peasantry. The support base of the latter, an Afro-Guyanese Attorney named Forbes Burnham, rested in the black urban proletariat. The radical faction of the PPP headed by Cheddi Jagan was elected to power in 1957. Britain agreed to the new elections with the hope of a victory by the moderates. Taking no chances, however, it restricted even further the exercise of executive authority enjoyed by the elected executive in 1953. While the working class continued to provide its overwhelming support to the nationalist leaders, such support began to rupture along racial lines.

With the victory of the radical faction of the nationalist movement, racial political alliances began forming across ideological and class lines, rendering invisible the hand of North Atlantic international capital. In 1959, Burnham's more moderate faction joined with a vehemently anti-Communist party representing the petite bourgeois Afro-Creole to form the Peoples National Congress (PNC). Around the same time, the United Force (UF) was founded as a right wing minority party. It received the bulk of its support from the country's Portuguese, Chinese, and lighter-skinned coloured population. The party relied for its survival upon the active backing of the country's business elite, international investors, and western governments. Finding themselves on the other side of the racial divide, most of the East Indian middle strata, including its business, professional and educated elite, threw their support behind Jagan's PPP, irrespective of the party's communist label.

By 1960, the country was politically divided into highly racialised camps. This was notwithstanding efforts by the United Force to present itself as a multi-racial flag bearer of anti-communism. But ideology took a back seat to the issue of race. Burnham's PNC began feeding the fires of anti-Indianism by exploiting the fears harboured by the predominantly black and coloured urban middle and working classes of an East Indian take-over of the urban sector. Racial politics assumed a new urgency as the PPP won elections held in 1960 and went on to lead a government under a new constitution of expanded self-government. The PPP won its victory on the strength of its almost exclusively Asian Indian support base.

By providing the mass base of support for the competing racialised parties, the working classes and peasantry became deployed against themselves in support of a system of global capital that dictated their continuing exploitation. Britain's explicit promise, made before the elections, that the country would be granted independence, intensified the racial struggle. Caribbean nationalist leaders began to impose their own understanding of nationalist belonging on the terms for the country's independence. From the inception, West Indian nationalist discourse acted to legitimise a pattern of regional interventionism in the country in the interest of Western capital. In pursuit of their ideological and Creole nationalist agendas, the leaders of the West Indies were prepared to violate the very principles of sovereignty and self-determination for which they had fought in their anti-colonial campaign. With the split in the nationalist movement, notions of West Indian belonging predisposed this political leadership to support the moderate faction of the Guyanese nationalist movement. Initially, their support seemed to be provided on ideological grounds as they rejected the

PPP's radical challenge to global capital. So, in the early sixties, they rallied around an anti-Communist coalition of the Peoples' National Congress (PNC) and the United Force (UF) notwithstanding the fair and free elections that brought the PPP to power and the campaign of violence unleashed by these two opposition parties to secure the PPP's ouster. In the process, they provided legitimacy to the campaign of intervention conducted and orchestrated by the United States and Great Britain against the party. This contributed significantly to the success of the campaign. Both governments justified their intervention by charges of communism. Reeling from a combination of covert activity, constitutional fiat and violent confrontation, Cheddi Jagan, the colony's premier, was forced to yield to demands for an imposed constitutional settlement that guaranteed electoral defeat. Under the terms of the settlement authored by Britain's colonial office, the Westminster-style constituency system for allocating seats in the colony's Legislative Assembly was to be replaced by an electoral system of proportional representation. This was guaranteed to give the combined opposition, supported by all of the racialised voting blocs except the Asian Indians, a legislative majority and the right to form the government. Elections were held in 1964 and a coalition government of the PNC and the UF was elected to executive office. [11]

The support base of the PNC rested firmly in the country's black and mixed proletarian working class and in the black and mixed salaried and professional middle classes whose members dominated the state sector, worked as functionaries in the private sector, or provided their professional services to both. The ideology of the former had been fashioned out of the radical nationalism of the fifties. This was reflected in the Fabianism of the party-leader, Forbes Burnham. The party's middle class support was much more conservative and apprehensive. Its commitment to nationalism stemmed from the clear expectation of power, authority, status and socioeconomic position to be inherited from the white coloniser. The interest of the United Force rested squarely in the continuation of relations of dependency with the global North, a policy highly favoured by its supporters in the commercial and productive sectors whose interests were inextricably linked to international capital. It used its strategic position in the coalition to impose its conservative pro-Western ideological agenda upon the government. Between 1964 and 1968, state policy explicitly favoured the domestic and international private sector. This demonstrated the considerable influence of the United Force in the coalition. Its leader, a businessman named Peter D'Aguiar, assumed the powerful portfolio of minister of finance. This gave him control over the state budget and the sole authority for authorship of fiscal policy. Commerce, industry, and the private professions became the primary beneficiaries of this policy. In 1966, with the coalition in power, Britain agreed to grant the colony its independence.

With the change of government, popular interests took a back seat to those of international capital. During its term of office, the PPP implemented policies that, even though far from socialist, were directed at ameliorating the conditions of the country's lower strata. Operating under the considerable political restrictions of colonialism between 1957-64, the party nonetheless managed an impressive array of domestic accomplishments. Its policies were focused on agriculture, health delivery, education, and social welfare. Development planning was introduced. Extensive and comprehensive surveys of the country's resources were made for the first time in its history. The country's electricity generating capacity was upgraded and expanded with state takeover of the Canadian-owned electric company. Agricultural production, particularly rice and vegetables, was expanded considerably. Malaria was eradicated and successful campaigns were introduced to control polio, typhoid and other forms of diseases. Numerous health centres, cottage hospitals, and maternity and child welfare clinics were built, particularly in the rural areas. Free medical care was also introduced. There was considerable expansion and upgrading of housing throughout the country and rent control ordinances were enacted to protect the rights of tenants. There was also considerable expansion of primary and secondary education with the state assuming full control and management of all primary schools in the colony. Technical education and teacher training were expanded and a University of Guyana was established.[12]

In the intensely political climate of the sixties, the opposition labelled these policies as racially biased. The party's effort at rural development was represented as favouring its rural Asian Indian supporters concentrated in the agricultural sector. As a result the middle and working-class supporters of the opposition opposed them. The prism of race through which everything was interpreted rendered irrelevant the considerable improvements that these policies brought to the life conditions of the working and middle classes. By 1967 when the PNC managed to gain full control of the government after enticing elected Members of Parliament from the United Force to 'cross the floor', it's policies were firmly locked into a racial agenda. This imposed upon the party an almost exclusive focus on the overwhelmingly black urban sector and foreclosed a rural agricultural emphasis that offered the best prospects for the country's development.[13] The politics of race imposed conditions upon the PNC that vitiated the democratic terms of legitimate governance. Without the support of the United Force, the PNC could not hope to win a national election. And by 1968 it had become increasingly the case that the PPP's support base was large enough to guarantee the party a majority even under the existing terms of proportional representation. In 1970 the black and mixed groups comprised 42 per cent of the country's population. With the exception of 'near whites', the mixed population comprising mostly descendents of black-white (coloured) and black-East Indian unions identified politically, socially, and culturally with the blacks. East Indians comprised slightly over 51 per cent of the population. Whites (including Portuguese) and Chinese comprised less than 2 per cent of the population respectively. And Amerindians comprised around 4 per cent of the population.[14]

To maintain its hold on power the PNC was forced rig the elections. Fraudulent electoral victories were secured in 1968, 1973, 1980 and 1985. A fraudulent referendum in 1978 paved the way for the establishment of an executive presidency in 1980. Beginning in the late seventies, coercive violence was deployed against the regime's opponents.[15] The PNC employed this combination of violence and electoral fraud to remain in power until 1992.[16]

Sovereignty, Democracy, and Interventionism

The issue of sovereignty cannot be divorced from terms of legitimacy. Nationalist discourse in the region was rooted in the idea of the free exercise of the will of the people. This was the very essence of the demand for self-determination by the anti-colonial movement. It was to be guaranteed through the practice of formalised democracy. When external political actors intervene to thwart democratic practice, then sovereignty became compromised.

Nationalist constructs of belonging in the rest of the English Speaking West Indies imposed particularly definitions of legitimacy upon the institutions of governance in post colonial British Guiana (now called Guyana). They supported forms of regional interventionism that undermined democratic practice. West Indian nationalism could not accommodate any claims to national belonging made by Asian Indians. In Guyana, however, the party supported by the latter was guaranteed to win any election that was freely and fairly conducted. The contradiction was resolved by replacing the requirements of majoritarian democracy with legitimacy constructs of belonging cast in racial terms of inclusion and exclusion.[17] Under these terms, regional governments refused to acknowledge the right of the PPP to rule, despite its majority support. The PNC, by virtue of its claim to represent the Creole population of Guyana, had, in the worldview of West Indian leaders, sole and legitimate rights to governance. They continued to recognise the party despite its resort to undemocratic practice and its deployment of coercion to stay in power. This bolstered efforts by Western governments in support of global capital, to keep the PPP out of power because of its left wing radicalism. The resolve to do so intensified considerably after party leaders openly committed the PPP to the ideology of

Marxism\Leninism and developed formalised relations with the communist parties of the Soviet Union and Eastern Europe.[18]

Thus, by the end of the sixties, three types of external impositions were acting upon the country political economy to undermine its sovereignty. First was the conservative orthodox ideology of pro-western capitalism imposed by the industrialised North Atlantic. Second was nationalist ideology of Creole belonging imposed by West Indian national actors. And third was the radical Marxism-Leninism of pro-Soviet communism imposed by Eastern European political actors upon the party that enjoyed the support of the majority of the country's population. The first two of these impositions combined to keep the PPP out of power. The third became a condition of its continued viability as it turned to Eastern Europe, its allies and its international sympathisers for support.

Isolation and Punishment as Instrumentalities of Interventionism

Soon the class dictates of the PNC's support base forced a confrontation with foreign international capital. The interests of the party's black lower class and black and coloured middle-class supporters were incompatible with the terms of participation of international capital in the country's political economy. The party's racial legitimacy rested with policies that improved the life conditions of these supporters. And these groups were certainly not the beneficiaries of a continuation of the policies inherited from the period of the coalition. This became quite evident during the early seventies as segments of the black working class began to mobilise against the ruling party. The visible benefits of party policy for the East Indian, white, and near-white elite produced a cleavage among the party's racial supporters. It led to the forced departure of leading Black Nationalist, Eusi Kwayana, who enjoyed considerable support among the younger members of the black middle class and a significant segment of the black lower class. In leaving, Kwayana pulled his African Society for Cultural Relations with Independent Africa (ASCRIA) out of the PNC. He accused the party of being 'a unity of the black political leaders with the Portuguese and Indian exploiting classes'.[19] The loss was quite significant since ASCRIA was a major recruiting and organising arm of the PNC.[20] Many blacks, reflecting ASCRIA's position, were no longer prepared to accept as legitimate the claims of the PNC to be the party representing the black population.

The PNC leadership responded with a series of policy initiatives. First, it attempted to wean the country away from the need for foreign imports by embarking on a campaign of national economic self-sufficiency in a Feed,

Clothes, and House Ourselves programme (FCH).[21] The programme was an attempt to deploy domestic productive resources to meet domestic consumer needs. The second strategy rested with an attempt to harness the savings of the black population through cooperative organisation. A programme of cooperative development was initiated to catapult blacks into agriculture, fishing, and small and mid-scale industry. Most importantly, however, the ruling party began to undertake efforts, through equity participation in the foreign-owned sectors of the economy, to gain access to the economic surplus generated by these industries for domestic redistribution. This began with an effort to enter negotiations with a subsidiary of Alcan Aluminium of Canada for equity participation. Western capital was willing to brook no challenge to its right to untrammelled operation in the country. The negotiations precipitated a campaign of economic retaliation, organised by Western governments led by the United States, which became so extraordinarily punitive that it eventually destroyed the country's economic viability and produced a crisis of poverty and despoliation.

With economic retaliation against the regime mounting, a decision was made in 1973 to forge a protective alliance with the eastern bloc and with socialist countries internationally. The ruling party began making ideological declarations in support of Marxism/Leninism and began to identify with radical causes internationally. Burnham made the decision to cast his lot with the radical anti-capitalist regimes of the global south. By 1976, most of the major holdings of foreign capital were nationalised placing the state in control of over 80 per cent of the productive assets of the country. The radical turn led, naturally, to efforts at restoring cross-racial class alliances. In 1973, attempts were made by the ruling party to recruit East Indians into its ranks. Between 1975 and 1976 the PPP provided the ruling party with 'critical support' after the latter made an unambiguous commitment to socialism.[22]

The problem for the country was its profound economic dependency and its inextricable ties to western capital. This made its economy vulnerable to punitive retaliation. And these came with a vengeance in the form of economic destabilisation efforts that combined with spiralling oil prices and a recession following the 1973 Middle East war to wreak havoc on the Guyanese economy. By 1978 an escalating economic crisis began to force the regime to cutback drastically on its capital projects, to curtail state spending, to retrench state employees, and to reduce the importation of essential commodities. A second oil shock in 1979 and an international recession during the early eighties contributed further to the country's rapid downward economic spiral. During the entire period of the eighties Guyana's economy was in a persistent state of near total economic collapse. Much more strident interventionist policies by United States and Great Britain, in the wake of the election of Ronald Reagan and Margaret Thatcher, led to further deterioration in the relations between these two countries and the PNC government. Their campaign of retaliation intensified, deepening an already severe economic crisis. The unemployment rate skyrocketed to 30 per cent and the country began to experience a severe health crisis leading to dramatic increases in mortality rates particularly among children and pregnant women. Its foreign debt ballooned dramatically.[23]

The government dealt with the crisis in two ways. First, it intensified its relationship with the Soviet Union, Eastern Europe, Cuba, and China in efforts to develop alternative sources of economic support. This produced intensified retaliatory action by Western governments. In 1983, Burnham strongly condemned the United States administration for its invasion of Grenada. In 1985, the United States suspended all economic assistance programmes to the government, closed the office of its Agency for International Development in the capital city, and began actively to bloc economic assistance from multilateral donors to the country. Second, the regime resorted to coercive measures and constitutional fiat to maintain its control of the state. These were added to its arsenal of electoral fraud. As the crisis escalated, the regime's effort at cross-racial alliance collapsed, and its own racial support began to erode. In 1976 PPP withdrew its offer of critical support and, in 1977 it began a campaign of 'non-cooperation and civil resistance' accompanied by strikes and demonstrations.[24]

The anti-Western and anti-capitalist turn of the PNC regime exposed the racial agenda of the West Indian nationalist leaders in their relations with Guyana. They continued to reject claims by the PPP to governance while supporting the legitimacy of the PNC regime. This was notwithstanding the new policy of state socialism and the regime's international alliances with the Communist bloc. The recognition of the PNC's legitimacy by the West Indian leadership resolved a dilemma faced by Western governments. The alternative to the PNC was the even more radical PPP with considerably stronger ties to the USSR. The best strategy was therefore one of isolation rather than regime change. This freed the ruling party to make economic policy and to reorganise the political system without the impositions of foreign international actors. At the same time, Western governments actively intervened to ensure the destruction of the country's economy. From the perspective of Western capitalist actors, economic retaliation without the prospect of regime change was the ideal solution to the imbroglio of Guyana. Both of the major parties were declared Marxist-Leninist and supporters of the Soviet Union and its socialist allies internationally. The deployment of the economic instrumentalities of punishment demonstrated the consequences of challenges to the hegemony of western capital. As an economic basket case and a cauldron of political coercion, crisis, and conflict.

Guyana could serve as a lesson in the consequences of challenging western capitalism. The country became a symbol of socialist degradation in the region. The fact that it seemed to be left to its own devices was all the more telling. This rendered invisible the pervasive interventionism that drove the political and economic crises as its government appeared free to choose the direction of its policy.

Globalism and New Instrumentalities of Control

By the latter half of the eighties, the deepening economic crisis in Guyana began to dictate an imperative of massive external assistance. This was at a time when the Soviet-led Eastern bloc countries and their allies were less able and less willing to provide economic and political support to sympathetic regimes. The PNC found itself with little option but to seek economic assistance from the West. The terms of access to external financing, however, were becoming subjected, increasingly, to the dictates of international financial institutions under the control of powerful capitalist western governments, particularly the United States. Countries seeking external financing were being forced to transfer authority over national economic policy to these institutions on terms authored by their international Boards of Directors. These terms were implemented by economic technocrats. Ideology became of little consequence in policy formulation.[25] Progressive and radical leaders found themselves with little option but to accept the dictates of international public policy that was driven by a resurgent neoliberal orthodoxy. Robbed of their autonomy, these leaders posed little threat to capitalist interests. The need for surveillance and intervention against radical governments and movements in the global South diminished as regimes were forced to give up autonomy in their economic affairs in exchange for access to external funding. The image of democratic governance could be preserved under conditions where global capital under the protection of multilateral financial agencies, was increasing its penetration of their respective political economies.

In 1988, after two years of negotiations, the World Bank and the International Monetary Fund (IMF) approved a policy framework paper for economic stabilisation for Guyana. At the time, the country's foreign debt totalled US $1.9 billion, an extraordinarily high figure relative to the country's GDP. Payment arrears on this debt had ballooned to US $1.1 billion. The policy framework laid the foundation for access to external funding.[26] It set the groundwork for a three-year Enhanced Structural Adjustment facility programme that led, in 1990, to a Structural Adjustment Loan. The policy framework has become the basis for the formulation of economic policy ever since.[27] Any government coming to power in Guyana has been forced to abide by its terms. Continued access to external financing has become contingent upon full satisfaction of its conditionalities.

Guyana was typical of countries of the Global South overcome with heavy debt burdens. Without access to external financing, economic integrity and political stability would be seriously imperilled. Increasing dependence upon multilateral financial institutions provided the opportunity for imposing, controlling, and regulating public policy in these countries. Policy formulation became sharply constrained by the dictates of the International Monetary Fund, the World Bank and other bilateral and multilateral funding agencies. Under these conditions, the ideology of the ruling regime was rendered irrelevant.

As the relationship between ideology and policy began to erode internationally, Western governments found a new cause in the popular movements of protest that began sweeping Eastern Europe. These were mounted in the name of democratic governance and civil and political rights. Western governments used the claim of the moral right of any populace to mount challenges against undemocratic regimes to justify strong support for these movements. As a result, democratic rule and the practice of civil rights became the new litmus tests of Western support for a regime and new justifications for intervention.

The interest of global capital can be shrouded by practices of democratic governance. The latter can give the appearance of popular will at a time when international actors are dictating national policy. In this manner, a democratically elected or popular government can sell to its supporters the outcomes of international negotiations as being best for the country and for their interests. Under these conditions, popular support for a government reduces the possibility of domestic opposition.

DEMOCRACY AND CIVIL RIGHTS: NEW INSTRUMENTS OF INTERVENTION

The collapse of Euro-communism at the end of the 1980s reduced considerably the anxieties, stemming from geo-strategic concerns. These centered on the threat posed to the West by ideological alliances between Eastern Europe and the Global South. The changing international climate in favour of civil and political rights in the Global South fostered by the United States and its Western allies in the wake of popular movements in Eastern Europe enhanced considerably the moral and ethical claim of the PPP to power. It combined with the new instrumentalities of economic control located in multilateral and bilateral financial institutions to impose new terms of political and economic organization in Guyana. Support for a PPP government would underscore the commitment of the United States and Western Europe to democracy under conditions where the party could pose little threat to Western and capitalist interests. For the first time, the persistent calls by the party's leaders for democracy began to get a sympathetic hearing by Western and West Indian governments. The PPP was no longer an international pariah in the Western world.

In the new technologies of interventionism, overt and covert use of violence and subversion by international actors has given way to dictates and impositions by those in charge of making and implementing international public policy. They use their control of access to foreign funding to secure compliance. Failure to satisfy the stipulated conditions under which these funds are delivered can prove economically and politically devastating for a government. Powerful western governments dictate these conditions in support of the interests of international capital. In 1985, Guyana became the first country in the history of the IMF to be declared ineligible for funding after rejecting the new economic orthodoxy.[28] The United States, whose intervention instigated this decision, also suspended bilateral economic assistance to the country. One year later, the regime was forced to enter into negotiations with the IMF and World Bank. Under the terms of a 'Policy Framework' for economic stabilisation, the ruling party agreed to reorganise the country's economy and dismantle most of the institutions of state socialism.[29] International financial agencies and aid donors began to demand a fundamental divestment of economic assets from the public sector and an expanded role for a viable private sector as the mainstay of the economy. They insisted upon deep cutbacks in the state bureaucratic sector. The government was forced to hire a British consulting firm to advise on restructuring the country's ministries with an aim of reduction of the state bureaucracy. The 18 ministries existing at the time were eventually reduced to eleven.[30]

As has been the case since the first nationalist government came to power in 1953, local bases of organisation were employed to impose the dictates of Western governmental and economic actors. A Patriotic Coalition for Democracy (PCD), formed in 1986 by five opposition parties, including the PPP, began acquiring a new international legitimacy. At their instigation, the restoration of democracy and civil and human rights soon became the basis for international political and economic support for the regime. By 1989, this unified, multi-party political opposition was able to demonstrate, unequivocally, that its cooperation was indispensable if the government's efforts to gain access to external funding were to succeed. In 1989 it used its control of the country's most powerful unions, representing workers in the country's major industries (sugar and bauxite) to call a series of crippling strikes at a pivotal point in negotiations between the regime and potential international aid donors and lenders, causing economic disruption.[31] The strikes proved critical in preventing the government from meeting the conditions stipulated by the IMF and World Bank to qualify for an enhanced structural adjustment facility and for other foreign exchange assistance that it desperately needed.[32] The opposition also called a successful boycott of local government elections in October 1989 and mounted a campaign petitioning for the intervention of western and Caribbean governments, particularly the 13 member English-speaking Caribbean Community.

The organised political opposition was joined by a civic coalition launched in 1990 that called itself The Guyanese Action for Reform and Democracy (GUARD). As a 'reform movement' it was able to add a voice of stridency to the PCD in demanding the restoration of democracy and human rights in the country. Organised by a Guyanese elite of trade union leaders, businessmen, religious leaders, public officials, and professionals, the movement was patterned directly after the protest movements of Eastern Europe.[33]

Whatever their ideological and racial divisions, the opposition parties and civic organisations remained united in their calls for fair and free elections. Their campaigns to bring this about were well coordinated, particularly in their overseas efforts. The latter crystallised with the formation of a 'World Union of Guyanese' by a former PPP attorney general, Dr Fenton Ramsahoye, who resided 'in exile' in the Caribbean. The Union made plans to approach the United Nations, the Organization of American States and the governments of the Caribbean, North America, and Western Europe.[34] It also began to mobilise the vast Guyanese migrant population overseas in support of calls for the restoration of democracy. In March, 1990, representatives of 10 Guyanese organisations in the United States organised a US chapter. Similar efforts were undertaken in Great Britain and the Caribbean where the bulk of the Guyana migrant population resides.[35]

The opposition's overseas campaign began to pay early dividends. The United States administration began to make forceful and unequivocal calls for electoral reform. As early as February, 1990, President George Bush Sr, using the occasion of a republic anniversary message to Guyana, openly called upon the Hoyte government to respect democratic values. This was quickly followed by a visit to the country, in March, of US State Department official, Sally Cowall. She emphasised, in no uncertain terms, her government's expectation that the Hoyte regime will be 'working towards ..... having an open, free and fair election.' She also made clear her administration's commitment to supporting an international observer team to monitor the country's electoral processes.

The United States backed up its words with a steep cut in foreign aid allocation. It provided the country with only US $1 million of an expected US $10-$13 million promised as part of a package of assistance from a multi-country support group. The group was formed to bail the country out of its economic woes. [36]

The United States Congress also got into the act. On March 19th, Senator Edward Kennedy issued a statement urging the government to ensure fair and free elections, to guarantee civil and political rights, and to restructure the party-controlled Elections Commission.[37] By August, members of both the United States Senate and House of Representatives, including most Democrats, began to call on the Secretary of State to 'seek to ensure that US taxpayer dollars do not support and entrench a regime that holds power only through electoral fraud'.[38] It was a call for the linking of economic assistance to the willingness of the regime to agree to free and fair elections. In September, The Hon. Stephen J. Solarz cited Guyana in the US House of Representatives as one of the countries 'whose governments do not yet permit fundamental political freedoms'.[39] Finally, in October, the US Congress managed to put a hold on US $600,000 in economic assistance to the country until 'the government has agreed to certain ground rules' for elections.[40] The calls for free and fair elections were also being pressed in other countries. In March, the Canadian Council of Churches called upon Prime Minister Brian Mulroney 'to use Canada's influence in support of democratic elections'.[41] There were similar appeals throughout the British Commonwealth, including the English-speaking Caribbean. The Washington-based Council for Hemispheric Affairs also joined in appeals for free and fair elections.[42]

In September, international pressures forced the Hoyte government to concede, after staunch resistance, to the monitoring of the elections by international observers. Finally, the government permitted visits by representatives of Americas Watch, the National Democratic Institute and the International Foundation for Electoral Systems, among other international human and political rights organisations, to assess the country's electoral system. It also extended an invitation to the Secretary General of the Commonwealth and to former US President Jimmy Carter's Council of Freely Elected Heads of Governments.[43] President Carter made the decision, in October, to visit Guyana for a meeting with the Hoyte government. He succeeded, during his talks with the government, in convincing the regime to agree to a number of electoral reform measures. These included the compilation of a fresh voters' list by house-to-house enumerations, the presence of party scrutinisers at these enumerations, and the preliminary counting of ballots at polling stations. These struck at the heart of the ruling party's machinery of fraud. The Elections Laws (Amendment) Bill and the Representation of the People (Amendment) Bill containing these provisions were tabled and passed in the country's parliament in December.[44]

The decision to demand fair and free elections by the international community was in keeping with the new morality of international support that rested with democracy and civil rights. It was made despite the pointed efforts by the new party leader, Desmond Hoyte who had succeed Forbes Burnham after his death in 1986, at compliance with the demands of the international funding agencies. A political rapprochement with the United States and a shift in policies away from socialism were not enough to stave off these demands for fair and free elections. The ruling party continued its efforts at reform, no doubt hoping for some reprieve. In 1990, it began wide-scale divestment of state holdings in both the export sector and in state-owned utilities and undertook a major effort to attract foreign private investments and to pursue export-led economic development. It began to make severe cuts in the state expenditure and in spending on state subsidies. It also implemented a series of massive devaluations. All these were in keeping with the demands of the IMF and World Bank. While these measures resulted in significant improvements in the country's relationship with the United States, they had little impact upon that country's new penchant for democracy. So, the regime's continued unwillingness to guarantee fair and free elections became a major obstacle in the country's international relations.[45] The administration and Congress of the United States became much more critical of the government's human rights record. As both bodies began to call pointedly for fair and free elections, the ruling party was forced to accept a formula for electoral reform worked out by former US president, Jimmy Carter.[46] He had intervened in the face of growing international pressure. The terms of reform were almost identical to those demanded by the country's opposition.[47] Elections under the terms of the new agreement were set for March 1991 but later postponed, provoking intense and wisespread protests. The regime's actions were met with strong US retaliation. The United States Senate quickly announced that it would appropriate no aid to the country without guarantees of a free and fair vote. In supporting the programme of electoral reform, the US senate called upon the Organization of American States and the United Nations to monitor the elections.[48] Finding itself with little option, the ruling party conceded, paving the way for elections in October 6, 1992 . Despite evidence of continued fraud, the PPP secured the majority of the vote and Cheddi Jagan went on to head a new government as Executive President. This was, certifiably, the first 'free and fair' election to be held in the country since 1968 when the PNC government won its first term in office without its coalition partner.

Even though enjoying support from the majority of the country's population, the leadership of the PPP fully recognised the new political reality. It could not hope to regain power without the intervention and support of international political and economic actors. Before the election, the party's leader, Cheddi Jagan embarked on several trips to the United States to engage in a concerted lobbying effort, meeting with administration officials, members of the US Congress, and ex-President Jimmy Carter. In attempts at appeasement, he declared in 1990 that 'the building of a so-called Communist state in Guyana is not on the agenda of the PPP and we have even dropped our insistence on a socialist-orientated (sic) program.' He publicly declared support for private enterprise and expressed a new commitment to welcome foreign capital into the country, and to divest publicly owned corporations in favour of foreign private investment.[49] These were the very terms stipulated by the IMF and World Bank for guarantees of continued access to foreign exchange support.

Democracy without Sovereignty: Race and Discipline

After the PPP was elected to power, the Carter Center organised and run by former President Jimmy Carter, began playing a central role in the country's international affairs and in its domestic policy. It was instrumental in organising and overseeing the 1992 elections that brought the PPP to power and had intervened with the United States Embassy in Georgetown and the International Foundation for Electoral Systems when the PNC started to show reluctance in handing over power when the votes were counted. After the elections, the Center was directly inserted into the country's decision-making process. It became instrumental in the fashioning of a National Development Strategy and began to serve as a conduit between the Guyanese government, international actors and multilateral aid donors. Its intervention was particularly important in relations with the United States. In effect, it became an international bargaining agent for the government.[50]

The idiom of race disciplines and regulates party-political support in Guyana. This explains the ability of the PPP and the PNC to retain popular support despite deteriorating social, political, and economic conditions and in the face of intensive penetration of the political economy by global capital. Legitimacy rests with racial control of the governing institutions of the state rather than with catering to popular interests. In the 1992 elections, the PPP received massive victories in areas of the country where the East Indian population was in the majority. The PNC's regional victories came in areas of black majorities. Between them, the two parties received 95.8 per cent of the votes with the PPP receiving 53.5 per cent and the PNC 42.3 per cent.[51] The electoral results demonstrated a continued salience of idiomatically defined racial identity. This allowed the PPP to retain support from the majority of the electorate.

On March 19th 2001, the electorate of Guyana again went to the polls. By the unanimous account of all neutral observers, including official foreign delegations, the elections could have served as the 'poster child' for fairness and transparency. Former United States President, Jimmy Carter, who led an observer mission for the Carter Center in Atlanta, declared that the elections were 'almost perfect'. With a full 88 per cent of the electorate voting, the PPP received 54 per cent of the vote to 42 per cent received by the PNC. The leader of the PPP became, once again, the country's Executive President.

It was the third electoral victory for the PPP since 1992. In elections held in December 1997 the party won with 55.3 per cent of the votes and in 1992 it won with 53.4 per cent. Yet, despite, the unanimous opinion of all electoral observers that the 2001 elections were fair, free, and devoid of fraud, the results were immediately contested by the People's National Congress (PNC), the country's major opposition party. This was despite the strong endorsement by its own appointed members to the Guyana Elections Commission as to its fairness and transparency. The Commission was charged with running the election under a Chairman who was considered, universally, to be neutral and impartial. Charges by the PNC that the elections were fraudulent were accompanied by an orchestrated campaign of violence. The campaign began even before the elections were contested, and escalated into mass mobilisation in the capital city. It was accompanied by politically motivated beatings and murder. On April 9th an area of the capital city of Georgetown was torched. Perceived supporters of the governing party owned many of the businesses that were burnt.

It was not the first time that the opposition employed tactics of protest and violence to contest the results of elections that were unquestionably free, fair, and 'transparent'. There was a similar campaign after the 1997 elections. While demands by the People's National Congress for a 'national front' government comprising itself and other opposition parties went unheeded, the campaign of violence and protest forced the ruling regime into making compromises that included agreements to consider establishment of joint committees of governance and joint management of parliamentary business and the working out of constitutional reform aimed particularly at reducing the power of the executive president.

The 2001 elections served as a stark reconfirmation of a racially polarised electorate. This has been the most pervasive feature of Guyanese politics since the racial splintering of the progressive nationalist Peoples Progressive Party (PPP) in 1956. The three electoral victories by the PPP beginning in 1992 came with solid support of the Asian Indian Guyanese majority, comprising over 51 per cent of the country's population. The PNC, solidly backed by the country's black and mixed population, comprising 39 per cent of the country's total, gained 42 per cent of the popular vote. The PPP ended up with 34 seats in the country's Legislature and the PNC with 27.

What is important in an analysis of the Guyana elections of 1997 and 2001 and their aftermath is the light it throws upon conditions of power in post-colonial political economies. Such an analysis raises the question of the relationship of effective power to the ideals of representative democracy. An increase in its percentage of the popular support, from 53.4 per cent in 1992 to 55.2 per cent in 1997, was not enough to guarantee the PPP's hold on political power. This had to be secured through international intervention. And despite such intervention, and an election outcome that was clearly incontestable, the post-election crisis in 2001 was much more violent and destructive. In the post-1997 political environment, PPP's ability to maintain control of the state was underwritten by international intervention and by clear demonstrations of international support. These served to counter the effective control by the PNC of the strategic domestic instruments of power. There were a number of ways in which international intervention negated the strategic power of the PNC in the domestic arena. In the highly racialised environment, PNC control of the judiciary was the first hurdle that the PPP had to overcome. It did so with the help of pressure and surveillance by the official body of Caribbean jurists that resulted in its neutralisation. The PPP's assumption of executive office was also underwritten by the intervention by western and regional governments.

The possibility of a coup by the country's uniformed services was certainly staved off by the threat of a regional and international military intervention. The PNC enjoyed overwhelming support among the ranks in the country's military and police. The potential for international intervention created the conditions for ensuring political neutrality given. By the 2001 elections, there was clear evidence of the depoliticisation of the military and police. The ruling party was confident enough to agree to the appointment of the former head of the Guyana Defence Force, Major General Joe Singh, to the position of chair of the Elections Commission. He was charged with the conduct of the elections. Even without this basis of support, however, the opposition PNC continued to demonstrate its ability to disrupt the social, political, and economic order, forcing the PPP into negotiated compromise.

In the strategic equation, the PPP could count on the absolute support of the predominantly East Indian private sector. The influence of this sector rested heavily on the relations it established with powerful international allies, particularly international business, international aid donors, and Western governments. In both 1997 and 2001, the influential East Indian dominated Private Sector Commission mounted a campaign that underscored the need for a 'stable economic environment'. It emphasised the destabilising consequences for the country's political economy of the opposition's campaign of protest and violence. This, undoubtedly, struck a resonant chord among the international actors concerned with the potential effects of political upheaval on the country's economy, particularly its international creditors concerned about repayment of a foreign debt of over US $2 billion. In the post-elections environment of 1997, the Private Sector Commission put its weight behind proposals for an international audit of the contested election returns, correctly anticipating that such an audit would confirm the PPP's victory. It also supported a negotiated political settlement as a basis for a return to political and social order. This, as it turned out, was precisely the solution imposed by the international community. Included was the decision for new elections in 2001. Through international mediation, the CARICOM Community (a common market comprising primarily English-speaking countries of the Caribbean) was given the official role of establishing binding terms for resolving the ongoing political crisis. In 1997, in the face of escalating violence and a refusal of the PNC to observe a ban on demonstrations and protest, the prime ministers of CARICOM countries negotiated s Herdmanston Accord, that was signed by members of the ruling party and the opposition. The accord formalised an official role for CARICOM. It committed both political parties to a process of negotiations and to the establishment of a Constitution Reform Commission under mutually acceptable terms. It also formalised the agreement to hold the general elections of 2001 under a new constitution.

The ruling party agreed to the terms of the accord in exchange for political order and stability. This included commitment to negotiate with the opposition to fashion a new constitution that came with the possibility of reducing its hold on power. These were the terms under which elections were held in 2001.

Clearly, it was the demonstration by the PNC of its ability to mobilise strategic sectors of power in the political economy that forced the PPP into making political concessions in exchange for political stability. But notwithstanding its strategic control, it was forced to give up its campaign of protest and non-cooperation with the government in 1997 in the face of considerable pressure from the international community that quickly moved to authenticate the results of the election. After some hesitation and resistance, the party's leadership decided, finally, to assume its place in Parliament and to agree to elections in three years under terms determined by the CARICOM accord.

The issue of legitimacy in Guyana rests with effective representation of the competing communal groupings. The consequences have been devastating. The dependence upon international intervention by racialised political parties has intensified the penetration of global capital and has eviscerated any semblance of sovereignty. Efforts at racial accommodation have been stymied by international intervention, first in 1953, then in the 1960s, and later in the first half of the seventies. Since then, economic decline and new technologies of intervention have tied the country even more firmly to international capital while elevating international decision makers in international financial agencies to positions of de facto governance, supported by Western and reginal governments. While conditions deteriorate, the popular segments of the Guyanese population continue to focus on racial control of the governing institutions of the state as they are regulated, controlled, and disciplined by regimes of racially organised political parties.

Endnotes

1. See Oswaldo de Rivero, *The Myth of Development*. (London and New York: Zed Books, 2001) pp. 11-31.
2. See Mandle 1996:57-71.
3. See Cary Fraser, *Ambivalent Anti-Colonialism*. (Westport, Conn and London: Greenwood, 1994). pp. 123-168.
4. This section is informed by a number of sources including Percy C. Hintzen, *The Costs of Regime Survival*. (Cambridge and New York: New York University Press, 1989), Thomas J. Spinner, *A Political and Social History of Guyana, 1945-1983*. (Boulder: Westview, 1984; Robert H. Manley, *Guyana Emergent.* (Boston, G.K. Hall, and Cambridge, Mass: Schenkman, 1979).
5. People's Progressive Party 1971:5.
6. See Fraser 1994, *passim*.
7. United States State Department, Decimal File: 1953.
8. Fraser 1994: ch. 6.
9. Jagan 1980: 124-46.
10. For a fuller discussion see Percy C. Hintzen, 'Racial and Ethnic Identity in the Caribbean' in *The Blackwell Companion to Racial and Ethnic Studies* edited by John Solomos and David Goldberg, (Oxford: Blackwell, 2001). pp.; and Percy C. Hintzen, 'Race and Creole Ethnicity in the Caribbean' in

Questioning Creole: Creolisation Discourses in Caribbean Culture edited by Verene A. Shepherd and Glen L. Richards. (Kingston: Ian Randle Publishers, London: James Currey Publishers, 2002).

11. This and the following discussions are covered in Hintzen 1989, *passim;* Spinner 1994, *passim;* Manley 1979, *passim, and* Fraser 1994, pp 123-68.

12. Jagan 1980: pp. 189-208.

13. See Population Census of the Commonwealth Caribbean 1970.

14. See Hintzen 1989. pp. 175-193.

15. See Hintzen 1989:52-56: Sheehan 1967; Pearson 1964; Lens 1965; Schlesinger 1965:779.

16. See Hintzen 1989, Hintzen and Premdas 1982.

17. See Hintzen 2002.

18. Hintzen 1989, pp. 63-70.

19. ASCRIA 1974.

20. See Hintzen 1989, *passim.*

21. Hintzen 1989:184.

22. Hintzen 1989:.183-192.

23. Hintzen 1989:170.

24. See Central Committee Document, Peoples Progressive Party, 1977.

25. See Hintzen 1995.

26. International Monetary Fund 1990:1.

27. See Ferguson 1995:50-55.

28. Ferguson 1995:1.

29. Hintzen 1989:*passim.*

30. *Latin American Regional Report: Caribbean,* January 24, 1991:2.

31. See Ferguson 1995:50.

32. Hintzen 1989b.

33. *Catholic Standard,* January 21, 1990:1-2.

34. *Trinidad Guardian,* April 12, 1990:7.

35. *Miami Herald,* March 26, 1990

36. *Caribbean Contact,* April 1990:6; *Catholic Standard,* March 11, 1990:2.

37. *Catholic Standard,* March 25, 1990:1.

38. Latin American Regional Reports: Caribbean, August 30, 1990.

39. US House of Representatives, September 11, 1990.

40. *Miami Herald,* October 8, 1990.

41. *Catholic Standard,* March 25, 1990.

42. *Catholic Standard,* April 29, 1990:1-8.

43. *Miami Herald,* October 8, 1990.

44. *Guyana Chronicle,* January 4, 1991:4-5.

45. Hintzen 1993.

46. Congressional Record 1990:1.

47. *Trinidad Guardian*, November 28, 1990:11; *Guyana Chronicle*, January 27, 1990:15.

48. Stabroek News, 15 January 1991:1-2; Latin American Regional Report: Caribbean, 28 February 1991:6-8.

49. See Bohning 1990; Miami Herald, 8 December; *Catholic Standard*, 13 May 1990, p. 5.

50. See Lynette Harvey 1996.

51. See Report of the Council of Freely Elected Heads of Government.

References

Bohning, D 1990. 'Ex-enemy seeks U.S. help to Gain fair Guyana Vote' *Miami Herald*, December 8.

Catholic Standard, May 13, 1990, p 5.

de Rivero, O. 2001. *The Myth of Development*. (London and New York: Zed Books)

Despres, L.. Cultural Pluralism and Nationalist Politics in British Guiana. Chicago, Ill: (1967).

Rand, McNally Economist Intelligence Unit. Country Report, No 1, 1990.

Ferguson, T., Structural Adjustment and Good Governance: The Case of Guyana. (Georgetown Guyana: Public Affairs Consulting Enterprise, 1995).

Fraser, C., *Ambivalent Anticolonialism* (Westport: Greenwood Press, 1994).

Harvey, L., 'Guyana's democracy, America's Policy'. *Guyana Review*. 42. (1996) July:10-11.

Hintzen, P., 'Reproducing Domination: Identity and Legitimacy Constructs in the West Indies'. *Social Identities*. Vol 3. No 1:47-75. (1997).

_____., *The Costs of Regime Survival*, (Cambridge and New York: Cambridge Univ. Press, 1989).

_____., 'Democracy and Middle Class Domination in the West Indies' in *Democracy in the West Indies*, edited by C. Edie, (Boulder: Westview, 1993).

_____., 'Structural Adjustment and the New International Middle Class' Transition, 24 (February, 1995) pp. 52-74.

_____., 'Creole Construction and Nationalist Ideology' in Goldberg, David T. and Soplomos, John, (ed) *The Blackwell Companion to Racial and Ethnic Studies* (Oxford: Blackwell, 2001).

_____., 'Race and Creole Ethnicity in the Caribbean' in *Questioning Creole: Creolisation Discourses in Caribbean Culture* edited by Verene A. Shepherd and Glen L. Richards. (Kingston: Ian Randle Publishers, London: James Currey Publishers, 2002)

Hintzen, P. C. and Premdas, R., 'Coercion and Control in Political Change'. *Journal of Inter-American Studies and World Affairs*, Vol. 24, no. 3, August (1982): 337-54.

Huberman, L and Sweezy, P. M., *Cuba: Anatomy of a Revolution*. (New York: Monthly Review Press, 1968).

International Monetary Fund, "Guyana: Enhanced Structural Adjustment Facility. Economic and Financial Policy Framework 1990-92", June 20, 1990, p. 1.

Jagan C., The West On Trial. (Berlin: Seven Seas, 1980).

_____., "President Cheddi B. Jagan on Independence". Guyana Review. 41. (1996) June. pp. 4-7.

Latin American Regional Reports: Caribbean, 5 April 1990, p. 4-5.

Lens, S., 'American Labor Abroad' *The Nation*, 5 July, (1965).

Mandle, J. R. 1996. *Persistent Underdevelopment: Change and Economic Modernization in the West Indies*. (Amsterdam: Gordon and Breach).

Robert H. Manley, 1979. *Guyana Emergent.* (Boston, G.K. Hall, and Cambridge, Mass: Schenkman).

Meeker-Lowry, S. 'Guyana Takes on the IMF'. In Context. 41.(1995) pp. 33-5.

Pearson, D., 'U.S. faces line holding decision.' *Washington Post*, 31 May, (1964).

People's Progressive Party, People's Progressive Party: 21 Years. (Georgetown: New Guiana Co., 1971).

Population Census of the Commonwealth Caribbean 1970. (Kingston, Jamaica: Census Research Programme, University of the West Indies, 1973).

Report of the Council of Freely Elected Heads of Government Observing Guyana's Electoral Process, 1990-92. Latin American and Caribbean Program, The Carter Center of Emory University. Atlanta, Georgia.

Schlesinger, A. Jr., *A Thousand Days*. (New York: Houghton Mifflin, 1965).

Sheehan, N. , 'C.I.A. men and strikers in Guiana against Dr. Jagan' *New York Times*, (February 22, 1967).

Spinner, T. J. *A Political and Social History of Guyana*, 1945-1983. (Boulder: Westview, 1984).

United States State Department. Decimal File, Telegram Maddox to Secretary of State, September 11. R.G. 59, Box 3542, (1953).

Weiner, T., 'Ghost of a Kennedy-C.I.A. plot has come back to haunt Clinton', *New York Times*, September 30, 1994: 1 and 4.(1994).

19

Which Way Forward: Constitutional Issues and Reform in the Twin-Island Federation of St Kitts and Nevis

Simon Jones-Hendrickson

This chapter's focus is on the constitutional issues in the Twin-island State of St Kitts and Nevis. Of central importance is the issue, which way forward should the State of St Kitts and Nevis go? Should the two islands continue to be the one unitary state that was put together, in a seemingly Machiavellian sense? Or should each island go its separate way? Should Nevis utilise its Damocles sword of 'secession' and sever its ties from St Kitts? Should St Kitts' political directorate follow the aspirations of some die-hard Kittitians and politicians and say, 'If Nevis wants to go, let it go?' I explore these ideas in this chapter. First I give an historical perspective on the links of St Kitts and Nevis. Second I look at the changing of the guardians of politics in St Kitts and Nevis. Third I consider a first pass of which way forward. Fourth, I consider accountability in St Kitts and Nevis and the way forward. Fifth I consider blood relations, cohesion and fragmentation. Sixth, I consider the constitutional significance andother consequences of separation and finally, I offer some conclusions on which way forward for St. Kitts and Nevis given the matrix of issues and the metrics of social and economic costs associated with separation.

HISTORICAL PERSPECTIVES ON THE LINKS BETWEEN ST KITTS AND NEVIS

In a paper written in 1980, aptly entitled 'The Dynamics of Fragmentation: The Case of St Kitts-Nevis' I noted that we had some serious concerns about what I saw as instability between the coalition of the political parties of St Kitts and Nevis. From that paper[1] I cite the following historical perspectives.

The earliest links between St. Kitts and Nevis seemed to have started on September 13, 1626. Then, Thomas Warner, the English adventurer to the Caribbean was made Lieutenant for the King of England for St Christopher

(St Kitts), Nevis, Barbados and Montserrat.[2] Nevis' links with St Kitts were further solidified as a result of the buccaneering, colonialistic and, ostensibly, the administrative experience of another Englishman. In 1828, Englishman Anthony Hilton established a colony in Nevis after his experience in St Kitts. By 1630, he had sufficiently impressed the Crown to be appointed Governor of Nevis. Even though he was eventually a failure, and even though he took recruits from St Kitts and Nevis to Tortugue to enter the service as buccaneers,[3] Hilton's governorship was the main point of solidarity in the links, which brought St Kitts and Nevis together.

Nevis lies two nautical miles, from end to end, southwest of St Kitts. Basseterre is the capital. Basseterre is also the administrative capital of the Federation of the State of St Kitts and Nevis. Charlestown, the capital of Nevis, is 12 nautical miles from the port of Basseterre. The short two miles of Nevis from St Kitts may have been one of the many rationales for the English and subsequently the British to link Nevis and St Kitts in an administrative unit. In 1871 when the Leeward Islands Federation (LIF) was formed, the islands were further secured in an administrative marriage. For British Administrative purposes, the LIF consisted of Antigua, Anguilla, Dominica, Montserrat, Nevis, St Kitts and the Virgin Islands. (The US Virgin Islands were then called the Danish West Indies).

The LIF did not progress as smoothly as Britain anticipated. Therefore in 1882, St Kitts, Nevis and Anguilla were linked in an arrangement termed a Presidency.[4] No economic rhyme or reason was given to the colonies for the arrangement. For Britain, the linking of the islands seemed to be one of administrative ease, and seemingly lower administrative costs. Although there may have been a rationale for the linking of Nevis to St Kitts over the two miles of water, there seems to be no strong reason for the linking of Anguilla to St Kitts, given that Anguilla is 70 miles away from St Kitts. This arbitrary federation-type linking seemed to have been the norm in British overseas diplomacy from the Caribbean to Africa, as Adedeji[5] notes in the case of Nigeria.

Over the years, the British made additional efforts to ensure that the St Kitts-Nevis (SKN) links remained intact. First, on July 1, 1956, the colony of St Kitts-Nevis and Anguilla (SKNA) was given official status. This colonial linkage permitted the British the levity to control Nevis and St Kitts from Basseterre. This pattern of administration was the bone of contention as far as Nevisians were concerned. Even after the British turned over the reins of government to the local political directorate in St Kitts and Nevis, this pattern of administration of Nevis from Basseterre has remained a sore spot and the central point of argument between the political directorates of the two islands. (Note we state the political directorates, as opposed to the ordinary Kittitians and Nevisians).

A second British initiative, which sought to forge stronger administrative links between Basseterre and Charlestown, was the outcome of the Federation. By 1957, when, by an Order in Council, Britain passed an Act to establish the West Indies Federation (WIF), and when all of the former British Caribbean countries, except British Guiana, British Honduras and the British Virgin Islands, decided to be members, SKN was further cemented into another administrative arrangement; this arrangement was again derived from external decision-making, and not from the wishes of the people concerned. The year 1957 was a critical threshold in the political relationship between St Kitts and Nevis.

In 1957, 17 years after the formation of the St Kitts-Nevis-Anguilla Labour Party and the St Kitts-Nevis Trades and Labour Union, Labour's control of the party machinery in the tri-island system was threatened. For the first time, candidates in Nevis and Anguilla won seats in the Assembly under a banner other than that of the Labour Party. Two 'Independents' were elected in Nevis and one Independent was elected in Anguilla.

Eugene Walwyn, an Attorney, and Wilmoth B. Nicholls, a teacher, were elected as Independents from Nevis to the Legislative Council (Legco) of St Kitts-Nevis and Anguilla. Kenneth Hazel, of Anguilla, was elected as and Independent to represent Anguilla in the Legco. According to Nicholls, both he and Walwyn

> argued during the election campaign that the Labour Party had adopted the same policies over the sister islands as did the British Government over her colonies. They maintained that the past neglects of Nevis could not be tolerated, and that another form of colonialism would not be tolerated.[6]

Robert Llewellyn Bradshaw, the acclaimed *First National Hero of St. Kitts*, the comrade leader of the St Kitts-Nevis-Anguilla Labour Party, was the Chief Minister at the time of Nicholls', Walwyn's and Hazel's entry into the Legco. Bradshaw did not take too kindly to the intrusion on his power in the political process. The opposition got a stormy reception when the Legco opened in 1957. According to Nicholls,[7] Nevisians saw the treatment of their representatives as a reaction on the part of the comrade leader, Robert Bradshaw. It was at this stage, therefore, notes Nicholls, that Nevisians began to seriously agitate for economic and political independence from St Kitts. There are, today, many variations on this theme of agitation. Some stories are shrouded in myth; some are embedded in partial facts. Some are embellished with a stretching of the truth.

From 1960 to 1980, there were a series of constitutional gaffes that brought the leadership of Nevis and St Kitts in contention. Among these was Bradshaw's dismissal of Walwyn from Nevis from sitting in the Executive Council. The

Executive Council was renamed the Cabinet in 1960. Walwyn's dismissal from the Cabinet was for breaching Cabinet secrecy. Bradshaw, who was sworn in as Chief Minister of St Kitts-Nevis and Anguilla after the July elections of 1966.

In the case of the expulsion of Walwyn from the Executive, Colonel Howard, the then British Administrator of St Kitts, Nevis and Anguilla reinstated Walwyn to the Executive Council. Bradshaw took to the streets of Basseterre to force Howard to demit office. This was similar to another Bradshaw-led 1950 huge demonstration, entitled Operation Blackburn, 'through the streets of Basseterre to focus attention on the Labour Movement's claim that the colonial office should consult with political representatives before the appointment of Governors and Administrators for Caribbean Colonies.'[7]

Three other features stand out. First, on the regional level, there was the collapse of the West Indies Federation in 1962. Second, on May 29, 1967, a number of Anguillians summarily expelled the police of St Kitts-Nevis and Anguilla from Anguilla. Third: On Saturday, June 10, 1967,

> a party of armed men from Anguilla (Anguillians and two American mercenaries) landed on St Kitts. They had two principal objectives which were interrelated. Firstly, the defense of the Anguilla Revolutionary (of May 29, 1967). Secondly, the overthrow of the Government of Premier Robert Bradshaw and the installation of a government sympathetic to the Anguilla cause.[8]

On the 27th of February 1967, Robert Bradshaw was sworn in as the first Premier of the Associated State of St Kitts-Nevis Anguilla, after he had returned from the Federal Parliament of the West Indies Federation in Trinidad. The Associated State was a state in association with Britain. St Kitts-Nevis and Anguilla was responsible for everything, internally while Britain was supposed to be responsible for external issues, particularly defense.'[9]

On that fateful day of June 10, 1967, according to Ronald Webster, latterly a chief minister of Anguilla, but who at that time was the leader of the revolutionaries who kicked out the civil authority from Anguilla, he:

> organised a small Anguillan invasion force and landed on St. Kitts. [Webster noted that] They were supposed to link up with Dr. (William) Herbert (who founded the PAM opposition in St Kitts) but somehow it didn't work out that way.[10]

With the help of the PAM party in St Kitts, members of a nascent political party in Anguilla threw out the rule of law in Anguilla, as that rule of law was implemented from St Kitts. Nevis saw the Anguilla move as a prelude for what should come for them. From that time onwards, the Nevisians started a sustained agitation for secession. The Labour Party dominated politics in St Kitts and Nevis up to 1980. With that dominance, there were a series of untoward clashes between the politicians in Nevis and the politicians in St Kitts. Many of these clashes were verbal in nature, and many of them were only fully exercised in the chambers of the House of Assembly. Things changed in 1980.

Changing of the Guardians of Politics in St Kitts and Nevis

On February 18, 1980, the electorate of St Kitts and Nevis went to the polls. When they had completed their civic duty, they presented the Caribbean with a stunning event. For the first time, in nearly three decades, the forces against Labour in St Kitts and Nevis were in a majority. The opposition forces of Dr Kennedy Simmonds' People's Action Movement (PAM) and Attorney Simeon Daniel's Nevis Reformation Party (NRP) combined to form a marginal majority of five (5) seats to Premier Lee L. Moore's St Kitts Nevis Anguilla Labour Party four (4) seats. This novel arrangement seemed to have lain to rest the theme of the NRP, namely, '*secession from St Kitts at all costs*'.

On June 21, 1984, the coalition government of PAM and the NRP called an election in SKN. The coalition won a resounding victory by capturing six of eight seats in the St Kitts districts. In Nevis, where the Labour party did not contest any seats, the NRP candidates won. But, whereas the NRP candidates were of pivotal importance in 1980 when their three seats made a difference, in the 1984 election, PAM's six seats in St Kitts were sufficient to put the NRP assistance on the sidelines. The NRP power brokers were no longer critical to the survival of the coalition government, as it was true in 1980[11]

In a sense, a new political style developed between St Kitts and Nevis. Once strong partners in a coalition, the former forces of Labour were now themselves in a lukewarm relationship. The new view of political leadership was one in which the PAM political directorate no longer saw opposition as a factor to be considered. They had marginalised both the Labour Party in St Kitts and had sidelined the NRP in Nevis.

On September 19, 1983, the coalition government of PAM and NRP had taken the country into independence form Britain. The Labour Party was adamantly opposed to the form of the constitutional provisions which gave Nevis move power in the Federation, and which gave Nevis the option to opt out of the Federation any time it wished. No such provision was made for St Kitts. Nevis was given a local Nevis Assembly. There was no provision for St Kitts to have a Local Island Assembly. In effect, the Federal government in St Kitts was the de jury government for St Kitts and Nevis and the de facto local government for St Kitts. Whereas Nevis was provided with a premier in the person of who commanded the majority of seats in the local elections in Nevis, there was no such provision in St Kitts. In a sense, again, the prime minister of St Kitts and Nevis was the federal prime minister and the de facto premier for St Kitts, although no such office exists.

From 1983 up to 1993 there was an uneasy calm in the country. The political directorate in Nevis got some benefits but there were not of the same scope as in 1980 when they were pivotal to decision-making. In the elections of 1993, there was very unstable conclusion. The ruling PAM government emerged from the elections with a total of 8,405 votes to 10,722 for the Labour Party. However, given the prevailing concept of who passes the post first wins, PAM claimed victory again with the help of the political directorate in Nevis. To many persons in St Kitts and Nevis, and definitely to the Labour Party leadership and supporters, this was intolerable. The Labour Party leadership and the rank and file felt that there was clear evidence that their convincing popularity victory was unequivocal evidence that the people wanted a change. This was not to be given the fact that the state of St Kitts and Nevis functions under a Constitutional arrangement that is commonly called the *Westminster model. This model is nothing more than who first passes the post wins.*

Central to this Westminster model is the fact that marginal candidates can enter the government, but a candidate who gets a massive numbers of votes is not able to give his or her excessive votes in the context of a plurality. This scenario developed in an unusual way in 1980 and 1984 when Labour got more popular votes, but was 'forced' on the sidelines as a result of the coalition of PAM and NRP. In 1984, Labour got nearly 500 more votes, but lost two seats.[12] When this scenario developed again in 1993, that is the scenario where there was a clear majority of votes for the Labour Party, but where Labour was again being forced to go on the political sidelines, the leadership of Labour decided that the will of the people should be respected. This meant, in the view of Labour leaders that the majority of the people did not want PAM, and hence PAM should not form the government. The data are presented in Table 2.

Chaos and confusion reigned for several days. The outcome of this was a series of violent clashes between the supporters on PAM and Labour. After several days of unrest, the Churches and other stakeholders, those members who are now called civil society, brokered a deal whereby the government would govern for two years and then go back to the polls in 1995.[13]

Table 1: Voting Patterns for Major Parties in 1980 and 1984

		Labour	PAM	Totals
1980		6,914	4,990	11,904
	%	58.1	41.6	99.70a
Seats		4	3	7
1984		7,463	8,596	16,059
	%	46.2	53.2	99.40a
Seats		2	6	8

Source: *Raw data were obtained from the Supervisor of Elections,* Election *Publications.*

Table 2: Voting Patterns for All Parties, 1993 and 1995

	Ballots Cast		Percentage	
Party	*1993*	*1995*	*1993*	*1995*
Labour	8,405	10,722	43.6	49.4
PAM	6,449	7,530	33.5	34.7
UPP	563	71	2.9	.04
NRP	1,641	1,521	8.5	7.0
CCM	2,100	1,177	10.9	8.2
Independents	1	3	0.0	0.0
Rejected Bal.	97	66	0.6	.03
Total	19,256	21,260	100.0	100.0

Source: *St Kitts and Nevis Digest of Statistics, 1999, p. 101.*

In the reelection called, the St Kitts and Nevis Labour party won seven of the eight seats in St Kitts. This St Kitts-based party ran no candidates in Nevis. Hence the election results pitted St Kitts political directorate against the Nevis political directorate.

The outcome of this issue was that the Nevis political directorate used their constitutional gift to raise the issue of secession, as is outlined in Section 113 of the Constitution. Once again, when Labour acceded to power, the political directorates in Nevis were of the disposition that they could not work with the

Labour Party Leaders in St Kitts. This idea has continued into the present. The present Labour Administration put in place a Constitutional Task Force, headed by Sir Fred Phillips, to look into the feasibility of where St Kitts and Nevis ought to go.

WHICH WAY FORWARD?

This idea of which way forward has been raised over the years by many persons. Sir Probyn Innis, a former Governor, raised that idea in several of his writings. One, in particular, entitled 'Whither Bound: St Kitts-Nevis?' makes the very poignant case that St Kitts is the burden bearer of Nevis. And even though Nevis was dragged into a forced union with St Kitts on January 1, 1883, 100 years, to the date, September 18, 1983, St Kitts and Nevis formed a union in independence. This prompted Innis[14] to ask the question:

> For how long will our beautiful island home of *St. Christopher* continue to groan beneath the thankless and hopeless task of being the *burden-bearer*?

Arising out of extensive interviews with the electorate and nationals in the Diaspora, the Phillips Task Force prepared four volumes detailing some scenarios of the way forward. Many persons in St Kitts, including persons in the ruling political directorate, are of the view that there is nothing that could be done to stop Nevis from leaving the Federation. In Nevis, in the USVI and in the USA, there are some die-hard persons who believe that Nevis has as much right and authority to go on its own, as any other state. In my deliberations with the political directorate in Nevis, and in my measured talks with very strong supporters and advisers of the ruling CCM party in Nevis, it was clear to me that while secession is an option, the cost of secession was not given the full weight that it ought to be given. Furthermore, many persons were not openly talking about the need for accountability in government. However, the people wanted to discuss accountability and wanted to see *more accountability* instituted. Below I reproduce *three* of the main points on accountability that was prepared for the Phillips' document.[15]

Accountability in St Kitts and Nevis and the Way Forward

1. Fundamentally, the general sentiment of the people who met the Constitutional Task Force is that in St Kitts and Nevis, there should be full disclosure of assets by all parliamentarians. This should be an

absolute necessity. Permanent Secretaries, Heads of Departments, and all senior persons in State Enterprises should also disclose their legal assets and their beneficial assets of equity. The latter are those assets that are in the name of someone else, and have been put in that scenario for the purpose of the person holding public office.

2. Safeguards should be put in place such that these officials never use government for unreasonable personal profit.

3. Ministers responsible for State Enterprises should make available to Parliament the reports (of the State enterprises) both on request (and) periodically. Furthermore, reports of State Enterprises should be debated on the floor of the legislature and all concerned should make themselves available for scrutiny.

In a nutshell, while persons on both sides of the Narrows (that is, the body of water that separates St Kitts and Nevis) want to move to secession, there is a prevailing sentiment that accountability is of paramount importance. In all of the issue of whither St Kitts and Nevis, there are other issues that are crucial. One of these issues is the question of bloodlines. We now turn to this issue of bloodlines in the context of cohesion and fragmentation.

Blood Relations, Cohesion and Fragmentation

This issue of bloodlines is of central moment in terms of where St Kitts and Nevis will go as a State, or if St Kitts and Nevis will go on their own, in their separate ways. In a 1985 paper[16] I considered the importance of relationships among the people of St Kitts and Nevis and other microstates and contended that this issue is of paramount importance. I noted that: There are Kittitians whose parents are Nevisians and there are Nevisians who parents are Kittitians. And there are variations on this social theme. In the (first) PAM/NRP government, a Kittitian-based Minister of Government (was) of Nevisian parentage. At the same time, a Nevisian-based Minister was born in St Kitts, of Kittitian parentage. In the government, over the years, Nevisians and Anguillians held prominent positions in the Civil Service. (A Dominican was one chief minister of St Kitts and an Antiguan held many positions including Attorney general, secretary of the Labour Party and minister of education. Indeed, it was his vision of education that today makes St Kitts one of the few Caribbean countries where the dreaded 11-plus examination system is not in place). Many Anguillians and Nevisians still hold prominent positions in the Civil service in St. Kitts today despite the fact that Anguilla broke away from St Kitts and

Nevis and returned to the colonial status with Britain. The substance of our point is this:

> In the context of Nevis and St. Kitts, history and blood relations (are) poised to play a critical role in the survivability of the state under (any form of government) ... (We venture) further ... We are of the view that the social relations endemic between the people of St. Kitts and Nevis are stronger than the politicians realise.[17]

In the context of the microstate of St Kitts and Nevis, the forces of cohesion deriving from blood-links seem particularly instrumental in keeping the state intact. Consequently, it is our view that the people will ensure that the forces of cohesion (will) dominate the forces of fragmentation. The members of PAM, NRP and CCM (the Concerned Citizens Movement) may play political games, and may engage in other political shenanigans, but in the long run, the blood relations would be causal in keeping the state together, as opposed to rending it apart. The social costs are too high at the moment. There may be short-run instabilities, but these will only be local instabilities. The instabilities will not be global in nature. The Federal level of the two islands, and at the island level, there are still people of good-will who want to see the state of St Kitts and Nevis remain as one entity. There is no doubt that the sword of Damocles could still be used any time by the political directorate in Nevis. But one can only hope that sound reason will prevail over irrational decision.

Constitutional Significance and Other Consequences of Separation

Before I conclude, we wish to quote, in extenso, from the Phillips Report, chapter 10, Volume IV on issues that are paramount in terms of separation.

1. The constitution of St Kitts and Nevis expressly recognises the rights of Nevis to secede in accordance with the provisions of section 113...Those provisions are designed to ensure that the issue of secession should be based on a full understanding of the implications of separation and a referendum which reflects the widespread and substantial support of the electorate of Nevis.
2. It is extremely important to recognise that the matter of secession involves far-reaching consequences and is much more complicated than the constitutional procedures for a referendum. The practical realities

arising from the close historical association of the economies and peoples of St Kitts and Nevis mean that there cannot be any serious resolution of differences merely by the constitutional act of separation and by a subsequent declaration of independence by Nevis. It would be simplistic to believe otherwise.

3. The significance of the implications of separation of Nevis from St. Kitts is fully recognised by section 113(2)(c) of the Constitution, and the provisions were designed by the Constitution-makers as the framework within which separation might legitimately take place. Subsections (1) and (2) of section 113 read as follows:

> (1) The Nevis Island Legislature may provide that the island of Nevis shall cease to be federated with the island of Saint Christopher and accordingly that this Constitution shall no longer have effect in the island of Nevis.
>
> (2) A bill for the purposes of subsection (1) shall not be regarded as being passed by the Assembly unless on its final reading the bill is supported by the votes of not less than two-thirds of all the elected members of the Assembly and such a bill shall not be submitted to the Governor-General for his assent unless -
>
>> (a) there has been an interval of not less than ninety day between the introduction of the bill in the Assembly and the beginning of the proceedings in the Assembly on the second reading of the bill;
>> (b) after it has been passed by the Assembly, the bill has been approved on referendum help in the island of Nevis by not less than two-thirds of all the votes validly cast on that referendum;
>> (c) full and detailed proposals for the future constitution of the island of Nevis (whether as a separate state or as part of or in association with some other country) have been laid before the Assembly for at least six months before the holding of the referendum and those proposals, with adequate explanations of their significance, have been made available to the persons entitled to vote on the referendum at least ninety days before the holding of the referendum.

4. A careful analysis of the provisions of section 113 demonstrates that it was the intention of the Constitution-makers to provide fundamental

safeguards designed to ensure that the electorate of Nevis would only be asked to make a decision on whether to separate from St. Kitts on the basis of:

    (a) an opportunity for *mature reflection* - hence the requirement for full an detailed proposals to be laid before the Assembly for at least six months before the holding of a referendum;

    (b) adequate explanations of the significance of those proposals, which must be made available to those persons entitled to vote at least ninety days before the vote.

Given the high level of 'test of separabilty' that the Constitution imposed on the Nevisians, if they want to secede, I now offer some concluding thoughts on whither St Kitts and Nevis.

CONCLUSION

In the final analysis, when all of the factors are considered, it is our view the current situation in St Kitts and Nevis could lead to a break in the long run. By long run, we mean over a ten-year period. Before such a situation is put into effect, however, men and women of goodwill in the state and out of the state will come to the table of understanding with a view of dissuading the members of the political directorate from taking the path of least resistance. From all observations, there are people in the political directorate of both dominant parties in St Kitts and Nevis, namely the St Kitts and Nevis Labour Party and the Concerned Citizens Movement, who would not put any barriers in the way if Nevis exercises its option to break from St Kitts and Nevis. This exercise of Section 113 will close the circle for those persons who are myopic. Persons, who have a long run, holistic and realistic view of the situation, would not wish to see the state fragment any more.

While one can appreciate the desire of some die-hards Nevisians and some die-hard Kittitians to see Nevis break from St Kitts, to seek secession, and ultimately to seek Independence, the underlying core *of this movement of grandeur could turn out to be a movement of delusion.* Some people do not want to believe that St Kitts and Nevis are twins. They see St Kitts and Nevis as a marriage of convenience; furthermore, they see that marriage as a marriage that did not work and will not work, no matter how long the situation. In the minds of the people of this point of view, it is better to have a separation now and end the marriage. Politicians and non-politicians hold this view alike. There are many in the private sector that believe that Nevis could stand on its own. And then there are those who believe that both Nevis and St Kitts will suffer after the break because St Kitts and Nevis are twins bound together by blood, economics and politics. When the separation occurs, these people believe that the separation will be a rupture that will have cancerous impacts on the body economics of both islands. For our part, it seems more sensible that both islands remain as a unitary state. Larger countries in Europe with greater and more solid economic platforms are coming together. CARICOM, right at home in the backyard, is coming together in a Caribbean Single Market and Economy (CSME). In the face of this barrage of commonness, this driving force to build unity for the sake of strength, to coalesce in numbers to face the onslaught of globalisation, the secession efforts of Nevis seem to be an anathema. But then again, Nevis has a right to make its own choice. Whither thou goest? Whither St Kitts and Nevis? Wherever each island goes the economic and political reality will be tough. Some members of the political directorate in Nevis feel that the international community will not let them fall. That view might have been borderline true prior to the cataclysmic day of September 11, 2001. Now, after 9/11 (September 11, 2001) the world, as we knew it, will not be the same. Now, more than ever, there is a need for small states and microstates to work together to resolve their differences, to build on their strengths, to forge a common bond to enable then them to move along a particular trajectory of survival. We have long said that size is not a constraint to survival. Size may sometimes be an impediment to survival, but in the long run small states could survive. The question is not survival. The question is what level of survival microstates intend to have, intend to live by, intend to implement, intend to institutionalise, if their people are to compete in the international arena. St Kitts and Nevis, whither thou goest? The minds of man cannot fathom where politics will take these two microstates. I am confident, however, that whatever road the two islands take, a unified state or a fragmented former state, accountability will be critical. That is the core problematique of the question: St Kitts and Nevis, whither thou goest? It does not follow that because St Kitts and Nevis split that automatically all will be 'hunky-dory' in the new nation states. This is not an easy issue. In the Caribbean today there are similar twin or multi-island situations: Antigua and Barbuda; Trinidad and Tobago; St Vincent and the Grenadines. Farther afield there is Quebec in Canada; the Basques in Spain, et cetera. The end result of a St Kitts Nevis split has far-reaching ramifications, far beyond the shores of the twin-island federation; far beyond the shores of a nation of 45,000 souls. And that is one of the determining factors of whether St Kitts and Nevis will go their separate ways. The internal and external forces of cohesion and fragmentation are in equilibrium. When that equilibrium becomes unstable, anything is possible. It is our long-held, perhaps overly optimistic view, that both islands will remain intact. And like a marriage that has its ups and downs, but in which the husband and the wife find ways of compromising, St Kitts and Nevis will find ways of compromising. New leadership may emerge that recognise that in unity there is strength. In unity microstates can build critical mass to combat issues of pessimism, parochialism and the cancer of insularity. This is the view of one man who has lived in the region for years, who has lived in the islands for years, and who is a Kittitian of Nevisian parents. While it might be said that I have a bias, as a result of my blood-links, I am still guided by reality, reason and some indicators of foresight as those indicators are orchestrated in the international arena.

Endnotes

1. Jones-Hendrickson, 1980, pp. 3-6; pp. 10-11.
2. See Acts of the Privy Council, Colonial Series, 1613-1680. No. 150. Cited in Merrill (1958). For all practical purposes, however, the first formal suggestion of a St Kitts-Nevis link came from Colonel John Hart, who was appointed Governor of the Leeward Islands in 1721 (Burns, 1954, p.458). The council of Trade and Plantations in the islands was opposed to Hart's suggestion. The members said:

   > We can by no means think of advising His Majesty to do an act this nature by the sole power of his Prerogative without the consent of the people. If the two islands are both of them convinced that it would be for their mutual convenience that such a Union should be made between them, let their respective Councils and Assemblies address His majesty for leave to make this alteration, which will bring this affair properly under his royal consideration, and in case the same should be approved of by His Majesty, they may then pass bills for this purpose. (*Calendar of State papers, CSP, Colonial Series*, 1722, p. 23, No. 7726, p. 7; No. 40, Burns, 1954, p. 458).

3. Merrill, 1958, p. 59.
4. H.M.S.O., 1959.
5. Adedeji, 1969.
6. Nicholls and Walwyn, 1979, p. 14.
7. Nicholls and Walwyn, 1979, p. 34.
8. Kelly, 1993, p. 50.
9. Bradshaw's Party, the St Kitts-Nevis Labour Party was always a stickler for a closer union of all of the states in the Caribbean. Bradshaw wanted to make sure that the trinity of St Kitts-Nevis and Anguilla remained intact.

To this end he endeavoured to keep the islands together, at all costs. For a perspective on this issue of the closer union of the islands, see Lee L. Moore 'Labour's Position On A closer Union of the OECS', The Labour Spokesman, June 13, 1987, reprinted in Jones-Hendrickson (1988, p. 75).

10. Colville Petty and Nat Hodge, 1987, p. 62.
11. Webster, 1987, p. 21.
12. Jones-Hendrickson, 1985, p.1.
13. We present the data for 1980 and 1984 in Table 1.
14. Innis, 1983: p. 5.
15. Phillips, 1998.
16. Jones-Hendrickson, 1985, pp. 23-24.
17. Jones-Hendrickson, 1985, p. 24.

Bibliography

Adedeji, Adebayo, *Nigerian Federal Finance: Its Development and Prospects,* (New York: African Publishing Corp., 1969).

Burns, Allan, *History of the British West Indies* (London: George Allen and Unwin, 1954).

Hubbard, Vincent K., *Swords, Ships and Sugar: A History of Nevis to 1900* (Placenta, California: Premiere Editions, 1992).

Her Majesty's Stationary Office (H.M.S.O), *Report of St. Kitts-Nevis and Anguilla, 1957 and 1958* (London: H.M.S.O., 1959).

Innis, Sir Probyn, *Whither Bound: St. Kitts-Nevis* (Antigua: Antigua Printing and Publishing, 1983).

Jones-Hendrickson, S. B. 'The Dynamics of Fragmentation: The Case of St. Kitts-Nevis.' (Paper presented at an Institute of International Relations, UWI, Trinidad Conference, at Halcyon Reef Hotel, Antigua, June 4-7, 1980).

Jones-Hendrickson, S. B. 'Forces of Cohesion and Forces of Fragmentation in St. Kitts and Nevis.' (Paper presented at the Caribbean Studies Association 10th Annual Conference, San Juan, Puerto Rico, May 29-June 1, 1985).

Jones-Hendrickson, S. B. (Editor), Lee L. Moore, 'Labour And Closer Union of the OECS' in *Interviews With Lee L. Moore*, Interviewer Dawud Byron, (Frederiksted: Eastern Caribbean Institute, 1988).

Kelly, Ida, *Step By Step from Nevis to Canada,* (Bird Rock Press: Ontario, Canada, 1993).

Merrill, Gordon C. *The Historical Geography of St. Kitts and Nevis, The West Indies* (Instituto Panamericano de Geographia E Historia, 1958).

Nicholls, Wilmoth B. 'Economic Conditions and Management Policies: An Analysis of the Secessionist Movements in the State of St Kitts-Nevis-Anguilla', Bachelor's Thesis, Sussex College of Technology, Sussex, England, 1979.

Petty, Colville L and Nat Hodge, *Anguilla's Battle For Freedom, 1967* (Anguilla: Petnat Publishing Company, 1987).

Phillips, Sir Fred, *Report of A Constitutional Commission, Appointed By His Excellency the Governor General of Saint Kitts and Nevis, Volumes i, ii, iii, iv,* July 1998.

Richardson, Bonham C., *Caribbean Migrants: Environment and Human Survival on St. Kitts and Nevis* (Knoxville: The University of Tennessee Press, 1983).

Webster, Ronald, *Scrapbook of Anguilla's Revolution* (Anguilla: Seabreakers, Ltd, 1987).

20

The Privy Council and the 1990 Insurrection in Trinidad and Tobago: Judicial Confusion and Implications for the Future

Hamid A. Ghany

ESTABLISHMENT OF THE JUDICIAL COMMITTEE OF THE PRIVY COUNCIL

The Judicial Committee of the Privy Council was established by virtue of the Judicial Committee Acts of 1833[1] and 1844[2] and its purpose at that time was to hear appeals from British colonial jurisdictions. The prerogative powers of the Crown to grant special leave to appeal from colonial courts to the Privy Council was therefore established by statute.

These powers were subsequently protected in relation to the colonies with the enactment of the Colonial Laws Validity Act 1865[3] which provided that no colony could legislate in a manner repugnant to British law. To this end, no colonial legislature could abolish appeals to the Privy Council. This matter was tested in relation to Canada when the Judicial Committee of the Privy Council ruled that the Canadian Parliament was incompetent to remove the appeal by special leave from Canadian courts in criminal cases.[4]

This would soon change under the provisions of the Statute of Westminster 1931[5] which established the British Commonwealth of Nations and recognised the Dominion status of the Commonwealth of Australia, the Dominion of Canada, the Dominion of New Zealand, the Union of South Africa, the Irish Free State and Newfoundland.

According to section 2 of the Statute of Westminster:

(1) The Colonial Laws Validity Act, 1865, shall not apply to any law made after the commencement of this Act by the Parliament of a Dominion. (2) No law and no provision of any law made after the commencement of this Act by the Parliament of a Dominion shall be void or inoperative on the ground that it is repugnant to the law of England, or to the provisions of any existing or future Act of Parliament of the United Kingdom, or to any order, rule or regulation

made under any such Act, order, rule or regulation in so far as the same is part of the law of the Dominion.[6]

This formula established in section 2 of the Statute of Westminster has been copied several times (albeit suitably modified) in the Independence Acts of a number of former colonies of Great Britain. This represents one of the ways in which independence can be granted, especially as far as the removal of legislative dominance through repugnancy is concerned. The decision to retain the Judicial Committee of the Privy Council after independence has been attained is a political one to be made by the former colony or dominion as the case may be. At the time of writing, there are eleven countries that use the Judicial Committee of the Privy Council as their final court of appeal in the Commonwealth Caribbean. These are Antigua and Barbuda, The Bahamas, Barbados, Belize, Dominica, Grenada, Jamaica, St Kitts-Nevis, St Lucia, St Vincent and the Grenadines, and Trinidad and Tobago.[7]

In this context, it can be argued that there is a strong judicial bond between the Commonwealth Caribbean and Great Britain. This is certainly reinforced by the fact that when Trinidad and Tobago became a republic in 1976, the government chose to retain the Judicial Committee in its new constitution[8] as the final court of appeal, while the Government of Grenada chose to reinstate the Judicial Committee as their final court of appeal in 1991.[9]

Composition of the Judicial Committee of the Privy Council

The Judicial Committee is comprised mainly of British Lords of Appeal who are appointed members of the House of Lords. These Lords of Appeal in Ordinary are appointed for life as members of the House of Lords under the provisions of the Appellate Jurisdiction Act 1876.[10] However, they serve in their judicial capacities until the age of seventyfive, while those Lords of Appeal who have been appointed after 1993 may now only serve until a retirement age of seventy under the provisions of the Judicial Pensions and Retirement Act 1993. In spite of this, they may be invited by the Lord Chancellor to sit in appeals before the Judicial Committee.[11] The Committee may also consist of judicial officers who are members of Her Majesty's Privy Council in Commonwealth countries from which appeals still lie to the Judicial Committee.[12] The Lord Chancellor is a Cabinet Minister, the head of the Judiciary, and the presiding officer in the House of Lords. He derives his appointment from advice tendered to the monarch by the prime minister and by convention he is a cabinet minister. By virtue of his office, he is head of the Judiciary as well as presiding officer in the House of Lords. In relation to the work of the Judicial Committee, it is the Lord Chancellor who is responsible for choosing the panel of judges that will sit and hear cases that come before the Judicial Committee.[13]

In this regard, it must be noted that the choices made by the Lord Chancellor as to which Lords of Appeal will sit in any particular case before the Judicial Committee must also be weighed against his other functions in relation to arranging the work of the House of Lords as the final court of appeal in Great Britain. It may not be possible to spare certain judges who are ideally suited for particular cases before the Judicial Committee, because they are involved in other matters before the House of Lords. This may have the effect of delaying proceedings before the Judicial Committee until such time as a particular judge or judges can be made available.[14]

In delivering its judgments, the Judicial Committee may reverse earlier opinions expressed in prior judgments. At the same time, it should be noted that before 1966 the Judicial Committee was required to give unanimous judgments as it was deemed improper for divided advice to be tendered to the Crown. This was changed in 1966 by the Judicial Committee (Dissenting Opinions) Order 1966[15] which made provision for dissenting opinions to be given in judgments delivered by the Judicial Committee.

In the case of those countries of the Commonwealth that became republics and retained the facility of appeals to the Judicial Committee, it should be noted that the process would be regulated by the constitution or local legislation. In such instances, the Judicial Committee would advise the Head of State of the republic as to its opinion and enforcement of the decision would be regulated in accordance with the constitution or the relevant law.[16]

THE 1990 ATTEMPTED COUP AND THE COURT PROCESS

On 27th July 1990, there was an attempted coup d'état by a group known as the JamaatalMuslimeen, which failed. One group of insurgents attacked the Parliament Building while the House of Representatives was in session, another group attacked the lone television station and seized control of it. In the aftermath of this failed attempt to overthrow the State, there was the commencement of criminal proceedings against the insurgents. It emerged that they had been given a general amnesty by the acting president of the Republic, which had been signed by him.

The acting president retained the original and initialed a copy, which was delivered to them by Canon Knolly Clarke of the Holy Trinity Cathedral who was acting as a mediator.[17] At the end of the crisis, the insurgents were charged with varying offences such as treason and murder as well as other offences related to the insurrection itself. However, they argued that the acting president of the Republic of Trinidad and Tobago had given them an amnesty document and to prosecute them was a violation of their constitutional rights.

The 114 insurgents commenced proceedings in the High Court by way of originating motion alleging that since they were the beneficiaries of a valid pardon the decision to detain and prosecute them was unconstitutional. To this the State entered an objection so as to allow the criminal proceedings, which had already commenced to continue to completion. Furthermore, eight of the insurgents applied to the High Court for leave to issue a writ of habeas corpus seeking their immediate release owing to the fact that they alleged that their detention was illegal.

Both matters were consolidated on appeal to the Judicial Committee in *Phillip and Others v the D.P.P. and Another* and *Phillip and Others v Commissioner of Prisons and Another.*[18] The Judicial Committee in allowing the appeals directed that the matters before them be consolidated for the determination by the High Court of the writ of habeas corpus as well as the validity of the amnesty granted to them.[19] What was amazing about this decision of the Judicial Committee was the fact that they accepted the validity of the amnesty document in the absence of any pleadings by the State on this issue. After all, the State was only entering an objection to the civil matters taking precedence over the criminal matters. Lord Ackner delivered the judgment of the Judicial Committee.

This course of events was commented upon by Michael de la Bastide, Q.C. in delivering the Anthony Bland Memorial lecture at the Cave Hill (Barbados) campus of the University of the West Indies on 23rd March 1995 (about two months before he was sworn in as Chief Justice of Trinidad and Tobago). In criticising the approach of Lord Ackner, de la Bastide said:

> At the stage at which Lord Ackner wrote his judgment, no evidence had been filed on behalf of the State for it was relying on a preliminary objection. Nevertheless, in the course of his judgment Lord Ackner made certain statements of fact based on the evidence filed by the Muslimeen without any qualification or reservation, as though the facts so stated had either been found or conceded.[20]

This was a most serious allegation and went to the issue of incompetence. Indeed, the central issue to be examined in this case was the view on the nature of the power of pardon when exercised on a pretrial basis. This apparent clarification of the view of the Judicial Committee on a pretrial pardon would have been instructive for the judges in Trinidad and Tobago who would subsequently determine the outcome of these cases that were now being returned to Trinidad and Tobago for adjudication. Indeed, it may be argued that the opinion expressed by the Judicial Committee regarding the pretrial power of pardon may have influenced judges in Trinidad and Tobago to some extent. In this context it will be useful to examine the issue of a pretrial pardon.

The PreTrial Power of Pardon

Section 87(1) of the Constitution of Trinidad and Tobago states as follows:

The President may grant to any person a pardon, either free or subject to lawful conditions, respecting any offences that he may have committed. The power of the President under this subsection may be exercised by him either before or after the person is charged with any offence and before he is convicted thereof.[21]

In the exercise of this power, the president is required to act on the advice of the Cabinet.[22] However, in their interpretation of this pretrial pardon, the Judicial Committee adopted the view that it resembled the pardoning power given in the Constitution of the United States to the President of the United States.[23] This is, perhaps, the point at which the Judicial Committee made a grave constitutional error insofar as they equated the exercise of a presidential power in a presidential system of government with the exercise of a presidential power in a parliamentary system of government. Clearly, the Judicial Committee was misled in their belief that the exercise of the power of pardon in both situations could be equated.

They relied upon observations made by one of the Founding Fathers of the United States Constitution, Alexander Hamilton. According to them:

It is interesting to observe that in the American case *Murphy v Ford* (1975) 390 F. Supp. 1372 decided in the United States District Court of Michigan, in which the validity of a pardon granted by President Ford to former President Nixon was challenged, there is quoted at p. 1373, the following observation of Alexander Hamilton in The Federalist No. 740 in 1788 explaining why the Founding Fathers gave the President a discretionary power to pardon: The principal argument for reposing the power of pardoning...[in] the Chief

> Magistrate Hamilton wrote, is this: in seasons of insurrection or rebellion, there are often critical moments, when a welltimed offer of pardon to the insurgents or rebels may restore the tranquillity of the commonwealth; and which, if suffered to pass unimproved, it may never be possible afterwards to recall ... [24]

This view was criticised by de la Bastide[25] on the ground that it amounted to bartering the lives of innocent people in order to bring an end to an insurrection. To that end, he surmised, this was tantamount to making deals with terrorists. It is difficult to accept that the Judicial Committee would promote the idea of making deals with terrorists in situations that would require delicate negotiations involving the lives of innocent people. However, on the face of the record, that is what they were advocating in this case.

The Judicial Committee must have been aware of the fact that Trinidad and Tobago operates a parliamentary system of government in which there is a Cabinet that is made up of a prime minister drawn from the House of Representatives and other ministers drawn from among the members of the House of Representatives or the Senate.[26] Furthermore, that in the exercise of his powers, the president acts, in general, on the advice of the Cabinet. Exceptions to this principle are that the president may, in constitutionally or legally stated situations, act on the advice of a person or authority other than the Cabinet, act after consultation, act in his own discretion or in his own deliberate judgment.[27] This is very different when compared to the system of government in the United States. Insofar as the power of pardon is concerned, the United States Constitution states as follows:

> The President shall be commanderinchief of the army and navy of the United States, and of the militia of the several States, when called into the actual service of the United States; he may require the opinion, in writing, of the principal officer in each of the executive departments, upon any subject relating to the duties of their respective offices, and he shall have power to grant reprieves and pardons for offenses against the United States, except in cases of impeachment.[28]

Clearly, under the United States Constitution, the president will take political responsibility for the grant of a pardon owing to the way in which it is exercised. Trinidad and Tobago's 1976 republican Constitution made a specific inclusion of a subsection providing for a pretrial pardon[29] largely because of the currency of events at the time of drafting the constitution arising out of the pardon granted by President Gerald Ford to former President Richard Nixon in 1974.[30]

However, political responsibility for the exercise of such a pretrial power of pardon clearly rests with the Cabinet, rather than with the president, having regard to the constitutional provisions surrounding the exercise of presidential powers in Trinidad and Tobago.[31] Did the acting president exercise his powers in respect of the amnesty document that was given to the Muslimeen by Canon Clarke in an extraconstitutional manner? That is to say, the document itself did not disclose the source of the president's authority and, in failing to do so, did not disclose where political responsibility for the decision lay. Having regard to the wording of sections 87(1) and 80(1) of the Constitution, the political responsibility ought to lie with the Cabinet if a pretrial power of pardon is exercised by the president. The amnesty document read as follows:

> Joseph Emmanuel Carter, as required of me by the document headed Major Points of Agreement hereby grant an amnesty to all those involved in acts of insurrection commencing at approximately 5.30 pm on Friday 27th July 1990 and ending upon the safe return of all Members of Parliament held captive on 27 July 1990. This amnesty is granted for the purpose of avoiding physical injury to the Members of Parliament referred to above and is therefore subject to the complete fulfillment of the obligation safely to return them.[32]

The acting president did not exercise his powers in accordance with the Constitution, but rather in accordance with the Major Heads of Agreement as required of him. Where was the source from which this power was exercised? Who was politically responsible for the grant of this amnesty? In the United States the president could have exercised his power to grant a pardon in this way because the power is vested in him and is exercisable by him directly.

In Trinidad and Tobago the president cannot exercise the pretrial power of pardon without reference to the Constitution and political responsibility for it must rest with the Cabinet. This raises the question about what was the collective responsibility of the Cabinet on this issue or whether the intention of the president, acting in his own deliberate judgment, was designed to deceive the insurgents by giving them what was an invalid amnesty document.

It is now clearly established that the State intended to give the Muslimeen a document that was not likely to be legally binding as a means of tricking them into a release in exchange for a pardon that could not stand up to court scrutiny.[33] Was it the collective responsibility of the Cabinet to deceive the Muslimeen by giving them a bogus amnesty in return for the release of the hostages? Or was it the deliberate judgment of the acting president to do so? There was never any intention to allow the Muslimeen to walk free. Indeed, the Prime Minister A.N.R. Robinson (who was one of the hostages in the Parliament

Building) urged the security forces to attack with full force before the negotiations with the Muslimeen had been completed.[34]

The Judicial Committee appear not to have taken into account the fact that A.N.R. Robinson continued to effectively hold the office of Prime Minister until August 4, 1990 when Mr Winston Dookeran was authorised to perform the functions of prime minister by the president acting on the advice of the prime minister.[35] The Judicial Committee failed to address the issue of political responsibility for the decision to offer an amnesty. Instead, they treated it as though the Acting President was competent to grant the Muslimeen a pardon as if he were acting in his own deliberate judgment. As far as can be seen, it was not the intention of the Cabinet to grant a valid amnesty to the Muslimeen insurgents[36] no more than it was the intention of the Cabinet to advise the Acting President to declare a state of emergency under sections 10(4) and 8(2) of the Constitution on the same day that the amnesty document was prepared and delivered to the Muslimeen.[37]

The Judicial Committee did not have the benefit of evidence filed by the State in *Phillip and Others v the D.P.P. and Another* and *Phillip and Others v Commissioner of Prisons and Another*[38] as they were relying on a preliminary objection, rather than making their substantive case.[39] Under those circumstances, it was improper and misleading for the Judicial Committee to have arrived at the following conclusion as expressed by Lord Ackner in delivering the opinion of the Board:

> If the applicants are only able to assert their pardon by way of a plea in bar at their eventual trial, as the Court of Appeal has held in both judgments the subject of these appeals, it follows that they are likely to remain in custody for many years on charges relating to offences for which, for the purpose of these appeals only, it must be assumed they have been validly pardoned.[40]

This was the most powerful signal that the Judicial Committee could have sent to the judges in Trinidad and Tobago that they believed (in 1992) that the Muslimeen insurgents had been validly pardoned. At the same time, it should be borne in mind that they were sending the issue of the validity of the pardon back to the courts in Trinidad and Tobago for determination. The way in which it was done was bordering upon giving instructions to the courts below to rule in a particular way as far as the validity of the pardon was concerned. When the courts in Trinidad and Tobago subsequently ruled in favour of the Muslimeen on the validity of the pardon, that substantive issue returned to the Judicial Committee on appeal from the Attorney General of Trinidad and Tobago and the Director of Public Prosecutions in 1994 in the case of *Attorney General of Trinidad and Tobago and Another v Phillip and Others*.[41]

Duress and the Validity of the Amnesty

The writ of habeas corpus issued to free the 114 insurgents on 30th June 1992 by order of Brooks, J. in the High Court of Trinidad and Tobago and the validity of the pardon was confirmed in those proceedings. On 9th November 1993, the Court of Appeal of Trinidad and Tobago (by a two to one margin) dismissed the State's appeal of the decision of Brooks, J. The Judicial Committee delivered its judgment on the State's appeal on 4th October 1994 in *Attorney General of Trinidad and Tobago and Another v Phillip and Others.*[42] The issue of the validity of the amnesty returned for a second opinion by the Judicial Committee. If the safe release of the hostages was a condition of the amnesty document being offered, then the issue of duress must arise. However, the Judicial Committee adopted a curious approach to this matter, which will impact on future judicial opinions should this issue ever arise again. Furthermore, the Judicial Committee was forced to search for a way out of their earlier opinion on the issue of a pretrial pardon. In the process of doing this, they have held out conflicting interpretations of the power to grant a pretrial pardon in the parliamentary democracies of the Commonwealth Caribbean where such powers exist (now or in the future). Perhaps, the factual contradictions that revealed the essence of how the Judicial Committee misled itself the first time around when compared to the second is best expressed by a comparison of the facts as stated by them in both cases on the issue of the amnesty itself as follows: 1992 Opinion:

> Canon Clarke witnessed the signing of the pardon by the Acting President, who retained the original. A signed copy was given to Canon Clarke for delivery to the applicants, one of who made a photocopy of it in the presence of the Honourable Mr. Kelvin Ramnath, Member of Parliament, who produced and identified that copy in the proceedings. The authenticity of the copy was proved by Canon Clarke.[43]

1994 Opinion:

> Initially, the acting president was not prepared to sign a draft of an amnesty, which had been prepared. But after Canon Clarke had expressed great fear for his life and those of the hostages, if he returned empty handed without some concrete response, the acting president was persuaded to change his mind. He signed the draft and initialled a copy, which he gave to Canon Clarke for delivery to the Muslimeen. He told Canon Clarke to tell them he had signed the original.[44]

These two statements of fact reveal the extent to which the Judicial Committee misled itself the first time around when they were relying only upon evidence filed by the Muslimeen. Having seen the evidence of the State in the second case, the Judicial Committee altered the facts to disclose the duress being placed upon the mediator for the State and the Muslimeen which they did not acknowledge the first time around. Furthermore, the signed copy of the pardon in the 1992 opinion became the draft of an amnesty of which the acting president; initialled a copy to be given to the Muslimeen in the 1994 opinion.

In spite of this obvious alteration of the facts, the Judicial Committee held that the amnesty document signed by the acting president was a valid pardon and could not be regarded as an offer of a pardon to end the insurgency. The fact that the Muslimeen did not comply with the conditions of the pardon, but rather sought to negotiate further with the State had the effect of invalidating the pardon. According to the Judicial Committee:

> Having received the pardon, they sought to achieve their other objectives, which were reflected in the Major Points of Agreement. Although the period of negotiation may have been protracted by the tactics perfectly properly adopted by Colonel Theodore to bring the insurrection to a peaceful conclusion, until the end of the second stage of the insurrection, the Muslimeen were still intent on achieving their broader objectives. They were certainly not surrendering or treating the insurrection as at an end. In doing this they were not complying with the condition to which the pardon was subject and as a result, even on the most charitable interpretation, the pardon was no longer capable of being brought into effect by complying with the condition to which it was subject. It follows that Brooks J. and the majority of the Court of Appeal was wrong in treating the pardon as valid.[45]

The Judicial Committee did a complete turnaround on the issue of the validity of the amnesty document signed by the acting president. Whereas in the earlier case (1992), Lord Ackner wrote as if the pardon were valid and that was not in dispute; in the second case (1994), the Judicial Committee had the benefit of pleadings by the State which substantially altered their view from the earlier position that the Judicial Committee seemed to have adopted. However, the ground on which they did their turnaround is dubious to say the least and offers good advice for future terrorists on how to commit the crime and structure their negotiations in order to escape any punishment.

The contrast can be seen in the following statement:

> that the applicants had established prima facie that they were the beneficiaries
> of a valid pardon which would render their detention and imprisonment on
> charges relating to offences covered thereby unlawful...[46]

When this is contrasted with the view expressed above[47] it is clear that the
preference shown by the Judicial Committee in the 1992 case could have
influenced the judges in Trinidad and Tobago to decide that the amnesty was
valid. This point of view was advanced by de la Bastide.[48] The overall effect of
these two judgments by the Judicial Committee has been to leave the Executive
in great doubt as to how to handle any future insurrection. The Judicial
Committee has shown great indifference on the key issue of whether or not the
lives of innocent people ought to be bartered by the welltimed issue of a pardon
with conditions attached to it.

Two major issues were not addressed by them satisfactorily. The effect of
duress on the grant of a pardon and the issue of ministerial advice being tendered
to the Head of State. These issues were treated in the following way by the
Judicial Committee:

> It is not necessary to decide on this appeal whether a pardon, which is formally
> granted, would ever be set aside for duress. For it to be capable of being set
> aside would require very exceptional circumstances, circumstances where, in
> the case of Trinidad and Tobago, it could be said that the document which
> records the purported grant of a pardon was not the president's document,
> notwithstanding that it bore his signature.[49]

The Director of Public Prosecutions also argued that the pardon had not
been properly constituted or promulgated. He was, however, refused leave to
advance a further argument, in support of which he had prepared a supplemental
case. This was that the pardon was also invalid or a nullity because under the
Constitution the power of pardon can only be exercised on the advice of the
cabinet and it had been issued without that advice.[50]

On the issue of duress, one cannot say that the pardon was formally
granted because the State led evidence to show that it was not. The Judicial
Committee was very aware of that evidence, but chose to circumvent it in the
following way:

> A striking feature of this case is that the acting president states that he never
> intended the pardon documents which he signed or initialled to take effect as a

pardon, unless and until he had received a recommendation from the duly appointed prime minister that a pardon should be granted. However, here the Board agrees with the approach adopted in the judgments in the lower courts that whether or not a pardon has been granted is to be determined objectively and in the circumstances which prevailed a pardon must be regarded as having been granted.[51] This was the escape route used by the Judicial Committee to get away from the fact that they had misled the courts in Trinidad and Tobago on their interpretation of a pretrial pardon in the 1992 case without the benefit of the evidence led by the State. Clearly the Acting President was trying to negotiate with the insurgents and was very conscious of the fact that he could not grant a proper pardon because he was not acting on political advice. It was never the intention of the State to grant a pretrial pardon and both the document and the evidence of the State proved that. The Acting President could not have been expected to take political responsibility for a power that he could not exercise in his own deliberate judgment, but instead had to be exercised on the advice of Cabinet. The duly appointed Prime Minister, A.N.R. Robinson, did not have his functions transferred to another Minister owing to illness until 4th August 1990.[52]

Under these circumstances, the acting president discharged his functions properly by not granting a pardon, but rather sent the draft of an amnesty with his initials as a negotiating tool. The acting president dealt with the situation by trying to negotiate a way out of the crisis in order to secure the release of the hostages (of whom one was the duly appointed prime minister). The only exercise of constitutional powers during this period was the declaration of a state of emergency on 28th July 1990,[53] that was based on the fact that the Prime Minister did not cooperate with the insurgents in the Parliament Building and was, therefore, in favour of military action as a response. The Judicial Committee were aware of this as stated by them as follows:

> The members of Parliament at the Red House were kept bound hand and foot and made to lie prone on the floor at gunpoint. During the Friday evening Abdullah wanted the prime minister to give orders for the troops to be withdrawn. He bravely did not cooperate and was shot and wounded.[54]

It is obvious that the duly appointed prime minister wanted to challenge the Muslimeen insurgents with force and his resistance to them was met with personal injury. The acting president did not need any further advice from the prime minister to exercise his constitutional powers to declare a state of emergency. Furthermore, he was clear in his mind that he was not going to grant them a pretrial pardon, but he was going to try to negotiate a settlement even if it meant using a ruse in order to restore stability and remove the immense pressure that had been placed upon the functioning of constitutional government in Trinidad and Tobago by the actions of the insurgents.

The judgment of the Judicial Committee in this case did not investigate the role of the Constitution in the exercise of presidential powers completely. On the one hand, the Judicial Committee addressed the issue of pretrial pardons on the basis of political thought in the United States on this subject; on the other hand, it sought to link the basis for such political thought on constitutional practice in the United Kingdom. However, the Judicial Committee missed the fact that the Constitution of Trinidad and Tobago cannot be compared to the United Kingdom owing to significant differences (as with other Commonwealth Caribbean constitutions).[55] Their ignorance or their coverup of their incompetence is recorded as follows:

> Both under English law and under the Constitution of Trinidad and Tobago a pardon should not be treated as being analogous to a contract. It does not derive its authority from agreement. It is not dependent upon acceptance of the subject of the pardon. In England its authority is derived from the prerogative and in Trinidad and Tobago its authority is dependent upon the Constitution.[56]

If the Judicial Committee is so clear as to the source of authority for a pardon in Trinidad and Tobago, why did they not rule that the document was unconstitutional and declare it null and void because the acting president improperly executed it? Instead they chose to deny the State the opportunity to argue this point before them.[57]

The only reason that they apparently could not declare it unconstitutional was to protect the mistake made by Lord Ackner and the Board in the 1992 case and so they voided the pardon on grounds that the Muslimeen did not discharge the socalled; lawful conditions in the amnesty document. The conditions in the amnesty document would have been rendered unlawful if the Judicial Committee had declared the amnesty unconstitutional.

As far as duress is concerned, the Judicial Committee chose to take a very literal view of this insofar as they refused to establish a precedent on the issue and used an analagous situation in Malaysia. They stated:

> No precedent has been found for any court setting aside a pardon on the grounds of duress. The closest analogous situation which has been identified is the decision of Tan J. in the High Court of Malaysia in *Mustapha v Mohammad* [1987] LRC (Const.) 16. In that case, in considering an allegation of duress in

relation to the appointment and removal of a chief minister, Tan J. (at p. 94) looked for guidance as to the meaning of duress from the *Oxford English Dictionary* and *Jowitt's Dictionary of English Law* (2nd edn., 1977) vol. 1, both of which referred to direct physical violence, or pressure, or actual imprisonment to the person whose act is being challenged and regarded that degree of duress as being required in the situation there being considered. In the case of a challenge to the validity of a pardon at least direct action of this nature would be required to establish duress. The conduct relied upon in this case is not of this direct nature and the decisions in the courts below were clearly correct on this issue.[58]

If this was the literal interpretation that they were prepared to use, why did they not see the duress facing Canon Clarke (the mediator) who told the acting president that he feared for his life if he returned empty handed to the Parliament Building?[59] Was it not clear to them that the mediator who was in a position to resolve the crisis was at personal risk if the Acting President did not send some kind of document? How much more direct pressure did the Acting President need to have exerted upon him for the standard outlined above to be satisfied? Why was the Judicial Committee reluctant to establish a new precedent for; setting aside a pardon on the ground of duress? Once again, this goes back to the initial error made by Lord Ackner and the Board in the 1992 case. The Judicial Committee had to engage in a coverup, rather than a correction.

CONCLUSION

The implications for the future are disturbing and terrorist insurgents have now been given a road map for such future actions with the compliments of the Judicial Committee of the Privy Council. The State is now constrained to negotiate within the confines of the Constitution when dealing with terrorists in the future. There is no extraconstitutional facility available to State officials by which to resolve similar situations. The balance has been tilted in favour of the insurgents of the future because the Judicial Committee chose to consider irrelevant facts and to ignore relevant facts in its two judgments surrounding the 1990 attempted coup in Trinidad and Tobago.

Endnotes

1. 3 & 4 Wm. IV, c.41.
2. 7 & 8 Vict., c.69.
3. 28 & 29 Vict., c.63.
4. See Nadan v R. [1926] A.C. 482.
5. 22 Geo. V, c.4.
6. 22 Geo. V, c.4., s.2.
7. See S. de Smith and R. Brazier, Constitutional and Administrative Law, (London: Penguin, 1994), p.170. It should also be noted that Grenada resumed appeals to the Privy Council in 1991 after they had been abolished by the People's Revolutionary Government in 1979.
8. Laws of Trinidad and Tobago, Ch. 1:01, Schedule, s.109.
9. See note 7 supra.
10. 39 & 40 Vict., c.59.
11. de Smith and Brazier, Constitutional and Administrative Law, p.334.
12. de Smith and Brazier, Constitutional and Administrative Law, p.169.
13. de Smith and Brazier, Constitutional and Administrative Law, p.410.
14. de Smith and Brazier, Constitutional and Administrative Law, p.334.
15. S.I. 1966 / No 1100.
16. For example, in the case of Trinidad and Tobago, section 109 of the 1976 republic constitution (Ch. 1.:01, Schedule) specifically provides that any appeal to the Judicial Committee with the special leave of the Committee itself shall lie in the same manner as if it had been brought with the special leave of Her Majesty to Her Majesty in Council. Furthermore, all prerogatives and privileges vested in Her Majesty in relation to Trinidad and Tobago were deemed to be vested in the State and exercisable by the President.
17. See *Attorney General of Trinidad and Tobago and Another v Phillip and Others* [1995] 1 AER 93 at 99.
18. [1992] 2 WLR 211.
19. [1992] 2 WLR 211 at 212 and 224.
20. Michael de la Bastide, Q.C., Anthony J. Bland Memorial Lecture, University of the West Indies, Cave Hill, Barbados, 23rd March, 1995, pp. 22-23.
21. Laws of Trinidad and Tobago, Ch. 1:01, Schedule, s. 87(1).
22. Laws of Trinidad and Tobago, Ch. 1:01, Schedule, s. 80(1).
23. [1992] 2 WLR 211 at 214.
24. [1992] 2 WLR 211 at 214.

25. Michael de la Bastide, Q.C., Anthony J. Bland Memorial Lecture, University of the West Indies, Cave Hill, Barbados, 23rd March,1995, p. 22.
26. Laws of Trinidad and Tobago, Ch. 1:01, Schedule, s. 76.
27. Laws of Trinidad and Tobago, Ch. 1:01, Schedule, s. 80.
28. Constitution of the United States of America, Article 2, section 2(1).
29. Laws of Trinidad and Tobago, Ch. 1:01, Schedule, s. 87(1).
30. See note 24 supra.
31. Laws of Trinidad and Tobago, Ch. 1:01, Schedule, s. 80(1).
32. [1992] 2 WLR 211 at 214.
33. See Ramesh Deosaran, *A Society Under Siege*, (Trinidad : ANSA Mc Al Psychological Research Centre, U.W.I., 1993), pp. 4748.
34. Deosaran, *A Society Under Siege*, p. 47.
35. *Trinidad and Tobago Gazette*, Vol. 29, No. 213, Gazette Notice 1616.
36. Deosaran, *A Society Under Siege*, p. 47.
37. Legal Notice No. 140, 28th July, 1990.
38. [1992] 2 WLR 211
39. See note 20 supra.
40. [1992] 2 WLR 211 at 215.
41. [1995] 1 AER 93.
42. [1995] 1 AER 93.
43. [1992] 2 WLR 211 at 214.
44. [1995] 1 AER 93 at 99.
45. [1995] 1 AER 93 at 107 and 108.
46. [1992] 2 WLR 211 at 212.
47. (note. 45 supra),
48. Michael de la Bastide, Q.C., Anthony J. Bland Memorial Lecture, University of the West Indies, Cave Hill, Barbados, 23rd March,1995, p. 27.
49. [1995] 1 AER 93 at 103.
50. [1995] 1 AER 93 at 97.
51. [1995] 1 AER 93 at 102.
52. See note 35 supra.
53. See note 37 supra.
54. [1995] 1 AER 93 at 98.
55. See Hamid Ghany, The Creation of Legislative Institutions in the Commonwealth Caribbean: The Myth of the Transfer of the Westminster Model5, Congressional Studies Journal, Vol. 2(1) 1994, pp. 3449.
56. [1995] 1 AER 93 at 102.
57. See note 49 supra.
58. [1995] 1 AER 93 at 104.
59. See note 44 supra.

* * *

21

'New Horizons in Caribbean Democracy'
Lecture Delivered to the Cave Hill Campus Law Society on: Governance and Democracy in the Caribbean in the 21st Century

Hon Dr Kenny D. Anthony, Prime Minister of St Lucia
In Celebration of Law Week, 15th March 2001

INTRODUCTION

The question of Democracy and Good Governance has become a burning issue in the Caribbean. Not only has the process of globalisation placed these issues at the centre of our political discourse, but the continuing process of economic liberalisation and integration has challenged fundamentally our old assumptions of democracy, the relationship of citizens to the structures of power, and our attitudes to fundamental questions like accountability, representation and participation.

It is these questions, which I assume have been sufficiently troubling to the Cave Hill Law Society, which accounts for our collective presence here today. I therefore wish to congratulate the Law Society for its vision and foresight, and for placing these questions before us.

THE PRESENT CONTEXT

It can be strongly argued that the present period marks a break with the past. The period has witnessed the transfer of power from the first generation of post-colonial leaders to a new generation, on whose shoulders have fallen the task of managing Caribbean societies into the new era of globalisation. Consequently, a new breed of politician has emerged, and enshrined in their personalities, is the blueprint for a new chapter in Caribbean politics.

We are currently witnessing the demise of the old traditional politicians who treated their politics as personal property. Many of these politicians created or inherited political parties in the 1960s, and have subsequently found it extremely difficult to relinquish or transfer power to younger politicians, even to those who had been their eager and loyal followers.

This was witnessed with Dame Eugenia Charles in Dominica, with Sir John Compton of St Lucia and with Sir James Mitchell of St Vincent and the Grenadines. The JLP of Edward Seaga will soon be undergoing a similar crisis of its own. In all of these cases the decision to relinquish power has been undertaken grudgingly, with the old leaders fighting valiantly to define the conditions under which their departure from the political scene would be affected. In most cases this has been reflected in their attempts to choose a successor over the heads of the populace and indeed against the wishes of their own party hierarchies.

In other instances, this is seen in the attempt to continue in the role of senior ministers, providing little room for the chosen successor to place his personal political stamp on the political process. Thus in many cases the office was relinquished while the power and privileges of Prime Ministership continued uninterrupted. One of the most telling failures of the old traditional politicians is the fact that their successors as well as the political parties which they left behind, have been unequivocally rejected by the populace at the first opportunity where public opinion has been called upon to adjudicate in these matters.

WORLD ECONOMY COMPELLING RE-ADJUSTMENTS

It is important to note that the demise of the old post-colonial politics and politicians and the emergence of the new breed of leadership coincide with major transformations in the world economy. These transformations, in themselves, are compelling re-adjustments in the internal civic relationships in our societies. Significantly, one of the urgent tasks of the new generation of Caribbean leadership is to manage the transition from the old political economy to the new, and to create a new democratic ethos for these new times.

It might be argued that we are beginning to see unusual political sophistry. Yet I should add that it is as yet too early to determine whether we are playing with form or substance. Whatever the truth of this question, it is clear that the emerging democracy involves a fundamental redistribution of political power. At its core, is the engagement of civil society, both in domestic and regional levels of power relations. On the negative side, we are also witnessing the emergence of an uneven and disproportionate spread of power among the social partners. In particular the period has witnessed the weakening of the trade union movement vis-à-vis the NGO movement and the private sector.

POLITICS OF INCLUSION

Despite these limitations, the redistribution of political power is seen in the conscious attempts by the new Caribbean leadership to engage civil society in the decision-making process. On one level this is reflected in a far greater tolerance towards political opponents and in the more genuine attempts to include opposition groups in decision making, and the 'politics of inclusion' or the 'politics of assimilation', is now becoming the order of the day.

One extraordinary example of this tendency can be seen in the case of Barbados where the ruling party has decimated the opposition by appropriating the personnel from the opposition DLP, further consolidating the power base derived from its huge parliamentary majority in the last election. We witness an almost similar approach in the case of Trinidad and Tobago.

These developments have led one regional political scientist to argue that the 'winner take all thesis is being refined'. Coming against a background where our recent electoral trends show an increasing tendency towards electoral landslides and one-sided parliaments, the end of 'winner take all politics' points to a growing degree of political sophistication on the part of the new Caribbean leadership. All in all, these developments create a context in which new features of Caribbean democracy are beginning to emerge.

NEW FEATURES OF CARIBBEAN DEMOCRACY

In the first place, there is a growing recognition that there are basic standards of democracy, which must be honoured and observed. Consistent with this, is the emergence of new mechanisms of political accountability, not only at the domestic level, but at the regional level as well.

At the domestic level, many of the islands have instituted measures to deepen and strengthen internal democracy. Thus, for example, Public Accounts Committees have been established in several islands to monitor the finances of public officials and as a safeguard against corruption. Most territories have witnessed far greater levels of public discussion and more open scrutiny of the work of governments. There have also been sustained efforts to engage the public in major policy reform efforts. Thus for example, in St Lucia, we have engaged in public consultations on Carnival, Sports, Youth policy, Public Sector reform, Education reform, and Labour reform. Discussions on Local Government reform are currently on-going, and new legislation will soon be put in place to modernise and democratise local government in St Lucia.

Many territories have also endeavoured to engage in Constitutional reform in order to create a new legislative super-structure consistent with the new democratic ethos. Thus, both Barbados and Jamaica have engaged in public consultations on Constitutional reform.

In Barbados, the question of republican status has been placed before the people and, as the constitution requires, await their verdict in a referendum. It is also important to note that whilst the question of the republican status is the current headline-grabber, there are other fundamental questions on Barbadian democracy now before the Barbadian people.

COMMITMENT TO CHARTER OF CIVIL SOCIETY

These efforts at deepening democracy find similar reflection at the regional level. All of the Caribbean territories have committed themselves to the CARICOM Charter of Civil Society, which is a fundamental statement on the region's governments' commitment to upholding human rights and the pursuit of good governance and democratic norms. The signatories to the CARICOM Charter of Civil Society have agreed to establish National Monitoring Committees made up of the leaders of the various branches of civil society, to monitor governments' compliance to the CARICOM Charter.

The new commitment of the region to democratic norms has meant that an atmosphere more conducive to the resolution of internal disputes has been facilitated. The interventionist role of CARICOM in resolving the internal political disputes in this period is unprecedented both in terms of frequency of intervention, as well as the level and outcomes of this involvement. Indeed, I am of the view that even CARICOM is not fully seized of the significance of its involvement, despite the fact that it has appointed a regional Prime Minister with responsibility for Justice and Good Governance in the region to undertake its regional responsibilities.

Thus far, CARICOM has engaged in dispute resolution in four member states, namely Guyana, St Vincent & the Grenadines, Haiti, and Trinidad and Tobago. The Trinidad example deserves special mention since this was the first time Trinidad, in living history, has called upon the region to assist in resolving an internal dispute.

A troubling question however, remains. How far should CARICOM's jurisdiction extend? More directly, is there the danger that in settling disputes, the democratic will of the electorate could be subverted? What is clear therefore is that the new generation of Caribbean leadership has endeavoured to refashion the internal democracy of Caribbean societies, albeit within the existing rules of engagement. Where such leadership inherited a tradition of periodic elections and a commitment to mass mobilisation within the political parties and trade union movement, the new leadership has sought to build on this foundation and to further deepen the fabric of Caribbean democracy.

Threats to Democracy

However, whilst we applaud the new efforts at democratisation it is also important to understand that the new global environment also possesses the potential to undermine the fabric of Caribbean democracy. My essential warning is that we should not take Caribbean democracy for granted.

There can be no question that Caribbean economies are under great pressure and if they fall apart, then the political changes, which are so badly needed, may fail to find expression. Already, we are beginning to find that the problems of crime, social banditry, and social decay are threatening to erode the economic gains made by Caribbean societies over the years. Increasingly, larger amounts of resources now have to be devoted to the task of law and order and social control. Our historical knowledge also teaches us that periods of economic crisis have been fertile soil for the growth of Fascism and other undemocratic extremist tendencies.

It is interesting to note that the old Caribbean democracy was sustained by the region's particular mode of insertion into the world economy. Preferential protection for the Caribbean's primary products on the European market resulted in a smug arrogance on the part of the traditional leadership, that the Caribbean's economic welfare was largely secure. This smugness was also reflected in their inability or unwillingness to include Caribbean populations in the decision-making structure beyond what was permitted under the Westminster parliamentary democracy. It was these tendencies, which Maurice Bishop described as 'two-second' democracy.

Similarly, such leadership was intolerant of criticism, and in many instances did not hesitate to use force to defeat political opponents. Eric Gairy's Grenada and Forbes Burnham's Guyana were only the most extreme examples of these tendencies. The rest of the Caribbean differed from these countries only in quantitative terms.

In contrast, the constant economic and political pressures under which Caribbean leadership currently operates leave them no choice but to include a wider cross-section of the population into the decision-making process. Indeed, the present period seems to validate the earlier warnings of political thinkers like C.L.R. James that Caribbean populations were clamouring for a new type of political democracy, which would render the post-colonial politics of the Caribbean obsolete. James had always insisted that 'every cook can govern' and that government should not be the preserve of a select few. In his view there was a growing need to include ordinary people in the decision-making process since our local parliaments were not the sole repositories of wisdom and vision.

James had spoken of 'free creative activity' as a new expression of Caribbean democracy, which would defeat the top-down leadership style evident in post-colonial political parties and trade unions. He warned, in his 'Notes on Dialectics', that the politics of the nation-state would be transcended by a new global politics, 'which embraced from the start, whole continents'. There has perhaps been no clearer validation of C.L.R. James' notion of 'free creative activity' than the struggle of the rainbow coalition against the WTO in the streets of Seattle in December of 1999.

However, just as the new global economy sustains more advanced types of democratic expression, it also threatens to reverse the political gains which have been made by our forefathers in the struggle for democracy and national self-determination. It is instructive that the leadership of the anti-colonial movements saw the struggle for democracy as being inextricably intertwined with the independence project and with the struggle for the economic and political development of the Caribbean social space.

New Forms of Imperialist Expression

Caribbean political thinkers have already begun to identify new forms of imperialist expression in the new global economy. They have coined the phrase 'recolonisation' to capture the extent to which the political space won by the early nationalist struggles are now being eroded by the increasing tendencies towards liberalisation. The main casualty, in all of this, is the idea of the nation-state as a mechanism to mediate the impact of the external economic environment upon the domestic political environment. Increasingly, internal sources of power now find themselves over-ridden by external sources of decision-making.

The more perceptive political observers have outlined clearly the implications of these realities for national self-determination and democracy. David Held for example, has presented one of the clearest arguments that globalisation has undermined national self-determination. According to Held, prior to the onset of globalisation, it was taken for granted that 'all the key elements of national self-determination ... could be neatly meshed with the spatial reach of sites of power in a circumscribed territory'. Whilst he does not argue that national sovereignty has been totally subverted, Held argues that this old assumption is increasingly being challenged by globalisation. In his view, 'the autonomy of democratically elected governments … is increasingly constrained by sources of un-elected and unrepresentative economic power'.

Other writers have argued that in the present context the old colonial problematic of 'power without responsibility', against which our forefathers struggled, has re-emerged in a new guise. Peck and Tickell, for example, have argued that whilst under classic colonialism the old colonial power exerted power over domestic populations to which they were neither responsible nor accountable, under globalisation the situation is one in which external sources of power enjoy 'power without responsibility', whilst domestic sources of authority enjoy 'responsibility without power'.

Anyone who has observed the number of governments which have fallen on the sword of IMF structural adjustment would agree that significant levels of domestic power have been lost to the external economic environment. What is interesting is that this has meant a corresponding weakening of the internal democratic environment to influence the domestic political environment.

Overcoming Defeatist Tendencies

Despite these tremendous external challenges, I have warned elsewhere that we need to overcome the defeatist tendency in which we fail to 'center ourselves as prime determinants of our common condition and our common destiny'. It is on this basis that I have proposed the need for both public sector and legislative reform for the region, as a means of overcoming the challenges to Caribbean democracy and as a necessary factor in the structural adjustment of the Caribbean region to the realities of the new global economy.

It is clear that a thriving internal democracy is required to overcome the challenges to Caribbean democracy. Quite apart from the redistribution of political power, one of our major challenges is to modernise our societies in order to reposition ourselves into the new global economy. Too often, persons see modernisation as being relevant only in the technological sense, but the modernisation I speak of refers to the upgrading of our institutional structures, redesigning our social infrastructure, and engagement in a process of aggressive legislative reform. It would no doubt surprise many of you to hear that the Civil Code, which has been largely operative in St Lucia, was enacted in 1879. This body of law continues to govern our private lives despite the tremendous technological and social changes, which have occurred since the nineteenth century. It is clear therefore that the Caribbean must resolve burning issues about its social institutions and must pay close attention to the legal formation, which must accompany the transformations to our social institutions and political economy.

However, whilst we modernise and reform our institutional and legal structures, it is critically important that we seek at all times to retain and strengthen the democratic fabrics of our societies. As I argued in a paper on Public Sector Reform in St Lucia, if our objectives are those of 'equity, justice and welfare maximization' then it stands to reason that 'the process should be based on the principles of inclusiveness and the constructive engagement of civil society'. This is made even more urgent given the small size of our societies and the fact that results of such reforms can be immediately discerned around us, in the various communities.

Further, in our efforts at institutional and legislative modernisation it is important that we do not contribute to social unrest in the region. If we accept that the aim of reform is to deliver higher levels of societal welfare, then it is vitally important that such reform is politically feasible. Indeed, as I reminded a previous audience, 'recent history is full of free-market heroes – all of them in developing countries – who saved the economy and lost the election. So reform with civil unrest is not an option'.

A Vital Barometer

The democratic index remains the most vital barometer against which we measure the success of the modernisation project in the Caribbean. To many, this emphasis on democracy might seem an expensive diversion from what may appear to be the more urgent tasks of economic development and ensuring social stability. In contrast, however, a deeper democratic environment is vital, not only for overcoming the problems of internal reform, but is also essential to confront the challenges to Caribbean sovereignty and independence.

In St Lucia, we have endeavoured to deepen the democratic impulse in major aspects of our public life. For instance, we have consistently invited comments and recommendations from key stakeholders prior to the formulation of our annual budgets. I can assure you that this is not an exercise in window dressing. In contrast, this serves to ensure that the internal environment continues to remain the prime determinant of our actions. In short, we see our democracy as the main defence against recolonisation. Without it, we would have no choice but to bow to the dictates of global economic forces, which are neither accountable to Caribbean populations nor constrained by popular intervention and choice.

The 'New Horizons in Caribbean Democracy' can only be reached through a skilful marriage between economic structural adjustment and institutional change and legal reform which widens the scope for public participation and further advances the process of redistributing political power in the region.

This is the essential and urgent task of this generation of political leadership in the Caribbean. I have all the confidence that we can meet these challenges boldly and confidently as a united Caribbean people. After all, many of you here tonight will be part of that great and historically necessary enterprise.

I thank you.

22

Governance in the Caribbean in the Age of Globalisation

Dr The Honourable Ralph E. Gonsalves
Prime Minister of St Vincent and The Grenadines

O n Friday, April 20, 2001 the leaders of all independent countries in the
Americas – North America, Central America and the Caribbean – with
the exception of Cuba gather in Quebec, Canada, for the Third Summit of the
Americas. Immediately prior to the Summit, non-governmental organisations
(NGOs) from across the globe will be meeting in the same city to reflect upon
and adopt action plans on some of the very same issues, and more, which
would be occupying the attention of the Summit itself. The focus of States of
the Summit will be on broad subject areas of great importance, touching upon
the strengthening of democracy, creating prosperity, free trade, the environment,
connecting the Americas through information technology and realising human
potential. The NGOs are undoubtedly and, in my view, rightly dissatisfied
with their 'omission' from the Summit process, the marginalisation of civil
society, and the adverse consequences of globalisation on hemispheric multilateralism. The debates which are currently raging in Quebec find resonance
here in the Caribbean. They prompt our consideration here tonight on the
matter of restructuring governance in the Caribbean in the age of globalisation.

Dr Jessica Bryon, a lecturer in the Department of Government of the
University of the West Indies, has drawn my attention in her essay 'The Impact
of Globalisation on the Caribbean' to the work of J.A. Scholte who has provided
us with a synthesis of the main elements of globalisation. Scholte focuses on
the following in this regard: deregulation of the financial markets and the
massive growth in trans-border financial transactions; the increase in
transnational production of goods and services and the liberalisation of
international trade; the growing number of transnational enterprises; the marked
tendency towards the globalisation of civil society movements, corporate entities,

---

The Prime Minister delivered this address at a public lecture organised by the Department of
Government, Sociology and Social Work, UWI, Cave Hill Campus.

criminal groups and regulatory bodies; the revolutionary impact of communications technology on the mobility of people, ideas and cultural goods; and finally, a sharp rise in the incidence of globalised environmental problems.

These central features of globalisation present opportunities and threats to our small and vulnerable societies in economic, political and social terms. The impact of globalisation is both combined and uneven, within and between countries, and presents enormous challenges to the governance of our Caribbean countries. The revolution in information technology which is part and parcel of the process and fact of globalisation has profound implications for the way governance is structured and manifests itself. Yet Caribbean governments have, by and large, conducted business as usual in the same worn-out political clothing as if nothing has changed fundamentally in the context in which they function.

In his fascinating book, *The Great Disruption: Human Nature and the Reconstitution of Social Order,* Francis Fukuyama addresses the impact of information on the polity and society as follows:-

> A society built around information tends to produce more of the two things people value most in a modern democracy: freedom and equality. Freedom of choice has exploded whether of cable channels, low-cost shopping outlets, or friends met on the Internet. Hierarchies of all sorts, whether political or corporate, come under pressure and begin to crumble. Large, rigid bureaucracies, which sought to control everything in their domain through rules, regulations and coercion, have been undermined by the shift toward a knowledge-based economy, which serves to 'empower' individuals by giving them access to information.

Clearly, the dissolution or breakdown of these hierarchies demand a restructuring of governance and full popular participation in the state administration.

The changes wrought by globalisation, modernity and demography in the Caribbean are quite profound on real flesh and blood people and thus summons corresponding alternations in the structures and practices of governance. Professor Trevor Munroe of the University of the West Indies in Jamaica speaks eloquently to this issue:

> The simple but critical fact is that the typical Caribbean person of the year 2000 is relatively young, urbanised, educated, informed and exposed to modernity and post-modernity in all its manifestations. Take one simple indicator: The amount of time which the average Caribbean citizen spent on international telephone calls in 1995 and 25 times the average for developing countries,

almost seven times the global average and, most surprisingly, 80 per cent higher than the industrialised states. This is no longer the old time cane cutter, small farmer or even civil service clerk! The needs and capabilities of this person are fundamentally different from the needs and capabilities of his parents and grandparents: typically rural, relatively uninformed, uneducated, unexposed, unconfident, for better or worse, living in a relatively practiced environment.

The new Caribbean persons, moreover, are organised in professional groupings, trade unions, community-based organisations, clubs and a range of NGOs like never before. They are demanding, quite correctly, far greater participation in government; they clamour, quite rightly, far more information from their governments; they are insisting on open, transparent governance stuffed with political hygiene; and they are calling for governments to show more creativity in tackling the extant malaise, for governments to be less in love with problems and more embracing of a faith in the people's capacities to address successfully their concerns in their own interest.

There is a loss of confidence in the political system by the people of our region. This loss of confidence manifests itself in a number of ways, including: increased voter apathy at general elections; a growing sense that the State does not possess the capacity to ameliorate, much less solve, the existing problems in the polity, economy and society; the mounting public disdain for politicians who are being increasingly perceived as corrupt and untrustworthy; and a gnawing skepticism with which the electorate greets almost every electoral promise made by the political parties.

There is merit in the perception of many that the State in the Caribbean lacks the capacity to address effectively the problems of joblessness, crime and violence, drug trafficking and drug abuse, family break-ups, run-down health and education services, the environment, youth alienation, the deteriorating physical infrastructure such as roads and public buildings and so forth. This increasing lack of capacity of the State is, in part, related to a scarcity of resources, material and non-material which is itself connected to the deleterious impact of aspects of globalisation, trade liberalisation and the process of the marginalisation of the Caribbean in the post-Cold War world. Then, too, some problems are of a family and community kind. Further, the State itself as an institution is losing some of its former pre-eminence in the international and domestic political systems consequent upon the revolution in information technology, globalisation, trade liberalisation, multi-lateral activities internationally, the extension of the power of business corporations, the proliferation of non-governmental organisations and their enhanced work in civil society, and the fall-out from what has been called 'the decline of ideology'.

To be sure, the State is still an authoritative institution in the international and national political systems but its old power which has been on the rise from the sixteenth century onwards, has recently been declining substantially.

A new and radically improved system of governance requires therefore an abandonment of statist or commandist approaches and an embrace of people-centred or communitarian strategies lodged within the realities of our Caribbean civilisation. Indeed our civilisation resonates with community consciousness. The American socialist, Amitai Etzioni, a passionate advocate or a community-based philosophy, argues in his *The Spirit of Community*, published in 1995, simply:

> Communitarians call to restore civic virtues, for people to live up to their responsibilities and not merely focus on their entitlements, and to shore up the moral foundations of society —
> Communities are social webs of people who know one another as persons and have a moral voice. Communities draw on interpersonal bonds to encourage members to abide by shared values. — Communities gently chastise those who violate shared moral norms and express approbation for those who abide by them. They turn to the state (courts, police) only when all else fails. Hence, the more viable communities are, the less need for policing.

The democratic state, with a reformed constitutional apparatus, and communities must work together in relative harmony so as to achieve good governance and an improved quality of life for people, individually and as a whole. But at least four requisites are to be put in place for this harmonious relationship between the democratic state and communities to be engendered and achieved.

First, the communities themselves must be viable in terms of a core of shared values – an ennobling stock of social capital – and appropriately organised community systems. Thus, partisan competitive politics, which has been shown to be necessary for the maintenance of democracy and individual liberties in our region, ought not to descend into political tribalism and so-called 'garrison constituencies' of the Jamaica type. Such a descent would undermine communitarianism. The competitive politics can be mature and tolerant and can properly co-exist with community-centred consensualism on practical issues (jobs, crime, corruption, education, health, the environment, culture, sports, gender concerns, and so forth) which matter dearly to people.

Secondly, the state structures must be profoundly democratised at the centre, and very importantly, too, at the decentralised levels for effective local government. The communities organised in recognised social partners or other non-governmental groupings ought to be allocated important roles and voices in the formal apparatus of government, centrally and locally, in addition to their traditional non-governmental functioning.

Thirdly, an appropriate conceptual and functional demarcation should be drawn up to manage efficaciously the relationship between the reformed, democratic state and the viable communities. The State, naturally, in such a model will focus its attention on the following:

(i) a cluster of subjects such as law and order, national security, foreign affairs, international trade, and the administration of the state bureaucracy;

(ii) matters which present a clear and present danger, for example, the AIDS epidemic; and

(iii) areas of activity in which there are no better full-scale alternatives available to state involvement such as public education, public health services and state social security arrangements.

Even in these three broad categories, the communities will work closely with the State; and private entities may supplement the efforts of the State in the domestic polity, society and economy. But in a wide range of activities which touch and concern people practically at the community or local level, the viable communities and the democratic local government bodies will carry the burden principally. Wherever the State acts in these areas, its involvement ought to be in the least intrusive way possible and should be a complement to, and not a subversion of, communitarianism. The history of community efforts and voluntarism in the Caribbean, including the magnificent contributions of NGOs in the region, suggests that there is a base upon which we can build.

Our creative imagination is capable of putting more on the agenda in this regard and in building it into our system of governance for national problem-solving. Peculiarly, the small size of our countries may be an asset in this regard. Take for example the maintenance and development of existing public schools. In St Vincent and the Grenadines there are some eighty primary and secondary schools owned and operated by the government. Most are in a run-down state with limited educational facilities. It should not be beyond us to have service clubs, community organisations, trade unions, private sector organisations, big businesses and even wealthy individuals, at home and abroad, adopt particular schools so as to keep the school plant in good repair, install computers and develop good school libraries, among other things. The schools will certainly be better off than they are now and the monies which the state would have had to expend on their upkeep could be put to other areas of national development. Importantly, too, a sense of community ownership will envelope the schools with consequential positive spin-offs.

The *fourth* requisite for this new partnership between the democratic state and viable communities and in the new circumstances of our modern, globalised life is a new and different kind of leadership. In my book, *History and the future: A Caribbean Perspective*, I sketched the principal elements of this new model of leadership. A prototype of such leadership was addressed by C. L. R. James in his 1963 classic, *Beyond a Boundary*, which is ostensibly a book about cricket but which is about more than cricket. In assessing Frank Worrell's leadership of the West Indies Cricket team on its 1960 - 1961 tour of Australia, James wrote:

> The West Indies team in Australia, on the field and off, was playing above what it knew of itself. If anything went wrong it knew that it would be instantly told, in unhesitating and precise language, how to repair it, and the captain's certainty and confidence extended to his belief of what he wanted to be done. He did not instill into but drew out of his players. What they discovered in themselves must have been a revelation to few more than to the players themselves.

The last two sentences of this Jamesian quotation point to the kernel of what is required of new leaders in our Caribbean civilisation.

The leaders too, must avoid a degeneration into authoritarianism and corruption. The Caribbean people do admire strong, authoritative leaders but they have grown tired of the authoritarian types who are frankly out-moded in the new milieu which I have earlier described.

The Caribbean people are rightly demanding that urgent and focused steps be taken to rid the body of politic corruption and corrupt leaders. New and resolutely-policed integrity, legislation to govern the conduct of politicians and senior public officials is needed. Illicit enrichment, that is the acquisition of wealth which cannot be honestly and reasonably explained by one's know assets and income, ought to be no compromise since corruption undermined cores values of good governance and distorts a fair and reasonable allocation of goods and services to the people.

Part of the corruption in the extant competitive party system relates to the very electoral system which is the mechanism for the validation of political change. Election in the Caribbean have become too expensive and something must be done about it. Both leaders and the electorate are on an ever-rising escalator of electoral expenditure madness. It must stop. Apart from an abuse of state resources, amounting in some cases to a 'rape of the Treasury', there is the ever-present concern that substantial campaign contributions may demand and secure return to their campaign 'investments' which are not in the public interest. New rules for campaign financing ought to be devised and the general public should be educated about inappropriateness of the delivery to them of electoral largesse by competing parties and candidates. This, I must confess, is a daunting exercise over the long haul!

It is fair to say though, that our inherited political institutions and home-grown political culture, though seriously flawed, have conspired to avoid the undemocratic political upheavals and dictatorships of Africa and Latin America. But our political system is in need of reform and change. We do not, however, require 'a re-invention of the wheel' or political engineering abstractly fashioned out of sync with our history, geographical size, experiences and civilisation's social capital.

There is a base upon which and enhanced governance can be built around the core political values of liberty, representative government, accountable democracy, the separation of powers, and independent judiciary, and an incorruptible, innovative, skilled and sensitive leadership. To this end, I have advanced some suggestions here and elsewhere for the marriage of a reformed, democratic constitution and a viable, people centred communitarianism within the over-aching framework of further ennobling our Caribbean civilisation. Hopefully, one day, this civilisation may express itself politically as one Caribbean nation. My entire life, has, in part, been dedicated to this. The political party, the Unity Labour Party (ULP), which I have the honour to lead and which formed the Government of St Vincent and the Grenadines just over two weeks ago in a landslide electoral triumph, published a document on July 31, 2000 entitled *Constitutional Reform: A Discussion*. In it the ULP advanced a number of ideas to restructure our country's system of governance.

At the very least the reformed governance formulae ought to rest on four pillars: the strengthening of the individual's fundamental rights and freedom; the developing and decentralisation of political democracy, including enhanced popular participation in government; making government much more honest, accountable and effective; and the consolidation and extension of the independence and quality of the judiciary.

In this restructuring exercise we build, I repeat, upon the solid liberal democratic foundation of our existing constitutions in the Caribbean while at the same time avoiding their glaring weaknesses. Every aspect of our structures of governance ought to come under intense scrutiny so as to make them function much better in the age of globalisation.

At the end of the day, a new structure of enhanced democratic governance must aid significantly in the solution of the complex, major problems of mass unemployment, escalating crime, endemic official corruption and an inappropriate educational system, among others. This issue naturally connects with a consideration of the role of the nation-state in the age of globalisation.

The British political economist, Will Hutton, in *The State to Come* is on target when he argues:

> Most analysis of globalisation is surprisingly glib, for while the nation state is clearly weaker in its capacity to run its national economy as it chooses, its capacity to initiate partnership, regulate activity, cut deals and even fix tax rates and spending levels is still significant. Indeed there is no other player on the horizon with the same power. In sum, nation states have palpably less autonomy that they did, but it would be wrong to portray, them as powerless. What has changed is the risks and rewards of particular kinds of conducts, and the ways they have to be executed. In other words there is a spectrum of possible policy manoeuvres open to national governments which can achieve their ends even in today's environment.

In the Caribbean context, the prime minister of Barbados, Owen Arthur, argued persuasively in this in a conference address at the University of the West Indies in Jamaica in September 1999, entitled 'Economic Policy Options in the Twenty-First Century'.

> It is [also] a very serious error to presume that the role of the state in the Caribbean should be marginalised. Such would prevent it from playing a creative role in the redesign of the Caribbean infrastructure that will enable it to move from the Industrial to the Information Age; from attending to long-standing deficiencies in the development of our human institutional and technological capabilities, from creating a framework within which non-traditional enterprise can emerge, and from carrying out those vital programmes to enhance and protect our environment in support of our sustainable development.
> After thirty (30) year of independence, the state cannot retreat as a force for good in Caribbean development. It must reform its way of doing business. It must reinvent itself to be fully relevant to today's purposes and tomorrow's needs. It must build new strategic alliances with the private sector, the non-governmental institutions, and all the institutions of our civil society to create a new good society, which can take its place among the family of nations in today's challenging age as a competitive, productive and prosperous region. But it cannot retreat.

In fashioning a new structure of governance and production in the Caribbean, the ethic of trust between and among the people, and between them and their leaders in their various organisations and in government, has to be built. One or two not-so-thoughtful commentators have scoffed at my articulation of this idea in several of my speeches. Perhaps I ought to answer them with Will Hutton's help who in *The State to Come* suggests:

> Trust is a 'soft' idea and economist instinctively recoil from the importance of its role. It cannot be reduced to algebraic equations, nor is it easy to build. It is part of a community's social capital, as Francis Fukuyama argues, had has deep historical and cultural roots; but that does not mean that we cannot act to shape institutions and patterns of behaviour which are more likely to generate trust than others. A community with a vigorous local democracy which allows plenty of opportunity to work cooperatively to produce local results is more likely to generate trust (and experience of how trust relationships are beneficial) which spills over into economic and social affairs than one without such opportunities.

Finally, it is my considered view that no meaningful and effective restructuring of government in the Caribbean is likely unless we act on the affirmation that we constitute an independent, authentic civilisation of a distinct type known as the Caribbean civilisation. It is from the well-spring of our civilisation that we will summon up the requisite creative energies to meet the challenges and threats of globalisation. It is the duty of each of us to be a living embodiment of the nobility of our civilisation and to pursue the quest for further advance our civilisation , including the finding of the most appropriate and efficacious political forms through which to fashion a new and better governance.

Part VI

※

*Recovering Caribbean History:
Discourse on Race and Plantation
Politics*

23

Plantalogical Politics: Battling for Space and the Jamaican Constitution

Taitu A. Heron

INTRODUCTION

The historical centrality of the plantation in Caribbean society has been visited time and time again because of its persistence in the institutions, value-systems and minds of Caribbean people.[1] Shortly after the granting of independence in Jamaica, it was clearly established that significant colonial baggage had been carried over.[2] In 1967, Sylvia Wynter argued that new world countries were bound to repeat the ills of their history if the baggage was not sorted and unloaded. 'A society', she noted

> reluctant to examine its premises, evasive of its past, uncertain of its identity, afraid of its own promise, worshipping its white heritage, despising its Black, or at best settling for ... being a multiracial, multicultural 'Out of Many, One', is in danger... For it is a society where the majority are still exiles in their own country. They are exiles too because for too long they have been made to deny one part or the other of their heritage.[3]

It is this colonial baggage that Wynter speaks of that I am also concerned with in exploring the centrality of the plantation in contemporary political realities in Jamaica. At the same time, this examination is undertaken by looking back in history, in order to make a more Caribbean-centred sense of the present, and to see further forward. The paper argues that the constitution upholds and legally seals, to a certain extent, the inherited colonial baggage. It is there, I argue, that it has to be tackled. If enslavement and colonialism were established to dehumanise and oppress groups of people on the basis of skin colour for profit, then the most natural human response to enslavement would be to struggle, resist, fight and survive. The conflict created spatial cross fires and tensions among the transplanted people (enslaved and enslavors), which, since formal independence, have made attempts at integration and consensus exceedingly difficult to achieve. The enslaving group upheld values and practices to maintain the exploitative relationship. Also, the enslaved/colonised people upheld their own values and practices, in spite of, in response to and as a result of, the actions of the enslaving/colonising group. This was expressed as a refusal to submit to an imposed inferior status and a demand for just treatment as human beings, whether through day-to-day resistance, subversive struggle and/ or by armed rebellion.[4]

The historical contradictions of this experience and its contemporary manifestations have perpetuated seemingly irreconcilable distortions, contradictions and fragmentations. Taking a cue from George Beckford, Louis Lindsay, Lloyd Best, CY Thomas and other members of the New World Group, whose studies concentrated on the problematique of development in plantation economies such as Jamaica, I am calling the colonial baggage, 'plantalogical politics'. In my view, efforts at governance and development that avoid plantalogical politics in neocolonial[5] societies will not create substantive positive change in democracy and development; neither will they answer our dilemmas of democracy and/or development. On the contrary, it is only by dealing with the reality of the plantalogical politics, negative and positive, may we begin to work through the distortions and begin to envisage integration and consensus in neocolonial societies. Jamaica, being a member of a wide group of neocolonial countries in the Americas, will have similarities and parallels of analysis. Thus this represents one of many perspectives that could be taken.

Rex Nettleford's conceptual framework on the battle for space in plantation societies such as Jamaica, provides a Caribbean-centred lens through which to analyse and interpret plantalogical politics.[6] Nettleford argues that by the use and abuse of space, we mean space to be a physical location each person has which "enables one to exist as a human in a common world'. Occupying space to exist as humans in a common world also means one has the ability, freedom and will to express oneself, to eat, to sleep, to worship, to have sex, to work, to think, to create, and to organise society as s/he deems fit. As such, space or the lack of space, encompasses the political, the social, the cultural, the economic and the personal of life itself. Finally, this idea of space also encompasses all that is in the universe for humankind to enjoy and coexist – from the heavens to the earth.[7] In this regard, the plantation represented the battlefield where the fight for space ensued, and where the politics of resistance against oppression was played out. Abuse of space meant fighting to get space, negotiate and manoeuvre space to regain that right as a member of the human family. In scenarios where human space is denied, questions and meanings of fundamental human rights loom large in the imagination – justice, freedom and identity.

The meanings of these ideals formed in the collective consciousness over time, takes on alterations as the society changes with each generation. Spatial dynamics change as well. The significance and weight that these meanings have will also change, negatively and/or positively, with the improvement or exacerbation of the space that a group of people occupy. Thus if there is a battle for space in a socially hostile environment, where one group dominates and rules over the other, the response is struggle. Thus it is to be expected that how much space . one occupies or is deprived of, will be contested at some point in time or another.

Charles Mills' idea on 'smadditization'[8] may also be seen as complimentary to Nettleford's 'battle for space'. Mills' sees the process of 'smadditizing' as African diaspora peoples struggle over time and space, to become and be recognised as *smaddy*/somebody within the context of the experiences of enslavement and colonisation. Essentially, it is process that one engages in at various existential levels to count as an equal human being. The response by the enslaved population was a long struggle. Mills points out that this has been a struggle on many levels (psychological, political, epistemological, cultural, ontological) where the ultimate goal has been to recognise one's personhood and membership in the human family, where it was (is) in question to begin with, and where because of ethnicity it was (is) denied.[9]

Efforts at smadditization are made by individuals or groups to reclaim their right to occupy space and exist as *smaddy*. The need for justice occurs when one's smadditizing efforts are impeded or oppressed by continuing hegemonic relations between the master and the enslaved, the colonised and the coloniser, the oppressed and the oppressor, the citizen and the neocolonial elite, man and woman. During enslavement and colonisation in the Americas, one experienced blatant abuse of space. In such an environment, the culture of the enslaved people was a contested culture and whose destruction was sought in a systematic fashion.[10] How does space operate in such an environment? How does one whose membership on the basis of skin colour is denied regain or reclaim space? How does the colonial power/neocolonial state/political and economic elite respond? How does they use space? And what does space have to do with a constitution?

The constitution upholds the ideals and laws of a country. It is supposedly the stepping-stone to nation building. Bearing that, and the battle for space in mind, what role does the constitution have, in neocolonial societies such as Jamaica? If, as I argue, the constitution is contentious, can we really say that the process of smadditization is complete? These questions will be explored here.

IN DEFENCE OF SPACE: PLANTALOGICAL POLITICS AND THE JAMAICAN CONSTITUTION

We may see 'Plantalogical politics' then, as the condition or situation in a society where the heritage of the slave plantation and the colonial experience manifest themselves in the politics of contemporary society. It has been pointed out before that the Caribbean plantation was specifically created for capitalist gain and in turn financed the advancement of the development process of European nations since the 1600s. The Caribbean plantation was the facilitating ground for global capitalism and the springboard for European modernity. The plantation became a human experiment in which two main groups – enslaved Africans and enslaving Europeans (followed by the indentured servitude of Indians and Chinese in the mid-nineteenth century) co-existed in a highly conflictual clash of cultures. In addition to the core economic function of the plantation, as George Beckford[11] noted, it functioned as a confined institution of social control and authority over all aspects of people's lives within it. In the Caribbean/the Americas, the plantation was the central location of the enslaved/enslaver, colonised/coloniser relationship and was organised in an all-pervasive way to ensure that the work on the plantation was done. This was done by the exploitation of one group of humans by another groups, by various means – physical torture, social control, psychological conditioning, sexual abuse and oppressive laws. This amounted to denying humanity to first the Africans, and then to the Asians, the right to self and space to exist in a common world. Simultaneously this gave the other group, the Europeans, group overarching and omnipotent space to control their environs and people within it for economic gain. The unequal and false binaries which enveloped the experience of enslavement and colonisation on the plantation – enslaved/enslaver, colonised/coloniser, white/person of colour, super ordinate/subordinate, Christian/heathen, civilised/primitive, superior/inferior, Europe/Africa – created and distortions within the existential reality of the Caribbean person. These binaries, which developed historically, are present in contemporary society.

The spatial dynamics involved in these relationships, using the idea of battle is captured in the Jamaican proverb – *two bull cyan rule ina one pen.*[12] Nettleford argues that this cultural conflict originating from the plantation created a continuous 'battle for space' between the dominator-European and the dominated-African.[13] For the dominator-Europeans, it was an effort to enslave a group of people and uphold a myth of superiority on the basis of skin colour. And at the same time, for the dominated-Africans, it was to refuse and rise above submission to the imposed inferiority. The spatial relationship between the dominator-European and the dominated-African was a relationship between two social groups, which were diametrically opposed. For the Africans, and later African and Indian Creoles, regardless of the dehumanising machinations of enslavement and indentured servitude, beginning with the Capture and Sale of Africans in the 1500s, have never accepted subpersonhood. An excerpt from Earl Lovelace's *Salt* captures this Battle for Space and deserves lengthy quotation:

Watch the landscape of this island... and you know that they coulda never hold people here surrendered to unfreedom...Things here have their own mind... after they settle in the islands... they begin to discover how hard it was to be gods... The heat, the diseases, the weight of armour they had to carry in the hot sun, the imperial poses to strike, the powdered wigs to wear, the churches to build, the heathen to baptize, the illiterates to educate, the animals to tame, the numerous species of plants to name, history to write, flags to plant, parades to make, militia to assemble, letters to write home. And all around them, this rousing greenness bursting in the wet season and another quieter shade perspiring in the dry... On top of all that, they had to put up with the noise from Blackpeople. Whole night Blackpeople have their drums going as they dancing in bush... they couldn't see them in the dark among the shadows but they could hear. They had to listen to them dance the Bamboula, Bamboula, the Quelbay, the Manding, the Juba, the Ibo... It was hard for whitepeople ... they try, but they had it very hard...they had to get people to fan them. People to carry their swords... They had to get people to beat people for them, people to dish out lashes – seventy-five, thirty-five, eighty-five. How else they coulda carry on The Work... No. Really, they try. They tried in administering the floggings to make sure and not to cause the effusion of blood or contusion; but what else to do? There was no natural subservience here. Nobody didn't bow down to nobody just so. To get a man to follow your instructions you had to pen him and beat him and cut off his ears or his foot when he runaway. You had was to take away his woman and child from him. And still that fellow stand up and oppose you... It had women there that was even more terrible... They had to ban them from walking and from raising up their dresstail and shaking their melodious backsides...The plantation people couldn't handle them. They beat them. They hold them down and turn them over and do them whatever wickedness they could manage; but they couldn't break them... And then it dawn on them that you can't defeat people... four hundred years it take them to find out that you can't hold people in captivity. Four hundred years! And it didn't happen just so. People had to revolt. People had to poison people. Port of Spain had to burn down. A hurricane had to hit the island. Haiti had to defeat Napoleon. People had to runway up to the mountains. People had to fight. And then they agree, yes, we can't hold people in captivity here.[14]

Nettleford[15] expands this where he describes the 'Battle for Space' as the:

> ...Phenomenon [which] turns on just about everything that informs the struggle to make sense of Caribbean existence whether one views from the point of politics, economics, social development or cultural dynamics... the Caribbean's own ancestral resort to marronage – retreats into safe psychic sanctums calling on inner reserves beyond the reach of external violators.

As one's outer or external space is violated, that is, by enslaved labour, physical, psychological and sexual abuse by plantation owners, officials and colonial authorities, one stretches inward to her/his inner space. This inner space is mental – the development of thoughts and ideas regarding one's existence. Further to that, this inner space may also be regarded as an immediate physical space that may offer no external interference – from the bushes and hills, to the expression of song, the use of musical instruments, food, dance, the *yawd*[16], to subversive resistance by poisoning, destruction of plantation equipment, and armed insurrection. What comes out of that 'inward stretch', that dig deep down for inner space, as a result of the battle, is the 'outward reach', which is determined by the opportunities for survival. Nevertheless, it was important to carve out a life and to improve one's, thereby beginning the process of smadditization.[17]

These spatial relations continue, not in the undisguised form of enslavement, but in more subtle snake-slithering ways, since Independence. Nettleford argues that the 'new perpetrators [are] to be found among the native governors, economic elite, the political bourgeoisie, and/or the neo-colonial superpowers brought in as allies in pursuit of hegemonic control of geographical spheres'.[18]

Spatial relations between the dominator-European and dominated-African was legitimated was through the country's constitution.[19] A country's constitution is supposedly the set of legal rules which hold sanctity and set out a framework for government; and which reflect and declare the principles on which that country should be governed. The constitution, it is argued, should reflect what the people, who make up that country, actually want; and contains the basic rules by which the people of a country agree to govern themselves. However, during the period of enslavement, the constitution was set up to govern that arrangement between planter and imperial interests, to ensure paramountcy of the plantation and the interests of sugar; and to regulate and agree upon a set of rules to govern the enslaved population. The constitution gave the colonial elite protection from, and entitlement to, the kind of lives they led and did not include any measure of accountability for the kinds of unjust acts that they committed in defence of the good life. The constitution denied the very existence of African human space:

Slaves hardly had any legal rights. They were treated in law as objects possessed by planters in the same way as their cattle and therefore were excluded from the constitutional process. They had no votes and were not represented.[20]

BATTLES FOR SPACE IN THE POST-EMANCIPATION ERA

Britain did not extend its own democratic project to the colonies. The amendments to the constitution further regulated the assurance of British imperial benefit and the exploitation of Africans and people of African descent. However, because the enslaved population resisted the idea of racial inferiority, the constitution also indicates the extent to which battles for space ensued.

Constitutional changes outlining the regulations for an entire 'free' society in 1838 were precipitated significantly by Jamaica's largest rebellion in the nineteenth century – the Christmas Rebellion of 1831-32, led by the Afro-Creole, Sam Sharpe. Arguably, an important marker as a battle for space was in 1838 with the passing of the Emancipation Act. The constitutional conventions enshrined thereafter, in this act, were to determine the rules of a 'free society'. Upon emancipation, the newly freed persons were not given political space to vote and/or represent themselves in government.[21] The planter class was practically hauled and dragged into accepting emancipation as a reality by the forces of pressure from below through the increasing agitation of the enslaved population. From above the pressure was manifested by increasing abolitionist activity in the metropole and on the islands, (albeit on ticket of a civilising mission to teach the newly freed people 'how to be civilised'). Internationally, pressure for emancipation was felt by encroachment of other European and American imperialist interventions. This was further exacerbated by the declining profitability of sugar. Augier pointed out that:

> Emancipation did not shock the white community into a posture of independence. To adopt such a stance they would have had to embrace the doctrine of social equality of all... what they chose to do, once they had stopped the trans-Atlantic debate with Great Britain about its invasion of their constitutional rights, was to use their political power to make of emancipation a mere word, without economic and social reality.[22]

As the British colonial power found another group of people of colour to exploit (in this case, the Indians and the Chinese), in the decade following emancipation, the Jamaican-African community tended to move away from plantations, and away from missionary activities, retreating into their own private space, which they had for the first time (although limited). As it was during enslavement, so it was in the post-emancipation era where religious practice also provided a necessary space for mental and cultural expressions in the process of smadditization. This meant that they became preoccupied with their own immediate smadditization by attempting to carve out their own self-sufficient social and cultural systems away from the plantation with the establishment of free villages. Additionally, they attempted to purchase their own land, or occupy land regardless of the reluctance of the white planter to class to relinquish their overarching space, including legal restrictions to land ownership enshrined in the constitution.[23]

It thus created an environment where it was felt that it was not so much that the British Government was to blame, but that rather the economic elite representing planter interests were frustrating the Jamaican-African community's efforts at smadditization.[24] Nonetheless, there was a relationship between local elites and imperial interests in which the latter had the potential or the right to contract or extend space. Wherever along the lines of the spatial dynamics, the battle for space for the Jamaican-African community was all the more frustrated by the continuing injustices of the planter class whose political power in the House of Assembly, could not accept Black, poor and landless as human. The constitution therefore, was not going to reflect otherwise.

Embodied in the constitution of this period was the obstruction of people of African descent in particular from entering political activity, whereby voting restrictions were placed on the basis of literacy and property ownership. The legislature adjusted these constitutional conventions (whenever) as more freed Jamaican-Africans began to meet the qualifications for entry into political office. These unjust relations supported by the constitution continued to impede the efforts by some aspiring Jamaican-African politicians, particularly by the 1850s and onwards, who became to become politically active and represent the interests of the Jamaican-African community.[25] As we have said, the main thrust behind the white community's strategy was to define entrance into the political game in classist and racist terms by only giving voice to 'property and intelligence'. And in this sense, were those who were 'human', who in their eyes was white, bourgeoisie, male, propertied and Anglican could enter into the political game.

There was further contraction of space on the economic level for Jamaican-Africans (and to a different degrees, for the Indians and Chinese later on) who attempted informal economic activity, such as petty trading and higglering. The colonial authorities responded by making further constitutional amendments that specified the rules of who could engage in economic activity, and how such activity should be organised. For the white planter class this was not regarded as a rightful search for space and an effort at independent socio-economic advancement. Instead, this was seen as a direct assault and a 'crime' against their own property rights and their domination of the island's economic productivity. Any colonised person or group who violated these laws, and committed these 'crimes' was met with harsh penalties by the magistrate courts. Offenders were sometimes met with punity and violence and were punished by inflicting lashes with the whip and/or sent to languish in the gaols at 'Her Majesty's Pleasure'.[26]

One of the greatest expressions in this period of the freedpeople's search and claim for space was the Morant Bay Rebellion of 1865. The rebellion was arguably a result of such irresponsible and unjust politics and economic deprivation, coupled with the condescending neglect of the welfare of the society after emancipation. This all-pervasive abuse of space by the white community, and the corresponding stretching inward to its auxiliary space the Jamaican-African community meant that their ideas and thoughts found congruence with their ancestral energies which allowed them to reach outward in response to the injustice.

After the Morant Bay Rebellion, significant changes were made to the constitution. We could argue here that this is perhaps a second marker, or indication as a battle for space in Jamaica's constitutional history.[27] The popular view held by white community in response to the rebellion was that it was 'one of the most horrid attempts that have been made to create a second Black republic in the western archipelago'. It was believed and that the Jamaican-African peasants were simply ungrateful and had not been 'sufficiently taught to enjoy the great blessings that white men have conferred upon them.'[28] Thus, it was no surprise that the main consequence of the Rebellion was to constitutional change marked by change from the oligarchic Old Representative System to the autocratic Crown Colony government, under the manipulative engineering tactics of the then notorious Governor John Edward Eyre[29].

This reflected a change in policy to 'imperial trusteeship' whereby, if left on their own, the white community would govern completely for their own interests and not protect and 'civilise' the Jamaican-African community, as they should. Left on their own, the Jamaican-African community, having only the 'rudiments of civilisation' would therefore need all the help they could get. Thus, through limited provision of education and health opportunities provided by the British Crown and its missionary appendages, the Blacks would become 'civilised'. Following this policy line, legal restrictions, which inhibited black Jamaicans from participating in the process was alleviated somewhat. At a marginal scale, some were able to purchase Crown lands at a subsidised cost and/or were given land titles for lands that they had occupied.[30] However, this was the exception rather than the rule, as the realities of trusteeship did not significantly assist in the improvement of the black Jamaican community. In this respect Munroe noted that,

> The failure of trusteeship to translate its theoretical intention into practice reflected in part a tendency inherent in constitutional orders set in contexts of grave disparities…[T]rusteeship allowed the natives to be exploited by 'every capitalist and private interest'.[31]

Spatial Battles from Morant Bay to Independence

Attempts at creating political space were markedly active again in the 1890s to early mid-1900s, whereby several Blacks, (including a few brown-skinned) attempted to enter the political arena and succeeded despite the constitutional restrictions.[32] In particular, calls were made by persons such as Robert Love, George Stiebel, Charles Campbell, Samuel Clarke, Gordon, Marcus Garvey and others, to mobilise the Jamaican-African community to becoming more politically aware, and to impart and understanding and importance of political representation.[33] Lumsden points out that these efforts were aimed at gaining support to lobby for constitutional change.[34] Efforts also were made to put the interests of the local Jamaican-African population on the agenda, and included issues aimed at alleviating some of the injustices meted out because of race – access to land, education opportunities and access and quality of health care. Some successful efforts were made where some Blacks, especially the brown-skinned, were able to elevate themselves to the middle class surmounting the racial restrictions. But in order to improve their social and economic spaces, some of them had to deny their cultural space. This meant suppressing their African heritage and to practice varying degrees of disassociation from their darker skinned counterparts. It also meant adopting and imitating the Anglophile tendencies of the white ruling class, in terms of education, values, norms, behaviour and mannerism; if one wanted to prove to be 'good British subjects' and 'civilised'; thereby and accruing the social and economic benefits thereof.[35] Social advancement was rarely allowed by any other means.

The efforts of most of the Jamaican community, who attempted to enter the political arena, were often stifled by the ever-present overarching space of the colonial elites whose interests continued to put the plantation and the myth of their own greatness first. Further to that, the stakes for attaining space on equal terms were so low and the colonial social mechanisms were so rigidly and divisively designed, that it often engendered survival tactics of intra-group fighting to claim individual and community space. At every turn that one attempted to carve out a space to be at liberty, the process of emancipation was persistently being thwarted. A battle for space continued to ensue because of the stubbornness inherent in the myth of superiority upheld by the white community, did not allow for objectivity, open-mindedness and humaneness to flow. It was not only the enslaved/colonised that had been dehumanised in the process but also the white colonial community. By participating in such an experiment with other human beings for financial self-aggrandisement, this could mean that a part of their heart/soul and mind had refused the idea that they could actually be wrong. If one accepts the myth of superiority on the basis of skin colour, to question it would mean endangering the economic benefits one accrues from it and would also mean admitting that a serious crime against humankind had been committed, and that justice would have to be done.

Thus, by the early twentieth century, it was clear that neither justice nor were efforts to facilitate smadditization were forthcoming. What instead was done was to continue to build around the myth of white superiority. For the overall Jamaican community of African and Indian descent, the ancestral self was also sacrificed in that it had to retreat into auxiliary or condemned spaces to continue to survive.[36] Specifically, the African-oriented culture was doomed to hidden spaces of those who were not ashamed to express it but at the same time, legal persecution for celebrating it was a reality. Also, in a strikingly real sense, exposing this ancestral self would not be beneficial to their social enhancement. By accepting accommodating somewhat to the colonial circumstances, (to varying degrees), African-adapted cultural expression was not deemed worthy of association by some of the very people from whom it sprang.[37] It is of course, not as straightforward as this. As Manoni and Memi and others have pointed out, the very nature of the colonial experience produces psychological disorders between both groups – the colonised and the coloniser. In this sense, any of the above scenarios could either be simple as 1. 2. 3, or mixed and matched, twisted, contorted, turned and squeezed to bring forth a variety of beliefs and positions of any colonial individual.[38] The colonial situation as it was systematically designed to do, did not only exploit and oppress a colonised people; it also duped a significant number of them.[39]

In the post-emancipation era, the church and the oppressive use of law increasingly took over where the whip could no longer enforce submission and dupe. Blackness presumed ignorance, barbarity and criminality before anything else. The laws of the colonial state were structured on these false premises. If one happened to be on the 'colonised' side of the fence, one was guilty before the game of making a life had begun. Law and order was maintained on this basis. Since there was no facilitation for human life within these confines of maintaining law and order, the practice of injustice in the post-emancipation era continued. A homeless person would be classified as a criminal. Stealing mangoes would warrant lashes of the whip. Walking in the 'wrong' neighbourhood brought suspicion and police harassment. As in many other post-emancipation societies (and indeed contemporary times), where one is born on the social/ethnic order may either classify a person as a 'criminal' or a 'law abiding citizen' – the state will correspond accordingly.

By the 1930s, the explosion of the labour riots reflected the need to address issues of poverty, illiteracy and chronic unemployment for the majority of the population. Space was being demanded again. From the colonial perspective, the 'native' in a situation like this, must once more be appeased in a manner keeping with the non-disturbance of the status quo. The 1938 labour riots signified another marker in Jamaican constitutional history. As a result of the riots, actions were further taken which eventually led to gradual constitutional decolonisation. A period of 'stewardship' in the arts of responsible politics was given to the emergent local political elite via the teachers of the 'Great British Empire'. Limited political space was given by granting of Universal suffrage in 1944. By 1962, after the Jamaica-induced demise of Federation of the 'West Indies',[40] independence was given in 1962. In this regard, Lindsay pointed out that:

[b]y gracefully appearing to concede the right of national sovereignty, the metropolitan government finds it easier to preserve the notion of a beneficent and non-exploitative mother country that has carefully and with much self-sacrifice prepared her colonial 'children' for ultimate independence and self-determination.[41]

While the move toward, and meaning of independence was different between the politicians from the People's National Party (led by Norman Manley) and the Jamaica Labour Party (led by Alexander Bustamante), deference to Britain, its culture and institutions was common among the leadership and among perhaps, the vast majority of the followers of both political parties. Both political parties reflected that Britain dominated their cultural and intellectual headspace. That was the route. In this historical context, it is understandable why independence in Jamaica was not achieved as part of an anti-colonial struggle or by large portions of the population mobilising to find their own ways to liberation.[42]

Lindsay noted that traditionally, independence has been historically connoted to mean liberation from the yoke of some external and oppressive force and the freedom of a community to define and pursue policies that reflect its own interests and values. Independence in Jamaica (and elsewhere in the Caribbean), in this regard, had no clear or decisive meaning, except that we would no longer be 'British subjects'. To a lesser extent, it did not mean a new beginning. Instead, independence meant handing over political power to a local Afro-Saxon elite, that perpetuated the plantalogical politics while attempting to build a 'new' nation; and manoeuvring to the local Afro-Saxon elite, the long neglected responsibility of providing the majority of the population with social and economic opportunities.[43]

Since both the colonial and local Afro-Saxon elite dominated the decolonisation process, the spatial domination of plantalogical ideologies were left untouched in the process of decolonisation. In turn, the so-called independence movement was such that the majority of the Jamaican masses fell prey to the idea of independence as meaning the guarantor of meeting the bread and butter issues that had plagued them so much since emancipation; and that the 'benevolent and caring' colonial 'mother' was finally departing. There was little agitation that could be called a significant anti-colonial struggle that spoke to independence as a means of liberation from an oppressive colonial mother and the building of a new nation on its own terms of reference. While one may argue that the need to address bread, butter, health and education were perhaps more critical to attend to at that time, we may also argue that this route was hegemonised by the Afro-Saxon elite. And is so doing, the cultural fundamentals of nation-building were left out, and gave way to the continued marginalisation of the cultural, social, political and economic spaces of the numerical majority.[44]

The spatial dynamics of specific aspects of the Jamaican Constitution

The overall framework of the Jamaican constitution, and specific aspects of it which I will point to here, do not appear to be significantly shaped by the culture, history and struggle of the Jamaican population. This in itself illustrates the extent to which the colonial authorities dominated space. The bias towards an economic elite and the protection of their way of life remains entrenched in the constitution. During the period of constitutional decolonisation, scant attention was paid to the granting of fundamental rights and freedoms for other citizens. In this respect, the fundamental rights and freedom of a Jamaican citizen are subject to respect for the rights and freedoms of others and for the public interest. Additionally, the protection of fundamental rights and freedoms in the constitution also includes a provision that preserves colonial laws that infringe upon these rights and freedoms. The neocolonial state and its branches, therefore has the power to oppress.

Parliament can also suspend the Fundamental Rights and Freedoms by passing a law by two-thirds majority in both Houses and no referendum will be needed. Legal representation provided by the Government is not considered. Anyone who seeks to challenge unconstitutional action by a public authority or officer is obligated to show that his/her personal interests are directly affected or threatened and that there is no other legal remedy available to him/her.[45] High levels of criminality and corruption notwithstanding, this leaves security forces of the neocolonial state with tremendous power that continues to be abused. Here, one can see the abuse of human space where spatial domination was tipped in favour of the (neo)colonial elite and where little respect was given for the space of the Jamaican community to exist as humans in a common world. Nevertheless, these constitutional conventions to date still have to be upheld by the Courts because it existed before the Independence constitution came into effect. It allows for the continued abuse of space for a significant number of the Jamaican population and demonstrates a fundamental lack of justice. That it does is no surprise, the constitution that Jamaica inherited was not founded with ideals of creating a just and equal society. That it still does is the contentious issue.

The constitution, as it was handed down upon formal Independence, also still has entrenched provisions, which pay homage to the British Throne. As such, the Head of State, which is supposed to embody a sense of national unity and pride, is still the British Monarch.[46] That these provisions were allowed demonstrates not only the overarching political and cultural space of Britain but also an acceptance of these spaces by the Jamaican leadership who participated in the process of constitutional decolonisation. This was done to the detriment of claiming to define their own political and cultural space according to common ideals and principles, real and symbolic to Jamaican history, culture, feelings and aspirations.

The Jamaican constitution and the meaning of retributive justice in contemporary society Constitutional changes did not occur out of free will or by a heartfelt need to improve the lives of the enslaved and the colonised. To this extent, changes in constitutional governance, was adjustment of what was interpreted as crisis – to do something 'before the natives massacre us all'. In other words, changes occurred to maintain law and order among the disenfranchised majority; and to maintain paramountcy of the colonial elite and its newly qualified neocolonial Afro-Saxons rather than to create and facilitate governing rules that would engender social equality and justice.

Since independence, successive governments have busied themselves with nation-building (among other things) and in some respects have attained relative success in the provision of social services, guaranteeing political and economic rights, education and health opportunities for its citizens. The generation that has been born since 1962 is far better off in this respect, than their forebears. At the same time, the need for constitutional changes have been recognised, and those in government since independence in 1962 have made attempts towards this effort.

Hence, constitutional changes were attempted, in 1974-1980 and then suspended after pressure from the International Monetary Fund (IMF) to cut back on 'non-essential' government programmes. The acceptance of those IMF impositions by the political elite by the Jamaican government, did not only reinforce the colonial baggage and the need for constitutional change but perpetuated an attitude of deference and mystification in the face of European power and authority. Rather than brave it anew, it was perhaps, easier to maintain illusions of progress via IMF and World Bank recipes, instead of taking hard, *independent* steps and make the bold decisions which genuine human progress demands.[47] There is also a selfish reality that one has to consider – abandoning the constitutional changes at that time, would also mean maintenance of the status quo which gave the political and economic elite the protection of being extended beneficiaries of neocolonial global capitalism, especially during the 1970s when the imperial posture of the USA lay heavily on the citizens of Jamaica.[48] It was not in their interest, locally and internationally, to further tamper with it.

Be that as it may, constitutional change has been on the agenda since the 1990s. Attention has been drawn to the need to create a Charter of Rights. This proposed Charter of Rights has been identified as the most important goal in changing the constitutional arrangements.[49] Further suggestions have been made to improve the nature of governing democracy and participation in political life to reflect national sentiments and to remove the foreign bias towards Britain.[50] However, the issue of removing the protectionist bias for the economic and political elite and the abuse of space has not been seriously tackled. Indeed, it has been argued as not having gone far enough in addressing the current deficiencies in the constitution.[51] In this respect, the draft Charter of Rights still does not grant citizens the right to bring offenders before the Constitutional court, whether other citizens or private entities, have violated their fundamental rights and freedoms. Additionally, the draft Charter does not grant citizens constitutional protection from other citizens or private entities. These omissions will continue to leave them vulnerable to large corporations, especially the contemporary space invaders, the multinationals; as well as the continuing coercive power of the state. Since both the economic protectionist bias and the abuse of space are directly related, one can argue that such a process will not be exhaustive and therefore not as effective.[52] To a large extent, there appears to be some kind of reluctance or maybe even fear, in upsetting the status quo that the colonial constitutional pass-down was able to establish and cement.

There is also perhaps, the ignorant arrogance often found among political elites that significant constitutional change does not really require wide-scale participation of the citizens of the nation, even if specific members representing some interest groups are involved in the process. As such, the monetary and human energies spent in the process do not reflect the idea that the constitution needs not reform, but rehauling and national prioritising.[53] This also points to a larger issue of governance in the Jamaican/Caribbean case, which has tended to be hegemonic and monopolistic in neocolonial times. In other words, the handling of constitution is itself fraught with plantalogical politics. Another issue that is reflected in the Constitution is the impression that Jamaica began in 1962 and not from the Tainos/Arawaks – to Columbus's piracy and erroneous navigation, through to transplantation of Africans, enslavement and colonisation etectera. It is not quite clear, from the constitution, how the rules for governance will be accepted and adhered to, if the constitution itself is not shaped by a revisionist history and culture of the country. It leaves one with the question – should the constitution reflect who the Jamaican people are? Does the constitution outline what the Jamaican people want, given its history and culture? Do the framers of the constitution understand what they are trying to build? Arguably, then, the process thus far reflects an emphasis on constitutional *reform* rather than on *transformation*, again spatially dominated by the (neo)colonial elite.

However, with accepting the colonial baggage that has been handed down without serious question or investigation, also means accepting and/or negating the fact that the constitution supports a fundamental lack of justice. What history has shown thus far is that several contradictions emanating from all social groups in Jamaican society occur because of a fundamental lack of justice. This lack of justice is inherited yes, but its perpetuation in the neocolonial era sews similar seeds of divide and conquer strategies of the colonial power. From the misguided perspective of the coloniser, that is what the enslavement and colonisation required. From the perspective of an ostensibly free society since Independence in 1962, its perpetuation belittles the smadditizing efforts of the ancestors to struggle, fight and survive, and to leave a presence to grow from, since the inception of enslavement. With a constitution that continues to not facilitate human life or the guarantee of justice as a human right, depending on where one is situated on the social/ethnic ladder, one may very well have to, *chuk it*, hustle or struggle to make a life. Thus battles for space continue among all groups which (i) perpetuates criminal behaviour; (ii) perpetuates aggressive measures both on the part of the protestor/actor or on the part of the law enforcement officers/punishers as the case may be (iii) and perpetuates feelings of defensive entitlement to space. Where is the space for discussion of how space can be equally shared? Where is the space to build national consensus?

With each generation, oral and written knowledge passes down that a great injustice has been done, and continues to do so. The denial of space to exist as humans in a common world is still prevalent in one's *yawd* . It has created the idea that retributive justice is necessary. The justice is considered to be retributive insofar as there is a feeling that there is need to gain an equality that injustice had overturned, and that the moral order is not balanced until this is administered. This continues in the collective consciousness and is perhaps most expressed in creative arts specifically in literature, music, song and dance – precisely the only spaces our forebears were able to significantly and visibly carve out during their enslaved and colonised circumstances. Here we may also recall the lyrical content of reggae in the 1960s and 1970s, especially by Peter Tosh, Bob Marley, Burning Spear, The Mighty Diamonds, The Abyssinians, Jacob Miller and so many other Jamaican cultural artists of that era, which spoke to the experience of living out an existence of denied human space, whereby it had to be demanded.[54] The aggressive and anti-political stance of many of the songs coming out of the dancehall era in the 1990s also illustrates a resort to claiming space where it is not legitimately given. At the same time, it illustrates that the proponents of dancehall reject the hegemony of neocolonial spatial allocations[55].

The lack of justice maintained in the status quo means a continued denial of legitimate space to exist as *smaddy*. Inclusive within this denial of space is also a lack of respect, legitimacy and value given to indigenous cultural expression. The way in which smadditization occurs, in contemporary times, is, like their forebears, a resort to auxiliary spaces of the creative imagination and auxiliary spaces of the dance, the roadside, the veranda, and the *yawd*. When pushed to a limit, in terms of the exploitative abuse of space, and/or non-facilitation to use that rightful space, one sees the same historical pattern of resistance being repeated. This takes the form of street protest, creative expression, increasing criminality and migration to other lands. The battle for space continues as Nettleford has noted, 'between the mass of the population and an oligarchic few who would wish to freeze their current occupation of political and economic space to timeless legitimacy'.[56]

Now they had another problem: it was not how to keep people in captivity. It was how to set people at liberty.[57]

CONCLUSION

'Smadditization' as mentioned earlier in the discussion was the process which one goes through to become 'somebody' in a world, largely denied because of one's ethnicity and class. But 'smadditization' is also a struggle to comfortably express and live with one's self in his/her own environment. The argument here is that the process of smadditization is not complete or has barely begun in Jamaica on several accounts. First, at a national level the historical development of the island, including the nature of the transfer of independence, had meant that how to define the Jamaican nation-self had not been undertaken. At an individual level, questions about its colonial past and the colonial baggage that are passed down, left un-addressed and allowed to fester, has not augured well for community and nation-building. The continuation of former colonial strategies of social stratification, divide and conquer behavioural tactics has not fostered consensus. And the majority of Jamaicans in the neocolonial era operate as cultural and political minorities, insofar as their space is not given as the dominant and legitimate space for expression and participation.

Jamaica's constitutional history has demonstrated that human life has not really been facilitated. Historically, the common interests of Jamaican people were not relevant. Subsequent constitutional reform has not applied surgery and penetrated the root of the problem – the plantalogical politics. The question of the perverse reality of colonial baggage and how it impedes nation-building was not considered in a 39-year old nation's previous attempts at building a new civilisation in the Americas. With the continuing difficulties experienced in Jamaican social and economic life, and the dissatisfaction expressed with neocolonial political practice, this idea of the need for retributive justice to attend to the continuing abuse/denial of space is significant. If one argues that this need for retributive justice is at least, almost nation-wide, the constitution would represent the point at which we could perhaps, address it seriously, if battles for space are to dissolve and if consensus is to emerge and flourish.

The suggestion is that the idea of a constitution should really be built in light of what is desirable for that nation and the *majority* of its citizens, and with an understanding of the past and the lessons learnt, and the mistakes that would be safe guarded to prevent repetition. If the European nations held the common interest to enslave and colonise groups of people from different corners of the earth for human exploitation and economic gains, why should independence, and therefore postindependence development, work in favour of a former colonised people when it was never meant to in the first place? This being the nature of plantalogical politics, at which point does one acknowledge and consciously attempt nation-building which at the heart of it begins with finding common interest? Following this line then, wouldn't the constitution be the best place to start?

One may argue that would be the project of an idealist population. Some would argue that such a process would also demand and require self-transformation. Secondly, while social progress may be initiated through constitutional change, it does not necessarily guarantee significant success. However, if one accepts that ideals are goals to work towards, then accepting the results that may and may not be beneficial would be part and parcel of a genuine attempt to create and build a just society. Not defining one's own rules to live by and not having them enshrined in a constitution may be considered more of an aberration, insofar as substantive positive change may not occur if one is not clear about the rules, if one is not clear about who and what the nation-self is. Constitutional transformation in this way would assist in the attempts of completing the process of smadditization, both at the individual level and at the national level.

Finally, constitutional transformation, as discussed here, would also allow for the emergence of common interest and consensus as an intrinsic part of the national psyche and necessary for the challenging task of nation-building. On this note, it is perhaps befitting to end with a quote from one of the Caribbean's most insightful intellectuals, C.L.R. James. In 1959, he wrote that in order for the Caribbean to grow beyond survival, it was necessary to prioritise the 'common' in *national* life:

> ... otherwise we have the flag and the national anthem and we have an enormous number of officials running up and down and in and out, but we remain essentially colonial, with the colonial mentality, because the social, geographical and even the historical surroundings of colonialism remain with us on every side.[58]

Endnotes and References

1. See in particular, George Beckford (1972, rpt. 1985, 1999), *Persistent Poverty Underdevelopment in Plantation Economies of the Third World*; Kamau Brathwaite (1971), *The Development of Creole Society in Jamaica 1770-1820* and Antonio Benitez Rojo (1997), *The Repeating Island: the Caribbean and the Postmodern Perspective.*
2. See Louis Lindsay, *Myth of Independence: Middle Class Politics and Non-mobilization in Jamaica.* (Kingston: Institute of Social and Economic

Research, University of the West Indies, Mona, 1975). Working Paper No. 6; Rex Nettleford *Mirror Mirror: Identity, Race and Protest in Jamaica* (1970).

3. See Sylvia Wynter (1967) 'Lady Nugent's Journal' in *Jamaica Journal*, Vol. 1, No. 1, December. pp. 23-34.

4. For such discussions see Richard Hart (1985) *The Slaves Who Abolished Slavery, Volume 2: Blacks in Rebellion*; Hilary Beckles, (1982) 'The 200 Years War: Slave Resistance in the British West Indies' in *Jamaican Historical Review*, No. 13; Hilary Beckles, (1993) 'Caribbean Anti-Slavery: the Liberation Ethos of Enslaved Blacks' in *Caribbean Slavery in the Atlantic World*, eds. Hilary Beckles and Verene Shepherd.

5. The preference is for the term 'neocolonial', rather than 'post-colonial'. 'Post-colonial' is problematic for in it implies that the 'colonial' (and all the connotations associated with it) does not exist, no longer exists, and that Europe can wipe its hands clean, clear its conscience of the dilemmas European imperialism created in the Caribbean and elsewhere it chose to destroy peoples and cultures for economic gain. My preference is for the term, 'neocolonial' which accepts that the colonial baggage persists locally and internationally.

6. For discussions on the battle for space, See Rex Nettleford (1993) *Inward Stretch Outward Reach: A Voice from the Caribbean*.

7. Ibid.

8. That is, 'smaddy', deriving from the English word, 'somebody'. This philosophical argument on the concept and process of 'smadditization' is developed in Charles. W. Mills, (1997), 'Smadditizin', *Caribbean Quarterly*, Vol. 43, no. 2, June, pp.54-55.

9. Ibid.

10. See Paget Henry, (1983) 'Decolonization and Cultural Underdevelopment in the Caribbean' in T*he Newer Caribbean: Decolonization, Democracy and Development*. Carl Stone and Paget Henry (eds.)

11. See George Beckford, (1972, rpt. 1985, 1999) *Persistent Poverty*, pp. 8-45.

12. Translates, as 'two bulls cannot rule in the same pen'.

13. Rex Nettleford (1993), pp. 80-86.

14. Earl Lovelace (1996) *Salt*. pp. 3-7.

15. Rex Nettleford (1993), p. 80.

16. Yawd is Jamaican for the English word, yard. Initially used to describe the 'Negro yard' – a small plot of land where the enslaved person could grow his/her agricultural provisions. In contemporary times it is used to refer to one's home, whether house or nation, that which one may call his/her own.

17. Nettleford, p. 81.

18. I concur with Nettleford that this continues at regional and international levels with the changing face of imperialism in the guise and 'headmanship' of the USA, in the current era of neo-liberal globalisation. Nettleford wrote in *Inward Stretch Outward Reach*:

> In the Caribbean world where colonial dependency, super ordinate/subordinate, powerful/powerless categories determined social realities from its modern beginnings.... Such dialectical relationships have been central to human existence as a matter of course. The ensuing battle for space, in both an elemental and physical sense, constitutes then, the force vitale, of a still groping society. To this day, the phenomenon of numerical majorities functioning as cultural and power minorities persists in the Commonwealth or Anglophone Caribbean...

Ibid.

19. Once the British captured Jamaica in 1655 a government based on the constitutional system in England was established for the benefit of the Englishmen who settled on the island. A governor was appointed and a Colonial Council was set up to advise him. A house of assembly was established for the purpose of passing laws and raising taxes. The colonial council became a second legislative house of the local Parliament. See Lloyd Barnett (1992), *The Jamaican Constitution: Basic Facts and Questions*.

20. Ibid.

21. Ibid.

22. Roy Augier, (1998) 'Before and After 1865' in *Before and After 1865: Education, Politics and Regionalism in the Caribbean*, eds. Brian L. Moore and Swithin Wilmot.

23. Ibid.

24. Ibid.

25. For further discussion on the participation of Jamaican-African politicians during this period see Joy Lumsden (1998) 'A Forgotten Generation: Black Politicians in Jamaica, 1884-1914' in *Before and After 1865: Education, Politics and Regionalism in the Caribbean*. Edited by Brian L. Moore and Swithin Wilmot, pp. 112-122.

26. Patrick Bryan, *The Jamaican People, 1880-1902: Race, Class and Social Control*, pp. 10-38.

27. Augier, (1998), p. 5.

28. The Falmouth Post, Oct 27, 1865; and Feb 16, 1866. Cited in Rosemary Mc. Nairn, 'From Panthers to Political Power: Evolution and Black Identity in Jamaica, 1865-1900'. In *Forging Identities and Patterns of Development in Latin America and the Caribbean*, edited by Patrick. M. Taylor et. al. p. 279.

29. Augier, (1998), p. 8.

30. Trevor Munroe *The Politics of Constitutional Decolonisation in Jamaica, 1944-1962*. (Kingston: Institute of Social and Economic Research, University of the West Indies, 1984) p. 13; Augier, (1998) p. 9.

31. Munroe, (1984) p. 13.

32. Joy Lumsden (1998) 'A Forgotten Generation: Black Politicians in Jamaica, 1884-1914' in *Before and After 1865: Education, Politics and Regionalism in the Caribbean*, pp. 112-122. The brown-skinned blacks were given some privilege to enter the political game, on the argument that their lighter hue of black caused by racial mixing (whether forced or voluntary) put them closer to the whites, therefore possibly more intelligent! For instance, they were allowed to occupy positions of petty officials and clerks. However, having the visible African heritage also meant that they could not occupy positions of authority or power and could only purchase land if European ancestry could be specifically traced back to a plantation, at least two generations back. Restrictions of educational qualifications also applied. Emanating from the plantation, the continuation of this colonial policy has created further tensions between these two groups of blacks. Patrick Bryan (1991) *The Jamaican People, 1880-1902: Race, Class and Social Control*; Derek Gordon (1991) 'Race, class and social mobility' in *Garvey: His Work and Impact*, eds. Rupert Lewis and Patrick Bryan; Patrick Bryan (1996) 'The Black Middle Class in 19th Century Jamaica' in *Caribbean Freedom: Economy and Society from Emancipation to the Present*, eds. Hilary Beckles and Verene Shepherd.

33. Lumsden, (1998) p. 113; Rupert Lewis (1988) *Marcus Garvey: Anti-Colonial Champion*; Tony Martin, (1993) 'Marcus Garvey, the Caribbean and the Struggle for Jamaican Nationhood' in *Caribbean Freedom: Economy and Society from Emancipation to the Present*, eds. Hilary Beckles and Verene Shepherd; Swithin Wilmot (2002) 'The Politics of Samuel Clarke' in *Questioning Creole: Creolisation Discourses in Caribbean Culture*, eds. Verene Shepherd and Glen Richards.

34. Lumsden (1998) p. 114.

35. Ibid.

36. This occurred to varying degrees for the Jamaican Indians and Chinese as well.

37. For elaboration, see Louis Lindsay (1981) *Myth of a Civilising Mission: British Colonialism and the Politics of Symbolic Manipulation*. Kingston: Institute of Social and Economic Research, University of the West Indies.

38. See especially, Albert Memi (1967) *The Coloniser and the Colonised* and O. Manoni (1956) *Prospero and Caliban: The Psychology of Colonialism*; Ashis Nandy (1994) *The Intimate Enemy*; and Kamau Brathwaite (1974)

Contradictory Omens; for detailed examinations on the psychological and cultural impact of colonialism on both the colonised and the coloniser.

39. For this paper, we are largely concerned with the condition of the (neo)colonised. However, Manoni (1956) and Memi (1967); among others, have pointed out that the (neo)coloniser carries within his/her consciousness and adopts its as apart of the cultural being of the European/ Euro-American and other derivatives, the idea of God-like superiority. This leaves two distortions worth isolating here. First is the idea that one is so great that mistakes naturally attributed to human behaviour is not possible or admissible. Second, that because of one's greatness, the value of life is greater, and thus one is entitled to more, even at the expense of other life forms (humans, animals, the universe and nature) and knowledge cultural bases. Therefore, one has to defend this life at all costs and with all available means. For extensive discussion see also Marimba Ani (1992) *Yurugu: An African-centred Critique of European Cultural Thought and Behaviour.*

40. For one discussion on the politics that led to the demise of the Federation, see C.L.R. James (1959), 'Federation: We Failed Miserably, How and Why'. Public Lecture delivered to the Caribbean Society, Kingston, Jamaica, November.

41. See Louis Lindsay, *Myth of Independence: Middle Class Politics and Non-mobilisation in Jamaica.* (Kingston: Institute of Social and Economic Research, UWI, 1975) p. 23.

42. Ibid. pp.16-17.

43. Ibid., p. 1; Roy Augier 'The Working of the Jamaican Constitution before Independence: A Commentary', *Caribbean Quarterly*, Vol. 8, no. 3, September 1962 p. 176.

44. Ibid. p. 52.

45. Barnett (1992) pp.6-7.

46. Ibid. p. 9.

47. Lindsay, p. 50.

48. Ibid. See also Michael Manley, (1982) *Struggle in the Periphery* for discussions on US interventionist imperial politics in Jamaica and other parts of the Americas at that time, with nations who chose to attempt reform in some way, reflecting a new kind of nation and politics – Grenada, Nicaragua, Chile etc.

49. 'Legislators want Charter of Rights to grant citizens more power', The Jamaica Observer. Online Version, May 21, 2001.

50. See Lloyd Barnett (1992); Report of the Reconstituted Constitutional Commission for Constitutional and Electoral Reform, (1994) Kingston: Government of Jamaica.

51. *Jamaica Observer*, Online version, May 21, 2001.

52. Lloyd Barnett (1992), p. 5.

53. 'No Cash Slows Reform' in *The Gleaner*, On-line version, November 12, 1999. Also, the Report of the Reconstituted Constitutional Commission for Constitutional and Electoral Reform, (1994) Kingston: Government of Jamaica.

54. See particularly, Erna Brodber (1985) 'Black Consciousness and Popular Music in Jamaica in the 1960s and 1970s' in *Caribbean Quarterly,* Volume 31, no. 2. 1985.

55. See for example, Anita M. Waters (1985) *Race, Class and Political Symbols: Rastafari and Reggae in Jamaican Politics.* For further discussion on the role of popular culture in Jamaican politics, particularly dancehall, see Taitu A Heron (1998) 'Political Manipulation and Popular Culture in Jamaica' in *Pensamiento Propio,* Vol. 3, no. 8, April.

56. Nettleford, (1993) p. 83.

57. Lovelace, (1996) p. 7.

58. James (1959) p.

***

24

Dèyè Mòn Gen Mòn
[beyond mountains are more mountains]
The Haitian Revolution and the
Discourse on Race and Slavery

David Granger

... Boisrond produced a second paper. The act of independence, which all the generals had signed, renouncing France, declaring the country free, and giving it the new but ancient name of Haiti. 'Long live independence!' shouted Dessalines. And the cannon began to boom, and the church bells pealed, and the crowd roared. Free at last, the world's first black republic, the hemisphere's second independent nation, Haiti, had been born.[1]

And what a birth. The fusion of ideologies, interests and actors that resulted in the establishment of the free state of Haiti, the emancipation of over a half million slaves,[2] and the collapse of the most profitable plantation economy of its era,[3] also engendered a fission of sorts, the impact of which would seem to be entirely out of proportion with Haiti's current place in the global hierarchy of nations. These days Haiti is a forgotten and forsaken place, apparently of little consequence to the powers that once struggled so mightily to bar its entry into our world. Is it possible that 200 years ago the British spent the lives of 60,000 men there, that, as WEB Dubois argued, the Haitian revolution strengthened the anti-slavery movement in Britain[4] and opened the way for serious debate on the subject in the United States; that it signaled the demise of Napoleon's designs on a North American empire, and prompted the southern states to end the African slave trade to their ports?

It is indeed possible. At the turn of the nineteenth century, Haiti was the epicenter of a shock that radiated like ripples on the surface of a Caribbean that so many wanted so desperately to remain calm. How is it then, that the Haitian revolution remains one of modern history's most under appreciated events? Why is it that the importance of Haiti's birth to the shaping of the discourse on race and slavery, or even the notion that the discourse was reshaped, goes virtually unacknowledged? These are the questions to be considered within this study.

It is difficult to argue that the Haitian Revolution was, in any way, a small event. The island endured nearly 13 years of virtually continuous armed conflict, beginning in earnest in 1791 with the revolt of the slaves of Haiti's northern plains, and culminating in the defeat of Napoleon's troops at the end of 1803. What began as a struggle by the affranchi caste,[5] to procure rights and recognition from France, a movement informed by the principles of the metropole's 1789 Revolution, but opposed bitterly by the colony's grand blancs,[6] ended with not only the near complete physical destruction of the colony, but the dismantling of the philosophical and psychological foundations of the colony as well.

A cursory history of the revolution is essential to a discussion of the discursive formations and manipulations surrounding the event.[7] In January of 1790, as the whites of St Domingo divided themselves into royalist and bourgeois factions, a delegation of mulattoes, led by Petion, Raimond and Oge, approached the assembly in France, invoked the Rights of Man, and petitioned for recognition of free coloured property owners as citizens with a vote. They were rejected. Seeing no hope for political flexibility in the colony, Oge resolved to return to St Domingo as the leader of an armed revolt.

Prepared and financed in London by Thomas Clarkson,[8] and armed during a stop in the United States,[9] Oge arrived in St Domingo on October 21, 1790. Too impatient to await reinforcements, he promptly attacked the city of Le Cap with only a few hundred men, and was just as promptly repelled, captured, tortured, and executed.[10] Not what he envisioned, but his actions were extremely important in that they began the armed conflict that, as James writes, 'woke the sleeping slaves.'[11]

Oge's action brought the metropole's revolution to the consciousness of the slave masses. Uprisings and desertions began slowly and in small scale, and were initially extinguished as easily as ever, but the slaves, well aware of the instability of the colonial administration and of the growing dissent between the petit blancs and grand blancs, continued to revolt and abscond in increasing numbers and with increasing intensity.[12] In July of 1791, a massive slave conspiracy, under the direction of a vodoun priest named Boukman, overran the northern plain. The revolution, while still amorphous and virtually directionless, was underway. The fighting continued in this relatively unorganised fashion for over two years, with ex-slaves holding the northern plain under the leadership of Bissaou, Jean Francois, and Toussaint L'Ouverture, all creole and former slaves, the mulattoes and their black allies controlling the southern peninsula under the direction of Rigaud, and the majority of the whites, still arguing amongst themselves, barricaded in the towns of the central plains and ports.

By the end of 1793, Toussaint was emerging as the most savvy, moderate, and respected of the black generals. In search of a position of power for him and his mostly ex-slave followers, and well aware of their precarious status under French control, he allied himself with the neighbouring Spanish army, and with a force of over 4,000 well-trained, disciplined and relatively well-provisioned men, began a campaign to subdue and stabilise large areas of northern St Domingo. By 1794, when the British, sensing an opportunity to regain an empire in the Americas and simultaneously stifle France's colonial expansion, sent seven thousand troops from Barbados to capture Martinique, St Lucia and Guadalupe, as well as threaten St Domingo, Toussaint, operating with the Spanish, and therefore an ally of the British, could only watch.

Sonthonax, St Domingo's incumbent Governor General, responded to the British incursion with his trump card; he freed all slaves willing to fight for France, giving the labourers an investment in staving off the British, and giving Toussaint his opportunity for a return to the French side. Toussaint immediately abandoned the Spanish, taking the supplies they had given him, drove them back into Santo Domingo, and directed his attacks at the British. By November of 1798, the British had been expelled from St Domingo, and by January of 1800, Toussaint, through armed struggle and political manipulation, had established himself as the military and political leader of St Domingo.

By most accounts, it was Toussaint's desire to govern St Domingo as a semi-independent protectorate of France, with slavery abolished, but the plantation system intact. In fact, he took steps to encourage, and in some cases force, his fellow ex-slaves to go back to work on the plantations. His own Black Code decreed that the former slaves would be expected to return to their plantations, or the nearest intact one, and work the fields. One half of the profit from the plantation would go to the interim government, one quarter to the owner, [13] and one quarter was to be divided among the labourers. In hindsight, this would have likely been the most peaceful and profitable plan for the colony and for France, but it proved unacceptable to Napoleon Bonaparte, who by this time had taken control of the French government. He was loathe to concede any power to what he described as 'gilded Africans', [14] and incensed by Toussaint's promulgation of a constitution and the implicit suggestion that St Domingo should be given Dominion status, [15] sent his brother in law Leclerc, in command of 20,000 troops, [16] to take the colony by force.

Toussaint's willingness to coercively return labourers to the plantations, an overwhelmingly economically motivated, and ostensibly short term plan, one designed to afford St Domingo some measure of financial autonomy, was nevertheless incompatible with the aspirations of many of the revolutionaries for freedom and land. [17] These ex-slaves were not willing participants in Toussaint's regime, and under the direction of bossale[18] generals like Sans Souci,[19] and maroon leaders like Macaya,[20] they were often active dissidents. The war for Haiti's independence raged for two years, and by its end, found the island ravaged, Toussaint extradited to France, and Dessalines, a leader less savvy, but more focused, and exponentially more harsh, at the head of a victorious army and a new nation. Along the way, the divisions between white, mulatto, and black, between creole and bossale had deepened, and the spectators had begun to shape their own version of Haiti's revolution and its repercussions.

It will be useful to establish a framework for the discussion of the discourse, which surrounds the Haitian Revolution. Michel Rolph Trouillot has attacked this question in his book *Silencing the Past,* and to put it very simply, he argues that the discourse is incomplete, and that what exists, has been misused. He uses the metaphor of 'silences' to describe this incompleteness, asserting that:

> Silences enter the process of historical production at four crucial moments: the moment of fact creation (the making of sources); the moment of fact assembly (the making of archives); the moment of fact retrieval (the making of narratives); and the moment of retrospective significance (the making of history).[21]

In all of these cases, the Haitian Revolution as an event, as well as a challenge to Western philosophy and colonialism, has been silenced. Trouillot points out that this silencing was facilitated in the first instance, the moment of fact creation, by the lack of literate sources within the revolutionary masses. He writes that the Revolution expressed itself through action rather than rhetoric, and therefore its advances could not be anticipated and accurately documented by the actors as they happened. The lack of literacy and (Western) political tradition among the revolutionaries, allowed them to make moves 'not overly restricted by previous ideological limits set by professionals in the colony or elsewhere',[22] but also inhibited their input at the moment of fact assembly, or the creation of archives. This meant that not only was the Haitian Revolution unimaginable to Western intellectuals who held negative images of Blacks or were simply intent upon denying the humanity of the slaves, it was apparently inconceivable to them even in the political context of the French and American Revolutions, and could not be recorded, evaluated, or narrated on the same terms. This refusal to place the Haitian Revolution on the same plane with the American and French Revolutions continues. Its retrospective significance has continually been silenced by its description as a revolt or insurrection in an age of revolutions.

Trouillot argues very convincingly that silencing is real, and that the Haitian legacy is a victim of this silencing, not only by non-Haitian contributors to the discourse, but by Haitians as well, who neglect episodes and themes of the

Revolution at odds with their subsequent nation building project. Where Trouillot is concerned with arguing the fundamentals of silencing, I am interested in the logistics of the process of silencing as it pertains to this specific case. Above I posed the question: How is it that the Haitian Revolution remains one of modern history's most under appreciated events? Trouillot answers this question, at least in a rhetorical sense: 'It was silenced.' I then go on to ask: Why is it that the importance of the Haitian Revolution to the reshaping of the discourse on race and slavery, or even the notion that the discourse was reshaped, goes virtually unacknowledged? I ask this because even as Trouillot and others argue that the Haitian Revolution was silenced, that the ambitions and achievements of Haiti's first leaders have been dismissed, they overlook the way in which that silencing took place. I would venture to point out that they fall into the very trap that Trouillot warns against. By asserting that individuals and institutions threatened by the Revolution coped with the threat by simply reinforcing the existing discourse on race and slavery, they silence the effect that the Revolution had on that discourse.

Trouillot argues that even as the size of the revolution became evident, the surrounding slave societies refused to acknowledge its importance. Rather than face the fact that the slaves were in search of freedom, they concocted alternate explanations, attributing agency to actors other than the slaves so as to 'force the rebellion back within their world-view, shoving the facts into the proper order of discourse.'[23] He argues, in fact, that for 13 years, the facts were tailored to fit the discourse. What then, when the facts finally overwhelmed that discourse and Haiti stood free? Trouillot offers no acceptable answer. He acknowledges, however, that 'The very deeds of the revolution were incompatible with major tenets of dominant Western ideologies.'[24] Ostensibly included among these tenets, are those which pertain to the construction of race and the rationalisation of slavery. Those aspects of existing ideology were in many cases no longer applicable. The events had outstripped any efforts to confine them within the parameters of the discourse. Indeed, it became impractical to attempt an explanation of the events of the Haitian Revolution using the existing discourse. Instead, the revolution as an event, and Haiti itself as a challenge to that existing discourse, were silenced. The reverberations of the Revolution were felt throughout the Caribbean and the United States, its ideals were absorbed by slaves and feared by slave owners, debated by legislatures and economic institutions, and consequently, the process of silencing Haiti was more complicated and confounding than has been acknowledged.

The silencing of the Haitian Revolution is confounding, though not surprising, largely because of the latent philosophical and ideological sentiments, which linked it with the French and American Revolutions. I pointed out above that Trouillot and others have argued that the common response to the Haitian Revolution was a reinforcement of the existing discourse on race and slavery; that slave owners in the United States and the British West Indies explained away the events in Haiti, the obvious transformation of individuals very much like the slaves and free colored people they were themselves in contact with, from, as James puts it, '[a mass], trembling in hundreds before a single white man, into a people able to organise themselves and defeat the most powerful European nations of their day,'[25] by clinging to characterisations of blacks as barbaric and sub-human and relying on the accompanying repression. Michael Dash shares this tenuous position, asserting that:

> In order to deal with the disturbing and threatening existence of a state founded by ex-slaves, Americans resorted to the discourse that had already stabilised the way the black race would be perceived. Relations between the United States and Haiti were the political articulation of such a discourse and to this extent, it could be claimed that the United States almost invented Haiti imaginatively in the nineteenth century.[26]

This is an oversimplification. Elsewhere, Dash argues for recognition of Haiti's symbolism as parallel with that of 'Said's Orient'. Whereas he states at one juncture that 'Americans resorted to the discourse that had already stabilised the way the Black race would be perceived,' at another he asserts that:

> Haiti emerges as an inexhaustible symbol designed to satisfy material as well as psychological needs. Images ... are not arbitrary in either case but constitute a special code, a system of antithetical values which establish radical, ineradicable distinctions between the subject and the other, west and east, the United States and Haiti.[27]

This emergence of Haiti as an 'inexhaustible symbol', ostensibly subsequent to the declaration of its independence, would indicate that perceptions of the Blacks who inhabited Haiti were subject to manipulation. Dash then suggests that 'this systematic network of images eventually hardens into unshakeable dogma that is based on the notion of the "other" as the negative of the subject, a zone of absence, a screen onto which the subject projects his repression.'[28] I find it difficult to reconcile this image of 'hardening' with the idea that Haiti was invented imaginatively by the United States. If the discourse was static, and the dogma unshakeable, what was the need for any invention at all? Alfred Hunt's evaluation of Haiti's influence agrees with my argument that this invention was necessary because the revolution did not prompt a solidification of the existing discourse, but rather forced a reshaping of it:

After St. Domingo, the South felt that it was perpetually under siege and it was increasingly aware of the instability that a slave society endured. One of the many lessons garnered from the events in 'hapless' St. Domingo was that supporters of slavery must develop a consensus on the ideological assumptions concerning white and black relations.[29]

I do agree that Haiti was in some sense, 'invented imaginatively' by the United States in the nineteenth century, and I also agree that much of the response to the Haitian Revolution consisted of attempts to reinforce the existing discourse. I must argue, however, that intellectuals all over the world, but especially in the United States and those European countries which held colonies in the region, were well aware of the similarities to be found between the American and Haitian Revolutions, both retrospectively, and during the Haitian Revolution itself. Furthermore, they were also aware, as were leaders in the United States, that not only was St Domingo absolutely pivotal in the struggle for North American empire, but that an independent Haiti under the leadership of Toussaint was a viable, if improbable, proposition. This knowledge, and the actions and policies, which it provoked, are part of the transformation of the discourse, which took place. The body of knowledge available to Western intellectuals with which to evaluate and characterise blacks was changed by the Haitian Revolution. Indeed, the scale of the Revolution forced that new body of knowledge to be considered. It would be naive to assume that contributors to the discourse were ignorant of this new perspective, or naive enough themselves to ignore its importance. Brenda Plummer, arguing along these same lines, points out the parallels between the revolutionary incubations of Haiti and the United States:

Though few countries were as dissimilar as the United States and Haiti, a furtive ideological bond linked eighteenth century republicanism in United States political culture with that articulated by the St. Domingo rebels. For the white yeomanry of the United States, the stability of the polity rested in free holders operating in their own interests, detached from the corruption engendered by dependence. Despite the efforts of indigenous rulers to perpetuate some form of unfree labor, Haitians also preferred the division of property in freehold. Land ownership and the right to bear arms remained crucial to the definition of liberty and personal honor in both societies.[30]

Carolyn Fick, also cognizant of the similarities shared by the American, French, and Haitian Revolutions, and also somewhat confounded by the silencing of Haiti's birth, expresses some skepticism that the lack of discourse to be found connecting the colonial question in general, and Haiti in particular, to the events of the French Revolution, is coincidental:

> When the events in St Domingo are examined from the vantage point of the colonial revolution, it becomes immediately evident that they are intertwined with, and even partially dependent upon those of the metropolitan revolution in France. Yet the sheer paucity, if not the near total absence, in French Revolutionary historiography of any substantive treatment of the colonial question, of the slave trade, or of slavery itself – indeed – of those interlocking spheres of activity forming the economic underpinnings of the rising French Bourgeoisie – would lead one to assume, that from the vantage point of the French Revolution, these issues were, at best, of only peripheral importance to the vital political and social problems facing a revolutionary France. That the abolition of slavery, the most radical step of the Haitian Revolution and perhaps even of the French Revolution, should occupy so trivial a place in the overall histories of the Revolution is no doubt a stubborn and persistent reflection of the inability of the French revolutionaries themselves to confront the issue of slavery head-on in the legislative assemblies, and to do so forthrightly in the name of those principles guiding the revolution – that is the universalist principles of liberty and equality.[31]

This silence is a reflection of the recognition by French intellectuals that the principles of liberty, equality and fraternity were shared by Haiti's revolutionaries, and of their inability to reconcile that recognition with the maintenance of slavery in other French colonies, or with the continued reliance on the existing discourse on race and slavery to justify it. There were members of the French government who recognised the transformation of the former slaves of St Domingo, as well as the futility of continued reliance on the existing discourse in governing evaluations of, and interactions with, those former slaves. This opinion was allegedly presented by an anonymous French Counselor of State:

> But now how different are our circumstances? Not only will there be no end to our detachments thither, but the life of ceaseless toil, in mountain marches and midnight skirmishes, with a lurking and marauding enemy, will give tenfold force to the unwholesome elements. Formerly a few hundreds were sufficient to guard the public peace, but now how many thousands will be requisite to dispossess an armed nation, fighting under a provident and valiant leader, for

their soil, their liberty, their very being? Do we not all know what our revolution has done on both sides of the ocean? It has changed a half a million of helpless and timorous slaves, the mere tools of the farmer and the artisan, the sordid cattle of the field, into men, citizens, and soldiers.[32]

Consider the following episode as further illustration of this consciousness: In 1792, as regiments of French soldiers prepared for departure to St Domingo, they were inspected by a General La Salle. Many of these units adopted slogans in accordance with the principles of the Revolution, and La Salle made it a point to evaluate the various slogans. When he came across the Loire battalion, he noticed that their chosen mantra was 'Live Free or Die'. Finding this unacceptable, he explained to the troops the danger of these words 'in a land where all property is based on the enslavement of Negroes, who, if they adopted this slogan themselves, would be driven to massacre their masters and the army which is crossing the sea to bring peace and law to the colony.'[33]

The effect of the dissemination of revolutionary ideals was recognised and feared not only by French scholars and military men, but also by the residents of the colonies surrounding St Domingo. In 1792, several refugee planters from St Domingo and their slaves requested a landing in Pennsylvania. The state refused and abolished slavery in the state immediately, as did Maryland in 1797.[34] In November of 1800, Representative Rutledge of South Carolina told Congress that the slaves of his constituency 'already had felt this new-fangled French philosophy of liberty and equality', and his state forbade the further immigration of blacks from Africa or the West Indies in 1803, as did Louisiana in 1806.[35] In October of 1802, the militia was called up to prevent the unloading of Haitian slaves from a French frigate in Georgetown, South Carolina.[36]

George Bridges, also demonstrating a cognizance of the effects of ideology in his *Annals of Jamaica*, argues that the planters of St Domingo were themselves to blame for the rising of the slaves; that their eagerness to reap the benefits of changes in France opened the door for the slaves to ingest the Rights of Man: 'As soon as the momentous secret was whispered in St Domingo, it converted the slaves, contented and happy, under the lightest of servile fetters, into implacable enemies and savage brigands'.[37] He later expresses his opinions on how Jamaica endeavored to avoid St Domingo's fate:

Jamaica had no security to expect but from its own exertions, and chiefly depended upon that fortunate and fair condition of its slave population, which rendered them content with their state, and unwilling to exchange a mild and easy servitude for the events of a hazardous rebellion. To keep them in ignorance of what was passing so near to them was impossible ... The most painful vigilance could not prevent the arrival of many seditious characters from the neighboring isle ... Every church, every house resounded with a fearful litany: 'save us from the example of St. Domingo, and from the daggers of our slaves.[38]

Obviously, we should not take Bridges' evaluation of the slaves at face value, but we can glean from his words the sentiment that the ideas of revolution certainly infiltrated St Domingo, and that the surrounding planters recognised that it was upon these ideas of equality and liberty that the revolution was based. The implication of these examples, of the refusals to accept the immigration of Blacks from Haiti, or in some cases, from anywhere in the West Indies; the recurring assertion that the ideas of the French Revolution had given the slaves the inspiration to revolt; was that those Blacks were inherently changed. They were no longer fit for servitude, and they had to be categorised and evaluated in a different way.

A variation on Bridges' argument was presented by another British observer, in an earlier evaluation of the revolution in St Domingo. He argues that the most significant message that the slaves absorbed from the struggle between the whites and mulattoes was that in spite of the ephemeral concepts of liberty and equality being invoked, they were to remain slaves. They realised that they would not be given the rights implied by the articulated universalising principles of the French Revolution, but would instead have to seize them. Like Bridges, this observer faults the whites for the dissemination of ideology, and the display of dissent, which he believed, emboldened the slaves:

The white colonists had just recovered their liberties ... The slaves had been resigned to their unlimited control; all that despotism can wish for they enjoyed: paramount and uncontrollable themselves, they exercised uncontrolled and undefined authority over others. Only one circumstance embittered their enjoyment of a power so gratifying to the perverted taste of man. They were required to share it with others, who, though equally free themselves, and equally competent, were unfortunately distinguished by a different shade of colour. Jealousy is inseparable from the lust of power, and a natural distinction served as a plea for restricting of all authority to the hands of a few. The people of colour remonstrated against this injustice ... In asserting their claim to a seat in the colonial assembly, they felt an impulse to danger and defiance, and cheerfully encountered death, even in its most horrid forms, what then, shall we conceive were the feelings of the Negroes? [39]

This evaluation concludes with the assertion that reform is the only viable avenue for the British West Indian possessions to avoid St Domingo's fate:

[Their experience] may demonstrate to us, that the preservation of our own islands, from similar disasters, depends on the early adoption of measures, which whilst they are vigorous and decisive, are just, conciliatory, and humane; and may caution us, that where we choose not to impart the beginnings of hope, we excite not the ragings of despair. [40]

Abolitionists seized upon the Haitian Revolution as irrefutable evidence that Blacks had the same capacity for revolt against injustice that the French and Americans exhibited in their respective revolutions, and that slavery was a misguided and inherently dangerous project. Spanish opponents of slavery, while apparently less effective in their arguments than their counterparts in Britain and France (Spain preserved slavery in Puerto Rico until 1873, and Cuba until 1880) used the actions of the slaves in Haiti to support their cause. Cuba in particular was a fertile ground for debate on the question of slavery. In the wake of St Domingo's collapse, Cuba became the world's largest sugar producer, with a commensurate growth in the slave population from 50,000 at the turn of the nineteenth century, to 350,000 fifty years later. [41] As early as 1822, Father Felix Varela y Morales referred to the 'republican slaves of St Domingo' as an example of the potential of the African labourers, as well as reminding Cuba's slave owners to learn from the example of St Domingo's Colons, many of who fled to Cuba during the revolution. As late as 1870, Emilio Castelas, another anti-slavery voice in Cuba, was still reminding Cubans of Haiti's revolution as part of his abolitionist arguments. [42]

Thomas Clarkson, on several occasions, reprimanded slave owners for their obtuseness in maintaining that the events of the Haitian Revolution were the result of outside agitation. By outside agitators, the French slave owners meant British abolitionists. As early as 1792, in his essay, *The True State of the Case, Respecting the Insurrection at St Domingo*, Clarkson, while demonstrating his own brand of obtuseness in omitting mention of his aid to Oge, made the case that the ideals of the French Revolution had infiltrated the collective consciousness of the slave masses independent of foreign messengers. Like Bridges, he reminds the slave owners that their own debates and quarrels over the events in France, were a ready source of information for the slaves. [43]

Long after the Haitian Revolution itself had been resolved, Thomas Clarkson maintained a correspondence with Henri Chistophe, Dessalines' successor as ruler of Haiti, and later with Boyer, who followed Christophe. Clarkson's letters to the Haitian leaders provide an illustration of the impact that the Haitian Revolution had on racialist thinking, both positive and negative:

I took the liberty of showing [the Emperor of Russia] one of your letters to me. This letter produced upon his Imperial Majesty the effect I had anticipated. He expressed his obligation to me for having shown it to him; for he confessed it had given him new ideas both with respect to Haiti and to your government. He had been taught by the French and German newspapers (and he had no other source of information) that Haiti was inhabited by a people little better than savages. He now saw them in a very different light.[44]

It is apparent from the Emperor's response that French and German newspapers were still reliant on the stock representations of Blacks as barbaric and inferior, but it is important that the tool for exploding the myth and enlightening him was furnished by a product of the Haitian Revolution. It is also apparent, in another of Clarkson's letters, this one to Boyer, that the existence of Haiti as an independent state, even in 1821, the year that France, in return for a large indemnity, finally recognised Haiti's sovereignty, was anathema to many French leaders, and continued to have an impact on colonial discourse in the metropole:

Your revolution in Haiti has changed the face of things here; and no doubt, this revolution will frequently force itself upon the consideration of the French government, with a view of inquiring whether it may not afford them new pretenses or new opportunities for completing their wishes in that quarter. It becomes you, therefore, to be on your guard, and more particularly when I inform you that the French Journals speak of Haiti more frequently than ever, and in such a way as to excite very unpleasant feelings among the friends of the African race.[45]

The abolitionist movement in the United States also made the connection between the Haitian Revolution and that of the American colonies. In the 1830s, William Lloyd Garrison repeatedly raised the ghost of the Haitian Revolution in an attempt to secure the support of the Northern states for abolition, as well as frighten southern slave owners with the prospect of revolt. Against their will, he attached Northerners to the maintenance of slave society:

So long as we continue as one body – a union – a nation – the compact involves us in the guilt and danger of slavery. If the slaves, goaded to desperation by their cruel masters, should rise en masse, do the citizens of New England reflect that they are constitutionally bound to assist the Southern taskmasters in subduing or exterminating the blacks and are liable to be drafted at a moments warning?

...What protects the South from instant destruction? Our physical force. Break the chain which binds her to the Union, and the scenes of St. Domingo would be witnessed throughout her borders.[46]

The discourse that emerged in Garrison's abolitionist newspaper, *The Liberator*, confirms that the Haitian Revolution was an event with a lasting impact on racialist debates, as were all slave insurrections. The overriding importance of the Haitian case, and the characteristic, which separated it from those various insurrections, however, was that it was so undeniably successful. This success, and the subsequent refusal of the leadership of the United States to acknowledge the Haitian achievement, exposed inconsistencies in Western ideology which were becoming more difficult to ignore or rationalise. Furthermore, as a review of the writings of David Walker, notorious for containing calls to slaves for revolt, points out, the proximity of Haiti to the United States made its example inescapable in subsequent evaluations of the potential of enslaved blacks:

> There are now about as many colored persons within the limits of the union as there were whites at the commencement of our revolution, and it seems to me impossible that they can be prevented from discovering their wrongs. All the laws that can be made cannot wholly exclude the rudiments of learning from among them. The name of Walker alone is a terror to the South, and it is probable there are more or will be more, like him. Negroes have shown their mental capacity in St Domingo, where, thirty-two years ago, they were as much or more debased than they are now in the United States. That example of bloodshed and misery is before the eyes of our slaves; that tragedy, it seems to me, will soon be enacted on an American stage, with new scenery, unless something is speedily done to prevent it.[47]

In arguing the hypocrisy of the continued reliance on slavery in the United States, the Anti-Slavery Record, an abolitionist publication, in 1837, invoked the Haitian Revolution as an embodiment of the republican principles supposedly underpinning the society of the United States. While this account of the Haitian's seizure of independence allowed American slave owners to distance themselves from those of St Domingo by emphasising the latter's brutality, and while it downplays the violence perpetrated by the slaves against their former owners, it does not fail to explicitly compare the inception of the two nations:

> Look at another exhibition which has been made before heaven and earth by a nation of slave holders – a nation that maintains the right of the majority to rule,

of a colony to throw off the yoke of a tyrannous mother country, and of every people who have vindicated their independence by the sword, to have it acknowledged and respected by other nations ... Slave holders themselves will not deny that the slaves of St Domingo, under the old French regime, were horribly abused. In the process of time, these slaves were made free men. Having tasted liberty, they scorned to be re-enslaved. They shivered the yokes, which their old masters sought to reimpose. They drove the minions of Bonaparte from their shores. After a war of less than two years, except the 60,000 in their graves, not a Frenchman of the invading host was left upon the island in the month of November 1803, to question their independence. They fortified that independence with a regular government. Where was our chivalric admiration of liberty and independence, which it did not step forth to welcome them to a standing among the nations of the Earth? [48]

This passage shows a clear understanding of the parallels between the two revolutionary struggles, as well as an outright celebration of the achievements of the Haitians in defeating a French army. Furthermore, it was found in a prominent publication at the center of the most important debate of the time. There is evident in this instance, a clear shift in discourse from a dogmatic characterisation of blacks as inferior and fit only for slavery, to one where Haitians, who have proven their merit, must be evaluated differently.

It was not only abolitionists who discarded the accepted discourse in favor of more pragmatic and realistic evaluations. The same British observer who above argued for reform of slave society, but not abolition, nevertheless concedes that the events of the revolution in St Domingo were neither surprising, nor inexplicable:

Let us be permitted a few reflections on the awful scenes that the island of St. Domingo has of late exhibited ... The destruction of flourishing plantations, the burning of houses, the slaughter of the whites by a secret treachery, or open revolt; the gross violations of female chastity; the dissolution of all the bonds of subordination, and all the attachments of society, contribute to fill the dreadful sketch. Are these enormities to be lamented? They surely are. Can they excite our wonder? By no means. [49]

In 1802, Henry Addington, Chancellor to the Exchequer in London, solicited an evaluation of the situation in St Domingo, and the effects that the upheaval would have on the British sugar isles. The report expressed the opinion that the French endeavor of recapturing St Domingo was an ill conceived one, both because of the perceived ideological fervor of the freed slaves, and because the likely result of more fighting would be an increasingly militarised and militarily competent black population: 'If I judge rightly of the approaching struggle, military skill and military habits will rise among them to a much higher pitch, and will be aided by a proved sense, not of equality merely, but of superiority, in war, to the troops of Europe.[50] Furthermore, it argued that while the existence of a free Black state was a dangerous example, the ideological dangers were outweighed by the likely material consequences:

> In contemplating [the failure of a French re-invasion], the public opinion seems so far to have anticipated my conclusion, as to regard the establishment of a Negro state, or even a community of free Negroes under the government of France in the West Indies, as likely to prove fatal in its consequences to our sugar colonies. The danger of such a political phenomenon in point of precedent is obvious. But that danger is not in my apprehension the greatest ground of alarm: for there is a state of extreme degradation in which man is little affected by political argument, even in the persuasive form of example; and a Jacobin would probably find the field Negro of Jamaica a marginally susceptible pupil.[51]

The author argues that the danger of a free Haiti to Jamaica and the other British colonies was not necessarily to be found in the exportation of ideology; indeed Bridges makes it clear that this ideology was being disseminated anyway, but in the inevitable formation of a militarily oriented state in the region. In the case that the French were somehow able to recapture St Domingo, holding the colony would necessitate a huge contingent of soldiers, always a threat to the British. If the expedition failed, it would leave a population of armed and battle tested, newly freed blacks, just miles from Jamaica's shores. This evaluation does not easily fit into the existing discourse on race and slavery. Rather than assuming that the French expedition would succeed based on the idea that Europeans were inherently superior to blacks, and that this superiority would translate into military dominance, the author, arguably heavily informed by the British failure to capture St Domingo, instead acknowledges the organisation and resolve of the blacks, and even the likely prospect of their victory. His conclusions on what he characterises as an inevitable threat to the British colonies, are based not on images of barbaric blacks exporting destruction to the surrounding islands, but on the likely policies of either an independent Haiti, or a reclaimed, but unstable St Domingo. Furthermore, he does not ascribe a relative value to either scenario, asserting only that in either case, the implications for Jamaica will be negative.[52] Ironically, it seems that just such a military presence precluded comparable revolts in Jamaica. David Geggus points out that:

In Jamaica, both the slave elite and the [African] maroon community responded positively to news of the St Domingo revolt, and an uprising was planned for Christmas 1791. However, the militia was then called up for the first time in nine years and the size of the garrison, already at a record level, was soon doubled. In fact, it was precisely the period 1776-1815 that saw British Garrisons in the Caribbean at their strongest.[53]

Further accounts from Jamaica also illustrate a shift towards an evaluation of the Haitians on a plane commensurate with their achievements rather than the usual reliance on negative racial stereotypes. It is again evident that the proven discourse on race and slavery, even for nearby slaveholders, was proving inadequate to explain the events in St Domingo. Several excerpts from the journal of Lady Nugent, the wife of a British General stationed in Jamaica, illuminate this point. These entries coincide with the commencement of Bonaparte's attempt to recapture St Domingo in 1802, and show that British subjects watching from Jamaica, perhaps also chastened by their own experience with Toussaint, were fully aware of his competency, and of the abilities of the ex-slaves to act effectively:

> Toussaint is determined to keep his command. This reminds me of a conversation General Nugent had with Colonel Charmilly, who said that General Toussaint, he was sure, would negotiate with France, and for a compensation, resign his command. General Nugent thought differently, and that he would retain his power as long as possible; that he would probably call upon the whites to join him, and, in case of their refusal, a general massacre of those unfortunate people would be the consequence, that is, if he found himself pressed at all by the French force sent to St Domingo. General Nugent thought also, that he would be likely to burn the towns, and retire to the mountains. At present, General Toussaint having declared exactly what General Nugent thought he would with respect to his government, had sent secret advice to all the white inhabitants, to come over to this island as soon a possible.[54]

Mrs Nugent gives updates of the condition in St Domingo throughout the year of 1802, most received from visiting French officers, refugee French planters, or gleaned from her husband's conversations with other military men. The various entries which mention St Domingo, when extracted from the journal and compiled, show a gradual development of Mrs Nugent's evaluation of the blacks in general, and Toussaint in particular. She seems impressed by the consistent correlation between Toussaint's actions, and her husband's predictions, and not at all convinced of either the inevitability of a French victory, or the validity of the assumption that Toussaint and his countrymen deserve to be re-enslaved:

The French have landed 20,000 men, and the consequence is just what General Nugent predicted. The whites have been taken into the mountains. Cap Francois has been burnt; it seems Toussaint's plan is to distress the French as much as possible, by burning the towns, and harassing them from the woods and mountains. How dreadful a business it is altogether; and indeed, it makes one shudder, to think of the horrible bloodshed and misery that must take place, before anything at all can be settled on that wretched island.[55]

Mrs Nugent's tone is almost neutral; there is no sense in this passage, or any of the others, that she assigns blame to the blacks for the situation in St Domingo. Neither is there, however, the sense that she supports the blacks in their revolution. She enjoys the services of slaves during her stay in Jamaica, but unlike her companions, she is aware of what she perceives as the strangeness of the arrangement. Her perception of the situation in the West Indies seems to be representative of the unavoidable shift in the wider collective perception of race and the institution of slavery in the wake of the Haitian Revolution:

I began the ball with an old Negro man. I was not aware of how much I shocked the misses Murphy by doing this. They told me afterwards that they were nearly fainting ... for in this country, and among slaves, it was necessary to keep up so much more distant respect. They may be right ... They seemed to think the example dangerous, as making the blacks of too much consequence, or putting them at all on equal footing with the whites, might make a serious change in their conduct, and even, as they think it must have in St Domingo, produce a rebellion in the island.[56]

It is apparent from Lady Nugent's journal entries that she is less conservative than her Jamaican cohorts; she finds no discomfort in dancing with an old black man at a ball; her somewhat detached vantage point damages her status as a model of colonial society. Nonetheless, her dealings with the more traditional members of her colonial society illustrate the impact of the events in St Domingo, if only by exposing her contemporaries' insecurities. From the evaluation solicited by the Chancellor, and Mrs Nugent's journal entries, which relate not only her perceptions, but the expectations of her husband (a general), and the attitudes of her cohorts, we may discern that the view from Jamaica was changing. The view was no longer the previously accepted one of islands made up of masses of inhuman, faceless slaves; but of a group of potentially revolutionary populations, and in the case of St Domingo, one possessing competent leadership and expressed goals. For the more intuitive observers, this reshaping of perceptions was conscious; for most it was expressed in the unconscious fear that St Domingo, and later Haiti, represented a new age.

When considering the discursive manipulation, which surrounded the Haitian Revolution, it would be remiss to examine the contributions of planters and abolitionists, without engaging in a reading of the reactions of the relevant governments. While British and French leaders attempted to subdue and silence the revolutionaries in overt and obvious ways, the more subtle policies of the United States in dealing with both St Domingo during the revolution, and Haiti immediately afterwards, are essential to understanding the process of silencing which took place. As suggested above, the shift in the discourse on race and slavery is quite clearly reflected in the responses of governments to the events in Haiti. Working within the model proposed by Trouillot and Dash, one where the common response to the Haitian Revolution was a reliance on the existing discourse to explain the events in St Domingo, or as Trouillot puts it, a manipulating of the facts to fit the discourse, one might expect that the government of the United States would dismiss the events as temporary or insignificant, and the leaders of the Revolution as either unintelligent and doomed to collapse, or as puppets controlled by white parties. To the contrary, the government of the United States, especially the Jefferson administration, was well informed about the revolution, its origins and its implications, and at several junctures, was intimately involved in the fighting through sales of arms and supplies, and in the politics of the conflict, through their dealings with France, Spain and Britain, as well as with Toussaint himself. It would be impossible to support an argument that the government of the United States, The president, his cabinet and advisors, as well as congressmen and representatives, many of them slave owning men, were ignorant of the scope and scale of the Haitian Revolution. Furthermore, their oration and legislation indicate that they internalised to some extent the implications of the revolution for their own situation, and their contributions to the discourse, in all their various forms, were similarly changed.

American involvement in the upheaval in St Domingo was immediate. Less than one month after the rising of the slaves in the northern plains, French colonial officials appealed to George Washington for aid. He agreed unconditionally:

> I have not delayed a moment since the receipt of your communication of the 22nd, in dispatching orders to the Secretary of the Treasury to furnish the money, and to the Secretary of War to deliver the arms and ammunition, which you have applied to me for. Sincerely regretting, as I do, the cause which has given rise to this application, I am happy in the opportunity of testifying how

well disposed the United States are to render every aid in their power to our good friends and allies the French to quell the alarming insurrection of the Negroes in Hispanola, and of the ready disposition to effect it, of the executive authority thereof.[57]

This reflex response to the insurrection fits within the discourse on race and slavery that existed at the time. Without further intelligence on the situation, the president made the decision to help repress a revolt. All he needed to know was that slaves were rebelling violently against a white regime. There is no evidence in any of Washington's presidential writings that he considered any alternative. This unquestioned adherence to policies attached to the existing discourse would not survive the turn of the century. Already apparent in Ternant's response to Washington, is the new difficulty in fitting the events of the revolution to the discourse. As early as 1791, the contributors to the discourse were being forced to reevaluate the ways in which they endeavored to explain the actions and perceived mentalities of slaves. Ternant's attempts to explain the origins of the revolt to Washington illustrate this phenomenon:

Early on the 24th (of August, 1791), Lieutenant Colonel Toussard ... took about 60 prisoners – 15 of these that had been taken in arms, were ordered to be shot; but before their execution every possible means was tried by cross examination and even promises of pardon to find out whether some white person or mulatto was not the chief promoter of the revolt – every effort was in vain; the prisoners continued to assert that it was the Negroes' own determination to exterminate the whites, their tyrants, and to destroy all sugar plantations, the produce of which they did not need, but which they on the contrary execrated as the cause of their miseries. 'This is our land.' said several of them. 'We have tilled and watered it long enough with our sweat and blood to seize it as our property.'[58]

The pragmatism of American leaders on the level of their political response to the Haitian Revolution was impressive, but it was not untainted by their concern over the precedent being set, and was of course mitigated by the larger political currents in the region.

The political climate of the era, especially surrounding the question of North American Empire, is integral to an understanding of the American role in the Haitian Revolution. In the last decade of the eighteenth century, the expansion of the United States had not yet become a forgone conclusion; the term 'manifest destiny' had not yet been coined. Spain owned roughly what is today Florida, Georgia and Alabama, and had acquired the Louisiana Territory, which covered one third of what is now the continental United States, from France. While the European powers were struggling over the lucrative colonies of the West Indies, the United States was interested in securing its own North American territories, and ensuring continued access to the trade routes and shipping lines, which were essential to its economic health. St Domingo would play an important role in those endeavors.

From 1798 to 1800, during the United States' quasi-war with the French, the government formed an unofficial alliance with Toussaint, giving him military aid that proved vital in his campaigns to subdue his mulatto rival Rigaud, in return for his promise that he would not allow France to use St Domingo as a base against the United States.[59] Britain also offered Toussaint aid, ostensibly in an attempt to pre-empt American hegemony. Neither state, however, would agree to recognise the independence of Toussaint's regime, fearing that such recognition might incite their slave populations to revolt. In fact, even as Jefferson agreed to an alliance with Toussaint and the resumption of trade with his administration, a move he felt was essential to national security; he expressed concern at the possible repercussions:

> 'Toussaint's clause' had received the approval of both houses of congress; even South Carolina in the House of Representatives voted for it. We may expect therefore black crews and supercargoes and missionaries thence into the Southern states; and when that level begins to work, I would gladly compound with a great part of our northern country, if they would honestly stand neuter. If this combustion can be introduced among us under any veil whatsoever, we have to fear it.[60]

With the rise to power of Napoleon Bonaparte, American security became decidedly less assured. Bonaparte's designs on North American Empire linked the future of St Domingo even more closely to the future of the United States. In September of 1800, unbeknownst to Jefferson, Bonaparte negotiated with Spain for the return of the Louisiana Territory. On September 30, 1800, before word of the transaction could leak, Bonaparte and Jefferson agreed on the Treaty of Morfontaine, in accordance with which, France would release the United States from its guarantee of French possessions in return for the abandonment of claims for French 'spoilation' of American merchant vessels.[61] Without knowledge of the Louisiana transaction, Jefferson was disposed to interpret this as a relaxation of tensions in the region. It meant that he no longer needed Toussaint's guarantee in St Domingo, and reneging on his promise, he conspired with France to help starve out its recalcitrant colony.[62]

Jefferson, of course, proved too trusting. Bonaparte had every intention of regaining St Domingo, and using it as a staging ground for a push up through the Louisiana Territory into North America. By the end of 1801, he was preparing Leclerc and his troops to carry out the first stage of this plan. It was at this juncture that Bonaparte made a contribution to the discourse on race and slavery. He made explicit in a letter to Talleyrand his concern that any outcome short of total victory for his troops would be a dangerous and irreversible precedent:

> Inform England that in taking my decision to liquidate Toussaint L'Ouverture's government in St Domingue I have not been guided by commercial and financial concerns so much as by the need to stamp out in every part of the world any kind of anxiety or trouble. The freedom of Negroes, if recognised in St. Domingue, and legalised by France, would at all times be a rallying point for the freedom-seekers of the New World.[63]

Jefferson, finally fully aware of Bonaparte's duplicity, expressed his grave concern over his nation's vulnerability:

> The single spot, the possessor of which is our natural and habitual enemy, is the port at New Orleans ... The day that France takes possession of New Orleans fixes the sentence which is to restrain her forever within her low water mark. From that moment we must marry ourselves to the British fleet and nation.[64]

Now that France had once again become a threat, Jefferson resolved that he would endeavor to halt Bonaparte's approach at St Domingo, and again offered assistance to Toussaint. He reopened trade to the colony, and when Toussaint was captured in late 1802, Jefferson continued to allow aid to be sent to Dessalines, Petion, and Christophe. It is difficult to say how instrumental this aid was to the revolutionaries, but it is safe to assume that it did not hurt them. The Jeffersonian Republicans were caught in a dilemma, which is tied closely to the issue of the discourse on race and slavery. Their pro-French and antiblack attitudes were in conflict with American national interests. By itself, Louisiana was not a viable possession for France; its productivity depended on French control of St Domingo. French control of St Domingo hinged on the defeat of Toussaint and the reestablishment of slavery, which Bonaparte had already instituted in Martinique and Guadeloupe. In this curious way, Jefferson found himself at least partially reliant upon a former slave in revolt against France to secure American interests in both the Mississippi Valley and the Caribbean. By late 1803, Bonaparte's campaign was blunted, and Haiti was independent. The cost of the failed campaign to re-enslave St Domingo, both in currency and lives, was so high for France, that by all accounts, it forced the sale of the Louisiana Territory to the United States.[65]

The resolution of war in Haiti, did not, of course, serve to resolve the controversy surrounding the establishment of a free state governed by former slaves. This presented a new dilemma for Jefferson; indeed, even before the outcome of the struggle was decided, he was preparing for the specter of an independent Haiti:

> The course of things in the neighboring islands of the West Indies, appear to have given a considerable impulse to the minds of the slaves in different parts of the United States. A great disposition to insurgency has manifested itself among them, which, in one instance, in the state of Virginia, broke out into actual insurrection.[66]

The actual immediate effect of the Haitian Revolution on the slaves of the United States is hard to gauge. To say that the increase in insurgency was directly caused by the events in Haiti, or even that there was an increase in insurgency, without the testimony of those involved, would be conjecture. The belief by slaveholders that there was an increase in rebelliousness, and that the increase could be attributed to the events of Haiti, does, however, indicate that the Revolution had a concrete effect on the thinking of those slaveholders. I would argue that the most important component of that effect was the new tendency of slaveholders to view blacks as political beings. Slaves were now evaluated on some level as conspirators, as planners, as susceptible to revolutionary ideology and propaganda.

This new attitude was reflected in the United States government's dealings with the newly independent Haiti. Trouillot argues that the outward attitude of the United States towards Haiti was contempt, but that this facade masked an anxiety caused by a weakening of the foundation of the existing discursive structure:

> ... European and United States leaders showed contempt for all Haitians, leaders and masses alike, and a total disdain for the independence they had so courageously won. The birth of an independent state on the ashes of a Caribbean colony was seen a major threat by racist rulers in Western Europe and in the United States. Given the climate of the times and the general acceptance of Afro-American slavery in the white world, the Haitian Revolution was equal to such modern day events as the Vietnamese victory, the 'loss' of French Algeria, or the rise of a socialist Cuba a few miles off the coast of Florida.[67]

The United States could not ignore the accomplishments of Haiti's own founding fathers. Instead it chose to cheapen them, and manipulate the way in which they were perceived by slaves and slaveholders. In its mildest form, anxiety over the disruptive potential of Haiti's revolution, created a persistent unwillingness among even the most progressive minds to recognise the parallels between Haiti and the United States. This can be seen in the ambivalence among those who believed in the ideal of revolution but could not bring themselves to accept the legitimacy of the newly independent black republic. In its more intense manifestations, this anxiety took the form of increased surveillance and repression of American slaves, and a demonising of the Haitian leaders, especially Dessalines, known for his animosity towards whites.

The refusal to evaluate the Haitian Revolution on the same plane as the French and American revolutions was matched by the fear shown to the ideas and information that now emanated from a free Haiti. In 1823, while addressing Congress on the question of whether Haiti should be recognised by the United Sates as an independent nation, Senator Monroe questioned the ability of the United States to absorb those ideas without dire consequences:

> The United States can receive no mulatto consuls or black ambassadors from Haiti, because the peace of eleven slave holding states will not permit black consuls and ambassadors to establish themselves in our cities, and to parade through this country, and give their fellow blacks in the United States proof in hand of the horrors which await them, for a successful revolt on their part.[68]

This question of recognition was central to the silencing of Haiti, and integral to the reshaping of the discourse. The United States could not deny the outcome of the revolution, but it could refuse to recognise the product as a viable nation. They withheld this recognition until 1862, when President Lincoln pushed it through after the secession of the Southern states. This timing is indicative of the reasoning behind the refusal. The Southern states, like Monroe, were wary of any unnecessary contact between Haitians and American slaves. The non-recognition limited trade and immigration, and allowed the Southern states to better filter the flow of information and people arriving from Haiti.

The United States' refusal to recognise Haiti's independence was easily identifiable as in conflict with the expressed tenets of American society. It exposed not only the hypocrisy of individual administrations, but of that entire society, and of the Western philosophy it was based on. It was representative of the continuing power of slaveholders over Haiti. Without recognition from the most powerful state in the region, Haiti had little hope of establishing national legitimacy, aid agreements or beneficial trade relationships. It was the official manifestation of all the private debate. Haiti may have won a battle, but they were hopelessly outgunned in the war. Beyond mountains are more mountains.

A practice that has proven to be part of both the silencing of the Haitian Revolution, and integral to the reshaping of the discourse on race and slavery which surrounded the events of the revolution, is the elevation of the creole generals, and Toussaint in particular, to the status of exemplary black figures, men to be admired as extraordinary, at the expense of both the rank and file of the revolutionary masses, and the bossale leadership. This elevation comes from sources both sympathetic to, and critical of, the insurgent slaves. Much of its effectiveness at silencing is to be found in this aspect of its character. Contributors to the discourse, C.L.R. James and Aime Cesaire among them, with their glowing biographies of Toussaint L'Ouverture, have reinforced the barriers, which hide the revolution's truths, by focusing on the adjusted discourse which surrounds Haiti's birth. The argument is as follows: unable to deny the facts of the Haitian Revolution, that is, the inherent inhumanity of slavery, the innate desire for freedom found within those Haitian slaves, the adoption in some form of the same revolutionary principles which drove both the American and French Revolutions, the resolve of the former slaves to remain former slaves, and their success in defeating both British and French troops in full scale warfare, observers instead settled on ways to explain the events which neither relied on the existing discourse, nor conceded the equality of blacks as a people. Unable to point to any white leadership, these observers chose instead to argue that the revolution consisted of a teeming mass of unintelligent and barely controlled blacks, led by a few extraordinary and admirable men, exhibiting the positive qualities of whites, but who happened to be black.

Toussaint and the new class he represented were reprehensible (or as Trouillot might say, unimaginable), to whites, but they possessed several attributes, which made them infinitely more palatable to those whites than their African born counterparts. As argued throughout this study, even as revolutions go, Haiti's was revolutionary. It was unthinkable even as it happened; but in many ways, it was like every other revolution. There was the typical internal conflict, and the emergence of an elite, which resorted to coercion in order to sustain its regime. Toussaint was an amazing individual, whose leadership enabled the slaves of St Domingo to secure their freedom, and it is obvious that he strove to act in the best interests of the collective. He was not, however, culturally representative of the revolutionary masses of Haiti. He and his Creole generals, Dessalines and Henri Christophe most prominent among them, aspired to be culturally more French than African. They subjugated the bossale leadership, opposed Vodoun in favor of Catholicism, and supported the rehabilitation of the plantation economy, even at the cost of ignoring the aspirations of most ex-slaves for autonomy and land.

As suggested above, this elevation of the Creole generals was not always done in a conscious attempt to silence the African born contributors, but it was part of a conscious change in the discourse. Both sides were engaging in this change. Those opposed to slavery, and impressed by the Haitian Revolution, used Toussaint, Dessalines, and Christophe as examples of Black equality. Dozens of biographies of Toussaint have been written since 1800, and at least ten of those were published before 1850.[69] In the 1840s Wendell Phillips used Toussaint as an example of black equality and capability, and during the civil war, invoked Toussaint again to argue for a place for black soldiers in the Union army.[70] In 1837. The Anti-Slavery record also held up Toussaint as an example of excellence. Their contribution illustrates the silencing effect of elevating Toussaint. They praised his successes against European enemies, and his ability in leading his cohorts, but above all, they praised his moderation; the fact that he had protected his former owners, and that he prevailed while playing by European rules.

This presentation may simply be a function of the abolitionists' need to reach both liberal and conservative audiences. They of course had to pick their examples carefully. But by seeking to ingratiate themselves to a moderate audience, they legitimate a moderate argument, one that says blacks may be considered equal because of this Europeanised example, rather than one that says blacks are equal as a whole because they are humans, regardless of culture. Furthermore, the elevation of Toussaint's version of revolution by abolitionists comes at the expense of Dessalines and Sans Souci, both of who were committed to freedom for their brethren at all costs, who explicitly denounced whites for their brutality towards slaves, and who exhibited no reticence in repaying that brutality. It not only silences their contribution, but implies disagreement.

An example of this phenomenon in later scholarship is found in the work of David Geggus. Geggus argues, like myself, that the creole and bossale factions of the revolution had different goals for Haiti. Geggus, however, oversimplifies the relationship, stating that the African born slaves were interested in a bloody revolution, an extermination of their oppressors, and eventual freedom and autonomy. The creoles on the other hand, were interested in overthrow, playing the role of an anti-colonial native elite. Once he establishes this relationship, he immediately diminishes its usefulness. He acknowledges that two thirds of the adult male slaves were bossales, but he concludes that since the revolution eventually succeeded, the tensions between creole and bossale could not have been significant. Furthermore, he concludes that the mixture of creole and bossale influence must have simply been in the right proportion. He homogenises the blacks even as he acknowledges their differences, and then goes on to more specifically silence the bossale contributions:

The St Domingo slave revolt certainly did exhibit tensions between creole leaders and African masses, which impeded its progress. Its success in overcoming them might simply testify to the strength of the other factors working in its favor. On the other hand, there could be something precisely in the mixture of African masses and creole elements; perhaps the combination of a suicidal fervor in battle with a sophisticated leadership, that goes a long way in explaining its success.[71]

This assumption that the competent leadership could only have come from the creole individuals, and that the eventual victory of creole principles indicates their superiority, is the epitome of the silencing process. By manipulating the history of the Haitian Revolution to include only creole contributions; by silencing the fact that African born slaves adopted the principles of equality and liberty, and participated actively in successful revolution against France, contributors to the discourse have weakened the impact of Haiti's birth. It was impossible to ignore the events of the revolution, but not impossible to manipulate their perceived meanings. By emphasising the creole element, contributors to the discourse, (American, European, and Haitian), make the revolution more acceptable, imaginable, and conceivable to western observers.

The Haitian Revolution is one of the most remarkable episodes in Western history. It is proof that even those events, which seem conclusive; black and white, as it were; are subject to the vagaries of interpretation. If Haiti was the epicenter of a shock that radiated across the Caribbean, the reshaping of the discourse on race and slavery, which accompanied its birth, was the seismic retrofit that lessened its disruptive impact on Western philosophy and colonialism. The lack of scholarship acknowledging this reshaping project is testimony to its effectiveness. It is not enough to win a revolutionary struggle; that struggle must also be legitimated, acknowledged and accepted, often by colleagues of the revolutionary losers. Beyond mountains are more mountains.

Endnotes

1. Genovese, Eugene, 1979, *From Rebellion to Revolution: Afro-American Slave Revolts in the Modern World.* This is one account of the public declaration of independence by Dessalines on January 1, 1804.
2. Estimates of the slave population range from 500,000 (James, C.L.R., 1938, *The Black Jacobins; Toussaint L'Ouverture and the San Domingo Revolution*) to 700,000, (*Journal of Negro History*, vol xxv no3, July 1940). The wide margin is due to the fact that planters' census reports are

notoriously unreliable. This misreporting was often intentional to avoid taxation, so that official numbers are most likely low. Deaths sustained by the revolting slaves are agreed to be in the 150,000 to 200,000 range.

3. 'By 1789, St Domingue was the world's largest producer of both sugar and coffee; its plantations produced twice as much as all other French colonies combined (and more sugar than all the British sugar islands combined); and French ships entering and leaving its ports accounted for more than a third of the metropole's foreign trade.' From Scott, Julius, 1986, *The Common Wind; Currents of Afro-American Communication in the Era of the Haitian Revolution* Dissertation, Department of History, Duke University. For economic numbers see also Williams, Eric, 1944, *Capitalism and Slavery*. For first hand descriptions of St. Domingue's pre-war opulence see Moreau St. Mery, 1798, *Description of St. Domingue, Vol 1*; Brown, Jonathan, 1836, *History and Present Condition of Haiti*; Candler, John, 1842, *Brief Notices of Haiti*.

4. Eric Williams complicates the issue by arguing that the Haitian revolution strengthened the British abolitionist movement by helping to make it an economically prudent policy. The British were unable to capture St Domingo themselves, in which case they surely would have continued slavery. If the French were to win it back, then the British would not help them rehabilitate the colony by selling them new laborers. (Williams, 1944, *Capitalism and Slavery*) Others, like Dubois, prefer to assert that the upheaval itself forced abolitionists to revise their arguments, and slave holders to give them weight. See Dubois, WEB, 1896, *The Suppression of the African Slave Trade to the United States of America, 1638-1870;* Harvard Historical Studies, number one.

5. The affranchi caste was the group of free mulatto and black persons of the colony. Most were the illegitimate offspring of wealthy planters, or had been manumitted by previous owners. Many owned slaves and the mulattos in particular, were often successful planters, much to the chagrin of the petit blancs (poor whites). In fact, by 1789, mulattoes owned one third of the cultivated land and one fourth of the slaves. (Moreau St Mery, 1798)

6. The grand blancs were the rich planter class. Most were temporary residents or absentee planters, interested in turning a quick profit and repatriating. The petit blancs were the poor whites, many of a lower economic station than mulattoes.

7. For an in depth history see James, C.L.R., 1938, *The Black Jacobins; Toussaint L'ouverture and the St. Domingo Revolution* or Fick, Carolyn, 1990, *The Making of Haiti.* The first gives an account from the perspective of the

revolutionary leadership, the second examines the role of maroons and other more marginalised black groups.

8. James, 1938, *The Black Jacobins.* James cites Lacroix, 1819, *Memoires pour Servir a l'Histoire de la Revolution de Saint Domingue,* Paris, Vol. 1 James asserts that while Clarkson would not have facilitated a revolt in a British colony, he was ardent enough in his conviction to want to see how it would play out in St Domingue, even at the expense of lives.

9. Brown, 1836, *History and Present Condition of Haiti,* London.

10. James, 1938, *The Black Jacobins;* Fick, 1990, *The Making of Haiti;* All historical accounts of the Haitian revolution note Oge's role, but the size of his force is recorded at anywhere from 300 - 500 men. An amusing, but apparently inaccurate variation on the story comes from Clarkson. As he tells it in his 1792 pamphlet, *The True State of the Case, Respecting the Insurrection at St. Domingo,* Oge was pursued and harassed by the whites without provocation and was forced to seek refuge in Spanish Santo Domingo, where he was extradited.

11. James, 1938, p.73; Debate before the British National Assembly emphasised the contribution of the mulattoes political actions to the consciousness of the slaves: 'The people of colour appealed to common justice, and common sense; it was to no purpose. The whites repelled them from their assemblies. Some commotion ensued, in which they mutually fell sacrifice to their pride and their resentment. The Amis des Noirs have not been accused of any interference in these dissentions, to which it is however probable that the slaves were not inattentive.' *An Inquiry Into the Causes of the Insurrection of the Negroes in the Island of St. Domingo,* read before the National Assembly, 29th February, 1792; London p.12.

12. Carolyn Fick, who argues that the importance of Toussaint, Dessalines, and Christophe (she, like most historians, is remiss in her neglect of the African born generals who fought alongside those creoles), was matched by that of the slave masses themselves, especially the ones reluctant to accept any creole leadership, emphasises the centrality of marronage to the success of the revolution and the forging of an independent identity for Haiti.

13. Toussaint encouraged the return of refugee planters to their land, hoping for the benefits of their expertise. In cases where the owner would not or could not return, Toussaint appointed a temporary protectorate, usually one of his officers.

14. James, 1938, *The Black Jacobins.*

15. The Constitution is printed in full in Nemours, *Histoire Militaire de la Guerre d'Lndependance de Saint-Domingue.* Vol 1, pp. 95-112. Paris, 1925. Interesting

points include the abolition of slavery; equality in employment to men of all colours; subordination of the church to the state; the appointing of Toussaint as Governor for life, with the power to name his successor; no provision for the existence of any French official within the government.

16. *The Unpublished Papers of Generals Leclerc and Rochambeau.* By the first wet season, even before they were exposed to Yellow Fever, Leclerc had already lost the majority of these troops, was begging for reinforcements, and had resorted to raising black regiments with payment and (false) promises of freedom. For more accounts of French casualties and troop movements see James, 1938, *The Black Jacobins*; Fick, 1990, *The Making of Haiti*; Ott, 1973, *The Haitian Revolution, 1789-1804.*

17. In a deviation from his pattern of praise and homage, James criticises Toussaint not for returning the laborers to the fields, but for doing it without explanation. Toussaint was concerning himself with state matters and neglecting to secure the support of the masses. James, 1938, pp. 276-288.

18. Bossale is the term used to denote a person born in Africa, as opposed to Creole, used for any person, regardless of race, who was born in one of the colonies.

19. In his text, *Silencing the Past; Power and the Production of History,* Michel Rolph Trouillot uses the case of Sans Souci, the most notable of the Bossale generals, as an example of the silencing of history.

20. Fick argues that these maroon bands simply chose not to participate directly in the revolution, other than to defend their own strongholds and raid plantations for supplies. They were interested only in maintaining their freedom and lifestyle, but attempts by both European and black troops to dislodge them had significant effects on the outcome of the conflict. Ultimately they were unable to remain neutral, but ironically enough, Haitian society has in many ways conformed to their wishes, allowing (or forcing) the majority of inhabitants into a peasant lifestyle. Fick, Carolyn, 1990, *The Making of Haiti.*

21. Trouillot, Michel, 1995, *Silencing the Past;* p.26.

22. Ibid., p.89.

23. Ibid., p.91

24. Ibid., p.95

25. James, 1938, preface to the first edition.

26. Dash, Michael, *Haiti and the United States; National Stereotypes and the Literary Imagination* (University of the West Indies, Cave Hill, London, 1988) p.5.

27. Ibid., p.2; For more on the construction of the other, see also Said, Edward, 1978, Orientalism; Memmi, Albert, 1951, The Coloniser and the Colonised; Fanon, Frantz, 1961, The Wretched of the Earth.
28. Ibid.
29. Hunt, Alfred, N., *Haiti's Influence on Antebellum America; Slumbering Volcano in the Caribbean* (Louisiana State University Press, 1988) p.115.
30. Plummer, Brenda Gayle, *Haiti and the United States; the Psychological Moment.* (University of Georgia Press, 1992) p.5.
31. Fick, Carolyn, 1990, *The French Revolution in St. Domingue; A Triumph or Failure?* In Gaspar and Geggus, eds., 1990, *A Turbulent Time.*
32. Brown, Charles Brockden, 1803, *An Address to the Government of the United States, on the Cession of Louisiana to the French; and on the Late Breach of Treaty by the Spaniards*; published by John Conrad; Baltimore; It has also been suggested that this report was fabricated by an American writer, maybe Brown himself, to emphasise the futility of the French expedition and the danger presented by St Domingo. Regardless of authorship, it was widely circulated in Southern newspapers, from Charleston to Baltimore; Hunt, Alfred, 1988, *Haiti's Influence on Antebellum America; Slumbering Volcano in the Caribbean;* Louisiana State University Press.
33. General La Salle to Governor-General Desparbes, July 11, 1792, reprinted in A. Corre, *Les Papiers du General A-N de La Salle,* pp.26-27 cited in Scott, 1986.
34. Ott, Thomas, *The Haitian Revolution; 1789-1804* (University of Tennessee Press, 1973) p.73.
35. Montague, Ludwell Lee, 1940, *Haiti and The United States, 1714-1938.* Duke University Press. Virginia prohibited immigration of Blacks from the West Indies in 1778, North Carolina followed in 1795.
36. Bridges, George Wilson, 1828, *The Annals of Jamaica*, vol 2, London; p214
37. Ibid., p.201.
38. Ibid., p.211.
39. *An Inquiry Into the Causes of the Insurrection of the Negroes in the Island of St. Domingo*; read before the National Assembly, 29th, February, 1792; London p.18.
40. Ibid., p.26.
41. Ott, Thomas, 1973, *The Haitian Revolution, 1789-1804,* University of Tennessee Press.
42. Ibid, p.216.
43. Clarkson, Thomas, 1792, *The True State of the Case, respecting the Insurrection at St Domingo;* London; Julius Scott discusses the surprising speed of communication networks in the West Indies in his dissertation, *The Common*

Wind; Currents of Afro-American Communication in the Era of the Haitian Revolution. He asserts that often slaves would receive information faster than the planters, and rumors of anti-slavery legislation or decrees would cover entire islands before planters were even aware of them.

44. Thomas Clarkson to Henri Christophe, October 30, 1818. Griggs, Earl and Prator, Clifford, eds, 1952, *Henri Christophe and Thomas Clarkson, A Correspondence* (Berkeley, Los Angeles: University of California Press).
45. Thomas Clarkson to Boyer, May, 25, 1821, Griggs and Prator, eds., 1952.
46. *We Are All Guilty;* The Liberator, January 7, 1832.
47. Nelson, Truman, ed., 1966, *Documents of Upheaval; Selections From William Lloyd Garrison's The Liberator, 1831-1865;* New York review by V, May 14, 1831, p.18.
48. The Anti-Slavery Record Vol. 3, no.3, March 1837 pp.2-.3
49. *An Inquiry Into the Causes of the Insurrection of the Negroes in the Island of St. Domingo;* read before the National Assembly; 29th February, 1792; London; p.3.
50. *The Crisis of the Sugar Colonies;An Inquiry into the Objects and Probable Effects of the French Expedition to the West Indies and Their Connection With the Colonial Interests of the British Empire.* In four letters to Henry Addington, Chancellor of the Exchequer, London, 1802 p.84.
51. Ibid., p.80.
52. Ibid., pp.80-85.
53. Geggus, David, 1983, *Slave Resistance Studies and the St. Domingo Slave Revolt; Some Preliminary Considerations;* University of Florida.
54. Cundall, Frank, 1939, *Lady Nugent's Journal;Jamaica one Hundred and Thirty Eight Years Ago.* Reprinted from a journal kept by Maria, Lady Nugent, from 1801-1815. Institute of Jamaica, London December 13, 1801.
55. Ibid., February 16, 1802.
56. Ibid., April 26, 1803.
57. *The Papers of George Washington; Presidential Series;* University Press of Virginia, 2000; Mastromarino, Mark, ed. Washington to Ternant, September 24, 1791.
58. Ibid., Ternant to Washington, September 24, 1791.
59. Logan, Rayford, 1968, *Haiti and the Dominican Republic,* University of North Carolina Press. pp.300-319 This was a no lose situation for Toussaint; he had no intentions of allowing France to establish a military presence in St Domingue independent of his command.
60. *The Writings of Thomas Jefferson,* 1853, Joint Committee of Congress, Albert Ellery Bergh, ed, Jefferson to James Madison, February 12, 1799.
61. Logan, 1968, p. 303.

62. Ibid., p.304.
63. Ibid., p.337.
64. *The Writings of Thomas Jefferson,* Jefferson to Robert Livingston, United States Minister to France, April 18, 1802.
65. Trouillot states explicitly that this question of the immediate effect on France of the Haitian Revolution is one of the most blatant sites of the silencing of Haiti. Like Carolynn Fick, he wonders at the lack of references to Haiti within the French Revolutionary discourse in general, but he expresses utter amazement that the connection is almost nowhere made, between the failure of Bonaparte to recapture St Domingue, the cost of the endeavor, and the abandonment of North American empire embodied by the Louisiana purchase. *Silencing the Past,* pp. 97-103.
66. *The Writings of Thomas Jefferson,* Jefferson to Rufus King, July 13, 1802.
67. Trouillot, Michel, 1995, *Silencing the Past,* p.5.
68. Logan, Rayford, 1941, *The Diplomatic Relations of the United States and Haiti, 1776-1891*; Chapel Hill, UNC Press; p.101.
69. These are results of my own searches for material on the Haitian Revolution. The majority of the biographies are from French and English authors, but there are also Spanish and Russian writers. I found ten from before 1850; there may be more.
70. Ott, Thomas, *The Haitian Revolution 1789-1804* (University of Tennessee Press, 1973).
71. Geggus, David, 1983, *Slave Resistance Studies and the St. Domingo Slave Revolt.* p.18.

Bibliography

Adams, Henry, *History of the United States During the First Administration of Thomas Jefferson,* (New York, 1889).

Addington, Henry, Chancellor of the Exchequer, London, *The Crisis of the Sugar Colonies; An Enquiry Into the Objects and Probable Effects of the French Expedition to the West Indies and Their Connection With the Colonial Interests of the British Empire.* In four letters *An Inquiry Into the Causes of the Insurrection of the Negroes in the Island of St. Domingo;* read before the National Assembly, 29th February, 1792; (London: Johnson, J., publisher, 1802).

Aptheker, Herbert, *American Negro Slave Revolts,* (New York, 1943).

———, ed., *And Why Not Every Man? The Story of the Fight Against Negro Slavery,* (1961).

———, *Anti-racism in US History; The First Two Hundred Years,* (1992).

Bell, Madison Smartt, *All Souls' Rising,* (Toronto, 1995).

Bellegarde-Smith, Patrick, *In the Shadow of Powers*, (Humanities Press International, 1985).

Bergh, Albert, ed., *The Writings of Thomas Jefferson*, 1 vol, (Joint Committee of Congress, 1853).

Bridges, George Wilson, *The Annals of Jamaica*, 2 vol (London, 1828).

Brown, Charles Brockden, *An Address to the Government of the United States, on the Cession of Louisiana to the French; and on the Late Breach of Treaty by the Spaniards*, published by John Conrad (Baltimore, 1803).

Brown, Jonathan, *History and Present Condition of Haiti* (London, 1836).

Candler, John, *Brief Notices of Haiti* (London, 1842).

Clarkson, Thomas, *The True State of the Case, Respecting the Insurrection at St. Domingo* (London, 1792).

Cundall, Frank, *Lady Nugent's Journal; Jamaica One Hundred and Thirty Eight Years Ago*. Reprinted from a journal kept by Maria, Lady Nugent, from 1801-1815 (London: Institute of Jamaica, 1939).

Dash, J. Michael, *Haiti and the United States; National Stereotypes and the Literary Imagination* (Barbados: University of the West Indies, Cave Hill Campus, 1988).

Dupuy, Alex, *Haiti in the World Economy; Class, Race, and Underdevelopment Since 1700* (Westview Press: Boulder, 1989).

Fanon, Frantz, *The Wretched of the Earth* (Paris, 1961).

Fick, Carolyn, *The Making of Haiti, the St Domingue Revolution From Below* (Knoxville: University of Tennessee Press, 1990).

————, 'The French Revolution in Saint Domingo; a triumph or failure?', Gaspar and Geggus, eds., *A Turbulent Time*, (1990).

Foster, Charles and Albert Valdeman, ed., *Haiti – Today and Tomorrow, an interdisciplinary study* (University Press of America, 1984).

Garrett, Mitchell Bennett, *The French Colonial Question 1789-1791; Dealings of the Constituent Assembly With Problems Arising From the Revolution in the West Indies* (Michigan: Ann Arbor, 1916).

Geggus, David, *Slave Resistance Studies and the St Domingue Slave Revolt: some preliminary considerations* (Gainsville: University of Florida, 1983).

Genovese, Eugene D., *From Rebellion to Revolution; Afro-American slave revolts in the making of the modern world* (Baton Rouge: Louisiana State Press, 1979).

————, *The World the Slaveholder Made; Two Essays in Interpretation* (New York, 1969).

Griggs, Earl and Clifford Prator, ed., *Henri Christophe and Thomas Clarkson, A Correspondence* (U.C. Press, 1952).

Hunt, Alfred N., *Haiti's Influence on Antebellum America; Slumbering Volcano in the Caribbean* (Louisiana: Louisiana State University Press, 1988).

James, C.L.R., *The Black Jacobins, Toussaint L'Ouverture and the San Domingo Revolution,* 2nd edn (Random House, 1938).

Jennings, Lawrence C., *French Reaction to British Slave Emancipation* (LSU Press, 1988).

Krantz, Frederick, ed., *History From Below: Studies in Popular Protest and Popular Ideology in Honour of George Rude* (Quebec: Concordia University, 1985).

Logan, Rayford, *The Diplomatic Relations of the United States and Haiti, 1776-1891* (Chapel Hill: UNC Press, 1941).

————, *Haiti and The Dominican Republic* (UNC Press, 1968).

Mackenzie, Charles, *Notes on Haiti* (London, 1830).

Mastromarino, Mark A., ed., *The Papers of George Washington; Presidential Series* (Virginia: University Press of Virginia, 2000).

Memmi, Albert, *Racism,* Translated, revised edition (Minnesota: University of Minnesota, 2000).

Montague, Ludwell Lee, *Haiti and the United States, 1714-1938* (Duke University Press, 1940).

Moreau St. Mery, *Description of St. Domingue, 1-2 vol* (1798).

Nelson, Truman, ed., *Documents of Upheaval; Selections From William Lloyd Garrison's The Liberator, 1831-1865* (New York, 1966).

Ott, Thomas, *The Haitian Revolution, 1789-1804* (University of Tennessee Press, 1973).

Plummer, Brenda Gayle, *Haiti and the United States; The Psychological moment* (University of Georgia Press, 1992).

Richardson, Ronald Kent, *Moral Imperium; Afro-Caribbeans and the Transformation of British Rule, 1776-1838* (New York Greenwood Press, 1987).

Said, Edward, *Orientalism* (New York: Toronto, 1978) *Secret History; or the horrors of St. Domingo, in a series of letters, written by a lady at Cape Francois to Colonel Burr* (Philadelphia, 1808).

Scott, Julius Sherrard, *The Common Wind; Currents of Afro-American Communication in the Era of the Haitian Revolution;* Dissertation (Department of history, Duke University, 1986).

Trouillot, Michel-Rolph, *Silencing the Past; power and the production of history* (Boston, 1995).

Williams, Eric, *Capitalism and Slavery* (North Carolina: North Carolina Press, 1944).

The Liberator, 13-16 vol, 1843-1846.

The Anti-slavery Record, 3:3, March 1837; 3:7, December 1837.

The Journal of Negro History, xxv: 3, July, 1940; xlvii: 1, January, 1962; xlvii: 3, July 1962.

Index